THE DUI BOOK:

A Citizen's Guide to Understanding DUI-DWI Litigation in America

By

William C. Head, Esq.

© 2006 by William C. Head

Published and Distributed by
HEADLINES MARKETING CORPORATION
750 Hammond Drive
Building 5-100
Atlanta, Georgia 30328-6116
E-mail: wchead@mindspring.com
(Fax: 1-404-250-1494)

INTRODUCTION

I wrote this book out of necessity. After representing thousands of citizens accused of "drunken driving," I know that no other book has ever been written that comprehensively addresses an accused citizen's questions about what happens during the typical DUI-DWI case, especially one that will be contested and will be prepared for trial. Because my practice over the past 30 years has focused upon contested cases involving people arrested for drinking and driving (or driving after having used drugs), I realized that only a handful of attorneys in America would have sufficient trial experience to be able to write this book. I also knew that most of them probably would not undertake the endeavor.

I have interviewed nearly 10,000 potential clients over my career. I have handled more than 1000 successful trials, and an even larger number of successful pre-trial motion hearings and negotiations for non-DUI-DWI dispositions for my clients. Many of these frightened and confused citizens have expressed the same or similar concerns about what happens to their driver's license, whether they would go to jail, and how a DUI-DWI conviction would impact their jobs, their ability to travel, or their ability to maintain or pay for automobile insurance. This book addresses those issues as well as hundreds of other issues relating to how to choose a qualified, experienced trial attorney and what to expect from each stage of a DUI-DWI case as it proceeds to trial and even beyond trial.

A person charged with a drunk or drugged driving offense faces an assortment of criminal and administrative court proceedings and potential penalties. On the criminal side, the defendant is usually charged with a traditional impaired driving offense (DUI, DWI, OWI, OUI, etc.) and may also be charged with a so-called "per se" alcohol offense [driving while having an illegal amount of alcohol in his or her system based on a breath, blood, or urine test], wherein it is not necessary for the prosecution to prove that the defendant was affected or influenced by the alcohol he or she consumed. On the legislative horizon are new presumptive "impairment" levels for contraband drugs, as America addresses an increasing problem with drivers impaired either by drugs alone, or in combination with alcohol. Plus, many states are now making refusal of a driver to submit to testing a crime, and putting these drivers in jail for up to one year (or possibly longer), simply because they refused testing.

If the person accused of DUI-DWI has one or more prior alcohol-related or drug-related impaired driving convictions during a specified period (the so-called "lookback" period), the severity of the criminal charge may be enhanced to a higher misdemeanor or even upgraded to a felony. Many states have dropped the "lookback" period and now consider ANY DUI-DWI in the person's LIFETIME in meting out harsh punishment. If the defendant was involved in an automobile accident that resulted in injury of or death to another person, he or she is likely to be charged with an aggravated driving under the influence offense, which is usually a felony. In several states, this type of offense can be accused and prosecuted as a MURDER charge.

The administrative penalties for either refusing to submit to testing requested by a police officer who believes that the person was drunk or submitting to testing and producing a test card "number" showing an unlawful blood or breath alcohol level can cripple a person's right to drive. Additionally, in the states that have passed laws calling for heavy monetary fines or even jail penalties of up to one full year for a person who refuses to submit to testing, these punishments are added to the administrative license suspension or revocation sanctions. Other states are using whatever force is required to collect a sample from accused drinking drivers who try to refuse testing, with several reported cases of DUI-DWI suspects being killed by police as they try to obtain a blood sample.

A defendant who refuses chemical testing is normally subjected to an administrative license revocation or suspension. In many states a defendant who submits to chemical testing and is found to have a blood or breath alcohol level above a specified limit (presently 0.08% for drivers age 21 and older in all American jurisdictions) is also subject to an administrative license revocation or suspension. These administrative penalties (which typically come *before* any criminal trial) are normally imposed after a cursory administrative hearing that barely affords many licensees the chance to address many issues concerning the legitimacy of the pullover or the arrest.

Public campaigns pursued and financed by MADD and other political activists seek to wipe out drunk driving and drugged driving, or (as some writers have stated) possibly seek to reinstitute Prohibition. These efforts have caused state legislatures to make our national DUI-DWI laws more punitive each year, changing the DUI-DWI laws in virtually every legislative session. In addition, the American courts, from the United States Supreme Court down, are generally unsympathetic to those accused of drinking and driving (or drugged driving) offenses.

Because these laws change constantly, the reader will need to go on-line to get current information about his or her state's laws on drinking and driving and drugged driving. A summary of the key provisions and code sections from the DUI-DWI laws of each American jurisdiction can be found on-line at http://www.theduibook.com/stateDUIDWIsummaries.htm.

In most states driving while intoxicated cases are being investigated, filed, and documented by police officers who specialize in such cases. Special training courses for prosecutors have been developed to try to assure that each DUI-DWI case concludes with a conviction. Armed with presumptively correct breath or blood test evidence, statutory presumptions (inferences) of impairment, the financial resources of the state, and a judge either sympathetic with (or whose campaign was largely funded by) MADD supporters, modern prosecutors do not take drinking and driving or drug-related impaired driving cases lightly. This fact complicates trials and makes the job of the criminal defense lawyer who undertakes the defense of these cases more difficult.

If nothing else, this book will assist the person accused of America's most common crime to learn more about the legal landscape in order to be prepared for what lies ahead of him or her. This book should provide most accused DUI-DWI suspects some peace of mind. Being able to read about how things work within the court system provides a valuable and calming advantage as opposed to not knowing what to expect next.

For criminal defense attorneys who are busy defending DUI-DWI clients on a daily basis, this book will act as a silent partner to them as their clients read the book to supplement the interviews and briefings that the attorney and his or her staff provide to their clients. This book will be a time-saver for the attorneys who discover it, and a valuable source of client comfort to those attorneys and their staff members who are typically deluged with questions about the topics covered in this book.

I have attempted to support each theory or tactic with a citation of legal authority or an authoritative article or research study, but the reader should understand that drunk driving is essentially a local matter, and that the statutes and appellate court decisions in each state are unique to that state, in many instances. Due to this situation, it is impossible to cite every applicable legal principle or authority or case on every issue discussed in this book.

William C. Head
Attorney at Law

DISCLAIMER

This book makes no claim to provide authoritative guidance in all criminal counts and every state. It is an overview of common procedures, tactics and stages of a DUI-DWI criminal prosecution. No person charged with impaired driving should rely upon this book as a do-it-yourself manual. This book is intended to be a written resource for accused drunken (or drugged) drivers to help supplement the readers' comprehension of the complexities of criminal litigation. Although every effort has been made to assure accuracy in these chapters, no warranty that every maxim or strategy will work in any particular case is claimed by the author. The reader should always defer to his or her local DUI-DWI specialist for the final word on how the reader's case should be handled.

TABLE OF CONTENTS

Chapter 3 - You've Been Arrested, and Now You Are Being Taken to Jail. What Do You Do Now?

3.3. What to do after securing your vehicle.

    3.3.1. Keep your arrest details to yourself.

    3.3.2. Staying out of trouble while the case is pending.

    3.3.3. If (or when) you have your license back, get busy.

Chapter 4 - Locating, Investigating, Interviewing and Hiring the Best Available Attorney to Handle Your DUI-DWI Case

4.0. Overview of this chapter.

4.1. Locate and contact a "top" DUI-DWI attorney immediately.

    4.1.1. References from friends or any lawyer you might know personally.

    4.1.2. Community and Courthouse Reputation.

    4.1.3. Advanced Training.

    4.1.4. Specialized Membership or Professional Affiliations.

    4.1.5. Disciplinary Actions.

    4.1.6. Seminar Speaker.

    4.1.7. Fees and Fee Structure.

    4.1.8. Focus of practice.

    4.1.9. Drunk Driving Specialists.

    4.1.10. Years in Practice.

    4.1.11. Lawyer-Paralegal ratio.

    4.1.12. Caseload.

    4.1.13. Use of Technology.

    4.1.14. Promising too much.

    4.1.15. Board Certified.

    4.1.16. Educational Background.

    4.1.17. Publications.

    4.1.18. Promotional Materials.

    4.1.19. Conflicts of Interest.

    4.1.20. Sub-specialization within the DUI-DWI Field.

    4.1.21. Engagement Letter.

    4.1.22. Language Skills.

    4.1.23. Ethics.

    4.1.24. Personality Compatibility.

    4.1.25. Communication.

4.2. What do I do if I just cannot afford the TOP DUI-DWI lawyer in my area?

4.3. Don't expect your attorney to be a magician.

4.4. Don't ask your attorney to be a crook.

4.5. Treat your attorney's staff like they are your family members.

4.6. Providing input to your attorney, but not being a pest.

4.7. After selecting an advocate, follow your attorney's advice.

4.8. Maintain a file with all your papers from legal counsel.

    4.8.1. Expect copies of all motions and filings.

    4.8.2. Expect any and all offers for a plea to be communicated to you.

4.9. Let your attorney decide which witnesses to interview.

4.10. Follow your attorney's advice on securing help from the best available expert witness(es) for your trial or motions.

4.11. Assist your attorney in locating & staying in touch with fact witnesses and helping procure medical or other records.

Chapter 5 - What Should You Be Doing to Prepare Your Legal Defense After Your Arrest?

5.0. Purpose of this chapter.

5.1. What happens if you get caught driving on a suspended license?

5.2. Is getting a "limited permit" the solution to your problems?

5.3. When can you get your license reinstated?

5.4. Can you just obtain a license in another state?

5.5. Can you drive on an "international" license here in the USA?

5.6. Once you are permitted to drive again, will things be back to normal?

5.7. Alcohol and drug assessment (and possible treatment) prior to going to trial.

5.8. Should you go to "DUI-DWI school" prior to trial?

5.9. Cleaning up your driving history before your case reaches trial or final disposition.

5.10. Make certain you have funds available to cover all costs.

5.11. Keep your schedule flexible for court proceedings — save all vacation days.

5.12. Community service is a good thing to do.

5.13. Anxiety can be a killer! Seek professional counseling if needed.

5.14. How will the judge or jury perceive you?

Chapter 6 - Potential Defenses, Strategies and Tactics for Your DUI-DWI Case

6.0. Purpose of this chapter.

6.1. Defenses related to the legality or sufficiency of the indictment, accusation, complaint, information, or other charging instrument (such as a uniform traffic citation).

6.2. Defenses relating to an illegal search warrant, if applicable.

6.3. Defenses related to the legality of a roadblock.

6.4. Defenses related to the legality of the stop of your vehicle.

6.5. Defenses related to the lawfulness of your arrest for DUI-DWI.

6.6. Defenses related to an unlawful search and seizure and exclusion of illegally seized evidence.

6.7. Defenses related to the violation by the police of your Fifth Amendment privilege against self-incrimination.

6.8. Defenses related to the violation by the police of your constitutional or statutory right to counsel once arrested.

6.9. Challenges to use of improper and non-standardized field sobriety evaluations.

6.10. Challenges relating to the officer's competence to administer field sobriety evaluations.

6.11. Challenges to the officer's ability and experience in distinguishing an impaired driver from an unimpaired driver.

6.12. Defenses relating to discovery abuse.

6.13. Defenses relating to exculpatory lost video evidence.

6.14. Defenses related to the failure of the police to comply with the requirements of the State implied consent statute.

6.15. Defenses related to the failure of the police to comply with the requirements of the state's independent test statute.

6.16. Defenses related to prosecution's ability to prove the elements of the offense, other than impairment.

6.17. Defenses related to the prosecution's ability to prove the required degree of intoxication other than by chemical testing.

6.18. Defenses related to the admissibility of the prosecution's breath testing evidence.

6.19. Defenses related to the failure of the police to comply with standard operating procedure during the arrest or forensic testing.

6.20. Defenses related to the credibility of the prosecution's breath testing evidence.

6.21. Defenses related to the admissibility of the prosecution's blood testing evidence.

6.22. Defenses related to the credibility of the prosecution's blood testing evidence.

6.23. Defenses related to police misconduct or perjury.

6.24. The defense of an unconstitutional or invalidly-adopted drinking and driving statute or related ordinance.

6.25. Defenses related to double jeopardy.

6.26. Defenses related to collateral estoppel or res judicata.

6.27. Defenses related to the denial of your right to a speedy trial.

6.28. The defense of necessity.

6.29. The defense of duress.

6.30. The defense of entrapment.

6.31. Ignorance defense.

6.32. The defense of the margin of error variance.

6.33. The defense that your partition ratio is substantially different than the breath machine is programmed to expect.

6.34. Defense of involuntary intoxication or lack of intent to drive.

6.35. Defenses related to preventing the enhancement of punishment for a drinking and driving offense.

Chapter 7 - Specific Challenges to Various Search and Seizure Issues That Can Force Total Dismissal of Your DUI-DWI Case

7.0. Purpose of this chapter.

7.1. Stopped based upon traffic offense or vehicle deficiency that is not actually an offense or deficiency.

7.2. Stopped based upon an observed equipment defect that is not a legally required item of equipment.

7.3. Stopped for a violation of law and the statute is unconstitutional.

7.4. Stopped for a drive-out tag being on the vehicle, and the temporary tag is in good order.

7.5. Stopped because vehicle is coming from an area where no residences currently are occupied.

7.6. Stopped based solely upon a "be on the look out" (BOLO) call from a concerned citizen, and the information given is legally insufficient.

7.7. Stopped at a roadblock that was illegally set up.

7.8. Stopped at a roadblock that was not overseen and selected by a properly trained supervisory officer.

7.9. Confronted by an officer in a legally parked car with no reason to suspect that a crime had been committed.

7.10. Stopped because person turned around near a roadblock location.

7.11. Stopped because officer had a hunch that a turn into an apartment parking lot was made to avoid a roadblock that was ahead.

7.12. Stopped because the officer saw an unusual but insignificant driving error that did not rise to the level of being reasonable suspicion of impaired driving.

7.13. Stopped after the officer's driving actions caused or "created" weaving due to the driver's preoccupation with the "threatening" actions of the police car in the rear view mirror.

Chapter 8 - The "Discovery" Process: How Your Attorney Learns What Evidence the Prosecutor Has and Decides How to Challenge or Explain It

8.0. Purpose of this chapter.

8.1. States vary in the comprehensiveness of the discovery allowed under local law, but the United States Supreme Court rulings set the "floor" below which no state can go.

8.2. Different tools can be used to uncover information relevant to your case.

8.2.1. Subpoenas.

8.2.2. Subpoena duces tecum (seeks documents or items to be brought with the person who is appearing pursuant to the subpoena).

8.2.3. Freedom of information act (F.O.I.A.).

8.2.4. Open records act requests.

8.2.5. Motion to produce.

8.2.6. Depositions (available in some states, and at some ALS/ALR proceedings).

8.2.7. Private investigator.

8.2.8. Officer's disciplinary file.

8.2.9. Officer's training records for state police academy central records.

8.3. A disclosure motion filed with the court and properly served upon the prosecutor will cause a list of prosecution witnesses to be produced.

8.4. Reciprocal discovery rules may require your attorney to also disclose to the prosecutor.

8.5. Videotapes are generally discoverable.

8.6. Look for private security video footage from a parking lot or business cameras where your car was stopped.

8.7. Police dispatch tapes and computer-aided dispatch (CAD) logs available from headquarters.

8.8. Any "BOLO" cases likely will have the actual "911" entirely recorded.

8.9. Accident reports from police department that investigated accident.

8.10. Possible use of an accident reconstruction specialist.

8.11. Court rules may allow a prosecutor to file certain special motions (e.g., motion to request to use "prior acts" evidence at trial of current DUI-DWI) to seek to have your judge allow harmful evidence to be used against you at trial.

Chapter 9 - Implied Consent (Informed Consent) (Expressed Consent) Laws: How to Use These Laws to Help You Win the Case.

9.0. Purpose of this chapter.

9.1 Explanation of implied (informed or expressed) consent laws in your state.

9.2. Can a law enforcement officer make the request for an implied consent blood, breath or urine test due to an accident, without gathering any traditional evidence of impairment due to the driver's injuries?

9.3. Does your state require the officer to give a formal, pre-formatted advisement?

9.4. Do your state laws require a valid arrest for DUI-DWI to occur prior to the implied consent advisements being read?

9.5. Does your state mandate when the officer is required to give the implied consent notification, or otherwise lose the right to use the test results against you?

9.6. Are there criminal penalties for refusing testing?

9.7. What are the driving restrictions or loss of license penalties for refusal?

9.8. Can you refuse testing in your state?

9.9. Does the procedure used in your state comply with *California v. Trombetta*?

9.10. Is the sample being requested for implied consent usable for possible other crimes?

9.11. Do you have the right of counsel before agreeing to submit to the state's test (or refusing to submit)?

9.12. Which instruments are approved in your state for roadside preliminary breath testing?

9.13. Is the preliminary breath testing device in your state part of the implied consent law, or is it a non-evidential test?

9.14. Is the officer required to advise you of your right to an independent test of blood, breath or urine?

9.15. If you request an independent test, does the officer have to reasonably accommodate that request?

9.16. If you want to request an independent test, do you have to first submit to the State's test?

9.17. For breath testing, what is your state's observation period (deprivation period) prior to taking the test?

9.18. How does implied consent law affect the administrative license suspension hearing in your case?

      9.18.1. Appeals from an Adverse Ruling from an Administrative Court.

      9.18.2. Winning or Losing the Administrative Hearing Will Not Affect the Criminal Case Afterward.

9.19. If you don't understand English, and the implied consent was read to you in English, how does this affect the state's tests?

9.20. If the officer misstates information or goes beyond the information required by your state's laws to be told to you, can this additional information result in your test result (or refusal) being excluded?

9.21. If you are forced to submit to testing after you verbally refused to cooperate, can the State seek to take away your driving privileges even though they have collected your blood?

9.22. If you are hearing-impaired, does it make a difference that the officer did not utilize an interpreter?

9.23. If you asked to be taken to Acme Hospital for an independent test, and the officer declines because there are closer hospitals, does this matter?

9.24. If you learn that the hospital requires cash or a check for an independent test, and you need to be taken by an ATM machine for money, can the officer decline to do this for you?

9.25. If you have been injured in a collision and (due to injuries) submitting to the breath test would be painful or difficult, does this constitute refusal?

9.26. If you just never answer by saying "yes" or "no" to the request for a forensic test, does this constitute refusal?

Chapter 10 - Understanding Breath, Blood, Urine, Saliva or other Forensic Testing and Your DUI-DWI Case.

10.0. Purpose of this chapter.

10.1. Breath test – most common form of testing.

10.1.1. Does your state require one sample collected or two for there to be a valid test?

10.1.2. If two samples are taken, how closely must the results (numbers) be to each other to constitute a valid test?

10.1.3. Regulations or statutes requiring testing officer to follow specified protocol.

10.1.4. Manner of blowing can alter final results.

10.1.5. Air bag residue may cause elevated readings.

10.1.6. Breath machine error readings and the importance of the follow-up by the testing officer.

10.1.7. Retention of all test cards is mandatory, because they are part of your evidence.

10.1.8. Computer database downloads and vital information from them.

10.1.9. Person doing the testing must be currently certified to run the test.

10.1.10. Periodic calibration checks and service records are critical to your defense.

10.2. Blood test – most reliable and accurate form of testing.

10.2.1. Gas chromatography for alcohol tests.

10.2.2. GC-MS (gas chromatography mass spectrophotometry) for drug analysis.

10.2.3. Get the entire set of records for the batch that was run, if possible.

10.2.4. Obtain discovery on how the standards were created for checking the alcohol accuracy for gas chromatography.

10.2.5. Get the retention time manual for the GC-MS device used to analyze drugs to assure that the peak was at the expected retention time.

10.2.6. Get service records for any blood test device.

10.2.7. Look for breaks in the "chain of custody" from collection to final analysis.

10.2.8. Independent tests to confirm or refute.

10.2.9. DNA is possible for comparing the blood allegedly collected by police and the defendant's.

10.2.10. Be cautious to not accept an immunoassay test for any "quantitative" drug results, without a confirmatory GC-MS.

10.3. Urine test – usually reserved for drugs and then only to determine presence of a class of drugs.

    10.3.1. If quantitative analysis of either drugs or alcohol is being used by the prosecutor, get expert witness to assist in refuting the results.

    10.3.2. Pooling is always a problem with urine testing.

    10.3.3. Urine will reveal low levels of contraband drugs longer than a blood test.

10.4. Saliva is not used for forensic alcohol testing, due to small volume, but is good for drug screening or DNA sampling.

10.5. Destruction of biologic samples of blood or urine prior to the defense being able to independently test the samples.

Chapter 11 - Understanding the Importance of Administrative License Suspension or Revocation Laws and their Interplay with Your DUI-DWI Case

11.0. Purpose of this chapter.

11.1. Administrative license suspension (or revocation) [ALS/ALR] proceedings almost always occur prior to criminal court date.

11.2. ALS/ALR proceedings are civil in nature, and often allow civil discovery usage.

11.3. ALS/ALR judges can be attorneys or non-attorneys (called "hearing officers" in some jurisdictions), so the fairness and due process compliance varies from state to state.

11.4. Your arresting officer may not be required to attend ALS/ALR hearings, so your attorney may need to subpoena the officer to force him or her to attend or to bring any records.

11.5. Your attendance at the ALS/ALR hearing may be waived in most jurisdictions, unless you need to testify.

11.6. Often, it is best not to show your "hand" to the state during the ALS/ALR hearings, and use the proceeding to obtain more information that may assist in winning the criminal case.

11.7. ALS/ALR proceedings may offer the chance to "negotiate" with the officer (or the state attorney handling the ALS/ALR) to withdraw the proposed suspension/revocation.

11.8. In some states, the same criminal prosecutor handles the ALS/ALR and the criminal proceedings, but in others this does not apply.

11.9. Use of a certified court reporter may be advisable, if the proceedings are merely tape recorded, so that a certified record of the sworn testimony can be used later in the criminal case.

11.10. Obtaining the video tape of the arrest or breath testing during the ALS/ALR hearing can be important to facilitate the criminal case.

11.11. The issues at the ALS/ALR hearing are limited, so your attorney may only be able to explore a limited number of points relating to the criminal case.

11.12. A knowledgeable attorney will know the pluses and minuses of holding the hearing versus possibly seeking to negotiate a withdrawal of the "hard" suspension that could occur.

11.13. Success rate for contested ALS/ALR cases varies from state to state, with some attorneys in some states reporting 80% or more retention of license, to 10% on low side.

Chapter 12 - Your Attorney's Pre-Trial Activities.

12.0. The purpose of this chapter.

12.1. Working behind the scenes.

12.2. Using an investigator to get answers that the attorney cannot.

12.3. Being "connected" without being a crook.

12.4. Timely and targeted filing of pleadings is critical.

12.5. Assisting you in hiring an expert to consult or testify.

12.6. Arraignment (where you plead guilty or not guilty) and a point in the case where certain motions and challenges might be required.

12.7. Pre-trial conferences with the prosecutor or the judge (with the prosecutor also participating).

12.8. Pre-trial motion hearings.

12.9. Being on a trial calendar.

12.10. Letting your attorney decide who (if anyone) testifies.

12.11. Preparing jury "charges" (instructions).

12.12. Being ready for the worst case scenario.

12.13. Your attorney's "time and expertise."

12.14. Be realistic and be flexible.

12.15. Compromise — it may be the best bet for you.

12.16. When "no deals" are available: your decision.

Chapter 13 - Opting For a Trial or Seeking a "Negotiated" or "Blind" Plea: Deciding What Option To Take?

13.0. Purpose of this chapter.

13.1. Getting a handle on your case.

13.2. Evaluating the "quality" of your case.

13.3. Evaluating the fairness of the assigned judge.

13.4. Evaluating the prosecutor's experience, "relationships" and "personal charisma."

13.5. In your jurisdiction, do you even get a jury trial?

13.6. Where do you find good jurors and bad jurors in your state?

13.7. If convicted, who sentences you?

13.8. Is a "deferred adjudication," diversion, "CWOF," "PBJ," or a "plea in abeyance" possible?

13.9. Is a "first offender" plea an option, to keep your long-term record clean?

Chapter 18 - Appeal, Motion for New Trial, Supersedeas Bond, Expungement and Other Post-Conviction Issues that Your Attorney May Assert on Your Behalf

Chapter 19 - Understanding Habitual Violator (Habitual Offender) Laws in Relationship to DUI-DWI Laws

Chapter 20 - Boating and Flying Under the Influence and Other Related "Impaired Operation" Laws.

20.0. Purpose of this chapter.

20.1. Boating under the influence or boating while intoxicated (BUI-BWI).

    20.1.1. Statutory wording — common law offense - alcohol.

    20.1.2. Statutory wording — per se offense — alcohol.

    20.1.3. Statutory wording — common law offense - drugs.

    20.1.4. Statutory wording — per se offense — contraband drugs.

    20.1.5. Statutory wording — inhalants or noxious vapors.

    20.1.6. Statutory wording — combination of two or more impairing substances.

20.2. "BUI-BWI - prescribed drugs" can call for a higher standard.

20.3. "Presumptions" (inferences) arising from test results.

20.4. Implied consent.

20.5. Implied consent not withdrawn by death or loss of consciousness.

20.6. Refusal admissible into evidence.

20.7. Underage boating under the influence.

20.8. "Nolo contendere" or "Alford" plea — are they allowed?

20.9. Child endangerment in a vessel.

20.10. Reckless operation of vessel or other water device.

20.11. Homicide by vessel.

20.12. Feticide by vessel.

20.13. Serious injury by vessel.

20.14. Implied consent warnings.

20.15. Administrative suspension/revocation of boating (and possibly driving) privileges for refusing to submit to testing.

20.16. Administrative suspension/revocation of boating (and possibly driving) privileges submitting to testing and being over the legal limit.

20.17. Requesting a hearing — timing and letter requirement.

20.18. Term of suspension.

20.19. Penalties if convicted.

20.20. What constitutes reasonable suspicion to stop a boat, versus stopping a motor vehicle on the highway?

20.21. Is reasonable suspicion even required to stop a boat?

20.22. Administrative regulations pertaining to boating use.

20.23. Flying under the influence.

    20.23.1. Federal law also has jurisdiction, so possible double judicial proceedings since two sovereigns.

Appendix E - Samples of Implied Consent (Informed Consent) Warnings

California

Michigan

Florida

Washington

Georgia

Appendix F - Types of Alcohol

Appendix G - Alcoholics Anonymous and Alternatives

Appendix H - Penalties for Refusal to Submit to State-administered Testing of Your Blood, Breath or Urine under Implied (Informed) Consent Laws

Appendix I - Checklist of Challenging Forensic (Blood or Breath) Tests in DUI-DWI Cases

A.   Whether the blood sample was timely withdrawn by a person legally qualified to do so.

B.   Whether an adequate chain of identification and custody can be established by the prosecution.

C.   Whether a legally authorized and scientifically reliable method of chemical testing was employed.

D.   Whether the chemical test employed in this case was properly performed by a qualified person.

CHECKLIST FOR DETECTION OF SCIENTIFIC ERROR IN BLOOD TESTING

A.   The withdrawal, preservation, and labeling of the defendant's blood sample.

B.   Whether the blood sample obtained from the defendant was representative of the blood needed for testing.

C.   Whether the integrity of the blood sample was maintained through the completion of testing.

D.   Whether the defendant's blood sample was properly and accurately tested.

E.   Whether adequate steps were taken to detect the presence of random or human error in the performance of the chemical test.

F.   Whether adequate steps were taken to detect the presence of systematic error in the laboratory or clinic where the blood sample was tested.

CHECKLIST FOR DETECTION OF FOUNDATIONAL ERROR IN BREATH TESTING

A.   Whether the method of testing used is scientifically accurate and reliable.

B. Whether the testing equipment used was in proper working order when the test was administered to the defendant.

C. Whether the breath testing equipment was properly operated by a qualified person.

D. Whether the breath test was administered within the required period.

CHECKLIST FOR DETECTION OF SCIENTIFIC ERROR IN BREATH TESTING

A. The defense of a lower partition ratio.

B. The defense of testing during absorption and the rising BAC defense.

C. Defenses related to the integrity of the breath sample.

D. The defense of simulator test error.

E. The defense of radio frequency interference.

F. Defenses related to the preservation of a sample of the defendant's breath.

Appendix J – Sample Client Questionnaire

Appendix K – Selected Provisions from the United States Constitution

DEDICATION

First, this book is dedicated to the thousands of clients who have entrusted their most serious legal problem to my care, seeking a favorable resolution. Their collective courage in putting their freedom, driving privileges and futures on the line by persevering through difficult and uncertain legal terrain, against all odds, have been an inspiration and a motivator for me to continue fighting these politically-charged cases. I hope that this book will inspire more citizens to fight for their legal rights through courts across America in the quest to assure that the Constitution is applied to impaired driving cases the same way that it is to a capital murder prosecution.

I also must thank my father, the late Louis B. Head, who convinced me early in life to not take the easy road to life's challenges. From extolling the importance and inherent value of hard work to fanatically training me to never quit at sports, he drilled discipline and competitiveness into my very psyche. His stories and words of praise about successful criminal defense attorneys winning difficult criminal trials through dedication and perseverance made quite an impression on me as a teenager.

Finally, thanks must be given to my wife, Kristen Campbell-Head, Esq., for sacrificing hundreds of nights and weekends of personal time for me to tackle this book. Her acceptance and understanding of the importance of this endeavor were essential to me being able to complete the book.

W.C.H.
April 17, 2006

"If it was easy, everybody would be doing it."
- Louis B. Head, 1915-1973

ACKNOWLEDGEMENTS

The original idea for this book arose from concern for the anxiety my clients expressed to me when they hired me to undertake their legal defense in DUI-DWI cases. Most of them have expressed similar concerns and asked similar questions over the 30 years that I have done this work. I felt that this book would provide a source of comfort to them by providing information and answers about the various stages of the trial process, including appeal.

Next, the person who helped me push the book to completion was Bob Baska, MD-JD. A talented author himself, Bob stumbled across my path as a third year law student assisting the prosecutor in a bench trial against me in a DUI trial of one of my clients in Gwinnett County State Court in early 2005. Bob's supervisor, Joe Loiselle, later called me to recommend that I hire Bob after his law school graduation in May of 2005, due to the fact that Bob could no longer assist the prosecutor's office under Georgia's "third-year practice act."

Another "thank you" goes to two law students who assisted me in the early phases of editing the book, Wes Jacobs and Chris Quin.

Julie Dymond-Donaldson, one of my stellar paralegals, assisted me tremendously through her close proofreading of the entire book, seeking to clarify any hard-to-understand passages. Her editing skills, derived from her training at the University of Georgia and at Georgia State University, were indispensable to me.

Further I would like to thank my wife, Kristen Campbell-Head, Esq., for her input and suggestions regarding changes to some of the legal and procedural provisions in the book. Her experience as a former prosecutor and criminal defense trial attorney in California helped me broaden my perspectives and resulted in improvement of many of the book's suggestions on how cases can be successfully fought.

In an effort to make the book easy to understand, I asked my 12-year old daughter, Lauren Ansley Head, to read over the text. She made numerous valuable suggestions regarding complex terms or legal jargon. I know that her input made the book more user-friendly.

I also want to thank Allison Valdes, my dedicated and loyal paralegal, who keeps me in court and (with Julie Donaldson's invaluable support and contributions) resolves my never-ending trial and seminar scheduling conflicts. Allison and Julie cover me when I am in court and coordinate the appearance of other attorneys who assist me in dozens of courts across Georgia. This assistance enabled me to finish this book.

William C. Head
Atlanta, Georgia
April 17, 2006

CHAPTER ONE

An Overview and Historic Perspective
of DUI-DWI Laws in America

In an attempt to explain DUI-DWI law to the non-lawyer in the most effective and understandable format, I chose simply to start from the beginning, with a review of the history and common terminology of this exploding area of criminal litigation. To explain to you how these cases are won and lost, I must review applicable case law (appellate court decisions) and examples of statutory law (legislative acts passed within each jurisdiction) relating to drunk driving defense. Changes to DUI-DWI law occur *daily* across America, and the first few years of the new Millennium have seen dramatic changes to this increasingly more important area of criminal law.

As the author of a treatise with daily changes in case law and statutory law, the task of staying current is daunting. Because a printed book cannot "stay current," this book identifies more than 250 helpful web sites, Internet resources, books available for purchase or from libraries, legal research tools and contact information for the user to be able to gather MORE information after identifying a topic or legal issue of interest. It is my purpose to provide an accurate overview of the laws applicable to DUI-DWI across America, and to help the reader locate top-notch legal counsel or written resources to help explain particular state law questions.

I hope that this "down-to-earth" treatment of a complex and ever-expanding subject will provide ready access to critical statutory wording and case law that may open an avenue of help to any person facing drunken driving charges. The book is written to be a "life line" for the person accused of this crime. For novice attorneys who are learning about the legal landscape of impaired driving and the unique legal concepts about this harshly punished body of law, the book (hopefully) will convince you to team up with an experienced legal expert in this field rather than attempt a trial against an experienced prosecutor who handles these cases daily. As many criminal defense veterans can attest, it is easier to defend a murder case than a DUI-DWI charge.

Because additional research or copies of legal cases may be needed, **Appendix A** of this book is provided to assist a non-lawyer to find more information from the case citations and statutory references set forth in this book. Over 1000 appellate cases from every jurisdiction in America are cited in these pages as well as approximately 300 statutory references and "linked" web pages. By following the "legal research tips" in **Appendix A**, you can get copies of key cases cited in this book, possibly locate an analogous case in your state, or locate local statutes at no cost or at a very reasonable cost.

Ultimately, hiring a skilled and experienced criminal defense lawyer who specializes or limits his/her practice to drunken driving defense is the wisest thing to do. (See **Chapter 4** for a review of how to select the best available driving under the influence trial attorney for your case). ***CAUTION:*** *A DUI-DWI case is not a good type of trial to try to handle alone!* No more than you would try to remove your own appendix should you try to be your own attorney in fighting your DUI-DWI case, with the stakes as high as they are in these cases. (See **Chapters 11, 13 and 17**).

Facing your drunk (or drugged) driving charges is a bewildering experience. You may be shocked by the aggressive attitude of the prosecutor in pursuing a case that you feel favors your innocence. Many clients ask *"Can't the prosecutor see that I'm a good person who deserves a break?"*

One of the primary purposes of this chapter is to explain why prosecutors are either extremely reluctant or possibly even legally prohibited by state statute from reducing or dropping a DUI-DWI case. Our laws have become so punitive and all-encompassing over the past quarter century that it is clear that this trend will only get worse. Once you understand and accept this, you can focus on taking the necessary steps to **WIN** your case and stop wasting valuable time pontificating on how unfair the laws on DUI-DWI are.

1.1. UNDERSTANDING THE OFFENSE. Today, you do not have to be "drunk" on alcohol or "stoned" on drugs to be convicted of DUI-DWI. You do not have to "intentionally" consume too much alcohol and then operate a car, truck or other "motorized" vehicle to be arrested for drunken driving. The vehicle you are in need not be moving, or the engine running for you to be at risk of being charged with and convicted of drunk driving.

None of the foregoing assumptions is true today in America. Our impaired driving laws have been continuously broadened over the past 25 years and have been made increasingly broad in their reach on an annual basis. Presently, in many states, you can be on a dirt road, sitting on your recreational 4-wheel ATV in the middle of your own private 4000-acre farm, with the key in the ignition and the engine off, and still be arrested for DUI-DWI.

One overriding "trend" has emerged nationwide in DUI-DWI law, and that is the steady erosion of a citizen's rights in the field of constitutional law, criminal law and criminal procedure. Egregiously bad case law and pro-conviction statutory enactments have created what one noted legal scholar and drunken driving guru calls ***"The DUI Exception to the Constitution."***[1]

1.1.1. A Brief History of the First 100 Years of Our DUI-DWI Laws. From the earliest days of wheeled transportation (or even when we only had four-legged beasts as vehicles), intoxicated "operators" have chosen to drink excessively and then try to travel to their chosen destination. An intoxicated cowboy who rode his horse back to the ranch after playing poker and swigging whiskey at the saloon seldom caused anyone a problem, but the *potential* to pose a danger to others certainly existed. If he drunkenly raced through town on his horse while pedestrians walked across the dirt streets of Dodge City, an innocent person could be killed or seriously injured by such action. In those days, no laws specifically prohibited such dangerous drunken acts, however.[2]

An English law passed in 1872 first made the operating of a steam-powered vehicle while intoxicated illegal and punishable by a prison sentence in Great Britain.[3] In 1904, the first reported news article in America appeared concerning automobiles and a drunken driving accident. From this inauspicious beginning approximately 10 years after "motorized cars" were introduced in America, an increasing number of news reports of impaired driving cases began to appear in periodicals. In England, the first vehicle death from an automobile-pedestrian collision (not involving alcohol) was reported in 1896:

---

[1] To read Lawrence Taylor's excellent treatment of this subject, go to: http://www.drunkdrivingdefense.com/general/lawrence-taylor.htm.

[2] Riding a horse while intoxicated today is defined specifically as not being DUI in certain states, PA [**Com. v. Noel,** 857 A.2d 1283 (Pa. 2004)] and Utah, [**State v. Blowers,** 717 P.2d 1321 (Utah 1986)].

[3] http://www.scienceservingsociety.com/ts/text/ch10.htm.

"On 17th August 1896 Bridget Driscoll was killed in Crystal Palace by a horseless carriage traveling at 4 m.p.h. This was the first reported traffic fatality to occur in Great Britain and the start of a problem that has now grown to epidemic proportions."[4]

Today, reports of accidents, particularly those involving suspected drunken drivers, dominate the police blotter and televised news reports of most media outlets across America. A DUI-DWI traffic accident with a fatality is far more likely to make the evening news today than a child molestation case.

In 1910, New York became the first state to enact "drunk driving" laws. Dozens of other states followed suit, with states such as New Mexico (in 1919) providing fines up to $1000 and one year in jail on a DUI-DWI conviction. An average year's income for many *families* in 1919 in New Mexico did not equal $1000! In current dollars, that would be the equivalent of $11,289.00 in 2005.[5]

In 1938, Professor Rolla N. Harger, chair of the Department of Biochemistry at the Indiana University School of Medicine, invented the first crude, analytical breath testing device, the "Drunkometer®." The early breath-testing devices required the person being tested to blow into a balloon (to regulate the size of the collected breath sample). The exhaled breath in the balloon was then passed over chemicals that changed color in the presence of alcohol. The extent of the color change, measured by photoelectric cells, revealed the approximate amount of alcohol in the sample. Professor Harger died in 1983.[6]

Over the succeeding seven decades, there have been six succeeding generations of breath alcohol testing instruments.[7] Current machines have dual wavelength testing capabilities and breath temperature adjustment technology available. The idea behind "improved" technology is that these devices are better at estimating a person's true blood alcohol level, without additive error (as a result of factors or conditions that increase the reported BAC level on the device) from a variety of sources, including operator error.

In 1939, following Dr. Harger's invention, Indiana became the first state in America to set a presumptive alcohol impairment limit at 0.15%. Other states did not immediately act to implement similar laws, until a national study in 1946 by a government agency suggested it for all states seven years later.

Shortly after Harger launched his new machine, another scientist released a second-generation machine. Dr. Glenn C. Forrester of St. Louis, Missouri, was working on a similar device, which he called the "Intoximeter®." After World War II, Michigan instituted the first statewide breath-testing program using the early model of the Intoximeter®, and Dr. Forrester founded a company called Intoximeters, Inc., which still provides a variety of breath testing instruments.[8]

In 1946, the first national highway safety conference was conducted by the National Committee on Uniform Traffic Laws and Ordinances.[9] The ever-increasing number of vehicles on the highway following World War II due to post-war production and full employment also led

---

[4]http://www.itsnottingham.info/ttart1.htm.

[5]http://data.bls.gov/cgi-bin/cpicalc.pl.

[6]*See* http://www.soundmedicine.iu.edu/archive/2003/quiz/drunkometer.html for more information on the Drunkometer or Dr. Harger.

[7]Dr. A. W. Jones, lecture on breath testing in Atlanta, GA, December 4, 2004, Intoxilyzer 5000 training program.

[8]http://www.intox.com/

[9]http://www.ncutlo.org/

to a staggering number of highway accidents involving injuries and deaths. The federal study recommended setting a standard level for blood alcohol impairment at 0.15%, so that states would have some "target" in determining when a driver was presumably impaired. This "number," incidentally, had been recommended as the correct standard by the American Medical Association (AMA). The AMA determined that this was the "accepted" level for impairment based upon their research. More about the AMA and its "research" will follow later in this chapter.

In 1953, New York was the first state in America to pass a new type of law aimed at forcing drunken drivers to submit to blood, breath or urine tests, if an officer who had stopped a car had sufficient evidence to support a reasonable belief that the driver was impaired by alcohol. Laws of this type became known as "implied consent" laws. The phrase "implied consent" or "informed consent" is used in virtually every state. The theory behind the New York statute was that any person who used the highways of New York "implicitly" consented to giving his or her permission for a blood sample to be collected for use as possible evidence at trial. Implied consent laws were based upon a legal fiction, however, because drivers had not, in fact, actually given such consent.

A refusal to submit to testing was possible under New York's law and similar laws of other states, but the driver would have his or her license suspended for 12 months for not submitting. Today, 100% of the jurisdictions in the USA have such laws with varying periods of license suspension or revocation for any refusal to submit to testing. Increasingly, however, more and more states no longer permit a person to refuse to be tested, and will resort to brute force to obtain a blood or urine sample when a "breath test" is declined. Other states have opted to not use force to take the sample, but may put the driver in jail for his or her "refusal" to give a sample.

In 1954, Robert Borkenstein of Indiana invented the Breathalyzer® breath testing instrument. This was a third generation device. This machine was a tremendous improvement over all prior designs and dominated sales of such devices in the United States for nearly 20 years. An improved version of his original device still remains in use in a few jurisdictions more than fifty years after its introduction.

Borkenstein, a former Indiana state trooper, became one of the best known and loved figures in alcohol-related highway safety. In 1962, he was appointed chairman of Indiana University's newly formed Department of Police Administration. He also started a well-known national training program on alcohol testing and the science behind the testing. The "Borkenstein" course, which is still attended by over one hundred state forensic scientists and police officers per year, continues today.[10] Dr. Borkenstein died in August of 2002 at age 89.

In 1956, President Dwight D. Eisenhower convinced Congress to authorize building the Interstate Highway System. Inspired by the German Autobahn when his troops occupied Germany during World War II, Eisenhower understood the immense value to national commerce and travel such a system would create. This highway system has created changes in mobility for Americans that was unheard of fifty years ago. As this relates to DUI-DWI, the transient drinking driver who has multiple DUI-DWI arrests in various states is now tracked via a national database of all state administrations of the 51 offices of DMV-DPS-BMV-SOS (driver's license issuance) offices.[11]

---

[10] http://www.indiana.edu/~lawactn/faculty/borkenstein/borkenstein.html

[11] http://www.drunkdrivingdefense.com/national/dps-offices.htm

A detailed study of accidents related to alcohol use was conducted in 1964 in the so-called "Grand Rapids" (Michigan) Study. The causal relationship between a higher incidence of motor vehicle crashes and elevated alcohol content levels was explored by this study. The report showed a significant increase in fatalities for drivers who had blood alcohol levels of 0.08 grams or more, and that the higher the BAC (blood alcohol content), the greater the percentage of deaths in DUI-DWI collisions. This set in motion state and federal legislative momentum to start lowering acceptable alcohol levels for drivers. The first two states to enact a BAC level lower than 0.15% for their respective states were Nebraska and New York in 1972.

In the late 1960s, the Department of Transportation and the National Highway Traffic Safety Administration had begun showing legislators and the public statistics (and graphic photographs) of the staggering number of deaths attributable to traffic crashes in general and alcohol-related crashes in particular. A few drunk driving laws were passed setting a lower alcohol level for drinking drivers, but these laws stipulated that a 0.10% BAC (or 0.12% BAC in some states) only created a "presumption" that an individual might be intoxicated; the charge of intoxication was still rebuttable (contestable) by the accused driver.

One public health scientist, Patricia Waller, summed up the prevailing nonchalant attitude of the American public in those days by observing:

"Drunk driving was considered more or less a 'folk crime,' almost a rite of passage for young males. Most adults in the United States used alcohol, and most of them, at some point, drove after doing so. This is not to say they drove drunk, but many of them undoubtedly drove when they were somewhat impaired. Although the law provided for fairly harsh penalties, they were rarely applied. Upon arraignment, defendants would ask for a jury trial, and because drinking and driving was so widespread, juries almost invariably acquitted the defendant, thinking, 'There but for the grace of God go I.'"[12]

In 1970, the federal government put out a proposal for bids to a variety of "research" scientists seeking to develop a standardized battery of "field sobriety tests" that could assist police across America in identifying DUI-DWI suspects who were proper candidates to arrest for suspected impaired driving from excessive alcohol consumption. NHTSA, a division of the United States Department of Transportation, eventually approved a group of scientists at the Southern California Research Institute (SCRI) based in Los Angeles, California. The primary authors of the final study and report were Dr. Marcelline Burns, Ph.D. and Dr. Herbert Moskowitz, Ph.D. Millions of taxpayer dollars were committed to this project, and the final product generated in 1983 was called the *National Highway Traffic Safety Administration's "Standardized Field Sobriety Tests."*[13] Attorneys in the DUI-DWI business call these the ***"NHTSA SFSTs."***

The first "SFST manual" was very short, and published in 1984. It received little attention at the time. Updated and "improved" NHTSA manuals were produced under NHTSA's authority in 1987, 1989, 1992, 1995, 2000, 2002 and 2004, with each manual systematically dropping the original study's safeguards to the public that were designed to prevent false arrests of persons who might smell of alcohol, but not be impaired at all. The protections for old and overweight citizens built in by Burns and Moskowitz, while incomplete and of questionable

---

[12]Waller, Patricia F., *Public Health's Contribution to Motor Vehicle Injury Prevention*, Am J Prev Med 2001;21. http://www.thecommunityguide.org/mvoi/mvoi-AJPM-c-pubhlths-contrib.pdf.
[13]http://www.nhtsa.dot.gov/people/injury/enforce/DESKBK.html#SFST.

value, have been all but ignored in the latest manuals for officers. See **Chapter 2** for more detail.

Yet, many police departments in many states do not utilize these evaluations or train their officers to follow the highly systematized "three test battery" of NHTSA's standardized evaluations. Parts of **Chapter 2** are dedicated to a thorough review of these standardized evaluations as well as the "other" field evaluations used by police that have no scientific studies to back up their reliability and no empirical foundation for claimed accuracy whatsoever. Arrests that are made using such evaluations are not even as reliable as flipping a coin in deciding whether to arrest a citizen based on random chance.

In 1972, Nebraska and New York passed the first laws stating that driving with a 0.10 blood alcohol content was conclusively "illegal per se." When thinking of this kind of DUI-DWI law, the phrase "driving while having an unlawful blood alcohol level" is more descriptive. No evidence of impaired ability to drive is needed to support a conviction under such laws. These laws were based on the fact that at 0.10%, any person, regardless of tolerance to alcohol, was (as a matter of state "public safety" policy) significantly less capable of operating a motor vehicle. By 1979, twelve states had set an illegal per se limit, all of them at 0.10% except New Hampshire which set that state's *per se* limit at 0.15%.

In 1976, Minnesota became the first state to enact an "Administrative License Revocation" law. Also called "Administrative License Suspension" laws in some states, this type of law had been recommended by NHTSA as a means of suspending or revoking an accused DUI-DWI driver's driving privileges before the case could come to trial on the underlying criminal charges. The concept for these laws was that any person who submitted to testing and rendered a test result equal to or greater than the state's presumed "impairment" level would be summarily suspended or revoked for a period of time. These proceedings were civil or administrative in nature, to avoid double jeopardy concerns. Now, whether a driver refused testing and suffered an implied consent penalty of loss of license for not taking the State's test, any driver who submitted and had a result equal to or greater than the state's legal limit would also suffer a suspension or revocation. *Damned if you do and damned if you don't.*

Neither the press nor the public paid much attention to the all the new activity of the dozen or more states that were passing new laws setting illegal *per se* limits. This lack of concern was reflected by a two-inch article printed in the October 16, 1979 edition of the *New York Times*, which noted that an all-time record number of people had been killed in "road accidents" in 1978 --- 50,145 people.

In 1980, the National Highway Traffic Safety Administration published its first "issue paper" on illegal *per se* and the benefits of using preliminary breath testing devices to screen drivers at the roadside. NHTSA also proposed model language for both types of "alcohol" based laws so that states could easily adopt new laws embracing these changes. A huge shift in the federal government's attitude toward "drunk driving" and accidents was about to occur, triggered primarily by some grieving mothers---and fathers---who spoke long and loud about the embarrassing lack of national attention being paid to "problem" drivers and DUI-DWI crashes causing serious injuries and fatalities.

1.1.2. The Ascendancy of M.A.D.D. and other Political Action Groups. A California woman named Candace (Candy) Lightner lost her 13-year old daughter, Cari, to a drunk driver in May of 1980. Cari was struck from behind and killed as she walked to a friend's house.

Candy Lightner soon heard about Cindy Lamb, a Maryland mother who --- six months before --- had survived a devastating accident with a drunk driver who struck her vehicle head-on while traveling at 120 miles per hour. In the November 1979 crash, her five-month old daughter Laura Lamb was rendered a quadriplegic. Both of the drivers in these cases had atrocious driving histories, including prior DUI-DWI convictions.

The efforts of these two mothers led to a national movement of citizens — mostly mothers of victims — that eventually became known as M.A.D.D. M.A.D.D. was originally named "Mothers Against Drunk Drivers," but the name was changed to focus on the *conduct* rather than the "person" behind the wheel. This group's success has led to at least a dozen other groups being formed with similar public awareness or political influence agendas (R.I.D.[14], S.A.D.D.,[15] R.A.D.D.,[16] etc.)

M.A.D.D. has been able to dramatically influence tougher DUI-DWI legislation in every jurisdiction in America. Raising $50,000,000 each year has facilitated M.A.D.D.'s political activities.[17] Lobbying efforts, letter-writing campaigns, picketing, fund-raising and similar activities have resulted in M.A.D.D. becoming one of the best-known and most widely funded non-profit groups in America. In the last 20 years, approximately 2500 legislative bills or laws have been submitted to legislators across America as a result of their movement. This source of pressure to increase punishment for all DUI-DWI offenders is the leading cause of the major changes in drunken driving legislation in America over the past twenty years.

Although M.A.D.D. denies being on a mission to re-institute Prohibition, many critics believe that this powerful group intends exactly for that to ultimately happen.[18] As recently as October, 2005, MADD was calling for the "per se" limit to be lowered to 0.05% on a national basis and in Canada.[19] Other politically motivated groups [such as the Mobil Eyes Foundation - which has Internal Revenue Code 501(c)(3) non-profit tax status] have started offering "bounties" ($50) for calling the "911" operator and reporting people who the caller believes are driving drunk, if such information leads to a DUI-DWI conviction.[20]

1.1.3. The Common Acronyms (Abbreviations) for "Drunk Driving" Used Across the USA. Although "DUI" is the most widely used acronym in the United States for the crime of "drunk driving," more than a dozen other abbreviated "names" for drunken driving are utilized across America. State legislatures write the impaired driving laws in each state, and there are 51 (including the District of Columbia) different sets of laws. While D.U.I. typically stands for "driving under the influence," other states have worded their laws differently, such as D.W.I. ("driving while intoxicated" or "driving while impaired"). In other states, the legislature defined the offense as "operating," not "driving." Hence, some states use "O.U.I." ("operating under the influence") or O.W.I. ("operating while intoxicated" or "operating while impaired").

One overriding concept should be understood: ***alcohol is NOT the only impairing substance of which a person is prohibited from being under the influence.*** All states prohibit impaired driving from almost all drugs --- illegal, prescribed, liquid, tablet, vapors, injected, snorted --- whether contraband or merely over-the-counter medications. Being given a prescription for medication by a doctor or merely picking up a bottle of liquid or tablet

---

[14]http://www.rid-usa.org/

[15]http://www.sadd.org/

[16]http://www.radd.org/

[17]http://www.duiblog.com/2004/10/20.

[18]See http://www.drunkdrivingdefense.com/publications-articles/anti-alcohol-madd.htm written by John Doyle and also Radley Balko's article "When Drunk Driving Deterrence Becomes Neo-Prohibition" which can be found at http://www.foxnews.com/printer_friendly_story/0,3566,171383,00.html.

[19]http://www.fftimes.com/index.php/2005-10-06/22975.

[20]http://www.advancetitan.com/story.asp?issue=11205&story=4182.

medication from the pharmacy section of your grocery store and taking a dose can constitute the basis for "intoxication" if you drive a car later. Even herbs and "health" formulas that you might pick up at a natural food store can reduce a person's awareness or cognitive ability and lead to a DUI-DWI arrest and possible conviction.

The following are the most common acronyms being used across America for various forms of "drinking and driving" acronyms, along with some state abbreviations showing where the acronym is used:

DUI [driving under the influence] (approximately 30 states use this acronym singly or in combination with other acronyms)

DWI [driving while intoxicated or driving while impaired] (TX, NC, LA, NY, MO, NM, KY, AK, AR, MN, NJ)

OWI [operating while under the influence or operating while impaired] (MI, WI, IA) [also sometimes referred to as "OVWI"]

OUI [operating under the influence] (MA, ME, RI) [also sometimes referred to as "OVUI"]

OMVI [operating a motor vehicle while impaired] (OH)

DWAI [driving while ability impaired] (NY, CO)

DUII [driving while under the influence of intoxicants] (OR)

DUI and **DWI** (MD, TN)

DUIL [driving while under the influence of liquor] (MI)

DWUI [driving while under the influence] (WY)

OVWI [operating a vehicle while impaired] (WI)

OVUI [operating a vehicle while under the influence] (MA)

OVI [operating a vehicle under the influence] (OH)

OUIL [operating under the influence of liquor] (NJ, MI)

UBAL [unlawful blood alcohol level] (MI)

In this book, these acronyms will be used interchangeably. Many times, the same acronym ("DUI" or "DUI-DWI") will be used when referring to both DUI-alcohol and DUI-drugs. Regardless of the acronym or the substance causing impairment, a conviction for "drunken driving" or "drugged driving" means TROUBLE!

1.1.4. The Coercive Involvement of the Federal Government. As awareness of the death toll and carnage on our highways obtained top priority in the press, the federal government began to pay close attention to the correlation between alcohol consumption and a driver's reduced ability to drive. In 1983, after President Ronald Reagan's Presidential Commission returned its findings, Congress took its first steps toward passing laws to "encourage" the states to enact laws prohibiting drunk driving. This initial assistance did not provide multi-millions of dollars for the states who took the lead in passing new laws, but suggested that this be done to protect their citizens from being victims of DUI-DWI drivers.

President Reagan then pushed Congress to put some financial incentives into strengthened DUI-DWI laws. A total of $125 million dollars was available to states for the period 1983, 1984 and 1985 *if* the states "conformed" to some mandatory changes in their DUI-DWI laws. This initial "coercion" plan has been followed in each succeeding presidency and by Congress, with money either being offered to implement tougher laws or money being taken away (i.e., withholding highway funds) if a state does not do what the federal government demands. The "strong arm" approach has worked and virtually 100% compliance by the states has been obtained through this method.

The Final Report of President Ronald Reagan's Task Force on Victims of Crime did not address drunk driving, even though this topic was one of the most frequently discussed issues in the nation at that time. That year 25,165 people were reportedly killed in crashes where some alcohol was involved in the accident, according to government statistics. The lack of national attention to victims of drunk drivers at that time was attributable, in part, to the fact that grassroots groups such as Mothers Against Drunk Driving (MADD) were in their infancy, and drunken driving was still considered by most of America to be unavoidable, if not acceptable conduct. The loss of life and injuries from these "accidents" were accepted by the majority of the unaffected American public as merely that --- an accident.

In 1983, however, after $125 million in federal dollars was allocated by Congress to help states fund countermeasures to drunk driving, the drive to end drunk driving began to pick up steam. These new laws became known as *the 410 program,"* based on the federal code section that provided funding (23 U.S.C. § 410). This was the first legislation on a federal level that created either a "carrot-and-stick" approach or (in later years) a "baseball-bat-over-the-head" approach to forcing states to enact laws that the federal government believed would reduce traffic deaths and injuries through lowering alcohol per se levels and adding Draconian punishment to sentences for DUI-DWI offenders. States would either comply or lose huge amounts of federal funding for not "playing ball."

The "Age 21 National Drinking Age Law" was enacted in 1984 to try to force states to increase the drinking age to 21 in all jurisdictions. Failure to do so would cost non-complying states millions in federal funds. Several states resisted this "strong arm" approach and refused to change the law in their state. Louisiana finally capitulated in 1996 and raised the drinking age to 21 after losing tens of millions of federal dollars in highway funding for "holding out" in protest to the federal government "coercion."

In 1986, two significant developments took place. MADD began its first training of volunteers for the purpose of supporting victims of drunk drivers and to serve as "victim advocates" in court proceedings. Also that year, the American Medical Association (the same group that had pushed the 0.15% BAC limit four decades earlier) now publicly supported a new lower BAC level for the United States at 0.05%. Apparently, drivers in America have become less and less capable of ingesting alcohol and then driving since 1946!

The year 1988 was a banner year for anti-DUI legislation in Washington and for several state legislatures. First, still more federal legislation under the "410 program" laws continued to threaten states with withholding funding of roads if they did not pass: (a) the "Age 21" drinking legislation, **plus** (b) pass open container laws **plus** (c) enact Administrative License Suspension/Revocation laws similar to the one first passed by Minnesota. This final part of the federal legislative landslide was the Drunk Driving Prevention Act of 1988, an amendment to the Anti-Drug Abuse Act of 1988. In addition, Congress passed another "funding will be withheld" law called the Transportation Equity Act of 1988.

That same year (1988), the state of Maine, acting on its own, passed one of the most strident laws in America when it became the first state to implement a new, even *lower* BAC "standard" for any repeat offender DUI-DWI suspects. After being first convicted, the new "presumptive" impairment level for those drivers age 21 and over previously convicted of DUI-DWI was 0.05%, not the 0.08% limit allowed for others. Also, to get your Maine driver's license reinstated at all, the previously convicted offender had to agree to consume NO ALCOHOL at all when driving for a period of 10 years. On top of that, additional penalties in the form of fines and possible jail were tacked on for any refusal to submit to testing if suspected of DUI-DWI.

While this flurry of federal and state legislative activity was afoot, the United States Supreme Court in 1990 ruled that "sobriety checkpoints" (roadblocks set up to nab drunk drivers) did not violate the United States Constitution's Fourth Amendment. This left only a state's constitution to protect its citizens from random searches and seizures that have not been authorized by a judge or magistrate (attorneys call these "warrantless searches and seizures," based on the lack of prior issuance of a warrant.)[21]

A national survey sanctioned by M.A.D.D. in 1994 showed that the American public was increasingly less tolerant of drunken drivers and that stiffer punishment for offenders was acceptable to the average man or woman on the street. The constant publicity in the media plus passage of annual federal and state laws increasing punishment had been noticed and embraced by the public.

In 1995, national drunk driving related fatalities rose for the first time in a decade. In response, President Bill Clinton publicly spoke out against impaired driving and announced that all states needed to embrace the 0.08% limit, and stop delaying enactment of such laws.

That same year, Maine swung into action again, passing the first "zero tolerance" law for drivers under the age of 21 who had been consuming alcohol. After this law was passed in Maine, federal legislation was enacted to "encourage" other states to follow Maine's example, and by 1999, every single state in America had done so, rather than lose millions of additional highway dollars.

To complicate this hotbed of federal activity on alcohol-impaired drivers, in 1997, the New England Journal of Medicine published findings from a lengthy study concerning the dangers of cell phone usage. Their conclusion was that a person using a handheld cell phone *was equally as dangerous as "a drunk driver."* Some critics, including leaders of MADD, scoffed at such claims. However, a 2001 study from Canada confirmed the results and demonstrated that a handheld cell phone user *was 38% more likely to be involved in a crash* when talking on the device.

In response, that same year, New York City and several other municipalities within that state enacted the nation's first laws prohibiting use of a handheld cell phone while driving. This legislation has now launched a *new* federal effort to prevent "distracted driving" that will soon rival DUI-DWI legislation. Several states have already passed such laws, with more to follow.

In passing the TEA-21 (Transportation Equity Act for the 21st Century) legislation in 1998, Congress amended the alcohol-impaired driving countermeasures incentive grant program (a successor to the "410" program), which provides extra funding for states that meet certain legislative enactment criteria. Beginning in federal fiscal year 1999, a state could qualify for a basic "410 program grant" by meeting five of seven criteria to qualify for a programmatic basic grant or a performance basic grant. The criteria for the basic grant included a program targeting drivers with a high BAC (blood alcohol content) levels.

According to the final rule issued by NHTSA in 2000, states qualifying under the high-BAC criteria must demonstrate the establishment of a graduated sanctioning system that assesses enhanced or additional sanctions (punishments) to drivers convicted of alcohol-impaired driving if they were determined to have a high BAC. To qualify as a high BAC system under this law, the state's BAC threshold must be higher than the BAC level for the standard DUI-DWI offense and also less than or equal to 0.20 percent BAC. Some states have passed laws making 0.15% their "number," while others passed laws holding 0.16% to 0.20% as their

---

[21]**Michigan Dept. of State Police v. Sitz,** 496 U.S. 444, 110 S.Ct. 2481, 110 L.Ed.2d 412 (1990).

"high number." More about enhanced punishment for high BAC offenders will be covered in **Section 1.7.1** of this chapter.

The enhanced sanctions must be mandatory, must apply to the first (and subsequent) DUI-DWI offense, and may include longer terms of license suspension, increased fines, additional or extended sentences of confinement, vehicle sanctions, or mandatory assessment and treatment as appropriate. The enhanced sanctions may be provided by state law, regulation, or binding policy directive implementing or interpreting the law or regulation. The majority of states have now enacted some form of "enhanced" punishment laws, and all will eventually pass such legislation.

In the year 2000, 41,821 people were killed in traffic crashes. Using government "statistics," 16,653 of these were related to alcohol.[22] Utah was the first state to voluntarily adopt the 0.08% BAC law in 1983. Twenty-two years later, after federal legislation was passed in October 2000 (at President Bill Clinton's request) threatening to withhold billions of additional federal dollars from states that did not enact new laws implementing the 0.08% standard, all states finally capitulated. Most states complied within the next two legislative sessions, with 100% of the states now falling into line with this federal mandate. Minnesota reluctantly became the final state to pass the law, effective August 1, 2005.

On June 16th, 2005, the Senate of the United States put forward another giant highway bill pushing states to adopt even stiffer penalties for three categories of drunken drivers: repeat offenders, those with very high blood-alcohol levels (greater than 0.15%), and those whose licenses were suspended for DUI-DWI but who kept driving anyway. The debate in the House has started. Expect new, tougher DUI-DWI laws to be passed soon and even more federal legislation in future years. One noted author, Lawrence Taylor, writes about his predictions for DUI-DWI laws at: http://www.duiblog.com/2005/02/23#a111.

Additionally, the Internet has provided a "pulpit" for various special interest groups to discuss pro-prosecution issues on web sites[23] as well as outspoken advocates against police officers that cheat and the Draconian punishments handed down in garden-variety DUI-DWI cases.[24]

Make no mistake - - - Big Brother has spoken. You will do as we say or your highway funds will die!

1.1.5. The Criminal Defense Bar Gets Organized. As the M.A.D.D. movement began rolling and gathering steam and political clout, every DUI-DWI law in America was radically changed. The 1983 legislation by President Ronald Reagan pushed states to meet the three mandatory "minimum standards" of that federal legislation: (1) pass a law making it illegal to operate a vehicle while the person's alcohol level was 0.10 or more, regardless of impairment; (2) imposition of a license suspension of not less that 90 days for any driver who refused to be tested for sobriety; (3) imposition of at least 48 hours in jail and 10 days community service on any repeat offenders within a 5-year period.

These new laws were a shocking change for many accused drinking drivers. In the past, a typical statute might contain provisions stating that drivers with alcohol levels of 0.15% or more would be "presumed" to be impaired. This new standard was considerably lower and a

---

[22]**Driving Under-the-Influence (DUI) Statistics**, California Dept. Of Alcohol and Drug Programs, November, 2004.

[23]http://www.stopduiaz.com/ [An Arizona prosecutor's web site showing prison sentences and photos of DUI-DWI offenders.]

[24]http://www.duigulag.com/ [A citizen's frank, critical discussion of over-the-top DUI-DWI enforcement].

new way of prosecuting the offense arose: *merely having this amount of alcohol in your system, with "impairment" being a non-essential part of the proof needed to convict the person.* Further, mandatory license suspension for ANY person who refused to be tested for alcohol content created a "legal coercion" that was designed to force a person to take the state's breath, blood or urine tests.

As punishment increased, criminal defense attorneys became "organized" to share strategy and trial techniques with other legal advocates trying to defend against this emerging new set of laws. In 1983, a 15-city, national tour was organized by the late Richard Erwin, Reese Joye, Dr. James Feldman, Lawrence Taylor, and Donald Nichols (to name a few) in order to share their knowledge of how to defend drunk driving cases in this exploding new segment of criminal defense law.[1] Books and seminars were started by numerous defense lawyers in the aftermath of this tour, including each of the named attorneys shown above.

Two newsletters were launched in the mid-1980s to help notify attorneys involved in drunk driving litigation. The first was the "Drinking and Driving Law Letter" started by Don Nichols of Minneapolis. This publication is now edited by Flem K. Whited, III of Daytona Beach, Florida. The second was the "DWI Journal," edited by John Tarantino of Providence, Rhode Island. This newsletter was edited by Mr. Tarantino for over twenty years before editorship of the publication was passed to the author in February of 2006. See http://www.DWIJournal.com.

Shortly after this, Don Nichols and other Minnesota DUI-DWI attorneys established the Minnesota Society for Criminal Justice. This organization formed a DWI Seminar Group that met monthly to discuss issues, and conducted the first annual, national seminar beginning in 1986 to train lawyers on how to fight for their clients' rights in these increasingly difficult cases. In 2005, the Minnesota group held its 20th annual seminar in Las Vegas. This appears to be its final national seminar.

In roughly the same time frame (1986 to 1991), several criminal defense attorneys helped spearhead efforts to organize DUI-DWI defense attorney "think tanks" within their states. Many of these groups, despite bringing competitors together, have also created strong associations of lawyers with a common goal---zealously representing their clients by sharing information on ways to win DUI-DWI cases. Doug Cowan and Steve Hayne in Washington, Reese Joye, Ronnie Cole and Jim Huff in South Carolina, Don Nichols, John Brink and Peter Wold in Minnesota, Billy Spruell and the author in Georgia, just to name a few. The bonds between members of such groups are very strong, and unity of action has helped "temper" harsh DUI-DWI legislation in several states. Additionally, these groups have teamed up to help improve appellate case law development in these states.

In 1994, the author began sponsoring a national seminar dedicated to training criminal defense attorneys about the ***science*** behind DUI-DWI cases. The program, "Mastering Scientific Evidence in DUI-DWI Cases," was the brainchild of Gil Sapir, a Criminalist/Attorney from Chicago. The emphasis of this program was to teach lawyers about breath, blood, urine and field sobriety training, to help combat prosecutors using "junk science" and "false science" in courthouses across America.

In 1995, the National College for DUI Defense, Inc. was started by twelve seasoned DUI-DWI defense attorneys from numerous states,[25] including the author. Following organizational meetings in Atlanta and Chicago in 1994, the group was incorporated as a non-profit organization in 1995. By invitation, 100 Founding Members were added to the rolls of the

---

[25]See http://www.theduibook.com/ncddoriginalregents.htm

organization in 1995. Today, nearly 500 defense attorney members have joined the group at a variety of membership levels.[26]

From the first 3-day summer training program conducted at Harvard University School of Law in July of 1995, the National College now conducts four programs, including assuming responsibility for the "Mastering Scientific Evidence" series from the author beginning in April of 2005. Presently, this organization has taken the lead in national training on both law and science for lawyers who endeavor to specialize in defending drunken driving cases at the highest level of skill. In a joint program with the NACDL [National Association of Criminal Defense Attorneys], the National College hosted its Fall Session in late September of 2005 (Las Vegas) where over 700 criminal defense attorneys attended.

The College now offers an ABA-approved Board Certification in "DUI DEFENSE." This is a designation of advanced legal knowledge in the field. With its own web site and busy defense-attorneys-only list serve, it now dominates the legal landscape in the DUI-DWI defense field.[27]

1.1.6. It Isn't Just About Alcohol Any More. In the last decade, a proliferation of DUI-DWI "drugs" cases have been decided at our local and appellate courts. Before 1980, fewer than 100 DUI-DWI appeals involving impairment by drugs can be found in all of American case law. More and more American motorists are taking prescribed or over-the-counter medications that can (and often do) make the driver less capable of reacting to sudden emergencies. Now over 1000 cases each year show up in appellate records. Furthermore, in the last 10 years or so, police officers have been trained on "drug recognition" techniques that assist them in identifying drivers who have taken drugs that impair motor skills. The course also focuses on "poly-drug" impairment, where a driver has used both alcohol and impairing drugs. (See **Sections 2.2, 2.4 and 2.15** for details about this highly complex "DRE" training.[28])

In 2003, Nevada became the first state to pass DUI-DWI-drug laws setting presumptive impairment levels for a variety of contraband substances such as marijuana,[29] followed in 2005 by a similar law in Virginia. Approximately 17 states now have some form of *per se* drug laws. These laws will be the first of many to be passed by state legislatures seeking to find additional ways to assure convictions of drivers accused in impairment cases involving illegal drugs, where there is a need to prove "impairment" (*i.e.,* in vehicular homicide cases caused by a person high on controlled substances). Georgia and Ohio are currently working to pass similar laws.

Use of common non-prescription medicine such as aspirin, ibuprophen or acetaminophen can have an additive effect to a person's impairment from alcohol. In addition, many non-prescription drugs (e.g., antihistamines) can impair a person who later consumes

alcohol. This "combination" of alcohol and many types of medications (or even illegal drugs, such as marijuana) can drastically increase the impairment effects on a driver.[30]

---

[26]See the College's web site at http://www.NCDD.com.

[27]http://www.ncdd.com.

[28]http://www.theiacp.org/

[29]NRS 484.379(3).

[30]http://www.drunkdrivingdefense.com/publications-articles/cannabis-marijuana-plus-alcohol-driving-performance-study.htm; http://www.drunkdrivingdefense.com/publications-articles/alcohol-and-marijuana-combined-impairment-effects.htm; http://www.drunkdrivingdefense.com/general/non-prescription-medication-alcohol.htm; http://www.drunkdrivingdefense.com/publications-articles/alcohol-and-other-prescribed-drugs.htm.

The explosion of illicit drug use cases in America is a point of major concern in the health and public highway safety arenas. The term "illicit" refers to types of drugs that have no medicinal use, such as LSD, "crystal meth" or crack cocaine. Annually, the federal government spends millions of dollars taking comprehensive surveys to determine how prevalent the illicit drug problem is. The information tabulated for 2002, set forth below, indicates a drug subculture in America that involves a substantial percentage of our citizens. The reality is that a significant number of illicit drug users drive while impaired, but (due to sporadic training of officers and the lack of roadside "drug detection" equipment) most are never detected, unless the smell of alcohol leads to a blood test.

The most overlooked impaired driving cases are those involving "controlled substances" (drugs and other chemicals and plants that are legally obtained through a prescription and are criminally regulated by the government when used without a prescription.) The number of people in America who take another person's medication is growing each year. Such usage is illegal in all states. Many of the people who use these drugs also consume alcohol at the same time.

Recent statistics from the United States Department of Health and Human Services (for the year 2002) indicate these troubling numbers about alcohol and illicit drug usage:
[All statistics and percentages are for total population of Americans aged 12 or older]

Current Alcohol Users	120 million (51.0%)
Current Illicit Drug Users	19.5 million (8.3%)
Admit Driving Under the Influence *of Alcohol* in 2002 [Drinkers at age bracket 21 were the highest percentage (70.9%)]	33.5 million (14.2%)
Number of illicit drug users who admit driving under the influence *of an illicit drug* in 2002:	11.0 million (4.7%)
Admit to Binge Drinking (5 or more drinks before stopping) within last 30 days	54.0 million (22.9%)
Most Commonly Used Illicit Drug:	
Marijuana/Hashish	14.6 million in prior 30 days
Cocaine (or Crack) Users	2.0 million
Hallucinogens (about ½ of these were Ecstasy users)	1.2 million
Psychotherapeutic Drugs (non-medical uses)	6.2 million
Pain Relievers	4.4 million
Tranquilizers	1.8 million

Stimulants	1.2 million
Sedatives	0.4 million
Heroin	0.166 million
Age bracket most likely to take illicit drugs, 18-25 years old	20.2% (of age group admits use)

The national survey also discovered additional troubling information. Over 3.5 million Americans received some type of substance abuse treatment in 2002. Of these, 2.3 million went to a specialty treatment facility versus utilization of "self help." However, approximately 22.8 million Americans *needed* treatment for an alcohol and/or drug problem.

Unemployed youthful substance abusers were *more than twice as likely* to abuse both illicit drugs and alcohol than youth under age 21 who were employed. Looking at all age brackets, Asians had the lowest percentage *of illicit drug use* while persons of native Americans/Alaskan descent had the highest (4.8% compared to 10.1%). Native American/Alaskan youths ages 12 -17 had a 20.9% abuse rate.

1.2. Definitions and Concepts You Need to Know To Understand This Book.
Most Americans know a little about the drunk driving and drugged driving laws in their respective states, but not NEARLY enough. In this field, a little knowledge can be a dangerous thing. That is why over one million DUI-DWI arrests continue to be made in the United States each year.

First, several different ways are available for a prosecutor to accuse a DUI-DWI case against a person. Assuming that only alcohol is involved, there are two general ways that virtually all alcohol based "drunk driving" cases get accused:

(1) *Traditional, common law DUI-DWI*, wherein the officer gathers evidence to support his or her "opinion" that you had consumed too much alcohol to drive safely. The exact legal standard used in each state varies, but this is the general idea. This type of DUI-alcohol case does not require any breath, blood or urine test, and (possibly) no field sobriety exercises either. In states where refusal to submit to testing is still permitted (e.g., Georgia, Florida, Connecticut), these "traditional" cases are common, whereas other states (e.g., Arizona, California, Michigan, Indiana) will use physical force and restraints to take a forcible blood or urine test (by catheter) if you refuse to voluntarily submit to testing.

(2) *A "per se" DUI-DWI* case is the type of drunk driving case that is based upon a "reading" or result from a blood, breath or urine test (or more than one type of test) indicating that the driver had consumed enough alcohol to put him or her at or above that state's legal limit for that person. For example, a driver under age 21 stopped in Georgia is allowed up to a 0.02 reading, whereas a driver in Georgia who is age 21 or more (who is not operating a commercial motor vehicle) is allowed to have up to a 0.08 reading. An adult driver stopped in North Carolina is allowed the same 0.08 result, but drivers under age 21 are held to a 0.00 reading

Then, drivers who have no alcohol in their systems, but are impaired by drugs are covered under different DUI-DWI provisions that prohibit driving while impaired by such drugs. In addition to the drug impairment DUI-DWI, most states also have another type of drug-related offense that allows prosecution if you have any measurable amount of a contraband (illicit) substance, such as PCP or marijuana in your system. Many states also have impaired driving statutes to deal with inhalants, such as glue or paint thinner vapors, as an impairing substance.

Finally, statutes in most jurisdictions cover a "combination" of alcohol and drugs, or alcohol and inhalants, or drugs and inhalants, etc. The bottom line is that if you get impaired on **anything**, expect to find that the state you are arrested in has a law that allows for your prosecution for the crime of drunk/drugged/impaired driving.

A GLOSSARY has been added to this book in **Appendix B.** This contains common terms and phrases used in criminal law, criminal procedure and some specific terms and acronyms for DUI-DWI related issues. Whenever a term or phrase stumps you, turn to the glossary for assistance. Due to the extremely large number of legal terms and concepts in the DUI-DWI field, the author has also added an extended glossary on line at http://www.theduibook.com/glossary.htm.

By explaining how broadly most states have defined the prohibited act of "driving under the influence" many misconceptions and miscalculations by the average citizen can be cleared up. For a drinking driver, trying to guess when he or she is at risk of being arrested for (and possibly convicted of) drunk driving (or drugged driving) is a dangerous and foolhardy game. The laws relating to these crimes are NOT always logical or fair. The laws, as presently written, are written so that every person who *consumes* alcohol or drugs is discouraged from not only utilizing any means of mechanized transport afterwards, but requiring harsh punishment if a violation occurs.

All states now have what is called a "per se" drinking and driving offense, which is typically defined as operating a vehicle with a blood alcohol concentration at or above a specified level (presently, 0.08 percent in all states for drivers of non-commercial vehicles who are age 21 or older). Two states (New York and Colorado) have a lesser offense called "driving while ability impaired" [DWAI] by an intoxicant. This offense is similar to driving while under the influence of alcohol, but a lesser degree of impairment is required to be proven to support a conviction. Additionally, license suspension/revocation implications and punishment for DWAI offenses are less severe under these statutes.

In addition to the simple misdemeanor drunken driving offenses (which applies to about 95% of all drunken driving cases), most states have what are called enhanced DUI-DWI offenses. These crimes are misdemeanor offenses that are **enhanced** to felonies or higher-level misdemeanors (examples: "gross" misdemeanor or "high and aggravated" misdemeanor) as a result of one or more prior convictions for DUI-DWI offenses. In most jurisdictions, the enhancement to a felony or serious misdemeanor is also triggered by virtue of the offenses occurring within a few years of each other. Typically this "window" is from 3 to 10 years, depending on how many DUI-DWI offenses have occurred, as defined in each state's laws. Remember, however, that a new but growing trend is to look back over your lifetime for prior offenses to enhance punishment, not just a certain number of years.

Finally, every state has what are referred to as aggravated, "serious" or enhanced offenses related to "drunk drivers," which are typically filed in instances where the defendant, while under the influence of an intoxicant, was involved in an automobile accident that resulted in serious injury to another person or persons or death to one or more persons. Enhanced and aggravated DUI-DWI offenses are discussed in **Section 1.7.1**, *infra*.

1.2.1 Misdemeanor DUI-DWI Offenses. Reduced to basic terms, most misdemeanor DUI-DWI offenses consist of four basic elements: (a) the prohibited vehicular activity - the operation or other use, (b) of a vehicle (usually a "motor vehicle"), (c) in a location identified as being covered by that state's laws, (d) while influenced by the consumption of an intoxicant. Typically, these four elements must be proven beyond a reasonable doubt to convict a person of any DUI-DWI offense except a "per se" offense. In a "per se" offense the prosecution does not have to prove that the consumption of the intoxicant affected the defendant's ability to operate a vehicle. A "per se" DUI-DWI case merely requires that the prosecution be able to put the test result into evidence and to convince the judge or jury that the result is reliable and trustworthy. Each of these elements is discussed separately below.

(a) The prohibited vehicular activity. DUI-DWI statutes employ a variety of terms to describe the prohibited vehicular activities.[31] Under some DUI-DWI statutes it is illegal to "drive" a vehicle while intoxicated, while under other statutes it is illegal to "operate" a vehicle while intoxicated. Some statutes combine the terms in their statutes using disjunctive language and make "driving or operating" the prohibited activity. Occasionally a DUI-DWI statute will also include the term "attempt to operate" or "attempt to drive" as a prohibited vehicular activity.

In the states that follow the Uniform Vehicle Code,[32] the prohibited vehicular activity is the "actual physical control" of a vehicle. In many states this activity is combined disjunctively with one or more other prohibited activities such as "driving" or "operating." In a few states the prohibited vehicular activity is the "physical control" of a vehicle, as opposed to "actual physical control." Some DUI-DWI statutes that use the term "drive" or "operate" as the prohibited vehicular activity define the term "driving" or "operating" to include actual physical control of a vehicle. To illustrate the variations in state laws defining the prohibited vehicular activity (e.g., "driving," "actual physical control") several state statutes are set forth in **Appendix C** in the back of this book.

Of the terms used to describe a prohibited vehicular activity, "actual physical control" is the most comprehensive wording used and the most inclusive. While some courts use the terms "operate" and "actual physical control" interchangeably, the term "operate" is usually less inclusive than the term "actual physical control," but broader and more inclusive than the term "driving," which is the narrowest and least inclusive of the commonly-used terms.[33] It is possible, for example, to have actual physical control of a vehicle while neither operating nor driving it.[34] Similarly, it is possible to operate a vehicle without driving it.[35]

The traditional definition of "driving" usually includes a requirement that the vehicle be in motion.[36] The vehicle's motion, however, need not come from its engine. Sitting behind the wheel of a coasting vehicle whose engine is not running may constitute a "driving" of the vehicle, even if the keys are not in the ignition.[37] Similarly, the steering of a vehicle that is being

---

[31]J. Pearson, *What Constitutes Driving, Operating, Or Being In Control Of Motor Vehicle For Purposes Of Driving While Intoxicated Statute Or Ordinance*, 93 A.L.R.3d 7 (1979 - 2005).

[32]The *Uniform Vehicle Code* is a proposed set of standardized "model" traffic laws prepared by the National Committee on Uniform Traffic Laws and Ordinances. The initial effort to standardize traffic codes came to fruition in 1926, when a committee under Commerce Secretary Herbert Hoover compiled the first national Uniform Vehicle Code.

[33]**State v. Wiles**, 26 S.W.3d 436 (Mo. App. 2000); **State v. Jones** 752 A.2d 1169, 714 So.2d 819 (La. App. 1998).

[34]**State v. Thurston,** 84 S.W.2d 536 (Mo.App. 2002); **Bodner v. State**, 752 A.2d 1169 (Del. Supr. 2000).

[35]**Ferguson v. State,** 198 Miss. 825, 23 So.2d 687 (1945); **McDuell v. State,** 231 A.2d 265 (Del., 1967); For an in-depth discussion of this subject, see *Annotation: What Constitutes Driving, Operating, or Being in Control of a Motor Vehicle for Purposes of Driving While Intoxicated Statutes, 93 A.L.R.3d 7 (1979 - 2005)..*

[36]**State v. Johnson**, 130 N.M. 6, 15 P.3d 1233 (2000); **People v. Swain**, 959 P.2d 426 (Colo. 1998).

[37]**State v. Fisher,** 57 Or. App. 776, 646 P.2d 652 (1982).

pushed or towed may constitute a "driving" of the vehicle for purposes of a DUI-DWI statute.[38] The vehicle's motion must be the result of an intentional act of the defendant, however, and not the result of an accidental or unintentional event. Thus, the accidental depressing of the vehicle's clutch by an intoxicated but sleeping defendant, causing the vehicle to move was held not to constitute "driving" of the vehicle for purposes of a DUI-DWI statute.[39]

The statutory definition of "driving" is usually broader and more inclusive than the common law definition. Accordingly, several courts, in applying a statutory definition of "driving," have held that direct evidence of vehicular motion is not a necessary element of "driving," especially if the vehicle's engine is running.[40]

The common law definition of "operation" usually includes the actual physical handling or manipulation of the electrical or mechanical controls of a motor vehicle, including the starting of the vehicle's engine.[41] A vehicle does not have to be in motion to be operated.[42] However, evidence must be present that the defendant exercised some control or manipulation over the vehicle, such as steering or braking, even if the vehicle is in motion. Evidence that the defendant was inside a moving but non-running vehicle, without more, does not constitute sufficient evidence of "operating" the vehicle.[43] However, it has been held that grabbing the steering wheel and stepping on the accelerator of a vehicle constitutes "operating" the vehicle even if another person is driving the vehicle.[44]

The "operation" of a vehicle requires the showing of intent by the defendant to set the vehicle in motion.[45] The starting of the vehicle's engine usually constitutes the showing of such intent and a person found alone in a non-moving vehicle whose engine is running is usually held to be "operating" the vehicle, even if the person was found asleep or unconscious.[46] Even if a vehicle whose engine is running is temporarily disabled or stuck in mud or snow, the person found behind the wheel may nevertheless be found to be "operating" the vehicle.[47]

Some courts, it should be noted, have held that a person found asleep behind the wheel of a non-moving vehicle whose engine was running was not "operating" the vehicle for purposes of a DUI-DWI statute.[48] In most cases of this sort, the defendant's vehicle was found parked in a parking lot or similar area and not on or next to the highway, thus lessening both the inference that the defendant recently drove the vehicle and the intent to set the vehicle in

---

[38]**State v. Thomas**, 28 Kan. App. 2d 655, 20 P.3d 82 (2001); **Williams v. State**, 884 P.2d 167 (Alaska 1994).

[39]**People v. Edwards,** 158 Misc. 2d 615, 601 N.Y.S.2d 539 (1993).

[40]**Johnson v. State**, 194 Ga. App. 501, 391 S.E.2d 132 (1990); **Boone v. State,** 105 N.M. 223, 731 P.2d 366 (1986); **State v. Fields,** 77 N.C.App. 404, 335 S.E.2d 69 (1985).

[41]**State v. Dubany,** 184 Neb. 337, 167 N.W.2d 556 (1969); **McDuell v. State,** 231 A.2d 265 (Del., 1967).

[42]**State v. Wymbs,** 10 Ohio Misc.2d 26, 462 N.E.2d 195 (1984); **State v. Morris,** 262 N.J. Super. 413, 621 A.2d 74 (1993).

[43]**State v. Rossi,** 734 So.2d 102 (La. App. 1999); **State v. Brister,** 514 So.2d 205 (La. App. 1987).

[44]**State v. Cruz,** 121 Or. App. 241, 855 P.2d 191 (1993).

[45]**Prudhomme v. Hults,** 27 A.D.2d 234, 278 N.Y.S.2d 67 (1967); **State v. Mulcahy,** 107 N.J. 467, 527 A.2d 368 (1987).

[46]**Commonwealth v. Williams,** 871 A.2d 254 (Pa. Super. 2005); **Oliver v. Commonwealth**, 40 Va. App. 20, 577 S.E.2d 514 (2003); **Villalobos v. Zolin,** 35 Cal. App. 4th 556, 41 Cal. Rptr. 2d 207 (1995).

[47]**People v. David "W,"** 83 A.D.2d 690, 442 N.Y.S.2d 278 (1981); **State v. Dubany,** 184 Neb. 337, 167 N.W.2d 556 (1969).

[48]**Wells v. Commonwealth**, 709 S.W.2d 847 (Ky. App. 1986).

motion.[49]   A defendant found asleep behind the wheel of a vehicle whose engine was not running but whose key was in the ignition and turned to the "on" position, was held not to be "operating" the vehicle.[50] See also http://www.duiblog.com/2005/04/18#a143.

Under many DUI-DWI statutes it is illegal to be in or have "actual physical control" of a vehicle while intoxicated. "Actual physical control" of a vehicle by a person is generally held to exist when the person is in a position to exercise influence, dominion, or regulation over the vehicle.[51] "Actual physical control" does not require the vehicle to be in motion or its engine to be running. All that must be shown is that the defendant had an immediate *potential* to operate the vehicle.[52]

To be in "actual physical control" of a vehicle, the defendant must normally be found inside the vehicle.[53] However, a defendant standing near the open trunk of a vehicle whose engine was running and that had a flat tire was held to be in physical control of the vehicle for purposes of a DUI-DWI statute.[54]

If it is shown that the defendant was inside a non-running vehicle, the location of the defendant inside the vehicle and location of the ignition keys are important issues. If the defendant was found behind the wheel and if the ignition keys were either in the ignition or in the actual or constructive possession of the defendant, a finding of "actual physical control" over the vehicle is likely to be upheld, even if one or more other acts (such as the fastening of a seat belt) had to be performed before the vehicle's engine could be started.[55]

The fact that the defendant was found asleep or unconscious does not prevent a finding of "actual physical control" if the defendant was found inside the vehicle and if the ignition keys were either in the ignition or in the possession of the defendant.[56] Courts following this line of cases frequently cite a legislative intent to apprehend drunk drivers before they can strike.[57]

Some courts, however, have refused to follow this approach. In several reported cases a finding of "actual physical control" was reversed where the defendant was found asleep or unconscious inside a non-running vehicle parked off the highway and where the ignition key was either disengaged or in the "off" position.[58] In such cases the courts often state that it is not feasible for an unconscious defendant to have actual physical control of a vehicle. The

---

[49]**City of Whitefish v. Large**, 318 Mont. 310, 80 P.3d 427 (2003); **State v. Telakowitz,** 61 Ohio Misc. 2d 499, 580 N.E.2d 101 (1991).

[50]**Harris v. Commonwealth,** 709 S.W.2d 846 (Ky. App. 1986).

[51]**State v. Robison,** 281 Mont. 64, 931 P.2d 706 (1997); **State v. Bugger,** 25 Utah 2d 404, 483 P.2d 442 (1971); **State v. Duemke,** 352 N.W.2d 427 (Minn. App. 1984).

[52]**State v. Kelton**, 168 Vt. 629, 724 A.2d 452 (1998).

[53]**Bearden v. State**, 430 P.2d 844 (Okla. Crim. App., 1967); **Overbee v. Commonwealth,** 227 Va. 238, 315 S.E.2d 242 (1984).

[54]**State v. Woodward,** 408 N.W.2d 927 (Minn. App., 1987).

[55]**Cincinnati v. Kelley,** 47 Ohio St.2d 94, 351 N.E.2d 85 (1976); **LaBeau v. Commissioner,** 412 N.W.2d 777 (Minn. App., 1987); **Petersen v. Dept. of Public Safety,** 373 N.W.2d 38 (S.D., 1985).

[56]**State v. Dawley,** 201 Ariz. 285, 34 P.3d 394 (2001); **Commonwealth v. Woodruff,** 447 Pa. Super. 222, 668 A.2d 1158 (1995); **State v. Williams,** 752 S.W.2d 454 (Mo. App. 1988); **Wiyott v. State,** 284 Ark. 399, 683 S.W.2d 220 (1985); **Adams v. State,** 697 P.2d 622 (Wyo. 1985); **Hughes v. State,** 535 P.2d 1023 (Okla. Crim. App. 1975).

[57]**State v. Smelter,** 36 Wash.App. 439, 674 P.2d 690 (1984).

[58]**State v. Zavala,** 136 Ariz. 356, 666 P.2d 456 (1983); **State v. Bugger,** 25 Utah 2d 404, 483 P.2d 442 (1971); **State v. Pazderski,** 352 N.W.2d 85 (Minn. App., 1984); **Roberts v. Commissioner,** 371 N.W.2d 605 (Minn. App., 1985).

appellate courts cite a legislative intent to encourage drinking drivers to pull off the road until they are sober.

The fact that a vehicle was temporarily immobile because it was stuck in mud or snow is insufficient to prevent a finding of "actual physical control."[59] Further, a finding of "actual physical control" has been upheld where the vehicle was out of gas or otherwise temporarily inoperable.[60] However, proof that the vehicle could not have been operated under any reasonable circumstance has been held to be a defense to the establishment of "actual physical control."[61] This defense must be raised by the accused driver, however, as the prosecution does not have to prove that the defendant's vehicle was operable to establish "actual physical control."[62] Each state's rules of criminal procedure control how this is done.

In a few states the operative term in the DUI-DWI statute is "physical control" of a vehicle, as opposed to "actual physical control." While the terms are similarly construed in most instances, it has been held that the term "physical control" is broader and more encompassing than the term "actual physical control."[63] Thus, an intoxicated person sitting in the right front passenger seat of a vehicle who reached over and stepped on the accelerator pedal was held to be in "physical control" of the vehicle for purposes of a DUI-DWI statute, even though the vehicle was being driven by another person.[64]

Regardless of the type of statute in a particular state, there must be some credible evidence that the defendant "operated" (or "had actual physical control of," etc.) a vehicle in order to sustain a DUI-DWI conviction. A DUI-DWI conviction was reversed on the grounds of insufficient evidence of operating the vehicle where it was shown that the officer investigating a one-car accident did not observe the defendant operating the vehicle and the defendant's admission of driving was suppressed because the officer failed to give the defendant a *Miranda* warning prior to questioning him about driving.[65] Insufficient evidence of actual physical control was found to exist where the defendant was found by police seated in the vehicle with the engine not running and where it was claimed that the defendant's girlfriend had been driving the vehicle at the time of the accident.[66]

A few states go even further to prosecute people who are drunk and ACT like they may try to drive. These states also have a separate crime of ***"attempted" DUI-DWI***.[67] Other states have ruled that there is no such crime possible.[68] See the following link for additional information: http://www.duiblog.com/2005/04/27#a152.

(b) The types of vehicles or devices covered. All DUI-DWI laws cover all forms of "traditional" motor vehicles, including automobiles, trucks, motorcycles, and vans. The

---

[59]**State v. Hendricks**, 586 N.W.2d 413 (Minn. App. 1998); **Lathan v. State,** 707 P.2d 941 (Alaska App., 1985)

[60]**State v. Smelter,** 36 Wash.App. 439, 674 P.2d 690 (1984).

[61]**Jones v. State,** 510 So.2d 1147 (Fla. App., 1987).

[62]**Toledo v. Voyles,** 14 Ohio App.3d 419, 471 N.E.2d 823 (1984); **Crane v. State,** 461 P.2d 986 (Okla. Crim. App. 1969).

[63]**State v. Juncewski,** 308 N.W.2d 316 (Minn. 1981).

[64]**Ives v. Commissioner,** 375 N.W.2d 565 (Minn. App. 1985).

[65]**Cook v. State,** 37 Ark. App. 27, 823 S.W.2d 916 (1992).

[66]**Commonwealth v. Price,** 416 Pa.Super. 23, 610 A.2d 488 (1992).

[67]Kansas: **State v. Kendall,** 55 P.3d 660 (Kan. 2002); Maine: [Me. Rev. Stat. Ann. Tit. 29 § 1312]; New Hampshire: [N.H. Rev. Stat. Ann. § 265.82]; Vermont: [Vt. Stat. Ann. Tit. 23, § 1201]; Maryland: [Md. Transp. Code Ann. § 8-1567].

[68]**Strong v. State,** 87 S.W.3d 206 (Tex.App.-Dallas 2002); **People v. Prescott,** 722 N.Y.S.2d 1334 (1997).

description of the types of vehicles or devices covered by a particular state statute normally becomes important only when a defendant is charged with operating an unusual device or vehicle while intoxicated.[69] Most DUI-DWI statutes refer to either "vehicle" or "motor vehicle" as the type of vehicle or device covered under state law.

Some statutes, however, contain additional language such as "automobile or other motor driven vehicle," "motor vehicle, aircraft, or watercraft," or "motor vehicle or other means of conveyance" in defining the types of vehicles or devices covered. In defining the term "vehicle" or "motor vehicle," the courts often refer to other chapters or sections of the motor vehicle laws. Thus, if a DUI-DWI statute does not contain a definition of "vehicle," "motor vehicle," or any other relevant term, reference should be made to the general provisions of that state's motor vehicle laws. See state law links at:
http://www.theduibook.com/stateDUIDWIsummaries.htm.

A "motor vehicle" is generally defined as any vehicle equipped with a motor or any vehicle that is self-propelled, except vehicles propelled solely by human power.[70] Accordingly, a tractor has been held to be a motor vehicle for purposes of a DUI-DWI statute,[71] as well as a Zamboni® being used at an ice skating rink.[72] A moped has been held to be a motor vehicle, even if its engine was not running and the driver was pedaling.[73] Similarly, snowmobiles are generally held to be "motor vehicles" under DUI-DWI laws, unless they are either specifically excluded under the DUI-DWI statutes or regulated under a separate statute.[74]

A "vehicle" is generally defined as any device in, upon, or by which a person or property is or may be transported or drawn upon a highway, except devices used exclusively on stationary rails or tracks.[75] It is readily apparent that the term "vehicle" is broader and more inclusive than the term "motor vehicle," and DUI-DWI laws covering "vehicles" are broader and more inclusive than those covering "motor vehicles."

In some states, a non-motorized bicycle has been held to be a "vehicle," but not a "motor vehicle or other means of conveyance."[76] Thus, in some states, you can be charged

---

[69]Even a Zamboni® - http://www.kvoa.com/Global/story.asp?S=3535801&nav=menu216_2_5.

[70]Uniform Vehicle Code, sec. 1-134.

[71]**Nemeth v. Commonwealth**, 944 S.W.2d 871 (Ky. App. 1997); **Commonwealth v. Hutchinson**, 423 Pa. Super. 571, 621 A.2d 681 (1993); **State v. Powell**, 306 S.W.2d 531 (Mo. 1957).

[72]http://www.kvoa.com/Global/story.asp?S=3535801&nav=menu216_2_5.

[73]**People v. Jordan,** 75 Cal. App.3d Supp. 1, 142 Cal. Rptr. 401 (1977); **State v. Senko,** 457 A.2d 824 (Me., 1983).

[74]**State v. Delap**, 237 Mont. 346, 772 P.2d 1268 (1989); **Melby v. Commissioner,** 367 N.W.2d 527 (Minn., 1985); **Annotation:** *Snowmobile Operation as DWI or DUI, 56 A.L.R. 4th 1092 (1987 - 2005); Annotation: What is a "Motor Vehicle" Within Statutes Making it an Offense to Drive While Intoxicated, 66 A.L.R.2d 1146 (1959 - 2005).*

[75]Uniform Vehicle Code § 1-134; **State v. Carr**, 761 So. 2d 1271 (La. 2000); **Commonwealth v. Lowe**, 31 Va. App. 806, 525 S.E.2d 636 (2000); **People v. Martinez**, 296 Ill. App. 3d. 330, 694, N.E.2d 1084 (1998); **City of Montesano v. Wells**, 79 Wash. App. 529, 902 P.2d 1266 (1995); **State v. Richardson**, 113 N.M. 740, 832 P.2d 801 (1992).

[76]*Compare* states holding that bicycling can be DUI-DWI - **State v. Shepard**, 1 Ohio App. 3d 104, 439 N.E.2d 920 (1981); **State v. Howard,** 510 So. 2d 612 (Fla. App. 1987) *with* states holding that bicycling cannot be DUI - **State v. Guidry**, 467 So. 2d 156 (La. App. 1985); **State v. Johnson,** 203 N.J. Super. 436, 497 A.2d 242 (1985); **Clingenpeel v. Municipal Court for Antelope Judicial Dist.**, 108 Cal. App. 3d 394, 166 Cal. Rptr. 573 (1980); **People v. Schaefer,** 274 Ill. App. 3d 450, 654 N.E.2d 267 (1995). See *Annotation: Operation of Bicycle as Within Drunk Driving Statutes*, 73 A.L.R. 4th 1139 (1989 - 2005).

with DUI-DWI for riding your bicycle while intoxicated.[77] Even a horse has been held to be a "vehicle" for purposes of a DUI-DWI statute in North Carolina, [78] while other courts, however, have ruled to the contrary.[79]

(c) The locations where DUI-DWI offenses may occur. Most DUI-DWI laws either do not specify the location where a DUI-DWI offense may occur or describe the location as "in the state" or "within the state." Statutes that specify particular locations where DUI-DWI offenses may occur typically employ phrases such as "any public highway or road," "a highway or private property used by the general public," "any public place," or "any way." Thus, publicly owned highways and areas are universally deemed to be covered locations for DUI-DWI offenses.

The major difference in the application of the various statutes is the extent to which they are deemed to cover offenses occurring on private or non-public areas. By way of example, the covered locations for offenses under the DUI-DWI statutes of several states are set forth in **Appendix C** in the back of this book, to give you some idea of how state laws vary.

DUI-DWI statutes that do not specify locations where offenses may occur are normally construed to cover offenses occurring anywhere in the state, whether on public or private property.[80] DUI-DWI statutes covering offenses occurring "in the state" or "within the state" are also construed to cover offenses that take place anywhere in the state, on either public or private property.[81] Further, the constitutionality of such statutes has been consistently upheld by the courts as a valid exercise of police power.[82]

In one state, a noteworthy exception exists to the general rule applying DUI-DWI statutes to conduct of this sort occurring on private property.[83] In that case an intoxicated defendant was arrested and charged with drunk driving for driving an unlicensed vehicle in circles in an enclosed remote field owned by the defendant's parents. Even though the DUI-DWI statute covered offenses occurring "within the state," the court ruled that the charged offense was not covered under the statute. The court stated that the defendant was posing no threat to the public, that his arrest did not further the purpose of the DUI-DWI statute, and that under the facts of the case it would be an unreasonable exercise of police power to prohibit the defendant's conduct.

When "public highways" or "public roads" are specified as the places where DUI-DWI offenses may be committed, offenses occurring on private property are not usually covered

---

[77]**State v. Shepard,** 1 Ohio App. 3d 104, 439 N.E.2d 920 (1981); **State v. Howard,** 510 So. 2d 612 (Fla. App. 1987); **State v. Davia,** 87 Haw. 249, 953 P.2d 1347 (1998); **State v. Woodruff,** 81 Or.App. 484, 726 P.2d 396 (1986).

[78]**State v. Dellinger,** 73 N.C.App. 685, 327 S.E.2d 609 (1985).

[79]**State v. Euton,** 77 Ohio Misc. 2d 19, 665 N.E.2d 775 (1996); **State v. Williams,** 449 So.2d 744 (La. App. 1984). See *Annotation: Horseback Riding or Operation of Horse-Drawn Vehicle as Within Drunk Driving Statute,* 71 A.L.R. 4th 1129 (1989 - 2005).

[80]**Madden v. State,** 252 Ga. App. 164, 555 S.E.2d 832 (2001); **State v. McColley,** 157 N.J. Super 525, 385 A.2d 264 (1978); **State v. Carter,** 424 N.E.2d 158 (Ind. App. 1981).

[81]**State v. Frank,** 2 Ohio App. 3d 392, 442 N.E.2d 469 (1981); **Highland Park v. Block,** 48 Ill. App. 3d 241, 362 N.E.2d 1107 (1977).

[82]**State v. Robbins,** 138 Wash. 2d 486, 980 P.2d 725 (1999); **Cook v. State,** 220 Ga. 463, 139 S.E.2d 383 (1964); **Kansas City v. Troutner,** 544 S.W.2d 295 (Mo. App. 1976).

[83]**State v. Day,** 96 Wash. 2d 646, 638 P.2d 546 (1981); **Sanders v. State,** 312 Ark 11, 846 S.W.2d 651 (1993); D. Okasinski, *Applicability, To Operation Of Motor Vehicle On Private Property, Or Legislation Making Drunken Driving A Criminal Offense,* 52 A.L.R.5th 655 (1997-2005).

unless the statute contains other language broadening the scope of its application.[84] However, under such statutes if the offense occurs on a publicly owned area, it is likely to be a covered offense, even if the area is not a highway. Thus, a road closed to the public because it was under construction and the portion of a public beach used for traffic have both been held to constitute a public highway or road for purposes of a DUI-DWI statute.[85]

For purposes of DUI-DWI laws, a "public highway" normally includes the entire platted or dedicated right-of-way, including the shoulder and any walkway or bicycle path included in the right-of-way.[86] Also, it is not necessary for the entire vehicle to be on the public highway for the offense to be covered under a DUI-DWI statute.[87]

DUI-DWI offenses occurring on private parking lots and other privately owned areas to which the public has access have been the subject of many reported cases. Many DUI-DWI statutes now specifically include parking lots and other public access areas as covered locations. In some jurisdictions, DUI-DWI laws cover offenses that take place at any location in the state. This coverage may be explicitly stated in the statute or because "location" is not described in the statute, such laws are typically construed (interpreted) by appellate courts in these states to cover offenses occurring on public roadways as well as private parking lots and other public access areas.[88]

DUI-DWI laws that specify "public highways," "public places" or similar areas as covered locations are generally, but not always, held *not* to cover offenses occurring on privately-owned parking lots and similar public access areas.[89] However, in a Vermont case, the parking lot of a restaurant was held to be a "highway" for the purpose of a DUI-DWI statute.[90]

If a DUI-DWI statute specifies "areas open to the public," "areas to which the public has a right of access," or similar descriptions of areas as being "covered locations," the extent of its application to offenses occurring on private property depends largely on the exact wording of the particular statute and the character of the private area in question. The location of the private area in relation to the public roads, the use of the area by the public in the past, and whether the access provided to the area is easy or difficult, are all factors considered by the courts in determining the applicability of such statutes.[91]

A privately owned parking lot with easy access to a major intersection was held to be a "way open to the public."[92] A ramp leading from a private lot that charged a fee for parking was

---

[84]**State v. Ball,** 264 S.E.2d 844 (W.V. App., 1980); **People v. Kissel,** 150 Ill. App. 3d 283, 501 N.E.2d 963 (1986), overruled on other grounds, 175 Ill. App. 3d 725 (1988).

[85]**Thurman v. State,** 167 Tex. Crim. App. 21, 317 S.W.2d 737 (1958); **Brown v. State,** 163 Tex. Crim. App. 170, 289 S.W.2d 942 (1956).

[86]**In re E.J.H.,** 112 Wis. 2d 439, 334 N.W.2d 77 (1983); **Melby v. Commissioner,** 367 N.W.2d 527 (Minn. 1985).

[87]**Commonwealth v. Ginnetti,** 400 Mass. 181, 508 N.E.2d 603 (1987), where a vehicle with its rear wheels on a private lot and its front wheels on the highway was deemed to on a "public way" for the purpose of a DUI-DWI statute.

[88]**State v. Carter,** 424 N.E.2d 158 (Ind. App. 1981); **State v. Frank,** 2 Ohio App. 3d 392, 442 N.E.2d 469 (1981).

[89]**Fowler v. State,** 65 S.W.3d 116 (Tex. App. — Amarillo 2001); **Rouse v. State,** 651 S.W.2d 736 (Tex. Crim. App. 1982); **People v. Kenyon,** 85 A.D.2d 916, 446 N.Y.S.2d 783 (1981).

[90]**State v. Jarvis,** 145 Vt. 8, 482 A.2d 65 (1984).

[91]**Annotation:** *Applicability, to Operation of Motor Vehicle on Private Property, of Legislation Making Drunken Driving a Criminal Offense,* 29 A.L.R.3d 938 (1970 - 2005).

[92]**Seattle v. Tolliver,** 31 Wash.App. 299, 641 P.2d 719 (1982).

held to be a "way open to the public."[93] A temporary parking area in a public park was held to be a "public vehicular area."[94] The parking lot of a restaurant was held to constitute a "public parking lot," while the parking lot of a state mental health facility was held not to constitute such an area.[95] Finally, the parking lot of a shopping center was held not to be a place to which there was a "public right of access."[96]

Finally, in a few cases, very foolhardy drivers have been foolish enough to test the resolve of TWO states in one crazed driving episode. Yes, if a person drives intoxicated in two different states while police officers are in pursuit, and evidence supports that fact, DUI-DWI cases in both states can be maintained against the driver.[97]

(d) The required degree of "influence" of consumed intoxicants. The DUI-DWI statutes of most states contain, in one form or another, the following three offenses: (1) an "under the influence of alcohol" offense; (2) an "under the influence of drugs" offense; and (3) a "per se" alcohol offense. Many states also have an "under the combined influence of alcohol and drugs" offense, and a few states have a "driving while impaired" offense, under which the required degree of functional impairment is less than that required in the "under the influence of alcohol" offense. A summary of the key provisions of the DUI-DWI laws of each American jurisdiction can be found on-line at http://www.theduibook.com/stateDUIDWIsummaries.htm. Trying to publish a summary of these mercurial laws in a printed book is like trying to sort through a box of feathers in a windstorm --- not very productive or useful.

Under many DUI-DWI statutes it is illegal to drive a vehicle "while under the influence of alcohol." In other statutes the term "intoxicant," "intoxicating liquor," "alcoholic beverage" or "impairing substance" is substituted for the word "alcohol." In some states it is illegal to drive a vehicle "while intoxicated" or "while in an intoxicated condition." The applicable terms used in several states are outlined in **Appendix C** in the back of this book.[98]

1.2.2. The Required "Degree" of Impairment: *State Standards Vary*. As indicated above, under most DUI-DWI statutes it is illegal to drive a vehicle while "under the influence" of alcohol or other intoxicants. However, the degree of physical or mental impairment required for a person to be "under the influence" varies considerably from state to state. Impairment "in any degree," "in some degree" and "to an appreciable extent" have each been held sufficient to render a person "under the influence."[99]

Other courts have held that the degree of impairment necessary for a person to be deemed "under the influence" is measured by the person's ability to operate a vehicle safely.[100] In such cases the standard is whether the driver's consumption of alcohol diminished his or her

[93]**Billings v. Peete,** 729 P.2d 1268 (Mont. 1986).

[94]**State v. Carawan,** 80 N.C.App. 151, 341 S.E.2d 96 (1986).

[95]**People v. Copeland,** 132 Misc. 2d 990, 506 N.Y.S.2d 249 (1986).

[96]**Commonwealth v. Langenfeld,** 1 Mass. App. 813, 294 N.E.2d 457 (1973).

[97]**Commonwealth v. Stephenson**, 82 S.W.3d 876 (Ky. 2002).

[98]Also see http://www.theduibook.com/stateDUIDWIsummaries.htm.

[99]**State v. Slater,** 109 N.H. 279, 249 A.2d 692 (1969); **Steffani v. State,** 45 Ariz. 210, 42 P.2d 615 (1935); **State v. Carroll,** 226 N.C. 237, 37 S.E.2d 688 (1946).

[100]**Thompson v. People,** 181 Colo. 194, 510 P.2d 311 (1973).

ability or capacity to operate a vehicle safely,[101] and it does not matter if other (even prescription) drugs assisted in the impairment ultimately caused by alcohol.[102]

Impairment of one's ability or capacity to operate a vehicle is usually linked to an impairment of the person's senses, judgment, and motor skills, although proof of actual erratic or unsafe driving is not normally required.[103] Thus, a person is "under the influence" when that person does not possess the clearness of intellect and control that he or she would otherwise have.[104]

It should be noted that some courts distinguish between the terms "intoxicated" and "under the influence," while other courts use the terms interchangeably. The courts that distinguish between the terms usually find "intoxicated" to be the stronger term and to require a greater degree of functional impairment.[105] Thus, it has been held that an intoxicated person is necessarily under the influence of alcohol, but one does not have to be intoxicated to be under the influence of alcohol.[106]

The degree of mental or physical impairment required for a person to be deemed "under the influence" or "intoxicated" varies not only from state to state, but often among the various types of DUI-DWI offenses within a state. It is obviously important to ascertain the degree of impairment required for conviction under each offense. Your qualified DUI-DWI defense trial attorney in your state will be able to explain your state's standard of proof.

Often the required degree of impairment is found in the pattern jury instructions approved for use in a particular state. In some states the degree of impairment required for conviction is set forth statutorily. Otherwise, the required degree of impairment must be ascertained from the state's case (decisional) law from its appellate courts. The degree of impairment required for conviction for a DUI-DWI offense in several states is set forth in **Appendix C** in the back of this book.[107]

1.2.3. Statutory Inferences for Common Law "Drunk Driving" Charges.
Most states have enacted statutory presumptions (inferences) for use in determining whether a person is under the influence of alcohol. This only applies to the traditional (common law) impaired driving offense, not the "per se" charges which require no proof of impairment at all. These presumptive statutes are intended for use in conjunction with chemical test evidence. Such "presumptive statutes" typically provide that when it is shown by chemical testing (a breath or blood test result that a trial judge has allowed to be admitted into evidence) that a person's blood alcohol concentration has reached a certain level, an inference arises that the person was under the influence of alcohol if sufficient proof can show this alcohol level when driving. This inference can be rebutted by your attorney at your trial, because no legal "inference" or "presumption" can be irrebuttable or (in effect) shift the burden of proof to you without leaving you the ability to refute that evidence. This type of DUI-DWI charge can always be challenged if fact witnesses (and possibly an expert witness such as a toxicologist or pharmacologist) can establish a lower alcohol level AT THE TIME OF DRIVING.

---

[101]**Commonwealth v. Connolly**, 394 Mass. 169, 474 N.E.2d 1106 (1985); **Harper v. State,** 91 Ga. App. 456, 86 S.E.2d 7 (1955).

[102]**Gray v. State,** 152 S.W.3d 125 (Tex.Crim.App. 2004).

[103]**Commonwealth v. Connolly**, 394 Mass. 169, 474 N.E.2d 1106 (1985).

[104]**State v. Knowles** 671 N.W.2d 816 (N.D. 2003); **State v. Steele,** 95 Ohio App. 107, 117 N.E.2d 617 (1952); **Commonwealth v. Buoy,** 128 Pa. Super. 264, 193 A. 144 (1937).

[105]**Cashion v. Harnett,** 23 A.D. 332, 255 N.Y.S. 169 (1932).

[106]**Jackson v. State,** 456 So. 2d 916 (Fla. App. 1984).

[107]For your state's summary, go to the Internet at: http://www.theduibook.com/stateDUIDWIsummaries.htm.

A typical presumptive statute provides that evidence of a blood alcohol concentration of 0.08% or more creates a presumption (inference) that the defendant was under the influence of alcohol. The presumptive level at which impairment is inferred varies, however. In most states it is .08%. Many presumptive statutes also provide that evidence of a blood alcohol concentration of more than .05% but less than 0.08% creates no presumption or inference of impairment, and evidence of a blood alcohol concentration of less than .05% creates a presumption (inference) that the person was not under the influence of alcohol. In most states, the prosecutor has the ability to try to rebut or challenge the issue of non-impairment, however.

A presumptive statute typically relieves the prosecution of the legal necessity of proving, through expert testimony, that a blood alcohol concentration at or above the presumptive level affected the defendant's ability to operate a vehicle.[108] A knowledgeable attorney representing a person facing such evidence will use witnesses (including expert witnesses) to rebut any such inference of impairment. Consult your DUI-DWI specialist to learn the applicable rules in your state.

As stated earlier, these presumptive statutes create a rebuttable "inference" of intoxication when evidence of the required alcohol concentration is admitted.[109] To be constitutional, however, a presumptive statute must not shift to the defendant the burden of proving his or her innocence as to any element of the offense.[110] Many courts have held that a presumptive statute merely creates a permissive inference upon which the jury may or may not find a defendant intoxicated upon proof of the required blood alcohol concentration, and shifts no affirmative burden to the defendant.[111]

It has been held that a judge's use of a jury instruction that fails to specify the rebuttable nature of the statutory presumption constitutes reversible error by the trial court.[112] Several courts have held that a permissive presumption alone, without other evidence of intoxication, will not support a traditional or "common law" DUI-DWI conviction.[113]

1.3.1. Understanding a "Per Se" DUI Case. The DUI-DWI laws of all states now contain a "per se" offense based upon a specified minimum *blood* alcohol concentration (all states now adhere to the 0.08% standard for drivers age 21 and over, as of August 1, 2005). Most states have also enacted legislation to prohibit driving with a specified *breath* alcohol concentration, and have set forth "grams of alcohol per 210 liters of breath." The alternative was needed to avoid the requirement of having an expert come to court on every breath test case and explain to the jury how much breath it took to convert the reading to the state's "blood" standard, which was worded in units of milliliters of blood, or some similar measurement.

Under a "per se" statute it is a crime for a driver to have a blood (or breath) alcohol concentration at or above the statutory level (whether determined by a blood or breath

---

[108]**State v. Ball,** 264 S.E.2d 844 (W. Va., 1980) [decided when that state's legal limit was 0.10%]

[109]**Salazar v. State,** 505 So. 2d 1287 (Ala.Crim.App. 1986); **Stepic v. State,** 226 Ga.App. 734, 487 S.E.2d 643 (1997).

[110]**Sandstrom v. Montana,** 442 U.S. 510, 99 S.Ct. 2450, 61 L.Ed.2d 39 (1979); **Mullaney v. Wilbur,** 421 U.S. 684, 95 S.Ct. 1881, 44 L.Ed.2d 508 (1975); **Vlandis v. Kline,** 412 U.S. 441, 93 S.Ct. 2230, 37 L.Ed2d 63 (1973).

[111]**State v. Hanks,** 172 Vt. 93, 772 A.2d 1087 (2001); **Barnes v. People,** 735 P.2d 869 (Colo. 1987); **Commonwealth v. Moreira,** 385 Mass. 792, 434 N.E.2d 196 (1982).

[112]**Anderson v. State,** 203 Ga. App. 118, 416 S.E.2d 309 (1992).

[113]**Petrie v. State,** 590 N.E.2d 603 (Ind. App., 1992); **People v. Allan,** 231 Ill. App. 3d 447, 595 N.E.2d 1317 (1992).

standard) while driving a vehicle, *regardless of the effect of the alcohol on the person.* Thus, under a "per se" statute the prosecution does not have to prove that the defendant was under the influence of the alcohol consumed. Impairment is not a required "element" of a per se alcohol DUI-DWI offense.

No expert witness is needed for the prosecution to correlate (to "match up") the alleged blood (or breath) alcohol concentration to any degree of impairment since a blood alcohol concentration at or above the level set forth in the statute is itself sufficient for conviction, *regardless of impairment.* Under a "per se" statute intoxication, in the traditional sense, is not a "guilt or innocence" issue. The issue of guilt or innocence depends upon whether the jury believes that the defendant had a prohibited blood alcohol concentration in his or her system at the time of driving (or, in some states, within 2, 3 or 4 hours after driving ended), from alcohol consumed before or during driving. To win your case against a per se alcohol reading at or over the applicable legal limit, a highly trained expert witness will be required in almost all instances.

In some states, it should be noted, the "per se" statutes proscribe (i.e., makes illegal) operating or driving with prohibited levels of alcohol in a person's blood, breath *or* urine. However, due to "pooling" issues, urine testing for alcohol content is notoriously unreliable to provide accurate "quantitative" results. A skilled DUI-DWI defense attorney and a qualified expert witness can devastate the reliability of such test results.

Under a "per se" statute, as under any DUI-DWI statute, it must be proven beyond a reasonable doubt that the defendant "drove" or "operated" "a vehicle" in "a prohibited area," as previously discussed in this section. However, instead of proving that the defendant was intoxicated or under the influence of alcohol at the time of the alleged offense, the prosecution need only prove beyond a reasonable doubt that the defendant's alcohol concentration (from a test of blood, breath or urine) was at or above the prohibited level *at the time of the driving.*[114] Some states have removed from their laws any "burden" on the State to prove what your BAC actually was **WHEN** driving, so long as your test was conducted within the statutory "window" set by your state's laws (typically 2 or 3 hours after the driving ended).

The constitutionality of "per se" statutes has been consistently upheld by the courts despite attacks on a number of grounds. "Per se" statutes have been most frequently challenged on the ground that they violate due process of law by creating an unconstitutional irrebuttable presumption of intoxication. The courts have rejected this assertion by holding that "per se" statutes create a new crime and not a presumption of intoxication.[115]

Several constitutional challenges have been taken regarding the "irrebutable" presumption set forth in statutes wherein a breath or blood test taken within 2, 3 or even 4 hours (depending on your state's laws) after you stopped driving would be "good evidence" under the statute. In other words, if the number obtained was "taken" from a test that was administered to you within the statutory time limit after the traffic stop, that was a violation of the *per se* law.[116] Such legal rulings ignore the "science" behind alcohol absorption and elimination and allow conviction of innocent people who can **PROVE** that their alcohol level was still rising when stopped by the police shortly after their last drink.

---

[114]**Yarbrough v. State,** 241 Ga.App. 777, 527 S.E.2d 628 (2000).

[115]**Commonwealth v. McMullen,** 756 A.2d 58 (Pa. Super., 2000); **Forte v. State,** 686 S.W.2d 744 (Tex. App. 2nd District, 1985) affirmed at 722 S.W.2d 219; **Seattle v. Urban,** 32 Wash. App. 634, 648 P.2d 922 (1982); **State v. Larson,** 12 Kan. App. 2d 198, 737 P.2d 880 (1987).

[116]**State v. Martin**, 174 Ariz. 118, 847 P.2d 619 (Ariz.App. Div. 1,1992); **Bohannon v. State**, 269 Ga. 130, 497 S.E.2d 552 (1998); **State v. Crediford**, 130 Wash.2d 747, 927 P.2d 1129 (Wash., 1996).

Because alcohol is absorbed over a lengthy period after being consumed, and then eliminated over an even longer period, the attack is based on the fact that proof of consumption whereby the person's alcohol level was still rising when stopped, and arguably HIGHER when tested (possibly 45 minutes to an hour later), this violated due process rights. Several states have ruled that the State has the burden to prove the "number" at the time of driving, and without such proof, the defendant wins on this issue.[117] These states have upheld the spirit of due process over abdicating the political pressure and public opinion by "legislating" science to obtain convictions of people who may NOT have had the prohibited amount of alcohol in their systems when driving.

It has been held that in protecting the safety of its citizens a state legislature may determine that a driver with a blood alcohol concentration of 0.08% or more constitutes a serious and immediate threat to the public safety, and that the passage of a "per se" statute is a reasonable means of protecting the public safety.[118] The constitutionality of such breath alcohol "per se" statutes has also been upheld.[119]

The constitutionality of "per se" statutes has also been challenged on a "void for vagueness" attack. Defendants have alleged that because they have no way of knowing when their blood alcohol concentration reaches the prohibited level, "per se" statutes fail to give adequate notice of the forbidden conduct and are therefore unconstitutionally vague. The courts have rejected this argument, ruling that the consumption of alcohol should put a person of ordinary intelligence on notice that he or she is in jeopardy of violating the statute and that any person who drives after drinking should reasonably be aware of the possibility of violating the statute.[120]

It has been held that the enforcement of a "per se" statute is not an unreasonable or unconstitutional exercise of police power.[121] It has also been held that a "per se" statute does not violate the equal protection clause of the Constitution.[122] Finally, the use of an implied consent law in conjunction with a "per se" statute has been upheld against a claim that the conclusiveness of the evidence of blood alcohol concentration violates a defendant's privilege against self-incrimination.[123]

Chemical tests can play an important role in the prosecution of most DUI-DWI offenses. However, because of the nature of a "per se" offense, the prosecution must prove the accuracy and reliability of the chemical test in "per se" cases more than in other types of DUI-DWI cases. Because a chemical test result is normally the only significant evidence required to provide proof of a person's guilt in a "per se" case, some fair-minded courts have held that a higher

---

[117]**Commonwealth v. Barud,** 545 297, 681 A.2d 162 (1996); **People v. Mertz,** 68 N.Y.2d 136, 506 N.Y.S.2d 290 (N.Y., 1986); **Forte v. State,** 707 S.W.2d 89 (Tex.Crim.App., 1986).

[118]**Lovell v. State,** 283 Ark. 425, 678 S.W.2d 318 (1984).

[119]**State v. McManus,** 152 Wis. 2d 113, 447 N.W.2d 654 (1989).

[120]**Burg v. Municipal Court,** 35 Cal.3d 257, 673 P.2d 732 (1983); **Smith v. Charnes,** 728 P.2d 1287 (Colo. 1986); **State v. Thompson,** 138 Ariz. 341, 674 P.2d 895 (1984), **State v. Rose,** 312 N.C. 441, 323 S.E.2d 339 (1985); **State v. Muehlenberg,** 118 Wis. 2d 502, 347 N.W.2d 914 (1984). See generally, **Annotation:** *Validity, Construction, and Application of Statutes Directly Proscribing Driving With Blood-Alcohol Level in Excess of Established Percentage,* 54 A.L.R. 4th 149 (1987 - 2005).

[121]**Commonwealth v. Mikulan,** 504 Pa. 244, 470 A.2d 1339 (1983); **Lowell v. Arkansas,** 283 Ark. 425, 678 S.W.2d 318 (1984).

[122]**State v. Woerner,** 16 Ohio App.3d 59, 474 N.E.2d 354 (1984).

[123]**Nawrocki v. State,** 235 Ga. App. 416, 510 S.E.2d 301 (1998); **State v. Franco,** 96 Wash. 2d 816, 639 P.2d 1320 (1982).

degree of testing accuracy should be required in a "per se" case than in other types of DUI-DWI cases.[124]

In most states, where a test result at or above the 0.08% limit has been obtained by police, a "per se" offense will be accused (charged) as a separate and distinct "count" (the way that the state claims that the DUI-DWI law has been violated) from the traditional or common law offense of "driving while under the influence" or "driving while intoxicated." More often than not, however, both offenses are based on the same conduct by the defendant, and it is common in many states for a defendant to be charged with both offenses (in alternative "counts") in the same complaint or information. Once again, the defense must bring to court an expert witness who can explain to the jury or judge why the alcohol test result is unreliable or not worthy of belief.

Multiple convictions resulting from the same conduct are not permitted in many states and in the states where multiple convictions are allowed, multiple punishments (for a single act of drunk driving) are not permitted. In a few states a "per se" offense is treated as a lesser included offense of driving while under the influence of alcohol or of driving while intoxicated, and multiple convictions are thereby precluded. This will be discussed further in **Section 17.3.1** of this book.

1.3.2. The issue of "while" in *per se* cases. It is important to note at the outset that in traditional DUI-DWI cases it must be proven beyond a reasonable doubt that the driving occurred "while" the defendant was intoxicated or under the influence of an intoxicant. The fact that the defendant was intoxicated at a later or earlier time does not necessarily prove that he or she was intoxicated when the driving occurred. The issue of "while" is important in cases where the prosecution cannot establish the approximate time of driving as well as in cases where the defendant consumed intoxicants after the completion of the driving but prior to the arrival of the police. Accident cases are prime examples of where this lack of proof commonly occurs.

A typical case involving the issue of "while" is the case where an intoxicated defendant is found alone (usually asleep or unconscious) off the road in his or her vehicle, often following a one-car accident, and there is no warm engine, fresh tire tracks, fluid trail following a front-end collision or any other evidence showing that the vehicle had recently been driven. In such cases it may be necessary for the prosecution to produce independent evidence that the defendant drove the vehicle while in an intoxicated state in order to sustain a conviction.[125] Much, however, depends on the particular DUI-DWI statute. If the statute specifies "actual physical control" as the prohibited vehicular activity, a showing of recent driving by the defendant may not be necessary.[126]

Another typical case in which the issue of "while" is likely to arise is the case where an intoxicated defendant is apprehended by the police a considerable time after the completion of the driving and the defendant has, since the completion of the driving, consumed some alcohol. In cases of this sort it is often difficult for the prosecution to establish the defendant's degree of intoxication at the time of driving.[127] For this defense to be applicable, however, the defendant's

---

[124]**State v. Murphy,** 7 Ohio Misc. 2d 1, 453 N.E.2d 1304 (1983).

[125]**People v. Hess,** 24 Ill. App. 3d 299, 320 N.E.2d 344 (1974).

[126]**State v. Williams,** 752 S.W.2d 454 (Mo. App., 1988), **Adams v. State,** 697 P.2d 622 (Wyo., 1985), and supra, this section.

[127]**Boyle v. Tofany,** 36 N.Y.2d 1012, 337 N.E.2d 127 (1975); **State v. Liebhart,** 707 S.W.2d 427 (Mo. App., 1986).

evidence of post-driving drinking must be credible.[128] See **Section 6.16** for a discussion of post-driving drinking as a defense to a BAC obtained through chemical testing.

In both types of "while" cases discussed above, much depends on the time interval between the completion of driving and the arrival of the police. If a police officer arrives only a few minutes after the completion of driving by the defendant, circumstantial evidence of recent driving can almost always be found and a conviction will usually be sustained.[129] However, if several hours or an indefinite period elapsed between the end of driving and the arrival of a police officer, the prosecution's case will be much weaker.[130]

1.4. Driving Under the Influence of Inhalants or Drugs. Most DUI-DWI state statutes contain provisions making it illegal to drive a vehicle while under the influence of either inhalants or drugs. This means that there must be some proof that the drug was hampering or lowering your normal ability to drive. This applies to ALL types of drugs, whether over-the-counter, prescribed or contraband (illicit).

Most states also have laws that prohibit driving AT ALL with any trace of any "contraband" substance or the "burn-off" (metabolites) products in your bloodstream. By **contraband**, this means "illegal for all purposes." Blood tests or urine tests can detect traces of contraband substances such as marijuana or cocaine for hours, days or weeks after the person has used the drug. For such laws, no proof of impairment by the contraband drugs (or the burn-off products from such drugs) is necessary.

This lingering evidence from drug usage is due to the fact that most drugs and chemicals that people ingest to "get high" are fat-soluble. This means that these are not washed out of the body by water, as alcohol is. These fat-soluble drugs are stored in the fatty tissue of the body so that the liver can slowly break them down and eliminate them over a period of days (or weeks) for heavy regular users of some drugs.

The length of time depends on the drug, the dosage amount taken and over what period of time it was ingested (smoked, injected, swallowed or inhaled). Conviction for DUI-DWI is constitutionally permitted if the contraband drug or the metabolites of the contraband drug can be found in the person's system.[131]

In many statutes the term "controlled substance," "impairing substance" or "intoxicating substance" is substituted for the term "drug." Statutes making it illegal to drive while under the influence of drugs are generally interpreted and applied in the same manner as DUI-DWI statutes, except that the presumptive "impairment" statutes do not apply.[132] At the time of publishing this book, Virginia and Nevada are the only states to specify quantitative levels for "presumptive" impairment by certain drugs, but others will surely follow this model. For a copy of Virginia's new law, see http://theduibook.com/VAdrugstatute.htm.

---

[128]**Akins v. State,** 176 Ga. App. 254, 335 S.E.2d 486 (1985); **Gilmore v. State**, 242 Ga.App. 470, 530 S.E.2d 221 (2000).

[129]**State v. Williams,** 752 S.W.2d 454 (Mo. App., 1988); **Commonwealth v. Devereaux,** 304 Pa. Super. 327, 450 A.2d 704 (1982); **Milwaukee v. Kelly,** 40 Wis.2d 136, 161 N.W.2d 271 (1968).

[130]**People v. Wells,** 103 Ill.App.2d 128, 243 N.E.2d 427 (1968), **Abelson v. State,** 269 Ga.App. 596, 604 S.E.2d 647 (2004) [lack of proof at trial that the breath test was obtained within three hours of the test being taken]. and **State v. Dodson,** 496 S.W.2d 272 (Mo. App., 1973).

[131]**Shepler v. State,** 758 N.E.2d 966 (Ind.App., 2001).

[132]**Annotation:** *Automobiles - Driving Under the Influence, or When Addicted to the Use, of Drugs as Criminal Offense,* 17 A.L.R.3d 815 (1968 - 2005).

Unless an applicable statute contains a restrictive definition of the term "drug," the term is likely to be given a broad definition by the court. In Oklahoma, toluene, a common substance found in paint, varnishes, polyurethane and similar products, was held to constitute a drug for purposes of a driving while under the influence of drugs statute.[133] Also, medically prescribed insulin was held to be a drug for purposes of a similar statute.[134] So, it is apparent that the fact that you may inadvertently inhale paint fumes while doing your job will not excuse a DUI-DWI offense caused by toluene. Furthermore, medically necessary drugs that you inject or ingest can lead to you being charged with DUI-DWI if that drug or chemical causes you to be impaired.

Some jurisdictions are strict about the State providing proof of which drug or drugs caused the person to be impaired. The *type* of intoxicant must be named in the charging document (indictment, accusation, etc.).[135] Other states really do not mandate such proof, so long as credible evidence can be placed in front of the jury to show clear impairment and "symptoms" consistent with sufficient dosage of some drug that has caused impairment.[136]

1.5. Proof of Consumption or "Presence" in Defendant's System. If a defendant is charged with the offense of driving while under the influence of a controlled substance, evidence must exist of either consumption of the substance by the defendant or the presence of the substance in the defendant's body. Evidence that the defendant was physically impaired and that pills and prescription bottles containing a controlled substance were present in the defendant's vehicle is not sufficient to support a conviction.[137] Further, even if there is evidence of the ingestion of drugs, if the defendant is charged with driving while under the influence of drugs, state law usually requires evidence that the defendant's driving ability was impaired by the ingestion of drugs in order for a conviction to be sustained.[138]

The courts are divided as to whether a charge of driving while under the influence of drugs can be based on the use of a medically required drug. A few courts have reversed convictions based solely on the defendant's use of a medically required drug, at least when it was shown that the defendant was unaware of the effects of the drug.[139] Other courts have held that the fact that the use of a drug is medically required is not a defense to a charge of driving while under the influence of drugs under any circumstances.[140] Several states have enacted statutes providing that the lawful or prescribed use of a drug is not a defense to a charge of driving while under the influence of drugs.[141]

1.6. Lesser-Included Offenses of DUI-DWI. The DUI-DWI laws in a few states contain an offense commonly referred to as "driving while ability impaired," or DWAI. This

---

[133]**State v. Broadrick,** 620 P.2d 450 (Okla. Crim. App., 1980).

[134]**People v. Keith,** 184 Cal. App. 2d Supp. 884, 7 Cal. Rptr. 613 (1960).

[135]**State v. Cordell,** 34 S.W.3d 719 (Tex. App. Ft. Worth 2000).

[136]**Walker v. State,** 239 Ga.App. 831, 521 S.E.2d 861 (1999).

[137]**State v. Chipman,** 176 Or.App. 284, 31 P.3d 478, (2001); **Roach v. State,** 30 Ark. App. 119, 783 S.W.2d 376 (1990).

[138]**State v. Kachwalla,** 274 Ga. 886, 561 S.E.2d 403 (2003); **Sparks v. State,** 195 Ga. App. 589, 394 S.E. 2nd 407 (1990), overruled on other grounds, **Green v. State,** 260 Ga. 625, 398 S.E.2d 360 (1990).

[139]**Commonwealth v. Wallace,** 14 Mass. App. 358, 439 N.E.2d 848 (1982); **People v. Van Tuyl,** 79 Misc. 2d 262, 359 N.Y.S.2d 958 (1974).

[140]**People v. Keith,** 184 Cal. App. 2d Supp. 884, 7 Cal. Rptr. 613 (1960); **State v. Tamburro,** 68 N.J. 414, 346 A.2d 401 (1975).

[141]Louisiana - LSA-R.S. 14:98; North Carolina - N.C.G.S.A. § 20-171.14; California - West's Ann.Cal.Vehicle Code § 23630; Guam - 16 G.C.A. § 18114; Idaho - I.C. § 18-8004; Tennessee - T. C. A. § 55-10-402; Utah - U.C.A. 1953 § 41-6a-504.

offense is similar to an "under the influence" offense except that the degree of impairment or intoxication required for conviction is less.[142]

Typically, under a presumptive statute, a blood alcohol concentration of 0.08% is required to establish a presumption of "under the influence," while a blood alcohol concentration of 0.05% is required to establish a presumption of "driving while ability impaired." The offense of "driving while ability impaired" is normally a lesser-included offense of the offense of "driving while under the influence."[143]

In concluding this section, it should be noted that criminal intent is not an element of any misdemeanor DUI-DWI offense. In other words, a person does not need to intend to "drive drunk" for the Prosecutor to be able to prove a DUI-DWI case against the person. The courts have consistently held that DUI-DWI offenses contain no element of *mens rea* (i.e., criminal intent; wrongful purpose; a guilty mind). Thus, in a DUI-DWI case the prosecution is not required to establish a criminal or wrongful intent by the defendant.[144] All that the prosecution needs to prove is that the person intended to drink alcohol (or take the drugs) and then later operated a vehicle. The person's knowledge that he or she is impaired is NOT required to be proven by the prosecution.

This rule not requiring the prosecution to prove "specific intent" applies to both "per se" cases and "under the influence" cases.[145] Finally, it is not necessary for the prosecution to prove that the defendant was aware that he or she was "under the influence" in order to obtain a conviction in a traditional DUI-DWI case.[146] Some courts have stated that the burden on the State is that the prosecution must merely show that the person consumed alcohol and then drove. Your intent to get "drunk" or impaired or to consume so much alcohol that you exceed the *per se* limit applicable in that state is not required to be proven.[147]

1.7. Enhanced and Aggravated Drinking-Driving Offenses. An enhanced DUI-DWI offense is an ordinary misdemeanor DUI-DWI offense that is transformed into a higher class of misdemeanor or even a possible felony offense by the allegation and proof of certain pre-existing conditions or circumstances, usually the existence of one or more prior drinking and driving convictions against the defendant. Enhanced offenses are punishable by more severe penalties than ordinary, first lifetime, misdemeanor drinking and driving offenses.

In most jurisdictions, due to federal "carrot-and-stick" legislation, the state laws relating to DUI-DWI have "minimum mandatory" punishment guidelines that prevent a judge from handing out a light punishment during sentencing. These guidelines also may call for moving repeat offender misdemeanors into a higher "classification" of misdemeanor, or even make repeat offenses a felony.

In Georgia, for example, a third DUI offense changes the simple misdemeanor offense into a "high and aggravated" misdemeanor DUI offense. The term **"high and aggravated misdemeanor"** requires jail time of not fewer than 26 days for each 30 days of the original

---

[142]**People v. McNamara,** 269 A.D.2d 544, 704 N.Y.S.2d 100 (2000), **State v. Gonzalez,** 14 Conn. App. 216, 541 A.2d 115 (1988).

[143]**People v. McNamara,** 269 A.D.2d 544, 704 N.Y.S.2d 100 (2000).

[144]**State v. Martinez** 268 Kan. 21, 988 P.2d 735 (1999); **State v. Tang,** 75 Wash. App. 473, 878 P.2d 487 (1994); **State v. Goding,** 126 N.H. 50, 489 A.2d 579 (1985); **State v. Pistole,** 16 Ohio App. 3d 386, 476 N.E.2d 365 (1984); **State v. West,** 416 A.2d 5 (Me. 1980).

[145]**Van Brunt v. State,** 646 P.2d 872 (Alaska App., 1982).

[146]**Morgan v. Anchorage,** 643 P.2d 691 (Alaska App. 1982).

[147]**State v. Martin,** 146 S.W.3d 64 (Tenn.Crim.App. 2004).

sentence. A person serving time for a simple misdemeanor can get "2 days-for-1 day" jail time credit for good behavior, but this option is not available for a person under a "high and aggravated" sentence.

In some states the enhancement of a drinking and driving offense may be caused by conditions or circumstances other than prior convictions (e.g., driving while already suspended, driving while having been declared an habitual violator for repeatedly being DUI, having had a prior implied consent testing refusal decided against you, or having a prior *per se* implied consent suspension imposed against you, etc.).

In response to federal legislation controlling highway funds, most states have added a type of enhanced DUI-DWI crime where the driver's blood or breath alcohol level exceeds a specified "number." For example, the state of Arizona has enacted a law describing "an EXTREME DUI as follows: "It is unlawful for a person to drive or be in actual physical control of a vehicle in this state if the person has an alcohol concentration of 0.15 or more within two hours of driving or being in actual physical control of the vehicle and the alcohol concentration results from alcohol consumed either before or while driving or being in actual physical control of the vehicle."[148] Punishments are increased dramatically over the penalty of a normal DUI-DWI in that state.

The following chart reviews Connecticut law, and will give some idea how enhanced penalties [for either refusing to be tested or having a high blood (or breath) alcohol level] cause mandatory loss of license periods to be increased.

Enhanced drinking and driving offenses should not be confused with aggravated DUI-DWI *criminal* offenses. An aggravated DUI-DWI criminal offense occurs when the defendant, while driving under the influence of alcohol, is involved in an accident wherein another person is seriously injured or killed. Aggravated DUI-DWI offenses are usually called "vehicular manslaughter," "homicide by vehicle," "serious injury by vehicle," and (in some jurisdictions) "murder."[149] These "aggravated" or "serious" driving cases are felonies in virtually every instance, and require some proof that the driver was either impaired by alcohol or drugs, or that the driver had a *per se* blood alcohol level equal to or above the applicable legal limit.

Administrative License Loss — Connecticut:

Blood Alcohol Level	1st offense	2nd offense	3rd offense
Refusal to be Tested	6 months	1 year	3 years
Under 21 0.02 Per Se	90 days	9 months	2 years
0.08 to 0.16 Per Se	90 days	9 months	2 years
Above 0.16 Per Se	**120** days	**10** months	**2.5** years

Additional Suspension if Later Convicted in the DUI Criminal Case (Connecticut):

License Loss:	1 year	3 years	5 years

The basic difference between the two types of offenses is that enhanced offenses are usually pursued against repeat offenders or those with elevated alcohol levels, while aggravated criminal offenses are filed in DUI-DWI cases involving injury or death. Aggravated drunken driving cases are discussed briefly throughout this book, but most details of the intricacies of such felony offenses, state-by-state, are beyond the scope of this national book on

---

[148]A.R.S. § 28-1382.
[149]**People v. Calderon**, 129 Cal.App.4th 1301, 29 Cal.Rptr.3d 277 (Cal.App. 5 Dist., 2005).

a basic DUI-DWI offense. Consult a highly trained and qualified DUI-DWI attorney in your state for this information.

Most aspects of felony drinking and driving cases are similar to misdemeanor DUI-DWI cases. In both types of cases the prosecution must allege and prove each element of the DUI-DWI offense charged. For example, the prosecutor may not only have to prove that the defendant was intoxicated (on either alcohol or drugs) but that due to that impairment, the defendant caused serious injury (or death) to other persons (either in defendant's vehicle, in another vehicle, or as pedestrians along the roadway).

For felony DUI-DWI cases, the range of jail punishment can be from 2 to 20 years in a state prison for homicide by vehicle (or manslaughter by vehicle) cases to *life imprisonment* in states that permit charging the driver with murder, after killing a person in an accident while drunk (or drugged). Alabama, North Carolina and California have such laws, to name a few.[150]

In an enhanced case, however, the prosecution must also allege and prove the conditions or circumstances that justify the "enhancement." This is usually derived from the existence of one or more valid prior impaired driving (DUI-DWI) convictions against the defendant, *or* possibly the existence of an elevated blood or breath alcohol level *or* (in California) where the driver has (at sentencing for a prior conviction) been apprised of the dangers of drinking and driving and the risk of serious injury or death, so that IF he or she does get involved in a crash, the person can be charged with murder.[151]

Due to national reporting of dangerous drivers (See **Section 17.3.4.**), convictions in other jurisdictions count as a "prior" offense virtually all the time, absent some flaw or statutory difference in the conviction from a different state. Providing your attorney with accurate information about your prior traffic and criminal history can be critical to your lawyer giving you accurate and dependable advice on possible plea alternatives and likely penalties if you opt for trial and are not successful. Be aware that your attorney is not going to report any prior offenses that the prosecutor is unable to locate on various criminal and motor vehicle databases. Plus, you can remain silent at sentencing pursuant to the holding in a landmark United States Supreme Court case, *Mitchell v. United States*, 526 U.S. 314, 119 S.Ct. 1307, 143 L.Ed.2d 424 (1999).

A skilled DUI-DWI defense attorney can sometimes make the difference between a murder conviction and a jury verdict for a lesser-included offense.[152] When a person's freedom is at stake in a felony case involving DUI-DWI and a death or a serious injury to another person in a related accident, getting the best available trial lawyer is critical.[153]

Be aware that when another person has died in a collision that occurred due to intentional bad driving, or driving with "reckless disregard" for the safety of others on the highway, most states also permit the prosecutor to seek felony enhancement of punishment for these other "predicate" (underlying) misdemeanor driving offenses that are "causally connected" to accidents causing death. The typical types of "serious" or "inherently dangerous" driving activity offenses in most states include "hit and run" (leaving the scene of an accident when

---

[150]**People v. Vanegas**, 115 Cal.App.4th 592, 9 Cal.Rptr.3d 398 (Cal.App. 2 Dist., 2004); **Richey v. State**, 853 So.2d 286 (Ala.Crim.App., 2002); **State v. Rich**, 351 N.C. 386, 527 S.E.2d 299 (N.C., 2000).

[151]**People v. Watson,** 30 Cal.3d 290, 637 P.2d 279 (1981).

[152]**Davis v. State**, 882 So.2d 884 (Ala.Crim.App., 2003).

[153]**State v. Collier,** 279 Ga. 316, 612 S.E.2d 281 (2005); **Crawford v. State,** 886 So.2d 846 (Ala.Crim.App., 2003**); Miller v. State,** 236 Ga.App. 825, 513 S.E.2d 27 (1999).

another person has been injured), attempting to elude a pursuing police officer,[154] aggressive driving (in some jurisdictions), racing (in some jurisdictions),[155] passing a stopped school bus (with visible signals to stop) that is discharging or picking up passengers[156] or possibly reckless driving.[157]

If you have committed one of these "serious" driving offenses (e.g., hit and run) and are also drunk at the time of the driving that led to the death, the prosecutor is allowed to charge the crime in *alternative* "counts" (separate paragraphs which set forth different alleged "causes" of the death of the person the defendant hit) within the indictment, information, accusation or other applicable charging papers. This means that the jury hearing the case against you will have more than one way (i.e., alternative ways) to consider the evidence and possibly find you "guilty" on one or more "counts.

1.8. The legal process. To provide a better baseline and roadmap for what any defendant faces in his or her particular state, sample misdemeanor flow charts of how a case proceeds from arrest through trial can be found in Section 5.11 of this book. One is from Michigan and the other from Georgia. Be aware that the process you face in your state may vary. This is yet another reason why every defendant facing any "drunk driving" charge should consult with a DUI-DWI specialist.

---

[154]**State v. Bethea**, 605 S.E.2d 173 (N.C.App., 2004) where Bethea was convicted of murder for attempting to elude and driving with reckless disregard of others at 100 m.p.h]

[155]**People v. Calhoun**, 20 Cal.Rptr.3d 537 (Cal.App. 4 Dist., 2004).

[156]O.C.G.A. § 40-6-393.

[157]Illinois - 625 ILCS 5/11-503; Virginia - Va. Code Ann. § 46.2-868.

Chapter 2

Being Confronted by the Police and Becoming a DUI-DWI Suspect —
Which Factors and Evidence Will Hurt or Help You?

2.0. Purpose of this chapter. The purpose of this chapter is to help you make the best possible decisions if you are facing a situation where you are being investigated by the police for suspicion of DUI-DWI. You may currently be facing a pending DUI-DWI charge, or perhaps have had a prior charge. If this is the case, you need to be fully aware of your legal obligations and your rights under both federal and state laws.

Millions of citizens routinely have made it a practice to have a glass of wine or a beer with dinner when they dine out. Others stop on their way home at a bar or club to have a drink or two with friends before driving home. These actions alone are not necessarily illegal for persons age 21 and over, although the police may use the odor of alcohol on your breath as their justification for your DUI-DWI arrest.

Also, certain factors may exist that make it much more likely that you will be stopped by a police roadblock. After living in a region for any period of time, you may recognize that because of an area's high concentration of late-night drinking establishments, certain sections of town will be more prone to police departments utilizing roadblocks. Similarly, certain main business highways are traffic arteries leading to and from "party areas" of towns or cities. It is common knowledge that the police are more likely to set up a DUI-DWI checkpoint on or near such arterial roads.

If you drive through these areas after 10 PM, you are much more likely to be stopped by the police than if you drive in these areas during daylight hours. Likewise, your chances of encountering a roadblock at 2 A.M. are 100 times more likely than they are at 2 PM in these areas. Hopefully, this chapter will be read by you before any such confrontation between you and the police occurs, so that you can make better choices that will help you avoid being accused of DUI-DWI.

However, if you have already gone through a situation where the police have arrested you for a DUI-DWI, in order to allow you and your DUI-DWI specialist to prepare your best defense, each of the subsections in this chapter should be considered and remembered in order to identify defenses or possible trial strategies for your attorney in preparing your case. By understanding the legal process, you will be better equipped to assist in your own defense.

The primary purpose of this chapter is to explain *when, where* and *how* you are most likely to be confronted by the police in situations where you may be suspected of impaired driving. If you are suspected of being impaired, you will be asked to submit to field sobriety evaluations. Whether you submit to these roadside evaluations or not, you will be asked to submit to implied consent testing. If you were previously arrested for DUI-DWI, it is critical that you be aware of these factors.

This information will not really help the person who gets trashed from alcohol or drugs (or both) to avoid being arrested (and probably convicted), so don't look for any "magic pill" or "super secrets" to cover that situation. Such grossly impaired drivers have no ability to recall the information in this book, much less use it when confronted by the police. For others who use moderation, knowing what to do, what to say (and NOT say) and how to respond to an officer can be of critical importance. Declining certain field evaluations, remaining silent or requesting the advice of an attorney may help win your case. For a substantial percentage of people who read this book, a potential DUI-DWI arrest situation WILL present itself in the future. Plus, it will likely occur when you least expect it.

Nothing in this book, or any book, can help a grossly impaired driver not be detected through simple observation of the typical manifestations that officers are trained to document when confronting a drunk or drugged driver. Honestly, a normal citizen can usually identify these same "symptoms," even if he or she is less capable than an officer of verbally describing the characteristics of a "drunk" at court. A basic premise of this book is that over 90% of the people who do consume alcohol and later drive do so with the full expectation that they pose no risk to the general driving public based on the amount of alcohol consumed.

The smell of alcoholic beverages or contraband (illegal) drugs such as marijuana will legally authorize any law enforcement officer who has "legally" come in contact with you to do further "investigation" to determine whether or not a crime has been or is about to be committed. Every state permits this "initial encounter" to take place with you (assuming the initial contact with you was legally made) and the laws of almost every jurisdiction consistently state that no *Miranda* or other advisement about your legal rights needs to be given AT THIS POINT. This could later be changed to a "custodial" (your arrest) situation by virtue of what is said and done between the officer and you. Then, *Miranda* warnings are required before other questioning by the officer can occur.

Be aware that your perception of what *Miranda* warnings protect is not the same perception of most American courts. Since its 1966 decision, *Miranda* advisements have been severely limited by our conservative courts. Most jurisdictions limit *Miranda* protections to situations where clear custody of you by the police exists and where the officer is questioning you in a manner that incriminating statements could be expected. In nearly all jurisdictions, *Miranda* has not been extended to cover field sobriety exercises or being asked to deliver a breath sample. Ironically, Canada has better protections of its citizens than we presently do in the United States.

2.1. The two general types of DUI-DWI. Police officers utilize two primary ways to charge you with "drunk" driving. These are "impaired driving" and "driving with an unlawful blood alcohol level" or "per se" DUI-DWI. These two types of offenses cover over 95% of all active DUI-DWI cases. The remaining cases involve "drugged" driving or impaired driving caused by other substances such as noxious vapors.

Impaired Driving is the *first* and most common type of DUI-DWI. This form of DUI-DWI has the usual components of a traditional (common law) drunk driving case involving these *elements* (essential parts of the crime that must be proven by the prosecutor to justify a conviction): **(a)** operating or being in actual physical control of a "vehicle;" **(b)** on a roadway, public way or other place prohibited by that state's laws (some states cover "any place within the state"); **(c)** while under the influence of an intoxicating beverage, substance, vapor or chemical, or some combination of these chemicals and substances.

This type of DUI-DWI requires proof of impairment through testimony of one or more witnesses, and (where available) a quantitative breath or blood test result for alcohol content. Only Virginia and Nevada have passed legislation establishing presumptive impairment levels based on certain contraband drugs. Nevada's law was enacted in 2003,[158] while Virginia passed their new law in 2005.[159]

A *second* major type of offense now exists that has absolutely *NO REQUIREMENT OF PROVING IMPAIRMENT* of the driver. It is sometimes called **"Driving UBAL"** or "driving with an unlawful blood alcohol level" when the driver has consumed enough alcohol to exceed the applicable legal limit for the driver's age group and vehicle type. Presently, as a result of the legal history set forth in Chapter 1, every state in America has very similar laws covering these various situations:

Drivers age 21 and over, in a non-commercial vehicle	0.08%
Drivers under age 21 [ZERO TOLERANCE *]	> 0.00 to 0.02%
Any driver of a commercial motor vehicle	0.04%

* State laws vary from a 0.00%, 0.01% or 0.02% standard for "zero tolerance." Go on-line to review your state's law for underage drivers: http://www.theduibook.stateDUIDWIsummaries.htm.

For those who take the state's test and render a sample with an alcohol level at or over the state's legal limit, this alone (assuming the test result gets into evidence and is believed by the jury or judge hearing your case) constitutes the separate offense of DUI-DWI **"per se"**. Note that quantitative impaired driving limits for contraband drugs have not YET been "established" by the federal government, but that this legislation will be enacted within the next 2 to 5 years. Hence, today, only ALCOHOL has quantitative impairment guidelines limits for traditional DUI-DWI.

2.2. Remain silent — it is your right! Your speech and other clues the police use to justify your arrest. The Fifth Amendment to the United States Constitution[160] has been found to include that you have an absolute right to remain silent and not incriminate yourself during your arrest and booking process.[161] This right applies to everyone,[162] is true in every state,[163] and it is true even if you are an alien or an illegal alien.[164] Once the arresting officer has read you your *Miranda* warnings, your silence after receiving the advisement cannot be used against you in court.[165]

You need to tell the officer(s) you have made the choice to remain silent.[166] This does not mean that you should not be appropriately polite with the law enforcement officers, using such terms as "please" and "thank you." Beyond providing the police identification information

---

[158]NRS 484.379(3).

[159]Va. Code Ann. § 18.2-269(A)(4).

[160]No person … shall be compelled in any criminal case to be a witness against himself… **U.S.C.A. Const. Amend. V.**

[161]**U. S. ex rel. Young v. Follette**, 308 F.Supp. 670 (S.D.N.Y. 1970); **U.S. ex rel. Parker v. McMann**, 308 F.Supp. 477(D.C.N.Y.1969); **U.S. v. Smith**, 31 F.R.D. 553 (D.C.D.C.1962).

[162]**Miranda v. Arizona**, 86 S.Ct. 1602, 384 U.S. 436, 16 L.Ed.2d 694 (1966).

[163]**Malloy v. Hogan**, 84 S.Ct. 1489, 378 U.S. 1, 12 L.Ed.2d 653 (1964).

[164]**U. S. v. Henry**, 604 F.2d 908 (5th Cir.(Fla.) 1979); **U.S. v. Brooks**, 284 F. 908 (E.D.Mich. 1922).

[165]**Smith v. Fairman**, 862 F.2d 630 (7th Cir.(Ill.) 1988).

[166]**Waldrop v. Thigpen**, 857 F.Supp. 872 (N.D.Ala. 1994).

such as your name and address, and showing them your driver's license, you do not have to answer any questions relating to why you were arrested. If you began answering some questions and decided that the questions are likely to incriminate you, the Miranda warnings also allow you to cease all answers if you demand to have your lawyer present.

If your stop was based on the officer's "reasonable suspicion," the police officer has the right to expect you to identify yourself,[167] and to have you produce your driver's license. Police officers receive training, including mock trial practice, during which they must recite sufficient information to support their decision to arrest a suspect. The training has led to officers spouting off a litany of these "common" symptoms of apparent intoxication so that the officer can survive a pre-trial motion to suppress challenging an arrest decision that lacked proper justification. A good defense attorney will argue lack of clear evidence of impairment if these symptoms are missing.

One handbook written for prosecutors and police officers provides this list:

The following facts and circumstances, not all of which will be present in any given case, are relevant to establish whether a person's driving ability was impaired, as demonstrated by indicia of observable intoxication and field "sobriety tests":

[A] Alcohol symptom checklist
-- Smell of alcohol
-- Impaired fine motor control
-- Impaired gross motor control
-- Slurred speech
-- Change in speech volume
-- Decreased alertness
-- Excessive sweating
-- Slow or shallow respiration
-- Inappropriate sleepiness
-- Changes in rate of speech
-- Bloodshot eyes

[B] Other factors possibly relating to observable signs of intoxication
-- Erratic operation of motor vehicle
-- Defective balance (e.g., staggering, stumbling, swaying)
-- Disheveled clothing
-- Flushed or pale face
-- Lack of coordination (e.g., staggering, fumbling with license)
-- Impaired memory (e.g., forgetting where registration is)
-- Impaired judgment
-- Impaired sight or hearing
-- Unusual attitude (e.g., hilariousness, combativeness)
-- Unusual physical acts (e.g., vomiting, belching, hiccupping)
-- Lack of awareness of surroundings or time of day

---

[167]**Hiibel v. Sixth Judicial Dist. Court of Nevada, Humboldt County,** 542 U.S. 177, 124 S.Ct. 2451, 159 L.Ed.2d 292 (2004).

[C] Factors relating to *alternative explanations* for indicia of observable intoxication

    -- Type and operating condition of vehicle
    -- Operator's familiarity with vehicle
    -- Sickness or injury at time of occurrence in issue
    -- Recent blows to the head
    -- Recent treatment by doctor or dentist
    -- Use of prescribed drugs or medicines
    -- Use of substance giving alcohol or beverage odor (e.g., mouthwash)
    -- Physical disabilities or defects (e.g., back condition)
    -- Pathological conditions having symptoms in common with those of alcoholic influence (e.g., diabetes, epilepsy)
    -- Speech defects (e.g., lisping, stuttering)
    -- Activities preceding occurrence in issue
    -- Fatigue

[D] Additional factors relating to field "sobriety tests"

-- Type of procedure administered
-- Precision of officer's directions
-- Understanding of directions
-- Performance by subject
-- Nervousness of subject
-- Presence or absence of witnesses
-- Scoring of tests and preservation of evidence (e.g., on videotape)
-- Quality of officer's memory
-- Quality of subject's memory
-- Time and place of administration of procedure
-- Factors affecting coordination (age, weight, training)
-- Clothing worn by subject (e.g., high-heeled shoes)
-- Characteristics of standing surface and location of procedure
-- Lighting, particularly stroboscopic or flashing lights
-- Other circumstances surrounding administration of procedure

Source: Kwasnoski, John B., Stephen, John, & Partridge, Gerald, ***Officer's DUI Handbook,*** Lexis Publishing (1998) at 3.

Category **[C]** above is a list of explanations (excuses) that officers sometimes ask the driver about in order to eliminate these alternative reasons for the bad driving or inability to perform field evaluations that has been observed. Remember that an officer WANTS to hear your speech patterns to determine if your speech is slurred, thick-tongued, disorganized or otherwise "impaired" sounding.

Certain drugs will also cause thick-tongued or very slow, halting speech patterns. If an officer can address any possible excuses for such symptoms during the first part of his or her conversation with you, it is more likely that you will not be able to assert a viable explanation of your errant driving or your unusual speech patterns when the case comes to court. Again, you should **REMAIN SILENT.**

When an officer approaches your vehicle's window, after asking for your license and possibly other documents, a question from the officer will usually start off the encounter. "Sir, do you know how fast you were going?" or "Is there some reason that you were not able to stay in your lane back there?" or "Miss, I clocked you with laser going 78 in a 45 miles per hour zone. Are you on your way to an emergency or something?"

The *content* of your answer is relatively unimportant to the officer. The *manner* of speech is what is being observed. Unfortunately, even officers with extensive training can be misled by what they hear. A large number of officers believe they can predict how much alcohol you have in your system through listening to your speech patterns.[168]

Engaging in lengthy excuses does nothing to improve the chances that you will be allowed to leave the scene, if the smell of alcohol or of contraband drugs is present. If the officer smells or suspects that he or she smells anything that might impair you, the next step of the officer's investigation is to ask you to step out of the vehicle.

Each aspect of this "exiting of the vehicle" maneuver will be noted by the officer in detail later, from how quickly you exit, whether you use the side of the car or door frame or arm rest of the car to assist your exit, whether you fumble with items in your hands, such as keys or wallet, whether you drop anything, how you balance yourself or possibly sway, once you get out---*anything and everything.* If you are crying, belligerent, pleading to be let go or exhibiting similar behavior that might possibly be associated with an impaired individual, the officer will note it in the report that he or she fills out later.

Although almost no one does this, you may be better off not immediately stepping out of the vehicle. If you politely ask the officer, "May I ask why I need to get out of the car?" he or she will usually advise you that impairment is suspected. If so, tell the officer that **you would like to call an attorney** to determine his or her advice about what to do. The officer will not usually allow this to be done and will insist that you need to step out. If you are "assisted" in exiting your vehicle (by the officer opening your door or touching your arm), then custody has likely occurred. DO NOT PHYSICALLY RESIST THE OFFICER, but **verbally try to decline getting out** of your vehicle.

2.3. Assume that everything is being recorded. A large number of police vehicles these days have the capability for either video or audio recording (or both) of everything that occurs in the general vicinity of the officer manning the vehicle. The camera usually is positioned to capture the scene in front of the vehicle, as is often attached by a bracket next to the interior rearview mirror. That is why the officer usually does any field sobriety testing in front of his car, or why the officer questions you in front of his car. Be aware, however, that most modern cameras can be rotated 360 degrees to be repositioned by the officer to focus on you sitting in the backseat of the car while at the roadside or while you are being transported to jail.

Audio microphones are located both on the officer's shirt or vest and inside his or her vehicle. The officer often has the capability to turn these microphones on and off individually, so that he or she can have private conversations with other officers, the dispatcher or a supervisor, yet catch any and every word you say on tape. **Remember: REMAIN SILENT even when you think you are alone and in a "private" place.**

If the officer is investigating you for DUI-DWI, it is then safe for you to assume that everything is being recorded from the time the officer first stops your vehicle through you either being delivered to the jail. This is especially true of anything you say, since the microphone in the back of the officer's patrol car can pick even a whisper that you utter under your breath.

---

[168]Fenella Sanders, **Straight Talk - R&D - News of science, medicine, and technology**, Discover, Vol. 21, No. 10 (Oct. 2000).

2.4. Common driving conduct or vehicle problems leading to traffic stops.

Today, officers assigned to a "DUI Task Force" team or similar special traffic enforcement unit will basically pull over any vehicle they see or come in contact with that gives them ANY explainable reason for confronting the driver. These special units typically operate at late hours (typically, 10 PM until 6 AM or 11 PM until 7 AM) and on high DUI-DWI days (Wednesday through Sunday, typically) when they know to expect a sizable percentage of drivers (1 or 2 out of every 10) to be drinking or using some substance that may impair them.

Except when DUI-DWI enforcement occurs through established roadside sobriety checkpoints (roadblocks) or at an accident scene, the first interaction with a police officer usually occurs when errant driving conduct or some defective item of equipment or an expired tag draws the officer's attention to your vehicle. This indicates to him or her that the vehicle can be stopped and legally investigated. Sometimes the "thing" that leads to your pullover may be unrelated to your driving actions, such as when an obvious equipment defect exists or an expired registration or inspection sticker is visible on your car.

However, the NHTSA (the National Highway Traffic Safety Administration, an arm of the federal Department of Transportation) has identified a number of visual driving cues (or clues, as they are sometimes referred to by officers) that NHTSA suggests police officers use to identify possible alcohol-impaired driving. Because this material is widely distributed to police agencies and included in the recommended NHTSA training program, it has become the initial basis upon which most officers begin to document their probable cause for stopping a vehicle in drunk driving enforcement.

This material was first published through NHTSA in 1981 as ***Visual Detection of Driving While Intoxicated - An Explanation of the DWI Detection Guide*** (DOT-HS-805711). The list is based upon 20 driving cues (clues) that NHTSA determined, from some detailed research, were the best ones for identifying likely night-time drunk drivers (.10 BAC or more) and setting them apart from night-time sober drivers. The clues were based on field studies where 4,600 patrol stops were correlated with BAC measurements. NHTSA published information suggesting that the 20 cues (clues) could be associated with 90% of all impaired driving detections.

This list was taught to every NHTSA "Standardized Field Sobriety Test" student for over twenty years. The list has been revised and placed in "groupings" recently to reflect newer "studies." See information on the new study at http://www.theduibook.com/NHTSAlist.htm.

The original 1981 NHTSA detection guide also assigned a probability to each of the cues purporting to indicate the relative probability (from a high of 65% to a low of 30%) that a driver exhibiting the cue was driving with a BAC of .10% or more. Seeing two or more of these cues in combination with each other increased the likelihood of the driver having a blood alcohol level of 0.10% or more. NHTSA warned users, however, that the probability values were intended primarily to emphasize the relative importance of a particular cue or clue and ***did not endorse using them when testifying in court.***

The list of clues or cues, as originally published,[169] is as follows:

1.	Turning with a wide radius	65%
2.	Straddling the Center or Lane Marker Line	65%
3.	Appearing to be drunk	60%
4.	Almost striking and object or vehicle	60%
5.	Weaving	60%
6.	Driving on other than designated roadway	55%
7.	Swerving	55%
8.	Slow speed (driving 10 mph or more under the speed limit)	50%
9.	Stopping, without cause, in the traffic lane	50%
10.	Following too closely	50%
11.	Drifting	50%
12.	Tires on center or lane marker	45%
13.	Braking erratically	45%
14.	Driving into opposing or crossing traffic	45%
15.	Signaling inconsistent with driving actions	40%
16.	Slow response to traffic signals	40%
17.	Stopping inappropriately (other than in traffic lane)	35%
18.	Turning abruptly or illegally	35%
19.	Accelerating or decelerating rapidly	30%
20.	Headlights off	30%

The foregoing list applies to cars, trucks, and other traditional vehicles. The list for motorcycle drivers is different. For an up-to-date consideration of the "cues" the officers are looking for to detect an impaired *motorcyclist*, check out a recent pamphlet outlining similar acts by motorcyclists published by the National Highway Transportation and Safety Administration.[170]

The two things that should immediately come to every reader's mind are **(1)** everyone has done some of these things, possibly on a daily basis, especially in the era of the hand-held cell phone, and **(2)** that the most common traffic offense, **speeding**, is _not_ on the list. Going back to what was stated before, ANY driving behavior, vehicle deficiency or activity that looks the slightest bit suspicious will usually result in an officer coming in contact with you, just to see if you display any signs of drinking or using drugs.

2.5. Driving a Vehicle that Invites Being Pulled Over. Equipment defects or vehicle safety problems sometimes provide the basis for an officer to pull you over. A dozen examples of such defects from reported appellate cases include the following:

(1) tires with insufficient tread;
(2) damaged, "starburst" or cracked windshield;
(3) outside mirror or other required equipment missing (e.g., fender or bumper);
(4) window tint too dark, vehicle glass in violation of state law;
(5) someone in vehicle not wearing seatbelt;
(6) tag not mounted in proper place, possibly in back window;
(7) dim or inoperable tail (brake, running) lights;
(8) excessive smoke coming from under the vehicle;

---

[169]NHTSA 1995.

[170]http://www.nhtsa.dot.gov/people/injury/pedbimot/motorcycle/610DWIMotorcyWeb/pages/index.htm.

(9) passenger hanging out window or gesturing to other motorists;

(10) honking horn inappropriately at night in residential area;

(11) improper dealer tag or "drive-out" tag on vehicle; and

(12) loud muffler or tail pipe extension (Glass Pack).

These correctable items (which likely would never merit a pullover during morning rush hour) have led to many late night traffic stops that ultimately resulted in DUI-DWI arrests. Remember, the officer only needs a single REASON for coming in contact with you and your vehicle. His or her REAL purpose in stopping you is to see if you are impaired or have other smells, visible or audible evidence of possible impairment.

If this sounds "unconstitutional" to you, it does NOT sound unconstitutional to the United States Supreme Court! In 1996, the high court *UNANIMOUSLY* approved of this type of tactic by police in a landmark decision that drastically reduced our legal and privacy rights as Americans.[171] Subsequent cases from our high court have further whittled away at the few remaining rights we have while driving our vehicles in 21st Century America.[172]

2.6. Avoiding roadblocks. Just like spiders looking for flies, DUI-DWI Task Force officers in major metropolitan cities set up their roadblocks where they are aware their "prey" is located. Therefore, they set up roadblocks at locations along major thoroughfares that have high numbers of restaurants and bars that lead to interstate highways and similar traffic arteries. See http://www.duiblog.com/2005/07/14#a205 for how governments get rich from DUI-DWI arrests.

The federal government will not allow roadblocks on interstate highways for a variety of reasons, starting with safety concerns. Hence, getting to the interstate for purposes of avoiding a roadblock is one basic strategy to avoid a roadblock.

However, the police know that most traffic will seek access to an interstate to travel home. Hence, the police will try to set up their sobriety checkpoints along one of these "feeder" roadways. Knowing or guessing which roadway has the roadblock set up is the gamble. The teams of sobriety checkpoint officers decide when and where they will establish the checkpoint and then converge at an appointed hour to block traffic on that street. Having the ability to allow cars to pull over to the shoulder or adjacent parking lots is a key safety concern of police at these roadblocks.

Virtually every roadblock has a "chase" car. This is an officer waiting in an idling vehicle at a strategic vantage point to see any vehicles that attempt to avoid the roadblock. These "chase" officers assume that ANY vehicle turning away from the roadblock is trying to avoid detection for possible impaired driving. Several cases across the USA have held that citizens who do not wish to be delayed at a roadblock, or citizens who believe they have happened upon an accident scene that is delaying traffic may find a safe, legal way to leave and not pass through the safety or sobriety checkpoint.[173] However, if you make an abrupt, unsafe or illegal maneuver in turning around, this will usually justify the chase car pulling you over.

---

[171]**Whren v. United States**, 517 U.S. 806, 116 S.Ct. 1769, 135 L.Ed.2d 89 (1996).

[172]**Ohio v. Robinette**, 519 U.S. 33, 117 S. Ct. 417, 136 L. Ed. 2d 347 (1996); **Atwater v. City of Lago Vista**, 532 U.S. 318, 121 S.Ct. 1536, 149 L.Ed.2d 549 (2001); **Hiibel v. Sixth Judicial Dist. Court of Nevada, Humboldt County**, 542 U.S. 177, 124 S.Ct. 2451, 159 L.Ed.2d 292 (2004); **Illinois v. Caballes**, 543 U.S. 405, 125 S.Ct. 834, 160 L.Ed.2d 842 (2005).

[173]**State v. Bryson**, 142 Ohio App.3d 397, 755 N.E.2d 964 (Ohio App. 8 Dist. 2001); **State v. Badessa**, 185 N.J. 303, 885 A.2d 430 (N.J. 2005).

Officers will usually position the roadblock location around a bend in a road, or over the crest of a hill, so that cars approaching the location will not have any side street to use to avoid passing through the checkpoint. Safety issues can pose a problem for the police if visibility of oncoming cars is limited or restricted by such hidden but dangerous locations. In one roadblock case handled by the author, the only roadway possible to turn upon as cars approached the roadblock was a horseshoe shaped road that emptied back onto the same roadway. Any car that made that turn, even if the turn was legal, was pulled over by the chase car. This roadblock was declared to be illegally set up by the trial judge when pre-trial motions were heard.

The great majority of cases that have declared certain roadblocks to be unconstitutional have been cases in which one of five scenarios occurred:

1. The person stopped turning away from the roadblock committed no crime, and the traffic stop was not supported by reasonable suspicion that any crime had been committed or was about to be committed.[174]

2. The roadblock was not established by supervisory personnel in accordance with federal or state constitutional law.[175]

3. The location of the roadblock or the approved date for the roadblock was different from the approved location or date set up by supervisory personnel.[176]

4. Lack of proof that cars were being stopped systematically, or lacking a consistent pattern of selected vehicles were being stopped (e.g., every 3rd vehicle) so that the pattern of checking cars was arbitrary.[177]

5. The officers at the roadway lacked sufficient training in DUI-DWI detection to assure that good probable cause decisions were being made at the checkpoint, so as to not inconvenience or delay innocent parties.[178]

Roadblocks have become a profit center for many municipalities. Although intended to deter drunk drivers, roadblocks usually result in many types of tickets being written other than DUI-DWI.[179] Beyond making a lot of money for their departments, many police officers now use roadblocks to facilitate arrests for DUI-DWI in order to meet quotas that their departments have ordered them to reach, or be demoted to a less desirable form of duty.[180]

2.7. When Being Followed by Police, Don't Pull Over Before Being Required to Do So. Intelligent people should not engage in conduct to "waive" or give up constitutional protections. One of the most basic of these constitutional protections is the right

---

[174]**State v. Bryson,** 142 Ohio App.3d 397, 755 N.E.2d 964 (Ohio App. 8 Dist. 2001).

[175]**State v. Rose,** 170 N.C.App. 284, 612 S.E.2d 336 (N.C.App. 2005); **State v. Morgan,** 267 Ga.App. 728, 600 S.E.2d 767 (Ga.App. 2004); **Com. v. Paes,** 862 A.2d 625 (2004); **Dale v. State,** 267 Ga.App. 897, 600 S.E.2d 763 (2004); **Com. v. Buchanon,** 122 S.W.3d 565 (Ky. 2003); **Kirby v. State,** 874 So.2d 581 (Ala.Crim.App. 2003); **State v. Kirk,** 202 N.J.Super. 28, 493 A.2d 1271 (1985); **State v. Reynolds,** 319 N.J.Super. 426, 725 A.2d 1129 (1998); **State v. Madalena,** 121 N.M. 63, 908 P.2d 756 (N.M.App. 1995); **State v. Tucker,** 19 Kan.App.2d 920, 878 P.2d 855 (1994); **State v. Parms,** 523 So.2d 1293 (La. 1988); **Ingersoll v. Palmer,** 43 Cal.3d 1321, 743 P.2d 1299 (1987); **Higbie v. State,** 723 S.W.2d 802 (Tex.App.-Dallas 1987); **Jones v. State,** 459 So.2d 1068 (Fla.App. 2 Dist. 1984); **State v. Garcia,** 489 N.E.2d 168 (Ind.App. 1 Dist. 1986); **State v. Downey,** 945 S.W.2d 102 (Tenn. 1997).

[176]**Com. v. Buchanon,** 122 S.W.3d 565 (Ky. 2003); **State v. Morgan,** 267 Ga.App. 728, 600 S.E.2d 767 (Ga.App. 2004).

[177]**State v. Hicks,** 55 S.W.3d 515 (Tenn. 2001).

[178]For additional information on this topic, see http://www.duiblog.com/2004/11/15#a37.

[179]http://www.duiblog.com/2005/05/11#a166.

[180]http://www.duiblog.com/2005/04/12#a142.

to be free from arbitrary traffic stops, based upon an officer's hunch rather than some traffic/criminal violation, equipment defect, missing or expired tag or decal, or other legally justified cause. So, how do you decide *when to pull over* when an officer is following your vehicle but has not signaled you to pull over?

A driver that sees a police car following his or her car (but without emergency lights flashing) may instinctively think that pulling over is the correct thing to do. *WRONG!* Keep proceeding within the speed limit, obey all traffic laws, stay entirely within your lane and make sure that no "outward" (visible) problems exist with your vehicle. Use turn signals to make any lane changes or turns, no matter how minor. Don't abruptly stop or suddenly turn into an adjacent parking lot without using a signal. Stay off the cell phone and do nothing to distract your attention from the roadway.

Court cases across the USA have consistently upheld the right of police officers who have not signaled or commanded that you pull over to come in contact with you without any legal justification when you are on foot, *or* if you pull over and stop your vehicle without being commanded to do so.[181] Legal farces that have helped perpetuate this practice, such as the legal theory known as the "community caretaking" doctrine. Basically, the theory goes, if an officer sees anything amiss in his or her community, he or she can and should investigate the "problem" area or suspicious behavior to clear up any problems.

If an officer sees you pull into a shopping center parking lot in an effort to get him or her to quit following you, the officer is hoping that you will come to a stop. Then, he or she is going to be able to legitimately come in contact with your car (and your face) without any legal basis to suspect a crime has been committed or is about to be committed. If you kept moving, and never pulled over until signaled to do so by the blue or red lights of the patrol car (or the siren or hand signals to stop), then any encounter created by the use of "color of law" (using the emergency equipment to force you to stop your vehicle) is what attorneys call a "tier one *Terry* stop."

The name *Terry* is derived from the landmark Fourth Amendment case, *Terry v Ohio*.[182] Pulling over a car stopped at a red light that takes an extra second or two to shift the manual transmission into first gear when the light changes to green does not justify a tier one Terry traffic stop because no offense was committed.[183]

The *Terry* decision embodies the Fourth Amendment's protection against stopping a vehicle without a legal justification for doing so. Beyond the protections of *Terry* in prohibiting use of police power to stop a vehicle on a mere hunch, and for no real traffic violation ("tier one" *Terry* stops), *Terry* further outlines the illegality of an officer fulfilling the original purpose of the stop and then (with no justifiable belief that criminal activity is afoot) start investigating for

---

[181]**State v. Lefevers**, 844 N.E.2d 508 (Ind. App., 2006); **State v. Underwood,** 257 Ga.App. 893, 572 S.E.2d 394 (2002); **State v. Percy,** 2006 WL 696134 (Ohio App. Dist.7 2006) [slip opinion].

[182]**Terry v Ohio**, 392 U.S. 1, 88 S. Ct. 1868, 20 L.Ed.2d 889 (1968). The U.S. Supreme Court has sculpted out three tiers of encounters between the police and citizens: (1) communication between police and citizens involving no coercion or detention, (2) brief seizures that must be supported by reasonable suspicion, and (3) full-scale arrests that must be supported by probable cause. In the first tier, police officers may approach citizens, ask for identification, and freely question the citizen without any basis or belief that the citizen is involved in criminal activity, as long as the officers do not detain the citizen or create the impression that the citizen may not leave. The second tier occurs when the officer actually conducts a brief investigative *Terry* stop of the citizen. In this level, a police officer, even in the absence of probable cause, may stop persons and detain them briefly, when the officer has a particularized and objective basis for suspecting the persons are involved in criminal activity.

[183]**Martin v. State**, 257 Ga. App. 435, 571 S.E.2d 459 (2002).

further potential crimes. This is a "tier two" *Terry* detention. A "tier three" *Terry* encounter occurs when sufficient evidence to arrest has been obtained from objective, particularized data.

Thousands of legal decisions across America have interpreted and made rulings on both tier one and tier two *Terry* issues. A recent case from Utah adequately states the rule for us. Any further temporary detention for investigative questioning after fulfilling the purpose for the initial traffic stop constitutes an illegal seizure, unless an officer has probable cause or a reasonable suspicion of a further illegality.[184]

2.8. If you don't take field (roadside) tests, will you lose your license? Since no requirement exists for you to take any of the field sobriety tests, there is no automatic mechanism for the police to suspend your driver's if you decline attempting these evaluations. Any state that is so misguided as to pass a law requiring citizens to perform agility exercises or be punished would (by such enactment of legislation) abandon the Constitution's protections for its citizens.

Having a driver's license is a qualified right for you, one that can and can be continuously reviewed by the State that gave it to you. So, some states have begun adopting laws that are designed to FORCE a person to submit to some roadside evaluations that do not involve agility exercises. The type of roadside evaluations that most of the states are seeking is a preliminary breath analysis on a hand-held alcohol sensor. If your state has such laws, failure to blow into such a device may cause a proposed administrative license action, but only with an adequate reason to believe you are impaired, and only with notice to you and an opportunity to be heard.[185]

Now, if you do not take the field sobriety tests, and you are eventually convicted of a DUI-DWI offense, you will lose your license as a part of that criminal court proceeding. However, that is likely months away from the time of your stop, and may never occur if an experienced DUI-DWI attorney helps you with your case.

2.9. If you refuse to be tested on the official state breath, blood or urine instrument, will you lose you license? Yes. A "summary" license suspendion (or revocation) for refusal is not part of each state's laws. However, you are entitled to a hearing to challenge the suspension or revocation. Every state has laws in place to take away your right to drive for refusing to submit to a legally authorized (i.e., the officer has reasonable cause to suspect impaired driving) implied consent breath, blood or urine test. You do, however, at the administrative hearing have the right to challenge the fact of whether or not you refused to be tested. If you lose the administrative hearing, your driver's license will be automatically suspended for a prolonged period of time, typically a year.[186] In many states, no "work permit" or limited license is available for such refusal suspensions.

In most states, if you refuse the blood, breath or urine tests asked of you by the police, and the police take your driver's license, you are still entitled to get a temporary driving permit after the officer takes your permanent license. This temporary permit is issued as a stop-gap authorization to allow you to drive until you can receive your administrative hearing. These

---

[184]**State v. Despain**, 74 P.3d 1176 (Utah Ct. App. 2003).

[185]Due Process clauses of the 5th Amendment, 14th Amendment, U.S.C.A.

[186]Alabama - Ala.Code 1975 § 32-6-49.13(g); Arizona - A.R.S. § 28-1321(I); California - West's Ann.Cal.Vehicle Code § 14100; Oklahoma - 47 Okl.St.Ann. § 754; Louisiana - LSA-R.S. 32:668; Georgia - O.C.G.A. § 40-5-67.1(g)(1); New Hampshire - N.H. Rev. Stat. § 265:91-b(1)(a); Washington - West's RCWA 46.20.308(8); Florida - West's F.S.A. § 322.2615(b)(6)(a); Texas - V.T.C.A., Transportation Code § 724.041, Guam - 16 G.C.A. § 18203; Hawaii - HRS § 291E-34; Kansas - K.S.A. § 8-1002(e); Texas - V.T.C.A., Transportation Code § 524.032; South Carolina -Code 1976 § 56-5-2951.

temporary permits are often good for only 30 days.[187] However, this legal period of time for you to drive on this temporary permit varies from state to state.[188] Almost always, the continuation of driving privileges only lasts until a decision is reached on your administrative license suspension or revocation AFTER you have properly and timely requested a hearing. Your DUI-DWI specialist can better advise you of the length of validity and restrictions applicable to any limited permit issued by your state.

2.10. If you take the state's "chemical" test(s), will you get to keep your license? Likely, at least for a while, you will keep your driver's license or at least some privileges to drive to and from work. In most states, if you take the offered blood, urine or breath test, the police have no authority to then completely take your driver's license (or at least your permit to drive to and from work) from you as they do if you refuse via the implied consent laws. By requesting an administrative hearing, you may be able to have the proposed license suspension set aside, or at least gain a "work permit" during any suspension period. You may certainly lose your driver's license if you plead guilty or are convicted of a DUI-DWI criminal offense at some later date.[189]

2.11. If you refuse the state's tests, can you obtain a "work" permit? Besides the temporary permit you may receive (if your permanent driver's license is taken by the police as noted above) as a result of a test refusal, another option may exist for you to be able to legally drive following a license suspension after a DUI-DWI stop. If available, you will be required to prove that you "qualify" for conditional or limited driving privileges.

In most states, if your arrest for DUI-DWI is a first one in your lifetime, there are circumstances under which you may have a limited or restricted driver's license reissued to you if you meet certain criteria (such as true necessity), no other travel sources are available to you, a lack of other circumstances attendant to your arrest, and/or to attend further alcohol or drug testing or treatment.[190] Often, the reissuance of a limited permit will only be allowed after 30, 60 or 90 days. One of the requirements may be for you to complete a drug and alcohol evaluation.[191]

In other jurisdictions, any refusal that occurs can be a basis for a total deprivation of driving privileges for a fixed period of time.[192] The length of total suspension (or revocation) can be 90 days, 180 days, one year or possibly younger, depending if this is your first alcohol related offense or a repeat offense (involving a prior administrative suspension or revocation).

You may be able to obtain a special exemption and get a restricted driver's license to continue traveling to work. The issuance of restricted privileges to drive may be at the discretion of the court, and not by your choice, and not within the control of your attorney. The

---

[187]Georgia - 30 days - O.C.G.A. § 40-5-67.1(f)(1); New Hampshire - 30 days - N.H. Rev. Stat. § 265:91-a(III); Kansas - 30 days - K.S.A. § 8-1002(e); Oklahoma - 30 days - 47 Okl.St.Ann. § 754(B); Louisiana - 30 days - LSA-R.S. 32:667(A)(1); Arizona - 15 days - A.R.S. § 28-1385(D);; South Carolina - 30 days - Code 1976 § 56-5-2951.

[188]Alabama - no temporary license issued - Ala.Code 1975 § 32-6-49.13; Washington - 60 days - West's RCWA 46.20.308(6)(d); Florida - 10 days - West's F.S.A. § 322.2615(b)(4); Texas - 41 days - V.T.C.A., Transportation Code § 524.011(f); Nevada - 7 days - N.R.S. 484.385; Texas - until the hearing - V.T.C.A., Transportation Code § 524.032

[189]Army Regulation 190-5.

[190]Tennessee - T. C. A. § 55-10-403; Alabama - Ala.Code 1975 § 32-5A-304.

[191]Florida - West's F.S.A. § 322.282; F.S.A. § 322.225; Texas - 180 days - V.T.C.A., Transportation Code § 521.377.

[192]625 ILCS 5/6-201; Code 1976 § 56-5-2951(I)(1).

issuance of restricted driving privileges may be set by state statute, with defined gidelines for eligibility. Certainly, the basic requirements are that you have a job that requires you to drive and that you have no other reasonable way to get around without a driver's license. However, such a restricted license also typically severely limits your ability to drive for non-work purposes, and determines where and when you can operate a vehicle.[193] Thus, a work permit may help you with some of the problems you face following your DUI-DWI arrest, but is seldom the solution to all of your problems.

If you have any other specific questions, ask the DUI-DWI specialist attorney handling your case regarding your state's rules. Your DUI-DWI specialist will be able to tell you the specifics regarding your limited driving rights, and the procedure for getting a limited license back if possible.

2.12. Who can refuse to be tested? In most states, unless someone was seriously injured or killed as a result of an accident related to your DUI-DWI arrest, you typically have the right to refuse to allow the police to take a blood, breath or urine sample from you.[194] In other words, the drawing of your blood, or the taking of a breath or a urine sample by the police must typically be voluntary.[195] However, if you are incapacitated, either because you are unconscious, incoherent or unable to consent for whatever reason (including being too intoxicated to consent or refuse), you lose your right to refuse such samples being taken from you in most states.[196] In Mississippi and Tennessee, although the police can still obtain blood or urine samples for testing if you are unconscious or incapable of refusing, these results may not be used against you in court.[197]

Florida's courts have ruled that absent a felony arrest, forcible draws of blood or urine are not authorized.[198] Georgia has recently handed down the most sweeping protections for the suspected DUI-DWI driver who has refused testing based upon either a felony arrest or a

---

[193]Georgia - O.C.G.A. §40-5-64; Tennessee - T. C. A. §§ 55-10-403 and 406; Alabama - Ala.Code 1975 § 32-5A-304.

[194]California - West's Ann.Cal.Vehicle Code §§ 23612, 13353; Florida - West's F.S.A. §§ 316.1932, 316.1939; Georgia - O.C.G.A. § 40-5-67.1(d); Indiana - IC 9-30-6-7; Mississippi - Miss. Code Ann. § 63-11-21; Tennessee - T.C.A. § 55-10-406(a)(4); Texas - V.T.C.A., Transportation Code § 724.013; Washington - West's RCWA 46.20.308(2).

[195]**Schneckloth v. Bustamonte,** 412 U.S. 218, 93 S.Ct. 2041, 36 L.Ed.2d 854 (1973). Several states have justified sidestepping the issue of "voluntariness" of providing an incriminating evidentiary sample to police when no arrest of the suspected criminal (many if these decisions are in felony cases carrying lengthy jail terms) has occurred. In **Combest v. State,** 981 S.W.2d 958 (Tex.App.-Austin, 1998), the officer used the Texas implied consent form, yet never advised Combest that he was under arrest. This scenario would not have been allowed to occur in Georgia, which (along with several other states) requires a valid arrest and probable cause to suspect impairment before any blood or urine tests could be requested. **Handschuh v. State,** 270 Ga. App. 676, 607 S.E.2d 899 (2004) [modified in **Hough v. State,** 279 Ga. 711, 620 S.E.2d 380 (2005)]; **Cooper v. State,** 277 Ga. 282, 587 S.E.2d 605 (2003).

[196]**Breithaupt v. Abram,** 352 U.S. 432, 1 L. Ed. 2d 448, 77 S. Ct. 408 (1957); California - West's Ann.Cal.Vehicle Code § 23612(5); Florida - West's F.S.A. §§ 316.1932(1)(c); Georgia - O.C.G.A. § 40-5-55(b); Texas - V.T.C.A., Transportation Code § 724.014; Washington - West's RCWA 46.20.308(4); **State v. Wight,** 765 P.2d 12 (Utah App., 1988), **State v. Tronolone,** 532 So.2d 1127 (Fla. App., 1988). It is also not necessary to give an unconscious driver an implied consent warning prior to chemical testing. **State v. Barefield,** 110 Wash. 2d 728, 756 P.2d 731 (1988).

[197]Mississippi - Miss. Code Ann. § 63-11-7; Tennessee - T.C.A. § 55-10-406(b).

[198]**State v. Slaney,** 653 So.2d 422 (Fla.App. 3 Dist. 1995).

misdemeanor so long as no injured victim of an accident you caused has visible serious injuries. "No" means "NO" in Georgia.[199]

A frightening trend, now seen in more than a dozen states, wherein a person who refuses breath testing can now be restrained or even physically harmed to forcibly draw blood or use a catheter in the person for a urine sample. Plus, some states will penalize the person who refuses testing by suspending or revoking his or her license, and still forcibly draw blood.[200] Typically this occurs when someone has been seriously injured or killed as a result of your motor vehicle accident. Case examples have all cropped up in the past 10 years and foreshadow problems ahead.[201] See also http://www.duiblog.com/2004/11/22#a47.

In numerous states, a person's initial refusal to submit to testing can be determined to be a "refusal" (causing total loss of driving privileges) even if the police ultimately obtain a test through force or threat of force.[202] In such situations, the driver suffers both an immediate license loss for the refusal and must face the blood or urine test results in court. This is why you must know the law in your state as it applies to implied consent.[203]

2.13. Who should refuse to be tested? In states where refusal is permitted, some people should refuse. This is sometimes true due to prior DUI-DWI convictions, or because even a single DUI-DWI conviction on their criminal record would be so devastating to their life that the punishment for a DUI-DWI conviction is significantly worse than anything they

---

[199]**State v. Collier,** 279 Ga. 316, 612 S.E.2d 281 (2005); **Hough v. State,** 279 Ga. 711, 620 S.E.2d 380 (2005).

[200]**State v. Bohling,** 173 Wis. 2d 529, 533, 494 N.W.2d 399 (1993).

[201]**People v. Jones,** 214 Ill.2d 187, 824 N.E.2d 239 (2005) [accident not involving death]; **Abney v. State,** 811 N.E.2d 415 (Ind. App. 2004) [accident involving death and hit & run afterward]; **State v. Espe,** 88 P.3d 807 (Kan. App. 2004) [accident involving non-fatal but serious injuries to passenger]; **State v. Rinard,** 2003 WL 21396703 (Ohio App. 9th Dist. 2003) [no accident]; **State v. Engesser,** 661 N.W.2d 739 (S.D. 2003) [no formal arrest had occurred, but vehicular homicide]; **State v. Worthington,** 138 Idaho 470, 65 P.3d 211 (Idaho App. 2002) [no accident, but felony arrest]; **State v. Faust,** 267 Wis.2d 783, 672 N.W.2d 97 (Wis.App., 2003) [leading case from Wisconsin]; also see **State v. Krajewski,** 255 Wis.2d 98, 648 N.W.2d 385 (Wis. 2002) [no accident; defendant feared needles and offered to submit to alternative type test; forcible blood draw okay anyway]; **State v. Mellett,** 642 N.W.2d 779 (Minn.App. 2002) [no accident, but a repeat offender DWI suspect; defendant acquitted for the DWI but convicted for criminal refusal and given jail sentence]; **People v. Sugarman,** 96 Cal.App.4th 210, 116 Cal.Rptr.2d 689 (Cal.App. 2 Dist. 2002) [defendant agreed to be tested by breath, but the effort was not successful; because she was a repeat offender, forcible blood draw was okay]; **State v. Hanson,** 588 N.W.2d 885 (S.D. 1999) [DUI-drugs; no accident; suspected marijuana from smell officer observed and drug dog sniffing the vehicle and driver; urinating is a "natural bodily function," so okay to gather without a warrant]; also see **State v. Nguyen,** 563 N.W.2d 120 (S.D. 1997) [vehicular homicide; non-English speaking defendant; no implied consent rights given; but, in felony cases, no right of driver to refuse testing]; **State v. Rains,** 574 N.W.2d 904 (Iowa 1998) [normal traffic stop for weaving; defendant was shot by the officer (in self defense) and then actively guarded by police at his hospital room, but this was not an arrest, for purposes of Iowa law; blood that was drawn at hospital was not done at the request of law enforcement, so okay to be used against defendant on DWI]; **People v. Hanna,** 223 Mich.App. 466, 567 N.W.2d 12 (Mich.App. 1997) [use of "Do-Rite sticks to choke a suspect]. **State v. Clary,** 196 Ariz. 610, 2 P.3d 1255 (Ariz.App. Div. 1 2000) [speeding only, no prior offenses, still okay for officer to hold defendant on the floor while a phlebotomist drew his blood].

[202]**Municipality of Anchorage v. Ray,** 854 P.2d 740 (Alaska App. 1993); **People v. Fite,** 267 Cal.App.2d 685 (Cal.App. 3 Dist. 1968); **State v. Clary,** 196 Ariz. 610, 2 P.3d 1255 (Ariz.App. Div. 1 2000); **State v. Baker,** 502 A.2d 489 (Me. 1985); **State v. Shantie,** 193 Or.App. 813, 92 P.3d 746 (Or.App. 2004); **Beeman v. State,** 86 S.W.3d 613 (Tex.Crim.App. 2002).

[203] http://www.theduibook.com/stateDUIDWIsummaries.htm.

face as a penalty from the refusal to be tested. It is certainly tougher for the police to prove most DUI-DWI charges against you when there is no scientific testing of any kind that the prosecution can use as evidence.

However, the punishment against you for a refusal (typically an administrative loss of your driver's license for a year or more) is automatic in most states,[204] while the punishment against you for the criminal charges of DUI-DWI must be subsequently proven in court by the highest legal standard in the world (proof beyond a reasonable doubt). Other reasons may justify a prosecutor dropping or reducing the criminal charges against you based on your attorney's challenges to the evidence. Also, if you go to trial and use a skilled criminal defense attorney, you might win.

Because state laws vary greatly insofar as loss of license penalties for refusal, no one rule exists relating to whether you can or should refuse testing. If the summary in **Appendix H** or the on-line data located at http://www.theduibook.com/stateDUIDWIsummaries.htm does not answer your questions, you need to contact a DUI-DWI expert in your state for guidance. With roadblocks being used in over 45 states, an arrest for impaired driving CAN happen to you even when you have not violated any traffic laws, so be ready if it does.

2.14. Will your "refusal" be used against you in court? Another factor to consider is that your refusal can typically be used against you in some way in your criminal drunken driving trial. Some states are passing laws that make the refusal to submit to blood, urine or breath samples in a DUI-DWI case punishable by criminal penalties, especially if you are subsequently convicted of a DUI-DWI offense.[205] Such a refusal in these states can be a criminal offense by itself, or might only enhance punishment of the underlying driving while impaired offense, if you are convicted. For example, in New Mexico, refusal makes the DUI-DWI an aggravated offense, with mandatory jail and enhanced sentence generally. Minnesota has similar enhanced penalties for DUI-DWI cases involving refusals.

Whether or not there are criminal penalties for refusing blood, urine or breath testing, such refusals often badly damage your DUI-DWI case. The admission into evidence by the prosecution of your chemical test refusal is invariably detrimental and this admission has been held to be constitutional.[206] Unless satisfactorily explained, the jury will normally assume that you refused to be tested because you had consumed too much alcohol and were afraid of failing the test, an assumption that the prosecutor seldom fails to bring to the jury's attention.

In addition, in many states the admission into evidence of a chemical test refusal entitles the prosecution to a "consciousness of guilt" jury instruction stating that the jury may consider the refusal as evidence of a consciousness of guilt by you. In those states, knowledgeable defense counsel should also submit a counterpart to the State's "consciousness of guilt" jury charge by submitting a "consciousness of innocence" jury charge (instruction) where you tried to take some type of test (i.e., blood) or offered to take any type of forensic alcohol test.

---

[204]Alabama - Ala.Code 1975 § 32-6-49.13(g); Arizona - A.R.S. § 28-1321(I); California - West's Ann.Cal.Vehicle Code § 14100; Oklahoma - 47 Okl.St.Ann. § 754; Louisiana - LSA-R.S. 32:668; Georgia - O.C.G.A. § 40-5-67.1(g)(1); New Hampshire - N.H. Rev. Stat. § 265:91-b(1)(a); Washington - West's RCWA 46.20.308(8); Florida - West's F.S.A. § 322.2615(b)(6)(a); Texas - V.T.C.A., Transportation Code § 724.041, Guam - 16 G.C.A. § 18203; Hawaii - HRS § 291E-34; Kansas - K.S.A. § 8-1002(e); Texas - V.T.C.A., Transportation Code § 524.032; South Carolina -Code 1976 § 56-5-2951.

[205]**State v. Morale**, 174 Vt. 213, 811 A.2d 185 (Vt. 2002); California - West's Ann.Cal.Vehicle Code §§ 23612(a)(1)(D), 23577; Florida - West's F.S.A. §§ 316.1932(1)(a), 316.1939; Indiana - IC 9-30-7-5; Mississippi - Miss. Code Ann. § 63-11-30(4); Tennessee - T.C.A. § 55-10-406(a)(3).

[206]**South Dakota v. Neville,** 459 U.S. 553, 74 L. Ed. 2d 748, 103 S. Ct. 916 (1983).

Also, as a practical matter when evidence of a refusal is admitted during the prosecution's case, it is sometimes necessary for you to testify at trial in order to effectively explain your reasons for refusing to submit. If your attorney gets to question you on all the things that may help your case, the prosecution gets to question you on all the things that may harm your case. Obviously then, the admission into evidence of a chemical test refusal should be avoided, if at all possible. Blocking the introduction of your "refusal" at trial is usually accomplished at pre-trial motions that are filed and pursued by your attorney. Most experienced trial lawyers handling DUI-DWI trials prefer to NOT put their clients on the witness stand at trial, unless absolutely forced to do so by the necessity to explain some indespensible point or establish some citical factual predicate for the case.

The important thing in your DUI-DWI prosecution is to have a prior plan in place after having talked to a DUI-DWI specialist. If you are meeting with a DUI-DWI specialist because you were arrested for DUI-DWI and you are attempting to best manage your situation, then remembering anything you said or did when the officer asked you to provide a blood, breath or urine sample might make all the difference in your defense. Details win cases, and your memory may be critical in cases where no video exists.

2.15. *Never* attempt to perform the SFSTs or other voluntary field tests. Police officers usually ask drivers whom they suspect of driving under the influence of either drugs or alcohol to perform "standardized field sobriety tests." The acronym for these psycho-physical tests is "SFST." Exactly what tests you are asked to perform varies, but may include the officer evaluating your eye tremors as you follow an object with your eyes (horizontal gaze nystagmus), asking you to perform a nine-step heel-to-toe maneuver down a line, turn and then return back down the same line in the same manner, and a leg lift exercise conducted in a specified manner while counting aloud in a manner described by the officer (e.g., "one-thousand one, one-thousand two, etc.). Other tests often include reciting parts or the complete (or a portion of the) alphabet (without singing), counting backwards, or adding or subtracting numbers in your mind. You may be asked "orientation" questions such as the time of day (without looking at your watch), the date, the day of the week or similar inquiries. You may also be asked to give a breath sample into a handheld alcohol detection device.

The field sobriety tests are, without a doubt, the greatest source of bad arrests and faulty convictions in DUI-DWI cases in this nation. There are only a few states where refusing to do these tests can be used against you at your trial if it goes that far,[207] while at least one has declared that to do so is a violation of your right against self-incrimination.[208] Virtually no Americans are aware that they have an absolute right to NOT attempt to perform these agility exercises and medically-created evaluations that are being offered by an officer who is marginally trained and often has an arrest quota to fill. Just to name a few reasons to NOT do these evaluations, or attempt to do them, consider the following information:

1. One scientist reports that *in excess of 98%* of the officers giving the three NHTSA standardized field sobriety evaluations do them (at least one of the three) incorrectly. The NHTSA training manuals---all of them---state that incorrect administration of the evaluations by the arresting officer "compromises the validity" of the tests.[209]
2. The original studies (and the so-called "validation studies" that were conducted in the mid-1990s to provide support for correlating NHTSA tests to the new 0.08% blood

---

[207]**Com. v. McGrail**, 419 Mass. 774, 647 N.E.2d 712 (1995); **Jackson v. State**, 681 S.W.2d 910 (Tex. App.-Fort Worth 1984).

[208]**State v. Fish,** 321 Or. 48, 893 P.2d 1023 (1995).

[209]J.L. Booker, *The Horizontal Gaze Nystagmus Test: Fraudulent Science in the American Courts*, Science & Justice, Vol. 44, No. 3, p. 133-139 (2004).

alcohol standard) *were NEVER subjected to "peer review,"* a process wherein other scientists review the hypothesis presented (i.e., that these evaluations can reliably predict which persons are at or above 0.10% (and in later "studies," at or above 0.08%). This would be equivalent to a company creating a new, potentially dangerous drug and putting on the market (with our government's stamp of approval) without a single *independent* laboratory source testing the reliability of effectiveness and its side effects or other problems.

3. Judges have "bought into" the claimed reliability of these field evaluations as "tests," believing, it would seem, that if the government promulgated and endorsed use of these evaluations, they must be "valuable" tools in the effort to deter DUI-DWI offenses. The proof of how much the courts have bought the "hook, line and sinker" is the horrifying fact that *more than 5200 reported appellate opinions* indicate that the words "fail" or "failed" AND "test" AND "field" show up in the same sentence. These evaluations were *NEVER* correlated to "impairment" levels, as has been stated in more than a dozen speeches by the principal creator of these field evaluations, Dr. Marcelline Burns, Ph.D.[210] Yet, court cases are allowed to be tried and convictions obtained on patently false evidence across America. Only recently have several courts across America called for extensive hearings to review these untouched claims of reliability and ultimately have declared that the "science" behind these evaluations is totally lacking. [211]

Nothing good happens if you attempt any of these tests. In a nutshell: **DON'T ATTEMPT FIELD EVALUATIONS!** They are all subjectively graded, and the only "judge and jury" of your performance at the scene is the police officer. If you are lucky, the tests are being audio and video recorded so that you have a defense as to your responses or the adequacy of the proper administration of the officer's testing protocols and instructions. Even in the best scenario, when you perform the tests correctly, with good excuses as to why your performance was not perfect, the police officer can claim that any mistake or miscue provided him or her with justification for your arrest for DUI-DWI. In most courts, these voodoo evaluations can be used at trial to convict you.

If you attempt any of them and allegedly "fail," the officer is going to testify to this at your trial. Your alleged failures may also be caught and recorded on any video or audio recordings. Judges and juries find such evidence very compelling in their decision whether or not to convict you of DUI-DWI. A video of you stumbling, bumbling and slurring your words gives great credence to the officer's contention that you were under the influence, even if no scientific evidence from a blood, breath or urine test result supports that conclusion.

Even if you somehow perform perfectly on all of the tests, or do not perform them at all, the officer can and likely will still arrest you for DUI-DWI. If all of this is recorded, this could be excellent ammunition in your eventual defense, but this may not help you at the scene. You can never expect to be absolutely perfect on these tests, especially at 3:00 AM, on the side of an interstate or other highway (that is *never* level), after you have been awake for 20 hours, and you are exhausted.

In the end, the chances of a field sobriety test helping you are so slight, and the chances of them hurting you so great, few situations exist where you should agree to performing the tests. Dozens of researchers and writers have pointed out that these agility exercises are designed for failure, to facilitate more arrests. See

---

[210]Speeches in San Francisco, California in 2000, and at Chicago in August of 2001 (ABA Convention).

[211]**United States v. Horn,** 185 F.Supp.2d 530 (D.Md. 2002); **State v. Lasworth,** 131 N.M. 739, 42 P.2d 844 (2001).

http://www.duiblog.com/2004/10/21. Also see the article recently by The Washington Post: Brigid Schulte, *Playing the DUI Hokeypokey: Police, Scientists Squaring Off over Field Sobriety Tests,* November 20, 2005.

Just say no - politely. Don't take any field evaluations, believing this will help you be on your way home. You will be better off remaining silent and letting the police process the case against you on little or no credible evidence.

2.16. Avoid "verbal gymnastics" or police officers' "Catch-22's." If you are stopped by the police, be polite and respond appropriately to showing your vehicle ownership documentation, license and proof of insurance. Don't discuss other issues such as where you are coming from, where you are going or attempt to justify the driving behavior that led to the pullover. You cannot and will not win in a battle of mental or verbal gymnastics with a law enforcement officer. He or she is not interested so much in your answers as the manner in which you give them. Remember your *right to remain silent.*

The more you talk, no matter what you say, the worse the situation is likely to become. You are not in charge of the situation. The officer is. Most officers take formal training on how to use questioning to keep you "off balance." One such police course is appropriately called "verbal judo." Remember that the officer is going to go home at the end of his or her shift, while you are trying to stay out of jail. Your adherence to these guidelines could prevent you from spending the next several years of your life straightening out a life-changing and potentially job-ending nightmare.

2.17. Don't lose your composure or use bad language. Police officers are in charge when they stop you and start an investigation for DUI-DWI. Most stops are in the middle of the night, when you are already tired. It is very easy to lose your composure or use harsh or bad language if you are stopped, especially if you think you have done nothing wrong. You may be upset, and the officer may not be willing to listen to explanations from you. In their eyes, you are either breaking the law or you are not. Excuses do not register with the officer.

Take a deep breath. Remember that everything you say or do is likely going to be recorded. You may be technically correct that the officer is not treating you well. However, the jury or the judge is not going to think highly of your bad language if you lose your composure. In their eyes, that is another sign that you may have been intoxicated.

In the brief minutes of your traffic stop, or the hours during the processing of your arrest, you **MUST** be on your best behavior. Always think of how you will appear to a jury. Getting mad or cursing at any law enforcement officer or jailer will almost always guarantee that the chances of obtaining a good result in your case will be diminished.

2.18. Politely attempt to leave by cab, on foot or with a friend, even if your car is towed. If you have been drinking **any** alcohol, or ingested **any** illegal drugs on the day before you have an accident, after you have traded insurance information with any other driver involved in a non-injury accident and before the police show up to investigate, politely attempt to leave the scene. Do this by walking away, calling a cab, or having a friend come and get you.

If you have traded insurance and license information with the other drivers, and no one needs medical help, departing the scene is not usually a criminal offense. This tactic only applies when no one is injured and needs medical assistance. If it takes hours for the police to find you after the accident, it will be very hard for them to prove you had any drugs or alcohol in your system at the time of the accident. If you are not at the scene when the police arrive, the first place they will look is at your address showing on your driver's license or tag number.

Staying at the scene until the police show up is asking to be tested, or to be punished through loss of your driving privileges if you refuse to be tested.

If you have been stopped by an officer who is asking you questions about drinking or the use of drugs, make no admission of any usage. Remain silent and request an attorney. If you are not detained after your refusal to perform any field sobriety tests, attempt to call a cab, call a friend to come get you or to start walking home. Tell the officer that you are willing to satisfy his or her concerns for safety by handing him or her your keys and either walking home or taking a cab home, but that you will not submit to testing that you do not trust to be reliable or accurate.

If he or she responds by asking, "So you don't think you are safe to drive?" or something similar, be sure to say, "That is absolutely not true. I am merely trying to satisfy you that I am cooperative in every way, even if I believe your concerns are not reasonable." If taking the cab results in your car being towed, that is a small price to pay to avoid being arrested and possibly convicted of DUI-DWI.

2.19. You are being arrested anyway — why is that? Under the "police" power inherent in the authority given to the States, the police officer has the right to arrest you if he or she feels that an articulable suspicion exists that you are committing a crime or have recently committed one. Please understand that you can be arrested in America for a routine traffic offense like speeding, a lane violation, or not wearing a seatbelt.[212] While such minor offenses do not usually lead to an arrest, it is within the officer's power to arrest someone rather than just give them a ticket at the scene unless your state laws provide otherwise.

The following list covers the seven ways or methods by which police typically come in contact with a suspected "driving while impaired" or "driving UBAL" (driving with an unlawful balance of alcohol) driver. This list contains the reasons for arrest in over 95% of the 10,000 plus DUI-DWI cases handled by the author's law firm since 1976:

1. Traffic offense or "moving" violation of some type is observed;
2. Accident of some type has occurred and police have been called;
3. Defective equipment or license tag or inspection decal problem observed;
4. Parked or non-moving vehicle with person sitting inside or standing next to vehicle that was recently driven;
5. Police receive a call from or direct, face-to-face contact with a concerned citizen to **B**e **O**n the **L**ook **O**ut (BOLO) for your vehicle due to alleged errant driving;
6. Roadblock, license check or sobriety checkpoint of some type;
7. Domestic argument or dispute arouses police attention to your vehicle departing from or arriving at home, or as a result of a police or dispatch to your home or some public location.

If the officer has stopped you, or if you have been detained at a DUI-DWI roadblock, certain conduct by you or items observed by the officer inside your vehicle or in your pockets will almost always get you arrested for DUI-DWI. First, if you admit that you have been drinking, even one or two drinks, the officer is going to believe you have been driving while impaired or under the influence. The low number of beverages that you claim to have consumed will not be believed by an officer, even if true. Most suspected drunk drivers tell the officer they have only had one or two drinks. Officers rarely believe a driver's claim to have had only one or two drinks even if the statement is absolutely true. The best rule is to not admit to anything - *remain silent*.

---

[212]**Atwater v. City of Lago Vista,** 532 U.S. 318, 121 S.Ct. 1536, 149 L.Ed.2d 549 (2001).

Secondly, if the officer can smell what he or she believes is alcohol on your breath, then he or she will likely arrest you whether or not you perform any field tests. The police are going to ask you to provide a blood or breath sample if they suspect the tests will reveal alcohol in your system. If they have any evidence of drug usage, a blood or urine sample will be requested. As you will read in other chapters, in some states you will be forced to give a sample even if you verbally (or physically) refuse to be tested.

2.20. You were given an advisement, and it was not the *Miranda* warning. What is it? The *Miranda* warnings are statements of your legal rights the police must give you when they arrest you.[213] In many DUI-DWI cases, officers may never give the *Miranda* warnings after custody is accomplished (by arresting you). It is much more likely that the advisement you are given in a DUI-DWI case is an "implied consent" (or informed consent) advisement. If you have ever heard implied consent warnings from a police officer before or after you were being arrested for some criminal offense, that offense is likely DUI-DWI.

By driving your vehicle on a public road in any state in the United States, you have (by using the state's highways) given your *implied consent* to have your blood, breath or urine tested to assure you are not impaired by some chemical substance (legal or illegal drugs, or alcohol). As with many other state laws, the wording of each implied consent statute varies somewhat from state to state.[214]

The types of warnings or advisements that may be required under an implied consent statute include: (1) a warning of the consequences of refusing to be tested; (2) a warning of the consequences of submitting to testing and yielding a result that constitutes a "per se" offense; (3) an advisement as to the alternate types of chemical tests to which the defendant may be asked to submit (i.e., breath test, blood test, urine test, etc); and (4) an advisement of the right to consult with an attorney before deciding whether to submit to chemical testing (in a minority of states). No state implied consent advisement has all these warnings. Most have two or three.

In most states, before the police officer can ask you for a blood, breath or urine sample based on your "implied consent" associated with your operating a vehicle on a public road, he or she must inform you of your rights. The timing of when the advisement must be given varies from state to state, but the timeliness may be strictly construed against the state if not given at the correct point in your DUI-DWI detention. In most states, police officers must substantially comply with a precise reading of the statutory warning or advisement provisions in order for the implied consent penalties to be invoked.[215] Warnings of the consequences of refusal typically must be clear and unequivocal.[216]

---

[213]You have the right to remain silent. Anything you say can and will be used against you in a court of law. You have the right to have an attorney present during questioning. If you cannot afford an attorney, one may be appointed for you. **Miranda v. Arizona,** 384 U.S. 436, 86 S.Ct. 1602, 16 L.Ed.2d 694 (1966).

[214]California - West's Ann.Cal.Vehicle Code § 23612(a)(1); Florida - West's F.S.A. § 316.1932(1)(a); Georgia - O.C.G.A. § 40-5-55(a); Indiana - IC 9-30-6-1; Mississippi - Miss. Code Ann. § 63-11-5(1); Tennessee - T.C.A. § 55-10-406(a)(1); Texas - V.T.C.A., Transportation Code § 724.011(a); Washington - West's RCWA 46.20.308(1), Wisconsin - W.S.A. 343.305(2).

[215]**State v. Bunnell,** 324 N.W.2d 418 (S.D., 1982); **Barnhart v. Dep't of Revenue,** 243 Kan. 209, 755 P.2d 1337 (1988); **Tarascio v. Muzio,** 40 Conn. Supp. 505, 515 A.2d 1082 (1986); **Kitchens v. State,** 258 Ga. App. 411, 574 S.E.2d 451 (2002); Georgia - O.C.G.A. § 40-5-67.1(b); Washington - West's RCWA 46.20.308(2); Wisconsin - W.S.A. 343.305(4).

[216]**Gargano v. Dep't of Motor Vehicles,** 118 A.D.2d 859, 500 N.Y.S.2d 346 (1986); **State v. Huber,** 540 N.E.2d 140 (Ind. App., 1989); **Graves v. Commonwealth,** 112 Pa. Commw. 390, 535 A.2d 707 (1988).

The effect of an inadequate or incorrect statements by an officer concerning the admissibility of a chemical test or a refusal in a criminal case can be the exclusion of any breath or blood tests or alleged refusal to be tested.[217] In some states, misleading or incorrect statements to you by the arresting officer can cause exclusion of these tests at administrative hearings,[218] and at your eventual trial.[219] How critical an EXACT reading of the precise advisements is depends on your state's laws, and your DUI-DWI specialist will know the standards for your state.

Because no constitutional or common law requirement exists mandating such advisements,[220] a small number of states have no "mandatory" reading of these warnings. In these states, no formalized advisement of the consequences of refusal or of testing over the legal limit is required.[221] Other states have very strict "warnings" to the driver.

The *correctness* or *completeness* of the implied consent warnings to fully communicate the consequences of refusal (or taking the state's test and having a per se alcohol level at or above the legal limit) may[222] or may not cause exclusion of the State's test results against you at a pre-trial motion hearing. Each situation is "fact-specific," meaning it all depends on what you were told and whether a normal person could understand the true and legitimate consequences of refusal. Even in states where refusal is a separate crime, generic or untargeted wording will be upheld by some courts.[223]

In Texas, you must sign a statement acknowledging you have been informed of your obligations and rights if you refuse to provide a sample.[224] However, even without the formal written statement, the officer must still inform you of all of your rights or your attorney can argue that you never legally gave your permission for the taking of your blood, breath or urine sample in a knowing and intelligent fashion. If your rights were violated, any results from the State's tests could be deemed not admissible against you, leading to the DUI-DWI charges against you being dismissed or reduced.[225] That is why it is critical for you to remember everything the officer told you (as close to word-for-word as possible) when you speak to your DUI-DWI specialist.

---

[217]**State v. Leviner,** 213 Ga. App. 99, 443 S.E.2d 688 (1994).

[218]**People v. Znaniecki,** 181 Ill. App. 3d 389, 537 N.E.2d 16 (1989).

[219]**State v. Downer,** 460 So.2d 1184 (La. App., 1984).

[220]**South Dakota v. Neville,** 459 U.S. 553, 74 L. Ed. 2d 748, 103 S. Ct. 916 (1983); **Brewer v. Motor Vehicle Div.,** 720 P.2d 564 (Colo., 1986); **Leiven v. Comm'r,** 370 N.W.2d 432 (Minn., 1985).

[221]California - West's Ann.Cal.Vehicle Code §§ 23612(a)(1)(D), 23612(a)(4), 23614(b), 23614(c); Florida - West's F.S.A. § 316.1932(1)(a); Indiana - IC 9-30-6-7; Mississippi - Miss. Code Ann. §§ 63-11-5(2), 63-11-5(4), 63-11-21; Tennessee - T.C.A. § 55-10-406(a)(3); Texas - V.T.C.A., Transportation Code § 724.015.

[222]**State v. Lubin,** 164 Ga.App. 689, 297 S.E.2d 371 (1982); **State v. Leviner,** 213 Ga.App. 762, 99, 443 S.E.2d 688 (1994); **Kitchens v. State,** 258 Ga.App. 411, 574 S.E.2d 451 (2002).

[223] **State v. Myers,** 711 N.W.2d 113 (Minn.App., 2006) [the implied-consent advisory administered to respondent violated respondent's due-process rights because it did not inform respondent that a test refusal is a gross misdemeanor that may result in harsher penalties than a test failure, but the court of appeals found the advisement that "refusal is a crime" to be sufficient].

[224]Texas - V.T.C.A., Transportation Code § 724.031.

[225]**Batliner v. Kansas Dept. of Revenue,** 90 P.3d 378 (Kan.App. 2004); **Nicholson v. Killens,** 116 N.C.App. 473, 448 S.E.2d 542 (N.C.App. 1994); **State v. Lubin,** 164 Ga. App. 689, 297 S.E.2d 371 (1982); **State v. Renfroe,** 216 Ga. App. 709, 455 S.E.2d 383 (1995); **State v. Terry,** 236 Ga. App. 248, 511 S.E.2d 608 (1999); **State v. Collier,** 279 Ga. 316, 612 S.E.2d 281 (2005); **Postlewait v. Dep't of Revenue,** 643 S.W.2d 314 (Mo. App., 1982); **Garrison v. Dothard,** 366 So.2d 1129 (Ala. App., 1979).

2.21. Can you obtain your own test(s)? If so, when and who pays? Every state has an independent test statute that is an integral part of the state's implied consent statutes.[226] An independent test statute typically provides that a person who submits to the requested chemical testing of the state may, at the person's own expense, have additional chemical tests performed. However, a failure to do so may not affect the admissibility of the blood or breath test performed by the police.

Most independent test statutes provide that only those who submit to chemical testing have the right to an independent test. The courts have generally upheld this proviso and have upheld the denial of any right to an independent test to those who refuse police testing.[227]

A few states, however, have ruled that restricting the right to an independent test to those who submit to police testing constitutes a denial of due process of law and that persons who refuse chemical testing also have the right to an independent chemical test.[228] Other courts have held that the right to an independent test may not be limited to those who submit to police testing. In such states, a refusal to be tested may be inadmissible if you were not given the required independent test advisement.[229]

Only a handful of states allow a person who has refused the State's test to request and receive an independent test. The majority of other states do not allow this, despite the obvious importance of an arrestee obtaining a contemporaneous sample of this evidence (blood alcohol level) for purposes of challenging the State's DUI-DWI case against him or her.[230]

In every state, if you get an independent test, you pay for it. In almost every state, if you request an independent test of your blood or urine, the law enforcement officer must do what he or she can reasonably do to accommodate that request.[231] A few states require exclusion of your test results if you are not allowed the chance to obtain an independent test.[232] Most states require that while the officer must give you a reasonable opportunity for a test, the failure to obtain a test does not affect the admissibility of the state's test.[233]

What happens if you do not have the necessary cash with you to pay for the test and you need to be taken to an ATM? Several cases from Georgia indicate why the Peach state may have the most driver-friendly case law in America. In one case, the arresting officer made a unilateral determination that the defendant could not afford an independent blood test based

---

[226]California - West's Ann.Cal.Vehicle Code § 23614; Florida - West's F.S.A. § 316.1932(3).; Georgia - O.C.G.A. § 40-6-392(3); Mississippi - Miss. Code Ann. § 63-11-13; Texas - V.T.C.A., Transportation Code § 724.019; Washington - West's RCWA 46.61.506(6).

[227]**State v. Larivee**, 656 N.W.2d 226 (Minn., 2003); **State v. Simmons**, 270 Ga. App. 301, 605 S.E.2d 846 (2004).

[228]**Snyder v. State**, 930 P.2d 1274 (Alaska, 1996); **State v. Swanson**, 722 P.2d 1155 (Mont., 1986).

[229]**Kintli v. State**, 325 Mont. 53, 103 P.3d 1056 (2004).

[230]**Puett v. State,** 147 Ga. App. 300, 248 Ga. App. 560 (1978).

[231]California - West's Ann.Cal.Vehicle Code § 23614; Florida - West's F.S.A. § 316.1932(3).; Georgia - O.C.G.A. § 40-6-392(3); Mississippi - Miss. Code Ann. § 63-11-13; Texas - V.T.C.A., Transportation Code § 724.019; Washington - West's RCWA 46.61.506(6); **Commonwealth v. Long**, 118 S.W.3d 178 (Ky. App., 2003), **Commonwealth v. King**, 429 Mass. 169, 706 N.E.2d 685 (1999); **State v. Anderson**, 258 Ga. App. 127, 572 S.E.2d 758 (2002); **Lau v. State**, 896 P.2d 825 (Alaska App., 1995).

[232]**State v. Peterson**, 739 P.2d 958 (Mont., 1987), overruled on other grounds by **State v. Waters**, 296 Mont. 101, 987 P.2d 1142 (1999), **State v. Sanchez**, 192 Ariz. 454, 967 P.2d 129 (Ariz. App., 1998).

[233]California - West's Ann.Cal.Vehicle Code § 23614; Florida - West's F.S.A. § 316.1932(3).; Georgia - O.C.G.A. § 40-6-392(3); Mississippi - Miss. Code Ann. § 63-11-13; Texas - V.T.C.A., Transportation Code § 724.019; Washington - West's RCWA 46.61.506(6);

solely on defendant's assertion that he only had $7.00 with him. The officer never tried to determine whether the defendant had other means to pay and never offered the defendant the opportunity to use the phone. The trial court held that the officer did not reasonably accommodate defendant's request for an independent test and this decision was upheld on appeal.[234]

Unfortunately, in other states, this extra step of the officer having to take you to an ATM machine may or may not be considered outside of what is a "reasonable accommodation." In the few cases that have addressed this issue, the officer was allowed to decline assistance and the State's test results were still admissible against the defendant in spite of the lack of the independent test,[235] while in another, when the suspect was short of the cash he needed for the blood test, he requested that the officer stop by an ATM machine to get the funds. The officer's refusal to accommodate this request caused the suspect's refusal to be excluded.[236]

2.22. Here are some things you can do if you are going out this evening and may have anything alcoholic at all to drink. Most people are so certain that being confronted by a police officer investigating a possible DUI-DWI offense will not happen to them that they make little or no preparation for the possibility. Over one million people make that error each year, and not a single one thought it could happen to him or her either.

A short list of items to prepare for the "worst case scenario" will be helpful. Before you depart, make sure you have the following:

1. The name and phone number for the top DUI-DWI attorney in your area.
2. The "hard line" phone number for a person who will be willing and able to bail you out of jail. Many jails only allow "collect" calls to be made, and cell phones can't take collect calls. Don't plan on using the stored numbers on your cell phone, because it will be confiscated by most jailers.
3. The phone number of a person who can come remove your vehicle from the roadway, if it can be done quickly, in order to avoid towing and storage charges. Due to potential liability, most police departments will not leave the vehicle along the road or even in a parking lot.
4. Clean your vehicle totally of any alcoholic beverage containers, including empties. Open container laws are written so broadly that you can be convicted of this offense even if the empty bottles or cans are weeks old and dry as a bone. Plus, when an officer sees these containers from peering through your vehicle's windows with his or her flashlight, this leads the officer to believe consumption occurred recently. Also, do not leave anything in your vehicle that is of high value or is irreplaceable when you go out. Some tow companies are not known for strict screening of the employees who load up cars at 3:00 AM. Plus, if you are not overly concerned about losing something of value, you might just opt to take a cab home (a opposed to driving your car) and retrieve your car the next day.
5. Take cash in the amount of $300 or more. This should be a sufficient amount to pay any required bonding fee for a drunken driving charge (typically, 10% to 15% of the total bond amount), if you need a commercial bonding company. If you have any prior criminal record or you are facing a felony charge, your bond amount may not be a fixed amount, nor be subject to being calculated from a printed "schedule." You may be stuck

---

[234]**State v. Anderson**, 258 Ga.App. 127, 572 S.E.2d 758 (2002).

[235]**Sheehan v. State,** 267 Ga.App. 152, 598 S.E.2d 873 (2004).

[236]**Butts v. City of Peachtree City,** 205 Ga. App. 492, 422 S.E.2d 909 (1992).

in jail until a judge looks at your prior criminal and driving history and sets an appropriate bond.

6. Take a credit card *and* a debit card. You may be forced to use one or the other (or both) to pay for bond fees or an independent test, if such a test is available. In some jurisdictions, you may be allowed to stop by an ATM machine to obtain needed cash for an independent test. Some jails will allow use of a debit card to let you bond out of jail, but not a credit card (due to higher bank fees on credit cards).

7. Because police have an unbelievable amount of latitude about towing your vehicle, do NOT have even the slightest amount (this includes ashes in the ash tray) of contraband drugs or any other medications in your vehicle that: (a) are not prescribed to you; (b) are not in their individual, proper containers (original pill bottles from the pharmacy); and (c) be sure to remove all paraphernalia (pipes, wrapping papers, bongs, clips, etc.) associated with any bad habits that may cause the police to tear apart your vehicle while searching for the hidden drugs that they KNOW must be there. Police can and will conduct an "inventory" search of all parts of your vehicle if it is to be towed. Some officers will illegally search it even if towing is not going to happen. The most commonly used legal excuse claimed by police is that they are "looking for evidence of your present crime (DUI-DWI)."

8. Keep in your possession the phone numbers of a co-worker who can cover for you with your employer if you do not get bonded out of jail in time for the next workday. Yes, you MAY be there for a couple of days.

9. Get the red out. Take Visine® with you to use after being in smoky rooms and harsh lights. Red eyes can be a symptom of a long, difficult day (not a DUI-DWI), so don't give this "symptom" to the police for them to use against you in court.

10. Use chewing gum or mints, or even brush and floss your teeth before leaving your drinking location to drive home. The odor of alcohol will be less prevalent if you take steps to freshen your breath before getting in your vehicle. Plus, even though having an open container of liquor, beer or wine in your vehicle can lead to legal problems, keeping a travel-size bottle of Scope® or mint-flavored Listerine® in the glove box can be a good explanation for the smell of alcohol in your car or on your breath.

2.23. Summary - what do I say and do if I am confronted by a police officer and suspected of DUI-DWI? No single answer will suffice for all people in all situations. For example, if an accident has occurred involving serious bodily injury or the death of another person, you may have no choice but to either voluntarily submit to testing or suffer forcible blood or urine extraction.[237] Plus, many jurisdictions will revoke or suspend your license for ATTEMPTING to refuse, plus forcibly take your blood and urine anyway.[238]

Also, advice for underage drivers in one state will not be good advice for underage drivers in another state. For example, knowledgeable DUI-DWI defense attorneys in California generally will tell drivers under age 21 to submit to the roadside PBT (preliminary breath testing) unit, yet tell drivers age 21 and over to NOT submit to it. The California DUI-DWI specialist will also advise all persons asked by law enforcement officers in that state to take a state-administered breath test to DECLINE it in favor of having blood drawn, so that the sample can later be independently analyzed.

For over 20 years, the author has utilized "Driver's Rights Cards" for clients stopped for suspected DUI-DWI in Georgia. These cards contain specific advisements that are also "variable," depending upon the situation. If Georgia law changes at the next legislative session,

---

[237]**Hough v. State,** 279 Ga. 711, 620 S.E.2d 380 (2005).

[238]**State v. Clary,** 196 Ariz. 610, 2 P.3d 1255 (Ariz.App. Div. 1 2000).

this advice might change, but it is applicable for now. A current copy is maintained on several web sites created by the author.[239]

CAUTION: No claim of accuracy for drivers in other states is made by referring to these Georgia-specific cards. Ask your local DUI-DWI specialist about how to handle an arrest situation in your state. In dealing with the police, here are five universally sound things to do that will protect your legal rights, if stopped:

1. If asked (or told) about an alleged traffic violation, do not try to appease the officer by agreeing with him or her that you committed some traffic offense. Don't get belligerent. Instead say, "Actually, sir (or ma'am), I believe I stayed entirely within my lane," or some other appropriate explanation. Remember, everything you are saying is being recorded, and your DUI-DWI attorney may be able to use the favorable things said by you in your favor.

2. If asked about alcohol use or drugs, either admit nothing, or blame it on your bottle of mouthwash. [E.g., "I just brushed my teeth!"] Don't incriminate yourself by admitting that you consumed "only two glasses of wine with dinner."

3. If asked for your license or any documents, have them ready to show the officer. Do not voluntarily get out of your vehicle for something stupid, like to go see the radar calibration to prove that your radar reading for a speeding ticket was correct. Stay inside the vehicle, seated, with your hands visible on the steering wheel. If the officer asks you to step out of the vehicle, explain that you prefer not to get out, due to safety concerns. If the officer claims to smell or detect alcohol or drugs, do not admit to having consumed anything. Just ask, "Am I under arrest?" The officer will say something like, "I need to give you some field evaluations to make sure you are safe to be on your way home." This seems rather innocuous until the officer "claims" that you failed or performed poorly on the field evaluations. Politely say, "Thank you officer, but unless I have my attorney present, I'd prefer NOT to try to perform agility exercises or medical tests that I am not familiar with." You can expect to be cajoled, prodded and verbally challenged as to why you are refusing to participate in these "simple tests." Do not let the officer start any evaluations. Only when he or she ORDERS you to get out, and physically opens your door should you reluctantly leave your car.

4. Once out of the car, *do nothing* and *walk nowhere other than where he or she insists, or forces you to go.* Explain your desire to not get out of the car at the roadside, and your desire not to be asked to walk, balance, count or perform any voluntary roadside evaluations of any type. If offered a hand-held breath analyzer, decline doing it, if you can. If asked, "Why not blow if you haven't been drinking?" tell the officer that you have no confidence in battery-powered devices that could either be inaccurate or carry bacteria, germs and diseases such as tuberculosis.

5. Ask to call your attorney on your cell phone as soon as the officer starts getting "pushy." Also state to the officer that you are willing to satisfy his concerns for safety by handing him your keys and either walking home or taking a cab home, but that you will not submit to testing that you do not trust to be reliable or accurate. If he says, "So you don't think you are safe to drive?" or something similar, be sure to say, "Absolutely not true. I am merely trying to satisfy you that I am cooperative in every way, even if I believe your concerns are not reasonable." If taking the cab results in your car being towed, that is a small price to pay to avoid being arrested and possibly convicted of DUI-DWI.

---

[239] http://www.theduibook.com/general/ga-drivers-rights.htm

CHAPTER 3

You've Been Arrested, and Now You Are Being

Taken to Jail. What Do You Do Now?

3.0. Overview of this chapter's purpose. Whatever the reason, the police officer has just made the decision to arrest you for DUI-DWI and has placed you in the back of his vehicle. This chapter covers what you should do at this point. Presumably, if you are reading this, it is because you have already gone through this experience or because your lifestyle may place you in this situation in the future. If you have already been arrested and if certain steps to start building a defense (as discussed in this chapter) have not already been done, it is time to begin them. Because critical factual details fade over time, and because valuable evidence could be lost due to delay, it is important to do the things covered in this chapter as soon as possible. Documenting all relevant facts within 12 hours of arrest is an excellent idea.

3.1. In the process of being arrested. In reviewing your DUI-DWI case, a skilled attorney reviews several distinct time periods during your arrest process: your time with the arresting officer(s), your time at the jail with other officers, and your time at the jail with anyone else. Although not as critical as the foregoing three time periods, the bonding process and your release from jail may also be important.

3.1.1. **In the police vehicle and your time with the arresting officer(s).** Once the arresting officer has placed you in his or her vehicle, or is transporting you to the jail for either processing your arrest or for further testing, the officer may attempt to strike up a "friendly conversation," or ask you further questions about your arrest. This may be a trap, so remain silent.

Once the adrenalin subsides, you might feel like talking, explaining yourself or trying to justify your actions. DON'T! After you have been arrested, the time for you to explain anything is over. The police officer has already made an arrest decision, or he or she would not have placed you in custody. Anything you say is likely being recorded, and possibly videotaped all the way to the jail and possibly inside the jail itself. Even if it isn't being recorded, what you say can and will be used against you in the prosecution of your case. Pleading to be let go, or to be "given a break" will usually not be well received by a judge or jury at trial.

In spite of this, some helpful details that you can discuss later with your criminal defense attorney may bolster your case. What did the officer say to you? Did the officer ever use threats of arrest or claims of "worsening" your situation if you did not cooperate? Did the police read you anything? When was this done? Was anyone else questioned by the officer either at the scene or while in route to jail? Who? If you do not obtain a name, what did this person look like or sound like? What did they talk about? Write down these details as soon as you can, and anything else you remember about the circumstances that arose during this time period.

3.1.2. Be polite with the jail personnel, but remain silent about your case facts. What you will endure during this entire arrest and jail process is rude, hurtful and embarrassing. However, you are not in charge. Lashing out at those around you will only make things worse. You will find that jail personnel are jaded to anyone who complains and that they can be both verbally abrasive and physically aggressive. You are not going to win a war of words with the jailers, breath test operator or law enforcement officers. At the end of the day, they are going home and you are in a concrete and steel structure that offers little opportunity for communication with the outside world.

The Fifth Amendment to the United States Constitution[240] provides that you have an absolute right to remain silent and not incriminate yourself during your arrest and booking process.[241] This right applies to everyone arrested, regardless of citizenship,[242] is true in every state,[243] and it is true even if you are an alien or an illegal alien.[244] Once the arresting officer has read you your *Miranda* warnings, your silence cannot be used against you in court.[245] You merely need to tell the officers you have made the choice to remain silent.[246]

Remaining silent does not mean that you should not be appropriately polite with the law enforcement officers, using such terms as "please" and "thank you." Beyond providing the police identification information such as your name, address and turning over your driver's license, insurance and registration papers, you do not have to answer any questions relating to what you did, where you were going or why you were arrested.

You may be asked to do different things by the law enforcement officers at the jail, including taking a breath test, answering personal questions, emptying your pockets, or removing jewelry, shoestrings or your belt. You may be asked to submit to a blood or urine test, and possibly to change out of your clothing into a uniform used at the jail. You do not have to answer their questions about other matters relating to your night's activities.

Do not talk to anyone else you meet in jail or at the testing facility about anything that happened related to your arrest. Once any words leave your lips, even if to a cellmate, over a telephone, or spoken to your wife and overheard by the police, this information can and likely will be used against you by the prosecutor and police in court.

3.1.3. Note the names of every jail person you see as well as sober and credible cellmates. A significant part of your case will come down to the word of the police against your word. In spite of "proof beyond a reasonable doubt" being the legal standard of proof in criminal cases, police officers' opinions can carry a lot of weight in a DUI-DWI prosecution. Your side of the story gains credibility with every witness and every single piece of favorable evidence you can gather for your defense. Even if someone you met with or saw in jail will not be able to add anything to your defense directly, they might be able to help in other ways.

However, to be able to get any help at all, your lawyer will need names of everyone you met at the jail. If possible, obtain telephone numbers or the names of their place of business so these witnesses can be called later. If you can accomplish it, write down names and contact information on your arm or hand. See Appendix J for a complete questionnaire that will facilitate processing your case when you see an attorney.

Any person at the scene of your accident or arrest may be a potential witness. Try to get their names and numbers immediately after you are released from jail. This applies to

---

[240]No person ... shall be compelled in any criminal case to be a witness against himself... **U.S.C.A. Const. Amend. V.**

[241]**U. S. ex rel. Parker v. McMann,** 308 F.Supp. 477 (S.D.N.Y. 1969); **U. S. v. Smith,** 31 F.R.D. 553 (D.D.C 1962); **U. S. ex rel. Young v. Follette,** 308 F.Supp. 670 (S.D.N.Y. 1970).

[242]**Miranda v. Arizona,** 86 S.Ct. 1602, 384 U.S. 436, 16 L.Ed.2d 694 (1966).

[243]**Malloy v. Hogan,** 84 S.Ct. 1489, 378 U.S. 1, 12 L.Ed.2d 653 (1964).

[244]**U. S. v. Henry,** 604 F.2d 908 (5th Cir.(Fla.) 1979)**; U.S. v. Brooks**, 284 F. 908 (E.D.Mich. 1922).

[245]**Smith v. Fairman,** 862 F.2d 630 (7th Cir.(Ill.) 1988).

[246]**Waldrop v. Thigpen,** 857 F.Supp. 872 (N.D.Ala. 1994).

anyone you met at the jail, including guards, janitors, nurses, or other people being processed for offenses while you were at the jail. If you are polite and not threatening, most people are willing to help you.

3.1.4. If "stonewalled" or ignored, use "911" to record your message. The law enforcement officers who are holding you may be too busy, or may say that they are too busy, for you to have access to your friends or family via telephone. Your jailers have different priorities than you do when you ask to use a telephone. If you have tried to get someone at the jail to help you obtain an independent test or need to give immediate information to someone because it is important to establish an indisputable timeline, dial "911" and record your message when the emergency operator takes your call.

This system records everything that you say and establishes a time that the call comes in. These tapes will be preserved for weeks if not months after your call. You might get reprimanded for wasting their time, but evidence of your clear voice and your "message" will be preserved for your defense. Remember, that anything you say will be accessible and useable by the prosecutor as well. Speak clearly, precisely and watch what you say.

3.1.5. Get bond posted and get out of jail ASAP. Nothing productive happens while you are in jail. Anyone who might be a witness in your favor is already forgetting details of what happened, because they have no need to write things down while these details are fresh in their memory. Your waiter or waitress will likely remember you the next day, but not 30 days later.

Any physical evidence at the scene of your arrest is being rained on, driven over or otherwise being altered by nature. Your car may be sitting by itself wherever you were stopped, unguarded and available to anyone but you, at least until you get out of jail. The police already have most if not all of their claimed evidence of impairment that is going to be used by the prosecution, while you are wasting time in jail rather than accumulating facts and information for your defense.

Different rules for bonding out of jail are applicable in different states. For example, in the state of Texas, your criminal defense attorney has the ability to help bond you out, once he or she is retained. In Georgia, a state Bar rule (that controls attorney conduct) and a state statute prohibit the attorney from acting in this capacity. Bailing a person out of jail is traditionally the responsibility of the person arrested and his or her friends and family.

3.1.6. Abiding by the Terms of Your Bond. Regardless of whether you post your own bond, use a family member or real estate equity value as the surety or hire a commercial bonding company, pay attention to the conditions and rules of your bond agreement. In some states, repeat offenders are required to not drive any vehicle that is not equipped with ignition interlock. In others, the judge setting bond can mandate that you can drive only for work-related purposes. Abide by the conditions that are imposed for your bond.

Commercial bonding companies can be very valuable to you in helping you get released from jail. In most jurisdictions, these same companies can act as your appellate bonding company, in the event you need to appeal an issue in your case and can remain out of jail on an "appeal bond." Be aware that these companies do not happily pay off your bond principal amount when you do not appear in court. If they need to locate you, they will. They are given extraordinary powers of detention once they locate you, and this can be a far less pleasant experience than the one involving your arresting officer. Stay in touch with your bonding representative. Keep them informed of the progress of your case, and communicate with them when they call you to remind you of a court date. Once your DUI-DWI specialist helps you get a reduction or a victory, always tell the bonding company about your excellent results, so they know who the best legal advocates are in your community.

3.2. What to do as soon as you are out of jail. Once out of jail, several critical things need to be done as soon as possible. Most important is writing down all the details of your arrest, detention, testing and jailing. Waiting even an extra day will cause loss of details. [See form questionnaire in **Appendix J**.] Besides contacting a DUI-DWI specialist to help you, you need to record your side of the story as completely as possible and have a close friend or relative take pictures of your vehicle, both inside and out, whenever any relevant evidence (e.g., open container inside the vehicle; body damage from a collision; deployed air bags) is in danger of being altered or lost.

3.2.1. Immediately write down all details of your events for the entire day of your arrest and the exact conversations between you and any law enforcement officer after the stop. Some of the most critical details that could help in your eventual defense happened not at the scene of your arrest, but in the minutes and hours before your arrest. Critical facts about your food or medication intake or possible exposure to interfering substances (e.g., paint fumes; glue) can be extremely important information.

Do not omit any details in your account of what happened. When did you get up? How long had it been since you had slept? Write down everything you ate, everything you drank, everywhere you went and everyone with whom you talked.

Writing down all the details such as the use of perfume, aftershave lotion or cologne prior to your arrest might be significant. Otherwise, if you finished dinner with a friend at a restaurant a half hour before your arrest, such information could provide a critical factor in your defense. Write these details down as soon as you can, before you forget a detail that may provide a good defense in your case, or at least offer facts that can create "reasonable doubt" about the accuracy of a breath test result or field sobriety evidence. [See questionnaire form in Appendix J.]

Next, write down everything any law enforcement officers said to you and anything you might have said back to them. Try to replay the conversations back in your mind and document the exact words. Was there anyone else who might have been present for any of these conversations? Write their names and contact information down for your attorney, but also have them write down every detail they can recall as soon as possible after the arrest occurs.

3.2.2. Photographing your car (inside and out) and any containers from which evidence was seized. As soon as you are released from your DUI-DWI arrest, you will want to retrieve your car. Valuable information can be derived from the condition and "contents" of your vehicle after the car has been towed away following the inventory search by the police officers at the roadway. By having a close friend or relative photograph the vehicle, he or she can be used as a witness at trial rather than put you on the witness stand.

Your car may have been left alongside a road, in a parking lot or near the location of your arrest. It may or may not have been parked in a safe area. If it has been left at such a location, secure it as soon as possible. The sooner you get your vehicle back under your control, the sooner you know that your property is safe and that your vehicle has not been tampered with by vandals or thieves.

If your license was already suspended before the current arrest, when you are released from custody do not risk driving away from the impound yard or location where it was parked. Have someone else drive it home for you. Police officers are prone to asking the owner of the impound lot to notify them if YOU drive away after retrieving your vehicle. A new arrest for driving while suspended only makes the initial DUI-DWI case more difficult to handle, and will almost guarantee a lengthy jail sentence for you.

No legal concerns arise from having pictures made of your vehicle and the inside of the vehicle as soon as you get it back into your possession. It does not matter if the pictures are made with a digital or traditional camera but retain any digital media cards in case the authenticity of this images are ever challenged. Be sure to include pictures of any alcoholic containers (bottles, glasses, etc.) or containers that held any alcohol (like cups, glasses, six pack cardboard containers or paper bags), that were left in your vehicle by the police. Take photos of where the containers are found inside the vehicle, including any liquids that remain in them.

You should get a friend or relative to videotape or photograph the scene of your arrest, with your car in its position where you were stopped. This person may need to be a witness later, so choose someone who will be highly credible and will also be available if your case goes to trial. If any roadway construction or hazardous conditions (e.g., potholes, dangerous driving grades, etc.) exist along the path your vehicle traveled, get good images of these. Be aware that some highway locations are extremely dangerous to film or photograph.

3.2.3. Can you record the officer's conversations with you? In this day and age of cell phones having cameras and audio recording devices reduced to the size of a ballpoint pen, you may have the means to record everything a law enforcement officer says to you and possibly conversations between two or more law enforcement officers in your vicinity. A passenger may be able to record a film clip or images on a cell phone from the scene of your arrest. In some instances, if your mobile phone is not confiscated, you may even be allowed to use your cell phone at the jail or breath testing location.

Having such information recorded could dramatically assist you in your defense, if it does not cause you more legal problems in obtaining it. Some jurisdictions prohibit "secret" recording of other people's conversations. It is critical that you know the statutes that apply in the state of your "confrontation" and detention with police, and be aware of your rights and responsibilities in this situation. You may be required to disclose to anyone being taped or recorded that you are making a recording of the conversation or that you are digitally capturing their images and voices.

When it comes to taping any conversations of others or between you and anyone else, including any law enforcement officers, either before, during or after your arrest, state laws vary enough that you should not do it unless you know for a fact that doing so is not illegal. Federal law (which generally applies to interstate communication devices like cell phones and regular phones) allows recording of phone calls and other electronic communications with the consent of at least **one party** to the call. A majority of the states and territories have adopted local wiretapping statutes based on our federal laws, although most also have extended their state laws to cover in-person recordings where at least one person to the conversation is aware of the fact of recording including phone calls and in-person tape or video recording.

Approximately thirty-eight states and the District of Columbia permit individuals to record conversations to which they are a party without informing the other person (or other parties) that they are doing so. These statutes are referred to as "one-party consent" statutes, and as long as you are a party to the conversation, it is legal for you to record it. (Nevada has a one-party consent statute, but the Nevada Supreme Court has interpreted the statute as requiring that ALL parties consent to the recording.)

Twelve states *require the consent of all parties to a conversation*, with some situational exceptions. Those jurisdictions (in alphabetical order) are *California, Connecticut, Florida,*

Illinois, Maryland, Massachusetts, Michigan, Montana, Nevada, New Hampshire, Pennsylvania and Washington. Although sometimes called "two-party consent" laws, if more than two people are involved in the conversation, all persons must consent to the taping. Ironically, some of these states have statutory exceptions for the POLICE to record you in situations such as traffic stops, without advising you of this recording. In fact, it is highly likely that the police recorded at least some, if not all or part of your actual arrest. Often, the driving behavior that lead to your stop and field sobriety evaluations that you took, plus all conversations between you and the officer, are recorded without notification to you or a request for permission from you.

Regardless of the state, it is almost always illegal to record a conversation to which you are not a party, do not have consent to tape, and could not naturally (i.e., without special electronic listening devices or equipment) overhear. So, it is likely illegal for you to record conversations between law enforcement officers if you are not also a direct party to the conversation. Federal law and most state laws also make it illegal to disclose the contents of an illegally intercepted call or communication. So, once illegal recording takes place, a new criminal act may arise every time the illegal recording is replayed or communicated, even to your lawyer.

Penalties for violations of the law are described in each applicable statute. These penalties include criminal sanctions (jail and fines) and possibly civil damages (money that a court may order the violator to pay to the subject of the taping). In dealing with phone calls, assume that cell calls and calls made on portable (wireless) units that are part of the hard-wired system within a home or business are covered by state law (and possibly federal law). In light of the differing state laws governing electronic recording of conversations between private parties, citizens are encouraged to be cautious when recording or disclosing information intercepted from an interstate telephone call. The safest strategy is to assume that the stricter state law will apply.

By way of example, Georgia is a "one-party" state. Nevertheless, under O.C.G.A. § 16-11-62, secretly recording or overhearing a conversation held in a private place (i.e., a rest room), whether carried out orally or by wire or electronic means, is criminally punishable as a felony under statutory provisions regarding invasions of privacy. However, the law expressly provides that it does not prohibit a person who is a party to a conversation from recording and does not prohibit recording if one party to the conversation has given prior consent.[247] So, in Georgia, you can secretly record the conversation between you and the police officer.

Georgia courts have declared that interception of a private cellular telephone conversation without the consent of at least one of the parties is a misdemeanor.[248] Furthermore, a federal court in Georgia has upheld a civil action for wiretapping offenses.[249]

One other note pertains to attorneys secretly tape recording conversations. State Bar rules (that control legal professionals and their conduct) may have special prohibitions against engaging in secretly tape recording a private conversation or advising a client to do so.[250]

---

[247] OCGA. § 16-11-66.

[248] **Barlow v. Barlow**, 272 Ga. 102, 526 S.E.2d 857 (2000).

[249] **Tapley v. Collins,** 41 F. Supp.2d 1366 (S.D. Ga. 1999), *rev'd on other grounds,* 211 F.3d 1210 (11th Cir. 2000).

[250] *See* Texas Disciplinary Rule 8.04 (a)(3) prohibits an attorney from electronically recording a telephone conversation with another party without first telling the other party that the conversation is being recorded. *See* Tex. Disciplinary R. Prof. Conduct 8.04 (a) (3) (1989). *Also see* State Bar of Texas Ethics Opinion No. 514, which acknowledged Rule 8.04(a) (3), and further stated that an attorney cannot circumvent his or her ethical

3.3. What to do after securing your vehicle. You have been arrested, booked, tested (or refused to be tested) and have posted a bond to get out of jail. You have spent several hours searching through your memory about everything that happened to you the day of your arrest, regarding the arrest itself and your time in custody, and have written all this down in as much detail as you can remember. You have put together a list of everyone you met during your arrest and your time in jail, what they might have said to you, and what you told them. You have even had a friend or family member take pictures or video footage of your car as soon as you could get back to the roadway where you pulled over. Possibly, you have spoken to a qualified criminal defense attorney and taken care of some preliminary matters. What should you do next?

3.3.1. Keep your arrest details to yourself. *Arrested* does not mean **_convicted_**. While being convicted of a DUI-DWI offense can have a possible effect on your job, your insurance rates, and on the rest of your life, being arrested and **not** eventually being found guilty, (or having the charges reduced or dropped), should not adversely impact your life. The best general rule to follow is to only discuss your case with people (such as your attorney's staff) who have a "need to know" these details. Plus, for anyone not associated with your attorney's office, the facts that they need to know are typically very limited and do not involve potentially inculpatory (i.e., admission of guilt or facts pointing to guilt) information.

In some instances, your employer may learn of your arrest because you cannot avoid telling them (e.g., you miss work the day after your arrest). In other instances, your employee handbook or employment contract may require disclosure of the arrest. In some instances, your use of a company vehicle may force you to discuss the arrest with a supervisor. Generally, however, the only person who typically needs to know the entire situation besides you is your DUI-DWI lawyer. Pilots and commercial truck drivers who have their CDL licenses may be legally obligated to report the arrest or any administrative license suspension. Check with a DUI-DWI expert in your state to see if this is a requirement for you and your situation.

This said, any words that leave your lips to anyone else can at least theoretically be used against you. Your conversation at the water cooler with the guy in the cubical next to yours can come back to haunt you when the prosecutor or an investigator from the prosecutor's office talks to this person and gets some detail that hurts your defense.

Although unlikely, a person that you speak with may have a legal problem going on as well that you don't know about and they may receive a better deal on their case from the prosecutor because they offer to give the prosecutor helpful information on your case. Your conversation at the gym could be overheard by a police officer, who can then take this information and use it against you. Remember that in our "Post-9/11" society, walls have ears, and **ANYTHING** you say to **ANYONE** can and will be used against you.

3.3.2. Staying out of trouble while the case is pending. As will be discussed elsewhere in this book, once arrested for DUI-DWI, you then face a legal process which could be over in as little as a few days (unlikely) to as long as year or more (too likely). During this time, while your case is still active and pending, you do not need to add to your problems. Any new infractions or legal problems can be disastrous, especially if it is a similar new offense.

First, while it might be legal or acceptable for anyone else in the world to have a glass of wine with dinner or a beer with a co-worker on the way home, it is not acceptable for you to

---

obligations by requesting that clients secretly record conversations to which the attorney is a party. *See* DR 8.04 (a) (1) (discussing violations of the disciplinary rules through the acts of others). **McWhorter v. Sheller**, 993 S.W.2d 781 (Tex.App.-Houston 1999).

drink any alcohol, in any form, and then drive. The absolute last thing you need to happen to you while you are pending a trial for a DUI-DWI is another drinking/driving arrest.

Second, if you use any illegal substance, don't drive. This includes marijuana, or any other illegal drug or prescription medicine that is not legally prescribed for you. If you are stopped and arrested for a second DUI-DWI offense while your original case is pending, you may prevent any possibility of negotiating away the initial charges, and the court system will come down upon you even harder.

Last, if there is any chance you are doing anything which could even possibly be considered illegal during this period of your life — DON'T. Pay your taxes, cross the street only at crosswalks, drive the speed limit and come to a complete stop at stop signs. Don't manhandle your spouse, hit your kids or beat your dog. Don't give the police any other chance to arrest you and to complicate your life further. For this time period, you and your life are under a microscope. The good news is that this harsh part of your life will eventually be over and you can get things back to normal, provided that you don't get into more trouble while your case is pending.

3.3.3. If (or when) you have your license back, get busy. Despite it being very easy for a DUI-DWI arrest to take over your life, don't let it. You need to concentrate on the other issues identified in this book to maximize your chances of winning your case or achieving a plea reduction. As your case progresses, your life must go on.

Once you hire a top DUI-DWI specialist, you should mentally shift responsibility for your fate to your attorney. Letting stress and sleeplessness overtake your life will do no good at all. You should focus on family issues, work responsibilities and following your attorney's recommendations. If you need a helpful DVD regarding "Dealing with Stress While Your Case Is Pending," go to this link: http://www.theduibook.com/stress-DVD.htm.

Staying employed is critical. This will help you maintain normalcy in your life. Furthermore, hiring a top DUI-DWI attorney is costly, plus court expenses and expert witness costs add to the financial burden. Other expenses directly relating to your case can arise in some cases (e.g., possible restitution costs for auto collision damages not covered by insurance). Talk to your lawyer about the expenses you face. Being prepared to pay fines and other expenses (in the event you lose your case), is also important. You could face monetary penalties (e.g., probation or treatment costs) having to do with sentencing if you are found guilty (or plead guilty) to either the DUI-DWI offense or a lesser offense.

Your hearings and your trial will likely result in you having to take time off from work so that you can not only attend, but assist your lawyer to prepare for court in the days and weeks before your upcoming hearings or trial. Due to other commitments of your lawyer's time, be flexible with meetings and agree to telephone consultations or e-mail communications when he or she suggests that a face-to-face meeting is not feasible.

Start taking positive steps in your life, becoming more active in your religious endeavors, performing volunteer work, or possibly enrolling in a drug or alcohol rehabilitation program or outpatient treatment, if recommended by your lawyer. Often, the need for such a program will already be on your agenda because you recognize a problem with alcohol in your life.

If you do begin attending a program like Alcoholics Anonymous, stay with it. If these sessions are not helping you, look into private counseling sessions. Keep a record of every meeting you attend, and have your sponsor, counselor or host sign off on your attendance sheet every time you attend a meeting. While these things will have no effect on any trial or decision of guilt or innocence, these steps provide your lawyer and you with some positive "evidence in mitigation" if your case is lost at trial. These steps may also assist your attorney to negotiate a reduced plea in your case.

Alcoholic's Anonymous offers several on-line questionnaires if you have any question as to whether or not alcohol is a problem in your life.[251]

---

[251] http://www.alcoholics-anonymous.org.

Chapter 4

Locating, Investigating, Interviewing and Hiring the

Best Available Attorney to Handle Your DUI-DWI Case

4.0. Overview of this chapter. If you have been arrested and charged with DUI-DWI, you should contact and retain the best available DUI-DWI trial lawyer to represent you. You should act quickly to retain counsel, but only make a hiring decision after looking at all of your options. Very few people automatically know the best DUI-DWI attorney in their area without some investigation.

By the time you have been arrested, the legal process has already started and the prosecution has already started to organize its case against you. The purpose of this chapter is to show you how to not only find the best possible DUI-DWI lawyer to represent you at this stressful time in your life, but to also advise you how to deal with the lawyer and his or her staff during the legal journey that you will need to take over the next year or so.

4.1. Locate and contact a "top" DUI-DWI attorney immediately. The situation you face when arrested and charged with a DUI-DWI crime is one of the most tangled legal webs in the entire criminal justice system, and gets literally more tangled with every passing day. In addition, the police and the prosecutor already have almost all the evidence they need to prosecute you for DUI-DWI before you are even allowed out of jail. From the first minutes after your arrest, you are fighting an uphill battle to assert your best defense to these charges. Because of this, it is vital to your defense to obtain the best possible attorney as soon as possible so he or she can start working for you.

Even if you are a lawyer, because of the constant changes and the hidden secrets that surround DUI-DWI law, you will not get justice unless you locate and contact a top DUI-DWI lawyer to take charge of your defense. These offenses carry too much public scrutiny to ask the prosecutor to "give you a break" and drop the charges, based on state Bar membership.

Would you want your *family* doctor to do your heart bypass operation? Would you want a heart surgeon who does one bypass a year to do your operation? Even worse, would you want for your open-heart surgery to be the doctor's first bypass ever? Would you choose your heart surgeon from the yellow pages, without checking out his or her credentials? The answers to all of these questions are obvious. How do you find the best DUI-DWI lawyer for you?

A number of factors need to be considered when hiring your DUI-DWI defense lawyer. With more than 50,000 so-called criminal defense lawyers practicing law in the USA, the process of selecting the right lawyer for you can be difficult. Only about 500 lawyers in the United States are "the best" in their geographic regions in defending drunken driving cases. Hence, you need to eliminate the 99 avowed criminal specialists to find the ONE "best" attorney for your DUI-DWI case. That means 1 in 100 criminal defense attorneys in your state is your BEST choice.

While there is no substitute for following the steps outlined below, a comprehensive Internet search for competent attorneys in your area may be helpful. Key word searches with any major search engine will generate several names of attorneys. Use the Internet to compare each candidate's qualifications. Also look at several top Internet directories. [252]

While there is no way in the mayhem, stress and hysteria of your life following an arrest for DUI-DWI you can use every possible resource, the following list of factors may prove helpful in narrowing the prospective candidates to two or three specialists.

4.1.1. References from friends or any lawyer you might know personally. A strong reference from a friend or colleague who has successfully referred or used the potential DUI-DWI attorney is often the best indicator of whether a lawyer is worthy of hiring. This gives you a starting place. Be sure, however, that the friend or colleague has seen the attorney's skill in court versus merely winning by default or by handling a guilty plea. Often, attorneys you may know personally in your "market area" who do NOT handle criminal cases will know the names of several top DUI attorneys in your area.

4.1.2. Community and Courthouse Reputation. Taking the following additional step may be *the very best measuring stick* that anyone can use to judge an attorney's "skill level." If your attorney has a sterling reputation within the legal community where your case is pending, chances are it was earned through hard work and over many years. Having *a great COURTHOUSE reputation* is more difficult than having a stellar community reputation. *Checking the attorney's COURTHOUSE reputation is the most direct and accurate litmus test of the GREAT drunk driving defense attorneys.*

Go to the courthouse in the county in which you were arrested, not necessarily the county in which you live. Very politely, talk with a person from the clerk of court's office, a bailiff, a deputy who is assigned to that courthouse or to a court reporter who is in court. Ask for their opinion about each "candidate's" skill in *fighting* cases.

Another good source for a referral is *law enforcement officers* who regularly face these lawyers in court, and will tell you their honest opinion. However, true "fighters" in the criminal defense bar may not be liked by some officers, due to the adversarial prior court proceedings between these officers and the best attorneys. If you know a police officer on a personal level, he or she may be more forthcoming.

Wearing clothes you would wear to your most important personal business, go in and watch court proceedings on a date before your first appearance date. Courts are usually open to the public. After the judge takes a break, try to politely speak to the court personnel near the front of the courtroom. Ask a bailiff, the court reporter, the calendar clerk or the deputy overseeing the courtroom WHICH one of the lawyers you are considering would he or she hire if they were facing a DUI-DWI prosecution and HAD TO TAKE THEIR BEST SHOT AT WINNING.

Be sure to give them any names you might already have in mind, because they may be hesitant to "recommend" or suggest any specific attorney or law firm. Also, the prosecuting attorneys may or may not give you an earnest opinion. Unless a prosecutor is a personal friend of yours, with your best interest at heart, do not blindly rely on a prosecutor's recommendation. It is only natural for any of them to try to steer you away from the Hell-bent DUI-DWI trial attorneys, to ease their workload.

4.1.3. Advanced Training. After finding possible attorneys that may fit your needs, check them out on-line with a Google or Yahoo search.[253] Search within the Internet profiles of the attorneys you are considering to confirm that he or she is a specialist in "drunk

---

[252]http://www.theduibook.com/internetdirectories.htm.

driving defense." The most highly trained DUI lawyers will have attended several of the following specialized courses which will be listed on their websites: the NHTSA Standardized Field Sobriety Test (Student or "Practitioner" Course), the NHTSA Standardized Field Sobriety Test (Instructor Course), the Breath Instrument Training Courses, the Drug Recognition Expert (or Drug Recognition Technician) Overview Course, and Blood and Urine Training.

4.1.4. Specialized Membership or Professional Affiliations. Once you have these names and have checked out their websites, before you call any one attorney, consider their "involvement" and "commitment" to the field of drunk driving defense once you have any names. What specialized professional membership standing does he or she maintain? Top attorneys are often found in special "founding member," "life member" or similar "special status" categories in these organizations.

This information will either be on each lawyer's website or on the websites of the professional organizations. In the DUI-DWI defense field, here are some places to examine to determine "proficiency":

a. National College for DUI Defense, Inc.[254]
b. The National Association of Criminal Defense Lawyers (NACDL).[255]
c. Many states and even a few large metropolitan cities have formed local affiliate branches of the NACDL.[256]
d. Martindale-Hubbell[257] is the oldest and most widely respected directory of attorneys in America. Their rating of "av" and/or their "Pre-Eminent Lawyers" designation signifies excellent reputation and credentials.

4.1.5. Disciplinary Actions. Once you have begun to narrow your search of whom to call, check out one last detail. Has the attorney ever been disciplined by the Board of Professional Responsibility of the state Bar of his/her practice location? This can be an obvious sign of problems. Also, some people falsely claim to be licensed attorneys, so be careful. The state Bar is also the place to check that the attorney is licensed and in good standing. Call your state Bar to see if your lawyer is in "good standing." Contact the American Bar Association on line to find links to all state Bar associations.[258]

Once you have the name of your top choice, and perhaps your number two choice, it is now time to interview them, to see if they fit YOUR needs. The supposed "best" DUI-DWI lawyer may not be the best one for you if your personalities clash. Write your questions down before you even go in and ask them about the following credentials.

4.1.6. Seminar Speaker. The top attorneys in each state are asked to speak for DUI-DWI-OUI-OWI seminars in their state and others. Being a regular invited speaker for several consecutive years is generally a great indicator of the "quality" of the attorney. Be sure to distinguish between "invited" speaking engagements versus self-promoting seminars. Ask about this "indicator" from any DUI / DWI attorney you are considering hiring.

---

[253]http://www.google.com; http://www.yahoo.com.

[254]http://www.ncdd.com/.

[255]http://www.nacdl.org/public.nsf/freeform/publicwelcome?opendocument.

[256]http://www.nacdl.org/public.nsf/freeform/affiliate_index?opendocument.

[257]http://www.martindale.com/xp/Martindale/home.xml.

[258]http://www.abanet.org/barserv/stlobar.html.

4.1.7. Fees and Fee Structure - How does the attorney set his or her fees? Most drunken driving lawyers work on a *flat fee basis*. An attorney cannot guarantee to win your case. Criminal matters cannot be handled on a "contingency" basis, due to Bar rules prohibiting this practice.

As you might expect, highly experienced attorneys often charge *much* higher fees than younger, less experienced lawyers. Additionally, a lawyer who fights each case cannot take the volume of cases handled by a "pleader" because trials and contested cases typically require 20 times as much legal time (or more) as handling a guilty plea. Thus, a GOOD trial lawyer typically will limit his or her caseload in order to do an excellent job for each client thoroughly and meticulously.

If an attorney prices him or herself much higher than MOST other DUI lawyers in the area, then do not hesitate to ask why. Don't be accusatory---just ask what distinguishes this lawyer from the other candidates you are considering who charge less. Conversely, a low fee quote usually means that you will get exactly what you paid for. One ex-State trooper turned DUI-DWI attorney from Louisiana, Glynn Delatte, ends each e-mail with this maxim: "Good lawyers aren't cheap, and cheap lawyers aren't good."

Comparison-shopping may serve a valuable purpose, but if you are looking for the attorney who can BEST handle your DUI-DWI successfully, the "pool" of super lawyers is often very small in every community. Their cost for handling your case may be more than you would have thought. For arrests in smaller cities, you may need to go to a suburban or larger metro area attorney to find a quality fighter. All of that said, for many persons facing the extreme penalties of a DUI-DWI conviction, price is secondary to an excellent track record for results.

4.1.8. Focus of practice - Most truly great DUI-DWI attorneys either restrict their cases to drunk driving (and drugged driving) or stay entirely within the field of criminal law. Some of these attorneys work within law firms that handle other matters, but the DUI-DWI specialist does nothing but drunk driving litigation. If the attorney that you are considering spends less than 80% of his or her legal time on criminal law, look further for an attorney.

Consider limiting your search for an attorney to a criminal defense attorney with a strong background or emphasis in DUI-DWI defense. Watch out for firms that sign you up with "any available" lawyers in the firm versus the experienced partners in the firm. If you pay premium dollars, this should be for the cost of retaining the best lawyer available. This is the person that should handle your DUI-DWI trial and (generally) the DUI-DWI pre-trial motions.

4.1.9. Drunk Driving Specialists - Nationally, only a few attorneys work 100% within the DUI-DWI field. However, some are primarily "pleaders" who are not TRIAL SPECIALISTS. Ask any prospective lawyer how many DUI-DWI **trials** they have tried in the last year. The lawyer who calls himself or herself "DUI-DWI attorney," yet has not tried *any* cases (or only a couple) in the past 12 months are either pleading guilty a great deal or not handling very many cases.

Ask pointed questions about why no trials have been conducted. Also ask the attorney about a percentage of ALL DUI-DWI cases that he or she handled in which the clients ultimately ended up with a favorable non-DUI-DWI disposition (on *all* the DUI-DWI counts, not just the common law count or just the "per se" charge).

4.1.10. Years in Practice - *There is no substitute for experience.* This rule is true in both warfare and in criminal trial practice. The longer one is involved in an active trial practice, the better one's litigation instincts generally become. But, the opposite can be true as well. Some lawyers who have been practicing for years may become lazy about staying up to date on the latest legal changes and trial strategies. So, look at the candidates' **RECENT** advanced DUI-DWI law training and recent seminar attendance or "invited speaker" record.

4.1.11. Lawyer-Paralegal ratio - A busy, experienced DWI-DUI trial attorney will have 1 to 2 paralegals assisting him/her. Trial preparation requires more time than processing guilty pleas. *A knowledgeable paralegal is worth his or her weight in gold.* Paralegals are like the HUB of a wheel, and assign tasks and responsibilities to many other support staffers, such as couriers, process servers, investigators and law clerks. An attorney who maintains a ratio of one to two paralegals per trial attorney may indicate that the firm is positioned well to process the work that is required for each case. It may also indicate that the attorney you thought you were hiring actually knows what is happening on your case and has the time to speak with you about your case when the need arises. However, a truly skilled trial lawyer relies on the trained paralegals to handle all routine inquiries in order to keep him or her *in court* trying to negotiate or win DUI-DWI cases.

4.1.12. Caseload - Is your lawyer taking on so much work that there is no way his or her cases can properly be handled? Too many lawyers don't know when to draw the line and say "no." Some attorneys hesitate to hire additional attorneys and staff to facilitate the pre-trial work that all cases require. A trial attorney may limit his or her caseload to between 40 and 100 cases per year, depending on these factors:

(1) What percentage must go to trial? In some states (e.g. Oregon and Kentucky), the prosecutor is legally barred from offering to reduce a DUI-DWI. In Georgia, the author gets about 65% to 70% of his cases resolved with non-DUI-DWI dispositions each year, without having to complete trials in each case. The fee charged is earned by the "win," despite the case not having to go through a two or three day trial.

(2) Can the case be resolved at a non-jury trial **or** pre-trial motion hearing? In some states, the "first level" of trial in any traffic law case is a non-jury trial. In states such as Mississippi, Arkansas and Virginia, if the first trial is lost, a completely NEW jury trial can be pursued at the next level. These quick bench trials may allow more than a 100 cases to be handled in a year.

In most states, however, this stage of a DUI-DWI case is relegated to pre-trial motions hearings, and a successful hearing can result in a victory or force the prosecutor to "cut a deal" for a non-DUI-DWI disposition. Lawyers who are successful at winning bench trials and pre-trial motions can handle a larger number of cases because DUI-DWI jury trials require 3 to 6 times the hours (or more) to resolve than these motions or quick trials.

4.1.13. Use of Technology - Technology has revolutionized the practice of DUI-DWI law probably as much as any other area in the legal profession. Does your attorney not only USE e-mail, but encourage its utilization by you? Does the attorney have the latest legal research and case management software? Does the attorney provide electronic newsletters and e-mail alerts to inform clients of breaking news about DUI-DWI and criminal law matters? Does the firm have an extranet (or a quick response e-mail plan) that allows you to log in to a private and secure web site to see what is happening on your case? Does the lawyer participate in state or national list servers or blogs?

Lawyers who master technology deliver legal services with better quality and can often leverage technology to deliver legal services less expensively. New legal developments are much easier to track due to e-mail notification, on-line legal research and instant electronic communication. Additionally, miscues such as missing a court date will typically be minimized by utilizing case management software to "calendar" all critical court dates.

4.1.14. Promising too much - *Be skeptical about lawyers who promise success.* An old wag among experienced DUI-DWI trial lawyers is "Show me a DUI-DWI lawyer who has never lost a DUI-DWI case, and I'll show you a lawyer who has never *TRIED* DUI-DWI cases." A lawyer who honestly presents the real risks and perils of trial without trying to talk you into an ill-advised plea of guilty is what you seek.

Be very wary of attorneys who claim to have special influence or "standing" with the judge or prosecutor in your case. An attorney who spends more time "name-dropping" impressive political or judicial names than explaining the favorable aspects of your case should be avoided like the plague!

Also, beware of lawyers who speak too negatively about their competitors. If the lawyer you are interviewing is worthy, he or she can stand on his or her own track record and reputation rather than tearing down the record of qualified competitors.

When you have your quest narrowed down to 2 or 3 potential attorneys who all seem to have the right credentials, go back to Section 4.2.2 above, and go to the COURTHOUSE for "the final answer." This provides the **BEST FINAL TEST** about who to hire.

4.1.15. Board Certified - As mentioned above, the National College for DUI Defense (NCDD) now offers the only national certification for DUI-DWI specialists. This rigorous examination and screening process has been approved by the American Bar Association. Of course, your attorney's state bar regulatory agency may or may not allow lawyers within that state to broadcast or "advertise" such certification. A few states certify lawyers in the area of *criminal law* (as opposed to "DUI-DWI defense"). If your lawyer practices in a state that *does* permit certification, ask whether he or she has obtained this credential.

Ironically, having criminal law designated as a specialty may not be a desirable designation in some states (i.e., in Texas, most criminal defense attorneys who specialize do NOT seek this Texas bar credentialing) due to the manner that it restricts the practitioner or potentially exposes him/her to additional financial liability. Board certification is no guarantee of quality, but it can certainly be an indicator of expertise, especially if obtained from NCDD.

4.1.16. Educational Background - While many fine lawyers have come out of mediocre or unaccredited law schools and many lousy lawyers come out of the Ivy League law schools, where a lawyer went to law school *can* still be an indicator of a person's ability to regularly achieve trial success. Most of America's top law firms acknowledge that the best law schools are "ABA-approved." This means that a branch of the American Bar Association has investigated the law school thoroughly for quality on dozens of "measuring sticks." You can go to the ABA web site to look up your prospective attorney's law school.[259]

4.1.17. Publications - Lawyers who frequently write scholarly articles relating to their area of law practice tend to keep themselves better informed about their field of specialization. The ability to get published in legal magazines or DUI-DWI trade journals is a good barometer of the lawyer's expertise. Writing the "book" on DUI-DWI law in the state where you were arrested is generally a great indicator of an advanced level of knowledge and expertise for a potential attorney. Authors of national treatsies on DUI-DWI law are considered to have achieved the highest level of peer recognition as experts in litigating DUI-DWI cases.

4.1.18. Promotional Materials - Pay attention to a law firm's client information package, marketing, Internet and promotional materials. Are they professional and polished or do they give the appearance of being "fly-by-night?" How the firm and its staff members deal

---

[259] http://www.abanet.org/legaled/approvedlawschools/alpha.html.

with clients and potential clients may be an indicator of how the firm will present itself - and, consequently, you - in court. Cheesy written materials usually come from sloppy law firms.

4.1.19. Conflicts of Interest - Some DUI-DWI defense lawyers may also act as part-time prosecutors in one or more inferior (entry-level courts of limited jurisdiction). Some DUI-DWI defense lawyers may even act as a part-time judge in an inferior court at the early part of their career. An attorney cannot act as a defense attorney in the same court that he or she works as a part time prosecutor or judge, however.

These lawyers typically will screen any potential "conflicts" and never interview any potential clients with cases pending in their courts. Usually, such conflicts are not a problem. Pay attention to this fact if the lawyer does not immediately "step out" of discussing ANY ASPECT of a case pending in his or her "court." This is a serious matter that is strictly prohibited by the State Bar Association.

4.1.20. Sub-specialization within the DUI-DWI Field - A number of "drunk driving defense lawyers" focus on particular types of matters within the DUI-DWI arena. For example, some lawyers only handle administrative license suspension or administrative license revocation matters. These practitioners never go to DUI-DWI criminal trials or conduct pre-trial motions in the criminal portion of these cases. Other criminal attorneys may only handle appeals of criminal law cases, including DUI-DWI appeals.

4.1.21. Engagement Letters - Read the fine print in your engagement letters or "fee agreements." Some lawyers load their agreements down with so much "legalese" and one-sided provisions that such agreements should raise suspicion. Consider using a lawyer who provides an agreement that is written in plain English that appears to be even-handed. Also make certain that you know what costs (beyond the fees) are your costs to pay and whether any appeals or potential re-trials (after a mistrial or "hung" jury) require additional fees.

4.1.22. Language Skills - Some clients who are not native English speakers may feel more comfortable working with a lawyer fluent in their language. A skilled DUI-DWI trial attorney who does not speak your language should have staff members available to translate for you or utilize telephone-based translation services. In trial, courts must make translation services available to accused citizens who are not fluent in English.

4.1.23. Ethics - Run as fast as you can from lawyers that tell you it is okay to lie or otherwise act dishonestly in your case. Run just as fast from any lawyer who agrees to lie for you. Aside from the obvious questions of ethics, professionalism and morality, you are risking jail time for any complicity in such shenanigans. The attorney is risking disbarment, jail time and potential civil litigation by suggesting this type of condct. RUN AWAY! It is not worth such aggravation and potential increased legal problems.

4.1.24. Personality Compatibility - Your interaction with your DUI-DWI lawyer in evaluating compatibility with your goals should be more than just an analysis of the lawyer's experience and competency. At the end of the day, a lawyer's "bedside manner" can mean a lot to how the overall relationship goes. Some clients are especially "on edge" and need more nurturing, due to the stress that a DUI-DWI puts them under.

Other clients merely want the attorney they hire to be a gladiator and go "slay the dragon" for them, and need no nurturing at all. They want an attack dog to represent them.

Find a lawyer who really cares about winning, and be realistic about your level of need in being "nurtured" (or not being nurtured) by the attorney. Since 90% or more of your communications will be with the attorney's staff, their supportiveness and attitude is also very important. Difficult or uncaring staff members are not being "team players" for your cause.

However, you must not constantly call the staff to ask for an update, when the progress of the case may be slow and somewhat plodding. If you are constantly knocking on an airliner cockpit door to ask, "How is the flight going?" you will be removed from the flight. Similarly, if you constantly interrupt your attorney or his or her staff, you will possibly lose your attorney. The author's staff is given full authority to "fire" any client who creates a continuing problem for office staffers through his or her incessant efforts to receive reassurance.

4.1.25. Communication - The *number one complaint against lawyers* in this country is not poor work quality. It is failing to communicate with their clients. You are paying a lot of money to hire a lawyer and it is your right to expect to be kept informed of developments and have your calls and e-mails returned in a timely manner.

Please note that this does NOT mean that the client and attorney's firm communicate daily. Busy trial attorneys cannot do that. Anxiety attacks that you suffer or excessive inquiries on your part can cause your attorney to terminate your relationship. A psychiatrist or psychologist is better suited to deal with such problems.

Calling your lawyer every day to inquire what is happening on your case is not "communication." It is a sign of extreme anxiety that may dictate a mental health evaluation and treatment for the stress that these difficult cases may cause.

With these parameters in mind, be cognizant of HOW the staff and the paralegals at prospective firms handle your calls and any personal visits. Are they polite and patient? Do they know what they are doing? Can they answer simple questions about where you can get information about DUI-DWI laws and penalties? All firms are **not** created equal, so pay attention to how are you treated. In the end, the question to consider should be, "Is this the attorney and staff I want spearheading my defense?"

4.2. What do I do if I just cannot afford the TOP DUI-DWI lawyer in my area? Many people will not be able to afford the top DUI-DWI lawyer in their area due to cost. Many lawyers who are excellent at fighting these difficult cases are *partners or associates* in the firm headed up by the top attorney in your market, and they usually charge less than the "senior partner."

Many of the attorneys in these firms have track records that are similar to the law firm's top DUI-DWI lawyer's record, because these attorneys have obtained advanced training, and share information about trial strategy with the senior partner. They stay up-to-date on the latest trial tactics. They will also know defenses to breath tests and field evaluations, the best expert witnesses, as well as judges' tendencies, prosecutors' weaknesses and police officers' lack of training or other problems. If the top attorney in your market is priced out of your financial reach, consider his or her partners, associates, or affiliated attorneys.

If you are considering using a public defender, keep in mind that you may need to be screened by the court administrator or similar organization handling indigent cases, if your financial resources are low. You may also be screened extensively by your judge or his/her staff to determine whether you truly are unable to pay a fee. Unfortunately, this evaluation by the judge may not take place for months after your arrest, thereby squandering critical time for mounting your defense while evidence is still fresh. Be aware that some courts may charge a nominal application fee to investigate your ability to pay legal fees, and that this cost may not be refundable.

While some public defenders are fantastic advocates for their clients, others are assigned far too many cases and often are given no budget to retain expert witnesses. For these attorneys, the revolving door of justice usually swings toward a jail cell.[260]

In an attempt to save you some money, or to appear cheaper, many lawyers may offer to "unbundle" their legal services and may offer "a la carte" legal work. In DUI-DWI practice, the first fee set may be for handling the ALS (ALR) administrative license suspension-revocation hearing. This is NOT a criminal matter, but is a related "civil" proceeding that determines whether you can continue to drive, operate on a restricted driver's license, or not drive at all. Such "line item" legal work or piecework really means that instead of the attorney handling a case from beginning to end, some attorneys will work on specific aspects of the case or simply provide the client with the lawyer's expertise or oversight. Depending on local practice in your area, this may be a reasonably safe plan or could be disastrous, causing you to end up with no legal representation when you need it the most.

The opposite of this practice of "unbundling" is the **super lawyer** who limits the number of cases he/she takes. In doing so, these attorneys may offer a flat, non-negotiable fee. If a client hires a TOP DUI-DWI attorney on this basis, relying upon a stellar "track record" at either winning DUI-DWI cases or getting charges reduced, the fee is a "results-driven" transaction where the attorney is committing to dedicating one of his or her time "slots" and his/her expertise in exchange for the agreed fee --- paid in full. If you hire such a specialist, either be completely comfortable expending the fee quoted to retain this super lawyer to obtain his or her best efforts, or look for a less expensive alternative.

4.3. Don't expect your attorney to be a magician. Your lawyer can only be your best possible advocate, not a miracle worker. If you decided to drink any alcohol and then drive, you may be held accountable for this in the form of a conviction. He or she cannot lie for you, perform some slight of hand and make the charges against you go away, or make you any guarantees as to the outcome of your case.

However, one of the reasons to obtain the best possible legal representation you can afford is that with greater experience and a known reputation for success, your lawyer may be able to help you through the legal process as smoothly as possible. After a full assessment of all evidence, this veteran trial lawyer may be able to utilize his or her experience to accurately predict what you can likely expect at any stage of the legal process. However, unless a negotiated plea is obtained for you by your legal counsel, your lawyer is not the one who makes the ultimate decision as to the result of your case. The jury and/or the judge decide this, depending on whether it is a jury trial or a non-jury (bench) trial.

4.4. Don't ask your attorney to be a crook. A lawyer has two dominant and almost absolute duties. He or she must zealously represent you as your advocate before the court and the rest of the world. However, your lawyer cannot lie or misrepresent the facts or the law to the court, even if doing so would be in your best interest. If your lawyer does lie to the court or misrepresent anything to the court, he or she could face disbarment and possibly face criminal charges.[261]

---

[260]See this article: http://www.duiblog.com/2005/08/30#a236.

[261]Where an attorney knowingly misrepresented a client's prior DUI-DWI history to a court, the lawyer was charged with and pleaded guilty to a felony [attempting to influence a public servant] and a misdemeanor offense [perjury in the second degree], and lost his right to practice law for the deception. **In the Matter of J.E.C.,** 50 P.3d 897 (Colo. 2002).

4.5. Treat your attorney's staff like they are your family members. For approximately six to eighteen months following your arrest, your attorney's staff will be like a part of your family. With little doubt, being arrested for DUI-DWI is one of the worst things that ever happened to you. It will seem like very few people are on your side, while the prosecution and the police seem to have endless resources. The best and most important asset you have on your side is your attorney and the people who work for and with your attorney to help him or her in this fight.

Although you may never see these activities, an experienced DUI-DWI attorney will have law clerks, paralegals, legal secretaries, other lawyers and investigators all coming together as a team to help you in your legal fight. Every part of this team is important. Those you do meet are there to help you. Some may work on your case and never meet you face-to-face.

This "closeness" or "family connection" does not mean you can abuse them. Remember, people work harder for people they like and respect. The best teams work like a family — with trust and caring tempered with being able to tell the other person honestly that certain conduct or behavior is not acceptable. Treat the other people working in your lawyer's office like you would want to be treated. An experienced trial attorney knows his or her staff's dedication and the attorney will support them in any disputes that arise from your boorish or offensive behavior. Don't lose your attorney by acting improperly toward his or her staff, because all TOP attorneys are dependent upon their TOP-NOTCH staff members.

4.6. Providing input to your attorney, but not being a pest. Your attorney, or some of the people who work for him or her, are going to ask you a lot of questions. They might ask you to help them contact witnesses, or go to the scene with an investigator. In the search for information, facts and identities of people who might be able to help you in your defense, there must be information flowing both from you and to you. Everyone recognizes that this bi-directional flow is very important.

Being arrested for a DUI-DWI is also scary, degrading and insulting. It is a painful time for you that may seem to never end. You will want the process to be completed so that you can move on with your life. You desire exoneration or at least that the DUI-DWI charge be dropped or reduced. Yet, you know that until a trial occurs, you can never be found guilty of DUI-DWI. This is the "dilemma" that both you and your attorney face.

However, little can be done to speed the process along by your involvement in the case. Your attorney is not in charge of 95% of the court scheduling process. The State, meaning the police and the prosecution, are much more in control of timing.

Your attorney is going to push to get you through the process as soon as possible, but must temper this with a knowledge that court proceedings must also be done at the time that is best for you. Therefore, although you may want a trial the day after your arrest, your defense is not going to be ready until your lawyer can gather all the pieces of information he or she needs to give you the best chance for obtaining a good outcome. The prosecution may be ready the day after your arrest to put you in jail, but your lawyer is going to need months of preparation and using tactical maneuvers to keep you out of jail, if possible.

All of this said, a quality lawyer keeps you involved when anything **changes**. You will get copies of all of the paperwork (filings, motions, judicial rulings or decisions) that passes between your lawyer and the court or the prosecution. Some attorneys may have someone on their staff call you once a week or so, even if nothing changes.

However, calling your lawyer on a regular (daily) basis just because you haven't heard anything for a few days only wastes your time, and your lawyer's time. Stop to think about the time it takes to answer your "anxiety" call, and ask yourself whether it is worth interrupting the attorney's staff from the important work that needs to be done on your case and cases of other clients being handled by your attorney. Even though some clients can abuse the use of email to try to micromanage their pending case, this is a less disruptive and more time efficient way to communicate.

If you are concerned that things are not being done in a way in which you think they should, call the lawyer's office and schedule an appointment with someone to talk things over. Make sure that the appointment has a purpose and is essential. After all, if your attorney is spending the time with you talking, he or she is not being able to work on your case with the court, with the prosecutor, or work with other clients to help them with their truly pressing legal problem.

If you absolutely have to have a "tickler" system in place to keep track of what is happening with your case, ask your lawyer or their paralegal when you might expect to hear about a change in status or something happening regarding your case. Only if you get beyond this date without hearing anything should you call and ask. The key is to be an active part of your defense, not a pest that hinders it.

4.7. After selecting an advocate, follow your attorney's advice. If you "second-guess" every step your attorney takes, you either have an incompetent attorney or you are obsessed with "control" issues. Either way, this tension will usually result in your attorney withdrawing as your legal counsel.

You should listen to your attorney's advice. For example, if you were involved in an accident with injuries to another person, your attorney will be mindful of the fact that any sworn testimony by you at sentencing or at pre-trial hearings will almost certainly be used against you at later court proceedings in a civil lawsuit for any injured party's claims for loss of earnings, pain and suffering, etc. Therefore, your attorney may advise you to remain silent at your sentencing based upon a recent U.S. Supreme Court ruling.[262] Other states have followed this precedent-setting case.[263] Such a strategy in accident cases may allow you to possibly save hundreds of thousands or millions of dollars in civil damages that may arise from a collision associated with your DUI-DWI arrest.

4.8. Maintain a file with all your papers from legal counsel. Right from the start of your arrest, you will have a large amount of paperwork coming your way. Expect to receive copies of forms used by the police, information from the jail, from your bondsman, and from court hearings in your case. You will also hear from your lawyer and his or her support staff. While your lawyer may want the originals or copies of some of the forms, it is critical to your defense that you keep at least a copy of everything, especially the court documents your lawyer sends you. That way, if your lawyer calls you and asks you a question about a specific document, you will be able to quickly give an answer.

4.8.1. Expect copies of all motions and filings. This is your case. The criminal charges are against you as the defendant. Your lawyer is your representative, your advocate, your voice, but is not charged with the crime. Your lawyer must send you a copy of all of the paperwork and documents either sent by the court or the prosecutor. If your lawyer

---

[262]**Mitchell v. United States,** 526 U.S. 314, 119 S. Ct. 1370, 143 L.Ed.2d 424 (1999), overturning a Third Circuit case in which Ms. Mitchell's refusal to be questioned by the judge resulted in harsher punishment.
[263]**Fuller v. State,** 244 Ga. App. 618, 536 S.E.2d 296 (2000).

asks you a question about a document or a videotape, be prepared to give him or her honest and straightforward answers. Spend the time to look at the evidence and be an active participant in your legal proceedings.

4.8.2. Expect any and all offers for a plea to be communicated to you. You have been charged by the state with a crime. Thus, it is **you** who must be told about all offers from the prosecutor to enter a guilty (or nolo contendere) plea to any of the charges in exchange for a reduced charge or a dismissal of some or all pending charges by the state. A lawyer who does not keep you adequately informed of such offers is subject to being disciplined by the state Bar. This failure to communicate a plea offer also might be the basis for you to win an appeal if you eventually lose your case.[264] Such misconduct might be the reason you could win a malpractice claim against your lawyer.

If you learn about an offer that was made but not communicated to you, this signifies a breakdown in communication. This is a serious matter to address with your attorney, or with a different attorney who handles claims against attorneys for malpractice.

4.9. Let your attorney decide which witnesses to interview. You have hired the best lawyer for your defense based on all the factors listed above. You have hired this highly trained professional who has years of experience with not only DUI-DWI charges, but who has also worked in the court where your case will be heard, and likely is very familiar with those who will be prosecuting your case. Let your attorney build a trial plan with whatever fact witnesses and expert witnesses he or she needs to mount a successful trial strategy. This is his or her arena, not yours. Even if following all of your attorney's advice involves a "leap of faith," you must not act to hinder his or her trial strategy.

Based on all of your attorney's expertise and the above factors, your lawyer will know which witnesses are the best witnesses to interview to give you the best possible defense. You may really want your Aunt Mabel to stand up and say how good a person you have been since birth, but this is not relevant for the question that is before the court. Once you have made the overall and critical decision as to who is going to be the best lawyer for you, let this person do his or her job. Second-guessing your legal representation only costs you more stress and wastes everyone's time. Your "doubts" about your attorney's strategy may actually be visible on your face, like a deer caught in the headlights.

4.10. Follow your attorney's advice on securing help from the best available expert witness(es) for your trial or motions. The reason you chose your attorney was based on all of the factors listed in the foregoing subsections. You have arranged to get the best possible person for you to be your champion at court. Why question his or her choice as to experts needed for trial? If your lawyer tells you he or she thinks that Expert X rather than Expert Y is best for your case, he or she is suggesting this based on years of expertise with DUI-DWI trials. Often, one particular expert has unparalleled knowledge and experience on the medical or scientific issue that is the lynchpin of your defense. Go with your attorney's choice and **HIRE THE BEST EXPERT AVAILABLE.**

---

[264]**Strickland v. Washington,** 466 U.S. 668, 104 S.Ct. 2052, 80 L.Ed.2d 674 (1984); **Muff v. State,** 210 Ga. App. 309, 436 S.E.2d 47 (1993); **Lloyd v. State,** 258 Ga. 645, 373 S.E.2d 1 (1998); **Avans v. State,** 251 Ga. App. 575, 554 S.E.2d 766 (2001); **Ex parte Wilson,** 724 S.W.2d 72 (Tex.Crim.App. 1987); **State v. Ludwig,** 124 Wis.2d 600, 369 N.W.2d 722 (1985); **In re Alvernaz,** 2 Cal.4th 924, 830 P.2d 747 (1992); **Lyles v. State,** 178 Ind.App. 398, 382 N.E.2d 991 (1978); **State v. Simmons,** 65 N.C.App. 294, 309 S.E.2d 493 (1983); **State v. Cameron,** 30 Wash.App. 229, 633 P.2d 901 (1981); **Cottle v. State,** 733 So.2d 963 (Fla. 1999); **Mott v. State,** 407 N.W.2d 581 (Iowa 1987); **Bates v. State,** 879 So.2d 519 (Miss.App. 2004); **Harris v. State,** 875 S.W.2d 662 (Tenn. 1994).

4.11. Assist your attorney in locating & staying in touch with fact witnesses and helping procure medical or other records. Your lawyer is going to ask you to assist in coordinating your defense because you are the best person to handle certain matters. You should obtain FULL contact information for any of your fact witnesses, including all phone numbers, e-mail addresses and the name and number of a close family member in case you lose touch with the witness. Due to very strict federal laws,[265] the process by which your medical records may be procured requires written consent. Hence, you may be asked to go to your doctor's office (or even to the hospital) to procure your full medical records that relate to an issue in your DUI-DWI case.

---

[265]http://www.hipaa.org.

Chapter 5

What Should You Be Doing to

Prepare Your Legal Defense After Your Arrest?

5.0. Purpose of this chapter. If you are facing a serious charge such as a DUI-DWI, the worst thing you can do is to get into additional legal troubles. This situation creates a nearly impossible "climate" for your skilled attorney to negotiate a reduced plea to your original DUI-DWI charge. Additionally, in some jurisdictions, the prosecutor can **COMBINE** both cases and let one jury hear both at one time if the charges at all relate to one another.[266] This is a losing proposition almost 100% of the time.

The rules pertaining to your administrative license suspension or revocation that occurs as soon as you are arrested for DUI-DWI vary greatly from state to state. Your right to drive in your state on such an administrative suspension/revocation will need to be discussed with your DUI-DWI attorney. See Chapter 11 for further information on this topic.

5.1. What happens if you get caught driving on a suspended license? Simply stated, driving on a suspended license is a new, additional crime.[267] In most jurisdictions, these added offenses will carry a mandatory jail sentence, especially if you are a repeat offender or have serious charges pending when you drive while suspended. These sentences can be very punitive. In one Texas case, the repeat drunken driver who kept driving while suspended received a 99-year jail sentence!

You might have an excuse for driving while your license is suspended if your driving was in light of a true emergency (i.e., to save someone's life), but it is the court that determines if your reason for driving really was a situation that rose to the level of a legal "necessity." Just having to get to work is not an emergency, nor is having to transport your children to school or to soccer practice. It takes little imagination to predict the consequences of such a situation.

Driving on a suspended license might also worsen your pending DUI-DWI case, particularly if the judge in that case is the same judge on the suspended license case. Such "repeat" offenses send the judge a message that you are not remorseful for your DUI-DWI because you violated an additional state law even before the first case was resolved.

5.2. Is getting a "limited permit" the solution to your problems? Depending upon your state's laws relating to a limited driving permit or restricted driver's license, the availability of such a restricted right to drive is almost always a matter controlled by statute, not

---

[266]**Noble v. State,** 275 Ga. 635, 570 S.E.2d 296 (2002); **State v. Lott,** 51 Ohio St.3d 160, 555 N.E.2d 293 (1990); **State v. Brunn,** 145 Wash. 435, 260 P. 990 (1927); **People v. Kemp,** 55 Cal.2d 458, 359 P.2d 913 (1961); **People v. Scott,** 24 Cal.2d 774, 151 P.2d 517 (1944); **Johnson v. State,** 29 Ala. 62 (1856); **State v. Hoffman,** 106 Wis.2d 185, 316 N.W.2d 143 (Wis.App. 1982); **Cash v. State,** 29 Tenn. 111, 10 Hum. 111 (1849); **Commonwealth v. Costello,** 120 Mass. 358 (1876); **Channell v. State,** 107 So.2d 284 (Fla.App. 2 Dist. 1958); Miss. Code Ann. § 99-7-2; **Irving v. State,** 8 Tex.App. 46, 1880 WL 8964 (1880).
[267]Washington - West's RCWA 46.20.005; Florida - West's F.S.A. § 322.34; Georgia - O.C.G.A. § 40-5-20; Texas - V.T.C.A., Transportation Code § 521.457; Tennessee - T. C. A. § 55-50-504; Idaho - I.C. § 18-8001; ; Indiana - IC 9-24-19-1; Missouri - V.A.M.S. 302.727; Minnesota - M.S.A. § 171.24; Alabama - Ala.Code 1975 § 32-6-19; Arizona - A.R.S. § 28-3316; California - West's Ann.Cal.Vehicle Code § 14601.1; Mississippi - Miss. Code Ann. § 63-1-57.

a judge's discretion. So, if a restricted permit to drive is available and you comply with the conditions to get such a permit, a restricted license should be available to you, at least for a first offense in an impaired driving case.

Limited driving permits are a creation of state statute and are not a "right" under any state or federal constitution. This means that the availability of such a permit is controlled by state law. Your DUI-DWI defense specialist will be able to guide you through the steps needed to obtain such a "work permit" or limited occupational license.

In most states, if your arrest for DUI-DWI is a first-time violation, there are circumstances under which you may have a limited or restricted driver's license available to you. Typically, if you meet your state's criteria, the limited license will identify what types of driving activity are permitted, and for what limited purposes.[268] Many states will allow a permit to first offenders who submit to testing, but will deny any limited permit to a person who refused to be tested for alcohol or drugs.[269]

Certainly, one of the most pressing questions you have is to determine if you can drive to and from work. Many people also travel out of state and need to rent cars when they get to remote destinations. Depending on your state's guidelines, you may be required to wait 10, 30 or 90 days to get a limited or restricted license after a DUI-DWI arrest or possibly after the criminal conviction. In some jurisdictions, certain drivers may be required to install an ignition interlock device prior to receiving their restricted license or work permit that allows restricted driving privileges (or must prove that they have contracted to install such a device).[270]

A restricted license or "work" permit severely restricts your ability to drive, determining where and when you can operate a vehicle.[271] Thus, a "work" permit may help you with some of the transportation problems you face following your DUI-DWI arrest, but is seldom the solution to all of your problems. For example, most rental car companies will not allow you to rent their vehicles without a full driver's license.

5.3. When can you get your license reinstated In most states, if your arrest for DUI-DWI is a first offense, there are circumstances under which you may have a limited or restricted driver's license issued to you. Typically, if you meet your state's criteria, the limited license will identify what types of driving activity are permitted, and for what limited purposes.

If your DUI-DWI arrest is your first offense, you may be able to get your full driver's license back after a few days (or possibly a few months) of administrative suspension if you

---

[268]Georgia - O.C.G.A. §40-5-64; Tennessee - T. C. A. § 55-10-403; Alabama - Ala.Code 1975 § 32-5A-304; Alaska - AS 28.15.201; Arkansas - A.C.A. § 5-65-104; Colorado - C.R.S.A. § 42-2-132.5; Florida - West's F.S.A. § 322.271; California - West's Ann.Cal.Vehicle Code § 13352; Washington - West's RCWA 46.20.391; Texas - V.T.C.A., Transportation Code § 521.221; Indiana - IC 9-24-15-2.

[269]New York - McKinney's Vehicle and Traffic Law § 530.

[270]Arizona - A.R.S. § 28-1461; Florida - West's F.S.A. § 316.1937; Georgia - O.C.G.A. §§ 42-8-111, 112; Illinois - 625 ILCS 5/6-205; Indiana - IC 9-30-5-7; Iowa - I.C.A. § 321J.4B; Kentucky - KRS § 189A.090; Louisiana - LSA-R.S. 32:378.2; Mississippi - Miss. Code Ann. § 63-11-31; New Hampshire - N.H. Rev. Stat. § 265:93-a; New Mexico - N. M. S. A. 1978, § 66-8-102; Oklahoma - 47 Okl.St.Ann. § 11-902; Oregon - O.R.S. § 813.600; Tennessee - T. C. A. § 55-10-412; Texas - Vernon's Ann.Texas C.C.P. Art. 17.441; Washington - West's RCWA 46.20.720.

[271]Georgia - O.C.G.A. §40-5-64; Tennessee - T. C. A. §§ 55-10-403 and 406; Alabama - Ala.Code 1975 § 32-5A-304; Alaska - AS 28.15.201; Arkansas - A.C.A. § 5-65-104; Colorado - C.R.S.A. § 42-2-132.5; Florida - West's F.S.A. § 322.271; California - West's Ann.Cal.Vehicle Code § 13352; Washington - West's RCWA 46.20.391; Texas - V.T.C.A., Transportation Code § 521.221; Indiana - IC 9-24-15-2.

complete a state-mandated course such as driving school or a drug and alcohol evaluation.[272] In some jurisdictions, both prerequisites must be met. This "right" to regain your FULL license is sometimes called an "early reinstatement."

The two preceding sections pertain to state action that takes your license AFTER losing your administrative license suspension (or revocation) hearing. You should ask your DUI-DWI specialist attorney handling your case regarding your state's rules on license reinstatement and limited permits to drive following an administrative "taking" of your license.

5.4. Can you just obtain a license in another state? The very short answer is no. Once your license is physically taken from you as a part of the DUI-DWI arrest process, an administrative license suspension (or revocation) action is started against your license. If any other state licensing office contacts your state, a "block" will be in place informing the other state that you have a pending license suspension or revocation proceeding that is unresolved.

Recent improvements to the National Driver's Registry have led to much better "tracking" of problem drivers. Today, any attempt to procure a license in any other state will likely be detected and acted upon by the state agency from which you are seeking the new license. If you offer the new state your plastic license to be surrendered for the new state's license, the agency representative in the new state where you are applying can confiscate the license if your existing state licensing agency notifies the new state that your license is suspended. For more detailed information on these new national rules and penalties for fraudulent procurement of a driver's license, read about current guidelines online.[273]

As a prerequisite for getting a driver's license in most states, you must not have your current license suspended or revoked in any other state.[274] Lying on an application form is always an additional crime.[275] Since the state's form is a type of affidavit, falsifying such reports can trigger additional license loss or serious criminal penalties. You can also lose your driver's license in your state for alcohol or drug offenses that you commit in another state.[276]

5.5. Can you drive on an "international" license here in the USA? If you are from another country and have a legitimate foreign license with an "international" license, you should be able to drive anywhere in the United States. If you get suspended or revoked here, that may change.

An international license is NOT a standard or a "standalone" license. It is merely a translation of your license from one language to the language of the nation where you will be visiting. You can drive in the United States with this license if you don't have a suspended state license from any jurisdiction in the United States.[277] Most states will not allow you to drive on

---

[272]Georgia - 30 - 180 days - O.C.G.A. §§40-5-84, 40-5-67.2; Florida - West's F.S.A. § 322.282; F.S.A. § 322.225; Texas - 180 days - V.T.C.A., Transportation Code § 521.377; Washington - West's RCWA 46.20.311; California - West's Ann.Cal.Vehicle Code § 13352; Tennessee - T. C. A. § 55-10-403; Mississippi - Miss. Code Ann. §§ 63-11-30, 63-11-31; Arkansas - A.C.A. § 5-65-104.

[273]http://www.lawschool.lexis.com/presscenter/hottopics/ECIReportFINAL.pdf.

[274]Alaska - AS 28.15.031; Arizona - A.R.S. § 28-3153; California - West's Ann.Cal.Vehicle Code § 12800; Florida - West's F.S.A. § 322.05; Indiana - IC 9-24-9-2; Mississippi - Miss. Code Ann. § 63-1-9; Tennessee - T. C. A. § 55-50-303; Texas - V.T.C.A., Transportation Code § 521.201; Georgia - O.C.G.A. § 40-5-65; Alabama - Ala.Code 1975 § 32-6-7; Washington - West's RCWA 46.20.091; Indiana - IC 9-24-2-3.

[275]Washington - West's RCWA 46.20.091; Indiana - IC 9-24-9-5.

[276]Alaska - AS 28.15.291; Georgia - O.C.G.A. § 40-5-52; Tennessee - T. C. A. § 55-50-504; Texas - V.T.C.A., Transportation Code § 521.306; Alabama - Ala.Code 1975 § 32-5A-195; Washington - West's RCWA 46.20.342; California - West's Ann.Cal.Vehicle Code § 13353.3.

[277]Alabama - Ala.Code 1975 § 32-6-10.

their roads if your license is suspended or revoked in any other state. Having an international license does not overcome this restriction.[278] Many international driver license sales pitches in bulk e-mail or on Internet sites are scams that seek to take desperate people's money. See this link for more information.[279]

5.6. Once you are permitted to drive again, will things be back to normal? The answer to this question depends on what you mean by "normal." In most states, if you are convicted of DUI-DWI in the criminal case, your license will be suspended for a first offense, or you can be forced to drive on a restricted license, for up to a year.[280] This may mean not being able to drive at all for some part of a full year in some states (e.g. Pennsylvania). In the alternative, a conviction can result in your license being restricted as to when and where you can drive. After the statutory suspension or revocation period is over, you can take the necessary steps set forth by your state's law to get your FULL license returned to you. Then, no restrictions on location and time of day for your driving remain.

Although getting reinstated after a first offense is relatively painless in most states, the opposite is typically true for second (or subsequent) offenses. All states have guidelines for determining what a "second" offense is, in terms of a mandatory suspension or revocation. However, most states have a five to ten year "look back" for prior offenses, for determining when you will be put through the ringer in trying to regain your full driving privileges.[281] Some states now have a lifetime "lookback" or review of your entire driving history.

5.7. Alcohol and drug assessment (and possible treatment) prior to going to trial. Once arrested for a DUI-DWI offense, most police officers assume that you may have an alcohol or drug problem. The same may be true for your employer, or even family or friends. Right or wrong, just being arrested says to the whole world that you *may* have a problem. Programs to screen you for problems are widely available, and most can be researched on-line.[282]

Your attorney may suggest that you undergo an alcohol and drug assessment, and possible treatment if such action is indicated. The first reason for this suggestion is if you do have an alcohol or drug problem, the sooner you face the problem, the sooner you are on the road to beating the problem. An arrest for a DUI-DWI can be a sign of a drug or alcohol problem. If a problem does exist, promptly addressing the issue is the best answer to not only

---

[278]Georgia - O.C.G.A. § 40-5-65; **Com. v. Allison,** 56 Mass.App.Ct. 1106, 778 N.E.2d 30 (2002); Mississippi - for 60 days - Miss. Code Ann. § 63-1-7.

[279]http://www.ag.state.mn.us/consumer/ylr/ylr_05_June.htm.

[280]Alabama - 90 days - Ala.Code 1975 § 32-5A-191(e); Arizona - no automatic suspension - A.R.S. § 28-1381(I); Arkansas - 120 - 180 days - A.C.A. § 5-65-104; Florida - no mandatory suspension - West's F.S.A. §§ 316.193, 316.655; Georgia - 1 year - § 40-5-67.2(a)(1) ; California - 6 months - West's Ann.Cal.Vehicle Code § 13352(a)(1); Indiana - 6 months - IC 9-30-4-6; Tennessee - T. C. A. § 55-10-406; Mississippi - 90 days - Miss. Code Ann. § 63-11-30(2)(a) ; Texas - 90 days to one year - V.T.C.A., Transportation Code § 521.344(a)(2); Washington - 90 days - West's RCWA 46.61.5055.

[281]5 years - Georgia O.C.G.A. §40-5-391(c)(2); Texas - V.T.C.A., Penal Code § 49.09(h); Florida - West's F.S.A. § 316.193(6)(b); Indiana - IC 9-30-5-3; Alabama - Ala.Code 1975 § 32-5A-191(f); Mississippi - Miss. Code Ann. § 63-11-30; 10 years - Tennessee - T. C. A. § 55-10-403(a)(3); California - West's Ann.Cal.Vehicle Code § 23560; South Carolina - Code 1976 § 56-5-2940; 7 years - Washington - West's RCWA 46.61.5055.

[282]http://www.drugandalcoholrehab.net/; http://www.caron.org/content.asp?section=seeking&cat=assess1&sub=seeking; http://www2.state.tn.us/health/A&D/assessment.htm.

the "problem," but is also the solution for not getting into more trouble while your case is pending.

Second, even if you do not have a drug or alcohol problem, the sooner you seek a private, independent assessment, the more likely this prompt action will impress your trial judge, in the event of a conviction or if your DUI-DWI attorney can arrange a favorable negotiated plea in your case. If you are appearing before the judge and have only started treatment two weeks prior to your final court appearance, this "last minute" effort to mitigate your punishment will not carry much weight. Address treatment issues early and show that you have investigated private treatment and aggressively addressed any problem that may be revealed by the assessment.

Furthermore, the results of your voluntary submission to treatment may also be used by your attorney in his or her discussions with the prosecutor. If this evaluation shows you have no drug or alcohol problems, this might give some credence to yet another reason why the charges against you might be lessened. In the alternative, if the counselor suggests some educational sessions that you complete, this can be a negotiating "chit" for your attorney to use to try to get a favorable negotiated plea or a non-DUI-DWI resolution in your case.

Your state may have a mandatory provision that all DUI-DWI convictions require evaluation for alcohol and drug dependency.[283] Your DUI-DWI specialist will know whether such evaluation and treatment is necessary in your case. If you have already completed this condition, the court will see that you have dealt with this possible problem in an assertive fashion and without being court-ordered to do it. Be sure that the counselor you choose is one of the state-approved providers of alcohol and drug rehabilitation, since your court or state law may only recognize state-approved counselors. Also make certain that your pre-trial (or pre-plea) attendance at an approved treatment program will be given full credit by your judge.

All in all, except for the expense of undergoing such an evaluation, and the little bit of time such an evaluation takes, you have little to lose by undergoing this assessment. If you do have a problem, then you can start therapy. If you don't have a problem, then you will receive a written confirmation from an independent expert that ongoing counseling is unnecessary.

5.8. Should you go to "DUI-DWI school" prior to trial? Finding a DUI-DWI school involves knowing which programs are approved in your state. Your attorney will know the approved schools in your area. Almost universally, successful completion of such a school is required for those who have been either convicted of, or who have pleaded guilty to, a DUI-DWI offense.[284] Completion of this school is typically a requirement to be able to regain your full driver's license. In many jurisdictions, even where a reduced plea to another offense other than DUI-DWI is obtained, attendance of this educational class may be mandated.

A special situation may exist for persons who live in a different state from the state where the DUI-DWI arrest took place. In such situations, you may be able to attend DUI-DWI school in your home state, complete only ONE course and be able to fully restore your driving

---

[283]Alabama - Ala.Code 1975 § 32-5A-191; Florida - West's F.S.A. § 322.291; Illinois - 625 ILCS 5/11-501; Louisiana - for second offense - LSA-R.S. 14:98; Oklahoma - 47 Okl.St.Ann. § 11-902(C); Wisconsin - W.S.A. 343.30; Georgia - for second offense - O.C.G.A. § 40-5-63.1; California - for second offense - West's Ann.Cal.Vehicle Code § 23646; Indiana - IC 9-30-5-15; Mississippi - Miss. Code Ann. §§ 63-11-30(2)(a), 63-11-32; Tennessee - for second offense - T. C. A. § 55-10-403(a)(1)(A); Texas - Vernon's Ann.Texas C.C.P. Art. 42.12; Washington - West's RCWA 46.61.5056, 46.61.5056.

[284]Louisiana - second offense - LSA-R.S. 14:98; Mississippi - Miss. Code Ann. §§ 63-11-30(2)(a), 63-11-32; Kentucky - KRS § 186.574; Tennessee - T. C. A. § 55-10-403.

privileges in both states. Ask your DUI-DWI specialist for advice on this before signing up for any course in a state different from the state where your arrest is pending.

However, if you attend this school at the recommendation of your attorney before either your trial or your plea of guilty, you may gain several significant benefits. First, if there has been an administrative suspension of your license, completion of this school may allow you to obtain reinstatement of your full driver's license again. If you have completed the course to secure the return of your license after an ALS/ALR license action against you, this DUI-DWI course is not usually required to be repeated after the criminal case has been completed, even if you ultimately plead guilty to DUI-DWI or are found guilty at trial.

Second, your attendance at this school may give your attorney some leverage with the prosecution in obtaining a reduced charge against you. Your attendance shows the prosecution your acceptance of a possible alcohol problem, and your willingness to accept responsibility for your actions. After all, one of the stated purposes of the course is to provide education that will assist you in not getting into similar trouble. Incidentally, your voluntary pre-trial attendance of a private counseling program is not a matter that must be disclosed by your attorney unless and until this issue relates to a negotiated plea in the case.

Finally, if you are found guilty of the DUI-DWI offense, attendance of the DUI-DWI school typically will be part of your sentence. If you have already successfully completed the school, this is one less thing you have to do when the case is resolved in court. Successful completion of the school can sometimes be used by your attorney to negotiate a lesser sentence on your behalf. Your attorney can submit to the prosecutor that you have taken this legal matter seriously, and have taken steps to address any "dependency" or safety issues.

Be aware that some states allow "advance" completion of the DUI-DWI school (e.g. Georgia) while others do not (e.g. South Carolina). You may have to wait until your case is over to start the driving school. Furthermore, a "DUI school" in one state may not be accepted by the state where your DUI-DWI charge is pending, so always confirm the acceptability of the course you plan to take before enrolling. Check with your DUI-DWI specialist before signing up for any course prior to disposition of your case.

5.9. Cleaning up your driving history before your case reaches trial or final disposition. As a part of taking on your DUI-DWI case, your lawyer will want to know about any of your past violations of the law, including any traffic infractions. You must also fully disclose to your legal counsel any pending criminal actions or traffic matters against you. This includes any speeding, reckless driving or any other traffic offenses you may be facing that are unresolved.

The reason for "cleaning" up your record is two-fold. First, if you have any other legal matters hanging over your head, it is far less likely your attorney will be able to make any deals with the prosecution regarding your DUI-DWI offense. When the prosecutor sees multiple pending offenses, he or she will surmise that your have probably committed several other acts of a similar nature without detection. Remember that the prosecutor has full access to all of the government's computer databases and can easily discover such matters.

Second, if you are found guilty of your DUI-DWI offense, almost anything in your life can be used either for you or against you in your sentencing. By cleaning up your record, you show the judge you are taking charge of your legal problems, your life and any impaired driving tendencies. The judge may then be inclined to consider a less punitive sentence. If you have other unresolved charges pending against you, it may appear to your judge that you are not deserving of leniency. He or she may take the position that a lengthy sentence in jail will facilitate resolution of the other pending cases. For certain, the judge will know that you will not be driving while you are in jail!

Finally, your attorney may be able to work out a "package" deal on all open charges, especially if all are pending within the same jurisdiction. This is a difficult undertaking, but at least let your attorney try to wrap up all pending matters. Don't be surprised if the prosecutor refuses to offer substantial reductions in penalties, however.

5.10. Make certain you have funds available to cover all costs. Once you have been arrested for DUI-DWI, you face significant expenses throughout the litigation process. Few people have enough money deposited in their checking account to be able to pay all costs and expenses at once. Typically, fee payments and related expenses occur over the entire length of your case, which may take a year or longer.

First, you will likely have to pay to be freed from jail after your arrest by posting an appearance bond. Some people do this with a cash bond, while others pledge real estate as "security" to assure that you will return for court. Typically, the sheriff or a clerk's office official will approve any such bonds that rely on the equity position in real estate that you have pledged. In a few states (e.g. Texas) a criminal defense attorney may be able to act as your bondsman.

Commercial bail bonding companies are an alternative to putting up your own cash or real estate. These businesses are paid a fixed percentage of the total amount as a "fee" for acting as your "surety." These percentages typically run from 10% to 15% of the face amount of the bond. If you fail to show up for court, the bonding company may be required to pay the full amount into court and "forfeit" the amount of your bond. If the bonding company's "bounty hunter" can locate you, however, you will be physically arrested and brought back to face charges. By bringing you back, the bonding company avoids losing the bond forfeiture amount.

Second, you need to retain the best DUI-DWI specialist attorney you can afford. Much like choosing a medical specialist for the purpose of performing delicate surgery, choosing a DUI-DWI attorney should be made in much the same fashion. At stake is your freedom, your right to drive, possibly a job or marriage, all depending on the outcome of your case. See Chapter Four of this book for full information concerning hiring an attorney for your case.

Third, you may be required to miss significant time from work during the days you will spend directly involved with your legal process. By carefully planning ahead, most of this time away from work can be covered by paid vacation time. If not, you still need to take the necessary time off to be able to defend your case. Other discretionary spending must be postponed until the case is over.

Fourth, in a typical contested DUI-DWI case, expenses will likely be added to the legal fees owed. Depending on the contract you signed with your lawyer, you may be expected to pay for investigators, accident reconstructionists, couriers, process servers, field sobriety experts and/or forensic experts to point out flaws in the police officer's adherence to his or her training, to procedural issues relating to your arrest, or to testify about your breath or blood testing procedures. Most of the top DUI-DWI experts will charge an initial fee to review the paperwork and any video recordings in your case. They may charge additional fees and request reimbursement for costs related to attending pre-trial hearings or trial such as needed to present your legal case. Your expert witness will be called upon to give his or her professional opinion about scientific or forensic issues that are critical to your defense.

Fifth, other expenses you may be expected to bear may include the cost for you to attend a DUI-DWI school recommended to you by your attorney. Also, you may incur some expenses out of your pocket for doing community service work or for cleaning up your driving record. Private alcohol or drug evaluation or treatment will also be a cost for you. If you have prior convictions or legal issues in another state, you may have to employ the services of an attorney in that state to track down certified records or copies of court documents that will be needed by your present attorney.

Finally, if worse comes to worse and you are convicted of a DUI-DWI offense, a monetary fine may be assessed that you will have to pay, either directly to the court or through your probation officer. Fines in DUI-DWI cases typically carry additional court costs and other "statutory surcharges" or assessments associated with being on probation. In some states (e.g., Texas and New Jersey) these costs can run into thousands of dollars. Other states (e.g., South Carolina) have an "integrated" automobile insurance system wherein every traffic violation, including DUI-DWI, leads to automatic increases in your insurance rates.

Considering all these expenses you face, it is best to look seriously at all possible avenues you have for generating the money you will need to cover these fees and expenses. Few people can simply pay for all of this out of their pockets. Many people have to borrow funds against their assets, or liquidate some assets to have money available. Some people have to borrow money from friends or family, or ask a family member to use his or her credit card to cover legal fees. Some will have to put as much as they can on credit cards, and then pay the balance over an extended time period. It is best to start exploring all of these possibilities at the beginning of your legal process in order to be able to meet these costs as they occur.

5.11. Keep your schedule flexible for court proceedings — save all vacation days. One of the most difficult issues that you may face is recognizing how little of the scheduling of court matters is within the direct control of your attorney. One of the things out of your control (and your attorney's) is determining when you will need to be present in court for different legal proceedings. It is the judge, and his or her clerks and assistants who set the court's schedule. If anyone has input, it is the prosecutor, in most jurisdictions. An attorney who is well versed in DUI-DWI practice will know the various methods for getting cases rescheduled or postponed if any way exists. Plus, a well-respected trial attorney who enjoys a stellar reputation for being prepared for trial may be able to obtain a change of court dates with your assigned judge in certain instances, where good cause for an "adjournment" or a "continuance" exists.

The legal process involves several steps that require you to clear your schedule. Some of these times include appointments when you will meet with your lawyer, your investigator or possibly your expert witnesses. You will likely have to go to the scene of your arrest for several reasons. Usually, these matters can be scheduled at times that will fit your schedule and the schedule of the expert witnesses.

Other times, you must make your schedule "fit" the court's schedule. In some states, you will need to be present any time your case is in court. In other states, a power of attorney given to your lawyer allowing him or her to act on your behalf or a written "waiver" (of your right to be present in court) signed by you can free you from attending certain court matters.

Assuming that you bond out of jail, no preliminary hearing will usually be needed in your case. A preliminary hearing is a legal proceeding wherein a judge (typically a magistrate judge) will be asked to review the evidence that led to your arrest to determine if your case should be bound over for further prosecution, or whether the existing evidence is too flimsy to support criminal charges. These hearings are not full discovery proceedings and usually offer little chance for your attorney to fully examine all witnesses. However, it is unlikely that your DUI-

DWI case will merit a preliminary hearing, unless a felony is involved, or unless you are held in jail for an extended period of time following your arrest.

The next sections of this chapter focus on the typical steps that will be followed in a typical DUI-DWI prosecution. State practice varies, so the steps may be slightly different in your state. The flow charts shown on the next few pages outline these steps in two different states.

Georgia Criminal Justice System Overview for Misdemeanor Arrests

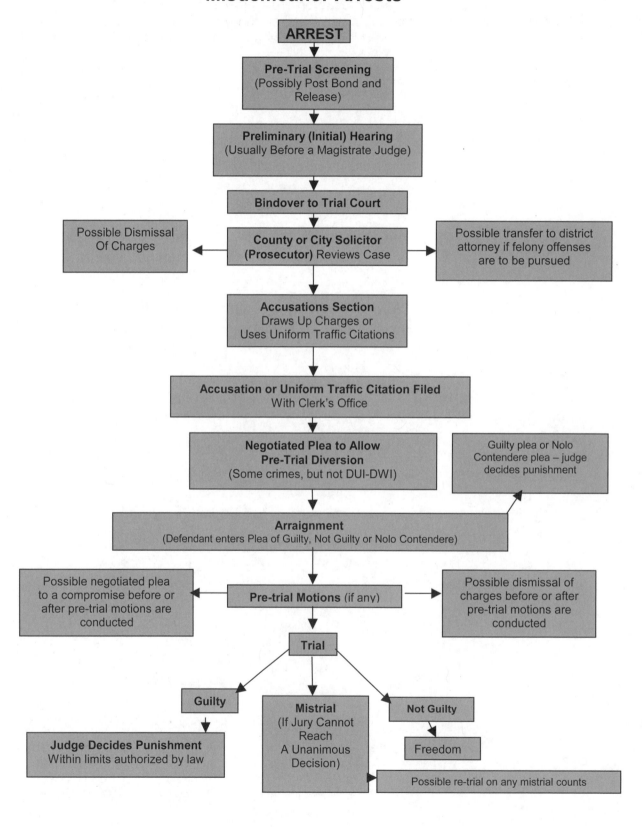

ARREST

Pre-Trial Screening
(Possibly Post Bond and Release)

Preliminary (Initial) Hearing
(Usually Before a Magistrate Judge)

Bindover to Trial Court

Possible Dismissal Of Charges ← **County or City Solicitor (Prosecutor)** Reviews Case → Possible transfer to district attorney if felony offenses are to be pursued

Accusations Section
Draws Up Charges or Uses Uniform Traffic Citations

Accusation or Uniform Traffic Citation Filed
With Clerk's Office

Negotiated Plea to Allow Pre-Trial Diversion
(Some crimes, but not DUI-DWI)

Guilty plea or Nolo Contendere plea – judge decides punishment

Arraignment
(Defendant enters Plea of Guilty, Not Guilty or Nolo Contendere)

Possible negotiated plea to a compromise before or after pre-trial motions are conducted ← **Pre-trial Motions** (if any) → Possible dismissal of charges before or after pre-trial motions are conducted

Trial

Guilty

Mistrial
(If Jury Cannot Reach A Unanimous Decision)

Not Guilty

Judge Decides Punishment
Within limits authorized by law

Freedom

Possible re-trial on any mistrial counts

Michigan Criminal Justice System Overview for Misdemeanor Arrests

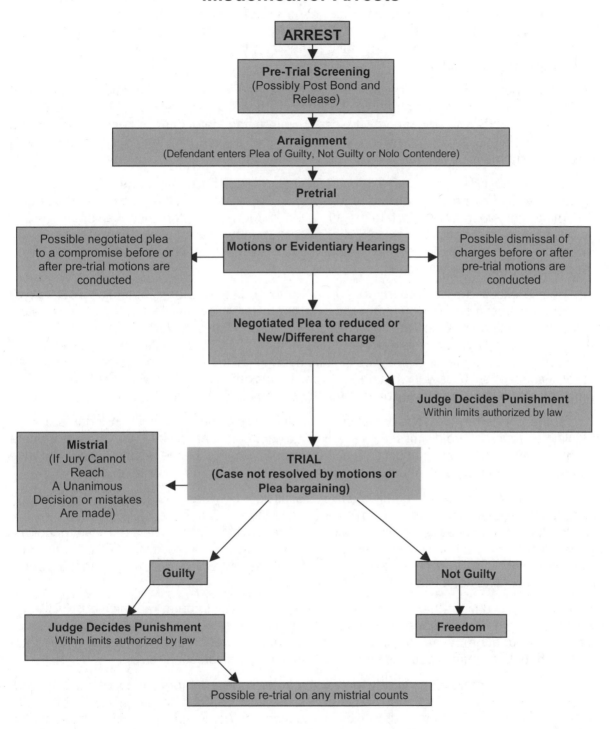

ARREST

Pre-Trial Screening
(Possibly Post Bond and Release)

Arraignment
(Defendant enters Plea of Guilty, Not Guilty or Nolo Contendere)

Pretrial

Possible negotiated plea to a compromise before or after pre-trial motions are conducted

Motions or Evidentiary Hearings

Possible dismissal of charges before or after pre-trial motions are conducted

Negotiated Plea to reduced or New/Different charge

Judge Decides Punishment
Within limits authorized by law

Mistrial
(If Jury Cannot Reach A Unanimous Decision or mistakes Are made)

TRIAL
(Case not resolved by motions or Plea bargaining)

Guilty

Not Guilty

Judge Decides Punishment
Within limits authorized by law

Freedom

Possible re-trial on any mistrial counts

Arraignment is commonly the first day that you will be expected to appear in court. Because many vital written "pleadings" may need to be prepared by your attorney and filed at, or prior to, your arraignment, do not wait until just prior to your arraignment to hire a lawyer. The arraignment is when the full, formal charges are read to you and your "response" to these charges entered. You can say "guilty," "not guilty," or offer to plead "no contest" (*nolo contendere*) to the charges, or you can stand mute and the judge will direct the clerk to enter a "not guilty" plea on your behalf.

While your particular arraignment will take less than ten minutes, you may need to be in court for the entire morning or afternoon because no one can assure when your case will be called. Many courts will give priority to cases where the defendant is represented by an attorney. Hopefully, you will be dealing with a court that allows pre-filing of all motions and a "waiver of arraignment." If so, this will excuse you from attending the arraignment.

You will most likely need to be in court for any pre-trial motion hearings. These hearings are also scheduled at the convenience of the judge. Some judges will not schedule these until the morning that your trial is set to begin, even though this often inconveniences jurors. Depending on what scheduling conflicts either your attorney or the prosecution may have, the date may be reset several times. The actual hearing can last as little as a few minutes or be heard over all or part of several days.

Unless excused by the court, you will need to be present at the hearing. Your lawyer may need your testimony or your "presence" in court, to review the testimony of the State's witnesses for accuracy. Also, your attorney may desire to have you testify at this hearing in order to try to win key evidentiary points in his or her quest to ultimately win your case. A typical favorable outcome at a pre-trial motion hearing might be the exclusion of some kep piece of evidence, such as your breath test result. Incidentally, your sworn testimony at this hearing cannot be used in any way at your trial if you opt NOT to testify then.[285]

Some courts require your presence at all scheduled court dates when legal issues or scheduling of your trial are discussed. This may include "calendar calls." If you are unfortunate enough to have your case pending in such a court, do not blame your criminal defense specialist for the court's petulant behavior that is almost always a huge waste of time.

A *calendar call* is an administrative discussion between the judge and all parties regarding the scheduling of trials and pre-trial hearings. The facts of your case are not presented and no witnesses or other evidence are typically presented at these hearings. However, if the court requires your presence in court, you will be required to sit through the proceedings while the prosecutor, the judge and all the lawyers representing various parties discuss the upcoming court schedule.

Finally, assuming that no resolution of your case through negotiations with the prosecutor or pre-trial motions is possible, trial is the next step in the court process. Surprisingly, your attorney may not know a precise date that your trial will start, due to the court trying to schedule as many cases as time will allow during a given court term.

It is not uncommon for ten or twenty trials to be scheduled for a one-week period, with all parties fully understanding that some of these trials will not occur. As the trial date approaches, some charges are dropped or reduced for some criminal defendants by the prosecutor at the last second. Other defendants decide to plead guilty or nolo contendere and

---

[285]**Simmons v. United States**, 390 U.S. 377, 88 S.Ct. 967, 19 L.Ed.2d 1247 (1968); **Hestley v. State**, 216 Ga. App. 573, 455 S.E.2d 333 (1995).

forego a trial. Occasionally, some of the lawyers or their witnesses may have other trials that conflict with your case's trial date.

For example, if you are scheduled to be the eighth case called to trial in a week, you could actually be the first trial on the first day of the trial week. In the alternative, your case might not start at all until the next available trial week, if an earlier case or cases use all of the available time.

You must be ready to proceed to trial at any time your case is scheduled for one of these trial weeks. Your attorney and all of your witnesses must also be ready to proceed, and often with very short notice. This means that you must be flexible and make yourself available to be present in court if your lawyer calls. For some types of employment, this is a task that is either impossible or extremely difficult. If you reside out of state when trial occurs, scheduling flights and time off from work can be very taxing.

Even more inconvenient to you, if your trial does not occur at all during the week when first scheduled, you will have been "on call" all week long. Employers do not understand or work well with such tentative scheduling of mandatory legal matters. Please understand that other than making the trial judge aware of the job difficulties that you are facing, your DUI-DWI attorney may have little control or authority to demand any accommodation of your work schedule or your need to come to court from another state.

Considering all of the above, it is possible that you will need to be able to take off a cumulative total of up to two weeks from work during the year after your arrest. Some matters can be handled without you being present at court. Other matters can be set for a fixed date as much as a month or two in advance. Others can be limited to a given week, but you and your attorney are not assured of being reached on the calendar on a given day.

For most people, this means possibly giving up your entire paid vacation time for the year. If given the choice between having to take unpaid vacation days off from work and using your paid days, considering the expenses you face, it may be better for you to forego other vacation and use your paid "leave" days to resolve your legal problems.

5.12. Community service is a good thing to do. Most DUI-DWI statutes require some community service work as a part of their mandatory punishment scheme. Most of these statutes require a "minimum" number of hours, depending on whether your offense is a first, second or subsequent offense within your state's "lookback" period. For example, in Georgia, the lookback period is five years, from the date of arrest to the next date of arrest. In South Carolina, the lookback period is ten years, creating a longer time frame within which to trigger mandatory, harsher punishment for repeat offenders. Nearly a dozen states have eliminated "lookback" periods and will review your entire driving history. This trend of reviewing your lifetime driving history will likely spread to other states in the next decade.

If your DUI-DWI attorney recommends that you begin doing community service hours, follow his or her advice. Getting these hours done at a charitable or non-profit organization may provide your attorney with a bargaining tool with which to approach your prosecutor.

An additional reason that your attorney may tell you to start community service hours is that your prompt and early commitment to do public service may be beneficial to you if you are required to go to trial and (unfortunately) lose the case. By showing the trial judge that you "took the bull by the horns" and got involved in a DUI-DWI school, alcohol assessment and treatment and performed community service hours, such actions can help mitigate your punishment at sentencing. In some courts, the judge may be inclined to permit you to serve all or most of the detention period on home confinement or "work release" (allowing you to go to work to protect your job).

Another benefit to performing community service in advance might be that the TYPE of service you are permitted to perform on your own might be far better than the work the judge may order you to perform after sentencing. Many jurisdictions have very unpleasant jobs for their "county" programs, including cleaning out the dog pound, collecting garbage or cleaning public toilets. Make sure you have chosen a knowledgeable DUI-DWI specialist who advises you regarding when, how and where to perform these hours in order to get full credit from your judge when you later appear in court to resolve your case (hopefully with a reduced or deferred plea of some type). Most courts require detailed records of all community service hours.

Yet another benefit to having all of the "conditions" required by that court completed in your case before the case is disposed of by a negotiated plea reduction or a trial is that you may be able to avoid "probation supervision fees." These are monthly costs for a probation officer to oversee and check up on your progress in completing any court-ordered punishment such as DUI-DWI school or community service. By having 100% of all conditions completed, your attorney can request the judge allow your probation to become "non-reporting," thereby possibly saving you from $15 to $60 per month, depending on the costs of this oversight in your state.

Although rare in DUI-DWI prosecutions, some states may terminate probation or "suspend" probation if you have performed all of the required "penalties" ordered by the judge. If your probation is terminated or suspended, you would no longer be "on probation" and subject to being re-arrested for a probation violation, if you fail to complete all ordered tasks. Even where your probation cannot be terminated or suspended (due to mandatory probation being part of your state's laws), your legal counsel may be able to negotiate with your court to allow your probation to become "non-reporting." This means that you may not need to travel to see your probation officer on a periodic basis and (possibly) not have to pay the monthly "supervision" fee.

If you have been proactive, having accomplished a large number of hours of community service at the time of your sentencing, this can be used by you and your attorney to show your remorse and your acceptance of responsibility for your actions. The sentence you are given by the judge might then be substantially reduced over what you would have received as a punishment if you had done nothing in advance. This is true for "reduced" pleas as well as when the case is resolved as a DUI-DWI.

Many people who get involved in community service find that they ENJOY it. If given an option, always try to choose a type of service that fits your personal "criteria." If you enjoy working with animals, look for a charity that protects or places pets. If you like working with children, find a project that taps into this preference. You may find that even when your term of service is over, you continue to provide volunteer hours for the same non-profit organization in the future.

5.13. Anxiety can be a killer! Seek professional counseling if needed. Being arrested and charged with DUI-DWI is the beginning of a long and often stressful process that can be the worst experience of your life. For people with no experience with the criminal justice system, your arrest and the time you spent in jail before you were released can be a source of nightmares and insomnia. Memories of the sounds, smells and discomfort of jail on the night of your arrest can be a difficult thing to shake.

If you find that you are having a tough time dealing with your stress, discuss this with your attorney. If you have chosen the right DUI-DWI attorney, he or she will understand what you are going through. He or she will likely suggest counseling, to assist you in the stressful times ahead.

When clients tell me about their stress, I always take it very seriously. In my thirty years of seeing people in these situations, I realize that this stress can make life miserable. Unfortunately, eight of my clients---all men---committed suicide before I could get their cases resolved. Never has anyone the author has represented committed suicide AFTER he went to trial. Hence, the stress of waiting for a resolution can be worse than the final outcome of the case.

One of the worst things about the entire situation is going to be the months of waiting while it seems like nothing is happening. You want to get through the process and get it completed. The anxiety of waiting and believing that everyone except you is in control of your life creates a great deal of anxiety. This is particularly true for people who are used to being in total control of their lives.

It is okay to ask for professional help through counseling. For many, it is the only answer to their problem. In fact, you can make your life worse by not seeking help.

Some people in your situation have an adequate support system, between their family, their religious affiliations, their friends, and possibly their employer. Many people find an excellent support system with their alcohol or drug counselor. Others will not have any similar support system, or may find that the support system they had is not adequate to help reduce the stress.

If you take out your anger or frustration on those who are close to you while you are under the legal microscope during this lengthy process, the destroyed relationships can be worse than anything that happens in court. In addition, if you cannot find ways of dealing with the distractions and anxiety of your situation, you may lose both personal and professional relationships as you try to "self-help" rather than turn the issue over to professionals.

Ask your DUI-DWI attorney to refer you to a counselor that he or she knows has both experience and compassion in these situations. Go for assistance sooner rather than later if there is any doubt in your mind that you need counseling. Sometimes, a single session or a couple of sessions with a counselor can point out a method of coping that will carry you through your case. If your issues or problems are more complex, you may be referred to a medical specialist such as a psychiatrist who can prescribe anti-anxiety medications or sleep medications.

The author has used a helpful DVD for his clients for the last fifteen years. If you want to know more about this DVD (entitled "How to Deal With Stress While Your Case is Pending"), check out this link for more information.[286]

5.14. How will the judge or jury perceive you? Often, just having been arrested for DUI-DWI is equivalent to being labeled in the minds of both judges and juries as having a alcohol or drug problem. Jurors tend to think that you "must have done something" if you are in court as the defendant. This section of the book will tell you how to put your best foot forward and (hopefully) increase your chances of being acquitted.

This is one of the most important reasons to hire the best DUI-DWI specialist attorney you can possibly afford and heed his or her advice. He or she will know how to prepare you for court and how to present you and your case in the best possible light when you appear before your assigned judge. An experienced DUI-DWI attorney also has extensive experience in the

---

[286]http://www.theduibook.com/stress-DVD.htm.

jury selection process, assuming that you have the right to a trial by jury in your state. Most experienced DUI-DWI trial attorneys understand what to ask the jurors (in *voir dire* - the jury selection process) and how to create an open dialogue to facilitate candid and honest answers about how jurors feel about certain issues.

Almost without exception, your jury "pool" will consist of fairly conservative individuals. Most of these people either work or are retired from an active work career. The jury should be a fairly good mix of the same ethnic and racial cross-section of that county. So, expect to see a jury pool that reflects the county's population diversity, not necessarily your race or ethnic origin.

Jurors also tend to like and react well to people who have a genuine smile. Jurors respond well to people who look them in the eye and communicate with facial expressions and appropriate physical reactions to situations that arise. When making eye contact, however, a good rule of thumb is to limit this to 3 to 5 seconds before moving your eye contact to another juror.

In many parts of trial, it will be appropriate to smile at some humorous verbal exchange or a comment by a witness or even the judge. Smiling, affable people get better results from jurors in trial situations where the outcome could go either way. Don't go overboard and "paste" a smile on your face for every phase of trial.

When dressing for the jury, it is best that your clothing and manner of dress be somewhat conservative, to reflect the composition of your likely jury pool. Also, remove any "body jewelry" or other visible symbols that you realize will make an immediate poor impression on a conservative, middle-aged, working-class juror. Tattoos need to be out of view of jurors, who may hold strong opinions about "body art."

The more conservative your hairstyle the better your chances will be with an average jury. Clean-shaven men can expect to be more readily accepted by the average jury. Similarly, women need to keep any skirt lengths "appropriate" and of course, no low-cut blouses. Remember, you are in a court of law. Listen to your DUI-DWI attorney when your "trial appearance" is in question.

Chapter 6

Potential Defenses, Strategies and Tactics

for Your DUI-DWI Case

6.0. Purpose of this chapter. The prosecution of a typical DUI-DWI case involves hundreds of facts and potential legal issues. The cornerstone of a successful defense is a full and open discussion of each aspect of your case with your experienced DUI-DWI attorney. Minor factual changes or revelation of certain "statements" by police during their investigation of your case or your arrest can lead to a favorable outcome.

A *legal defense* is a general term for the effort of an attorney representing a defendant during trial and in pre-trial maneuvers to defeat the prosecution in a criminal case such as a DUI-DWI.[287] In some cases, your attorney may identify a "complete defense" (a legal excuse) to the alleged DUI-DWI charges, called an *affirmative defense*, to counter, defeat or remove all or a part of the contentions of the State (the prosecution). In other cases, your highly qualified defense attorney will be looking for shortcomings in the police evidence that create a "failure of proof" on some aspect of the case.

The first of these general considerations is whether or not the prosecution has any evidence at all on all the requisite "elements" of each DUI-DWI count. (A *count* is a legal term for each separate crime the state has charged you with committing.) For example, if you have a single vehicle accident and you are only found later at your home drinking a beer, the prosecution may not be able to prove that you had been drinking *before* the accident occurred, which is a key "element" of the proof required for a DUI-DWI charge.

It does not matter if you were wildly intoxicated last Thursday evening when a vehicle fitting your car's description was seen driving erratically, if you can't be placed behind the wheel. If you were sitting at home, and never even got in any motor vehicle that night, you may have a good defense to the traffic offenses. If somehow the police charged you with DUI-DWI (based upon a **B**e **O**n the **L**ook **O**ut or BOLO call of a partial tag number) and the police lack proof that you were outside of your home at the time of the alleged driving, it is highly likely the DUI-DWI charges against you will be dropped.

Another consideration is whether or not during your arrest the police violated any state statutes, constitutional provisions, regulations or other legal authority (such as decisional law from an appellate court that has ruled on the same evidentiary issue). If they did, was the violation of such a type or "degree" that it will offend the notion of fair play and justice from the point of view of the trial court? An example of this would be if you are a minority, and the police were simply stopping every person of your race, and only these drivers, as they passed through

---

[287]http://dictionary.law.com/default2.asp?typed=defense&type=1&submit1.x=49&submit1.y=12.

a small town.[288] Another example of illegal police conduct would be a roadblock that is illegally set up without supervisory authority, as required by state law.[289]

Although very few DUI-DWI cases involve an "affirmative defense" or "legal justification," your attorney may be able to defend certain cases on this basis. The affirmative defense of "necessity" could be one such answer to criminal charges. For example, if you had consumed six beers while sitting at home but your wife cut her hand in the kitchen, severing an artery, you might have to drive her to a hospital for emergency care if the bleeding was excessive and an ambulance was twenty minutes away. Such an "affirmative defense" is not an absolute bar to prosecution, but it can be asserted as a complete defense to the crime of drunk driving in most states, if the circumstances of the emergency are found to have justified the driving with an unlawful blood alcohol content in your system.

This chapter discusses some of these possible defenses, strategies and tactics to the DUI-DWI charges against you. The more complete your knowledge of these issues and legal matters, the more helpful you can be to your attorney in fighting for your legal rights in your DUI-DWI case. You need to give your attorney ALL the facts so that he or she can uncover potential defenses, strategies and legal challenges in your case.

6.1. Defenses related to the legality or sufficiency of the indictment, accusation, complaint, information, or other charging instrument (such as a uniform traffic citation). In a criminal prosecution, you start with a presumption in your favor that you are innocent until and unless proven guilty.[290] You also have the right to be accurately and completely informed precisely what the charges are that the State is bringing against you.[291] Such information is vital to protect your constitutionally guaranteed right to a fair trial.[292] For example, if you cannot read or only speak a different language, you must usually still receive a written copy of the official charges against you. However, at your first appearance before the court to announce whether you plead guilty or not guilty (called your "arraignment"), the charges will be read to you in a manner and language that you can comprehend.

The paperwork starting a DUI-DWI case can be as simple as the written citation or traffic ticket that the law enforcement officer gave you at the time of your arrest. Some

---

[288] **State v. Payne,** 759 S.W.2d 252 (Mo.App. E.D. 1988); **State v. Loyd,** 530 N.W.2d 708 (Iowa 1995); **State v. Rose,** 170 N.C.App. 284, 612 S.E.2d 336 (N.C.App. 2005); **Lee v. Com.,** 2000 WL 1219429 (Va.App. 2000).

[289] **Com. v. Paes,** 862 A.2d 625 (2004); **Dale v. State,** 267 Ga.App. 897, 600 S.E.2d 763 (2004); **Com. v. Buchanon,** 122 S.W.3d 565 (Ky. 2003); **Kirby v. State,** 874 So.2d 581 (Ala.Crim.App. 2003); **State v. Reynolds,** 319 N.J.Super. 426, 725 A.2d 1129 (1998); **State v. Madalena,** 121 N.M. 63, 908 P.2d 756 (N.M.App. 1995); **State v. Tucker,** 19 Kan.App.2d 920, 878 P.2d 855 (1994); **State v. Parms,** 523 So.2d 1293 (La. 1988); **Ingersoll v. Palmer,** 43 Cal.3d 1321, 743 P.2d 1299 (1987); **Higbie v. State,** 723 S.W.2d 802 (Tex.App.-Dallas 1987); **Jones v. State,** 459 So.2d 1068 (Fla.App. 2 Dist. 1984); **State v. Garcia,** 489 N.E.2d 168 (Ind.App. 1 Dist. 1986); **State v. Downey,** 945 S.W.2d 102 (Tenn. 1997).

[290] **Iowa v. Tovar,** 541 U.S. 77, 124 S.Ct. 1379, 158 L.Ed.2d 209 (2004); **In re D.C.,** 2004 WL 2492278 (Tenn.Ct.App. 2004); **Sun Co. of San Bernadino v. Superior Court,** 29 Cal.App.3d 815, 105 Cal. Rptr. 873 (4th Dist. 1973); **McLaurin v. State,** 882 So.2d 268 (Miss.App. 2004); **State v. Durio,** 878 So.2d 700 (La.App. 3 Cir. 2004); **State v. Snow,** 2003 WL 21663683 (Tenn.Crim.App. 2003); **State v. Schmitz,** 2003 WL 21384857 (Minn.App. 2003); **Garcia v. State,** 2005 WL 1991729 (Tex.App.-Austin 2005); **Petrie v. State,** 590 N.E.2d 603 (Ind.App. 3 Dist. 1992); **State v. Bolton,** 68 Wash.App. 211, 842 P.2d 989 (Wash.App. 1992).

[291] 21A Am. Jur. 2d Criminal Law § 979.

[292] **Spencer v. State of Tex.,** 385 U.S. 554, 87 S. Ct. 648, 17 L.Ed.2d 606 (1967); **Griffin v. Camp,** 40 F.3d 170 (7th Cir. 1994); **State v. Wallace,** 258 Kan. 639, 908 P.2d 1267 (1995).

jurisdictions authorize the use of such documents (and only these documents) to proceed all the way to your trial. Other jurisdictions will permit such "charging documents" to be used, or permit a prosecutor to draw up a more precise accusatory document, or even accuse you of additional criminal charges, by way of a typewritten *accusation, information* or *complaint* that more clearly states how and when the offenses occurred. In such a case, the ticket or citation is "superceded" or replaced by the new "formal" document.

The State might use other types of written notification to officially notify you of all of the charges against you. While you may have received a copy of the paper citation or ticket at the time of your arrest delineating the specific charges against you, the State has the option of bringing additional (or different) charges against you if their investigation of the facts of the case reveal that amended or alternative counts should be pursued against you.

Any new charges that were not originally made against you must be filed by the prosecutor within the "statute of limitations" period. Many states have laws that madate that the prosecutor assert all available charges against you when the case is "accused."[293] This prevents a prosecutor who gets miffed after losing at a trial of one or more DUI "counts" from drawing up a new charge or charges against you (e.g., reckless driving) during the applicable statute of limitations period.

For misdemeanor DUI-DWI cases, the most common time limit for filing charges against you after the commission of the offense is two years. Felonies usually have longer statutes of limitations, going all the way to "no time limit" for murder cases.

Hence, you may arrive at your arraignment and learn that not only have you been charged with DUI-DWI (which you knew), but several alternative counts of DUI-DWI, and possibly other traffic or criminal violations as well. For example, if the search of your vehicle uncovered marijuana, you may face charges (beyond possession of controlled substances – drugs) for DUI-DWI (alcohol), plus a separate charge of DUI-DWI (contraband drugs), plus DUI-DWI (alcohol and drugs, in combination).

The name of this charging document can vary depending upon local practice rules and custom. In some states this document is called an accusation, an indictment, a complaint or an "information." However, the term "indictment" usually refers to a felony prosecution, not a misdemeanor prosecution.

Because this charging document must inform you adequately of the charges against you, deficiencies in the *form* of the document or in the *contents* (substance) can be used by your attorney as means to either cause the documents to be redrawn or possibly (in certain circumstances) to completely bar (prevent) prosecution of the person charged in the event that "jeopardy" has attached and the State did not correct the flawed charges before jeopardy "attached." A demurrer (or motion to quash) is an attack by the defendant on the form or the content of the accusatory document.

A special demurrer (or special motion to quash) is an attack on the FORM of the document. One such attack might be that the crime with which you are charged cannot be specified on this kind of document. Another could be that it lacked a key signature by the prosecutor or the grand jury foreperson.

A general demurrer (or general motion to quash) is a challenge to the SUBSTANCE or content of what is written in the document. In other words, the accusatory document must be drawn correctly, in unambiguous language. It must contain the correct information and the

---

[293]Cal. Penal Code §654; O.C.G.A. §16-1-7

correct name of the defendant, otherwise the attorney representing the person accused of the crime can ask the judge to grant a complete "discharge and acquittal" of criminal charges against him or her if the prosecutor goes forward with trial and jeopardy "attaches" by virtue of you being put on trial for which your liberty and other eights are at stake.

The timing for asserting and form of filing this kind of legal challenge is very important, and requires an extensive knowledge of state law and criminal trial practice to succeed. This is a prime reason why you need a DUI-DWI specialist who knows when, how and by what written filing of documents to best use this little-known legal challenge.

6.2. Defenses relating to an illegal search warrant, if applicable. In 99% or more of drunken driving arrests, "warrantless" arrests are made. Therefore, it is highly unlikely that you were arrested and have been charged with DUI-DWI based on an illegal search warrant. However, the Fourth Amendment to the United States Constitution guarantees to every citizen the right not to have to defend himself or herself against an illegal search warrant.[294] See **Appendix I** for more on the federal constitution's protections.

In some situations following a collision causing a death or serious bodily injury, the police may seek a search warrant to procure a blood sample of the driver for suspected drugs or alcohol in his or her system. Also, some DUI-DWI arrests may be made after you have already reached your residence and have been inside for a period of time. If you (or any other occupant) do not respond to the doorbell or knocking at your door, any entry of your home by the police without a search warrant may constitute an illegal search. Opening the door – even a small crack – will usually result in overzealous officers barging right into the residence.

If the police do obtain a warrant, which can be done via a telephone call to a magistrate judge, they will come into the home. If there is evidence of possible recent alcohol consumption (e.g. empty cold beer cans, empty wine bottles, an opened bottle of liquor), then the police will never be able to determine when any alcohol within your system was consumed. REMAIN SILENT.

A search warrant is a written order by a judge which permits a law enforcement officer to search a specific place (e.g., "112 Magnolia Avenue, Apartment 3, Atlanta, Georgia," or a "2004 Pontiac Trans-Am, Texas license number 123ABC") and identifies the persons in possession of the real estate or vehicle (if known) and any illegal articles intended to be seized (often specified by type, such as "weapons," "drugs and drug paraphernalia," or "evidence of instruments used to cause bodily harm"). Such a search warrant can only be issued upon a sworn written statement of a law enforcement officer (which may also include a prosecutor), setting out his or her good faith belief that the evidence being sought is at the place and in the possession of the person(s) specified in the sworn document.

The 14th Amendment of the United States Constitution applies the rule embodied in the 4th Amendment to the states. Evidence unconstitutionally seized by the police cannot be used against you in court, nor can evidence "resulting from or growing out of an illegal search be utilized as evidence."[295]

However, since few if any DUI-DWI arrests have anything to do with a search warrant, this is a very rare defense when compared to other crimes. Accident cases and situations

---

[294]The right of the people to be secure in their persons, houses, papers, and effects, against unreasonable searches and seizures, shall not be violated, and no warrants shall issue, but upon probable cause, supported by Oath or affirmation, and particularly describing the place to be searched, and the persons or things to be seized. U.S.C.A. Const. Amend. IV.

[295]http://dictionary.law.com/default2.asp?typed=search+warrant&type=1&submit1.x=52&submit1.y=7.

where a person gets to his or her home after being involved in either a "hit and run" or "evading a police officer" cases are the most common fact patterns that trigger this type of legal analysis. If police come to your home, don't talk. REMAIN SILENT.

6.3. Defenses related to the legality of a roadblock. Many roadblocks set up by the police are illegal. These are controlled by the 4th Amendment of the United States Constitution or a similar state constitutional provision or state statute that limits "searches and seizures."[296]

The police must have a legally sufficient reason to stop your vehicle as a general rule. This reason can be based upon an observation of a traffic offense, defective equipment, an expired tag or inspection sticker, or some observable evidence that a crime is being committed or is about to be committed. In most states, however, roadblocks have been approved for use in stopping "impaired" drivers, so long as the roadblock is LEGALLY established and operated under strict, established guidelines that assure no discrimination or profiling has occurred.[297]

Roadblocks are valid under the ambit of a State's police powers to insure that the roads are safe from drunk drivers. The United States Supreme Court upheld this authority under the federal constitution in the case of *Michigan v. Sitz*.[298] The standards set in this case cannot be ignored by any state, since federal law is superior to all state laws. A state may add additional, more protective standards for citizens' rights for roadblocks in that state, or even ban roadblocks as being violative of the state constitution.

The exact legal parameters of a valid roadblock vary from state to state. However, most states that allow roadblocks have developed rules that include the following: (1) the decision to implement the roadblock must be made by supervisory personnel rather than by law enforcement officers in the field; (2) the roadblock operation must be carried out pursuant to specific, prearranged procedures requiring all passing vehicles to be stopped; and (3) the delay experienced by passing motorists must be minimal.[299]

Decisional law (appellate law) in some states has added other requirements. For example, Massachusetts requires adequate lighting at the roadblock site and the visible presence of signs that warn motorists of a roadblock ahead.[300] Several states have held these

---

[296]The right of the people to be secure in their persons, houses, papers, and effects, against unreasonable searches and seizures, shall not be violated... U.S.C.A. Const. Amend. IV.

[297]**Illinois v. Lidster,** 540 U.S. 419, 124 S.Ct. 885, 157 L.Ed.2d 843 (2004); **State v. Golden,** 171 Ga.App. 27, 318 S.E.2d 693 (1984); **Com. v. Beaman,** 880 A.2d 578 (Pa. 2005); **State v. Varner,** 160 S.W.3d 535 (Tenn.Crim.App. 2004); **People v. Sears,** 2 Misc.3d 447, 769 N.Y.S.2d 708 (N.Y.Just.Ct. 2003); **State v. Thomas,** 372 N.J.Super. 29, 855 A.2d 17 (2002); **State v. Tarlton,** 146 N.C.App. 417, 553 S.E.2d 50 (2001); **State v. Jones,** 483 So.2d 433 (Fla. 1986); **Banks v. State,** 681 N.E.2d 235 (Ind.App. 1997); **City of Seattle v. Mesiani,** 110 Wash.2d 454, 755 P.2d 775 (1988).

[298]**Michigan Dept. of State Police v. Sitz,** 496 U.S. 444, 110 S.Ct. 2481, 110 L.Ed.2d 412 (1990).

[299]**Illinois v. Lidster,** 540 U.S. 419, 124 S.Ct. 885, 157 L.Ed.2d 843 (2004); **State v. Golden,** 171 Ga.App. 27, 318 S.E.2d 693 (1984); **State v. Deskins,** 234 Kan. 529, 673 P.2d 1174; **Kinslow v. Commonwealth,** 660 SW2d 677 (Ky. App. 1983); **State v. Coccomo,** 177 N.J. Super. 575, 427 A.2d 131 (1980); **U.S.A. v. Prichard,** 645 F.2d 854 (10th Cir. 1981); **Com. v. Beaman,** 880 A.2d 578 (Pa. 2005); **State v. Varner,** 160 S.W.3d 535 (Tenn.Crim.App. 2004); **People v. Sears,** 2 Misc.3d 447, 769 N.Y.S.2d 708 (N.Y.Just.Ct. 2003); **State v. Thomas,** 372 N.J.Super. 29, 855 A.2d 17 (2002); **State v. Tarlton,** 146 N.C.App. 417, 553 S.E.2d 50 (2001); **State v. Jones,** 483 So.2d 433 (Fla. 1986); **Banks v. State,** 681 N.E.2d 235 (Ind.App. 1997); **City of Seattle v. Mesiani,** 110 Wash.2d 454, 755 P.2d 775 (1988); **State v. Dearman,** 54 Wash.App. 621, 774 P.2d 1247 (1989).

[300]**Commonwealth v. McGeoghegan,** 389 Mass. 137, 449 N.E.2d 349 (1983).

DUI-DWI roadblocks to be inherently unconstitutional under their state constitutions, including Michigan, Oklahoma, Arizona and South Dakota.[301]

Thus, if the police did not follow precisely the legally required guidelines set forth in your state, or if these DUI-DWI roadblocks are not allowed in your state, your criminal defense attorney can use this as a defense to the charges against you. To win a case based upon an illegal roadblock, you will likely need to have one of the top DUI-DWI specialists in your state when you make your legal challenge. See this informative article: **http://www.duiblog.com/2005/05/03#a159**.

6.4. Defenses related to the legality of the stop of your vehicle. For any law enforcement officer to have a valid reason to stop you in your vehicle there must be a "articulable and reasonable suspicion" that:

(1) you are an unlicensed driver;
(2) that your vehicle is not registered;
(3) either you are a "wanted" person on a criminal charge or the vehicle you are driving is in violation of the law.[302]

"Articulable" means the law enforcement officer is able to verbalize specific facts and reasons to the court, through testimony, a reason why he or she believed a violation of the law existed that would justify the stop of your vehicle. What constitutes "reasonable" is analyzed on a case by case basis,[303] but it typically has to be more than a mere "hunch" or guesswork on the part of the officer.[304]

As an example, the following traffic stops by police officers have been ruled to be NOT reasonable: (1) if you stopped near a construction site where crimes had occurred before, got out of your car and walked around for a few minutes;[305] (2) if you were just driving below the posted speed limit but not impeding traffic;[306] or (3) if you were weaving slightly in your vehicle

---

[301]**State v. Smith**, 674 P.2d 562 (Okla.App.1984); **State ex rel. Ekstrom v. Justice Court**, 136 Ariz. 1, 663 P.2d 992 (1983); **State v. Olgaard**, 248 N.W.2d 392 (S.D.1976); **State v. Van Dorne**, 139 Idaho 961, 88 P.3d 780 (2004); **Sitz v. Department of State Police**, 443 Mich. 744, 506 N.W.2d 209 (1993).

[302]**Delaware v. Prouse**, 440 U.S. 648, 99 S.Ct. 1391, 59 L.Ed.2d 660 (1979); **Brisbane v. State**, 233 Ga. 339, 211 S.E.2d 294 (Ga. 1974); **State v. Payton**, 344 So.2d 648 (Fla.App. 2 Dist. 1977); **Hoag v. State**, 728 S.W.2d 375 (Tex.Crim.App. 1987); **State v. Watkins**, 827 S.W.2d 293 (Tenn. 1992).

[303]**State v. Holton**, 205 Ga. App. 434, 422 S.E.2d 295 (1992); **Woods v. State**, 956 S.W.2d 33 (Tex.Crim.App.1997); **State v. Andrews**, 57 Ohio St.3d 86, 565 N.E.2d 1271 (Ohio 1991); **State v. Watkins**, 827 S.W.2d 293 (Tenn. 1992); **Berge v. Commissioner of Public Safety**, 374 N.W.2d 730 (Minn. 1985); **Popple v. State**, 626 So.2d 185 (Fla. 1993); **People v. Cantor**, 36 N.Y.2d 106, 324 N.E.2d 872 (N.Y. 1975); **State v. Kennedy**, 107 Wash.2d 1, 726 P.2d 445 (Wash. 1986); **State v. Kowal**, 31 Conn.App. 669, 626 A.2d 822 (Conn.App. 1993).

[304]**Hanson v. State**, 222 Ga. App. 537, 474 S.E.2d 735 (1996); **State v. Carlson**, 102 Ohio App.3d 585, 657 N.E.2d 591 (Ohio App. 9 Dist. 1995); **People v. Young**, 241 A.D.2d 690, 660 N.Y.S.2d 165 (N.Y.A.D. 3 Dept. 1997); **State v. Farabee**, 302 Mont. 29, 22 P.3d 175 (Mont. 2000); **State v. Parker,** 84 Conn.App. 739, 856 A.2d 428 (2004); **State v. Haskell**, 645 A.2d 619 (Me. 1994); **State v. Burgess**, 876 So.2d 263 (La.App. 2004); **State v. Alexander**, 2005 WL 2276913 (Wis.App. 2005); **State v. Glover**, 116 Wash.2d 509, 806 P.2d 760 (1991); **Johnson v. State**, 146 S.W.3d 719 (Tex.App.-Texarkana 2004); **State v. Simpson**, 968 S.W.2d 776 (Tenn. 1998); **Denton v. State**, 805 N.E.2d 852 (Ind.App. 2004); **Anderson v. State,** 864 So.2d 948 (Miss.App. 2003); **Bordelon v. State**, 908 So.2d 543 (Fla.App. 1 Dist. 2005).

[305]**State v. Sevy**, 129 Idaho 613, 930 P.2d 1358 (Ct.App. 1997).

[306]**Richardson v. State**, 39 S.W.3d 634 (Tex.App.-Amarillo 2000).

when no other vehicles were around.[307] "Laying drag" (white smoke coming from squealing and spinning tires) in the midst of heavy vehicular and pedestrian traffic *is* an adequate reason to stop your vehicle.[308] The officers must have some reasonable and articulable suspicion that you are committing a crime before they decide to stop you, not just develop this suspicion *after* your stop.

In your DUI-DWI case, you thus have a possible legal challenge to the basis of the "stop" or confrontation by the police if the law enforcement officer who initially stopped you, or discovered you intoxicated in your stationary vehicle, cannot give the court a good reason for the stop or for interrupting your privacy. Because each case is fact-specific, most of these challenges are won on extremely minor evidentiary points that are brought out by your criminal defense specialist at a pre-trial motion.[309]

A specific example of this type of affirmative defense is the "stationary shelter" defense. Used mostly in northern states, this is the situation where you may have left a bar or tavern in a very intoxicated state. You have to go somewhere at four in the morning after you have been drinking, and the warmth of the inside of your car may be the difference between freezing to death and surviving until you are sober enough to drive. While you may be found by the police in the front seat of your vehicle, and still in an intoxicated state, some courts have suggested that the appropriate legal test should be whether you posed a threat to the public by your exercise of present or imminent control over your vehicle while impaired, rather than simply using your vehicle as a stationary shelter.[310] If your well-seasoned DUI-DWI attorney is able to show the weather conditions that evening were such that your car was the only shelter between you and death, and that there was no evidence that you intended to drive until you were sober, the actions of the police in interrupting your privacy may not have been valid.

6.5. Defenses related to the lawfulness of your arrest for DUI-DWI. The Fourth Amendment to the United States Constitution also protects you against any illegal or unlawful seizure (arrest) by the government.[311] A temporary non-custodial traffic stop turns into an "arrest" when a reasonable person in your position would think that the traffic stop was no longer temporary.[312]

Certainly, when you have been put in the back seat of a police car with no interior handles to open the doors, or if you have been handcuffed and are no longer free to leave, you

---

[307]**Jordan v. State**, 831 So.2d 1241 (Fla. 5th Dist. 2002) - Maintaining a single lane is a matter of safety, not precision, sayeth the court.

[308]**State v. Armstrong**, 223 Ga. App. 350, 477 S.E.2d 635 (1996).

[309]**Martin v. State**, 257 Ga.App. 435, 571 S.E.2d 459 (2002); **Bowers v. State,** 221 Ga.App. 886, 473 S.E.2d 201 (1996); **State v. Downs**, Slip Copy, 2004 WL 1293403 (Ohio App. 6 Dist. 2004).

[310]William C. Head, Holly Morris, *Stationary Shelter as an Affirmative Defense*, DWI Journal Law & Science, Vol. 18, No. 1, Jan. 2003; **State v. Love**, 182 Ariz. 324, 897 P.2d 626 (1995).

[311]The right of the people to be secure in their persons, houses, papers, and effects, against unreasonable searches and seizures, shall not be violated... U.S.C.A. Const. Amend. IV.

[312]**Berkemer v. McCarty**, 468 U.S. 420, 104 S.Ct. 3138. 82 L.Ed.2d 317 (1984); **Hughes v. State,** 259 Ga. 227, 378 S.E.2d 853 (1989); **Hutto v. State,** 977 S.W.2d 855 (Tex.App.-Hous. (14 Dist. 1998); **Nash v. Com.,** 12 Va.App. 550, 404 S.E.2d 743 (1991); **Morrissette v. State,** 229 Ga.App. 420, 494 S.E.2d 8 (1997); **State v. Martin,** 543 N.W.2d 224 (N.D. 1996); **City of Strongsville v. Minnillo,** 2003 WL 125128 (Ohio App. 8 Dist. 2003); **State v. Evans,** 692 So.2d 305 (Fla.App. 4 Dist. 1997); **State v. White,** 674 N.W.2d 683 (Iowa App. 2003); **State v. Thomas,** 843 So.2d 834 (Ala.Crim.App. 2002); **Williamson v. State,** 876 So.2d 353 (Miss. 2004); **State v. Craig,** 115 Wash.App. 191, 61 P.3d 340 (2002).

are under arrest.[313] In most states, when the police draw weapons and point them at you, you have no expectation that this will be an ordinary, temporary traffic citation,[314] while this is not true in all circumstances.[315] Whether or not you are under arrest depends *not* upon the opinion of the officer, but upon existing facts and circumstances that support a normal person's subjective sense of lack of freedom.[316]

The rules outlining what constitutes sufficient "probable cause" or reasonable grounds for a custodial arrest for DUI-DWI vary from state to state.[317] Whether or not there was sufficient probable cause or reasonable grounds for your arrest for DUI-DWI will depend on your state's case law, statutes and constitution, plus the circumstances surrounding your arrest. Having the smell of alcohol on you alone is typically not enough "probable cause" for a custodial arrest for impaired driving, unless you are under age 21 and alcohol is a prohibited substance for you to possess.[318] In Texas, where no "open container" law exists, just because the police see the driver with an open bottle of beer in his hand, it is not by itself a sufficient reason to stop you.[319] This is why your DUI-DWI specialist attorney will need to know all of the minor details of your arrest. These details may well provide the basis of a legal challenge that convinces your judge to declare the custodial arrest to have been illegally made.

6.6. Defenses related to an unlawful search and seizure and exclusion of illegally seized evidence. It is a very rare DUI-DWI case that revolves around physical evidence that has been taken from you by the government in an unlawful manner. Most DUI-DWI cases revolve around the officer's testimony as to what he or she observed, video tapes or audio recordings made by the officer in the line of duty, and physiological testing (blood, breath or urine) performed on you to establish the presence and quantity of alcohol or drugs in your system at the time of your arrest.

Unless you are arrested, or willingly consent to a search, you have the Fourth Amendment protection against an unlawful search of you or your vehicle.[320] The police cannot

---

[313]**Morgan v. State,** 195 Ga. App. 732, 394 S.E.2d 639 (1990); **State v. Nelson,** 261 Ga. 246, 404 S.E.2d 112 (1991); **Hopkins v. State,** 799 So.2d 874 (Miss. 2001); **Alford v. State,** 22 S.W.3d 669 (Tex.App.-Fort Worth 2000); **State v. Craig,** 115 Wash.App. 191, 61 P.3d 340 (2002).

[314]**State v. Jones,** 2005 WL 1950292 (Tenn.Crim.App. 2005); **Levi v. State,** 147 S.W.3d 541 (Tex.App.-Waco 2004); **People v. Aless,** 2002 WL 819858 (Cal.App. 4 Dist. 2002); **State v. Raker,** 883 So.2d 887 (Fla.App. 1 Dist. 2004); **Shirley v. State,** 803 N.E.2d 251 (Ind.App. 2004); **Bearden v. State,** 662 So.2d 620 (Miss. 1995); **State v. Rivard,** 131 Wash.2d 63, 929 P.2d 413 (1997); **People v. O'Neal,** 32 P.3d 533 (Colo.App. 2000); **People v. Carlson,** 307 Ill.App.3d 77, 716 N.E.2d 1249 (1999); **Basnueva v. U.S.,** 874 A.2d 363 (D.C. 2005); **State v. Theetge,** 171 Vt. 167, 759 A.2d 496 (Vt. 2000).

[315]**People v. Smith,** 13 P.3d 300 (Colo. 2000).

[316]**Stansbury v. California,** 511 U.S. 318, 114 S.Ct. 1526, 128 L.Ed.2d 293 (1994).

[317]**Baptist v. Lohman,** 971 S.W.2d 366 (Mo.App. E.D. 1998); **State v. Kasian,** 207 Wis.2d 611, 558 N.W.2d 687 (Wis.App. 1996); **State v. Olson,** 342 N.W.2d 638 (Minn.App. 1984); **State v. Kiefer,** 2004 WL 2244553 (Ohio App. 1 Dist. 2004); **Cann-Hanson v. State,** 223 Ga.App. 690, 478 S.E.2d 460 (1996); **Lopez v. State,** 936 S.W.2d 332 (Tex.App.-San Antonio 1996); **Moran v. North Dakota Dept. of Transp.,** 543 N.W.2d 767 (N.D. 1996); **State v. Taylor,** 648 So.2d 701 (Fla. 1995); **State v. Baue,** 258 Neb. 968, 607 N.W.2d 191 (Neb. 2000); **Scully v. City of Watertown, NY,** 2005 WL 1244838 (N.D.N.Y. 2005); **Martin v. State,** 176 Ind.App. 99, 374 N.E.2d 543 (1978); **Watson v. State,** 835 So.2d 112 (Miss.App. 2003); **State v. Harrison,** 2003 WL 882379 (Tenn.Crim.App. 2003); **State v. Avery,** 103 Wash.App. 527, 13 P.3d 226 (2000).

[318]**Domingo v. State,** 82 S.W.3d 617 (Tex. App.-Amarillo 2002).

[319]**Jackson v. State,** 681 S.W.2d 910 (Tex. App.-Fort Worth 1984).

[320]The right of the people to be secure in their persons, houses, papers, and effects, against unreasonable searches and seizures, shall not be violated... U.S.C.A. Const. Amend. IV.

delay you too long before they either have to arrest you, or let you go.[321] Furthermore, having a dog sniff your vehicle while it is stopped, as long as it does not delay the process of you being ticketed, is not an illegal search.[322] This is why you should never have ANY illegal drugs in your vehicle, in case your routine speeding ticket is being issued by an officer who just happens to have a drug-sniffing dog in his or her vehicle.

Being placed in the back of a police car before being "officially" arrested, and then waiting until another officer arrives to perform your field sobriety evaluations, allowing the original police officer to search your vehicle and find evidence leading to your DUI-DWI arrest, is an illegal search and unconstitutional.[323] Once stopped, your refusal to consent to a search before your arrest cannot factor into the reasonable suspicion to detain you. It is not probable cause by itself to search you and your vehicle.[324]

Certainly, anything illegal or contraband that is "in plain sight" within or on your vehicle (such as an illegal attachment or faulty piece of equipment) can be cited by the police as justification for a further search and used against you in your case.[325] Then, at the time of your arrest, the police have certain rights to search not only you, but also the passenger compartment and any containers found in the passenger compartment of your vehicle.[326] The purpose of such a search is typically justified by claiming that such a search was needed to determine if other evidence of the criminal act is present.

In traffic arrests following a DUI-DWI investigation, a different kind of search takes place in almost all cases. If no "sober" driver is available to drive your vehicle away, it will likely be towed, by order of the police. A search done prior to your vehicle being towed away (called an "inventory search") is supposed to be done to assure that if valuables inside the vehicle disappear while the vehicle is impounded, the police department will not be held accountable.[327]

Because almost every custodial arrest leads to a vehicle impound and the "inventory search," you should never keep any contraband items in your vehicle. Most common are illegal

---

[321]55 minutes of questioning at the scene of your car stop too long - **State v. Garcia,** 123 S.W.3d 335 (Tenn. 2003); **Florida v. Royer,** 460 U.S. 491, 103 S.Ct. 1319, 75 L.Ed.2d 229 (1983).

[322]**Illinois v. Caballes,** 543 U.S. 405, 125 S.Ct. 834, 160 L.Ed.2d 842 (2005).

[323]**O'Boyle v. State,** 117 P.3d 401 (Wyo. 2005).

[324]**U.S. v. McKneely,** 6 F.3d 1447 (10th Cir.(Utah) 1993).

[325]**Illinois v. Andreas,** 463 U.S. 765, 103 S.Ct. 3319, 77 L.Ed.2d 1003 (1983); **State v. Allen,** 762 So.2d 92 (La.App. 4 Cir. 2000); **Grinberg v. Safir,** 181 Misc.2d 444, 694 N.Y.S.2d 316 (N.Y.Sup. 1999); **State v. Trudeau,** 165 Vt. 355, 683 A.2d 725 (1996); **Ervin v. State,** 630 So.2d 115 (Ala.Crim.App. 1992); **State v. Romero,** 224 Mont. 431, 730 P.2d 1157 (1986); **Marryott v. State,** 263 Ga.App. 65, 587 S.E.2d 217 (2003); **State v. Pike,** 139 N.C.App. 96, 532 S.E.2d 543 (2000); **Wright v. State,** 932 S.W.2d 572 (Tex.App.-Tyler 1995); **State v. Halla-Poe,** 468 N.W.2d 570 (Minn.App. 1991); **Comby v. State,** 901 So.2d 1282 (Miss.App. 2004); **Watson v. State,** 533 So.2d 737 (Ala.Crim.App. 1988); **State v. Bryant,** 678 S.W.2d 480 (Tenn.Crim.App. 1984); **Guidi v. Superior Court,** 10 Cal.3d 1, 513 P.2d 908 (1973); **State v. Parnell,** 221 So.2d 129 (Fla. 1969); **Lance v. State,** 425 N.E.2d 77 (Ind. 1981); **State v. Lair,** 95 Wash.2d 706, 630 P.2d 427 (1981).

[326]**New York v. Belton,** 453 U.S. 454, 101 S.Ct. 2860, 69 L.Ed.2d 768 (1981).

[327]**Whren v. U.S.,** 517 U.S. 806, 116 S.Ct. 1769, 135 L.Ed.2d 89 (1996); **Sheppard v. Aloisi,** 384 F.Supp.2d 478 (D.Mass. 2005); **State v. Volkman,** 675 N.W.2d 337 (Minn.App. 2004); **Bratton v. State,** 77 Ark.App. 174, 72 S.W.3d 522 (2002); **U.S. v. Stewart,** 149 F.Supp.2d 236 (E.D.Va. 2001); **Ray v. State,** 798 So.2d 579 (Miss.App. 2001); **State v. Reid,** 2000 WL 502678 (Tenn.Crim.App. 2000); **People v. Needham,** 79 Cal.App.4th 260, 93 Cal.Rptr.2d 899 (2000); **State v. Robinson,** 743 So.2d 814 (La.App. 4 Cir. 1999); **State v. Dickey,** 152 N.J. 468, 706 A.2d 180 (1998); **Gaston v. State,** 155 Ga.App. 337, 270 S.E.2d 877 (1980); **Urquhart v. State,** 261 So.2d 535 (Fla.App. 2 Dist. 1971).

drugs such as cocaine and marijuana, but sometimes the police will seize prescription painkillers or anti-anxiety medications that are not in a proper container or that are prescribed to someone else. Other types of "contraband" items might include child pornography, an unlicensed weapon, an illegal (profane) bumper sticker, or obviously stolen merchandise.

Additionally, if you wreck your vehicle and leave it off the shoulder of the road, the police may be able to legally search the vehicle without the necessity of a warrant. The existence of the wrecked vehicle will authorize a search for victims or identification of the owner of the vehicle. A purse found inside an abandoned vehicle can be searched.[328] However, a passenger's purse (after she was asked to step out of the vehicle) cannot legally be searched.[329]

In almost every DUI-DWI case, this is the sequence of events. In most cases, little chance exists that any other evidence will be "seized" by the police in order to be used against you later at your DUI-DWI trial. However, if for any reason, the DUI-DWI case against you involves physical evidence that was taken from you in unlawfully, your attorney may then be able to have this harmful evidence excluded from consideration at your trial. One of the more common successful challenges has been when police open locked or closed containers to look for illegal items.

6.7. Defenses related to the violation by the police of your Fifth Amendment privilege against self-incrimination. The Fifth Amendment to the Constitution of the United States outlines a citizen's protection against self-incrimination: *"nor shall be compelled in any criminal case to be a witness against himself..."* Once you have been placed under arrest, if you are to be questioned further, you have to receive from the law enforcement officers a notification of this right.[330] Not only should you be notified of this right, but if you say something self-incriminating before you receive this warning, these statements may not be used against you.[331] However, spontaneous utterances to police (especially those statements captured on videotape) can be devastating to the case against you if they are ruled to be unprotected by the Fifth Amendment. Once again, use your **RIGHT TO REMAIN SILENT**. See more on your federal Constitutional rights in Appendix K.

6.8. Defenses related to the violation by the police of your constitutional or statutory right to counsel once arrested. Under the Fifth Amendment right against self-incrimination and your Sixth Amendment right to have an attorney be available for your defense,[332] you have a right for your attorney to be present any time the police are questioning you after your arrest.[333] It is best, however, for you to invoke this right to have counsel present

---

[328]**State v. Rynhart,**125 P.3d 938 (Utah 2005); **City of St. Paul v. Vaughn,** 237 N.W.2d 365 (Minn. 1975).

[329]**State v. Celusniak,** 135 N.M. 728, 93 P.3d 10 (N.M.App. 2004).

[330]**Miranda v. Arizona,** 384 U.S. 436, 86 S.Ct. 1602, 16 L.Ed.2d 694 (1966); **State v. O'Donnell,** 225 Ga.App. 502, 484 S.E.2d 313 (1997); **Hutto v. State,** 977 S.W.2d 855 (Tex.App.-Hous. (14 Dist.) 1998); **Nash v. Com.,** 12 Va.App. 550, 404 S.E.2d 743 (1991); **Com. v. Mahoney,** 400 Mass. 524, 510 N.E.2d 759 (1987); **State v. Martin,** 543 N.W.2d 224 (N.D. 1996); **State v. Kiefer,** 2004 WL 2244553 (Ohio App. 1 Dist. 2004); **Hopkins v. State,** 799 So.2d 874 (Miss. 2001); **State v. Easler,** 327 S.C. 121, 489 S.E.2d 617 (1997); **State v. Evans,** 692 So.2d 305 (Fla.App. 4 Dist. 1997); **State v. Thomas,** 843 So.2d 834 (Ala.Crim.App. 2002); **People v. Forster,** 29 Cal.App.4th 1746, 35 Cal.Rptr.2d 705 (1994); **City of College Place v. Staudenmaier,** 110 Wash.App. 841, 43 P.3d 43 (2002).

[331]**Berkemer v. McCarty,** 468 U.S. 420, 104 S.Ct. 3138, 82 L.Ed.2d 317 (1984); **Hughes v. State,** 259 Ga. 227, 378 S.E.2d 853 (1989).

[332]In all criminal prosecutions, the accused shall enjoy the right ... to have the Assistance of Counsel for his defense. U.S.C.A. Const. Amend. VI.

[333]**Escobedo v. Illinois,** 378 U.S. 478, 84 S.Ct. 1758, 12 L.Ed.2d 977 (1964).

and to remain totally silent until your attorney arrives. Once you have unambiguously requested that your counsel be present, the police can no longer interrogate you without your permission. Nor can the police get someone else to ask their questions for them once you have requested the presence of your counsel.[334]

The right to counsel and the related privilege against self-incrimination described above must be told to you as a part of the police reading of your "Miranda" rights.[335] These rights also apply to actions of the states (not just to officials of the federal government) because of the extension of these Fifth Amendment rights by way of the Fourteenth Amendment.

Once you have been informed of your right to have your attorney present during questioning, and you unequivocally refuse to speak to the police unless your lawyer is present, anything you say cannot be used against you.[336] If the police persist in questioning you, all such evidence obtained in violation of your Fifth and Sixth Amendment rights will be thrown out by your trial judge.[337] Once custody is clear and the police push forward with field sobriety tests in order to gather evidence of DUI-DWI, you are first entitled to be told your *Miranda* rights.[338]

When you appear in court, the judge will also inform you that you have a Sixth Amendment right to counsel. You can "waive" (give up) the right to be represented. However, the trial court does not, before accepting your waiver of counsel at a hearing at which you are going to plead guilty, have to give you a rigid and detailed admonishment of the usefulness of an attorney, tell you that an attorney may provide an independent opinion concerning whether it is wise to plead guilty and inform you that without an attorney, you may risk overlooking a defense.[339]

Thus, to provide for your best defense, it is critical that *you* remember exactly what was told to you by any law enforcement officer, at any time. The timing of questioning or statements made by you is also important, so be certain to note when anything was said to you by the police or asked of you by the police. It is also very important to tell the police early in their investigation of you that you want your attorney present any time you are to be questioned by them.

If you were not informed (immediately following your arrest) as to your right to legal counsel, the right to remain silent and the right to be told that anything you say can and will be used against you, this is a clear violation of your constitutional rights. A "conversation" with you that is started by the police may be deemed to have been a contrivance to deprive you of your legal rights. If you were refused access to an attorney after you asked for one and the police continued to question you in spite of your request, proof of such a violation can be used by your attorney in your defense, or possibly used to get the entire charges against you dismissed. See **Appendix K** for more information on your federal constitutional rights.

---

[334]**Messiah v. United States,** 377 U.S. 201, 84 S.Ct. 1199, 12 L.Ed.2d 246 (1964).

[335]**Miranda v. Arizona,** 384 U.S. 436, 86 S.Ct. 1602, 16 L.Ed.2d 694 (1966). **State v. Slette,** 585 N.W.2d 407 (Minn.App. 1998); **State v. Dunn,** 108 Wash.App. 490, 28 P.3d 789 (Wash.App. Div. 2 2001); **Com. v. Falvey,** 2004 WL 3090745 (Mass.Super. 2004); **State v. Harmon,** 131 Idaho 80, 952 P.2d 402 (Idaho App. 1998); **Floyd v. State,** 710 S.W.2d 807 (Tex.App.-Fort Worth 1986); **State v. Nece,** 206 N.J.Super. 118, 501 A.2d 1049 (1985); **State v. Jones,** 457 A.2d 1116 (Me. 1983).

[336]**Edwards v. Arizona,** 451 U.S. 477, 101 S.Ct. 1880, 68 L.Ed.2d 378 (1981).

[337]**State v. Rosengren,** 199 Ariz. 112, 14 P.3d 303 (2000).

[338]**State v. O'Donnell,** 225 Ga.App. 502, 484 S.E.2d 313 1997).

[339]**Iowa v. Tovar,** 541 U.S. 77, 124 S.Ct. 1379, 158 L.Ed.2d 209 (2004).

6.9. Challenges to use of improper and non-standardized field sobriety evaluations. It is highly likely that the police officer who stopped you, or found you behind the wheel in your stationary car, administered field sobriety tests to you before he or she arrested you. These evaluations can include a wide variety of agility exercises, mental acuity drills, plus the most common "standardized" three evaluations: the horizontal gaze nystagmus evaluation, the one leg stand, and the nine-step walk and turn. Other evaluations such as reciting the alphabet (or partial alphabet) and anything else the officer may ask you to do in the time between your first encounter with the police officer and your arrest, are being done for one purpose: *to gather further alleged incriminatory evidence against you in order to later use it at your trial.*

The "standardized" field sobriety evaluations refer to a set of roadside evaluations that were created and implemented by NHTSA (the National Highway Traffic and Safety Administration). This federal agency is an arm of the Department of Transportation. These NHTSA field tests have been in use across the United States for over twenty years. Most DUI-DWI "task force" officers use and rely upon these evaluations to assist them in deciding on whom to arrest. When performed, demonstrated and instructed correctly, in fair conditions and to a healthy subject with no physical defects or impairments, these evaluations can help identity a driver whose blood alcohol level is over 0.10 in the majority of cases. They are in no way close to being reliable in identifying drivers at or near the 0.08 level any better than 50% of the time, despite police officers' claims (based on the so-called "validation studies.")[340]

In some jurisdictions, certain types of field sobriety evidence are not permitted to be used by the prosecutor at trial to prove impairment or even to show the presence of alcohol in a person's system.[341] In other states, such field sobriety (roadside sobriety) test information is limited to proving the presence of alcohol.[342]

If these evaluations are allowed into evidence in your state, but were done incorrectly,[343] or if the officer's decision to arrest you for DUI-DWI was based on non-standardized field sobriety procedures that have no proven reliability,[344] your lawyer may be able to argue that this evidence be excluded or (possibly) that the entire arrest for DUI-DWI was invalid due to the unreliable "evidence of impairment" based on flawed field testing. If the arrest

---

[340]See http://www.theduibook.com/hlastala.htm

[341]**State v. Chastain**, 960 P.2d 756 (Kan. 1998); **Young v. City of Brookhaven**, 693 So.2d 1355 (Miss. 1997); **State v. Murphy**, 953 S.W.2d 200 (Tenn. 1997); **Pennsylvania v Bruder**, 488 U.S. 9 (1988); **Pennsylvania v Muniz**, 496 U.S. 582 (1990); **Allred v State**, 622 So. 2d 984 (Fla. 1993).

[342]**Schultz v. State**, 664 A.2d 60 (Md.App. 1994).

[343]**U.S. v. Horn**, 185 F.Supp.2d 530 (D.Md. 2002); **State v. Lasworth**, 131 N.M. 739, 42 P.3d 844 (N.M.App. 2001); **Hawkins v. State**, 223 Ga.App. 34, 476 S.E.2d 803 (1996); **State v. Homan**, 89 Ohio St.3d 421, 732 N.E.2d 952 (Ohio 2000); **People v. Buening**, 229 Ill.App.3d 538, 592 N.E.2d 1222 (Ill.App. 5 Dist. 1992); **Schultz v. State**, 106 Md.App. 145, 664 A.2d 60 (1995); **Ex parte Malone**, 575 So.2d 106 (Ala. 1990); **Cann-Hanson v. State**, 223 Ga.App. 690, 478 S.E.2d 460 (1996); **Kerr v. State**, 921 S.W.2d 498 (Tex.App.-Fort Worth 1996); **James v. State**, 260 Ga.App. 536, 580 S.E.2d 334 (2003); **State v. Tousley**, 271 Ga.App. 874, 611 S.E.2d 139 (2005); **State v. Baity**, 140 Wash.2d 1, 991 P.2d 1151 (2000).

[344]**State v. Tousley**, 271 Ga.App. 874, 611 S.E.2d 139 (2005); **Harper v. State**, 249 Ga. 519, 292 S.E.2d 389 (1982); **State v. Dille**, 258 N.W.2d 565 (Minn. 1977); **Reed v. State**, 283 Md. 374, 391 A.2d 364 (1978); **Hartman v. State**, 946 S.W.2d 60 (Tex.Crim.App. 1997); **Brim v. State**, 695 So.2d 268 (Fla. 1997); **State v. Porter**, 241 Conn. 57, 698 A.2d 739 (1997); **Ex parte Dolvin**, 391 So.2d 677 (Ala. 1980); **McGrew v. State**, 682 N.E.2d 1289 (Ind. 1997); **Crawley v. State**, 219 Tenn. 707, 413 S.W.2d 370 (Tenn. 1967); **State v. Baity**, 140 Wash.2d 1, 991 P.2d 1151 (2000); **Paty v. Director of Revenue**, 168 S.W.3d 625 (Mo.App. E.D. 2005).

was invalid, then the drunken driving charges against you must typically be dropped. This is why it is critical for you to remember every detail of all of the conversations and activities between you and the police officer that occurred in the time before your arrest. As soon as possible after your arrest, write down each and every detail of the entire involvement of the police officers, breath test operators, hospital personnel, etc.

6.10. Challenges relating to the officer's competence to administer field sobriety evaluations. Simply put, if the officer who administered the field sobriety tests is not able to prove that he or she was well trained and competent to give you those tests, your attorney may possibly be able to get the results of those tests thrown out of your case.[345] If the results cannot be thrown out due to the officer not being proven to be incompetent to give the tests, then demonstrating (at trial) his or her lack of experience or competence in properly administering, demonstrating or "grading" these evaluations may be used to challenge the weight and credibility of the evidence.[346] If your field sobriety evaluations are thrown out, it is likely the officer did not have enough probable cause to arrest you for DUI-DWI. Where probable cause is found to be lacking for your custodial arrest, the DUI-DWI charges must typically be dropped.[347]

Even the national media has begun understanding the unfairness and subjectivity of the so-called "field sobriety tests." After top-rated researchers have empirically shown that the evaluations are "designed to fail," the media has begun to reveal the soft underbelly of this mainstay of police work. See http://www.georgiacriminaldefense.com/dui-hokeypokey-sfst.htm.

A national effort to FORCE citizens to submit to field sobriety screening tests will be evident over the next decade. One primary focus will be to mandate roadside screening with portable alcohol screening devices. Manufacturers are presently making more portable devices for this purpose, including devices that print out a written score or result. Two of such devices are depicted below.

Intoximeter Alco-Sensor IV XL

---

[345]**People v. Bostelman,** 325 Ill.App.3d 22, 756 N.E.2d 953 (Ill.App. 2 Dist. 2001); **U.S. v. Kawa,** 25 F.3d 1059 (10th Cir.(Utah) 1994); **Davis v. State,** 2005 WL 1539710 (Tex.App.-Hous. (1st Dist.) 2005); **State v. Homan,** 89 Ohio St.3d 421, 732 N.E.2d 952 (Ohio 2000); **State v. Superior Court In and For Cochise County,** 149 Ariz. 269, 718 P.2d 171 (Ariz. 1986); **State v. Reisner,** 584 So.2d 141 (Fla.App. 5 Dist. 1991); **Kerr v. State,** 921 S.W.2d 498 (Tex.App.-Fort Worth 1996).

[346]**Cann-Hanson v. State,** 223 Ga.App. 690, 478 S.E.2d 460 (1996).

[347]**State, City of St. Louis Park v. Quinn,** 289 Minn. 184, 182 N.W.2d 843 (1971); **State v. Sickles,** 25 Ohio App.2d 1, 265 N.E.2d 787 (Ohio App. 5 Dist. 1970); **State v. Ellison,** 271 Ga.App. 898, 611 S.E.2d 129 (2005).

Draeger Alcotest 7410 Plus DOT

Depending on the state where your case is pending, your attorney may or may not be able to obtain information regarding the police officer's training and experience prior to trial or at a pre-trial hearing. However, it is usually available during trial. Until your attorney gets to question the officer who performed the field evaluations during your DUI-DWI stop, the flaws in his or her training or proper administration of the tests may not appear.

If proof of the officer's departure from or non-compliance with the proper procedures is to be established, your attorney will usually need an expert witness who is an instructor on these psycho-physical tests. An experienced DUI-DWI attorney likely knows the majority of the law enforcement officers in the geographic region in which he or she practices law, and will typically know which officers are deficient in administering the standardized field sobriety evaluations. Follow your attorney's advice in retaining an expert to neutralize this evidence against you by telling the jury how and why it was done incorrectly. Even hand-held breath alcohol screening tests can be exluded from evidence where police officers cannot prove compliance with mandatory periodic calibration checks or with establishing that the particular device used was an "approved" screening device.[348]

6.11. Challenges to the officer's ability and experience in distinguishing an impaired driver from an unimpaired driver. Certainly, a law enforcement officer with years of DUI-DWI arrests and with advanced extensive training in DUI-DWI evaluations and arrests is much more likely to be able to distinguish an impaired driver from a driver who is unimpaired and safe to drive. However, absent proof of advanced training, an officer's years of experience are not a guarantee of the officer's competence level.

Some officers will arrest ANY motorist who has the smell of alcohol on his or her breath when the person declines to participate in so-called "voluntary" field sobriety evaluations. Sometimes these arrests are made out of spite or in an abundance of caution, to assure that no impaired person drives away from the scene and kills someone else further down the road. Such arrests can be overturned and the DUI-DWI case dismissed as a result of pre-trial proceedings.[349] If not resolved pre-trial, your chances of acquittal at trial are probably excellent.

Any arrests that are made with little or no proof of the typical "manifestations" of drunken behavior or symptoms should be challenged by your attorney. The usual items cited by the police point out the smell of alcohol, admission to drinking, slurred speech, loss of balance, and

---

[348]**Turrentine v. State,** 176 Ga.App. 145, 335 S.E.2d 630 (1985); **Sharber v. State,** 750 N.E.2d 796 (Ind.App. 2001); **State v. Damon,** 328 Mont. 276, 119 P.3d 1194 (Mont. 2005); **State v. Doerr,** 229 Wis.2d 616, 599 N.W.2d 897 (Wis.App. 1999).

[349]**State v. Batty,** 259 Ga.App. 431, 577 S.E.2d 98 (2003) [driver had 0.143 and 0.158 test results]; **State v. Gray,** 267 Ga.App. 753, 600 S.E.2d 626 (2004) [single car accident with retaining wall and high breath test results]; **State v. Burke,** 230 Ga.App. 392, 496 S.E.2d 755 (1998) [motorcycle accident].

glazed or red bloodshot eyes. Reviewing this list will reveal why REMAINING SILENT can be critical in your quest for acquittal.

Your attorney may or may not be able to obtain background information regarding the law enforcement officer who made the determination to arrest you for DUI-DWI. This information may be unavailable at a pre-trial hearing or prior to your trial beginning. Many specialists in this field share transcripts on officers and assist fellow criminal defense lawyers in an effort to assure that all citizens obtain justice in these politically charged and often unfair legal proceedings.

6.12. Defenses relating to discovery abuse. Discovery is the use of statutorily established procedures in a criminal case to obtain information before trial through written demands for production of documents, for pre-trial depositions of parties and potential witnesses (where permitted), through written interrogatories (questions and answers written under oath)(if permitted), through written requests for admissions of fact, by undertaking an examination of the scene along with the petitions and motions employed to enforce these discovery rights. The prevailing theory of liberal rights of discovery in most states is that all parties will go to trial with as much knowledge of relevant information or key facts as possible. This entails an exchange of basic information such as a witness list from each side of the case. The laws of most states provide that neither party should be able to keep secrets from the other.[350] Most jurisdictions permit both sides to obtain fairly equal access to any information that is not privileged (meaning that certain evidence is protected from disclosure based upon some confidentiality, or upon a recognized privilege to not make disclosures).

In your DUI-DWI case, discovery is the formal process by which your side and the prosecution exchange information in accordance with state guidelines regarding evidence that will possibly be used at trial and previously recorded statements or testimony regarding your case. Depending on whether you have been charged with a misdemeanor DUI-DWI offense or a felony, your state may have different rules regarding discovery. In most states, the prosecution **must** release some basic information. This may entail releasing as little as the results from any scientific (blood, breath or urine) tests that the state proposes to admit at your trial,[351] a copy of the police report,[352] the names of any witnesses they plan on using at trial,[353] any statements you allegedly made to the police,[354] and any exculpatory evidence (evidence in the possession of the prosecution which shows or tends to show that you did not commit the crime of which you are charged.) This is the mandatory minimum of information the prosecutor must release to you and your attorney in accordance with the landmark United States Supreme Court decision in *Brady v. Maryland*.[355]

How much more information is mandated that the prosecution release to your attorney depends upon the law in your state. Florida[356] and Indiana[357] are among the most liberal of

---

[350]http://dictionary.law.com/default2.asp?selected=530&bold=discovery‖.

[351]Georgia - O.C.G.A. § 17-16-23; Fla. R. Crim. P. Rule 3.220(b)(1)(J); Tenn. R. Crim. P., Rule 16(a)(1)(D); Indiana - Trial Procedure Rule 26(B)(1); Washington - Rule CrRLJ 4.7(a)(1)(iii).

[352]Fla. R. Crim. P. Rule 3.220(b)(1)(B); Tenn. R. Crim. P., Rule 16(a)(1)(C); Vernon's Ann.Texas C.C.P. Art. 39.14(a); Indiana - Trial Procedure Rule 26(B)(1); Washington - Rule CrRLJ 4.7(a)(1)(iv).

[353]Georgia - O.C.G.A.§ 17-16-21; Fla. R. Crim. P. Rule 3.220(b)(1)(A); Indiana - Trial Procedure Rule 26(B)(1); Washington - Rule CrRLJ 4.7(a)(1)(i).

[354]Georgia - O.C.G.A. § 17-16-22; Fla. R. Crim. P. Rule 3.220(b)(1)(C); Tenn. R. Crim. P., Rule 16(a)(1)(A); Vernon's Ann.Texas C.C.P. Art. 39.14(a); Indiana - Trial Procedure Rule 26(B)(1); Washington - Rule CrRLJ 4.7(a)(1)(ii).

[355]**Brady v. Maryland,** 373 U.S. 83, 83 S.Ct. 1194, 10 L.Ed.2d 215 (1963).

[356]Fla. R. Crim. P. Rule 3.220.

states with regards to having to release as much as possible, while in Georgia and Virginia, only the minimum mandated by *Brady* is grudgingly released, and (in Virginia) often only at trial. How much is released depends on your state. Your DUI-DWI specialist can better explain your discovery rights under your jurisdiction's laws to you. He or she may utilize discovery at the administrative hearing to augment discovery for your upcoming criminal trial or to get a preview of what is to come later in your criminal case.

6.13. Defenses relating to exculpatory lost video evidence. In some DUI-DWI arrests, the arresting officer will have a video recording of all or part of the roadside conversation, field evaluations and chronology of the arrest process. If any law enforcement officer had a working camera at the arrest location, his or her department likely had in place a written departmental policy that the entire arrest should be recorded in order to be used later at trial. In the event a video was made at the scene, yet none can be located later, your attorney can likely use the loss of this potentially exculpatory evidence as a defense in your case. Depending on State law and decisional case law, the loss of this evidence may result in a significant strategic advantage in your case.

Combine this with your constitutionally guaranteed presumption of innocence until and unless proven guilty beyond a reasonable doubt and the best DUI-DWI specialists can attempt to get the charges against you reduced or totally dropped.[358] However, like with any defense, there are no guarantees of such a result, and your attorney must still demonstrate that the missing tape was favorable to you or that it may have shown your innocence.[359] States that shift this burden of proof to an accused citizen who is stopped along the side of the highway are more interested in processing criminal cases than in requiring the State to prove the case beyond a reasonable doubt. See also: http://www.duiblog.com/2005/04/24#a151.

6.14. Defenses related to the failure of the police to comply with the requirements of the State implied consent statute. In most States, once you have been arrested for DUI-DWI, the police officer making the arrest must inform you of specific rights under state law relating to your obligation to take a state-administered test of your blood, breath or urine, as well as other rights to refuse this testing. In some states, the officer may also be obligated to advise you of any independent test rights that you may have under state law. In these states, failure to strictly comply with the law will cause the State's test results to be excluded.

The practice among states varies regarding whether any formal advisement of your obligations and rights must be given by the officer. When it must be given, where it must be given, and what happens if you decline testing, covers the entire spectrum of likely legal challenges in your state. These rights are commonly known as "implied consent" rights. In some states, no advisement is formalized by state law. In others, it is part of state statute. In other states (like Arizona and Wisconsin), mere refusal of a first lifetime offense DUI-DWI from

---

[357]Indiana - Trial Procedure Rule 26.

[358]**State v. Benton,** 136 Ohio App.3d 801, 737 N.E.2d 1046 (Ohio App. 6 Dist. 2000).

[359]**State v. Ferguson,** 2 S.W.3d 912 (Tenn. 1999); **State v. Nelson,** 399 N.W.2d 629 (Minn.App. 1987); **Chissell v. State,** 705 N.E.2d 501 (Ind.App. 1999); **State v. Belgarde,** 289 Mont. 287, 962 P.2d 571 (1998); **People v. Camp,** 352 Ill.App.3d 257, 815 N.E.2d 980 (Ill.App. 2 Dist. 2004); **State v. Rivers,** 837 So.2d 594 (Fla.App. 2 Dist. 2003); **Spaulding v. State,** 195 Ga.App. 420, 394 S.E.2d 111 (1990); **State v. Benson,** 152 Ohio App.3d 495, 788 N.E.2d 693 (2003); **State v. Benton,** 136 Ohio App.3d 801, 737 N.E.2d 1046 (Ohio App. 6 Dist. 2000); **State v. Ward,** 17 P.3d 87 (Alaska App. 2001).

a roadblock stop will authorize the police officer to draw blood by force, *plus* seek to take away your license for your refusal.[360]

Of course, if you do refuse, in most states, this can be used against you by the prosecution at trial. Plus, you will likely then have your license suspended or revoked for a period of time as a result of having refused. In some states, a refusal can carry jail time or other penalties beyond a license suspension. (**Appendix H**)

It is common for the implied consent warning to be tied to either your age or your possible status as a holder of a commercial driver's license (CDL). Examples of these implied consent warnings from several states can be seen in **Appendix D**.

Your state may give you no option but to submit to a test, even resorting to physical force to extract blood or gather urine through a catheter. Furthermore, states vary greatly in their allowance of an independent test of your own choosing. For example, Georgia will allow liberal accommodation of an independent test or tests, but only if you have first submitted to the state's test. A very few courts, however, have ruled that restricting the right to an independent test to those who submit to police testing is a denial of due process and that persons who refuse chemical testing still have the right to an independent chemical test.[361]

In states that require the officer's strict compliance with reading a specific implied consent advisement, non-compliance by the officer will result in exclusion of the State's test result. In some states (e.g., Georgia) even evidence of your "refusal to be tested" will be excluded if non-compliance with the strict rules controlling the implied consent advisement are not followed.[362]

In other states, very loose rules exist regarding when and what must be told to you as a DUI-DWI suspect. Plus, many states place no obligation upon the police to transport you to a testing facility or otherwise accommodate a request for independent testing of your blood, breath or urine. If denied this important right, collect the names of all who denied you this opportunity to collect evidence, plus call "911" on a pay phone to ask the operator to assist you in obtaining your independent test.

If you were not read the correct implied consent warning at all, your attorney is likely to argue that you were denied a reasonable explanation of your implied consent testing options. If you did not understand your legal rights, any action you took with regard to submitting to or declining the state's chemical tests was not made with a full understanding of your options. Your attorney may be able to get any unfavorable test results excluded from being introduced at trial. Without these test results showing a scientific measurement of either drugs and/or alcohol in your system at the time of the testing, the DUI-DWI charges against you may be dismissed or reduced to a lesser offense.

6.15. Defenses related to the failure of the police to comply with the requirements of the state's independent test statute. One of the usual requirements of the implied consent law is that you have the right to obtain an independent test of your blood, breath or urine taken after you submit to the State-administered test.[363] This sample can be

---

[360]**State v. Clary**, 196 Ariz. 610, 2 P.3d 1255 (Ariz.App. Div. 1 2000); **State v. Bohling**, 173 Wis.2d 529, 494 N.W.2d 399 (Wis. 1993).

[361]**Snyder v. State**, 930 P.2d 1274 (Alaska, 1996); **State v. Swanson**, 722 P.2d 1155 (Mont., 1986).

[362]**State v. Leviner,** 213 Ga.App. 99, 443 S.E.2d 688 (1994).

[363]Georgia - O.C.G.A. § 40-6-392(a)(3); Texas - V.T.C.A., Transportation Code § 724.019; Tennessee - T. C. A. § 55-10-410(e); Florida - West's F.S.A. § 316.1932(3); Mississippi - Miss. Code Ann. § 63-1-84;

tested independently by a laboratory of your choice (and at your expense) in order to permit you to challenge the State's test result that will be used against you at trial.

Your independent test also protects against the possibility of a switched sample by the police and state crime lab. Numerous examples of samples of one person being switched with another person's sample have been reported in several states. Lawsuits have been filed to collect damages for such negligence. If your State statute requires that you be given this opportunity for independent testing, and you were not accommodated by the police, most states provide for exclusion of the State's tests.

In some states, the protection of the right to an independent test by a facility of your choosing is strictly applied against the police. For example, in Georgia, even if you obtained an independent test at a hospital, if the hospital was *a different one* than you selected, the State loses the ability to introduce its tests.[364] Georgia also has decided that just because the police help you get your blood drawn for your independent test, they must also reasonably accommodate you in getting that blood tested or the State's test results will not be able to be introduced at your trial (for example, at the hospital, the hospital cannot simply draw your blood, then simply hand you the vial).[365]

However, there are states where non-compliance with the implied consent statute does not negate the scientific reliability or admissibility of the results of your tests at trial.[366] These states have abandoned reasonable protection of their citizens' rights in favor of prosecuting cases even where the evidence cannot be fairly challenged by the citizen due to police non-compliance.

6.16. Defenses related to prosecution's ability to prove the elements of the offense, other than impairment. To be convicted of a DUI-DWI charge, the State has to prove each of the "elements" of each offense against you beyond a reasonable doubt. An "element" (one of the essential components of the criminal offense) is an essential part of the offense charged. For example, "driving" is a central element in most common law DUI-DWI cases, even though many states have expanded "driving" by also covering "actual physical control" to cover situations where driving has ceased, but strong evidence exists that the car was recently driven (or is observed with the engine still running).

This means, even if the State can prove that you were intoxicated, they still have to prove that you were either "driving," "operating" or in "actual physical control" of your vehicle at the time of your intoxication. Thus, while it is illegal to be driving while intoxicated, it may not be a crime in your state to be "sleeping off" your intoxication in the driver's seat of your car if it doesn't move, the engine is not running, or the key is not in the ignition. Decisional law indicates that being out of the driver's seat (sleeping in the rear passenger area) or not having access to the ignition key (possibly locked in the trunk) will create better facts to show lack of "actual physical control" of the vehicle.

If your criminal defense attorney can show to the court that the State cannot prove any one element of a DUI-DWI charge against you, then the entire charge typically can be defeated. Often, prosecutors are hesitant to reduce or dismiss these cases. This is why the best DUI-DWI attorneys challenge any inconsistencies in the police reports and investigate

---

Alabama - Ala.Code 1975 § 32-5A-194; Washington - West's RCWA 46.61.506(6); California - West's Ann.Cal.Vehicle Code § 23158(b).

[364]**Joel v. State,** 245 Ga.App. 750, 538 S.E.2d 847 (2000); **State v. Hughes,** 181 Ga.App. 464, 352 S.E.2d 643 (1987).

[365]**Koontz v. State,** 274 Ga.App. 248, 617 S.E.2d 207 (2005).

[366]**State v. Zielke,** 137 Wis.2d 39, 403 N.W.2d 427 (1987).

these cases thoroughly. Your attorney will need to know every fact that you can remember about the entire day leading up to your arrest.

6.17. Defenses related to the prosecution's ability to prove the required degree of intoxication other than by chemical testing. If the State lacks any scientific test results of your blood, breath or urine (either because you refused, the police did not perform such a test, or possibly due to a machine or lab malfunction), the State may still attempt to prove you were DUI-DWI by other means.[367] These "means" may include your poor performance on any voluntary field sobriety tests, any physical evidence observed, detected or seized by the police at the time of your arrest (*examples:* smell of alcohol, open container of alcohol, observing red, blood-shot eyes, hearing slurred speech). These manifestations or observable symptoms can form the basis of "opinion" testimony from either the police or other witnesses that assert that you looked or acted somewhat "drunk." Each year, thousands of citizens are convicted on such questionable "opinion" evidence.

Remember, in most states, if a chemical test indicates an alcohol level at or over the legal limit, there is both a *per se* DUI-DWI and a separate common law (traditional) driving under the influence charge [where the State must prove that the presence of alcohol (or possibly drugs) in your system caused impairment]. When the State does not have a scientific test "number" or illegal substance (such as marijuana in the blood), the only type of DUI-DWI charge that can be prosecuted is a common law alcohol impairment offense or drug impairment offense based largely on smell of these substances and possible admissions by you of use of these substances (or maybe both, if sufficient evidence supports this).

In different states, this other scientific evidence may or may not be available to your attorney as a part of the pre-trial discovery process. You may have to wait until a pre-trial hearing or the beginning of your trial to uncover exactly what this other evidence will be. Such procedures hamper your attorney's ability to prepare for your trial. Your attorney will likely need to anticipate the State's evidence and subpoena your own witnesses to help prepare your defense if he or she has found issues with the State's scientific testing. Remember, it is still the State's burden to prove beyond a reasonable doubt each and every element of any charge against you.

The best DUI-DWI attorneys know the names and expert training background of an array of expert witnesses, and the location of manuals or regulations that can provide ammunition to challenge the State's scientific evidence. Such witnesses or evidence will cost money to bring to court, but will be essential to your case. These witnesses charge for their time in preparing for court, reviewing your case file and being available to provide expert opinion evidence about some disputed aspect of your case.

6.18. Defenses related to the admissibility of the prosecution's breath testing evidence. If you did submit to a State administered breath test, in light of your presumption of innocence, the prosecution must prove that at the time of your test the electronic equipment was in proper working order, that it had been properly maintained and that the breath test was conducted in a proper fashion.[368] This is an area of DUI-DWI law that is a

---

[367]D. Shinar, E. Schechtman, R. Compton, *Drug identification on the basis of observable signs and symptoms*, Accident Analysis and Prevention, 2005.

[368]**Luginbyhl v. Com.,** 46 Va.App. 460, 618 S.E.2d 347 (Va.App. 2005); **Nivens v. State,** 832 N.E.2d 1134 (Ind.App. 2005); **City of Columbus v. Childs,** 2005 WL 1693624 (Ohio App. 10 Dist. 2005); **Gumma v. White,** 216 Ill.2d 23, 833 N.E.2d 834 (Ill. 2005); **Bozarth v. Director of Revenue, State of Missouri,** 168 S.W.3d 78 (Mo.App. E.D. 2005); **Belvin v. State,** 2005 WL 1336497 (Fla.App. 4 Dist. 2005); **State v. Palmaka,** 266 Ga.App. 595, 597 S.E.2d 630 (2004); **State v. Sensing,** 843 S.W.2d 412

hotbed of appellate litigation on both the federal level and the state level. See news of a challenge in Florida at http://www.abanet.org/journal/ereport/n18breath.html and a different type of challenge in Texas at http://www.duiblog.com/2005/10/29 for two very recent examples of this trend.

If the prosecution fails to provide all of this proof, the test results may be excluded (not allowed) as part of the trial evidence against you. In most states, however, discrepancies in the manner that the breath test operator conducted the test may go only to the weight of the State's chemical test evidence. This means that the test result comes into evidence and then your attorney puts up evidence to counter it. For example, you may have excellent proof that your breath test was taken during the absorptive stage of alcohol intake and metabolism (burn off), and this can cause falsely high readings.[369] If these test results are barred from being used against you, it is likely the DUI-DWI charges against you may be dismissed, or a "reduced" charge (to a less serious offense than drunk driving) may be negotiated by your attorney. If this is not possible, then at least your chances for acquittal are improved because you can show flawed evidence (by use of expert testimony) at trial. Another possibility is that the State's representatives simply cheated at reporting breath test accuracy reports.

6.19. Defenses related to the failure of the police to comply with standard operating procedure during the arrest or forensic testing. Since every state has breath testing equipment that is used in the great majority of DUI-DWI cases, each state has put into place some type of "shortcut" method by which the prosecution can introduce the breath test into evidence. This saves costs, since the person who checked the machine's calibration may not be required to appear at court to prove the underlying scientific theory and reliability of the breath machine used in your case. If such detailed proof is provided, this is called "laying the foundation" for admission of the breath test results.

This cost-saving procedure may be subject to a challenge by your criminal defense specialist on grounds that your Sixth Amendment right of confrontation is violated when a certificate of inspection is permitted to admit the breath test results against you. Your attorney cannot cross-examine a piece of paper. Recent case law from the United States Supreme Court and several state courts around the country may cause these "short-cut" methods of establishing a foundation to be deemed insufficient,[370] while other states have declared these methods valid.[371]

The best DUI-DWI attorneys know the procedures that are utilized by the various police departments in their area. These experienced legal advisors also know the reasons behind the steps in the calibration checking procedures. Failure to follow the proper procedures for either your DUI-DWI arrest or for handling the scientific or documentary evidence collected from your arrest (blood, urine or breath samples, the police video, any photos taken by the police of the

---

(Tenn. 1992); **Howes v. State,** 120 S.W.3d 903 (Tex.App.-Texarkana 2003); **City of Seattle v. Allison,** 148 Wash.2d 75, 59 P.3d 85 (2002); **Robertson v. State,** 604 So.2d 783 (Fla. 1992). There is a report out of the March 30, 2005 *Toronto Sun*, by Ian Robertson, that a man attempted to foil the breathalyzer machine by stuffing his mouth full of his own feces. This is likely outside of the police protocol.

[369]See http://www.duiblog.com/2005/03/22#a129.

[370]**Crawford v. Washington,** 541 U.S. 36, 124 S.Ct. 1354, 158 L.Ed.2d 177 (2004); **Belvin v. State,** 922 So.2d 1046 (Fla. 4th DCA 2006); **Shiver v. State,** 900 So.2d 615 (Fla.App. 1 Dist. 2005); **People v. Orpin,** 8 Misc.3d 768, 796 N.Y.S.2d 512 (N.Y.Just.Ct. 2005).

[371]**Pierce v. State,** 278 Ga.App. 162, 628 S.E.2d 235 (2006); **Brown v. State,** 268 Ga. 76, 485 S.E.2d 486 (Ga. 1997); **State v. Cook,** 2005 WL 736671, 2005-Ohio-1550 (Ohio App. 6 Dist. 2005); **Napier v. State,** 820 N.E.2d 144 (Ind.App. 2005); **State v. Godshalk,** 381 N.J.Super. 326, 885 A.2d 969 (N.J.Super.L. 2005); **Harkins v. State,** 735 So.2d 317 (Miss. 1999).

scene or of you, etc.) can result in your attorney successfully arguing pre-trial motions that can either cause the case to be dismissed or be the basis for exclusion of key State evidence.

Missing videotapes or the loss of other critical evidence may be fatal to the State's case.[372] While protections are put in place to protect the police officers during the arrest by allowing them to make video and audio recordings, a breach of the rules for storage and retention of video evidence may be held against the police, due to the defense lawyer's argument that the destroyed or lost evidence would be favorable to you. Such destruction of evidence or mishandling of evidence is called "spoliation" of evidence, and operates to the State's detriment in most situations. The concept, simply stated, is that the State had control and custody of this critical evidence and somehow squandered it or destroyed it, leaving you less able to fully defend your case.

Your memory of the events and sequence of the arrest process can be critical to identifying this type of issue for your defense. Recounting the chronological progression of what transpired in the hours surrounding your arrest for DUI-DWI can be critical to your attorney if a videotape disappears.

6.20. Defenses related to the credibility of the prosecution's breath testing evidence. To be allowed to tell the jury your breath tests results, the prosecution must first "lay a foundation" to support the introduction of the "numbers" that are to be considered by the jury. The prosecutor must establish that the machine was in good working order and that it had been used in the manner approved by the State.[373]

One of the most important "science" lessons you need to know if you are facing a breath test (or even a blood test) is how the human body ingests, circulates and processes alcohol. When you understand that issue better, you can see how a knowledgeable attorney can challenge ANY case involving indirect testing devices that are often purchased or approved for state use due to a LOW BID process. Read this excellent article by Dr. David Benjamin, a Ph.D. Pharmacologist: http://www.drunkdrivingdefense.com/how-we-process-alcohol.htm.

In the United States, there are fewer than 10 versions of evidential breath testing instruments in use today. This includes various models or "generations" of machines known by the same "trade" name. For example, the Intoximeter EC-IR has a series I and a series II machine. The Intoxilyzer 5000 has its most recent "EN" version of its 68 series, plus the older generation 68 series, the 66 series and the 64 series. See this informative article about the constant changes in "state-of-the-art" breath devices: **http://www.duiblog.com/2005/10/06#a254**.

One of the devices used in some states (the Draeger) is a German-designed machine and the other nine versions are owned by three American companies. Your knowledgeable DUI-DWI attorney MUST know detailed information on how the machine used in your case operates to have a realistic chance of winning ANY trials that involve a breath test reading that has an alcohol content reading OVER THE PER SE LIMIT.

---

[372]**State v. Benson,** 152 Ohio App.3d 495, 788 N.E.2d 693 (2003). **State v. Benton,** 136 Ohio App.3d 801, 737 N.E.2d 1046 (Ohio App. 6 Dist. 2000); **State v. Ward,** 17 P.3d 87 (Alaska App. 2001).

[373]**City of Seattle v. Allison,** 148 Wash.2d 75, 59 P.3d 85 (2002); **Luginbyhl v. Com.,** 46 Va.App. 460, 618 S.E.2d 347 (Va.App. 2005); **Nivens v. State,** 832 N.E.2d 1134 (Ind.App. 2005); **City of Columbus v. Childs,** 2005 WL 1693624 (Ohio App. 10 Dist. 2005); **Gumma v. White,** 216 Ill.2d 23, 833 N.E.2d 834 (Ill. 2005); **Bozarth v. Director of Revenue, State of Missouri,** 168 S.W.3d 78 (Mo.App. E.D. 2005); **Belvin v. State,** 2005 WL 1336497 (Fla.App. 4 Dist. 2005); **State v. Palmaka,** 266 Ga.App. 595, 597 S.E.2d 630 (2004); **State v. Sensing,** 843 S.W.2d 412 (Tenn. 1992); **Howes v. State,** 120 S.W.3d 903 (Tex.App.-Texarkana 2003).

The information in this book is not intended to provide you with detailed information about the intricacies of how these devices work, or how and why they can be proven to be inaccurate or unreliable, under certain circumstances. Your highly trained criminal defense specialist who handles these impaired driving cases will be able to advise you on challenges that can be made in your case, based upon your state's regulations, your personal health issues, your "contamination or interference" issues, or possible challenges to your state's shoddy breath testing program.

For more information on specific ways to challenge a breath machine result, see these excellent and informative sources: (1) Drunk Driving Defense [http://www.duicenter.com/books/order.html]; (2) Free Internet Overview of the Intoxilyzer [http://www.science.howstuffworks.com/breathalyzer4.htm]; (3) Basic science history and overview [http://www.ncdd.com/dsp_articledetails.cfm?article=2]; (4) Infrared spectroscopy basic information: [http://www.science.howstuffworks.com/breathalyzer.htm]; (5) Weaknesses in the Intoxilyzer 5000: [http://www.drunkdrivingdefense.com/publications-articles/intoxilyzer-5000-weaknesses.htm] and in the author's state law book through Thomson-West: [http://www.drunkdrivingdefense.com/publications-articles/georgia-dui-trial-practice.htm]; (6) "Breath Testing Equipment: What Every Citizen Must Know," by the Author - [http://www.drunkdrivingdefense.com/general/breath-testing-information.htm]; (7) *Annotation, **Trial Defenses to a Breath Test Score,*** 70 Am. Jur. Trials 1 (2006); and (8) the second edition of "101 Ways to Avoid a Drunk Driving Conviction," which features over 40 separate technical challenges to breath testing devices, due to be published July 4, 2006: [http://www.theduibook.com/101waysbook.htm].

Police in most jurisdictions are permitted by statutes or regulations to utilize battery-powered fuel cell devices to screen suspected intoxicated drivers at the roadside. The numerical results from these devices usually cannot be admitted into evidence (i.e., put in front of a jury). In the states that do not allow the "number" to be introduced, most allow the officer to say that the result obtained was "positive" or "negative" for alcohol. These devices are referred to by the acronym "PBT" (preliminary breath tester, or portable breath test).

Other states, (e.g., California and Iowa) allow the number to be admitted as part of the evidence at trial. A few devices that are portable and battery powered also have portable printer connections and capability, so that a printed result can be generated, and (if state law permits) these results be introduced into evidence in your criminal case. (See RBT model below, right).

Intoximeter Alco-Sensor IV [DOT]

Intoxilyzer S-D2

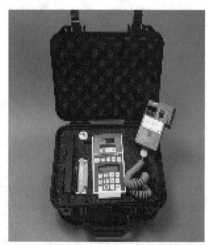
Intoximeter RBT IV (with printer)

On the next three pages are photos of the various evidential breath testing devices in use across America in 99% of all cases prosecuted today. Also included with the manufacturer's images of its devices is the URL to show where you can go to obtain more information on a particular brand of evidential breath test. Remember that each manufacturer is using these web sites to "hype" its breath testing machine, so read each site's claims with a grain of salt.

America's Evidential Breath Testing Devices

National Patent Analytical Systems (NPAS) has three primary models of equipment in current use. NPAS is the ONLY manufacturer that opens its doors and its maintenance records for review by criminal defense attorneys, without being forced by a court of law to do so. The three devices are shown below, starting with the oldest device (BAC DATAMASTER) and moving to the most recently released. See their web site at: http://www.npas.com/

BAC DATAMASTER

Datamaster CDM

Datamaster DMT

http://www.npas.com/

German-made Draeger 7110 Mark III-C

http://www.draeger.com/

CMI, Inc. from Owensboro, Kentucky, makes two versions of the Intoxilyzer. The 8000 is the newer device, and was designed for better portability and dual-wavelength confirmation of alcohol.

Intoxilyzer 8000

Intoxilyzer 5000

http://www.alcoholtest.com/

Intoximeter EC-IR (Models I and II)

http://www.intox.com/

In most states, you will have been asked to give two breath "exhalations" within a specified time period on one of these devices. These two results must "agree" (must be close enough to the same number) and be close enough to demonstrate reliability.[374] The printed results MUST be saved and preserved to prove the results for your test; otherwise, all results should be suppressed. In states that use and save all test results by way of computer database, a lost test card may be replaced by the computer data. For those that do not save results or use a computer, any attempt to introduce the "number" is subject to several constitutional challenges, including confrontation and due process.

In a few states, only one breath exhalation is mandated, and this faulty procedure ("faulty" because the result has not been repeated to show that the initial reading was a reliable reading) is "good enough for government work."[375] From a scientific reliability standpoint, single analysis of a forensic sample without verification or replication is scientifically deficient. Any college chemistry professor will testify to the inherent scientific lack of reliability of single analysis "forensic" samples.

Issues of "specificity" relating to infrared or fuel cell breath testing devices have been the Achilles heel of many devices. Solvents that are inhaled by way of work-related contamination of workplace air laced with solvents have produced many false results. Common chemicals (such as toluene) found in many oil-based paints, varnishes, paint thinners, cleaning solvents in auto repair businesses, glues, mineral spirits, stains and similar products can produce false high "readings" on some breath testing devices under certain conditions. Be sure to advise your qualified DUI-DWI defense attorney of any such issues that might relate to your case.

The author has had clients with reported exposure from working in the field of floor refinishing, auto body repair, chemical companies (sold small package products after being purchased in bulk) and even cases where common household solvents such as Formula 409™ were used. Most exposure comes from inhalation, versus absorption through the skin. However, both types of absorption are possible with certain volatile chemicals.

---

[374]Georgia - **State v. Kruzel,** 261 Ga.App. 90, 581 S.E.2d 711 (2003); O.C.G.A. § 40-6-392(a)(1)(B); Washington - West's RCWA 46.61.506(4)(a)(vi).

[375]Texas - **Fulenwider v. State,** 2004 WL 1585286 (Tex.App.-Hous. (1 Dist.) 2004); Tennessee - **State v. Korsakov,** 34 S.W.3d 534 (Tenn.Crim.App. 2000); Florida - West's F.S.A. § 316.1932; **State v. St. Amant,** 504 So.2d 1094 (La.App. 5 Cir. 1987).

See the article on the next page from a case the author handled nearly 20 years ago, where a worker's exposure to floor finishing products elevated his breath test results to more than 4 times the true alcohol result. This device, the Intoximeter 3000, has now been replaced by the Intoximeter EC-IR machine, but a considerable portion of the mechanical underpinnings of the new machine are all but identical to the older 3000 series instrument.

New Drunken-Driving Defense Causes a Stir

BY ANDREW BLUM

National Law Journal Staff Reporter

IN A NEW TWIST to drunken-driving cases, a handful of defense attorneys have begun challenging the validity of "driving while intoxicated" (DWI) tests by arguing that their clients were not legally under the influence of alcohol but had instead inhaled chemical solvents on the job.

Attorneys in Georgia and Minnesota have claimed that their clients' inhaling vapors from solvents used in such products as paint, floor finish and cement had given a false indication on Intoximeter® devices. The devices are intended to test how much a person has been drinking by measuring the alcohol content of his or her breath.

Others in the DWI defense bar had not come across any such cases in their practice but said it seemed plausible. "There's no doubt in my mind it can happen," said John A. Tarantino of Providence, R.I.'s Adler Pollack & Sheehan, Inc.

However, a prosecutor in one of the cases derided the defense, calling it a new "tactic for creating reasonable doubt" in the jurors' minds.

In Georgia, where the drunken-driving statute is known as DUI (driving under the influence), William C. Head defended a man who had been putting a finish on a gymnasium floor and was arrested later that day for drunken driving. *State v. Keating*, ST-86-TM-0867 (State Ct., Clarke Cty.).

University Town

The Athens, Ga., case at first seemed typical; the University of Georgia is located there, and police are tough on drunken driving, Mr. Head explained.

"But this was not a student," he said, adding [that] his client [who] was in his 40s, was able to prove he was working with solvents, and had "1 ½ beers" after work -- not enough to make him drunk.

Mr. Head of Athens' McDonald, Head, Carney & Haggard, asked the judge handling the case to allow him to conduct an experiment to recreate the job situation. The judge agreed, but only if a police officer monitored the defendant, James Keating, the entire day.

The officer chosen, a 25-year-old "teetotaler," was an athlete and "looked like Hercules," said Mr. Head. At the end of the day with Mr. Keating, the officer tested with a higher "alcohol" reading than the defendant.

The judge dismissed the charges before trial, said Mr. Head, adding that even the state prosecutor -- a former pharmacist -- did not object to the dismissal after learning of the officer's test. The prosecutor was unavailable for comment.

[Adapted from *The National Law Journal*, Monday, April 18, 1988, p.7]

The State's failure to "lay a proper foundation" will result in the test results not being admitted into evidence. Such a failure of proof of a key part of the DUI-DWI case can either end the case or render the remaining "proof" inadequate to support your conviction. [See more ideas from the checklist contained in **Appendix I.**]

6.21. Defenses related to the admissibility of the prosecution's blood testing evidence. Blood testing procedures are entirely different from breath testing measures. For a blood test to be admissible as evidence, the prosecutor has to demonstrate the reliability of the test by putting forth various witnesses. For the results of the State's test to be admissible, the State must show that it was performed in such a way that the results obtained should be considered accurate and that the substance being tested (i.e., blood, breath or urine) came from you and no one else.[376]

The first area of proof focuses upon whether or not the test machine itself was properly calibrated, whether or not the test was run correctly and run by someone capable, trained and authorized to operate the machine. If the blood test results being used against you were drawn as a part of a medical evaluation following an accident (in a hospital), rather than those drawn at the express direction of the police for evaluation in a crime lab, the testing must still have been done in compliance with the statutory standards for such "forensic" tests.[377]

The second area of inquiry focuses on the State's ability to establish the **chain of custody** for your sample. This issue may be raised in virtually all blood test cases due to the fact that any sample of a bodily substance can "decompose" (spoil). This decomposition process can actually generate (create) ethyl alcohol, which is the type of alcohol in all alcoholic beverages. Your attorney focuses upon whether the sample was collected properly, whether the sample was stored properly, whether the collection tubes were the correct type required for forensic testing, whether your arm was swabbed with a non-alcoholic pad, when and where the samples were stored in a refrigerated receptacle, whether the nurse or phlebotomist properly inverted the vial of blood before sealing the package for shipment to the crime lab, and similar issues that involve the "integrity" of the sample.

Even when grossly improper handling of your blood sample is shown by your attorney, the lab results may not be automatically excluded from evidence at trial. In some states, any discrepancies in the chain of custody may go to the *weight* of the evidence, and not cause the lab results to be excluded.[378] In others, the judge acts as gatekeeper and decides what evidence is too tenuous to be allowed to be used by the State in its prosecution of a case.[379] In the states that require the prosecution to establish a full and unbroken chain of custody, the lab results may be kept out of evidence. Such an exclusion by a trial court often ends the "per se" alcohol case, due to a "lack of evidence" to support that DUI-DWI charge against you. [See more ideas from the checklist contained in **Appendix I.**] Such exclusion of this critical evidence in an accident case can cause the State's entire case to fail.

6.22. Defenses related to the credibility of the prosecution's blood testing evidence. Before a blood test result may be admitted by your trial judge into evidence against you, the prosecutor must be able to cross several "hurdles" that your defense lawyer may raise. At each point in the prosecutor's offer of proof that the blood test was properly collected, stored, refrigerated and tracked (as it goes in and out of the laboratory's refrigeration units), your defense attorney will be challenging the completeness of the State's record-keeping and the scientific propriety of each step.

---

[376]**Taylor v. State,** 855 So.2d 1 (Fla. 2003); **Serrano v. State,** 936 S.W.2d 387 (Tex.App.-Hous. (14 Dist.) 1996); **Self v. State,** 232 Ga.App. 735, 503 S.E.2d 625 (1998); **State v. Goodman,** 643 S.W.2d 375; **Parris v. Zolin,** 12 Cal.4th 839, 911 P.2d 9 (Cal. 1996)); **Nix v. State,** 276 So.2d 652 (Miss. 1973); **Hayes v. State,** 514 N.E.2d 332 (Ind.App. 3 Dist. 1987); **Cole v. State ex rel. Dept. of Transp. & Development,** 755 So.2d 315 (La.App. 3 Cir. 1999); **City of Cleveland v. Byers,** 1997 WL 10149 (Ohio App. 8 Dist. 1997); **State v. Goodman,** 643 S.W.2d 375 (Tenn.Crim.App. 1982).

[377]**State of Ohio v. Mayl,** 106 Ohio.3d 207 (2005).

[378]Ala.Code 1975 § 12-21-13; **Self v. State,** 232 Ga.App. 735, 503 S.E.2d 625 (1998); **Tennant v. Roys,** 44 Wash.App. 305, 722 P.2d 848 (1986); **State v. Morales,** 170 Ariz. 360, 824 P.2d 756 (Ariz.App. Div. 2 1991).

[379] **Whitfield v. State,** 524 A.2d 13 (Del. 1987).

For blood alcohol tests (as opposed to blood tests for drugs), it is essential that the blood be drawn in a correct manner, using a brownish-red colored solution (Betadine) or white (Hibaclens) soap rather than an alcohol pad or swab. If alcohol is used to prepare your skin before the needle insertion, then this may artificially raise the alcohol content in the sample due to contamination by the alcohol on the surface of your skin. The additive effect from such an alcohol-based swab has been reported to be as high as 0.16%.

Next, the receptacle in which a "legal" blood alcohol must be collected and held is a grey-top tube. These tubes are most often "Vacutainers®," a product manufactured by Becton-Dickinson.[380] The color of the top (the rubber stopper) is very important in this blood collection process.

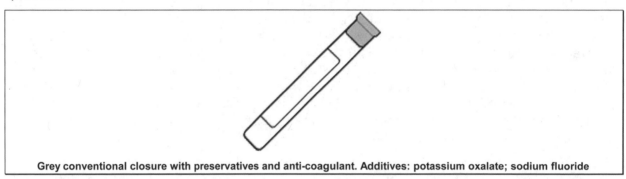

Grey conventional closure with preservatives and anti-coagulant. Additives: potassium oxalate; sodium fluoride

Red-stopper tubes are also used by hospitals (for many of their testing procedures) for a determination of your blood alcohol level, and also for some drug screens. However, because these tubes have no chemicals added as preservatives or anti-coagulants, any tests must be run on the blood samples in these tubes within a few hours due to the fact that the blood will clot and otherwise become putrid and decompose very quickly. As mentioned in the previous section, when blood putrefies, it decomposes into a variety of by-products. One of these by-products generated is the production of ethanol (alcohol). This alcohol is indistinguishable from any alcohol (ethanol) that you drink.

One of the differences in a grey-top tube is that these vials contain one of several powdered or liquid preservatives. Scientists call these chemicals, as a category, "bacteriastats." A properly mixed vial of your blood and these bacteriastats will be "stable" for several days or even weeks, especially if properly refrigerated.

Whoever draws (collects) your blood must gently invert the tube to mix this preservative with your blood immediately after drawing it. This is typically done by gently inverting and rocking the grey-topped tube 12 to 15 times to assure dissemination of the powder or liquid throughout your blood. Incomplete mixing of all of the powdered or liquid preservative can lead to putrefaction and decomposition. Shaking the tube too vigorously can cause the structural components of the blood cells to break down. Such "breaking open" of the cell structures can lead to flawed results when the sample is analyzed.

Another defense your attorney may raise deals with using the incorrect type (colored stopper) of tube. Most state crime labs mandate the color of the stopper in the test tube so that decomposition of samples that sit in the lab for a long time is minimized due to being mixed with powdered or liquid chemicals designed to retard bacterial growth. Your DUI-DWI defense attorney will know what your state's regulations or rules mandate for the blood collection vial's stopper color.

---

[380]http://www.bd.com.

If the blood was not inverted correctly so as to mix with the preservative and anti-coagulant, then any results can be challenged by your defense attorney. The attorney will use cross-examination of the prosecutor's witnesses to start creating "reasonable doubt." Then, expert witnesses may be called to testify on your behalf to show how the flawed handling of the blood likely could result in a falsely elevated blood alcohol reading. If the tests are not scientifically credible, then the alleged alcohol reading should not be used against you at trial. [See more ideas from the checklist contained in **Appendix I.**]

6.23. Defenses related to police misconduct or perjury. For a variety or reasons, police and crime lab workers sometimes cheat. Often, it is to save time or money. Other times, neglect or sloppiness is the problem. This misconduct overshadows and taints the State's "forensic" test results that are sought to be used against you. Your skilled defense attorney will know how to focus the jury's attention on the false testimony or shoddy laboratory work of the State crime lab and move the jury's attention away from your "alleged" blood alcohol (or drug) tests.

Perjury is the crime of intentionally lying after being duly sworn (to tell the truth) by a notary public, judge, court clerk or other official.[381] Also, modern statutes often make certain types of government documents (such as police officers' reports) "sworn" documents even without a notary witnessing the officer's signature or swearing to an oath. One of the most serious acts of misconduct a law enforcement officer can do is to commit perjury. Jurors and judges tend to discredit all testimony of any witness who can be proven to have departed from telling the truth on any issue involved in a criminal prosecution.

Showing perjury or a prior inconsistent statement is an important first step in convincing a jury (or a judge) that the officer or lab technician is not worthy of belief on any issue. Your defense attorney will ask the judge for a jury instruction that tells the jurors that if they find a lack of credibility of any witness, they can disregard the witness' entire testimony.

6.24. The defense of an unconstitutional or invalidly-adopted drinking and driving statute or related ordinance. In order for you to be guilty of a crime, you have to have violated a law that is constitutionally valid. As an example, if the government attempted to pass a DUI-DWI law that eliminated the requirement that some type of "actual physical control" for driving or operating a motor vehicle be presented by the prosecutor, this law would certainly be found unconstitutional. If a statute is ruled to be unconstitutional, it cannot be used as the basis of charging you with a crime.

An example of such a statute in DUI-DWI law can be seen in a recent statute in the State of Washington. In 2005, Linda Callahan, a prominent Washington DUI-DWI attorney, challenged Washington's new statute [RCW 46.61.506(4)], which *requires* a judge to admit a breath test when the prosecution meets the factors listed there as prima facie proof of a reliable BAC. Under the Washington statute, the judge is *required* to assume the truth of the prosecution's evidence and the defense is not allowed to challenge the evidence in a pre-trial hearing. She challenged the constitutional fairness of the law that made legal challenges to the State's evidence before this key prosecution evidence is revealed in the presence of the jury. This law, she argued, violates the separation of powers doctrine and due process of law to a person accused of a crime. Many state courts have already ruled this type of law unconstitutional.

In another example of a constitutionally infirm traffic stop from Indiana, the defendant was stopped because the music coming from his car was judged to be too loud by the police,

---

[381] http://dictionary.law.com/default2.asp?selected=1508&bold=perjury‖.

based on a "noise" ordinance. The Indiana Court of Appeals found that the ordinance itself was invalid because it was unconstitutionally too vague. The statute was ruled to be constitutionally invalid. Hence, the stop under that state law was illegal.[382]

6.25. Defenses related to double jeopardy. It is a violation of the Fifth Amendment of the United States Constitution for anyone to be held criminally accountable twice for the same issue by the same sovereign (legal entity).[383] What this means is that you cannot be made to stand trial a second time for any of your actions in a state court if the first trial in a state court has already had a final ruling in your favor. Believe it or not, in some countries, the government **can** start over and keep trying until they get a conviction.

Several important exceptions to "double jeopardy" exist. Each state is a separate and distinct sovereign (independent government) from our federal government. With certain types of crimes, each sovereign may try you for the same set of circumstances if your actions are violative of different laws of each "sovereign." However, for this to occur in a DUI-DWI case is highly unlikely because in almost all prosecutions for DUI-DWI, the federal government has no "jurisdiction" since it is a state crime that almost always occurs on state property (as opposed to crimes occurring on federal lands).

Next, be aware that double jeopardy applies only at a certain point in the legal proceedings. If your proceedings get stopped by the judge before a verdict or judgment is rendered, you may have no constitutional protection against a second trial. In most jurisdictions, this point in time is after the jury has been impaneled and sworn in,[384] or after any testimony or evidence has been started after the jury is sworn in. In a non-jury (bench) trial, the usual time for jeopardy to attach is once the first witness begins testifying at the trial.[385]

A mistake made by raising an issue too early may allow the prosecutor to ask the judge to delay the proceedings, correct the error, and begin your trial again – with the error resolved. This is yet another reason to have the best DUI-DWI attorney you can afford, because he or she will know exactly when and how to raise the double jeopardy issue that may win your case on this highly specialized legal issue.

It is not a double jeopardy situation for your license to be taken from you in an administrative hearing, and for you then to have to stand trial for DUI-DWI in a criminal court

---

[382]**Lutz v. City of Indianapolis**, 820 N.E.2d 766 (Ind.Ct.App. 2005).

[383] ... nor shall any person be subject for the same offence to be twice put in jeopardy of life or limb... U.S.C.A. Const. Amend. V.

[384]**U.S. v. Jorn**, 400 U.S. 470, 91 S.Ct. 547, 27 L.Ed.2d 543 (1971); **Jones v. Kiger**, 194 Ariz. 523, 984 P.2d 1161 (Ariz.App. Div. 1 1999); **Stevenson v. State**, 404 So.2d 111 (Ala.Crim.App. 1981); **Larios v. Superior Court**, 24 Cal.3d 324, 594 P.2d 491 (1979); **State v. Heaven**, 127 Wash.App. 156, 110 P.3d 835 (2005); **State v. Roberson**, 888 So.2d 727 (Fla.App. 5 Dist. 2004); **Laster v. State**, 268 Ga. 172, 486 S.E.2d 153 (1997); **Domangue v. State**, 654 N.E.2d 1 (Ind.App. 1995); **Steen v. State**, 92 Tex.Crim. 99, 242 S.W. 1047 (Tex.Crim.App. 1922); **State v. Huskey**, 66 S.W.3d 905 (Tenn.Crim.App. 2001); **King v. State**, 527 So.2d 641 (Miss. 1988).

[385]**Holcomb v. State**, 858 So.2d 1112 (Fla.App. 2 Dist. 2003) - When evidence is begun to be presented; **Hall v. State**, 722 N.E.2d 1280 (Ind.App. 2000) - when the first witness is sworn in; **State v. Czaplinski**, 956 S.W.2d 839 (Tex.App.-Austin 1997) - when both sides have announced ready and the defendant has pled; **Ahern v. Ahern**, 15 S.W.3d 73 (Tenn. 2000) - when the first witness testifies; **People v. Superior Court**, 28 Cal.Rptr.3d 529 (Cal.App. 5 Dist. 2005) - when the court begins to hear evidence; **Perkinson v. State**, 273 Ga. 491, 542 S.E.2d 92 (2001) - when defendant has been "put to trial" before the trier of fact; **State v. Graham**, 91 Wash.App. 663, 960 P.2d 457 (1998) - when the first witness is sworn; **Beckwith v. State**, 615 So.2d 1134 (Miss. 1992) - when first witness is sworn.

and possibly lose your license again.[386] Although the hearing at which your driver's license is suspended immediately following a DUI-DWI arrest may seem like a criminal trial, the only question determined at such proceedings is whether or not you should lose a property interest (that is, your driver's license).[387]

You have no constitutional or statutory right to drive. You merely have a privilege from the state that granted your license to you. The administrative hearing is provided after your DUI-DWI arrest to determine if your driving privilege should be suspended or revoked. This is a different issue than the legal issues involved in your criminal case, when your liberty interests are at stake (you could be put in jail or penalized with fines, be forced into alcohol or drug treatment for rehabilitation purposes, or be required to perform a substantial number of community service hours.) Because different interests are at stake, the issue being litigated in the two related (but different) proceedings is not the same. Courts across the United States have ruled that being put through both proceedings is not double jeopardy.[388]

6.26. Defenses related to collateral estoppel or *res judicata*. "Collateral estoppel" is a legal doctrine related to *issue preclusion*. This means that the issue being raised by a party already has gone to trial or been settled in another court proceeding and there no reason exists to try it again in your court.[389] In fact, one of the precepts of our legal system is that all parties are bound by that earlier decision.

An example of issue preclusion in a vehicular homicide trial could involve attempting to prosecute the death case against you after a judge has already acquitted you of the DUI-DWI charge. In such a case, because the DUI-DWI charge is an essential element of the vehicular homicide case, the defense attorney's challenge based upon collateral estoppel (issue preclusion) will be successful.[390]

---

[386]**United States v. Ursery,** 518 U.S. 267, 116 S.Ct. 2135, 135 L.Ed.2d 549 (1996); **Ex parte Mata,** 925 S.W.2d 292 (Tex.App.-Corpus Christi 1996); **Davidson v. MacKinnon,** 656 So.2d 223 (Fla.App. 5 Dist. 1995); **State v. Sneed,** 8 S.W.3d 299 (Tenn.Crim.App. 1999); **Murphy v. State,** 267 Ga. 120, 475 S.E.2d 907 (1996), **State v. Brabson,** 976 S.W.2d 182 (Tex.App.-Corpus Christi 1998); **State v. McClendon,** 131 Wash.2d 853, 935 P.2d 1334 (1997); **Baldwin v. Department of Motor Vehicles,** 35 Cal.App.4th 1630 (Cal.App. 1 Dist. 1995); **Schrefler v. State,** 660 N.E.2d 585 (Ind.App. 1996); **Miles v. City of Gulfport,** 735 So.2d 1012 (Miss. 1999).

[387]**United States v. Ursery,** 518 U.S. 267, 116 S.Ct. 2135, 135 L.Ed.2d 549 (1996).

[388]**Department Of Highway Safety and Motor Vehicles v. Brandenburg,** 891 So.2d 1071 (Fla.App. 5 Dist. 2004); **Goodman v. Com.,** 37 Va.App. 374, 558 S.E.2d 555 (2002); **State v. Kerr,** 330 S.C. 132, 498 S.E.2d 212 (S.C.App. 1998); **State v. Ellenburg,** 283 Mont. 136, 938 P.2d 1376 (1997); **State v. Hill,** 555 N.W.2d 697 (Iowa 1996); **People v. Dvorak,** 276 Ill.App.3d 544, 658 N.E.2d 869 (1995); **State v. Kerr,** 330 S.C. 132, 498 S.E.2d 212 (S.C.App. 1998); **Ex parte Reyna,** 947 S.W.2d 313 (Tex.App.-Fort Worth 1997); **State v. McClendon,** 131 Wash.2d 853, 935 P.2d 1334 (1997); **Brennan v. Kmiotek,** 233 A.D.2d 870, 649 N.Y.S.2d 611 (N.Y.A.D. 4 Dept. 1996); **State v. Sonnier,** 679 So.2d 1011 (La.App. 1996); **Baldwin v. Department of Motor Vehicles,** 35 Cal.App.4th 1630, 42 Cal.Rptr.2d 422 (Cal.App. 1 Dist. 1995); **Schrefler v. State,** 660 N.E.2d 585 (Ind.App. 1996); **Miles v. City of Gulfport,** 735 So.2d 1012 (Miss. 1999).

[389]http://dictionary.law.com/default2.asp?typed=collateral+estoppel&type=1; **Walton v. State,** 831 S.W.2d 488 (Tex.App.-Hous. (14 Dist.) 1992); **Dorsey v. State,** 251 Ga.App. 640, 554 S.E.2d 278 (2001); **State v. Carter,** 452 So.2d 1137 (Fla.App. 5 Dist. 1984); **State v. Esco,** 911 So.2d 48 (Ala.Crim.App. 2005); **Holloman v. State,** 656 So.2d 1134 (Miss. 1995); **Zapata v. Department of Motor Vehicles,** 2 Cal.App.4th 108, 2 Cal.Rptr.2d 855 (Cal.App. 1 Dist. 1991); **Christensen v. Grant County Hosp. Dist. No. 1,** 152 Wash.2d 299, 96 P.3d 957 (2004).

[390]Commonwealth v. States, 891 A.2d 737 (Pa.Super. 2006).

"Res judicata" is Latin for "the thing has been judged," and is ***claim*** *preclusion*. That is, between the State and you, a specific issue has already been decided in a court of law and there is no reason to debate this issue again your DUI-DWI trial.[391]

For example, in Mississippi or Arkansas, if you start at a non-jury, inferior court level and had specific rulings made that were in your favor (for example, that your traffic stop was illegal because the officer made a "mistake of law" about the lack of an outside, rearview mirror being a mandatory piece of equipment for your truck,[392] this may be a ruling that is "res judicata" if the State attempts to begin prosecution again in a higher (Circuit or Superior) court.

6.27. Defenses related to the denial of your right to a speedy trial. Speedy trial is a protection derived from the United States Constitution relating to the State not being allowed to unreasonably delay your trial. This right is especially important for people who are incarcerated. Unreasonable delay is a violation of the "due process" provision of the Fifth Amendment (applied to the states by the Fourteenth Amendment).

Each state may also have its own statute or constitutional provision limiting the time an accused person may be held in custody before trial (e.g. 45 days).[393] Some states have an excellent statutory right to a speedy trial (Georgia) while others have no rights beyond what is guaranteed to you by the United States Constitution (South Carolina).

Charges must be totally dismissed and the defendant released from any further legal obligation if the stated period for trial to be started expires without the State bringing you to trial. However, defendants often waive the right to a speedy trial in order to have additional time to prepare a stronger defense. If you are free on bail, you will not be harmed by the waiver of a speedy trial, since you are free from incarceration.[394]

When an excessive amount of time has passed before the State charged you with a crime,[395] or (after being indicted or accused) the process of getting to trial has been too slow,[396] your attorney might be able to get the charges dropped because of this excessive delay. This type of "speedy trial" challenge is based on a "constitutional" denial of speedy trial. Four critical facts need to be shown by your attorney; (a) the length of the delay; (b) that the delay was not caused by your side, but by the State; (c) that you asked for a prompt trial (in some written filing

---

[391]Res judicata - http://dictionary.law.com/default2.asp?typed=res+judicata&type=1; **State v. Carter,** 452 So.2d 1137 (Fla.App. 5 Dist. 1984); **Swain v. State,** 251 Ga.App. 110, 552 S.E.2d 880 (2001); **Ex parte Culver,** 932 S.W.2d 207 (Tex.App.-El Paso 1996); **Com. v. Stephenson,** 82 S.W.3d 876 (Ky. 2002); **State v. Bacote,** 331 S.C. 328, 503 S.E.2d 161 (1998); **Young v. City of Seattle,** 25 Wash.2d 888, 172 P.2d 222 (1946); **Zapata v. Department of Motor Vehicles,** 2 Cal.App.4th 108, 2 Cal.Rptr.2d 855 (Cal.App. 1 Dist. 1991); **Ex parte Myers,** 68 S.W.3d 229 (Tex.App.-Texarkana 2002).

[392]**United States v. Chanthasouxat,** 342 F.3d 1271 (11th Cir. 2003).

[393]Tennessee - T. C. A. § 40-15-105 - 14 days; Georgia - O.C.G.A. § 17-7-170 within this term or the next term of court; California - Pen. C. § 1382 - 30 days; Florida - Fla. R. Crim. P. Rule 3.191 - 60 days; Texas - **Zamorano v. State,** 84 S.W.3d 643 (Tex.Crim.App. 2002) - multi-factorial analysis; Washington - **State v. Williams,** 85 Wash.2d 29, 530 P.2d 225 (1975) - 60 days; California - West's Ann.Cal.Penal Code § 802 - one year.

[394]http://dictionary.law.com/default2.asp?typed=speedy+trial&type=1

[395]Tennessee - one year total from the time of the offense - T. C. A. § 40-2-102; Florida - three years - **Ehrlick v. State,** 898 So.2d 237 (Fla.App. 4 Dist. 2005); Georgia- two years - O.C.G.A. § 17-3-1(d); Texas - two years for misdemeanor DUI - Vernon's Ann.Texas C.C.P. Art. 12.02, three years for felony DUI - Vernon's Ann.Texas C.C.P. Art. 12.01; California - one year - West's Ann.Cal.Penal Code § 802.

[396]"In all criminal prosecutions, the accused shall enjoy the right to a speedy and public trial..." U.S.C.A. Const. Amend. VI. "In criminal cases, the defendant shall have a public and speedy trial by an impartial jury." Georgia Const. Art. 1, § 1, ¶ XI; **Bass v. State,** 275 Ga.App. 259, 620 S.E.2d 184 (2005).

with the court); and (d) that your ability to defend the case has been harmed or compromised in some way. Sometimes a fourth factor, the length of the delay, is also an issue considered by the courts.[397]

However, your right to a speedy trial can be lost through trickery by your attorney or deceptive lawyering.[398] Courts are protective of the criminal justice system when it appears that "manipulation" of court guidelines has occurred. This is yet another reason to have a seasoned DUI-DWI attorney representing you.

6.28. The defense of necessity. Necessity in a DUI-DWI case is where you admittedly drove while impaired, but that you had a good (emergency) reason for doing so. An example is if you were at home drinking, with no intention to drive, when your wife cut her arm very badly. Ten minutes after your "911" call for emergency help, an ambulance has still not arrived at the scene to help save your wife from bleeding to death. Rather than let your wife die, you drive her to the hospital, despite knowing that you have had too much to drink before driving. You acted upon this serious emergency and drove while intoxicated since you had "no other choice" if you wanted to save her. Whether or not society would consider this justified is a question for the jury to decide.[399]

To raise this "affirmative defense," most states require that you notify the State that this will be part of your case. Some states require that the defense admit being impaired to be allowed to assert this "affirmative defense" or another type of affirmative defense. That way, the burden of proof typically shifts to the State to DISPROVE your assertion that "necessity" excuses you from being legally responsible for DUI-DWI.[400]

Raising such a defense may put the State to a nearly impossible task of disproving the "affirmative defense." You may get a reduction in charges offered, to avoid trial on the more serious charge of DUI-DWI. One possible "negotiated" reduction of the DUI-DWI charge might be reckless driving where no loss of driving privileges is involved. Furthermore, even if you lose

---

[397]**Barker v. Wingo,** 407 U.S. 514, 92 S.Ct. 2182, 33 L.Ed.2d 101 (1972); **People v. Taranovich,** 37 N.Y.2d 442, 335 N.E.2d 303 (1975); **State v. Yates,** 223 Ga.App. 403, 477 S.E.2d 670 (1996); **State v. Bishop,** 493 S.W.2d 81 (Tenn. 1973); **Emery v. State,** 881 S.W.2d 702 (Tex.Crim.App. 1994); **Jaco v. State,** 574 So.2d 625 (Miss. 1990); **People v. Gilmore,** 222 Mich.App. 442, 564 N.W.2d 158 (1997); **People v. Lawson,** 67 Ill.2d 449, 367 N.E.2d 1244 (1977); **State v. Bazemore,** 249 Ga.App. 584, 549 S.E.2d 426 (2001); **People v. Archerd,** 3 Cal.3d 615, 477 P.2d 421 (1970); **State v. Nims,** 180 Conn. 589, 430 A.2d 1306 (1980); **Hatcher v. State,** 83 Wis.2d 559, 266 N.W.2d 320 (1978); **State v. Mende,** 304 Or. 18, 741 P.2d 496 (1987); **State v. Bound,** 43 Ohio App.2d 44, 332 N.E.2d 366 (1975); **State v. James,** 394 So.2d 1197 (La. 1981); **Cosco v. State,** 503 P.2d 1403 (Wyo. 1972); **State v. Christensen,** 75 Wash.2d 678, 453 P.2d 644 (1969); **McCallum v. State,** 407 So.2d 865 (Ala.Crim.App. 1981); **State v. Roundtree,** 438 So.2d 68 (Fla.App. 1983); **Collins v. State,** 163 Ind.App. 72, 321 N.E.2d 868 (1975).
[398]**Linkous v. State,** 254 Ga. App. 43, 561 S.E.2d 128 (2002).
[399]**Tarvestad v. State,** 261 Ga. 605, 409 S.E.2d 513 (1991); **People v. Gross,** 21 A.D.3d 1224, 801 N.Y.S.2d 430 (N.Y.A.D. 3 Dept. 2005); **Rodriguez v. State,** 2005 WL 2313567 (Tex.App.-El Paso 2005); **Marquardt v. State,** 164 Md.App. 95, 882 A.2d 900 (Md.App. 2005); **Stodghill v. State,** 892 So.2d 236 (Miss. 2005).
[400]**Laravie v. Battle Creek Mut. Ins. Co.,** 2005 WL 2007200 (Neb.App. 2005); **Zulli v. Coregis Ins. Co.,** 910 So.2d 437 (La.App. 5 Cir. 2005); **State v. Champagne,** 879 A.2d 1147 (N.H. 2005); **Babb v. Graham,** 615 S.E.2d 434 (N.C.App. 2005); **State v. Buehler-May,** 279 Kan. 371, 110 P.3d 425 (2005); **Willis v. State,** 191 Ga.App. 251, 381 S.E.2d 416 (1989); **Knowles v. Robinson,** 60 Cal.2d 620, 387 P.2d 833 (1963); **State v. Lopez,** 676 N.E.2d 1063 (Ind.App.1997); **Madison v. DeSoto County,** 822 So.2d 306 (Miss.App. 2002); **Fountain Parkway, Ltd. v. Tarrant Appraisal Dist.,** 920 S.W.2d 799 (Tex.App.-Fort Worth 1996); **Braun v. State,** 90 Wash.App. 1048 (Wash.App. Div. 1 1998); **State v. Johnson,** 1996 WL 526845 (Tenn.Crim.App. 1996); **State v. Romano,** 355 N.J.Super. 21, 809 A.2d 158 (N.J.Super.A.D., 2002).

this trial, the judge's punishment will typically be less severe than in a normal case, due to your honest perception that you needed to act to address whatever the "necessity" was that prompted you to drive.

In other states (e.g., California), raising an affirmative defense merely shifts the burden of proof to the defendant to **PROVE** that defense. Therefore, due to the rule in that state putting the burden of proof on the defense, no pre-trial notice is required to be given to the prosecution.

6.29. The defense of duress. Duress, in a legal sense, is breaking a law because something or someone else is making you break the law. It is the use of force, false imprisonment or threats (and possibly psychological torture or "brainwashing") to compel someone to act contrary to his/her wishes or interests.[401] An example of duress in a DUI-DWI case would be if someone put a gun to your head and made you drive them to another location even though you protested that you could not drive safely because you were intoxicated.

This is a very rare "affirmative defense" in a DUI-DWI case. Furthermore, notice of such a defense to the prosecutor may be required prior to trial. Your DUI-DWI specialist will know the applicable rules in your state in the event this affirmative defense is being considered on your behalf.

6.30. The defense of entrapment. In criminal law, entrapment is the act of law enforcement officers or government agents inducing or encouraging a person to commit a crime when the accused party indicates no prior intent or action to commit the crime on his or her own accord. The key to entrapment is whether the idea for the commission of a crime or encouragement of the criminal act originated with the police or government agents instead of with the supposed "criminal."[402] Entrapment, if proved, is a complete defense to a criminal prosecution.

Like duress, entrapment is an unlikely defense in a DUI-DWI case. Again, pre-trial notice of this affirmative defense is likely part of your state law. Your experienced DUI-DWI attorney will know how and when to raise it. See http://www.duiblog.com/2004/12/13#a66 for a discussion of such questionable police tactics.

One example of "entrapment" might be found in this DUI-DWI fact pattern. An intoxicated man walks out of a bar, having consumed all of his alcohol after he stopped driving earlier. An officer sees the man and says, "If you don't get off the street this minute, I am going to arrest you for public intoxication." The driver says, "Okay, if you insist, but I am not going to try to drive anywhere" and walks to his car and sits in the front seat behind the wheel. The bar has closed and it is freezing outside. The man sits behind the wheel and starts the engine to use the heater in the vehicle. If the police officer arrests him for DUI-DWI, this could be a foundation to assert the legal defense of "entrapment."

6.31. Ignorance defense. With some criminal laws, not knowing what you are doing, or ignorance, is a defense to being punished for the crime. This is not true for DUI-DWI offenses. No good case law exists in any jurisdiction for such a defense to impaired driving. However, a person may NOT intend (or even know) that he or she is driving, if certain prescribed medication is taken and the person begins "sleep driving."

This rare and somewhat difficult defense is based on "lack of intent to drive." [http://www.georgiacriminaldefense.com/some-sleeping-pill-users-range-far-beyond-bed.htm;

---

[401] http://dictionary.law.com/default2.asp?selected=597&bold=duress||
[402] http://dictionary.law.com/default2.asp?typed=Entrapment&type=1&submit1.x=73&submit1.y=12.

Ambien Users are Waking Up and Smelling the Lawsuits, Lawyers Weekly USA, April 10, 2006, p.1.] Your attorney should always inquire about any medications or pills that you may have taken prior to driving. See the Questionnaire in **Appendix J.**

6.32. The defense of the margin of error variance. Some breath test programs euphemistically call breath machine error "sampling variability." With any scientific or electronic test, a margin of error in the machine being able to precisely measure a sample will always exist.

In most states, the acceptable "difference" between two breath exhalations is 0.020 or less between the two samples. If the breath test results are "borderline," then your attorney may be able to present the defense to the "per se" DUI-DWI charge that the State cannot prove beyond a reasonable doubt that your breath alcohol level was actually at or above the requisite alcohol level. Usually, an expert witness is needed to assert this defense, as well as thorough discovery about the reliability of the State's calibration checks on the particular breath machine.

6.33. The defense that your partition ratio is substantially different than the breath machine is programmed to expect. The basic breath machine is set up to "estimate" a blood alcohol level based on a standard ratio of breath to blood of 2100 units of breath to 1 unit of blood in your body. A defense can be raised as a legitimate, scientific attack if your ratio is always lower (e.g., 1400 to 1) and this can be documented. Again, to establish the "partition ratio" defense requires the use of one or more expert witnesses.[403] Most experienced DUI-DWI trial attorneys will only assert this attack if no better explanation of an errant breath test result is available to your defense lawyer. In at least a few states, this defense has been legislatively eliminated or determined to be irrelevant and upheld by appellate courts in that state.[404]

6.34. Defense of involuntary intoxication or lack of intent to drive. This defense has been frowned on by almost all courts as being untenable. However, certain situations do arise wherein the person may legitimately be unaware that a fruit punch was spiked, or where a person who had no plan to drive inadvertently caused an alcohol "blackout" through heavy drinking. This can cause a total lack of awareness of volitional acts, especially after taking certain prescribed medications that interacted badly with the alcohol.[405]

6.35. Defenses related to preventing the enhancement of punishment for a drinking and driving offense. All states have statutes that can "enhance" or increase the mandatory minimum punishment for a DUI-DWI offense based upon either: (a) your extremely high blood alcohol level at the time of your arrest; (b) due to your alleged prior DUI-DWI convictions; or (c) [in a few states] for refusing to submit to the State's chemical test of your blood, breath or urine. Such statutes put a premium on your defense attorney being able to mount a successful challenge to this "enhancement" evidence that could cost you a much longer jail sentence.[406] These challenges may focus on proving one or more of the prior cases

---

[403]**People v. Thill,** 297 Ill.App.3d 7, 696 N.E.2d 1175 (Ill.App. 2 Dist. 1998); **Trillo v. State,** 165 S.W.3d 763 (Tex.App.-San Antonio 2005); **State v. Downie,** 117 N.J. 450, 569 A.2d 242 (N.J. 1990).

[404]**State v. Storholm,** 210 Ariz. 199, 109 P.3d 94 (Ariz.App. Div. 1 2005); **State v. Hardesty,** 136 Idaho 707, 39 P.3d 647 (Idaho App. 2002); **State v. Allen,** 104 Or.App. 622, 802 P.2d 690 (Or.App. 1990); **State v. Downie,** 117 N.J. 450, 569 A.2d 242 (N.J. 1990); **People v. Ireland,** 33 Cal.App.4th 680, 39 Cal.Rptr.2d 870 (Cal.App. 6 Dist. 1995).

[405]For additional information about these defenses, see these sources: **State v. Prine,** 1991 WL 35156 (Ohio App. 9 Dist. 1991); **Larsen v. State,** 253 Ga.App. 196, 558 S.E.2d 418 (2001); and http://www.duiblog.com/2005/04/27#a152 http://www.duiblog.com/2005/04/06#a139.

[406]Enhanced DUI offenses - Alabama - Ala.Code 1975 § 32-5A-191 - **Altherr v. State,** 2004 WL 1909277 (Ala.Crim.App. 2004); Georgia - O.C.G.A. § 40-6-391(c); Texas - V.T.C.A., Penal Code § 49.09; Florida -

should not be used against you to enhance the penalties in the current case, or may focus on deficiencies in the current DUI-DWI case.

In states with an "extreme DUI-DWI" law (e.g., Arizona), using expert testimony to show that the State's "breath number" is not credible can mean a substantial difference in your punishment.[407] You may not win the lesser DUI-DWI charge, but a finding of not guilty on the "extreme DUI-DWI" charge can save your right to drive and keep you from serving a longer jail term.

A specific example from Texas of eliminating "prior offense" evidence might be that you are accused of having a second DUI-DWI offense within 10 years of a prior conviction from another state.[408] If your attorney can prove that the other conviction was a DIFFERENT type of statute and not substantially similar to your state's statute, this argument might prevail. This would mean that your minimum mandatory punishment could be substantially lessened.[409]

West's F.S.A. § 316.193; Tennessee - T. C. A. § 40-35-114; South Carolina - Code 1976 § 56-5-2940; Kentucky - KRS § 189A.010; Washington - West's RCWA 46.61.5055; California - West's Ann.Cal.Vehicle Code §§ 23540, 23546, 23550; Mississippi - Miss. Code Ann. § 63-11-30.

[407] A.R.S. § 28-1383.

[408] Texas - V.T.C.A., Penal Code § 49.09(e)(1)(2).

[409] **Bruno v. Director, Dept. of Public Safety,** 673 So.2d 445 (Ala.Civ.App. 1995); **Com., Dept. of Transp. v. McCafferty,** 563 Pa. 146, 758 A.2d 1155 (2000); **Anderson v. State, Dept. of Public Safety and Dept. of Transp.,** 305 N.W.2d 786 (Minn. 1981); **State v. Bergh,** 679 N.W.2d 734 (Minn.App., 2004); **Rigney v. Edgar,** 135 Ill.App.3d 893, 482 N.E.2d 367 (1985); **Draeger v. Reed,** 69 Cal.App.4th 1511, 82 Cal.Rptr.2d 378 (1999); **Keith v. Capers,** 362 So.2d 130 (Fla.App. 3 Dist. 1978); **Hardison v. Haslam,** 250 Ga. 59, 295 S.E.2d 830 (1982); **Druen v. Shook,** 540 N.E.2d 48 (Ind. 1989).

Chapter 7

Specific Challenges to Various Search and Seizure Issues
That Can Force Total Dismissal of Your DUI-DWI Case

7.0. Purpose of this chapter. Based on the Fourth[410] and Fourteenth[411] Amendments to the United States Constitution, the police must have an adequate reason before they stop your vehicle. All states, other than California, have state constitutional protections that offer equal or better protections to those found in the federal constitution. California lacks such protections due to the voters being hoodwinked into voting to give up any state constitutional protections that offer greater protection of their liberties than the rights that exist under the United States Constitution.

Once stopped by the police, any indication of possible impairment from alcohol or drugs will lead to a DUI-DWI investigation. A very minor tag irregularity or vehicle equipment problem will authorize an officer to pull the car over, even if the officer's real purpose is to look for other possible criminal activity.[412]

If the "reason" for the stop is not proper (i.e., not legally sufficient), then from the start of your detention, all further evidence gathered by the police is not admissible in court and all alcohol or drug related charges arising from this incident can be dismissed if a proper motion is filed by your criminal law specialist. Once a motion is filed [typically a "motion to suppress" or a "motion in limine" (a motion to limit the use of evidence)] the trial judge will be asked to review the legitimacy of the traffic stop. This chapter discusses some of the most common legal challenges your attorney might raise on your behalf at a pre-trial motion hearing. Your chances of success will often be based on all of the details you provide during your interview process when you tell your attorney your version of what happened at the time of your arrest.

In addition to your account of the incident details, the officer's video or audio tape (if any), police report, traffic citations, other documents of your arrest, detention, vehicle towing and bonding out of jail will be of great value to your attorney. If you took any breath test, the printed evidential cards showing these results will also be important.

7.1. Stopped based upon traffic offense or vehicle deficiency that is not actually an offense or deficiency. The police officer must have a valid and proper reason to stop your vehicle.[413] If the officer who pulled you over made a MISTAKE OF LAW (i.e., thought

---

[410]The right of the people to be secure in their persons, houses, papers, and effects, against unreasonable searches and seizures, shall not be violated... U.S.C.A. Const. Amend. IV. **People v. Luedemann,** 357 Ill.App.3d 411, 828 N.E.2d 355 (Ill.App. 2d Dist. 2005); **United States v. Chanthasouxat,** 342 F.3d 1271 (11th Cir. 2003); **Crooks v. State,** 710 So.2d 1041 (Fla. App. 1998); **State v. Cerny,** 28 S.W. 3d 796 (Tex. App. 2000); **State v. Tarvin,** 972 S.W. 2d 910 (Tex. App. 1998); **State v. Gullett,** 78 Ohio App. 3d 138, 145; 604 N.E.2d 176 (1992); **State v. Holler,** 224 Ga. App. 66, 479 S.E.2d 780 (1996); **State v. Aguirre,** 229 Ga. App. 736, 494 S.E.2d 576 (1997); **Martin v. State,** 257 Ga. App. 435, 571 S.E.2d 459 (2002).

[411][N]or shall any State deprive any person of life, liberty, or property, without due process of law... U.S.C.A. Const. Amend. XIV.

[412]**Whren v. United States,** 517 U.S. 806, 116 S.Ct. 1769, 135 L.Ed.2d 89 (1996).

[413]**Delaware v. Prouse,** 440 U.S. 648, 99 S.Ct. 1391, 59 L.Ed.2d 660 (1979); **Brisbane v. State,** 233 Ga. 339, 211 S.E.2d 294 (1974); **State v. Payton,** 344 So.2d 648 (Fla.App. 2 Dist. 1977); **Hoag v. State,** 728

that an offense had been committed or that some equipment deficiency was "required" equipment), then the entire stop and all evidence recovered or collected by the police will be suppressed (excluded from evidence) at the time of the pre-trial motions hearing.

Specific examples of "mistake of law" cases will help illustrate this point. In the first case, during the very early morning, the police decided to run a license tag number through their system to check it. The officer entered the wrong number and the tag came up invalid. The officer then stopped the driver, who was later accused of DUI-DWI. The Kentucky Court of Appeals determined that because there was a mistake of law, that the driver really did not have an invalid plate, and since the mistake was the officer's, there was no valid justification for the stop.[414]

In an Ohio case, the reason for the stop was a mistaken warrant out on the defendant who was subsequently charged with DUI-DWI. When the warrant was found to be mistaken, no other reason existed for the stop, and the court determined that all evidence gathered by the police because of the stop could not be introduced.[415]

In a third case, an officer pulled over the defendant after he had made a U-turn over a double yellow line on federal property, when this was not a crime. The court ruled that all evidence obtained because of the stop must be suppressed.[416]

As a last example, an officer stopped a young, black male driving an apparent rental or loaner car because the officer noted a "disabled placard" hanging from the rear-view mirror. Even after a response from his dispatcher that the vehicle had not been reported stolen, the officer considered it so abnormal for a young person to be displaying this placard, that he stopped the vehicle. The court found that this "hunch" was not an adequate reason for the stop.[417]

7.2. Stopped based upon an observed equipment defect that is not a legally required item of equipment. One valid and common reason a law enforcement officer may stop your vehicle is if he or she observes a missing piece of equipment on your vehicle or sees that a part of your vehicle is defective.[418] Common examples are if your brake lights are burned out, your tires are bald, or one of your headlamps is not working. However, if a law enforcement officer stops you because your rearview mirror is too small, and there is no law specifying the size of your rearview mirror, then the officer's pretext for the stop is invalid.[419] If

---

S.W.2d 375 (Tex.Crim.App. 1987); **State v. Watkins,** 827 S.W.2d 293 (Tenn. 1992); **United States v. Chanthasouxat,** 342 F.3d 1271 (11th Cir. 2003).

[414]**Waldrip v. Com.,** 2005 WL 1593702 (Ky.App. 2005).

[415]**State v. Coleman,** 108 Ohio Misc.2d 48, 739 N.E.2d 419 (Ohio Mun. 2000).

[416]**U.S. v. Beckman,** 3 F.Supp.2d 654 (D.Md. 1998).

[417]**U.S. v. King,** 244 F.3d 736 (9th Cir. 2001).

[418]Georgia O.C.G.A. §40-8-20 et seq.; Florida West's F.S.A. § 316.001 et seq.; Tennessee T. C. A. § 55-9-201 et seq.; Texas V.T.C.A., Transportation Code § 547.001 et seq.; Alabama Ala.Code 1975 § 32-5-210 et seq.; Mississippi Miss. Code Ann. § 63-7-1 et seq.; South Carolina Code 1976 § 56-5-4410 et seq.; **United States v. Chanthasouxat,** 342 F.3d 1271 (11th Cir. 2003).

[419]**People v. Luedemann,** 357 Ill.App.3d 411, 828 N.E.2d 355 (Ill.App. 2d Dist. 2005); **United States v. Chanthasouxat,** 342 F.3d 1271 (11th Cir. 2003); **Crooks v. State,** 710 So.2d 1041 (Fla. App. 1998); **State v. Cerny,** 28 S.W. 3d 796 (Tex. App. 2000); **State v. Tarvin,** 972 S.W. 2d 910 (Tex. App. 1998); **State v. Gullett,** 78 Ohio App. 3d 138, 145; 604 N.E.2d 176 (1992); **State v. Holler,** 224 Ga. App. 66, 479 S.E.2d 780, (1996); **State v. Aguirre,** 229 Ga. App. 736, 494 S.E.2d 576 (1997); **Martin v. State,** 257 Ga. App. 435, 571 S.E.2d 459 (2002).

that pretext is based on anything other than a published, existing law, then the stop itself will be declared invalid.

7.3. Stopped for a violation of law and the statute is unconstitutional. In order for you to be guilty of a crime, you have to violate a law that is not unconstitutionally vague. Sometimes, state legislators pass laws that are too vague or ambiguous to be legally enforceable. In such situations, if the law is struck down by your appellate courts, this frees you of all charges, since the law under which you were arrested was not constitutional.

As an example, the Georgia legislature passed a law making it unlawful to drive while you had any marijuana in your system at all. The courts found this unconstitutional because no connection existed between the very low levels of any legally used marijuana and any concerns for driver safety and protecting the public.[420] In Texas, where a motor vehicle law was written in such a complicated fashion as to not be able to be understood, it was declared unconstitutional. The wording of the statute was "forbidding the operating or driving of motor vehicles on any public highway 'where the territory contiguous thereto is closely built up, at greater rate of speed than 18 miles per hour,' was too indefinite and ambiguous as to the places where it is to apply to be operative."[421] On the other hand, just because "driving under the influence" is defined in two different ways by statute in many states, this does not make this term vague and thus unconstitutional.[422]

If you have been charged under a DUI-DWI statute or ordinance that is later declared unconstitutional or otherwise invalid, or has already been declared unconstitutional at the time of your arrest, your attorney can raise the defense that you had not in fact violated the law, as the law itself was not valid. Although such challenges are rare, top criminal defense attorneys raise such challenges when it may win your DUI-DWI case. Recent aggressive law enforcement activity has increased the chances of unconstitutional acts occurring in the effort to arrest more "drunk drivers." **http://www.duiblog.com/2005/01/09#a82**.

7.4. Stopped for a drive-out tag being on the vehicle, and the temporary tag is in good order. It is certainly a lawful reason for a law enforcement officer to stop you if your drive-out tag or temporary license is no longer valid, or if it is not displayed in a valid manner. However, if the officer made a mistake and the tag was valid, or if the tag was in fact displayed in a valid manner, then in some states, the pretext for the stop was then invalid.[423] In other states, such a stop would be upheld as being valid.[424] In Florida, appellate decisions exist on both sides of this issue.[425] If the pretext for the stop is invalid, so is the stop. In such an event, the charges may be dismissed at a pre-trial hearing.

7.5. Stopped because vehicle is coming from an area where no residences currently are occupied. Police officers certainly have a duty to protect the public as a whole.

---

[420]**Love v. State,** 271 Ga. 398, 517 S.E.2d 53 (1999).

[421]**Ex parte Slaughter,** 92 Tex.Crim. 212, 243 S.W. 478 (Tex.Crim.App. 1922).

[422]**Cargile v. State,** 244 Ga. 871, 262 S.E.2d 87 (1979).

[423]**State v. Swords,** 258 Ga. App. 895, 575 S.E.2d 751 (2002); **State v. McCulloch,** 906 S.W.2d 3 (Tenn.Crim.App. 1995).

[424]**In re Forfeiture of ($28,000.00) in U.S. Currency in Various Denominations and a .380 Handgun,** 124 N.M. 661, 954 P.2d 93 (1997); **English v. State,** 603 N.E.2d 161 (Ind.App. 1 Dist. 1992); **People v. Altman,** 938 P.2d 142 (Colo. 1997); **State v. Bowers,** 250 Neb. 151, 548 N.W.2d 725 (1996); **State v. Mitchell,** 731 So.2d 319 (La.App. 4 Cir. 1999); **State v. Poindexter,** 941 S.W.2d 533 (Mo.App. W.D. 1997).

[425]**Diaz v. State,** 800 So.2d 326 (Fla.App. 2 Dist. 2001); **State v. Bass,** 609 So.2d 151 (Fla.App. 5 Dist. 1992).

Part of this duty would be to protect areas under construction from thievery. However, just because you are driving on a public road out of one of these areas is not by itself sufficient reasonable suspicion for a law enforcement officer to stop your vehicle, even if it can be one factor out of several to establish articulable suspicion.[426] If the stop was unlawful, then any other evidence arising from the stop (such as evidence of driving under the influence of alcohol) cannot be held against you.

7.6. Stopped based solely upon a "be on the look out" (BOLO) call from a concerned citizen, and the information given is legally insufficient. Now that cell phones are so common, the police get a lot of calls from concerned citizens regarding what these citizens believe is an ongoing criminal offense. However, for the police to act on this information, it must be sufficiently detailed so as to allow the police to do something more than stop everyone in a similar vehicle on the highway. Basically stated, the United States Supreme Court has held that no corroboration (verification of the accuracy) of the anonymous tip equals an illegal seizure.[427]

As an example, the police likely could not legally stop your vehicle based only on a call from an unknown citizen who said that "a person" was getting into a blue Ford in downtown Columbus, Ohio and that the driver "looked" drunk,[428] although such a call can be one of many pieces which could lead to adequate sufficiency.[429] On this flimsy information, any blue Ford in Columbus, Ohio could be pulled over, since no model of Ford or tag number was given. If you were stopped solely on the basis of this call, it is likely the court would consider such a stop legally lacking in sufficient detail. If declared to have been illegal, then other evidence developed following the traffic stop would also be excluded by the trial court (such as the State's DUI-DWI evidence).

If, on the other hand, the police received a call describing some alleged violation of state law regarding an older white male, driving a red 1997 Ford Ranger pick-up truck, eastbound on Broad Street near the Municipal Court Building in Columbus, Ohio, bearing tag number BRG 319, and with the driver's side door painted silver, and your vehicle's description matched all of these criteria and you were stopped, such specific detail would likely be enough to give the police a legitimate reason to stop you. So, the law allows warrantless traffic stops when sufficient details are given by the concerned citizen to the police dispatcher.

7.7. Stopped at a roadblock that was illegally set up. For certain "emergency" situations (usually the commission of a felony in the vicinity), the police can set up roadblocks to prevent specific criminal activity. Also, in more than 45 states, the police can also

---

[426]**State v. Goodenough,** 1996 WL 649130 (Ohio App. 11 Dist. 1996); **Edwards v. State,** 2003 WL 22248850 (Tex.App.-Austin 2003); **State v. Smith,** 2003 WL 22309485 (Tenn.Crim.App. 2003).

[427]**Alabama v. White,** 496 U.S. 325, 110 S.Ct. 2412, 110 L.Ed.2d 301 (1990); **VonLinsowe v. State,** 213 Ga.App. 619, 445 S.E.2d 371 (1994); **State v. Webb,** 398 So.2d 820 (Fla. 1981); **Baldwin v. State,** 606 S.W.2d 872 (Tex.Crim.App. 1980); **Florida v. J.L.,** 529 U.S. 266, 120 S.Ct. 1375, 146 L.Ed.2d 254 (2000); **State v. Morales,** 137 N.M. 73, 107 P.3d 513 (2004); King v. State, 157 S.W.3d 656 (Mo. App. W.D. 2004); **Postell v. State,** 264 Ga. 249, 443 S.E.2d 628 (1994); **Lowenthal v. State,** 265 Ga. App. 266, 593 S.E.2d 726 (2004); **State v. Ludes,** 27 Kan.App.2d 1030, 11 P.3d 72 (2000); **Anderson v. Director, North Dakota DOT,** 696 N.W.2d 918 (N.D. 2005).

[428]**Vansant v. State,** 264 Ga. 319, 443 S.E.2d 474 (1994); **Mix v. State,** 893 P.2d 1270 (Alaska App. 1995).

[429]**State v. Stolte,** 991 S.W.2d 336 (Tex.App.-Fort Worth 1999); **State v. Luke,** 995 S.W.2d 630 (Tenn.Crim.App. 1998).

set up DUI-DWI roadblocks.[430] If the police follow their training procedures manual, such DUI-DWI roadblocks in most states are typically found to be valid extensions of each state's police powers to serve and protect the public's health, welfare and safety.[431]

These police department training protocols are typically established based on each state's individual requirements for legality that will typically track the guidelines of the United States Supreme Court's holdings, with possible other more restrictive rules being added by each state. To refine and interpret these rules, and determine if the police followed all of them, various state appellate decisions have established what police conduct at such roadblocks is permissible.

During the investigation of your DUI-DWI case, your attorney may discover that the police did not follow their training protocol. This may mean that the roadblock was illegal, and that your detention and arrest may be thrown out by the judge at a pre-trial motion hearing.

7.8. Stopped at a roadblock that was not overseen and selected by a properly trained supervisory officer. One of the more common statutory or court-ordered requirements for the establishment of a roadblock is that a trained and experienced supervisory officer must oversee and select the location of the roadblock. Furthermore, the time and location of the "sobriety checkpoint" must be selected by this supervisor.[432] If during the investigation of your DUI-DWI case, your attorney finds this requirement was not met, then the roadblock would be declared illegal. Then, any arrests that were made as a result of the illegal roadblock would be thrown out.

7.9. Confronted by an officer in a legally parked car with no reason to suspect that a crime had been committed. In most circumstances, it is not illegal for you to be sitting in your parked car, as long as you are legally parked in a place that is open to the public. The cases that have ruled in favor of the police have generally involved a car parked in a high crime area or a place where burglaries had been occurring recently. Unless the police can verbalize a legitimate reason for confronting you in your parked car, any evidence gathered of DUI-DWI will be suppressed.

For the police to begin their investigation of a possible crime by confronting you as you sit otherwise legally in a parked car, they must have some other evidence that a crime is occurring.[433] This goes back to you having a constitutionally guaranteed right found in the Fourth Amendment[434] to be free from illegal searches and seizures and applied to actions of the

---

[430]**State v. Smith,** 674 P.2d 562 (Okla.App. 1984); **State ex rel. Ekstrom v. Justice Court,** 136 Ariz. 1, 663 P.2d 992 (1983); **State v. Olgaard,** 248 N.W.2d 392 (S.D.1976).

[431]**Brent v. State,** 270 Ga. 160, 510 S.E.2d 14 (1998); **State v. Abelson,** 485 So.2d 861 (Fla.App. 4 Dist. 1986); **Fink v. State,** 866 S.W.2d 333 (Tex.App.-Hous. (1 Dist.) 1993); **State v. Downey,** 945 S.W.2d 102 (Tenn. 1997); **Ex parte Jackson,** 886 So.2d 155 (Ala. 2004); **State v. Jackson,** 764 So.2d 64 (La. 2000).

[432]**LaFontaine v. State,** 269 Ga. 251, 497 S.E.2d 367 (1998); **Brent v. State,** 270 Ga. 160, 510 S.E.2d 14 (1998); **State v. Abelson,** 485 So.2d 861 (Fla.App. 4 Dist. 1986); **Fink v. State,** 866 S.W.2d 333 (Tex.App.-Hous. (1 Dist.) 1993); **State v. Downey,** 945 S.W.2d 102 (Tenn. 1997); **Ex parte Jackson,** 886 So.2d 155 (Ala. 2004); **State v. Jackson,** 764 So.2d 64 (La. 2000).

[433]**State v. Westbrooks,** 594 S.W.2d 741 (Tenn.Crim.App. 1979); **People v. Luedemann,** 357 Ill.App.3d 411, 828 N.E.2d 355 (Ill.App. 2d Dist. 2005); **United States v. Chanthasouxat,** 342 F.3d 1271 (11th Cir. 2003); **Crooks v. State,** 710 So.2d 1041 (Fla. App. 1998); **State v. Cerny,** 28 S.W.3d 796 (Tex. App. 2000); **State v. Tarvin,** 972 S.W. 2d 910 (Tex. App. 1998); **State v. Gullett,** 78 Ohio App. 3d 138, 145; 604 N.E.2d 176 (1992); **State v. Holler,** 224 Ga. App. 66, 479 S.E.2d 780, (1996); **State v. Aguirre,** 229 Ga. App. 736, 494 S.E.2d 576 (1997); **Martin v. State,** 257 Ga. App. 435, 571 S.E.2d 459 (2002).

[434]The right of the people to be secure in their persons, houses, papers, and effects, against unreasonable searches and seizures, shall not be violated... U.S.C.A. Const. Amend. IV.

officers who work for State agencies through the Due Process Clause of the Fourteenth Amendment.[435] Prior to this investigation of you in your DUI-DWI case, if the officer only had evidence of your *legal* actions, the officer's actions (and investigation that led to an impaired driving arrest) were unconstitutional, and any intoxication test results that flowed from this unconstitutional act should not be used against you. In this situation, your attorney's job is to prove that you committed no illegal acts.

7.10. Stopped because person turned around near a roadblock location. The Fourth Amendment also protects citizens against the police pulling your car over on a hunch.[436] If the only reason the police officer stopped you was that you appeared to turn around (or down a side street) near a DUI-DWI roadblock, this is not a sufficient reason for the stop.[437] If this is the **only** reason the police stopped you, then everything that follows (including your DUI-DWI arrest) would not be admissible against you.

7.11. Stopped because officer had a hunch that a turn into an apartment parking lot was made to avoid a roadblock that was ahead. For any law enforcement officer to have a valid reason to stop your vehicle there must be an "articulable and reasonable suspicion" that you are an unlicensed driver, that your vehicle is not registered, or that either you or the vehicle you are driving is in violation of the law.[438] "Articulable" means the law enforcement officer is able to give the court, through his or her testimony under oath, a reason why he or she believed there was a violation of the law justifying the stop of your vehicle. What constitutes "reasonable" is analyzed on a case-by-case basis,[439] but it typically has to be more than a mere "hunch" on the part of the officer.[440] Certainly, an otherwise legal turn into an apartment parking lot does not rise to "articulable suspicion" if based only on an officer's hunch. Nor does police observation of you driving (otherwise lawfully) through an unlit area, late at

---

[435][N]or shall any State deprive any person of life, liberty, or property, without due process of law... U.S.C.A. Const. Amend. XIV.

[436]The right of the people to be secure in their persons, houses, papers, and effects, against unreasonable searches and seizures, shall not be violated... U.S.C.A. Const. Amend. IV; **Jorgensen v. State,** 207 Ga.App. 545, 428 S.E.2d 440 (1993).

[437]**Stanley v. State,** 191 Ga.App. 603, 382 S.E.2d 686 (1989); **Boyd v. State,** 751 So.2d 1050 (Miss.App. 1998); **Steinbeck v. Com.,** 862 S.W.2d 912 (Ky.App. 1993); **State v. Badessa,** 185 N.J. 303, 885 A.2d 430 (N.J. 2005).

[438]**Delaware v. Prouse,** 440 U.S. 648, 99 S.Ct. 1391, 59 L.Ed.2d 660 (1979); **Brisbane v. State,** 233 Ga. 339, 211 S.E.2d 294 (1974); **State v. Payton,** 344 So.2d 648 (Fla.App. 2 Dist. 1977); **Hoag v. State,** 728 S.W.2d 375 (Tex.Crim.App. 1987); **State v. Watkins,** 827 S.W.2d 293 (Tenn. 1992).

[439]**State v. Holton,** 205 Ga. App. 434, 422 S.E.2d 295 (1992); **Woods v. State,** 956 S.W.2d 33 (Tex.Crim.App. 1997); **State v. Andrews,** 57 Ohio St.3d 86, 565 N.E.2d 1271 (Ohio 1991); **State v. Watkins,** 827 S.W.2d 293 (Tenn. 1992); **Berge v. Commissioner of Public Safety,** 374 N.W.2d 730 (Minn. 1985); **Popple v. State,** 626 So.2d 185 (Fla. 1993); **People v. Cantor,** 36 N.Y.2d 106, 324 N.E.2d 872 (N.Y. 1975); **State v. Kennedy,** 107 Wash.2d 1, 726 P.2d 445 (Wash. 1986); **State v. Kowal,** 31 Conn.App. 669, 626 A.2d 822 (1993).

[440]**Hanson v. State,** 222 Ga. App. 537, 474 S.E.2d 735 (1996); **State v. Carlson,** 102 Ohio App.3d 585, 657 N.E.2d 591 (Ohio App. 9 Dist. 1995); **People v. Young,** 241 A.D.2d 690, 660 N.Y.S.2d 165 (N.Y.A.D. 3 Dept. 1997); **State v. Farabee,** 302 Mont. 29, 22 P.3d 175 (2000); **State v. Parker,** 84 Conn.App. 739, 856 A.2d 428 (2004); **State v. Haskell,** 645 A.2d 619 (Me.1994); **State v. Burgess,** 876 So.2d 263 (La.App. 3 Cir. 2004); **United States v. Colin,** 314 F.3d 439 (9th Cir. 2002); **State v. Brite,** 120 Ohio App. 3d 517, 698 N.E.2d 478, (1998); **State v. Lafferty,** 291 Mont. 157, 967 P.2d 363 (Mont. 1998); **Wilson v. State,** 874 P.2d 215 (Wyo. 1994); **United States v. Gregory,** 79 F.3d 973 (10th Cir. 1996); **United States v. Smith,** 799 F.2d 704 (11th Cir. 1986).

night, and where the officer is aware that burglaries have occurred in the immediate area in the recent past,[441] rise to articulable suspicion.

Some cases get decided on a minor fact, such as the vehicle stopping abruptly and then suddenly turning into a parking lot, thereby creating "reasonable suspicion" of the driver seeking to avoid the roadblock versus visiting someone who lived there. This is why the detailed account of your arrest that you give to your criminal defense specialist is so important.

7.12. Stopped because the officer saw an unusual but insignificant driving error that did not rise to the level of being reasonable suspicion of impaired driving. For the police to begin their investigation of a suspected crime (like DUI-DWI), by confronting you (i.e., using emergency lights or a siren to pull you over) as you are driving, they must have some other evidence that a crime is occurring.[442] To stop your car without justification violates your constitutionally guaranteed right to be free from illegal searches and seizures protected by the Fourth Amendment[443] and applied to actions of the States through the Fourteenth Amendment.[444]

For you to have a good challenge to an unconstitutional pullover, the driving behavior may be unusual, but not illegal. Each of these cases is fact-specific and will be determined by how well your DUI-DWI attorney can use cross-examination at the pre-trial motion hearing to uncover the officer's baseless decision to pull you over.

In a pair of Georgia cases, where one defendant took a few extra seconds to get going when a traffic light turned green,[445] or where another defendant and the passenger switched places at a stop sign,[446] neither act alone formed reasonable suspicion for a pullover when there were no other vehicles affected and each defendant did not impede other traffic. In a Minnesota case, just because a driver appeared startled at the appearance of a police officer, this did not form enough reasonable suspicion for a stop.[447] A similar situation occurred in Florida when the police approached a defendant legally sitting in his parked car, and asked the driver to step out of the vehicle and start an investigation merely because the defendant appeared somewhat startled at the officer's approach.[448]

7.13. Stopped after the officer's driving actions caused or "created" weaving due to the driver's preoccupation with the "threatening" actions of the police car in the rear view mirror. Some courts recognize that the presence of a law enforcement officer "tailgating" you, or aggressive driving or approaching rapidly from the rear of your vehicle (leading to your constant observation of the officer in your rearview mirror) may reasonably

---

[441]**City of Minot v. Johnson**, 603 N.W.2d 485 (N.D. 1999).

[442]**People v. Luedemann**, 357 Ill.App.3d 411, 828 N.E.2d 355 (2005); **United States v. Chanthasouxat**, 342 F.3d 1271 (11th Cir. 2003); **Crooks v. State**, 710 So.2d 1041 (Fla. App. 1998); **State v. Cerny**, 28 S.W. 3d 796 (Tex. App. 2000); **State v. Tarvin**, 972 S.W. 2d 910 (Tex. App. 1998); **State v. Gullett**, 78 Ohio App. 3d 138, 145; 604 N.E.2d 176 (1992); **State v. Holler**, 224 Ga. App. 66, 479 S.E.2d 780, (1996); **State v. Aguirre**, 229 Ga. App. 736, 494 S.E.2d 576 (1997); **Martin v. State**, 257 Ga. App. 435, 571 S.E.2d 459 (2002).

[443]The right of the people to be secure in their persons, houses, papers, and effects, against unreasonable searches and seizures, shall not be violated... U.S.C.A. Const. Amend. IV.

[444][N]or shall any State deprive any person of life, liberty, or property, without due process of law... U.S.C.A. Const. Amend. XIV.

[445]**Martin v. State,** 257 Ga.App. 435, 571 S.E.2d 459 (2002).

[446]**Streicher v. State,** 213 Ga.App. 670, 445 S.E.2d 815 (1994).

[447]**State v. Johnson,** 444 N.W.2d 824 (Minn. 1989).

[448]**Popple v. State,** 626 So.2d 185 (Fla. 1993).

cause you to weave while trying to drive lawfully. Some states have held that weaving caused by the officer's goading or "threatening driving conduct" by itself does not establish an articulable suspicion of a crime that gives the police a legitimate basis to stop you and subject you to a search and seizure unless the movements of your vehicle are also unsafe.[449]

Brief lapses of staying in your lane are not necessarily violations of the law.[450] If such acts by the police car behind you triggered your errant driving in your DUI-DWI stop by the police, and this weaving was the officer's only reason for stopping you, it is possible that (with the proper proof) the court will declare the stop to have been unjustified and not allow any evidence against you that arose out of the stop.

This situation, like those in several other subsections of this chapter, depends on excellent representation by a quality DUI-DWI attorney and fair consideration by a judge who truly honors and follows our Constitution. Unfortunately, finding a top-quality attorney is usually easier than finding such a judge.

---

[449]**Rowe v. State** 363 Md. 424, 437; 769 A.2d 879 (2001); **Crooks v. State**, 710 So.2d 1041 (Fla. App. 1998); **State v. Cerny**, 28 S.W. 3d 796 (Tex. App. 2000); **State v. Tarvin**, 972 S.W. 2d 910 (Tex. App. 1998); **State v. Gullett**, 78 Ohio App. 3d 138, 604 N.E.2d 176 (1992).

[450]**Frasier v. Driver and Motor Vehicle Services Branch (DMV)**, 172 Ore. App. 215 (2001); **State v. Livingston**, 206 Ariz. 145, 75 P.3d 1103 (Ariz.Ct.App. 2003); **United States v. Gregory** 79 F.3d 973 (10th Cir. 1996).

Chapter 8

The "Discovery" Process: How Your Attorney Learns What Evidence the Prosecutor Has and Decides How to Challenge or Explain It

8.0. Purpose of this chapter. In fighting your DUI-DWI case, your side has the right to know some, if not all, information about your arrest and the chemical testing the prosecutor is preparing to use against you at your trial. In some jurisdictions, the disclosure of some facts is mandatory, while in other states, disclosure is not as easy to obtain. The process by which this information is released to your attorney by the prosecution, and also (in most states) from your side to the prosecution, is called "discovery."

The best DUI-DWI trial specialists know what to expect to receive from the prosecutor in a typical case. They also know what they should be provided, and more importantly, when something important appears to be missing. This chapter explains part of the discovery process that applies to your case.

8.1. States vary in the comprehensiveness of the discovery allowed under local law, but the United States Supreme Court rulings set the "floor" below which no state can go. The minimum discovery that must be provided to you in a criminal prosecution (if properly requested by your attorney) has been established by the United States Supreme Court. In a case known as *Brady v. Maryland,* if the prosecution has any exculpatory evidence (evidence that tends to be favorable to you), he or she must eventually provide this evidence. In some jurisdictions, however, this can be withheld until your trial.[451]

When a prosecutor fails to divulge such important data in a timely fashion, this is called a "discovery violation." There are three components of a true *Brady* violation: the evidence at issue must be favorable to the accused, either because it is exculpatory, or because it tends to impeach the police officer; the evidence must have been suppressed or withheld by the State, either willfully or inadvertently; and prejudice to your case must have occurred.[452]

The "floor" of discovery has other limits. The Sixth Amendment compulsory process clause may be violated if a trial judge blocks a defense witness's ability to testify if that ruling entirely excludes the testimony of a material defense witness.[453] If your DUI-DWI case is pending in federal court, the discovery rules are covered in Federal Rules of Criminal Procedure, Rule 16. Otherwise, rely upon your DUI-DWI trial specialist to understand your state's laws. He or she will be fully aware of how strong the discovery laws are in your state.

8.2. Different tools can be used to uncover information relevant to your case. Many different tools may be utilized by your attorney in a criminal prosecution in order to "discover" information regarding the evidence the prosecutor will use to try to prove your guilt. Either side can require people to come to court to testify (through issuance of a subpoena), or require them to come to court and bring documents or other items with them to be used as possible evidence in your trial. (This is called a "subpoena *duces tecum*"). A motion to produce (similar to the device used in a civil case) may be used in your state, too. These and other possible tools are discussed below.

---

[451]**Brady v. Maryland,** 373 U.S. 83, 83 S.Ct. 1194, 10 L.Ed.2d 215 (1963).

[452]**Strickler v. Greene,** 527 U.S. 263, 119 S.Ct. 1936, 144 L.Ed.2d 286 (1999).

[453]**Taylor v. Illinois,** 484 U.S. 400, 108 S.Ct. 646, 98 L.Ed.2d 798 (1988).

In some states, a pre-trial deposition (sworn testimony from key state witnesses taken down verbatim by a court reporter), can be requested by your attorney. Also, as part of your administrative license suspension (or revocation) hearing, your attorney may be able to use civil "discovery" tools such as a "notice to produce" (to compel documents or tapes to be turned over), "requests to admit" certain facts, or other civil forms of discovery to uncover favorable evidence. In some jurisdictions, the use of pre-trial "civil" depositions of police officers may be available for your attorney to use.

The primary purpose of forcing the state to reveal or turn over 100% of any available items that will (or could be) used to help prove your case at trial is that your skilled DUI-DWI defense attorney knows that the "smoking gun" that wins your case may be found in these materials. Additionally, any pre-trial hearings or depositions that require your police officers to give sworn testimony "locks in" key testimony from them for your trial when it later gets scheduled. This can lead to the impeachment of the officer and possibly cause his or her total collapse on the witness stand.

8.2.1. Subpoenas. A subpoena is an order of the court handling your case for a witness to appear at a particular time and place, for the purpose of giving sworn testimony. A subpoena may also be used in some states to obtain pre-trial testimony from a witness at scheduled depositions (testimony under oath taken outside of court), pre-trial motions, or administrative license suspension/revocation hearings and at trial. Subpoenas are issued by the court clerk or the judge of the tribunal you are in (e.g., criminal court or administrative license suspension hearings) under the authority of the court, but must be served personally on the party being summoned. Failure to appear as required by the subpoena can be punished as contempt of court if it appears the absence was intentional or occurred without justifiable excuse for non-attendance.[454]

8.2.2. Subpoena *duces tecum* (seeks documents or items to be brought with the person who is appearing pursuant to the subpoena). A subpoena duces tecum[455] (sometimes referred to by attorneys by the acronym "SDT") is a court order requiring a witness to bring documents in his or her possession (or under the control of the witness) to a certain place at a certain time. This subpoena must be served personally on the person who possesses or has control of the documents and whose appearance at court is commanded. The list must be clear in stating what items are being requested. If such a SDT is overly broad or oppressive, the prosecutor may seek a protective order from the judge that restricts or limits the scope of the SDT.

Issuance of a subpoena duces tecum is the common way to obtain potentially useful evidence, such as police reports or videotapes that are in the possession of a third party. A subpoena duces tecum must specify the documents or types of documents (e.g. "All roadblock records and supervising officer authorization records for the sobriety checkpoint established September 21, 2005 at the intersection of Smith Street and Jones Avenue, Peoria, Illinois at or about 2:00 A.M.") or it will be subject to an objection that the request is "too broad and burdensome."

---

[454]http://dictionary.law.com/default2.asp?typed=subpena&type=1; Tennessee - T. C. A. § 40-2-107; Texas - Vernon's Ann.Texas C.C.P. Art. 24.01 et. seq.; Florida - West's F.S.A. § 914.04; Georgia - O.C.G.A. § 24-10-20 et. seq.; Washington - Superior Court Criminal Rules, CrR 4.7; Indiana - Trial Procedure Rule 45; Mississippi - Miss. Code Ann. § 99-15-9; California - West's Ann.Cal.Penal Code § 1326 et. seq.

[455]Tennessee - T. C. A. § 40-17-123; Texas - V.T.C.A., Government Code § 552.0055; Vernon's Ann.Texas C.C.P. Art. 24.02; Florida - West's F.S.A. § 914.04; Georgia - O.C.G.A. §§ 9-11-35, 9-11-45, 24-10-20 et. seq.; Washington - Superior Court Criminal Rules, CrR 4.7; Indiana - Trial Procedure Rule 26 et. seq.; Mississippi - Miss. Code Ann. § 99-15-9; California - West's Ann.Cal.Penal Code § 1054 et. seq.

To obtain documents from the opposing party, a "Request for Production of Documents" is more commonly used in some states. Failure to respond to a subpoena duces tecum (or in some states, a motion or request for the production of documents) may expose the non-complying party to punishment for contempt of court for disobeying a court order.[456] Fines or even jail sentences, or both, can be imposed by the judge. In some instances, the judge may order reimbursement of costs and attorney's fees to you for the State's non-compliance.

8.2.3. Freedom of information act (F.O.I.A.). The Freedom of Information Act, as codified in 5 U.S.C.A. § 552 is a federal law that requires any federal agency to make available and provide to the party requesting disclosure certain information that those agencies have in their possession. This may include documents such as copies of police department records and administrative staff training manuals.

Certain records may be protected from disclosure, such as records in an ongoing investigation by the police. Depending on whether or not there was any federal involvement in your DUI-DWI (such as federal training manuals for law enforcement officers or any information from federal law enforcement agencies), this information must be provided to you and your attorney.

Many states have adopted state disclosure statutes that track the F.O.I.A. law in their jurisdiction. For example, South Carolina has a very powerful "F.O.I.A." type statute known as "Rule 5" that allows you to get virtually any state record or other tangible piece of favorable or potentially favorable evidence that may be used in your case. Your DUI-DWI defense specialist will be thoroughly knowledgeable about your state's discovery tools and the scope of your state's laws in reaching hidden records.

8.2.4. Open records act requests. Other states have adopted statutes that are somewhat similar to the Freedom of Information Act. These laws are sometimes called "open records act" laws and allow for the public inspection of documents, papers, letters, maps, books, tapes and other materials in the possession of public agencies and officers. However, as a part of these open records requests, certain materials may be restricted from such disclosure - like information from ongoing investigations and the names of confidential informants.[457]

8.2.5. Motion to produce. A motion to produce (or "notice to produce") is a formal written request filed by your attorney, asking the court to order the prosecution to release a copy of some item of evidence or document to you that the prosecution possesses. Many states utilize this form of discovery in both civil and criminal cases. A motion of this type can also come from the prosecution asking your side to produce some evidence, as long as it is not confidential or protected under the "attorney-client privilege" or another privilege such as marital or psychiatric privilege. Whether or not the judge grants the motion depends on what is being asked for, and if the side asking for the evidence has some clear legal right to obtain the evidence.

8.2.6. Depositions (available in some states, and at some ALS/ALR proceedings). A deposition is where both sides get a chance prior to trial or hearings to question a person, while the witness is under oath, and with the proceedings being recorded

---

[456]http://dictionary.law.com/default2.asp?typed=subpena+duces+tecum&type=1.

[457]Georgia O.C.G.A.§50-18-70; Alabama - ARE Rule 508; California - West's Ann.Cal.Gov.Code § 6253; Florida - West's F.S.A. § 119.07; Indiana - IC 5-14-3-1 et. seq.; Mississippi - Miss. Code Ann. § 25-61-1 et. seq.; Tennessee - T. C. A. § 10-7-503; Texas - V.T.C.A., Government Code § 552.021 et. seq.; Washington - West's RCWA 42.17.260.

either as a transcript by a court reporter, by a videotape (or digital recording), or by a video recording. It allows either side's attorney to send written notice to require witnesses to appear at a specific time and place and provide sworn testimony.

If any laws make these discovery devices available to you, this means that you may not have to wait until trial to ask very important questions of key witnesses against you relating to your case. Such early disclosure of vital information can assist your attorney in seeking a possible compromise resolution of the drunken driving accusation (reduced charges) or possible dismissal of your case. Remember that depositions are much more common in civil litigation than in criminal cases. A few states allow depositions in DUI-DWI or other criminal cases as a part of the discovery process,[458] while most do not.[459] Most states have provisions for taking depositions in administrative license suspension (or revocation) hearings that are related to a criminal charge for DUI-DWI. These ALS/ALR hearings are civil in nature, not criminal.

The other benefit to taking a deposition is that if a witness later changes his or her story, and your attorney catches them in this discrepancy, then this change of sworn testimony can be used against this witness to impeach him or her. The impeachment of a key witness can be a large part of your favorable evidence at trial. Judges and juries do not appreciate witnesses who change their "version of the truth" on important issues. These witnesses are not trusted when their stories change. This is a tactical step during trial that can be critical for you when it is your word against the officer's and the jury has to decide who is a credible witness and who is not.

In criminal proceedings, since you are charged with a crime, you cannot be compelled to testify. It is your choice (under the direction and guidance of your experienced trial attorney) whether you ever provide any testimony at trial or at pre-trial matters. Any sworn testimony that you give at a pre-trial hearing for purposes of proving an issue relating to suppression of illegally obtained evidence cannot be introduced at your trial if you and your attorney decide to have you remain silent at trial. The police officers and other witnesses cannot opt out of giving sworn testimony, if properly subpoenaed.

8.2.7. Private investigator. Your attorney may feel that the use of a private investigator might be beneficial for your defense. This typically involves an additional cost for you, but these professionals can be worth their weight in gold. Such investigators often are retired law enforcement officers who have good contacts with the local police officers who are still on the job and they know how the other side thinks and operates. Most of the best DUI-DWI trial lawyers across America use one or more private investigators, where the investigator's input or investigation could be vital to finding a way to win.

Private investigators also know how to evaluate the scene of your stop (the roadway location) for problems with the fairness of your field sobriety evaluations. An investigator might be able to uncover other discrepancies in the police report (or the video records) and may help explain to the judge or jury some "problem" with your balance (that occurred during field testing

---

[458]New York - **People v. Rose,** 8 Misc.3d 184, 794 N.Y.S.2d 630 (N.Y.Dist.Ct. 2005); Florida - Fla. R. Crim. P. Rule 3.220, **Russ v. City of Jacksonville,** 734 So.2d 508 (Fla.App. 1 Dist. 1999); Iowa - **Iowa Supreme Court Bd. of Professional Ethics and Conduct v. Apland,** 577 N.W.2d 50 (Iowa 1998); Georgia - **Keef v. State,** 220 Ga.App. 134, 469 S.E.2d 318 (1996); Kansas - **Angle v. Kansas Dept. of Revenue,** 12 Kan.App.2d 756, 758 P.2d 226 (1988); Texas - Vernon's Ann.Texas Const. Art. 1, § 10.
[459]New Mexico - **Dente v. State Taxation and Revenue Dept., Motor Vehicle Div.,** 124 N.M. 93, 946 P.2d 1104 (N.M.App. 1997).

on the roadside video made by the officer) in order to help sway the ultimate "fact finder" (jury or judge) to enter a "not guilty" verdict.

If your experienced DUI-DWI attorney recommends the hiring of a private investigator for your case, it is because your attorney is looking after your best interest, not just wanting to spend your money. Many times, the input of the private investigator can help uncover a "smoking gun" in the arresting officer's reports or in his or her prior disciplinary history. Other times, this investigator can provide the winning evidence in your DUI-DWI trial by testifying about the arresting officer's violation of training or breat testing protocol.

8.2.8. Officer's disciplinary file. If any of the law enforcement officers involved in your DUI-DWI stop and arrest have had disciplinary problems in the past which could be relevant to your situation, this information can be obtained by your legal counsel as a part of the state's open records act, discovery obligations or similar disclosure laws.[460] If the last five of the officer's DUI-DWI stops and arrests were all thrown out due to sloppy or refuted police work, why should the jury believe the officer for your arrest? Or, if the officer was disciplined for not being truthful, this may be ammunition to challenge his or her credibility at trial. Once an officer has been officially sanctioned, disciplined, fired, suspended or otherwise "written up" as a liar, his or her ability to continue in work as a "street cop" is going to be short-lived.

8.2.9. Officer's training records for state police academy central records. In some states, all of the training records for the local law enforcement officers are available to your attorney as a part of the state F.O.I.A. or open records act.[461] Two important details might come from these employment records.

First, it allows your attorney to prepare to more fully question law enforcement officers who will be testifying against you at either a pre-trial hearing or at your trial. The better prepared your attorney is, the more likely the questions asked of the police officers will provide answers for the possible legal issues in your case. Having ALL the critical information derived from discovery is the best way to win a DUI-DWI case – either during a motions hearing or at the trial of the case.

For example, in one trial the author handled, the officer was shown on videotape "bullying" the author's client both verbally and through physical "posturing." The author used his training records to point out to the jury that he had taken four courses on the topic of "verbal judo," and had recently been made an instructor in how to verbally overpower a suspect under investigation. In part, the case was won by pursuing a 20-minute line of questions on this "skill" that he used on a young man frightened half to death.

Second, if any police officer on the witness stand at either trial or at a pre-trial hearing states something on the record regarding his or her training or experience, especially if it is in regard to their DUI-DWI experience or training, and the records do not reflect similar information, the officer's candor with the judge or jury can be put in doubt. The more the police officer is proved to be mistaken, or not be able to tell the truth, or demonstrates a lack of adequate training, the more the judge and jury have reason to believe you over the officer.

---

[460]Georgia O.C.G.A.§50-18-70; Alabama - ARE Rule 508; California - West's Ann.Cal.Gov.Code § 6253; Florida - West's F.S.A. § 119.07; Indiana - IC 5-14-3-1 et. seq.; Mississippi - Miss. Code Ann. § 25-61-1 et. seq.; Tennessee - T. C. A. § 10-7-503; Texas - V.T.C.A., Government Code § 552.021 et. seq.; Washington - West's RCWA 42.17.260.

[461]Georgia O.C.G.A.§50-18-70; Alabama - ARE Rule 508; California - West's Ann.Cal.Gov.Code § 6253; Florida - West's F.S.A. § 119.07; Indiana - IC 5-14-3-1 et. seq.; Mississippi - Miss. Code Ann. § 25-61-1 et. seq.; Tennessee - T. C. A. § 10-7-503; Texas - V.T.C.A., Government Code § 552.021 et. seq.; Washington - West's RCWA 42.17.260.

8.3. A disclosure motion filed with the court and properly served upon the prosecutor will cause a list of prosecution witnesses to be produced. One of the most important things that is obtained as a result of your discovery request of the State is that the prosecutor's office must release vital information about its witnesses against you at trial, such as name, phone number, address and similar information. Typically, this is required for any of their potential scheduled witnesses.[462] This information greatly increases the preparedness of your attorney, giving him or her valuable preparation time in order to best plan your defense.

Most experienced DUI-DWI specialists know the police officers in their jurisdictions, the usual state experts, as well as what kind of witnesses these people make when they are in front of a jury. Many experienced DUI-DWI attorneys maintain previous transcripts of these officers and experts. Your defense is often designed around the strengths and weaknesses of the prosecutor's case, starting with their list of witnesses and your attorney's understanding of how the State will attempt to prove the case against you.

Following these rules of disclosure, if your state has a statutory legal requirement for the release of the list of witnesses, and the prosecution does so, but later attempts to introduce a "surprise" witness at trial, such a move is seldom permitted by the judge. Most states have strict court rules or "case" law (decisional law) that prohibit the use of "surprise" witnesses absent proof that the name or location of the witness was only discovered that day (or the day before trial).

8.4. Reciprocal discovery rules may require your attorney to also disclose to the prosecutor. Depending on the discovery rules of your state and the exact charges against you, certain information regarding documents and your expert or fact witnesses must be released by your side to the prosecutor as well. Depending on your state's laws, you may have to disclose a limited amount of information about the "substance" of your witnesses' testimony. This release in some cases is mandatory and in some cases, occurs only if the court grants a motion sought by the prosecution for the state to receive the information from your attorney.[463] In other states, no meaningful reciprocal discovery from the defense to the prosection exists, at least for a misdemeanor DUI-DWI case.[464]

8.5. Videotapes are generally discoverable. If the police officer who stopped you took videotape recordings on either analog or digital recording devices, a copy of this video is generally available for your defense.[465] This is not true in all states, such as Georgia or Virginia, where the tape must only be made available at trial.[466] Unless allowed to be withheld by statute, failure of the prosecution or the police to release these tapes to your attorney prior to (or within a fixed number of days prior to trial) trial usually means the withheld information cannot be used against you in your trial.

---

[462]Georgia - O.C.G.A.§ 17-16-21; Fla. R. Crim. P. Rule 3.220(b)(1)(A); Indiana - Trial Procedure Rule 26(B)(1); California - West's Ann.Cal.Penal Code § 1054.1; Tennessee - T. C. A. § 40-17-106; Texas - Vernon's Ann.Texas Const. Art. 1, § 10; Vernon's Ann.Texas C.C.P. Art. 39.14; Washington - Rule CrRLJ 4.7.

[463]Tenn. R. Crim. P., Rule 16(b); Washington - Superior Court Criminal Rules, CrR 4.7; California - West's Ann.Cal.Const. Art. 1, § 30; Indiana - Trial Procedure Rule 26; Washington - Rule CrRLJ 4.7.

[464]Georgia, Texas.

[465]Washington - Superior Court Criminal Rules, CrR 4.7, West's RCWA 5.45.020, West's RCWA 9.73.100; California - West's Ann.Cal.Penal Code § 1054.1; Indiana - Trial Procedure Rule 26(B)(1); Mississippi - MS Const. Art. 3, § 26; Texas -Vernon's Ann.Texas C.C.P. Art. 39.14; Washington - West's RCWA 10.58.010, West's RCWA 5.45.020.

[466]O.C.G.A. §17-7-210, **Orr v. State,** 209 Ga. App. 832, 434 S.E.2d 723 (1993).

Be aware, however, that video recordings are not universally used in all police stops. In California, video is rare. In South Carolina, video recordings exist in virtually any traffic stop. In Georgia, Texas and Tennessee, most DUI-DWI "task force" officers have cameras in their cars.

8.6. Look for private security video footage from a parking lot or business cameras where your car was stopped. One thing you can do, or a private investigator may do for you, is to investigate the vicinity of your stop and arrest. While the police may or may not have a video recording of your encounter with the police, other video cameras may have been positioned on buildings, in parking lots, or even set up on tall poles by private security services hired to maintain security for a mall or shopping center. If the police have a short video showing only what occurred *after* your car was pulled over, it may be helpful to your defense to locate an independent, and sometimes more comprehensive, video of the entire driving path leading up to your arrest location. Such evidence can reveal inappropriate actions or even constitutional violations by the police that can help your attorney obtain a favorable resolution to your case.

An example where this might help is if the police officer testifies that the only reason your vehicle was stopped was because you were weaving illegally in and out of traffic or crossing the lane lines. Often, a police video is only activated at the time the officer decided to stop you, which is usually after these alleged traffic violations occurred. An independent video from an adjacent parking lot camera or an interstate monitoring camera will be devastating to the state's case if it proves you didn't change lanes or weave.

Since the September 11, 2001 terrorist attacks in America, the federal government has gained enormous power to spy on all of America, including your vehicle while it is driving upon the highways of your state. Billions of dollars have been spent by the state and federal government to erect cameras along interstates and on some state thoroughfares and freeways. Footage from one or more of these cameras may be discoverable as part of your defense if these records exist and are subject to subpoena or F.O.I.A. requests. If the reason for the traffic stop is thrown out, then so are all the subsequent charges such as charges for DUI-DWI that are only discovered by the police after the illegal arrest. This is called "lack of reasonable suspicion" (or "lack of articulable suspicion") to believe a crime or traffic violation has been committed.

8.7. Police dispatch tapes and computer-aided dispatch (CAD) logs available from headquarters. Most police departments maintain taped copies of their dispatch radio communications and computer-aided dispatch (CAD) logs for several days to several months after they are created. Even after recordings are disposed of, a printout or written account is usually maintained for a lengthy period of time. Under the F.O.I.A. or Open Records Act in each state, this information may be available to you and your attorney.[467]

These tapes and logs may confirm or may refute what the police officer at the scene of your DUI-DWI arrest wrote down about the incident. In the alternative, these records might give your attorney a "smoking gun" as an independent source of highly credible data. The best DUI-DWI specialists will refuse to leave any stone unturned in their investigation of your arrest, and this information might help your case. In some instances, the tapes may not be favorable to you. This type of exhaustive search for **ANY** helpful information is what justifies higher fees for the best DUI-DWI attorneys.

---

[467]Georgia O.C.G.A.§50-18-70; Alabama - ARE Rule 508; California - West's Ann.Cal.Gov.Code § 6253; Florida - West's F.S.A. § 119.07; Indiana - IC 5-14-3-1 et. seq.; Mississippi - Miss. Code Ann. § 25-61-1 et. seq.; Tennessee - T. C. A. § 10-7-503; Texas - V.T.C.A., Government Code § 552.021 et. seq.; Washington - West's RCWA 42.17.260.

One example of how these CAD logs can assist your DUI-DWI defense attorney is to help challenge the time of the stop. Because virtually all "per se" alcohol DUI-DWI statutes contain a 2, 3, or 4-hour "window" after you stopped driving within which the police must obtain a breath, blood or urine test. Delays in procuring this test may cause this type of drunk driving prosecution to fail, based on a lack of proof that your "chemical test" was taken within the designated period of time.[468] Beyond winning the "per se" count in your case, proof of false testimony by the officer may convince the jury (or your trial judge) to find you "not guilty" on all charges.

8.8. Any "BOLO" cases likely will have the actual "911" entirely recorded. A "**B**e **O**n the **L**ook**O**ut" or BOLO call is where a concerned citizen has typically called the 911 operator or the police department directly to report a possible criminal violation. These emergencies calls between the operator and the police are likely to have been recorded.[469]

Under the F.O.I.A. or the Open Records Act in your state, this information may be available to you.[470] Finding errors or inconsistencies in the "reported" information can cause the entire police "stop" to be declared illegal. If the information given by the concerned citizen is not specific or detailed enough to have allowed the police to stop you, or if there were significant details regarding identification of you or your vehicle that were very different than described in the emergency call by the concerned citizen, your case can be won.

The author actually won a vehicular homicide case in which the driver was described as a black male in a Ford Explorer, blue in color, and no tag numbers or predicted path of travel given. Two miles away, on a different city street, a green Jeep Cherokee driven by a blonde, blue-eyed male was pulled over and charged with the crime. The entire case was dismissed at a pre-trial motion hearing, despite his 0.23 blood alcohol content.

8.9. Accident reports from police department that investigated accident. If you were involved in a motor vehicle accident as a part of your DUI-DWI arrest, a police investigation of the accident likely exists. Either the officers at the scene, or a special team of police accident investigators, may have measured physical markings, ruts or skid distances, collected physical evidence at the scene, taken photographs or video footage, and may have performed chemical or scientific analysis of certain items collected at the accident scene.

Whatever the police did, or if done by official representatives of the police or the crime lab, it is usually possible for your attorney to get copies of these investigative reports if it is not already part of the regular police report regarding your arrest for DUI-DWI.[471] Furthermore, your attorney may be able to get this information under an F.O.I.A. request or Open Records Act demand.[472]

---

[468]**Abelson v. State,** 269 Ga.App. 596, 604 S.E.2d 647 (2004); **Yarbrough v. State,** 241 Ga.App. 777, 527 S.E.2d 628 (2000).

[469]**Page v. State,** 250 Ga.App. 795, 553 S.E.2d 176 (2001).

[470]Georgia O.C.G.A.§50-18-70; Alabama - ARE Rule 508; California - West's Ann.Cal.Gov.Code § 6253; Florida - West's F.S.A. § 119.07; Indiana - IC 5-14-3-1 et. seq.; Mississippi - Miss. Code Ann. § 25-61-1 et. seq.; Tennessee - T. C. A. § 10-7-503; Texas - V.T.C.A., Government Code § 552.021 et. seq.; Washington - West's RCWA 42.17.260.

[471]Fla. R. Crim. P. Rule 3.220(b)(1)(B); Tenn. R. Crim. P., Rule 16(a)(1)(C); Vernon's Ann.Texas C.C.P. Art. 39.14(a); Indiana - Trial Procedure Rule 26(B)(1); Washington - Rule CrRLJ 4.7.

[472]Georgia O.C.G.A.§50-18-70; Alabama - ARE Rule 508; California - West's Ann.Cal.Gov.Code § 6253; Florida - West's F.S.A. § 119.07; Indiana - IC 5-14-3-1 et. seq.; Mississippi - Miss. Code Ann. § 25-61-1 et. seq.; Tennessee - T. C. A. § 10-7-503; Texas - V.T.C.A., Government Code § 552.021 et. seq.; Washington - West's RCWA 42.17.260.

Be aware that blindly relying on police measurements, photographs, interviews and "conclusions" drawn from such physical evidence and witness statements falls short of being "independent." Hiring your own accident reconstruction expert as soon as possible could mean the difference between acquittal and conviction. [See Section 8.10 of this book.]

At times, your attorney may have to file a motion asking your court to require the prosecution to provide your side with copies of these reports. If timely and properly requested and not provided by the prosecutor before trial, the court can exclude this non-disclosed information from being used against you. Additionally, if it is later discovered (after your conviction) that the prosecutor hid "exculpatory" (favorable) information that would have aided your attorney in the defense of your case, a motion for a new trial, motion in arrest of judgement or similar "post-conviction" filing may overturn your conviction.

8.10. Possible use of an accident reconstruction specialist. If your situation involved a motor vehicle accident, your attorney may recommend that you hire an accident reconstruction specialist. Such a witness will typically be most valuable to your case at the earliest possible date after the collision in order to document and measure any skid marks, existing obstructions of your view (such as hedges at an intersection) etc. An accident reconstruction specialist will almost always have either police or engineering training (or both) that allows him or her to look at the report of your accident and apply engineering standards and other scientific principles (i.e., physics) to reconstruct or recreate what likely caused the accident.

These reconstruction experts may even be able to determine who was "at fault," and other critical details such as the speed of the vehicles at the time of the accident, the braking pattern of all vehicles, or even identify the relative positions of passengers inside the vehicles prior to the collision. Sometimes these details make the difference between a guilty verdict and an acquittal, or a reduction from a felony vehicular homicide charge to a misdemeanor offense.

Your DUI-DWI attorney may suggest the use of a specific accident reconstruction specialist due to a number of factors. The attorney's recommendation may be based on who is best for your particular type of accident, or possibly based upon who might have the best courtroom presence at your trial, or who has the best credentials. With experienced legal counsel, the choice of an expert on reconstruction ultimately might be determined by evaluating who best counters the proposed experts that the State has indicated that it will call upon to testify against you.

8.11. Court rules may allow a prosecutor to file certain special motions (e.g., motion to request to use "prior acts" evidence at the trial of current DUI-DWI) to seek to have your judge allow harmful evidence to be used against you at trial. In some states and in some courts, prosecutors may be able to admit some (or all) of your prior DUI-DWI arrests or other criminal convictions as part of the evidence in the current DUI-DWI case. These "prior acts" (or "similar transactions") can be considered by the judge or jury as part of the evidence they consider in trying to reach a verdict.[473] It can be devastating evidence for a jury to hear at trial.

Usually, the accusation for each crime stands by itself, the theory being that just because you robbed a store three years ago does not mean you committed the robbery offense for which you currently stand accused. Introduction of such information is typically considered

---

[473]California - West's Ann.Cal.Evid.Code § 1101; Georgia - Uniform Superior Court Rule 31.3; Florida - West's F.S.A. § 90.404(2)(c); Indiana - Rules of Evid., Rule 404(b); Texas - Rules of Evidence, Rule 404(b); Washington - West's RCWA 10.58.010, Washington Rules of Evidence, ER 404(b).

too inflammatory to be allowed into evidence. However, the prosecution may be allowed the opportunity to introduce evidence of your prior "similar" acts in your current DUI-DWI trial.

In some states (like Georgia), court rules liberally allow prosecutors to introduce ANY prior DUI-DWI conviction, if the correct witnesses can be brought to court. In other states (like South Carolina), the use of such "prior acts" evidence is virtually never allowed to be heard or considered by the current jury, absent its use for impeachment (when you have testified on your own behalf) or to provide an "element" of the current crime that you are disputing. (Example: if you are charged as a felon due to having two prior drunk driving convictions, you may dispute the prior convictions. Such dispute of this fact allows the prosecution to bring in proof of these prior convictions to provide a foundation for establishing the State's "third offense" evidence.)

When prosecutors seek to use "similar acts" evidence, most state statutes or rules of court require the prosecutor to tell you and your attorney a reasonable amount of time before your trial that the State wants to introduce such evidence at your trial and state the reasons why.[474] This gives your attorney time to fight the introduction of this potentially damaging information at trial and to prepare challenges concerning the information. Usually, a special hearing will be held outside the jury's presence to determine the admissibility of such "prior act" evidence. In the State of Washington, no advanced written notice is required.[475] In Georgia, a 10 day advance notice is required as a general rule.[476]

Your experienced trial attorney will know the available methods of trying to block that evidence of "prior acts" from coming into your trial. Common challenges that may be asserted by your criminal defense lawyer (and more than one may be asserted on your behalf) include:

(1) any probative value that this evidence is far outweighed by its prejudicial harm; or

(2) the age of the prior offense is so old that the two events are not truly similar or connected in any way; or

(3) the circumstances of the two cases are so completely different that the State cannot, in good faith, claim that proof of the prior act sheds any light on the likelihood that the new act was committed.

---

[474]California - West's Ann.Cal.Evid.Code § 1101; Georgia - Uniform Superior Court Rule 31.3; Florida - West's F.S.A. § 90.404(2)(c); Indiana - Rules of Evid., Rule 404(b); Texas - Rules of Evidence, Rule 404(b).

[475]Washington - West's RCWA 10.58.010, Washington Rules of Evidence, ER 404(b).

[476]Uniform Superior Court Rule 31.1; Uniform Superior Court Rule 31.3.

Chapter 9

Implied Consent (Informed Consent) (Expressed Consent) Laws:
How to Use These Laws to Help You Win the Case.

9.0. Purpose of this chapter. Just by driving or controlling your vehicle on any public road in any state, you have given that state your **implied consent** (in some states, referred to as **expressed consent** or **informed consent**) to have law enforcement officers who develop a reasonable suspicion of impairment to seek to test your blood for drugs or alcohol. However, as it is with most laws, the State is held to specific standards as well, if they are going to exercise this option of requesting that you be tested. This chapter describes these "implied consent" laws, and how you can use them to your advantage if you and your attorney have been arrested for DUI-DWI.

These laws, and the standards to which the State and law enforcement officers are held, can be very specific and technical. A time difference of plus or minus ten minutes one way or another, or in what order things were done in your DUI-DWI arrest, might be critically important for your defense.[477] If the police did not follow the established implied consent procedures in your state, your attorney may be able to get the charges against you dismissed even before a trial. This is why your attorney will need to know as precisely as possible what happened between you and any law enforcement officer, what was said by anyone at the arrest location, at what point in time it was said, and when anything was done (such as placing you in handcuffs or calling a tow truck). If your attorney's questions seem overly critical or nit-picky, his or her efforts to build your defense are the reason.

9.1 Explanation of implied (informed or expressed) consent laws in your state. Breath testing in DUI-DWI cases began in the United States in the late 1930s. Shortly after, in 1939, Indiana became the first of several states to pass laws permitting the introduction of breath test results as well as blood test results in DUI-DWI cases. Not surprisingly, "chemical" testing (referring to blood, breath or urine testing of any *chemicals* within these biological samples taken from a subject) quickly gained the favor of the law enforcement establishment. Just as quickly, however, drinking drivers learned to refuse to submit to such tests.

To overcome these refusals, the concept of **implied consent** was adopted, wherein the states embraced the fiction that a person who drives a motor vehicle on the State's highways is **deemed to have consented** to the chemical testing of his or her body fluids upon being lawfully arrested for a DUI-DWI offense. Initially, all states permitted the person's "implied" consent to be withdrawn (in other words, if asked to take a test by a police officer, the person could say "no"). However, when this happened, license loss penalties (or loss of the privilege to use the highways of the state where you refused) would be imposed by that state. The first implied consent law was passed in New York in 1953, and by 1971 all states had enacted similar laws.

As with many other DUI-DWI state laws, the wording of the statutes varies somewhat

---

[477]**Hough v. State,** 279 Ga. 711, 620 S.E.2d 380 (2005).

from state to state.[478] The types of warnings or advisements that may be required under an implied consent statute include: (1) a warning of the consequences of refusing to be tested; (2) a warning of the consequences of submitting to testing; (3) an advisement of the right to consult with an attorney before deciding whether to submit to chemical testing; and (4) an advisement as to the alternate types of chemical tests to which the defendant may choose to submit (i.e., breath test, blood test, urine test, etc). No state has all of these warnings. Most have at least two or three.

More importantly, when appellate courts within each state undertook to interpret the meaning of certain language in their state's laws, a wide range of legal holdings were rendered by the various states that related to the implied consent law of that jurisdiction. Today, the same holds true. In pro-citizen states such as Georgia, the courts have made implied consent rulings that are comparatively liberal in terms of constitutional and statutory protections.[479] In others, such as Arizona, the legal rulings on implied consent are dismally pro-prosecution.[480] See this article about Utah police officers forcibly taking your blood, and doing it themselves: http://www.duiblog.com/2005/02/01.

Why is all of this important? In most states, police officers must substantially comply with the statutory warning or advisement requirements in order for implied consent penalties to be invoked.[481] Warnings of the consequences of refusal typically must be clear and unequivocal.[482] The effect of an inadequate warning on the admissibility of a chemical test refusal in a criminal case can be exclusion at trial of any alleged refusal to be tested,[483] or erroneous advisements can affect the use of these tests at administrative hearings,[484] or at your eventual criminal trial.[485]

9.2. Can a law enforcement officer make the request for an implied consent blood, breath or urine test due to an accident, without gathering any traditional evidence of impairment due to the driver's injuries? Certainly, there may exist reasons for a law enforcement officer to request that you undergo a blood, urine or breath analysis if he or she observes you commit a traffic violation. Symptoms such as red, bloodshot eyes, slurred speech, poor performance on your field sobriety evaluations, the smell of alcohol on your breath and your other physical manifestations at the time of your stop may provide circumstantial evidence of possible intoxication. These questions and field tests form "reasonable grounds" or "probable cause" for you to be subjected to the scientific blood, urine or breath testing. In most states, your submittal to such testing **MUST** be preceded by proper, timely and complete implied consent advisements.

In some states, this "reasonable grounds" or "probable cause" element has been

---

[478]California - West's Ann.Cal.Vehicle Code § 23612(a)(1); Florida - West's F.S.A. § 316.1932(1)(a); Georgia - O.C.G.A. § 40-5-55(a); Indiana - IC 9-30-6-1; Mississippi - Miss. Code Ann. § 63-11-5(1); Tennessee - T.C.A. § 55-10-406(a)(1); Texas - V.T.C.A., Transportation Code § 724.011(a); Washington - West's RCWA 46.20.308(1), Wisconsin - W.S.A. 343.305(2).

[479]**State v. Collier,** 279 Ga. 316, 612 S.E.2d 281 (2005); **Hough v. State,** 279 Ga. 711, 620 S.E.2d 380 (2005).

[480]**State v. Clary**, 196 Ariz. 610, 2 P.3d 1255 (Ariz.App. Div. 1 2000).

[481]**State v. Bunnell**, 324 N.W.2d 418 (S.D. 1982); **Barnhart v. Dep't of Revenue**, 243 Kan. 209, 755 P.2d 1337 (1988); **Tarascio v. Muzio**, 40 Conn. Supp. 505, 515 A.2d 1082 (1986); **Kitchens v. State,** 258 Ga. App. 411, 574 S.E.2d 451 (2002).

[482]**Gargano v. Dep't of Motor Vehicles**, 118 A.D.2d 859, 500 N.Y.S.2d 346 (1986); **State v. Huber**, 540 N.E.2d 140 (Ind. App., 1989); **Graves v. Commonwealth**, 112 Pa. Commw. 390, 535 A.2d 707 (1988).

[483]**State v. Leviner,** 213 Ga. App. 99, 443 S.E.2d 688 (1994).

[484]**People v. Znaniecki**, 181 Ill. App.3d 389, 537 N.E.2d 16 (1989).

[485]**State v. Downer**, 460 So.2d 1184 (La. App., 1984).

specifically applied to vehicular homicide (vehicular manslaughter) statutes that purport to allow police to draw blood from every individual involved in a DUI-DWI fatality or serious injury crash. That is, if you are involved in a serious accident, with either very significant damages, visible serious injuries to anyone, or someone has died, in these states the law enforcement officers can require or ask every driver involved in the collision to undergo the scientific testing of their blood, breath or urine based on the implied consent statutes.[486]

However, the courts of some states have found that merely being in a serious accident or the fact that there has been a death in an accident does not amount by itself to enough reason for you to be forced to undergo such testing based on the implied consent statutes. The Mississippi Supreme Court declared the law in that state unconstitutional since it did not require that an officer develop a good faith belief that the cause of death was based upon evidence of another driver's impairment.[487] In a similar case in Georgia, the Supreme Court of Georgia also found a necessity of gathering basic evidence to support the belief that impairment resulted from alcohol, drugs or some impairing substance,[488] although a more recent case found that if there is any other evidence that a driver was under the influence of drugs or alcohol, a warrantless taking of your blood or urine is likely justified to protect the public.[489]

9.3. Does your state require the officer to give a formal, pre-formatted advisement? No constitutional or common law requirement compels the police to give such advisements.[490] These advisements, and the requirements to give them, come from state statutes. In some states, the law enforcement officer asking you to give a breath, urine or blood sample for the purposes of scientific testing under the implied consent statute must give you a very formal, pre-formatted advisement or explanation of your rights.[491] In other states, instead of a strict, formatted advisement, the officer must cover a list of items or steps for the implied consent issues to be covered adequately.[492] In Texas and South Carolina, you must sign a form acknowledging you have been informed of your rights if you refuse to provide a sample.[493]

The importance of this advisement is at least two-fold to you as a DUI-DWI defendant. First, the words coming from the officer give you *some* idea of your rights and your testing obligations. However, this statement does not inform you of all of your rights, nor is the topic or subject matter commonly known to the average citizen. Hence, its meaning is not fully understandable to most people, especially if they are not afforded access to legal assistance before deciding what to do. Typically, the police officer has little or no more knowledge of the meaning of this formal statement than you do, and any explanation they try to give you cannot be relied upon. In fact, his or her verbal "interpretation" of what the warning means can cause

---

[486]Florida - West's F.S.A. § 316.1933(1)(a); Georgia - O.C.G.A. § 40-5-55(a); Indiana - IC 9-30-7-3(a); Mississippi - Miss. Code Ann. § 63-11-8; Texas - V.T.C.A., Transportation Code § 724.012(b); Washington - West's RCWA 46.20.308(3).

[487]**McDuff v. State**, 763 So.2d 850 (Miss., 2000).

[488]**Cooper v. State**, 277 Ga. 282, 587 S.E.2d 605 (2003).

[489]**Hough v. State,** 279 Ga. 711, 620 S.E.2d 380 (2005).

[490]**South Dakota v. Neville**, 459 U.S. 553, 103 S. Ct. 916, 74 L. Ed. 2d 748 (1983); **Brewer v. Motor Vehicle Div.**, 720 P.2d 564 (Colo., 1986); **Leiven v. Comm'r**, 370 N.W.2d 432 (Minn., 1985).

[491]Georgia - O.C.G.A. § 40-5-67.1(b); Washington - West's RCWA 46.20.308(2); Wisconsin - W.S.A. 343.305(4).

[492]California - West's Ann.Cal.Vehicle Code §§ 23612(a)(1)(D), 23612(a)(4), 23614(b), 23614(c); Florida - West's F.S.A. § 316.1932(1)(a); Indiana - IC 9-30-6-7; Mississippi - Miss. Code Ann. §§ 63-11-5(2), 63-11-5(4), 63-11-21; Tennessee - T.C.A. § 55-10-406(a)(3); Texas - V.T.C.A., Transportation Code § 724.015.

[493]Texas - V.T.C.A., Transportation Code § 724.031; South Carolina Code 1976 § 56-5-2934.

the implied consent warning to be misleading and legally defective.[494]

Second, if a requirement exists in your state to give such an advisement, if the law enforcement officer failed to give it to you, or gave it in an incomplete or inaccurate fashion, any test results which were obtained after this flawed advisement may be excluded from evidence at trial after the issue is raised by way of a motion in limine by your DUI-DWI specialist.[495] The general rule is that if a warning of the consequences of refusal is required by statute and is not properly and timely given, you did not commit an implied consent violation.[496] In addition, the warning must be given by the proper person.[497] Without these test results, most DUI-DWI cases fall apart and the charges against you may well be dismissed or reduced.

9.4. Do your state laws require a valid arrest for DUI-DWI to occur prior to the implied consent advisements being read? The order in which the steps of your arrest and the advisement was given to you can make a very significant difference in your case, which is yet another reason why your attorney will ask you to work very hard at remembering everything that happened to you in the hours surrounding your DUI-DWI arrest. In most states, you must be officially arrested before the implied consent is read to you.[498] In other states, the order or sequence of steps required to invoke implied consent is not as important to these states' appellate judges, or it is not specified in the statute.[499]

9.5. Does your state mandate *when* the officer is required to give the implied consent notification, or otherwise lose the right to use the test results against you? In most States, the law enforcement officer must give you some form of implied consent notification before the blood, breath or urine sample is taken from you. Otherwise, the prevailing rule is that the test results will likely have to be thrown out.[500] The admonishment of your obligations and rights under implied consent may not have to be done word for word to match the precise words in the statutes. Instead, in most situations, it must inform you only of the true and legitimate consequences of your refusal as well as the implications of testing and rendering a result over the legal limit. In other states, the prosecution does not lose your test

---

[494]**City of Waupaca v. Javorski,** 198 Wis.2d 563, 543 N.W.2d 507 (1995); **Sponar v. South Carolina Dept. of Public Safety,** 361 S.C. 35, 603 S.E.2d 412 (S.C.App. 2004); **Kitchens v. State,** 258 Ga.App. 411, 574 S.E.2d 451 (2002); **People v. Franciskovich,** 202 Ill.App.3d 693, 560 N.E.2d 19 (1990).

[495]**State v. Lubin,** 164 Ga. App. 689, 297 S.E.2d 371 (1982); **State v. Renfroe,** 216 Ga. App. 709, 455 S.E.2d 383 (1995); **State v. Terry,** 236 Ga. App. 248, 511 S.E.2d 608 (1999); **State v. Collier,** 279 Ga. 316, 612 S.E.2d 281 (2005).

[496]**Postlewait v. Dep't of Revenue,** 643 S.W.2d 314 (Mo. App., 1982); **Garrison v. Dothard,** 366 So.2d 1129 (Ala. App., 1979).

[497]**Tartaglia v. State,** 753 S.W.2d 833 (Tex. App., 1988).

[498]Georgia - O.C.G.A. § 40-5-67.1(a); California - West's Ann.Cal.Vehicle Code § 23612(a)(1); Florida - West's F.S.A. § 316.1932(1)(a); Indiana - IC 9-30-6-7; Tennessee - T.C.A. § 55-10-406(a)(3); Washington - West's RCWA 46.20.308(1); **Commonwealth v. Nazzaro,** 112 Pa.Cmwlth. 543, 535 A.2d 761 (1988); **People v. Collins,** 154 Ill. App. 3d 149, 506 N.E.2d 963 (1987).

[499]Mississippi - Miss. Code Ann. §§ 63-11-5(2), 63-11-21; Texas - V.T.C.A., Transportation Code § 724.015; Washington - West's RCWA 46.20.308(2); **Westendorf v. Dep't of Transp.,** 400 N.W.2d 553 (Iowa, 1987); **Wood v. Motor Vehicles Div.,** 93 Or. App. 575, 763 P.2d 190 (1988); **Handschuh v. State,** 270 Ga. App. 676, 607 S.E.2d 899 (2004); **Hough v. State,** 279 Ga. 711, 620 S.E.2d 380 (2005).

[500]**Batliner v. Kansas Dept. of Revenue,** 90 P.3d 378 (Kan.App. 2004); **Nicholson v. Killens,** 116 N.C.App. 473, 448 S.E.2d 542 (N.C.App. 1994); **State v. Lubin,** 164 Ga. App. 689, 297 S.E.2d 371 (1982); **State v. Renfroe,** 216 Ga. App. 709, 455 S.E.2d 383 (1995); **State v. Terry,** 236 Ga. App. 248, 511 S.E.2d 608 (1999); **State v. Collier,** 279 Ga. 316, 612 S.E.2d 281 (Ga. 2005); **Postlewait v. Dep't of Revenue,** 643 S.W.2d 314 (Mo. App., 1982); **Garrison v. Dothard,** 366 So.2d 1129 (Ala. App., 1979).

results if at least some version or part of the correct notification is given.[501]

9.6. Are there criminal penalties for refusing testing? Several states are now making refusal to submit blood, urine or breath samples in a DUI-DWI a *criminal* act carrying criminal penalties. Some of these states only make it criminal if you are subsequently convicted of your DUI-DWI offense.[502] Such a refusal in these states can be a criminal offense by itself, or might only enhance your punishment beyond the regular penalties if you are convicted of the underlying DUI-DWI offense and are deemed to have refused to be tested..

Whether or not criminal penalties are imposed for refusing to take a blood, urine or breath test, such refusals often badly damage your DUI-DWI case. The admission into evidence by the prosecution to undergo chemical testing is often detrimental in the eyes of a jury. The admission of your refusal of your refusal against you at trial has been held to be constitutional by the United States Supreme Court and by nearly all states.[503] Unless satisfactorily explained, the jury will normally assume that you refused to be tested because you had consumed too much alcohol and were afraid of failing the test, an assumption that the prosecutor seldom fails to bring to the jury's attention. Experienced DUI-DWI attorneys know ways to neutralize the impact of a refusal in the eyes of either a judge (sitting without a jury) or a jury.

In addition, in many states the admission into evidence of a chemical test refusal entitles the prosecution to a "consciousness of guilt" jury instruction stating that the jury may consider the refusal as evidence of a consciousness of guilt of drunken driving by you. In those states, knowledgeable defense counsel may also submit a counterpart to the state's "consciousness of guilt" jury charge by submitting a "consciousness of innocence" jury charge (instruction) where you tried or offered to take some type of test, but were denied the opportunity to take a test by the officer.

Also, as a practical matter when evidence of a refusal is admitted during the prosecution's case, it is often necessary for you to have to testify in order to effectively explain your reasons for refusing to submit. Most experienced trial lawyers handling DUI-DWI trials prefer to NOT put their clients on the witness stand. Obviously then, the admission into evidence of a chemical test refusal should be avoided by seeking its exclusion at a pre-trial motion hearing, if at all possible.

9.7. What are the driving restrictions or loss of license penalties for refusal? Significant penalties typically exist for refusing to take the breath, blood or urine test when officially and properly requested to submit to such test or tests by the law enforcement officer. The specific automatic penalties depend on whether this is your first arrest for DUI-DWI. If it is not your first offense, the amount of time since your prior DUI-DWI offense(s) may determine the severity of any penalties for a second or third "refusal" to be tested under implied consent.[504]

---

[501]**Head v. State,** 137 Idaho 1, 43 P.3d 760 (2002); **Shoemaker v. Ohio Bur. of Motor Vehicles,** 78 Ohio App.3d 425, 604 N.E.2d 1386 (1992).

[502]**State v. Morale**, 174 Vt. 213, 811 A.2d 185 (Vt. 2002); California - West's Ann.Cal.Vehicle Code §§ 23612(a)(1)(D), 23577; Florida - West's F.S.A. §§ 316.1932(1)(a), 316.1939; Indiana - IC 9-30-7-5; Mississippi - Miss. Code Ann. § 63-11-30(4); Tennessee - T.C.A. § 55-10-406(a)(3).

[503]**South Dakota v. Neville,** 459 U.S. 553, 103 S. Ct. 916, 74 L. Ed. 2d 748 (1983).

[504]California - One year license suspension - West's Ann.Cal.Vehicle Code § 23612(a)(1)(D); Florida - One year suspension of license - West's F.S.A. § 316.1932(1)(a)1.a.; Georgia - One year suspension of license - O.C.G.A. § 40-5-67.1(d); Indiana - One year suspension of license - IC 9-30-6-9(b); Mississippi - 90 day suspension of license Miss. Code Ann. § 63-11-5(2); Tennessee - One year suspension of license - T.C.A. § 55-

9.8. Can you refuse testing in your state? In most states, unless someone was serious injured or killed as a result of an accident related to your DUI-DWI arrest, you typically have the right to refuse to allow the police to take a blood, breath or urine sample from you.[505] In other words, the drawing of your blood, or the taking of a breath or a urine sample by the police must typically be voluntary.[506] However, if you are incapacitated, either because you are unconscious, incoherent or unable to consent for whatever reason, you ordinarily lose your right to refuse such samples being taken from you in the majority of states.[507] In Mississippi and Tennessee, although the police can still obtain blood or urine samples for testing if you are unconscious or incapable of refusing, these results may not be used by the prosecution in its case against you in court.[508]

Florida's courts have ruled that absent a felony arrest, forcible draws of blood or urine are not authorized.[509] Georgia has highly protective guidelines for the suspected DUI-DWI driver who has refused testing based upon some felony arrests and for all misdemeanor arrests. When you refuse, the police in most states do not have the authority to force you to submit to a blood or urine test in a normal DUI-DWI case, even by seeking a search warrant.[510] A new statute enacted in 2006 seeks to change Georgia law on this issue.[511]

A troubling and growing trend, now being used in more than a dozen states, is being permitted by some appellate courts. These courts have held that a person who refuses breath testing can be restrained or even physically harmed to forcibly draw blood or use a catheter in the person for a urine sample. Typically this occurs when another person in a suspected drunk driving accident case has been seriously injured or killed as a result of the accident. Case

---

10-406(a)(3); Texas - 180 day license suspension - V.T.C.A., Transportation Code § 724.015(2); Washington - One year license suspension - West's RCWA 46.20.308(2)(a).

[505]California - West's Ann.Cal.Vehicle Code §§ 23612, 13353; Florida - West's F.S.A. §§ 316.1932, 316.1939; Georgia - O.C.G.A. § 40-5-67.1(d); Indiana - IC 9-30-6-7; Mississippi - Miss. Code Ann. § 63-11-21; Tennessee - T.C.A. § 55-10-406(a)(4); Texas - V.T.C.A., Transportation Code § 724.013; Washington - West's RCWA 46.20.308(2).

[506]**Schneckloth v. Bustamonte,** 412 U.S. 218, 93 S.Ct. 2041, 36 L.Ed.2d 854 (1973). Several states have justified sidestepping the issue of "voluntariness" of providing an incriminating evidentiary sample to police when no arrest of the suspected criminal (many if these decisions are in felony cases carrying lengthy jail terms) has occurred. In **Combest v. State,** 981 S.W.2d 958 (Tex.App.-Austin, 1998), the officer used the Texas implied consent form, yet never advised Combest that he was under arrest. This scenario would not have been allowed to occur in Georgia, which (along with several other states) requires a valid arrest and probable cause to suspect impairment before any blood or urine tests could be requested. **Handschuh v. State,** 270 Ga. App. 676, 607 S.E.2d 899 (2004); **Hough v. State,** 279 Ga. 711, 620 S.E.2d 380 (2005); **Cooper v. State,** 277 Ga. 282, 587 S.E.2d 605 (2003).

[507]**Breithaupt v. Abram,** 352 U.S. 432, 77 S. Ct. 408, 1 L. Ed. 2d 448 (1957); California - West's Ann.Cal.Vehicle Code § 23612(5); Florida - West's F.S.A. §§ 316.1932(1)(c); Georgia - O.C.G.A. § 40-5-55(b); Texas - V.T.C.A., Transportation Code § 724.014; Washington - West's RCWA 46.20.308(4); **State v. Wight,** 765 P.2d 12 (Utah App., 1988), **State v. Tronolone,** 532 So.2d 1127 (Fla. App., 1988). It is also not necessary to give an unconscious driver an implied consent warning prior to chemical testing. **State v. Barefield,** 110 Wash. 2d 728, 756 P.2d 731 (1988).

[508]Mississippi - Miss. Code Ann. § 63-11-7; Tennessee - T.C.A. § 55-10-406(b).

[509]**State v. Slaney,** 653 So.2d 422 (Fla.App. 3 Dist. 1995).

[510]**State v. Collier,** 279 Ga. 316, 612 S.E.2d 281 (2005); **Hough v. State,** 279 Ga. 711, 620 S.E.2d 380 (2005).

[511]To authorize forcible blood draws, the 2006 Georgia General Assembly added a new subsection to O.C.G.A. § 40-5-67.1, which becomes became effective July 1, 2006:

(d.1) Nothing in this Code section shall be deemed to preclude the acquisition or admission of evidence of a violation of Code Section 40-6-391 if obtained by voluntary consent or a search warrant as authorized by the Constitution or laws of this state or the United States.

examples have all cropped up in the past 10 years and foreshadow likely problems ahead.[512]

Because Arizona has one of the broadest statutes [A.R.S. § 28-1388] authorizing forcible blood draws in every suspected DUI-DWI case, their statute is reproduced here for the reader to examine.

> **D.** If a person under arrest refuses to submit to a test or tests under § 28-1321, whether or not a sample was collected pursuant to subsection E of this section or a search warrant, evidence of refusal is admissible in any civil or criminal action or other proceeding. The issue of refusal is an issue of fact to be determined by the trier of fact in all cases.
>
> **E.** Notwithstanding any other law, if a law enforcement officer has probable cause to believe that a person has violated § 28-1381 and a sample of blood, urine or other bodily substance is taken from that person for any reason, a portion of that sample sufficient for analysis shall be provided to a law enforcement officer if requested for law enforcement purposes. A person who fails to comply with this subsection is guilty of a class 1 misdemeanor.

What is apparent is the harsh, criminal penalties for refusal coupled with an easy, approved statutory method of obtaining a telephonic search warrant for a forced blood draw. Even more disturbing is the practice by Arizona to allow police officers to attend a course lasting a couple of hours to restrain you and then permit the **OFFICER** to draw your blood. This is covered by the language in §28-1388 (A) after it discusses doctors and nurses drawing the blood. Note that § 28-1338(F) gives the officer who harms you or kills you immunity from being sued! *This is American Justice at its best!*

9.9. Does the procedure used in your state comply with *California v. Trombetta?* In 1984, The United States Supreme Court decided that the constitutional

---

[512]**People v. Jones,** 214 Ill.2d 187, 824 N.E.2d 239 (2005) [accident not involving death]; **Abney v. State,** 811 N.E.2d 415 (Ind. App. 2004) [accident involving death and hit & run afterward]; **State v. Espe,** 88 P.3d 807 (Kan. App. 2004) [accident involving non-fatal but serious injuries to passenger]; **State v. Rinard,** 2003 WL 21396703 (Ohio App. 9th Dist. 2003) [no accident]; **State v. Engesser,** 661 N.W.2d 739 (S.D. 2003) [no formal arrest had occurred, but vehicular homicide]; **State v. Worthington,** 138 Idaho 470, 65 P.3d 211 (Idaho App. 2002) [no accident, but felony arrest]; **State v. Faust,** 267 Wis.2d 783, 672 N.W.2d 97 (Wis.App., 2003) [leading case from Wisconson]; also see **State v. Krajewski,** 255 Wis.2d 98, 648 N.W.2d 385 (Wis. 2002) [no accident; defendant feared needles and offered to submit to alternative type test; forcible blood draw okay anyway]; **State v. Mellett,** 642 N.W.2d 779 (Minn.App. 2002) [no accident, but a repeat offender DWI suspect; defendant acquitted for the DWI but convicted for criminal refusal and given jail sentence]; **People v. Sugarman,** 96 Cal.App.4th 210, 116 Cal.Rptr.2d 689 (Cal.App. 2 Dist. 2002) [defendant agreed to be tested by breath, but the effort was not successful; because she was a repeat offender, forcible blood draw was okay]; **State v. Hanson,** 588 N.W.2d 885 (S.D. 1999) [DUI-drugs; no accident; suspected marijuana from smell officer observed and drug dog sniffing the vehicle and driver; urinating is a "natural bodily function," so okay to gather without a warrant]; also see **State v. Nguyen,** 563 N.W.2d 120 (S.D. 1997) [vehicular homicide; non-English speaking defendant; no implied consent rights given; but, in felony cases, no right of driver to refuse testing]; **State v. Rains,** 574 N.W.2d 904 (Iowa 1998) [normal traffic stop for weaving; defendant was shot by the officer in self defense and then actively guarded by police at his hospital room, but this was not an arrest, for purposes of Iowa law; blood that was drawn at hospital was not done at the request of law enforcement, so okay to be used against defendant on DWI]; **People v. Hanna,** 223 Mich.App. 466, 567 N.W.2d 12 (Mich.App. 1997). **State v. Clary,** 196 Ariz. 610, 2 P.3d 1255 (Ariz.App. Div. 1 2000) [speeding only, no prior offenses, still okay for officer do hold defendant on the floor while a phlebotomist drew his blood]; **Carleton v. Superior Court,** 170 Cal.App.3d 1182, 216 Cal.Rptr. 890 (Cal.App. 4 Dist. 1985); **Cox v. State,** 473 So.2d 778 (Fla.App. 2 Dist. 1985). http://www.drunkdrivingdefense.com/general/blood-tests.htm.

protections against the destruction of breath test evidence by the prosecution or by law enforcement did not apply to the States by forcing them to preserve samples of your breath at the time they were also having you breath tested for your blood alcohol limit. This ruling was made despite the fact that it is technically possible for the law enforcement system and the State to capture a sample of the breath for later analysis.[513] The theory was that what was being admitted as evidence against you in a DUI-DWI case were the results of electronic reading from the breath test, not the breath samples themselves.

Most experienced DUI-DWI trial attorneys are fully aware that *Trombetta* may be correct for California's implied consent procedures, but not for other states where less protection is offered to the DUI-DWI suspect. In California, the statute compels the officer to request a breath test in a misdemeanor DUI-DWI case, but requires the officer to tell you that because a breath test does not retain a sample for later independent analysis, you can opt to have blood drawn instead.[514] Moreover, the State pays for this blood test in California, not you.

More importantly, under *Trombetta*, before you would have ann Constitutional right to demand preservation of these samples, you would have to show these samples had a possible chance of showing you were not guilty, and if so, that you had no other means of showing this. Because almost every state gives you the right to obtain an independent sample, your state likely does not have to preserve any of your breath samples to be used as possible favorable evidence at your trial. The reality is that your state may not even require the police to **TELL YOU** about the right to independent testing, or even provide meaningful assistance in seeing that you get the testing done.

9.10. Is the sample being requested for implied consent purposes also usable for possible other crimes? The unfortunate answer is in some states, yes. However, in other states, the answer is no. Once the police have your blood, breath or urine sample, in some states it becomes evidence that can be used against you for other crimes. Like any other evidence in their possession, law enforcement can use it to investigate any crime, especially if it relates to your DUI-DWI offense.[515]

Other states do not allow its use in prosecuting you in non-DUI-DWI situations. In Georgia, the consent you give is limited to prosecution of DUI-DWI offense and cannot otherwise be used for police investigation of other crimes.[516] The same is true in Michigan.[517]

9.11. Do you have the right of counsel before agreeing to submit to the state's test (or refusing to submit)? In most states, you do not have the right to have your lawyer present (or to even call an attorney on the telephone) while making your decision to either accept being tested or to refuse the blood, breath or urine testing.[518] This means the

---

[513]**California v. Trombetta,** 467 U.S. 479, 104 S.Ct. 2528, 81 L.Ed.2d 413 (1984).

[514]West's Ann.Cal.Vehicle Code § 23612.

[515]**State v. Dahl,** 247 Wis.2d 499, 633 N.W.2d 279 (Wis.App. 2001); **State v. Coyle,** 2000 WL 283073 (Ohio App. 4 Dist. 2000); **Radcliffe v. State,** 234 Ga.App. 576, 507 S.E.2d 759 (1998); **State v. Krantz,** 174 Ariz. 211, 848 P.2d 296 (Ariz.App. Div. 2 1992).

[516]**State v. Jewell,** 228 Ga.App. 825, 492 S.E.2d 706 (1997); **Turpin v. Helmeci,** 271 Ga. 224, 518 S.E.2d 887 (1999).

[517]**State v. Jewell,** 228 Ga.App. 825, 492 S.E.2d 706 (1997); **People v. Keen,** 396 Mich. 573, 242 N.W.2d 405 (1976).

[518]**Kunzler v. Miller,** 154 Ariz. 570, 744 P.2d 671 (1987); California - West's Ann.Cal.Vehicle Code § 23612(a)(4), Mississippi - Miss. Code Ann. § 63-11-5(4); **Com., Dept. of Transp., Bureau of Traffic Safety v. O'Connell,** 521 Pa. 242, 555 A.2d 873 (1989); **People v. Gursey,** 22 N.Y.2d 224, 239 N.E.2d 351 (1968);

police do not have to give you access by phone or in person to an attorney when you are being pressed to make this critical decision. Such a request to speak to legal counsel can even be considered a refusal of this testing in some states,[519] while not in others.[520] In a few states, you have a reasonable amount of time in which to consult with counsel while you are making up your mind whether or not to submit to the test.[521]

9.12. Which instruments are approved in your state for roadside preliminary breath testing? In most states, alcohol analyzers may be used as a part of the screening or preliminary procedure used by police as a part of his or her roadside evaluation to determine whether or not to arrest you for DUI-DWI. These are smaller, hand-held devices that are battery-powered. While most devices give a numerical value as to an estimated blood alcohol level, this number is so unreliable as to not be accepted as admissible evidence at trial in most states. Such preliminary breath test results typically are used only for a determination as to whether you have the presence of or an absence of any alcohol on your breath.

Even in states that allow an officer to use a hand-held roadside breath analyzer, an evidentiary foundation usually has to be made by the prosecution in order to be able to use ANY results,[522] but this is not true in every state.[523]

9.13. Is the preliminary breath testing device in your state part of the implied consent law, or is it a non-evidential test? In some states, the use of a roadside or handheld alcohol sensing devices is a part of the implied consent testing allowed by statute.[524] In most states however, it is not the value that comes up on the machine that is important. Rather, if the test shows alcohol on your breath, this is yet another indicator to the officer that he or she might have sufficient circumstantial evidence of possible impairment to request a blood or an "evidential" breath test at the jail or precinct (police station). The numerical value that is indicated on the digital screen on these hand-held machines after your breath test is a non-evidentiary result in the majority of states. However, most states that prohibit mentioning numerical results do permit the officer to say whether the screening device was positive for alcohol or not. Unfortunately, these hand-held devices can be fooled into giving a "positive" result for alcohol if you have recently used a commonly-sold cough drop.[525]

In some instances, the preliminary analyzer results will be LOWER than the official state breath testing device. If this is a key part of your defense, the favorable "low" results may be

---

Department of Highway Safety and Motor Vehicles v. Farr, 757 So.2d 550 (Fla.App. 5 Dist. 2000); Schmidt v. State, 816 N.E.2d 925 (Ind.App. 2004); State v. Frasier, 914 S.W.2d 467 (Tenn. 1996).

[519]Dikeman v. Charnes, 739 P.2d 870 (Colo. App., 1987); Floyd v. State, 710 S.W.2d 807 (Tex. App., 1986); Standish v. Department of Revenue, 235 Kan. 900, 683 P.2d 1276 (1984); *See generally*, Debra T. Landis, Annotation, *Request Before Submitting to Chemical Sobriety Test to Communicate With Counsel as Refusal to Take Test Under Implied Consent Law*, 97 A.L.R.3d 852 (2005).

[520]Commonwealth v. Doherty, 88 Pa. Commw. 482, 490 A.2d 481 (1985); Baillie v. Moore, 522 N.W.2d 748 (N.D., 1994); State v. Mason, 99 Ohio App. 3d 165, 650 N.E.2d 164 (1994).

[521]Friedman v. Commissioner of Public Safety, 473 N.W.2d 828 (Minn. 1991); State v. Vietor, 261 N.W.2d 828 (Iowa 1978).

[522]Turrentine v. State, 176 Ga.App. 145, 335 S.E.2d 630 (1985); Sharber v. State, 750 N.E.2d 796 (Ind.App. 2001); State v. Damon, 328 Mont. 276, 119 P.3d 1194 (Mont. 2005); State v. Doerr, 229 Wis.2d 616, 599 N.W.2d 897 (Wis.App. 1999).

[523]People v. Rozela, 345 Ill.App.3d 217, 802 N.E.2d 372 (Ill.App. 2 Dist. 2003).

[524]Indiana - IC 9-30-7-2; California - West's Ann. Cal. Vehicle Code § 13388.

[525]http://www.ananova.com/news/story/sm_1552495.html?menu=news.quirkies.strangecrime - **Sucking on a Fishermen's Friend could get you into trouble.**

admissible at your trial, under the federal constitution.[526]

9.14. Is the officer required to advise you of your right to an independent test of blood, breath or urine? In almost every state, one of your rights is to have an independent test of your own performed at a laboratory of your choice and at your own expense.[527] However, in some states, this right is not one the officer must tell you of before asking you for a sample of your breath, blood or urine.[528] In a few states, failure of the officer to inform you of this right or to you in obtaining this test does not preclude the State from using the evidence it gets from its testing.[529] Other states have a more "pro-citizen" view of the importance of independent test advisements and require that the notice be verbally stated in a manner that communicates all options for an independent test.[530]

9.15. If you request an independent test, does the officer have to reasonably accommodate that request? Most states have an independent test statute that is an integral part of the state's implied consent statutes.[531] An independent test statute typically provides that a person who submits to chemical testing may, at the person's own expense, have additional chemical tests performed, but a failure to do so does not affect the admissibility of the test performed by the police. The specific provisions of independent test statutes vary considerably from state to state. Your DUI-DWI specialist counsel will be intimately familiar with the statute in your state.

In almost every state, if you request an independent test of your blood or urine, the law enforcement officer must do what is reasonable to accommodate that request.[532] A few states throw out the test results obtained by the police if you are not allowed the chance to obtain an independent test,[533] while most say that while the officer must give you a reasonable opportunity, that failure does not affect the admissibility of the State's test.[534]

Some state statutes mandate that the police officer must assist the defendant in

---

[526]**Rock v. Arkansas,** 483 U.S. 44, 107 S.Ct. 2704, 97 L.Ed.2d 37 (U.S.Ark. 1987).

[527]California - West's Ann.Cal.Vehicle Code § 23614; Florida - West's F.S.A. § 316.1932(3).; Georgia - O.C.G.A. § 40-6-392(3); Mississippi - Miss. Code Ann. § 63-11-13; Texas - V.T.C.A., Transportation Code § 724.019; Washington - West's RCWA 46.61.506(6); Wisconsin - W.S.A. 343.305(5)

[528]Texas - V.T.C.A., Transportation Code §§ 724.019, 724.062; Mississippi - Miss. Code Ann. § 63-11-5(2), **Green v. State,** 710 So.2d 862 (Miss. Apr 16, 1998); Florida - West's F.S.A. § 316.1932.

[529]California - West's Ann.Cal.Vehicle Code § 23614(d); Mississippi - Miss. Code Ann. § 63-11-13; Texas - V.T.C.A., Transportation Code §§ 724.019, 724.062; Washington - West's RCWA 46.61.506(6), 46.20.308(2).

[530]**Nelson v. State,** 135 Ga.App. 212, 217 S.E.2d 450 (1975); **State v. Stary,** 187 Wis.2d 266, 522 N.W.2d 32 (Wis.App. 1994).

[531]California - West's Ann.Cal.Vehicle Code § 23614; Florida - West's F.S.A. § 316.1932(3).; Georgia - O.C.G.A. § 40-6-392(3); Mississippi - Miss. Code Ann. § 63-11-13; Texas - V.T.C.A., Transportation Code § 724.019; Washington - West's RCWA 46.61.506(6).

[532]California - West's Ann.Cal.Vehicle Code § 23614; Florida - West's F.S.A. § 316.1932(3).; Georgia - O.C.G.A. § 40-6-392(3); Mississippi - Miss. Code Ann. § 63-11-13; Texas - V.T.C.A., Transportation Code § 724.019; Washington - West's RCWA 46.61.506(6); **Commonwealth v. Long,** 118 S.W.3d 178 (Ky. App., 2003), **Commonwealth v. King,** 429 Mass. 169, 706 N.E.2d 685 (1999); **State v. Anderson,** 258 Ga. App. 127, 572 S.E.2d 758 (2002); **Lau v. State,** 896 P.2d 825 (Alaska App., 1995); **Municipality of Anchorage v. Serrano,** 649 P.2d 256 (Alaska App. 1982).

[533]**State v. Peterson,** 739 P.2d 958 (Mont., 1987), overruled on other grounds by **State v. Waters,** 296 Mont. 101, 987 P.2d 1142 (1999), **State v. Sanchez,** 192 Ariz. 454, 967 P.2d 129 (Ariz. App., 1998).

[534]California - West's Ann.Cal.Vehicle Code § 23614; Florida - West's F.S.A. § 316.1932(3).; Georgia - O.C.G.A. § 40-6-392(3); Mississippi - Miss. Code Ann. § 63-11-13; Texas - V.T.C.A., Transportation Code § 724.019; Washington - West's RCWA 46.61.506(6);

obtaining an independent test. Other statutes state that the police shall not deny the defendant the right to obtain an independent test. Still other statutes are silent on the subject of the police officer's obligation.[535] In determining the reasonableness of police conduct in failing to assist the defendant in obtaining an independent test, much may depend on the reason given by the police for not assisting the defendant.[536]

9.16. If you want to request an independent test, do you have to first submit to the State's test? The independent test statutes in most states provide that only those who submit to chemical testing offered by the police have the right to an independent test. The courts have generally upheld this proviso and have denied the right to an independent test to those who refuse police testing.[537]

A few courts, however, have ruled that restricting the right to an independent test to those who submit to police testing constitutes a denial of due process and that persons who refuse chemical testing also have the right to an independent chemical test.[538] Other courts have held that the right to an independent test may not be limited to those who submit to police testing. In such states, a refusal to be tested may be inadmissible if the defendant was not given the required independent test advisement.[539]

Only a handful of states allow a person who has refused the State's test to request and receive an independent test. Despite the obvious importance of you being permitted to obtain a contemporaneous sample of this evidence (blood alcohol level) for purposes of challenging the State's DUI case against you, the appellate courts in a majority of states maintain this legal position.[540]

Especially in states where the right to an independent test is limited to persons who submit to police testing, the denial of the right to an independent test cannot be used as a defense in implied consent proceedings. However, it would seem that the denial by the police of your right to submit to a different form of testing than the type requested by the officer might be raised as a defense by you in an administrative "refusal" proceeding where the state seeks to administratively suspend your driving privileges for refusal of the officer's test. Consider the situation where an officer insists on blood testing and you (due to a fear of needles) say "I'll take any type of tests that do not involve needles."

If an independent test statute does not require the police to notify you of the right to an independent test, it is generally held that the right must be affirmatively asserted by you to be

---

[535]Police need only provide telephone access - **Pollock v. Comm'r of Pub. Safety**, 1995 WL 46209 (Minn. App., 1995); Police officer must provide reasonable transportation to a defendant who wishes to obtain an independent test - **State v. Hughes**, 181 Ga. App. 464, 352 S.E.2d 643 (1987); **Ward v. State**, 758 P.2d 87 (Alaska, 1988); **State v. Nicastro**, 218 N.J. Super. 231, 527 A.2d 492 (1986); **Fiegel v. Cabot**, 27 Ark. App. 146, 767 S.W.2d 539 (1989).

[536]Officer had to spend three hours investigating serious accident - **Commonwealth v. Horne**, 56 Mass. App. Ct. 1105, 776 N.E.2d 1040 (2002); Officer arbitrarily refused to permit the defendant to go to another room in the hospital to obtain change in order to pay the receptionist for the test, the officer was deemed to have refused to permit the defendant to obtain an independent test - **Gordon v. State**, 190 Ga. App. 55, 378 S.E.2d 362 (1989); Department policy is found to be reasonable and was followed, a denial of the right to an independent test is not likely to be found. **State v. Jalkiewicz**, 303 N.J. Super. 430, 697 A.2d 155 (1997).

[537]**State v. Larivee**, 656 N.W.2d 226 (Minn., 2003); **State v. Simmons**, 270 Ga. App. 301, 605 S.E.2d 846 (2004).

[538]**Snyder v. State**, 930 P.2d 1274 (Alaska, 1996); **State v. Swanson**, 722 P.2d 1155 (Mont., 1986).

[539]**Kintli v. State**, 325 Mont. 53, 103 P.3d 1056 (2004).

[540]**Puett v. State,** 147 Ga. App. 300, 248 S.E.2d 560 (1978).

effective and that a police officer has no duty to advise you of the existence of the right.[541] In such jurisdictions, it is essential that an accused "drunken driver" know his or her rights and assert these rights. On the theory that you cannot be held to have waived rights of which you are not aware, a few courts have required police officers to advise you of the right to independent chemical testing even if the statute does not so require. These courts have suppressed the prosecution's chemical test evidence in the absence of such an advisement.[542]

9.17. For breath testing, what is your state's observation period (deprivation period) prior to taking the test? In most states, when a breath test is requested, you must remain under observation of a law enforcement officer for a certain period of time to ensure you have not vomited, burped, smoked, put anything in your mouth, or not had anything more to drink, immediately before you take the evidential breath test.[543] This rule is designed to ensure that a false breath test is not created through mouth alcohol contamination or similar interference with the testing device's "measurement" of deep lung air.

Washington law requires a fifteen-minute observation period and two samples to be taken.[544] Other states either call for a 15 or 20 minute observation time period to eliminate defense challenges to "mouth alcohol" contamination.[545] Some states call this a "deprivation" period. Your DUI-DWI specialist will know the limits and proper terminology for your state. [See more ideas from the checklist contained in **Appendix I.**]

In some states, proof of starting the test too soon will cause the total exclusion of the State's breath test.[546] In others, such proof only permits your attorney to argue that the results are unreliable.[547]

9.18. How does implied consent law affect the administrative license suspension hearing in your case? The issues to be resolved at implied consent

---

[541]**Ruffenach v. Comm'r of Pub. Safety**, 528 N.W.2d 254 (Minn. App., 1995); **Green v. State**, 710 So.2d 862 (Miss., 1998).

[542]**State v. Karmen**, 150 Vt. 547, 554 A.2d 670 (1988); **Montano v. Superior Court**, 149 Ariz. 385, 719 P.2d 271 (1986), which held that a defendant who is not subjected to chemical testing must be advised of the right to an independent test.

[543]Delaware - 20 minutes - **Clawson v. State,** 867 A.2d 187 (Del.Supr. 2005); Texas - 15 minutes - **State v. Mechler,** 153 S.W.3d 435 (Tex.Crim.App. 2005); Alaska - 15 minutes - **Kinneen v. State,** 2004 WL 2914978 (Alaska App. 2004); Kentucky - 20 minutes - **Culver v. Com.,** 2004 WL 1301318 (Ky.App. 2004); Utah - 15 minutes - **State v. Vialpando,** 89 P.3d 209 (Utah App. 2004); Mississippi - 20 minutes - **Graham v. State,** 878 So.2d 162 (Miss.App. 2004); Ohio - 20 minutes - **State v. Rennick,** 2003 WL 21134848, 2003-Ohio-2560 (Ohio App. 7 Dist. 2003); Tennessee - 20 minutes - **State v. Korsakov,** 34 S.W.3d 534 (Tenn.Crim.App. 2000); Idaho - 15 minutes - **State v. Charan,** 132 Idaho 341, 971 P.2d 1165 (Idaho App. 1998), South Carolina - 20 minutes - Code 1976 § 56-5-2950(a)..

[544]West's RCWA 46.61.506(4)(a)(ii).

[545]Delaware - 20 minutes - **Clawson v. State,** 867 A.2d 187 (Del.Supr. 2005); Texas - 15 minutes - **State v. Mechler,** 153 S.W.3d 435 (Tex.Crim.App. 2005); Alaska - 15 minutes - **Kinneen v. State,** 2004 WL 2914978 (Alaska App. 2004); Kentucky - 20 minutes - **Culver v. Com.,** 2004 WL 1301318 (Ky.App. 2004); Utah - 15 minutes - **State v. Vialpando,** 89 P.3d 209 (Utah App. 2004); Mississippi - 20 minutes - **Graham v. State,** 878 So.2d 162 (Miss.App. 2004); Ohio - 20 minutes - **State v. Rennick,** 2003 WL 21134848 (Ohio App. 7 Dist. 2003); Tennessee - 20 minutes - **State v. Korsakov,** 34 S.W.3d 534 (Tenn.Crim.App. 2000); Idaho - 15 minutes - **State v. Charan,** 132 Idaho 341, 971 P.2d 1165 (Idaho App. 1998); South Carolina - 20 minutes - Code 1976 § 56-5-2950(a).

[546]**State v. Sensing,** 843 S.W.2d 412 (Tenn. 1992); **U.S. v. Plumer,** 920 F.Supp. 151 (D.Kan. 1996); **People v. Haney,** 155 Ill.App.3d 44, 507 N.E.2d 230 (Ill.App. 4 Dist. 1987).

[547]**State v. Palmaka,** 266 Ga.App. 595, 597 S.E.2d 630 (2004).

administrative hearings are usually limited by statute to the following:

(1) Whether the defendant was lawfully arrested for a DUI-DWI offense;[548]

(2) Whether the arresting officer had reasonable cause to believe that the defendant was operating a motor vehicle while under the influence of alcohol or drugs;[549] and

(3) Whether the defendant refused to submit to chemical testing when requested to do so.[550]

The independent test defenses described in this chapter generally are applicable to administrative "per se" proceedings because the denial of the right to an independent test also prevents the defendant from effectively challenging the accuracy of the police chemical tests relied on by the State in the administrative proceeding. Challenging the accuracy of the state's chemical test evidence (on a variety of grounds) is one of the few defenses available in administrative "per se" proceedings.[551]

In hearings under an administrative "per se" statute, the State must normally prove that you drove or operated a vehicle, that your breath or blood alcohol content (BAC), as established by chemical testing, was at or above the prohibited level, and that the chemical testing equipment was functioning properly when the test was performed. Some state guidelines require proof that the state's chemical test was taken within a certain time period after the driving ended, typically within 2 or 3 hours. Again, the specific issues may vary in a particular state, and your DUI-DWI defense counsel should be totally aware of your state's requirements.

The burden of persuasion at an implied consent hearing is always on the state to prove by a preponderance of the evidence that a violation of the implied consent statute occurred. This burden is typically met by introducing the report, statement, or testimony of the arresting officer to establish a few basic facts to support the license suspension or revocation action being taken. In some states, e.g., California, your defense attorney must subpoena the officer to come to court in order to cross-examine him or her. In other states, e.g., Georgia, Texas and South Carolina, the officer's failure to appear will result in any proposed administrative license suspension or revocation being "rescinded" or lifted.

It is important that the defendant vigorously cross-examine the arresting and testing officers at this hearing, and get a transcript of the sworn testimony from a certified court reporter, because it is often the only evidentiary hearing allowed prior to trial. Especially if the hearing is held under the state administrative procedure act, liberal discovery may be permitted in implied consent cases, and the testimony or other evidence produced here might provide a winning defense strategy for your attorney.

9.18.1. Appeals from an Adverse Ruling from an Administrative Court. In most states the hearing officer's decision may be appealed to another court for review of the administrative judge's decision. The court hearing the appeal must review the case based on the record established at the implied consent hearing. This is yet an additional reason to use a court reporter at the hearing. Again, the exact procedure varies from state to state and procedures followed by your state should be ascertained through your DUI-DWI specialist.

9.18.2. Winning or Losing the Administrative Hearing Will Not Affect the

---

[548]**People v. Luedemann,** 357 Ill.App.3d 411, 828 N.E.2d 355 (Ill.App. 2 Dist. 2005); **Bristol v. Com.,** 45 Va.App. 534, 612 S.E.2d 244 (2005).

[549]**State v. Ellison,** 271 Ga.App. 898, 611 S.E.2d 129 (2005); Arizona - A.R.S. § 28-1321(E)(1); Delaware - 21 Del.C. § 2742(f); Oregon - O.R.S. § 813.410(2).

[550]**Brown v. Director of Revenue, State of Missouri,** 164 S.W.3d 121 (Mo.App. E.D. 2005).

[551]**Charnes v. Lobato,** 743 P.2d 27 (Colo., 1987).

Criminal Case Afterward. Many of the issues determined at the implied consent hearing are identical to those faced in the criminal trial of the DUI-DWI offense. However, because the implied consent proceeding is deemed to be a civil proceeding and because of the differences in the burden of proof in the two proceedings, the doctrines of res judicata and collateral estoppel have consistently been held not to be applicable to the proceedings. Neither the prosecutor nor you are bound in one case by a finding in the other.[552]

Finally, the Double Jeopardy Clause in the Fifth Amendment does not prevent the state from imposing implied consent sanctions upon you even if you are later acquitted of the criminal DUI-DWI offense.[553] However, a few states have passed statutes that provide that winning the criminal case or having the DUI-DWI charge reduced or dismissed will allow immediate reinstatement of your license, regardless of the remaining suspension period of the administrative license action.[554]

9.19. If you don't understand English, and the implied consent was read to you in English, how does this affect the state's tests? The results are mixed on this issue, depending on the state in which you were arrested for your DUI-DWI. In some states, you can avoid having the penalties of implied consent applied to your driving privileges if you can prove you did not comprehend English. If it can be shown that you did not understand English at the time of your arrest, and that you did not understand that you were being asked to perform a test, then some state appellate courts have decided that a refusal of testing did not occur.[555]

Other states are unconcerned by your inability to speak or understand a word of English, and the refusal is allowed to punish you anyway.[556] States like Wisconsin, who protect the truly non-English speaker, will not protect anyone who can "get by" in English when conversing with an officer.[557] However, while in other states it has been held that while a non-English-speaking defendant must be able to understand the consequences of a refusal in order to have validly refused chemical testing of their breath or blood, such a defendant is not entitled to have the request to submit the chemical testing under the implied consent law made in his or her native language.[558]

At least in states where your refusal to submit must be "knowing and conscious" (many states do not so require), it may be a defense to show that you, because of your physical or mental condition, were physically or mentally incapable of knowingly and consciously refusing to be tested.[559] This defense must be established by competent medical evidence, however, or it will not be accepted.[560] It is not a defense to show that your physical or mental inability to

---

[552]**Gibson v. Faulkner**, 132 N.C. App. 738, 515 S.E.2d 452 (1999); **Swain v. State**, 251 Ga.App. 110, 552 S.E.2d 880 (2001); **Medrow v. Taxation and Revenue Dep't**, 126 N.M. 332, 968 P.2d 1195 (N.M. App., 1998).

[553]**Neil v. Peterson**, 210 Neb. 378, 314 N.W.2d 275 (Neb. 1982).

[554]Georgia – O.C.G.A. § 40-5-67.1(g)(4).

[555]**State v. Begicevic**, 270 Wis.2d 675, 678 N.W.2d 293 (2004); **Martinez v. Peterson**, 212 Neb. 168, 322 N.W.2d 386 (1982).

[556]**Rodriguez v. State,** 275 Ga. 283, 565 S.E.2d 458 (2002).

[557]**State v. Bruestle**, 691 N.W.2d 927 (Wis. Ct. App. 2004).

[558]**Furcal-Peguero v. State,** 255 Ga. App. 729, 566 S.E.2d 320 (2002); **Yokoyama v. Comm'r**, 356 N.W.2d 830 (Minn. App., 1984).

[559]**Higgins v. Dep't of Motor Vehicles**, 101 Nev. 531, 706 P.2d 506 (1985); **Dep't of Licensing v. Sheeks**, 47 Wash. App. 65, 734 P.2d 24 (1987).

[560]**Laurita. v. Dep't of Transp.**, 158 Pa. Commw. 576, 632 A.2d 611 (1993); **Villeneuve v. Comm'r**, 417 N.W.2d 304 (Minn. App., 1988).

refuse testing was caused by excessive intoxication.[561]

9.20. If the officer misstates information or goes beyond the information required by your state's laws to be told to you, can this additional information result in your test result (or refusal) being excluded? It depends which state your DUI-DWI offense occurred in, and exactly what the officer said. If the additional comments by the officer are considered misleading or coercive, making it impossible for you to make an informed decision regarding the independent test, even if the rest of the implied consent advisory was read correctly, your test results may be excluded.[562] In other states, too much information (or erroneous information) being issued by the officer will not lead to evidence being excluded.[563] The burden may shift to your attorney at a pre-trial motion hearing to show that these improper warnings likely made a difference on your decision to submit (or not submit) to testing in the case.[564]

9.21. If you are forced to submit to testing after you verbally refused to cooperate, can the State seek to take away your driving privileges even though they have collected your blood? This is the situation in several states. Numerous states allow for the forcible drawing of your blood in some or all DUI-DWI cases,[565] but the question of whether you are administratively suspended for not immediately consenting to be tested may of may not be applicable in your state. Even if the police obtained your blood by force, the state can seek to take away your driving privileges through the implied consent law based on your *attempt* to not give a sample. Hence, the state gets its "cake" and your license, too!

The basis for the Arizona court's decision is that the refusal is a refusal, while the blood can be drawn by force based on either the power of a "warrant" that is inherent in the implied consent law, or if the blood was drawn forcibly for a medical purpose. Either way, the results of the scientific test can be used against you at trial, as can evidence of your attempted refusal to allow the sample.[566]

9.22. If you are hearing-impaired, does it make a difference that the officer did not utilize an interpreter? Persons who are legally deaf may have a defense to non-compliance with implied consent laws. In Georgia, statutory protections require a sign language specialist to be summoned to translate the advisements.[567] However, other states,

---

[561]**State v. Superior Court of Pima County,** 155 Ariz. 403, 747 P.2d 564 (Ariz.App. Div. 2 1986).

[562]**State v. Terry,** 236 Ga. App. 248, 511 S.E.2d 608 (1999); **County of Ozaukee v. Quelle,** 198 Wis.2d 269, 542 N.W.2d 196 (Wis.App. 1995); **State v. Bartels,** 112 Wash.2d 882, 774 P.2d 1183 (1989); **State v. Young,** 483 So.2d 31 (Fla.App. 5 Dist. 1985).

[563]**State v. Collins,** 166 S.W.3d 721 (Tenn. 2005).

[564]**Schafer v. State,** 95 S.W.3d 452 (Tex.App.-Hous. (1 Dist. 2002); **State v. Myers,** 711 N.W.2d 113 (Minn.App., 2006).

[565]Illinois - **People v. Jones,** 214 Ill.2d 187, 824 N.E.2d 239 (2005); Indiana - **Abney v. State,** 811 N.E.2d 415 (Ind. App. 2004); Kansas- **State v. Espe,** 88 P.3d 807 (Kan. App. 2004); Ohio - **State v. Rinard,** 2003 WL 21396703 (Ohio App. 9th Dist. 2003); South Dakota - **State v. Engesser,** 661 N.W.2d 739 (S.D. 2003); Idaho - **State v. Worthington,** 138 Idaho 470, 65 P.3d 211 (Idaho App. 2002); Wisconsin - **State v. Faust,** 267 Wis.2d 783, 672 N.W.2d 97 (Wis.App., 2003); Minnesota - **State v. Mellett,** 642 N.W.2d 779 (Minn.App. 2002); California - **People v. Sugarman,** 96 Cal.App.4th 210, 116 Cal.Rptr.2d 689 (Cal.App. 2 Dist. 2002); Iowa - **State v. Rains,** 574 N.W.2d 904 (Iowa 1998); Michigan - **People v. Hanna,** 223 Mich.App. 466, 567 N.W.2d 12 (1997).

[566]**State v. Clary,** 196 Ariz. 610, 2 P.3d 1255 (Ariz.App. Div. 1 2000).

[567]**Yates v. State,** 248 Ga. App. 35, 545 S.E.2d 169 (2001).

such as Kansas, lack any such niceties in its laws.[568]   Your DUI-DWI specialist will know the case law in your state, and after meeting with you, if this is an appropriate defense, he or she will know the likelihood of a successful challenge for your case.

9.23. If you asked to be taken to Acme Hospital for an independent test, and the officer declines because there are closer hospitals, does this matter? It all depends on your state's definition of what would be a reasonable accommodation by your officer in obtaining your independent test. In some states, it makes no difference which hospital drew and analyzed your blood. In others, the test must be truly your independent choice of hospitals.[569] Some states do not allow you a choice of where your independent blood sample is drawn.[570]

Several cases from Georgia indicate why Georgia may have the most comprehensive protections of driver's rights in America. In one case, where the arresting officer made a unilateral determination that defendant could not afford an independent blood test, based solely on defendant's assertion that he only had $7.00 on his person, but without determining whether defendant had other means to pay or offering defendant the opportunity to use the phone, the court held that the officer did not reasonably accommodate defendant's request for an independent test.[571] In another, after requesting an independent blood test, the defendant was taken to the **nearest** hospital where a blood "sample" was taken, but the hospital would not perform an alcohol test on the blood sample, so the sample was not admissible as evidence. The Georgia Court of Appeals determined that the officer had failed to reasonably accommodate the defendant's request for an independent test.[572] In a third case, an officer's refusal to wait 15 to 30 minutes until someone could bring money for the suspect's independent testing violated his right to an independent test.[573]

9.24. If you learn that the hospital requires cash or a check for an independent test, and you need to be taken by an ATM machine for money, can the officer decline to do this for you? Unfortunately, this extra step of the officer having to take you to an ATM machine may or may not be considered to be beyond what was a reasonable "accommodation." In the few cases on point, the officer was allowed to decline assistance and the state's test results were still admissible against the defendant in spite of the lack of the independent test,[574] while in another, when the suspect was short of the cash he needed, he requested that the officer stop by an ATM machine to allow him to get funds for the blood test at the hospital. The officer's refusal to accommodate this request caused the citizen's alleged refusal to be excluded from evidence.[575]

9.25. If you have been injured in a collision and (due to injuries) submitting to the breath test would be painful or difficult, does this constitute refusal? The answer is maybe yes, maybe no. Your inability to provide a breath sample suitable for testing may

---

[568]**State v. Bishop,** 264 Kan. 717, 957 P.2d 369 (1998); **Kim v. Kansas Dept. of Revenue,** 22 Kan.App.2d 319, 916 P.2d 47 (1996).

[569]**Joel v. State,** 245 Ga.App. 750, 538 S.E.2d 847 (2000); **Lockard v. Town of Killen,** 565 So.2d 679 (Ala.Crim.App. 1990); **People v. Dicks,** 190 Mich.App. 694, 476 N.W.2d 500 (1991).

[570]**State v. Hilditch,** 36 Or.App. 435, 584 P.2d 376 (1978); **State v. Ettore,** 228 N.J.Super. 25, 548 A.2d 1134 (1988); **Com. v. Rosewarne,** 410 Mass. 53, 571 N.E.2d 354 (1991).

[571]**State v. Anderson,** 258 Ga.App. 127, 572 S.E.2d 758 (2002).

[572]**State v. Button,** 206 Ga. App. 673, 426 S.E.2d 194 (1992).

[573]**Brady v. City of Lawrenceville,** 206 Ga.App. 395, 425 S.E.2d 404 (1992).

[574]**Sheehan v. State,** 267 Ga.App. 152, 598 S.E.2d 873 (2004).

[575]**Butts v. City of Peachtree City,** 205 Ga. App. 492, 422 S.E.2d 909 (1992).

constitute a refusal, unless it can be established that you were improperly instructed by the breath test operator, the instrument was improperly operated, or unless you can prove that your inability was caused by a valid physical or medical condition.[576]

It is generally held by appellate-level courts that a refusal does not occur if you were unable to provide a sample or specimen for testing because of the presence of a medical or physical condition that made it impossible for you to provide the sample or specimen.[577] However, unless the condition is obvious, the existence of the medical or physical condition and its effect on your ability to provide a sample must be established by credible medical evidence, and not simply on your word.[578] Your attorney will need to fight this issue by producing evidence of the medical problem at a pre-trial hearing. It should be noted that the courts do not consider intoxication to be a valid reason for an inability to provide a sample for testing.[579]

9.26. If you just never answer by saying "yes" or "no" to the request for a forensic test, does this constitute refusal? A defendant does not have to expressly refuse chemical testing to be deemed to have refused. If you failed to respond "yes" or "no" to a request for testing, your silence may be considered a refusal in some states,[580] while not in others.[581]

In other words, in the absence of an explicit (e.g., an overt, verbal "NO") refusal, your words or your conduct may be deemed to constitute a refusal to submit to chemical testing. It is generally held that a refusal occurs when a defendant displays conduct that would lead a reasonable person in the police officer's position to believe that the defendant is unwilling to submit to testing.[582]

Occasionally, a citizen will initially refuse chemical testing and later decide to consent to testing. In some states the person who initially refused testing may, under certain conditions, "cure" the refusal by subsequently consenting to testing.[583] It is generally held that a refusal

---

[576]**Reibel v. Curry**, 38 Ohio Misc. 71, 313 N.E.2d 26 (1974); **Huber v. Comm'r**, 382 N.W.2d 573 (Minn. App., 1986). For two emphysema cases, which should be adaptable to COPD or lung cancer patients, see **Burson v. Collier,** 226 Ga. 427, 175 S.E.2d 660 (1970); **Department of Public Safety v. Orr,** 122 Ga. App. 439, 177 S.E.2d 164 (1970).

[577]**Lamay v. Commonwealth**, 29 Va. App. 461, 513 S.E.2d 411 (1999); **Drake v. Kan. Dep't of Revenue**, 272 Kan. 231, 32 P.3d 705 (2001).

[578]**Tullo v. Commonwealth**, 837 A.2d 605 (Pa. Commw., 2003); **Flanigan v. Commonwealth**, 806 A.2d 524 (Pa. Commw., 2002).

[579]**Malkowsky v. Dep't of Pub. Safety**, 53 S.W.3d 873 (Tex. App., 2001); **Corum v. McNeill**, 716 S.W. 2d 915 (Mo. App., 1986). *See generally* Russell G. Donaldson, Annotation, *Sufficiency of Showing of Physical Inability to Take Tests for Driving While Intoxicated to Justify Refusal*, 68 A.L.R. 4th 776 (2005).

[580]**Ruth v. Director of Revenue**, 143 S.W.3d 741 (Mo. App., 2004); **Anderson v. Commissioner of Public Safety,** 379 N.W.2d 678 (Minn.App. 1986); **Lampman v. Department of Motor Vehicles,** 28 Cal.App.3d 922, 105 Cal.Rptr. 101 (Cal.App. 2 Dist. 1972); **McRoberts v. Kansas Dept. of Revenue,** 17 Kan.App.2d 680, 843 P.2d 280 (1992); **Rains v. Director of Revenue, Missouri Dept. of Revenue,** 728 S.W.2d 649 (Mo.App. S.D. 1987); **Mayo v. Moore,** 527 N.W.2d 257 (N.D. 1995); **State v. Gardner,** 52 Or.App. 663, 629 P.2d 412 (1981).

[581]**Mills v. Swanson,** 93 Idaho 279, 460 P.2d 704 (Idaho 1969); **State v. Sherwin,** 236 N.J.Super. 510, 566 A.2d 536 (N.J.Super.A.D. 1989); **Mathis v. North Carolina Div. of Motor Vehicles,** 71 N.C.App. 413, 322 S.E.2d 436 (N.C.App. 1984);

[582]**Dace v. Director of Revenue,** 123 S.W.3d 252 (Mo. App. 2003); **Tornabene v. Bonine ex rel. Ariz. Highway Dep't,** 203 Ariz. 326, 54 P.3d 355 (Ariz. App.2002).

[583]**Noland v. State,** 151 Ariz. 466, 728 P.2d 685 (Ariz. App., 1986); **Larmer v. State,** 522 So.2d 941 (Fla. App., 1988).

may be cured by a subsequent consent only if: (1) the consent was given within a reasonable time after the refusal and while the defendant was still in custody; (2) the delay caused by the initial refusal would not have affected the accuracy of the chemical test; and (3) honoring the request would not have caused an undue inconvenience or an additional expense to the police.[584] At least one state adds the requirement that the officer still be at the location and not have left the presence of the person in custody.[585]

---

[584]**Fugere v. State**, 120 N.M. 29, 897 P.2d 216 (1995); **In re Smith**, 115 Idaho 808, 770 P.2d 817 (1989).
[585]**Department of Public Safety v. Seay,** 206 Ga.App. 71, 424 S.E.2d 301 (1992).

Chapter 10

Understanding Breath, Blood, Urine, Saliva

or other Forensic Testing and Your DUI-DWI Case.

10.0. Purpose of this chapter. As a part of your DUI-DWI case, it is almost certain that you have either gone through a scientific evaluation of your blood, urine, breath saliva or hair, or that you refused. If you refused, this chapter is otherwise irrelevant unless a biologic sample was forcibly taken from you. If you have gone through one of these tests, this chapter will help you understand the tests themselves, as well as their strengths and weaknesses.

10.1. Breath test – most common form of testing. In a DUI-DWI case, two general types of breath analysis "tests" may have been offered to you. The first may have been a preliminary, roadside, hand-held field breath analyzer that typically runs off a 9-volt battery. Some devices can also run from a power cord that inserts into the police car's cigarette lighter. [See three examples of these in Section 6.20 of this book.] The other may have been a more scientific machine (like an Intoxilyzer®, a BAC Datamaster®, an Intoximeter® or a Draeger®). The roadside test is the handheld device, which an officer can use like other "field sobriety" screening tests in his or her quest for enough evidence to be able to arrest you.

All states will allow the use of these devices to test you if you consent to being screened. In almost all states, since the screening tests at the roadway are non-evidential, you may decline taking the field breathalyzer without any penalty. Further, in the overwhelming majority of states, the battery-powered devices are only allowed to determine the *presence of* or *absence of* alcohol in your system. Other states allow the officer to disclose the number from such portable screening breath analyzers to the jury at trial and to guess at your possible level of physical impairment due to the "number" reported on the device.

Some states have specifically declared the use of these hand-held devices to be a part of their implied consent law.[586] Due to the lack of regular calibration checks for accuracy on these devices, any numerical values on the machine at the time of your testing are legally irrelevant in most states except for establishing the presence or absence of alcohol on your breath.

The more sophisticated and more scientifically dependable EVIDENTIAL breath test is the machine used at the police station or at the jail (like an Intoxilyzer®, a BAC Datamaster®, an Intoximeter® or a Draeger®). [See Section 6.20 of this book.] These are usually table-top machines that plug into a 110-volt outlet and produce a print-out of the results after the testing. Some jurisdictions have purchased mobile testing vans that may contain these devices inside. Several of the major breath testing manufacturers sell these portable devices in both evidential models and non-evidential versions. The rest of this subsection deals with these machines, inasmuch as the numbers produced by these devices are the results that can be used against you in a typical court case as evidence by the prosecutor to establish your actual blood (or breath) alcohol level at the time of your arrest.

A new movement is occurring with all of the major breath testing machine manufacturers to make the evidential testing devices portable. [See Section 6.10 of this book.] Then, an

---

[586]Indiana - IC 9-30-7-2; California - West's Ann. Cal. Vehicle Code § 13388.

officer can test you immediately at the roadside with a full-fledged, evidential (meaning, that the printed result can be used in court) breath analyzer that prints out a test card for later use against you at trial. In many states, non-evidential, hand-held roadside testers are allowed for use by officers, but any results observed on the digital readout are not admissible in court.[587]

Any experienced DUI-DWI specialist either has his or her own breath testing devices that can be used to run experiments, or has access to the breath machine used in your state through one or more expert witnesses. These devices are subject to giving false high readings due to a variety of problems with the machines, including the presence of common items such as the residue of peppermint Altoids®, pizza (especially with onions), carbonated soda containing fruit flavoring and sugar (such as Sprite®) or even white bread in your mouth. For more information on this topic, see: http://www.duiblog.com/2004/11/20#a51 and http://www.duiblog.com/2005/03/08#a121.

10.1.1. Does your state require one sample collected or two for there to be a valid test? In some states, you will be asked to give two breath exhalations to be tested, and the results must be close enough to each other to demonstrate a reasonable degree of consistency.[588] In the other states, any one test result is adequate for "legal" purposes, if properly performed.[589]

Mouth alcohol detection is a feature that many manufacturers claim will help prevent false high readings. However, these detectors are not routinely calibrated for proper performance and do not work in even half of the cases where some mouth alcohol is present.[590] Some devices will actually print a false, elevated test result when some alcohol is in your body and other alcohol from your mouth or esophagus gets added to the sample when you deliver a breath sample.[591] [See more ideas from the checklist contained in **Appendix I**.]

10.1.2. If two samples are taken, how closely must the results (numbers) be to each other to constitute a valid test? For the test results of either of the samples to be considered accurate enough to be used against you, most states (except a few such as New Jersey and Wisconsin) require multiple tests, and also require that the two results be close enough to each other to demonstrate some measure of scientific "precision" to confirm an appropriate agreement or the results are thrown out. This limit of difference on human subject breath testing is typically 0.02 grams, or 0.03 grams in one or two states.[592] This difference is allowed because most states require an accuracy of no more than 0.01 in the machine's

---

[587]**State v. Holler,** 224 Ga.App.66, 479 S.E.2d 780 (1996); Schoolfield v. State, 251 Ga.App. 52, 554 S.E.2d 181 (2001).

[588]Two samples required - Georgia - **State v. Kruzel,** 261 Ga.App. 90, 581 S.E.2d 711 (2003); O.C.G.A. § 40-6-392(a)(1)(B); Washington - West's RCWA 46.61.506(4)(a)(iv); Minnesota - M.S.A. § 169A.51(Subd. 5(a)); Nevada - N.R.S. 484.386(1); Wisconsin - W.S.A. 343.305(6)(c)(1); Arizona - A.R.S. § 28-1323(A)(3); More than one sample- New Jersey - N.J.S.A. 39:4-50.2(a).

[589]One sample required - Texas - **Fulenwider v. State,** 2004 WL 1585286 (Tex.App.-Hous. (1 Dist.) 2004); Tennessee - **State v. Korsakov,** 34 S.W.3d 534 (Tenn.Crim.App. 2000); Florida - West's F.S.A. § 316.1932.

[590]See http://www.duiblog.com/2005/03/30#a134 and http://www.duiblog.com/2005/03/31#a135.

[591]See http://www.theduibook.com/hlastala.htm.

[592]Georgia - samples must be within 0.02 grams of each other - O.C.G.A. § 40-6-392(a)(1)(B); Minnesota - samples must be within 0.02 grams of each other - M.S.A. § 169A.51(Subd. 5(d)); Washington - samples must be within 10% of their mean - West's RCWA 46.61.506(4)(a)(iv); Nevada - samples must be within 0.02 grams of each other - N.R.S. 484.386(1)(a); Arizona - samples must be within 0.02 grams of each other - A.R.S. § 28-1323(A)(3); Oklahoma – 0.03 - **Morgan v. State ex rel. Dept. of Public Safety,** 882 P.2d 574 (Okla.App. Div. 1993); Massachusetts – 0.02 - 501 CMR 2.56.

variance from a tested simulator sample to a known chemical standard.[593] Variances in human breathing patterns will not allow reliable dual sample testing with less than a 0.02 grams (plus or minus) variability.

10.1.3. Regulations or statutes requiring testing officer to follow specified protocol.

Because scientific breath testing occurs so frequently and a variety of issues are constantly litigated, most police departments have specific protocols with regard to performing this testing. If you did take a State-administered breath test, in light of your presumption of innocence, the prosecution must typically prove that at the time of your test this equipment was in working order, was properly maintained and that the test was administered in a proper fashion, typically according to their protocol.[594] These protocols are commonly designed out of their experience, and in consultation with the prosecutors, as to what is required for an arrest for DUI-DWI to be successfully followed by a conviction.

The best DUI-DWI specialists in your state know your state's protocols for the breath testing, and more importantly, the reasons behind the steps in the protocol. If the protocol for your breath test was not followed, this may imply to the court that there is a problem with either the arrest or with the collection of the evidence. While the protocols are put in place to protect the reliability of breath test results collected by the police officers during your arrest, a breach of these protocols may be used in your benefit to have the charges against you be dismissed, reduced or to win at trial. [See more ideas from the checklist contained in **Appendix I.**]

10.1.4. Manner of blowing can alter final results.

The manner in which you deliver your breath sample may affect the results of your breath test results.[595] First, if you attempted to comply with the breath test, but there was a problem with the plastic mouthpiece, this might cause your machine to malfunction. The same can be true of the machine not working if you "over blow" (blow too hard or with too much air being rapidly forced through the breath collection tube). A malfunction in the pressure switch may cause a false reading.[596] If the officer does not realize what is causing the problem, he or she might jump to the conclusion that you refused the test by intentional non-compliance.

Next, you can hyperventilate by crying or by having a "panic attack." As the air is circulating into and out of your lungs too quickly, the results of the amount of alcohol it reads in your breath does not accurately reflect what amount of alcohol is in your blood stream. Likewise, hypoventilation (holding your breath) can cause a false, elevated test result.

If your body is overheated for any reason such as after exercise or from being in a steam room, this can elevate a breath test reading. Women typically have greater fluctuations in their body temperature due to their menstrual cycle. Also, a simple fever that elevates your body temperature a few degrees can cause a higher breath test alcohol reading that is higher than the real "number."[597] During menopause, middle-aged women experience wide swings in

---

[593]Mass. 501 CMR 2.56; .Y. Comp. Codes R. & Regs. tit. 10, § 59.4; Wis. Admin. Code § Trans 311.10; **People v. Orth,** 124 Ill.2d 326, 530 N.E.2d 210 (Ill. 1988).

[594]**Luginbyhl v. Com.,** 46 Va.App. 460, 618 S.E.2d 347 (2005); **Nivens v. State,** 832 N.E.2d 1134 (Ind.App. 2005); **City of Columbus v. Childs,** 832 N.E.2d 1134 (Ohio App. 10 Dist. 2005); **Gumma v. White,** 216 Ill.2d 23, 833 N.E.2d 834 (Ill. 2005); **Bozarth v. Director of Revenue, State of Missouri,** 168 S.W.3d 78 (Mo.App. E.D. 2005); **Belvin v. State,** 2005 WL 1336497 (Fla.App. 4 Dist. 2005); **State v. Palmaka,** 266 Ga.App. 595, 597 S.E.2d 630 (2004); **State v. Sensing,** 843 S.W.2d 412 (Tenn. 1992); **Howes v. State,** 120 S.W.3d 903 (Tex.App.-Texarkana 2003).

[595]Head, William C., *The Georgia DUI Trial Practice Manual* (2005 Ed.), § 5.1.2.5.

[596]**Walker v. State,** 262 Ga.App. 872, 586 S.E.2d 757 (2003).

[597]http://www.duiblog.com/2005/03/28#a133.

body temperature in a matter of minutes.

Last, if you took the test while seated and leaning forward, this position may have caused a reflux (movement of stomach contents up your esophagus) of some of your stomach contents, including any alcohol in your stomach gases or free in your stomach. Because the machine automatically considers a ratio of alcohol in your breath as compared to your blood alcohol level, liquid alcohol or alcohol in this stomach gas can markedly increase the reported breath test results.

10.1.5. Air bag residue may cause elevated readings. In some DUI-DWI cases, there is an automobile accident involved. Most automobiles on the road today have air bags.[598] Most air bags are packed either in baking soda or talc, or both. Some newer vehicles have air bags that are packed in a two-stage baffle system. These powdery substances prevent "sticking" of the bag when it deploys. This fine powder inhaled as a result of an air bag crash can create the "Tyndall" effect, which may cause a false reading on any infrared breath testing machine if this powder is exhaled by you into the infrared breath machine, causing erroneously high readings by your breath testing device. Depending on the recency of inhalation and the quantity of powder emitted, all infrared breath analyzers used in America are susceptible to this same "contamination" of the breath sample chamber issue, if baking soda or talc were part of the air bag system's packing materials.

The propellants used to launch the air bags are gasses that may also affect the readings of infrared breath analysis devices, depending on which propellant was used in your car. To discover which propellant was used in your air bag, your attorney may have to contact the manufacturer of your car.[599]

The important thing about all of this is to remember if your air bag deployed during any accident, and you submitted to a breath test, you should report this to your DUI-DWI attorney. Other details such as how much time between the accident and any breath test, or the make and model of your car may also be important.

10.1.6. Breath machine error readings and the importance of the follow-up by the testing officer. If, during your testing, the breath machine came up with an "error" reading on the monitor or the print-out, and you were subsequently considered to have refused to provide a sample, there are several possible reasons. First, you may not have been delivering the breath sample correctly, either because the instructions were not given correctly, they were given correctly but you did not understand them, or they were given correctly and you chose not to perform. If the problem was with either of the first two possibilities, you may have a possible defense to the claim that you refused the test.

Second, if it was not one of these problems that caused an error reading to register on the machine, was there a problem with the machine itself? Did the officer just stop trying to obtain an adequate sample after the first attempt, or did the officer try to reset the machine and start over? Details you remember about these few minutes may lead to the assertion of a defense that you tried to perform, but that the reported result was the fault of the machine.

Last, if the machine came up with an error reading, or several error readings, but the officer and you were still able to finally come up with a sample or samples that the machine found acceptable, these added steps may place enough reasonable doubt in the mind of a judge or a jury to win your case. A victory likely depends on what the officer had to do to get an adequate sample, or what you said or attempted to do that will make the difference in your

---

[598]http://inventors.about.com/library/inventors/blair_bags.htm

[599]Head, William C., *The Georgia DUI Trial Practice Manual* (2005 Ed.), § 5.2.

defense.

In some states, when two or more "error" readings have caused the device to not capture a valid test, the breath testing officer may be authorized to request an alternative type of test, such as a blood test. Also, some error readings may indicate an "interfering substance" has been detected, indicating a possible medical emergency.

10.1.7. Retention of all test cards is mandatory, because they are part of your evidence. Any results from blood, breath or urine tests are be very important to any defense in your DUI-DWI case. First, immediately after you were tested on the desktop breath analysis machine at the jail or precinct/station house, the machine produced several copies of the results. You should have been given a duplicate copy of every one of these printed results. While this test result is typically obtainable by your attorney from the prosecution in your case,[600] if you have your copy, this assists in the prompt evaluation of your case.

The second test report you may have received is if for any reason you had a blood alcohol test taken by a doctor, nurse or paramedic, they may have given you a copy of that test result as well. If nothing else, you may have already received a bill or a receipt from the charges of the hospital for them to perform a blood or urine test for you. If you do not have a copy of these results, your lawyer may ask you assist to obtain a copy. Due to federal privacy laws, it is usually much easier for you to get this copy than for your lawyer to do so.

With either set of test results (police or medical), the defenses you may be able to raise can be based on these documents. Particularly if there are significant discrepancies between these results, the sooner your attorney knows of all of these results, the sooner he or she can raise these defenses.

Last, there is always the chance that the prosecution will mistakenly charge you using someone else's test results, even if the other results have your name on their cards. Clerical errors **do** occur. If you have your copy of any test cards or test results that you know are from you, and the tests the State attempts to admit in evidence do not match up, you may be able to get the entire case dismissed. [See more ideas from the checklist contained in **Appendix I.**]

10.1.8. Computer database downloads and vital information from them. All infrared breath testing devices have a built-in computer, with a microprocessor and a serial port that can be downloaded either by a modem or by an on-site computer. Software has been created for each different machine to capture and organize this data. This allows in some states for a complete and accurate history of all defects and aborted tests to be maintained. However, some state's laws do not hold their crime labs accountable to the public and purposely refuse to keep such a database.[601]

In other progressive states, such as South Carolina, Wisconsin and Minnesota, this information may lead to a successful defense to your DUI-DWI case if it can be shown the machine upon which you were tested has a history of multiple failures or a systemic error in its functionality. Your DUI-DWI specialist will know your state's regulations and laws and will know if it is possible to hire an expert to analyze this data. See this article about a challenge in Texas to such information: http://www.duiblog.com/2005/10/29.

10.1.9. Person doing the testing must be currently certified to run the test. In most, if not all of the states, for any breath test on you to be considered valid, the person who

---

[600]Georgia - O.C.G.A. § 17-16-23; Fla. R. Crim. P. Rule 3.220(b)(1)(J); Tenn. R. Crim. P., Rule 16(a)(1)(D); Indiana - Trial Procedure Rule 26(B)(1).

[601]Head, William C., *The Georgia DUI Trial Practice Manual* (2005 Ed.), § 5.1.2.1.

ran the test on you must have been certified to run the machine at the time you were tested.[602] If the prosecution cannot bring that proof to your hearing or trial, the test results will likely have to be thrown out.

10.1.10. Periodic calibration checks and service records are critical to your defense. The breath testing machines used by the police go through months of frequent use between "tune-ups." In order for the breath test results to be used against you in court, the prosecution not only has to be able to show the numerical results, but also that the machine was in good working order and that it had been operated appropriately.[603] You may have grounds to exclude your breath test if your attorney can show the machines were not adequately maintained and frequently calibrated. A similar attack may be possible on results from a blood analysis device, too. [See **Appendix I** for a more complete guide to breath and blood test challenges.]

Part of the routine maintenance on infrared devices involves checking each machine's calibration and testing the device against known samples of either liquid solutions or "dry gas" cylinders to assure the accuracy of the machine. This may be done both at the time of your testing and on a periodic basis such as monthly or quarterly. It is often considered a requirement for the prosecution to prove, by the admission of these periodic calibration "checks" and maintenance records, that the machine was in optimal working order if the results of your breath test are to be used against you in your DUI-DWI case. The records may be offered to prove that the machine was capable of rendering accurate results.[604] Absent these documents, your breath test may be excluded or your case may be dismissed. In other states, these records are not a necessary part of your prosecution, meaning there are no grounds for an automatic dismissal if these records are not produced by the State.[605]

This is why your attorney will likely request these records from the prosecution as a part of the discovery process. Your attorney or an expert assisting your attorney may want to

---

[602]Arizona - A.R.S. § 28-1323(A)(2); Wisconsin - W.S.A. 343.305(6)(a); Connecticut - C.G.S.A. § 14-227a(b); Georgia - O.C.G.A. § 35-3-154; Indiana - IC 9-30-6-5; Kansas - K.S.A. § 8-1002(a)(3); Kentucky - KRS § 189A.103(3)(b); Maine - 29-A M.R.S.A. § 2524(3); Missouri - V.A.M.S. 306.114(2); Montana - MCA 61-8-404(1)(b)(i); New Mexico - NMRA, Rule 8-603(2)(a); Rhode Island - Gen.Laws 1956, § 31-27-2(c)(5); South Carolina - Code 1976 § 56-5-2950(a); Vermont - 23 V.S.A. § 1203(a); Virginia - Va. Code Ann. § 18.2-268.9; West Viriginia - W. Va. Code, § 17C-5-4(f); Arkansas - A.C.A. § 5-65-206(D)(1)(B)(2).

[603]District of Columbia - DC ST § 50-2205.03; Missouri - V.A.M.S. 306.114(2); Rhode Island - Gen.Laws 1956, § 31-27-2(c)(5); **Luginbyhl v. Com.,** 46 Va.App. 460, 618 S.E.2d 347 (2005); **Nivens v. State,** 832 N.E.2d 1134 (Ind.App. 2005); **City of Columbus v. Childs,** 2005 WL 1693624 (Ohio App. 10 Dist. 2005); **Gumma v. White,** 216 Ill.2d 23, 833 N.E.2d 834 (Ill. 2005); **Bozarth v. Director of Revenue, State of Missouri,** 168 S.W.3d 78 (Mo.App. E.D. 2005); **Belvin v. State,** 2005 WL 1336497 (Fla.App. 4 Dist. 2005); **State v. Palmaka,** 266 Ga.App. 595, 597 S.E.2d 630 (2004); **State v. Sensing,** 843 S.W.2d 412 (Tenn. 1992); **Howes v. State,** 120 S.W.3d 903 (Tex.App.-Texarkana 2003).

[604]Colorado - C.R.S.A. § 42-4-1303; Arizona - A.R.S. § 28-1323(A)(5); Arkansas - A.C.A. § 5-65-206(D)(1)(B)(2); Georgia - **Dougherty v. State,** 259 Ga.App. 618, 578 S.E.2d 256 (2003); **State v. Ofa,** 9 Haw.App. 130, 828 P.2d 813 (1992); Illinois - **State v. Knapp,** 690 N.W.2d 698 (Iowa App. 2004); Kentucky - **Com. v. Davis,** 25 S.W.3d 106 (Ky. 2000); Mississippi - Miss. Code Ann. § 63-11-19; **Callahan v. State,** 811 So.2d 420 (Miss.App. 2001); Missouri - **Sullivan v. Director of Revenue, State of Mo.,** 980 S.W.2d 339 (Mo.App. S.D. 1998); New Jersey - **State v. Maida,** 332 N.J.Super. 564, 753 A.2d 1240 (N.J.Super. 2000); New Mexico - **State v. Smith,** 128 N.M. 467, 994 P.2d 47 (N.M.App. 1999).

[605]Alabama - **Lum v. City of Brewton,** 883 So.2d 241 (Ala.Crim.App. 2003); Missouri - **Duckworth v. Director of Revenue, State of Mo.,** 11 S.W.3d 658 (Mo.App. E.D. 1999); Ohio - **State v. Black,** 2004 WL 88857 (Ohio App. 6 Dist. 2004); South Carolina - **State v. Salisbury,** 330 S.C. 250, 498 S.E.2d 655 (S.C.App. 1998).

closely inspect these records at the time of any hearing or at trial. As one national expert on DUI-DWI laws noted about breath machines, the government has changed them constantly, which indicates that these machines are in no way perfect.[606]

10.2. Blood test – most reliable and accurate form of testing. If drawn correctly, handled correctly and tested properly, a blood test is the most accurate and reliable direct measure of your blood alcohol level. The State considers your blood level in its determination of whether or not you are *per se* driving under the influence (e.g., over the legal alcohol limit) as well as in a "common law" driving while intoxicated case. Breath testing is only a "second best" approximation, with numerous factors going into the breath device's ability to produce accurate and reliable results.

As opposed to a blood test, which cannot be contaminated by mouth alcohol or a test subject's "health" issues (such as diabetes), all breath tests are subject to "limitations" on their accuracy and reliability. It is this unavoidable difference that creates numerous challenges to breath testing devices and their accuracy.

10.2.1. Gas chromatography for alcohol tests. Gas chromatography takes a small quantity of your blood (after it is mixed with another chemical in the lab) and (using a small flame) turns this liquid into a vapor.[607] Depending on how quickly this vapor diffuses through a packed column (usually using diatomaceous earth), the machine is able to determine not only the presence or absence of ethyl alcohol in your blood, but the amount as well. A gas chromatograph can also indentify other alcohols and similar "chemicals" such as acetone.

10.2.2. GC-MS (gas chromatography mass spectrophotometry) for drug analysis. GC-MS is the accepted "standard" for precision and accuracy in drug analysis when it is the amount of any drug in your bloodstream is suspected.[608] This test vaporizes a small quantity of your blood, then analyzes a wide spectrum of possible drugs based on how long the "retention" time is before a substance (drug) is indicated on the spectrum. By determining the pattern of this entire process, comparing it to known standards and retention times kept in the laboratory, the lab technicians and chemists running the test can then determine not only what drugs are in your blood, but how much.[609]

10.2.3. Get the entire set of records for the batch that was run, if possible. Because GC-MS is a very sophisticated test to run, using a complex and expensive machine, the samples from all over the state are often brought to a central location (like the state crime lab) and run on a weekly or monthly basis as batches.

One defense for you in your DUI-DWI case might be if there were problems with any part of the batch, or if the test results for the entire batch appeared skewed. By looking at the entire "batch" of tests that were run with your samples, an expert may be able to identify some problem with the GC-MS device such as a failure of the "column" or some other malfunction.

10.2.4. Obtain discovery on how the standards were created for checking the alcohol accuracy for gas chromatography. Before any sample is run on the gas chromatography device, standards (samples with known concentrations alcohol) are run through the machine to help guarantee the machines accuracy. These are typically checked at three, four or five different levels from 0.02 to 0.20. Scientists refer to this as "checking for linearity." If the results derived from running these standards do not correspond with the known

---

[606]http://www.duiblog.com/2005/10/06#a254.

[607]http://www.online-medical-dictionary.org/omd.asp?q=gas+chromatography.

[608]http://www.drugfreeworks.com/DFW%20FAQ.htm#How%20reliable%20are%20the%20drug%20tests?

[609]http://www.online-medical-dictionary.org/omd.asp?q=gas+chromatography.

levels of alcohol in the sample, then the machine is out of calibration and inherently unreliable.

This accuracy is based upon the assumption that the standards are truly "standard." How these standards were created, how they are maintained and how they are used during testing may affect their reliability. If they were unreliable, or if there is any just a question of their reliability, this may cast enough doubt on the test results to get them thrown out of your DUI-DWI case. [See more ideas from the checklist contained in **Appendix I.**]

10.2.5. Get the retention time manual for the GC-MS device used to analyze drugs to assure that the peak was at the expected retention time. Each GC-MS machine is a little different, with each one having "retention time" results that might be a little different. Because a defective column may "drift" and cause the reported retention time to be reported incorrectly, looking at all of the paperwork and retention time manuals could be very helpful in revealing a flawed test. Your attorney may also procure a court order to have independent analysis to verify (or refute) the State's test.

10.2.6. Get service records for any blood test device. No matter what device was used to analyze your blood, you may have a defense if that machine was not correctly maintained, or if it has a history of frequent breakdowns or false readings. For that reason, your attorney may attempt to get these records, if the State is obligated to surrender or disclose this information.

10.2.7. Look for breaks in the "chain of custody" from collection to final analysis. For any blood, urine or other biologic sample that is being used against you in your DUI-DWI case other than the breath test (including any blood which was drawn from you), in order to use any results from these samples against you, the prosecution must prove that your sample was always in possession of someone connected with State. In other words, the prosecution must be able to demonstrate to the court the various custodians (who had actual physical possession) of this sample from the moment the sample left your body until it was actually analyzed in the appropriate analytical machine.[610] This is what is called the "chain of custody."

If there is a break in this chain of custody, your attorney will try to use this in order to get the results of these tests suppressed, so that it cannot be used against you. In some states, the laws are very protective of sloppy and unreliable "chains of custody" by the State and let a jury or judge consider such evidence for whatever "weight and credibility" it may have.[611] [See more ideas from the checklist contained in **Appendix I.**]

10.2.8. Independent tests to confirm or refute. In almost every state, one of your rights if you are arrested for DUI-DWI and the police take any blood, breath or urine samples from you, is to have an independent blood or urine test of your own performed at a laboratory of your choice and at your own expense.[612] The benefits to you undergoing this

---

[610]**People v. Sugarman,** 96 Cal.App.4th 210, 116 Cal.Rptr.2d 689 (Cal.App. 2 Dist. 2002); **Pittman v. State,** 110 Ga.App. 625, 139 S.E.2d 507 (1964); **People v. Lach,** 302 Ill.App.3d 587, 707 N.E.2d 144 (Ill.App. 1 Dist. 1998); **Jones v. State,** 761 So.2d 907 (Miss.App. 2000); **State v. Carney,** 219 Mont. 412, 714 P.2d 532 (1986); **Com. v. Arizini,** 277 Pa.Super. 27, 419 A.2d 643 (1980); **Ex parte Department of Health and Environmental Control,** 350 S.C. 243, 565 S.E.2d 293 (2002); **Tonnan v. State,** 171 Tex.Crim. 570, 352 S.W.2d 272 (Tex.Crim.App. 1961); **Avila v. State,** 18 S.W.3d 736 (Tex.App.-San Antonio 2000).

[611]**Lewis v. State,** 215 Ga.App. 486, 451 S.E.2d 116 (1994); **Bailey v. State,** 229 Ga.App. 869, 494 S.E.2d 672 (1997); **Swanson v. State,** 248 Ga.App. 561, 545 S.E.2d 713 (2001).

[612]California - West's Ann.Cal.Vehicle Code § 23614; Florida - West's F.S.A. § 316.1932(3).; Georgia - O.C.G.A. § 40-6-392(3); Mississippi - Miss. Code Ann. § 63-11-13; Texas - V.T.C.A., Transportation Code § 724.019; Washington - West's RCWA 46.61.506(6); Wisconsin - W.S.A. 343.305(5).

independent test are several.

First, if the results of your test do not correlate with those drawn at the direction of the police, this is very significant evidence as to the invalidity of all of the test results. Without any reliable test results, most DUI-DWI cases fall apart and must be reduced or dismissed.

Next, if your independent test only confirms the results of the prosecution's tests, this may give your attorney important information when it comes to negotiating with the prosecution for a possible settlement of the charges against you without trial. On the other hand, if the result is the same number as the breath test, but blood was drawn nearly three hours *after* driving, an error in the less reliable breath test may be provable, since the human body is in a constant state of elimination of alcohol even before alcohol consumption stops.

10.2.9. DNA is possible for comparing the blood allegedly collected by police and the defendant's. If there is a question about whether or not the sample the State is attempting to use against you is truly your sample or not, then if the State's sample has been properly preserved, the DNA in this sample can be compared to your DNA. The benefit to you in this ability is if the DNA does not match up, then no matter what any chain of custody paperwork may say, it is very unlikely that the sample the State has is from you. This additional information can then be used very strongly in your defense.[613]

10.2.10. Be cautious to not accept an immunoassay test for any "quantitative" drug results, without a confirmatory GC-MS. The GC-MS is a highly accurate way of determining not only the *presence* of drugs in your system, but also the quantitative *amounts* of those drugs as well. While it is likely as good at detecting the presence or absence of drugs, an immunoassay is not nearly as accurate for determining how much of these drugs were there. Immunoassay analysis is much more commonly used as a *screening* test. Because drugs can be detectable in either your blood, or especially in your urine, for prolonged periods of time, you may be losing a defense to the DUI-DWI charges against you if you not determine the actual blood or urine levels or concentrations of these drugs.[614]

As an example, just because you smoked pot a month ago does not mean you were in any way impaired to drive today. Yet, if all you have is an immunoassay for THC or the breakdown or marijuana, this result may come out positive, leading to the false impression that you were impaired while driving. On the other hand, if you can prove by the admission into evidence of GC-MS results showing a very accurate and very low level of these same by-products, this may lead to you winning at trial or the DUI-DWI charges being thrown out.

10.3. Urine test – usually reserved for drugs and then only to determine presence of a class of drugs. Urine testing does not reflect a measure of your blood alcohol because alcohol is one of the substances that is broken down by your liver instead of your kidneys.

However, testing your urine is one of the most common methods of testing your for the presence of drugs, with simple dip-stick tests commonly available for screening tests for cocaine, amphetamines, methamphetamines, marijuana (THC), methadone and other opiates (narcotics), phencyclidine (PCP), barbiturates, benzodiazepines and tricyclic anti-

---

[613]**State v. Nickelson,** 2003 WL 22952740 (Minn.App. 2003); **State v. Templeton,** 148 Wash.2d 193, 59 P.3d 632 (2002); **Com. v. Blasioli,** 454 Pa.Super. 207, 685 A.2d 151 (1996).

[614]http://www.nacdl.org/public.nsf/0/7e2489f2d3cca065852568480073b12f?OpenDocument; Beverly Potter and Sebastian Orfal, **Drug Testing At Work: A Guide For Employers and Employees** (Ronin Publishing, 1995; ISBN: 0-914171-70-4) 35; Bryan S. Finkle, *Drug-Analysis Technology: Overview and State of the Art*, **Clinical Chemistry,** 33.11(B) (1987).

depressants.[615] These tests are as easy as you urinating in a cup, and the officer then placing the test strip in your urine for one to three minutes. If the strip changes to the right color, your urine is considered a positive test for that class of drugs. Once again, this is merely a "presumptive" (or screening) test that needs to be confirmed by GC-MS.

10.3.1. If quantitative analysis of either drugs or alcohol is being used by the prosecutor, get expert witness to assist in refuting the results. Quantitative analysis means the prosecution is attempting to demonstrate the exact level of the prohibited substance in your blood rather than just the presence or absence. This type of analysis is not uncommon for alcohol, to determine if the level of alcohol in your system is at or above a certain level, (0.08 for adults or 0.02 grams for drivers under age 21 [in most states], depending on your age and circumstances), it is a crime in and by itself. This is the "per se" alcohol DUI-DWI charge.

However, there can be times when a specific level of marijuana or barbiturates, or any other drug may be important to the State in its prosecution. An example might be if you admit to having smoked marijuana a week ago, but none since. While you may have a positive screening urine or blood test, the prosecution must typically also prove that you were under the influence of these drugs while you were driving for you to be liable for a DUI-DWI charge.

That being the case, the prosecution may try to prove that your blood or urine level was high enough or sufficient to demonstrate to a judge or jury that your defense of not being impaired cannot or should not be believed. To do this, the prosecution will want to perform one of these quantitative analyses on your sample, and then present the results at your trial.

Because these tests have inherent problems, an expert on your side may be able to attack the accuracy of the results. If the results cannot be considered accurate, then this may lead to them either being thrown out, or to them being discounted by the jury. This expert may be the difference between you winning or losing.

10.3.2. Pooling is always a problem with urine testing. Urine pooling means that your body is always making urine in your kidneys, then delivering that fluid to your bladder. Depending on how much you make, how big your bladder is, and how often you decide to do so socially, you empty your bladder anywhere from a couple times a day, to many times. Between these times, your urine is pooling in your bladder, waiting to be peed out.

If you haven't urinated for ten to twelve hours prior to being tested, and you had used some of those drugs in the recent past, the urine sample that is tested will have drug residue in it, even if those drugs were not affecting your mind or your reactions while you were driving. Of course, to use this defense against a DUI-DWI charge, you may have to admit to the use of the drug. Depending on the drug and whether or not it was prescribed for you, having this prohibited drug in your system could also be a crime.

10.3.3. Urine will reveal low levels of contraband drugs longer than a blood test. Your kidneys slowly and constantly remove the breakdown and waste products of most chemical substances from your body.[616] Because your kidneys concentrate these waste products from your bloodstream, the residue of any drugs is detectable in your urine for much longer than in your blood.

Depending on how critically the State wants to analyze a urine sample from you, drugs you may have taken months ago may cause your urine test to be positive. If all the police do is dip a test strip into your urine (the most common form of drug testing which can be done

---

[615]http://www.drugteststrips.com/info_pages.php/pages_id/23/?ref=GO330.

[616]http://www.gotmo.net/info/urine.htm.

216

anywhere), illegal drugs such as marijuana, amphetamines, narcotics and barbiturates may all be detected in your urine sample for weeks after you were exposed to the drugs. If the police send the urine sample off for a more critical analysis to a crime lab, even more minute amounts of these drugs can be detected for months after your exposure.

10.4. Saliva is not used for forensic alcohol testing, due to small volume, but is good for drug screening or DNA sampling. Yet another type of bodily fluid or tissue you might be asked to give to law enforcement may be some of your saliva. This can be done either by having you spit into a collection cup, or by swabbing the inside of your mouth. Either way, the amount of sample they get is too little to do any of the routine alcohol testing on it.

However, even this amount of saliva can be used to test for drugs in your system, or to check your DNA patterns. It is important for your defense to remember if you gave such a sample, as the prosecution may use any information so gathered to search for other crimes with which to charge you, or as a basis for the DUI-DWI charges against you.

10.5. Destruction of biologic samples of blood or urine prior to the defense being able to independently test the samples. Most states' crime laboratories either have an internal policy or regulations or statutes that control how long they will retain biologic samples. Unless a person's blood or urine sample has been identified and set aside to NOT be destroyed, all samples are eventually incinerated. Some states destroy samples after 6 or 12 months. Others send a notice to the defendant along with the crime laboratory's results, and such notice may notify of proposed destruction in a matter of 60 to 90 days, absent a request for preservation or additional testing.

Top DUI-DWI defense attorneys will seek independent analysis of such samples in many cases. Also, your drunk driving defense specialist may notify the crime lab to NOT destroy your blood or urine samples. This request is typically sent in a manner that will assure proof of delivery (e.g., certified mail or hand delivery by a courier). Such a request, if followed by the destruction of the sample being held at the crime laboratory, could lead to a successful challenge to your biologic test results.

Two keys cases control most litigation on this subject. The United States Supreme Court ruled in *Arizona v. Youngblood*, 488 U.S. 51, 109 S.Ct. 333, 102 L.Ed.2d 281 (1988) that proof of intentional destruction of exculpatory evidence (or potentially exculpatory evidence) can result in a violation of the federal constitution. Unfortunately, the burden of showing that the evidence was intentionally destroyed AND that it was likely to provide some exculpatory information for an accused person was placed upon the defendant.

Another key case from the United States Supreme Court is *California v. Trombetta*, 467 U.S. 479, 104 S.Ct. 2528, 81 L.Ed.2d 413 (1984), which says that the state need not preserve every breath sample so long as the accused is afforded an opportunity to get an independent test or a type of alternative test that allowed the accused to seek a separate analysis of the forensic test.

Proving intentional destruction of a blood or urine test by the agents of the State is all but impossible. Unless your state has a statute or constitutional provision that gives its citizens better protection against police and crime laboratory destruction of blood or urine samples, challenges to destruction of a biologic sample are likely to fail.

One "step" that your attorney may take to improve your chances of winning such a challenge is to obtain a court order wherein the judge handling your case orders that the biologic sample not be destroyed. In *Blackwell v. State*, 245 Ga.App. 135, 537 S.E.2d 457 (2000), a court order for preservation did not save Mr. Blackwell's blood sample from being destroyed at the GBI crime laboratory. This case was dismissed by the trial judge largely due to the fact that a probation officer's drug screening test for drugs showed "negative" results, despite a subsequent crime lab analysis reporting "positive" results. In two other cases, however, the results were not even excluded by the trial court and offered no chance of total dismissal of the charges, despite highly questionable conduct by the State.[617]

---

[617]**Swanson v. State**, 248 Ga.App. 551, 545 S.E.2d 713 (2001); **Shoemaker v. State**, 266 Ga.App. 342, 596 S.E.2d 805 (2004).

Chapter 11

Understanding the Importance of Administrative License Suspension or Revocation Laws and their Interplay with Your DUI-DWI Case

11.0. Purpose of this chapter. Almost every state's DUI-DWI law requires that you will automatically have your driver's license suspended if you are arrested for DUI-DWI and a resulting chemical test of your blood, breath or urine yields a numeric result at or above the applicable legal limit (e.g., 0.08 for adults who are not operating a commercial vehicle), or if you refuse the blood, urine or breath testing requested by your arresting officer. While you may or may not get a temporary license to provide limited driving privileges for you after your arrest, if you want to get your license back, you face an administrative process that is separate from your criminal case.

In the various states, these civil hearings may be referred to as hearings for "administrative license suspension" or ALS, or "administrative license revocation" or ALR. Your ALS/ALR hearing and your criminal hearing or trial may seem to you to be similar type legal proceedings. In fact, the decisions reached usually involve some of the same facts that surround your arrest. Your criminal case involves whether or not you broke the law, and whether the State can prove you broke the law *beyond a reasonable doubt.*

However, the administrative license suspension often has little to do with whether or not you broke the law. Instead, it is based on the limited right you have to be allowed to drive a vehicle, conditionally granted to you at some time in the past by the State, and whether or not this right has been taken away from you in a constitutionally approved manner. This chapter discusses this administrative license suspension/revocation procedure, and how this interacts with your criminal case.

11.1. Administrative license suspension (or revocation) [ALS/ALR] proceedings almost always occur prior to criminal court date. For reasons explained in other sections of this book, it is unlikely any hearing or your trial will be held within many weeks, if not many months after your DUI-DWI arrest. It will typically take that long for your attorney to investigate your case, gather all the information he or she can, and then organize experts and your defenses. Even if you have a constitutional right to a speedy trial, such rapid trials typically benefit only the prosecution because they usually have all their information for your prosecution within hours of your arrest. Except for the scheduling hassles, the prosecution expects you to show up for your trial unprepared and without any adequate or organized defense to the pending charges.

On the other hand, most state administrative hearings have to be held by statute within weeks, and rarely more than thirty days after your arrest.[618] It is typically not a question of

---

[618]Alabama - 30 days - Ala.Code 1975 § 32-6-49.13(g); Arizona - 30 days - A.R.S. § 28-1321(I); California - must apply within ten days - West's Ann.Cal.Vehicle Code § 14100; Oklahoma - 30 days - 47 Okl.St.Ann. § 754; Louisiana - no time limit - LSA-R.S. 32:668; Georgia - O.C.G.A. § 40-5-67.1(g)(1); New Hampshire - N.H. Rev. Stat. § 265:91-b(1)(a); Washington - West's RCWA 46.20.308(8); Florida - 30 days - West's F.S.A. § 322.2615(b)(6)(a); Texas - no more than 26 days - V.T.C.A., Transportation Code § 724.041, Guam - 30 days - 16 G.C.A. § 18203; Hawaii - 39 days - HRS § 291E-34; Kansas - 30 days - K.S.A. § 8-1002(e; Texas - no sooner than 11 days after the incident - V.T.C.A., Transportation Code § 524.032; South Carolina - 30 days - Code 1976 § 56-5-2951.

whether or not you lose your license. Commonly, at the time of your arrest, the law enforcement officer took your regular driver's license and gave you a temporary driving permit, which is valid for thirty days or less.[619] Your state's license agency may delay this hearing for a lengthy period (60 or more days), so long as your limited privilege to drive is protected until the hearing. The ultimate question is usually whether your license to drive should be returned to you by the state or whether it will be suspended or revoked.

11.2. ALS/ALR proceedings are civil in nature, and often allow civil discovery usage. These ALS/ALR proceedings are civil in nature, not having anything to do with any criminal penalties. Losing your license in one of these hearings may seem like a criminal penalty, but it is not.[620] Beyond taking away your ability to drive, an ALS/ALR hearing does not also generate penalties such as fines or jail, or performance of community service hours. Additionally, in these civil proceedings, federal and state constitutional protections may not apply. [See Appendix K for a listing of these protections.]

Because it is a civil proceeding and not a criminal proceeding, your state's civil discovery rules may be used to obtain information from the state, not the criminal rules of procedure. While misdemeanor criminal discovery in your state may be very limited, civil discovery is universally more extensive in its reach and scope. Depositions are more readily available in civil cases. In preparation for depositions, the State has to disclose certain information. Depositions are pre-trial meetings between the parties with a court reporter present. Depositions allow your attorney to be able to question witnesses for the State under oath, and to create a certified transcript of such testimony for later use at trial or pre-trial motion hearings.

11.3. ALS/ALR judges can be attorneys or non-attorneys (called "hearing officers" in some jurisdictions), so the fairness and due process compliance varies from state to state. In almost every state, no requirement exists that the "judge" for these administrative hearings be an attorney.[621] That being the case, and considering the legal nature of the proceeding, the fairness and the "due process" compliance varies greatly, not only state to state, but also from judge to judge. Your DUI-DWI specialist lawyer may have to assist these judges on legal research to facilitate these hearing officers' understanding of the law.

In a recent case from Florida, an appellate court actually ruled that the non-attorney judge had departed from her neutral role as a "referee" in hearing license suspension cases. This upheld a lower court's determination of the judge's improper actions in making evidentiary rulings in favor of the State of Florida and against the licensee. [622]

11.4. Your arresting officer may not be required to attend ALS/ALR hearings, so your attorney may need to subpoena the officer to force him or her to attend

---

[619]Georgia - 30 days - O.C.G.A. § 40-5-67.1(f)(1);New Hampshire - 30 days - N.H. Rev. Stat. § 265:91-a(III); Kansas - 30 days - K.S.A. § 8-1002(e); Oklahoma - 30 days - 47 Okl.St.Ann. § 754(B); Louisiana - 30 days - LSA-R.S. 32:667(A)(1); Arizona - 15 days - A.R.S. § 28-1385(D); Alabama - no temporary license issued - Ala.Code 1975 § 32-6-49.13; Washington - 60 days - West's RCWA 46.20.308(6)(d); Florida - 10 days - West's F.S.A. § 322.2615(b)(4); Texas - 41 days - V.T.C.A., Transportation Code § 524.011(f); Nevada - 7 days - N.R.S. 484.385; Texas - until the hearing - V.T.C.A., Transportation Code § 524.032; South Carolina - 30 days - Code 1976 § 56-5-2951.

[620]**United States v. Ursery**, 518 U.S. 267, 116 S.Ct. 2135, 135 L.Ed.2d 549 (1996); **Ex parte Mata,** 925 S.W.2d 292 (Tex.App.-Corpus Christi 1996); **Davidson v. MacKinnon,** 656 So.2d 223 (Fla.App. 5 Dist. 1995); **State v. Sneed,** 8 S.W.3d 299 (Tenn.Crim.App. 1999); **Murphy v. State,** 267 Ga. 120, 475 S.E.2d 907 (1996); V.T.C.A., Transportation Code § 524.012(e)(1).

[621]California - West's Ann.Cal.Vehicle Code § 14104.2; Guam - 16 G.C.A. § 18203; Hawaii - HRS § 291E-38.

[622]**Dept. of Highway Safety and Motor Vehicles v. Griffin**, 909 So.2d 538 (Fla.App. 4 Dist., 2005).

or to bring any records. Because of the limited questions that are to be asked or answered at an ALS/ALR hearing, it is not uncommon for the State to want to treat this as a nuisance procedure, pushing it through with as little effort as possible. One aspect of this is that the police officer who took your license may not automatically have to attend these hearings, as often the submission of his or her paperwork answering the required questions is enough proof of the alleged civil violation to allow the hearing officer to uphold the suspension or revocation.

However, one benefit to you in these proceedings may occur if your attorney subpoenas this officer to attend, and then has the opportunity to ask him or her questions while the officer is under oath and on the record. If other police officers were involved in the arrest or breath testing process, they may be also forced to attend and testify. This information can then be used against your arresting officer, who is usually the key witness for the prosecution in your criminal case. Knowing what this person is going to say, what other officers in your case may have to say, and "locking them in" on their answers, gives your attorney an idea of which of your possible challenges and defenses have the best chance of success.

Further, if any officer changes his or her sworn statements and testifies differently at your trial, this is very much in your favor as the officer's truthfulness and candor are placed directly into question. When it is your word against the officer's, if the officer is shown to not always remember details, or not always tell the truth, this commonly swings the judge or jury to your side.

11.5. Your attendance at the ALS/ALR hearing may be waived in most jurisdictions, unless you need to testify. In most states, unless you request such a hearing, your license suspension is automatic.[623] Those states that give you a temporary license allow you to have this document until it expires, and you are then without authority to operate a motor vehicle.

If there is an ALS/ALR hearing, due to the limited issues the proceeding must answer, the judge does not usually have any questions to ask you. (See Section 11.11 below in this chapter.) In most states, the hearing is held whether or not you are there, so your attendance may be waived.

If you do request a hearing for whatever reason, because most questions will be posed to other witnesses, your presence is not typically required unless your lawyer feels it important for you to be present. You may have to refute an alleged refusal to submit to testing. Alternatively, your presence may assist your attorney with questions to factual matters that arise in the hearing, when your attorney is allowed to cross-examine the State's witnesses.

11.6. Often, it is best not to show your "hand" to the state during the ALS/ALR hearings, and use the proceeding to obtain more information that may assist in winning the criminal case. It may be very useful to your criminal case to put your arresting law enforcement officer on the stand in the ALS/ALR hearing and "lock in" the officer's testimony on key issues. If you take the stand, or you have your experts testify on your behalf at the ALS/ALR hearing, the prosecution may be able to do the same to you. This may be detrimental to your criminal case later.

---

[623]Alabama - Ala.Code 1975 § 32-6-49.13(g); Arizona - A.R.S. § 28-1321(I); California - West's Ann.Cal.Vehicle Code § 14100; Oklahoma - 47 Okl.St.Ann. § 754; Louisiana - LSA-R.S. 32:668; Georgia - O.C.G.A. § 40-5-67.1(g)(1); New Hampshire - N.H. Rev. Stat. § 265:91-b(1)(a); Washington - West's RCWA 46.20.308(8); Florida - West's F.S.A. § 322.2615(b)(6)(a); Texas - V.T.C.A., Transportation Code § 724.041, Guam - 16 G.C.A. § 18203; Hawaii - HRS § 291E-34; Kansas - K.S.A. § 8-1002(e); Texas -V.T.C.A., Transportation Code § 524.032; South Carolina -Code 1976 § 56-5-2951.

If you have good defenses to your DUI-DWI charges, giving the prosecutor knowledge of these issues allows him or her more time to try to refute them. Unless getting your license back immediately is critical to your life, and you have rock-solid defenses in your criminal case, taking the stand is seldom a wise move. Many states have a mandatory suspension of your license if you are convicted, so giving the prosecution any useful information at this administrative hearing may win a battle but lose the war. The ultimate objective is to avoid a DUI-DWI conviction.

11.7. ALS/ALR proceedings may offer the chance to "negotiate" with the officer (or the state attorney handling the ALS/ALR) to withdraw the proposed suspension/revocation. Any time you can get your attorney and the prosecutor in the same room, with the facts of the case before both of them, a chance always exists for negotiation. Both sides have likely seen similar cases many times. Both know the courts, the judges and the local laws. If the prosecutor from the criminal case does not have to attend your hearing, then the facts of the case are also before the state attorney who is assigned to assist the police officers to present their case facts.

The best DUI-DWI specialists have worked with these people for years, with hundreds, if not thousands, of similar cases to provide a basis for anticipating how the judge may rule. He or she knows how to negotiate with either the presiding officer or the state attorney to obtain your best chance at getting your license back. For some clients, being able to continue driving may be of greater importance then trying to win the DUI-DWI criminal case. If this is your situation, speak to your attorney about this to see what options you may have.

11.8. In some states, the same criminal prosecutor handles the ALS/ALR and the criminal proceedings, but in others this does not apply. In some states, the same prosecutor who will be trying your criminal case will also be handling the administrative license suspension or revocation hearing. In other states this is not true. In a few states, no attorney acts as a representative for the police officers, leaving them to litigate their own cases.

If it is the same prosecutor in both situations, then this may be all the more reason **not** to bring forth any of your "best" evidence because while you might get your license back sooner, you may ultimately lose your criminal DUI-DWI case. However, any time you get the prosecutor in the same room with your attorney, with the evidence in front of both of them and the testimony of your arresting officer now having been presented and recorded, this may be an excellent opportunity for negotiation regarding the criminal charges against you.

11.9. Use of a certified court reporter may be advisable, if the proceedings are merely tape recorded, so that a certified record of the sworn testimony can be used later in the criminal case. Not every court or hearing has a court reporter or stenographer (someone sitting at the front of the courtroom or just off to the side), who is taking down a word-by-word transcript of the proceeding as it happens. Your attorney is listening to every word, but cannot write down everything. To have one of these people at an ALS/ALR hearing will cost you some money.

However, because you may have the chance for your attorney to question the testing officer if your attorney can require them to attend, locking in their side of the story, a transcript of this testimony can be worth its weight in gold to your case. This is far better than simply having the proceeding tape-recorded, because having the testimony written in a transcript gives your attorney a better chance to prepare more thoroughly. Plus, a typed, certified transcript can be used in the criminal case to impeach the witness if he or she changes their story about your arrest or test. This testimony may also confirm defenses available to you, or may show your attorney which ones might require another expert witness to testify to refute the officer.

11.10. Obtaining the video tape of the arrest or breath testing during the ALS/ALR hearing can be important to facilitate the criminal case. In spite of the limited issues which must be proven in an ALS/ALR hearing, the best proof for your side in either this hearing or for your criminal trial may be the video tape of your arrest or the admission of your breath test. A picture may be worth a thousand words, but a video recording may mean the difference between acquittal and a criminal conviction.

Of greater importance is the likelihood that your attorney can argue your side from only this video evidence and use of your expert witnesses. This means you do not have to take the witness stand in your defense. Taking the stand allows the prosecutor to also ask you questions, which can be very damaging at your criminal case. Thus, whether for the administrative hearing or for your criminal case, obtaining any videotape of your arrest or the administration of your breath test is very important.

If your license can be returned to you based on these video recordings, your attorney may require them to be produced and shown to the judge or hearing officer at your ALS/ALR hearing. More often than not, however, the videotapes are needed for purposes of trying to win the criminal case.

The administrative hearing may serve this additional important function. In states with limited discovery, this could also be the first time your attorney has access to these video recordings, something critical to the presentation of your defense in your criminal case. Thus, obtaining these videos by use of a subpoena can be the main reason to go through an ALS/ALR hearing. A DUI-DWI specialist knows the laws of your state and has experience with the courts and these type hearings, to know exactly the best path for you to take.

11.11. The issues at the ALS/ALR hearing are limited, so your attorney may only be able to explore a limited number of points relating to the criminal case. The issues that can be discussed at your ALS/ALR hearing are very limited. Typically, the only issues presented at these hearings revolve around: (1) whether or not the police officer had a reasonable cause to believe that you were intoxicated to a degree that you were violating the state law by driving; (2) that you had been placed under arrest and lawfully detained; (3) that you had failed or were unable to complete the blood, breath or urine test that the officer had requested; and (4) whether or not you had been informed of the loss of your license when you refused your test. The standard of proof placed upon the State in administrative (civil) hearings is not nearly as high as at your criminal trial, being only "preponderance of the evidence" rather than "beyond a reasonable doubt." [624]

In some states, challenges by the petitioner (the licensee) have been permitted at these hearings where it was shown that the officer handling the arrest violated the driver's rights to an independent test, or similar rights under that state's implied consent laws. [625] Other states are more restrictive of legal challenges that can restore driving privileges.

In most states, the initial burden of proof is on the State, not the motorist.[626] However, a substantial minority of states have shifted that initial burden of proof to the motorist.[627] This is

---

[624]Arizona - A.R.S. § 28-1385(I); Oklahoma - 47 Okl.St.Ann. § 754(3); Alabama - Ala.Code 1975 § 32-6-49.13(f); California - West's Ann.Cal.Vehicle Code § 13557(a); Texas - V.T.C.A., Transportation Code §§ 524.012(b), 524.035; Hawaii - HRS § 291E-38; South Carolina - Code 1976 § 56-5-2951(f).

[625]**Connolly v. State**, 79 Wash.2d 500, 487 P.2d 1050 (Wash. 1971); **Field v. State off Nevada, Department of Motor Vehicles and Public Safety,** 111 Nev. 552, 893 P.2d 380 (1995); **Hardison v. Chastain,** 151 Ga.App. 678, 261 S.E.2d 425 (1979).

[626]**Rain v. Director of Revenue,** 46 S.W.3d 584 (Mo.App.2001); **Byler v. Com., Dept. of Transp.,** 883 A.2d 724 (Pa.Cmwlth. 2005).

possible to legislate in these matters, and not in criminal matters, due to the CIVIL nature of the proceedings. The United States Constitution protects against shifting the burden of proof in any criminal case to an accused person facing criminal charges. A sample list of the specific, limited issues that are allowed to be discussed in several states' individual hearings is set forth in **Appendix D**.

11.12. A knowledgeable attorney will know the pluses and minuses of holding the hearing versus possibly seeking to negotiate a withdrawal of the "hard" suspension that could occur. After investigating the facts of your case, the most experienced DUI-DWI attorneys know the pluses and minuses of holding an ALS/ALR hearing in your situation. If a hearing takes place, the attorney will know what evidence (if any) your side should present. Based on his or her years of experience with criminal law and the history of such hearings in your particular region, these DUI-DWI specialists know what can be accomplished (and more importantly), what you may lose by going through a contested administrative hearing.

The sworn hearing process may reveal defenses for your case through the questioning of the police officers involved in your arrest at this hearing. On the other hand, taking the stand to get your license back at the hearing may produce a very short-term gain, and may cause you to lose your criminal case and ultimately have to go to jail.

11.13. Success rate for contested ALS/ALR cases varies from state to state, with some attorneys in some states reporting 80% or more retention of licenses, to 10% on the low side. Each state conducts these proceedings differently, based on the hearing officers (or judges) who preside over them, the specific jurisdiction where your hearing will be held and how they have been run in the past. Some attorneys report an 80% to 90% (or better) success rate of getting your license (or full driving privileges) back, while in some states, this success rate may be as low as 10% to 15%.

Depending on the laws of your state, the licensee may be saddled with the burden of proof at the administrative license suspension hearing.[628] In other states, the use of pro-prosecution hearing officers (who are often glorified state police officers) and a very restricted set of legal issues that can be raised at ALS/ALR hearings can greatly diminish your chances of winning one of these hearings.

The most important thing is for you and your DUI-DWI specialist to sit down and discuss what is most important to you. It may not be a "win" if you fight to immediately get your license restored only to later lose your criminal case due to disclosures at the ALS/ALR hearing that compromise your criminal case. Some attorneys who claim a high rate of success at administrative hearings may be sacrificing the more important victory on the criminal case.

---

[627]**People v. Orth**, 124 Ill.2d 326, 530 N.E.2d 210 (Ill. 1988); **People v. McClure**, 218 Ill.2d 375 (Ill. 2006); **Minnich v. Administrative Director of Courts**, 109 Hawai'i 220, 124 P.3d 965 (Hawai'i 2005); Indiana Code §§ 9-30-6-2; and 9-30-6-3.
[628]IC 9-30-6-10(f).

Chapter 12

Your Attorney's Pre-Trial Activities.

12.0. The purpose of this chapter. You will likely meet or communicate by phone or e-mail several times with your DUI-DWI specialist during the months between your arrest and your trial or your pre-trial hearings. You may also spend time with experts or with your attorney's office staff and paralegals, but the scattered hours you spend with your attorney may make it seem as if you are not getting your money's worth. The purpose of this chapter is to help you understand just how much work is involved by your attorney in the preparation of your case, and in managing it properly.

12.1. Working behind the scenes. The vast majority of what goes on in your DUI-DWI case happens behind the scenes. You spend hours with your attorney at different stages of the case. However, what you do not see are the long hours of preparation, legal research, telephone calls and face-to-face conversations your attorney has with members of his or her staff, experts, witnesses for the prosecution, even with the prosecutors, and perhaps with the judge. The best DUI-DWI attorneys know everyone in your court system, including the judges, the clerks, the court reporters, and the prosecutors. All of these participants in the court system have support staff members too.

No one should promise you that they can obtain a "deal" for you because of who he or she knows. That is not the way the court system works. Prosecutors do not have to offer deals, and state law may prohibit the prosecutor from reducing a DUI-DWI.[629] However, if your attorney can make things work as smoothly as possible, then this is part of why you have hired your DUI-DWI specialist.

12.2. Using an investigator to get answers that the attorney cannot. Private investigators typically have been law enforcement officers themselves in the past. Many have decades of law enforcement experience, usually with one or more of the local police departments. They still have friends on the force and know how each department works. They know who to call to obtain documents or videotapes and who is in charge. They can ask questions of police officers that others (including your attorney) cannot, and can often get answers to important questions more readily than your attorney can. The best investigators can see details that others may miss.

These are reasons your attorney may recommend the use of a private investigator to help in preparing your defense. If you want to put forward your point of view at your trial or hearings, and if you want to leave no stone unturned in your defense, then listen to your attorney and use the investigator he or she recommends.

12.3. Being "connected" without being a crook. One of the reasons you need an experienced DUI-DWI trial expert to represent you is his or her knowledge of the court system, the judges, and the prosecutors. You should take it as a very good sign when the judge or the prosecutor warmly or humorously greets your attorney by his or her first name or nickname. It is typically a sign of respect, or even positive personal feelings between them. These favorable connections may lay the groundwork for the judge to be receptive to your attorney's arguments.

---

[629]**State v. Moen**, 110 Wn. App. 125, 38 P.3d 1049 (2002); **State v. Nelson**, 166 Or.App. 189, 999 P.2d 1161 (2000).

However, just because of this respect, do not expect miracles, or for your lawyer to try to swing things in your favor based on anything "shady" or illegal. Your attorney must work within the law as it applies to your case. All you should expect is what the law allows him or her to do ethically.

12.4. Timely and targeted filing of pleadings is critical. The less experienced criminal defense attorney may file generic, untargeted pleadings with the court and the prosecution during pre-trial proceedings. Often, these pleadings have nothing to do with any particular defense and may be boilerplate, untargeted challenges with no chance of success. While these pleadings cannot be ignored, if they are not specific enough or are not filed at the right time, they may have the effect of either being returned unanswered, or rejected by the court as being untimely filed. Such poorly drafted motions aggravate judges, waste costly court resources and time, plus may squander a trategic opportunity to win your case.

Your DUI-DWI attorney takes the facts from your case, closely examines all the evidence he or she can uncover, and then prepares specific and timely pleadings or requests of documents or witness production from the court and the prosecutor. He or she knows what should have been received from the police and prosecutor, and is familiar with the time required to obtain it. Your attorney will know the proper language to put in a written motion to cause the prosecutor to disclose the needed information.

By filing pleadings that are both specific and timely, the prosecution is less likely to be able to argue to the court that the information or evidence being sought should not be released to your side. If your pleading is requesting the court to do something, and if the request is targeted, specific, reasonable and backed by the law, it is hard for the court to refuse. Because the information requested to be disclosed is often critical to your case (e.g., video recordings, or asking the court to deny admission of certain evidence), making these requests in a timely and targeted fashion is critical as well. If not correctly done, your side can lose access to this material, or fail in the effort to exclude harmful evidence.[630]

12.5. Assisting you in hiring an expert to consult or testify. Because your DUI-DWI specialist knows the courts, knows the likely makeup of juries in the county of your arrest, and knows your best defenses, he or she also knows why an expert is needed to testify in building your case. Based on decades of DUI-DWI trial experience, your lawyer knows who is best for your situation among the dozens of available experts to testify at your trial or hearing. He or she knows each expert's range of knowledge, as well as his or her weaknesses and strengths.

12.6. Arraignment (where you plead guilty or not guilty) and a point in the case where certain motions and challenges might be required. Early in your case (a few days or even weeks after your arrest), yet months before any hearing or trial, you will be brought before a judge and asked how you want to plead - guilty or not guilty. If you need to ask the court to appoint an attorney for your defense, this is usually done at this proceeding or shortly afterward.

Most states have a specific timetable for the filing of any motions or challenges by your side. State law can require that this filing be accomplished a specific number of days before your trial. Some motions and challenges must be filed at or before your arraignment, or the opportunity will be lost. The time limit applicable to your case may also depend on the issue you are raising. If your attorney does not make certain challenges in a timely manner, you usually

---

[630]**State v. Grandison**, 192 Ga. App. 473, 385 S.E.2d 139 (1989); **Waller v. State,** 251 Ga. 124, 303 S.E.2d 437 (1983).

lose the opportunity to do so. Defenses that you might have could then be lost. This is yet another reason to hire a well-seasoned DUI-DWI trial attorney so that you do not lose your case due to lost opportunities.

12.7. Pre-trial conferences with the prosecutor or the judge (with the prosecutor also participating). A pre-trial conference is a meeting with the trial judge, the prosecutor and your attorney, at which neither you nor the prosecutor will need to present witnesses or seek to submit evidence. You should think of this meeting as the "staging meeting" for planning your trial. This is a situation where your attorney, the judge and the prosecutor get together, often in the chambers (office) of the judge. It is unusual for a court reporter to be present, but some courts require recordation of this conference too.

Because these "planning" conferences are not always recorded or transcribed, some courts may conduct a conference call by telephone with your attorney and the prosecutor. Other judges may require that a written document summarizing all of the usual issues at the pre-trial conference be agreed upon between the attorneys and turned in to the judge for review. Any disputed evidentiary issues may have to be settled by the judge.

Examples of issues that might be handled or discussed at a pre-trial conference may include: marking and identifying the anticipated exhibits, the order in which witnesses will be heard, discussion of how long the trial may take, negotiations for sentencing recommendations, determining if a possible plea bargain may be reached, or similar issues relating to making the trial more efficient. These meetings may also be used to discuss any unresolved motions or evidentiary rulings, or any atypical or unusual sentencing considerations which the judge would have to review or approve.

12.8. Pre-trial motion hearings. In some cases, pre-trial motions may result in your case being dismissed or reduced to a non-DUI-DWI disposition. Examples of issues at motion hearings include whether or not your stop by the police was legal, whether or not your blood, breath or urine tests, or your refusal to be tested can be part of the evidence that the jury is allowed to hear, and whether or not all of your constitutional rights were observed by the police. These are issues that are presented and argued without a jury being present, with rulings on all issues being rendered by the judge.

The procedure for raising these issues before trial is to schedule a pre-trial hearing with your attorney (and likely you), the prosecutor and the judge. A court reporter always should be present at motion hearings to take down all testimony and court rulings. At the conclusion of the hearings, the judge will be rendering one or more rulings that will set the ground rules for the trial. The court reporter also takes down the testimony of the witnesses for either side, and this sworn testimony can be used to impeach officers who change their testimony at trial.

A major difference between a pre-trial motion hearing and a conference with the judge is the presence of witnesses being sworn and questioned by both sides. Any evidentiary rulings made by the judge will control the admissibility of the evidence at trial. If your case reaches trial, certain portions of the motions hearing may become a pivotal battleground between your attorney and the prosecutor. Any rulings made by the judge that were challenged by your legal counsel may be the basis of a successful appeal later.

The winning of a pre-trial hearing by your side gives your attorney great leverage in getting the charges against you either lessened or even dropped. Because they are so much shorter than a trial, your attorney may place much effort into winning such important points in your favor. Such hearings also "lock in" the testimony of the prosecution's witnesses, giving your attorney a better chance to prepare to question them at your trial.

One aspect of winning critical rulings at pre-trial motion hearings is that almost every state provides the prosecution with the absolute right to stop the case before trial and seek appellate review of any adverse rulings by the judge. The reason for the availability of an immediate appeal is that if the trial goes forward without key evidence against you being available to the prosecution, no appeal can be brought if you are acquitted. So, state statutes allow the prosecution to halt the proceedings and seek appellate review of rulings at motion hearings.

12.9. Being on a trial calendar. A trial calendar is the entire list of all the cases that may be handled by a particular court over a particular session or trial "term" of court. A trial term or session usually lasts from one week to a month. A typical calendar may have three to ten times more cases on it than can be accommodated because many cases will be resolved by a plea to some offense or offenses as part of negotiations between the prosecutor and defense attorneys representing accused citizens. Most jurisdictions give priority to the oldest cases first unless other "priority" issues cause newer cases to be called first. Two possible categories of "special" priorities can be a pending demand for a speedy trial or to accommodate an incarcerated defendant.

Thus, just because your case has been placed on a trial calendar does not mean your trial will be held during that term of court. On the eve of trial, your attorney may be able to negotiate an acceptable deal with the prosecution. A technical problem (such as witness availability) may arise with your case (or with the prosecution's case), such that the trial will be postponed. Another possible scenario is that the court may not be able to reach your case by the time the trial term is over.

Be prepared mentally, emotionally and financially for your case to be called by the judge as early as the first day of the trial calendar. Also, be aware that you could have to wait through several calendars. An experienced DUI-DWI attorney knows how to "read" the trial calendar, giving you a reasonable estimate of your chances of being reached on the calendar during a particular trial term.

12.10. Letting your attorney decide who (if anyone) testifies. If you are starting your DUI-DWI trial, it is important at this point to accept that your attorney "knows best" in regard to how to conduct your trial. He or she will have a game plan for how the case should proceed and how the evidence will "play out." The plan remains flexible until he or she sees what the prosecution puts forward as far as testimony and evidence. Your attorney then proceeds to present to the judge and jury whatever evidence is needed (if any) to refute the State's case against you.

Part of your attorney's job is deciding who should testify on your behalf. As a defendant, you have no duty to put up any evidence whatsoever. You are innocent until and unless proven guilty.[631] Most experienced criminal defense attorneys do not put their clients on the witness stand unless the client's testimony is absolutely essential to winning the case.

If your attorney does think it advisable for you to present witnesses, he or she does so based on decades of experience with the court you are in, with the judge who is running the court, with the same type juries you now face. Your DUI-DWI specialist knows the law and is familiar with the smallest details of your case. Your attorney knows what evidence or testimony may be able to be introduced in your favor, and has evaluated how much damage the prosecutor may be able to inflict on your case by way of cross-examination. After all of the months of preparation, it is best for you to trust your attorney's judgment. Your job at trial may

---

[631]**Sun Co. of San Bernadino v. Superior Court,** 29 Cal.App.3d 815, 105 Cal. Rptr. 873 (4th Dist. 1973).

be to remain attentive and "likeable" so that the jurors remain open to entering a not guilty verdict on your charges.

Many defendants in your position want to testify. They want to tell their side of the story. They want their day in court. However, if the defendant in a criminal case takes the witness stand, the entire dynamic of the trial changes for the jury. It often becomes a popularity contest between a law enforcement officer, who is trained on how to be a good witness and often has over 100 trials under his or her belt, and you - - - an accused "drunk driver."

An experienced DUI-DWI attorney takes endless factors into account before he or she recommends that you take the stand in your defense. He or she may insist that you not take the stand. First, what do you have to say? Juries may be less willing to believe you because they may believe that you might say anything to save yourself. It may be much more powerful for the friend you had been with all evening to take the stand and say you had had only two drinks during the entire evening, and showed no sign of impairment whatsoever.

Second, after months of working with you, your attorney likely has a good idea of how you will be perceived by a jury. Most accused citizens are not able to endure a grueling cross-examination by a seasoned prosecutor. An experienced trial attorney can evaluate this aspect of your case better that you can.

Third, if you take the stand in your defense, while you get to tell your side of the story, the prosecution gets to cross-examine you. The prosecutor's job is to ask you difficult questions, making you appear to be a liar or a fool. There is an art to cross-examination, and some prosecuting attorneys are very good at it.

In conclusion, while you may make a few points by testifying on your own behalf, the prosecutor usually damages your case in some respect. In the worst-case scenario, the prosecutor may torpedo your entire case by making you look bad on the witness stand. The decision of whether or not you testify is ultimately yours. However, not following your expert attorney's advice is similar to not heeding your physician's health recommendations.

12.11. Preparing jury "charges" (instructions). At the end of your trial, the judge reads to the jury a series of instructions called "jury instructions" or "jury charges." These instructions are the legal rules that the jury must apply to the evidence they have heard. Jury charges have several components.

First, the judge will once again read to the jury the charges pending against you, word for word, from the accusatory document. The judge then reads the statutes under which you have been charged. That is, if you have been charged with DUI-DWI, he or she reads to the jury the statute which sets out each of the elements of each type of DUI-DWI offense you face.

Next, the judge also reads to the jury the legal meanings of all of the important words or phrases involved with your case. He or she will read to the jury an explanation of what "beyond a reasonable doubt" means, and will explain to the jury your state's definition of "impairment" required to be proven by the State to support a drunk (or drugged) driving conviction.

Furthermore, the judge must explain other general instructions, such as how to select a foreperson, how to fill out the verdict form, and how the verdict must be unanimous. The judge will also advise the jury how to ask questions in the event issues about how to proceed arise during deliberations. The jury is then excused to deliberate your fate.

These jury charges, or jury instructions, come to the judge as suggestions from both your attorney and the prosecutor. In most states, these instructions are in binders or manuals containing "pattern" instructions, or instructions on specific points that have been given in the past and have been found acceptable by higher courts. The suggestions from the prosecutor and from your attorney are usually based on favorable language from one or more appellate cases. The decision as to exactly which jury charges will be given is made by the judge, after conferring with both attorneys outside the presence of the jury. This always occurs prior to the lawyers delivering their closing arguments (summation).

The most experienced DUI-DWI attorneys know just how critical it is to get the best possible jury charges in your case. Sometimes getting the judge to change a word or two, or accept your attorney's suggested modification can make a huge difference in the outcome of your case. These same DUI-DWI specialists know your state's laws, and know when and how to object to the instructions that the judge is giving that do not conform to your state's required standards for jury instructions.

The denial of your attorney's suggested jury charges can be important. If your lawyer makes a written suggestion for a jury charge which is denied by the judge, this could form the basis of a successful appeal if you are found guilty by the jury. Your attorney will also "reserve" any objections to the judge's final jury charge until any post-trial motions or possible appeal, when an objection can be specifically made and applicable legal precedent cited to the judge.

12.12. Being ready for the worst case scenario. In spite of a good case, a skilled litigator on your side, and a rock solid defense, you may still be found guilty of DUI-DWI. One reason that the best DUI-DWI attorneys look for a negotiated plea for reduced charges (a non-DUI-DWI) is to eliminate the possibility of a trial ending with a conviction for drunken driving on your record.

It is important for you to be prepared for this eventuality, even if your attorney tells you that the chance of it is slight. If you have a family, prepare them for what might happen in the event of a conviction. Ask your DUI-DWI defense attorney what to expect and put your affairs in order. Follow his or her advice about how to be prepared to file an immediate appeal if a conviction occurs.

In most misdemeanor convictions, by filing an appeal and posting a "supersedeas bond" (an appeal bond that delays enforcement of all or most of the punishment given in the sentence), you may have the right to "delay" all or most of the punishment imposed by the judge (or jury) after a conviction. This issue should be discussed with your DUI-DWI specialist prior to trial. Take steps to be prepared to file the appeal in your case where your incarceration can be delayed.

12.13. Your attorney's "time and expertise." Hopefully, you have chosen your DUI-DWI specialist because he or she is the best criminal defense attorney available for your case. One of the reasons you have hired your attorney is his or her reputation for winning DUI-DWI cases. Your attorney actually sets his or her fee based upon the estimated time that will be required to handle your case as well as charging for his or her "expertise" in this area of law.

Time. You will spend hours with your attorney and his or her staff members prior to your trial. If trial takes place, you may spend several days together. However, you never see the long hours, late night and early morning preparation sessions your attorney goes through reviewing your file and police reports, consulting with the experts, with his or her staff, or in reviewing legal research. You will not be present when PowerPoint presentations or large closing boards are being created for presentation to the jury. All you see is a polished professional putting decades of experience to work on your behalf. Your attorney's overriding concern is to help you find a way to avoid a DUI-DWI conviction by bringing to bear all of his or her talents at trial practice.

Unfortunately, a portion of the cost for your attorney includes "wait time" at court while the judge handles legal matters. You and your attorney must make court appearances sometimes when the case may not go forward for a variety of reasons. This is part of your attorney's job - - - to be ready when called to trial. Hence, if it sometimes seems like your attorney isn't doing much on your case while you are waiting, this is the reason why.

While your attorney is in court, other legal matters for other clients cannot be handled. You and your lawyer are expected to sit in court and wait until it is your turn for trial. That typically means no talking, no use of cellular phones and being able to do little else but wait.

Expertise. The best way to know your attorney's level of expertise is to watch the lack of expertise among lawyers without extensive DUI-DWI experience attempt to handle a case. Much like watching a professional athlete make a spectacular play look too easy, you don't see the years of training and experience that went into making the seasoned defense attorney's command of a courtroom look natural. In court, when you see a polished attorney by your side, it is a great source of comfort in a nerve-racking ordeal.

You only see the end result of your attorney's years of trial experience. You can't see their connections or the relationships your attorney has spent time cultivating among the judges, courtroom staff and prosecutors. Do not expect your lawyer to get favorable treatment for you because of who he or she is and who he or she knows. However, if a judge or the prosecutor knows and respects your attorney because of his or her expertise, they may concede certain legal issues in deference to your attorney's excellent reputation for knowing the law. This asset - - - an excellent reputation for thorough knowledge of the law - - - can help your attorney win tough DUI-DWI cases.

12.14. Be realistic and be flexible. Even the best DUI-DWI specialists are not magicians. Even the most experienced DUI-DWI attorney can only portray the best aspects of your case, setting forth the facts and the opinions of experts in a way that puts your case in the best possible light for the jury. Likewise, any negative factors in your case will be highlighted by the prosecutor for the jury. Any statements you made on videotape or as noted by the officer in his or her report will be the subject of much attention, as will your performance on any field sobriety evaluations.

Your attorney is not in charge of all aspects of your case. The prosecutor has much to do with the timing of hearings, the scheduling of any trial, deciding upon charges to bring you and similar matters. The prosecutor also decides when to agree to a non-DUI-DWI recommendation and will recommend any punishment you may face.

Last, the court system is set up for the convenience of the court, not for you or your attorney. It is not unusual for hundreds of cases to be scheduled for the same day as your arraignment, for thirty or more cases scheduled for the same week as your trial or motion hearing. This "overbooking" is commonly utilized in the event that some cases cancel, settle or are not ready to proceed. It keeps the court busy, even if you are forced to sit around and wait your turn, or are asked to come back another week or month because they did not reach your case this time. Neither your schedule nor your attorney's schedule is of much concern to the court.

You know the importance of the charges you face and how they will affect your life. You need to evaluate your financial situation and what fees and costs you can afford. After listening to your side of the story, investigating the facts and the evidence for and against you, your attorney can inform you as to what you realistically face as far as likely punishment. Your attorney will also explain fees and estimated costs of the case. He or she may give you news or opinions that you do not want to hear. Sometimes, no technicalities exist to terminate the charges, and the facts and evidence against you are unfavorable. When you meet with your attorney, be prepared to hear the unvarnished truth.

12.15. Compromise — it may be the best bet for you. Compromise is defined as a settlement of differences by arbitration or by consent reached by mutual concessions.[632] The prosecution and the police believe you have committed a crime or they would not be pursuing the prosecution against you. Sometimes, the middle ground of accepting a guilty or nolo contendere plea against you for some lesser offense than DUI-DWI satisfies the need of the prosecutor and police that you have learned your lesson. This means you will have a record of conviction, and you will face some penalty, even if the punishment will likely be much less than what you faced for a DUI-DWI conviction.

Many times, the most difficult mental battle is for you to accept the condition of a proposed compromise. You may have to make decisions that are not totally satisfying to you but may be better for your family and your job outlook. You may face a decision where your desire for a complete exoneration at trial is outweighed by the certainty of a compromise plea arrangement that assures damage control for your future.

A number of factors go into these decisions. The facts of your case, the expense you face to continue the fight, the ramifications of any criminal offenses on your record (even if less serious than a DUI-DWI), your attorney's experience with your court, the competence level of your prosecutor, the credibility of your arresting officer, all must be weighed and considered by you (with your attorney's guidance) in deciding whether or not to accept a compromise.

12.16. When "no deals" are available: *your decision*. In the end, no "deal" may be available to you. This may be the situation because the evidence against you is strong, because the prosecutor is legally prohibited from reducing a DUI-DWI (or does not want to deal), or as a result of the facts of your case being so favorable that you want to take your chances for a total win. If you have any prior history (such as a prior alcohol or drug related arrest), prosecutors often refuse to offer much of a deal. In such instances, you can either plead guilty to the DUI-DWI offense or roll the dice with your jury (or judge) at trial.

In the end, the final decision is yours to make. Your attorney can only explain the options and possibly explain the odds of winning. The best DUI-DWI attorneys are experts at explaining to you the repercussions and benefits of any decision at any point in your case, but the ultimate decision is yours and yours alone. Once you make your decision, move forward with a positive attitude and do not second-guess your decision.

---

[632]http://www.m-w.com/cgi-bin/dictionary?book=Dictionary&va=Compromise&x=11&y=16.

Chapter 13

Opting For a Trial or Seeking a "Negotiated" or "Blind" Plea:

Deciding What Option To Take

13.0. Purpose of this chapter. From the first court appearance on your DUI-DWI case, you always have the option to plead guilty to the charges against you. Often, clients who call the author's office are so overcome with a feeling of guilt that the idea of admitting to their guilt consumes much of their analysis of how to proceed with their case. If any criminal case deserves to be further explored before pleading guilty, it is the typical DUI-DWI case. Therefore, always have your case analyzed by a top criminal defense attorney who specializes in DUI-DWI law before making a final decision. This chapter will explore the typical consequences and options if you do plead guilty.

If you elect to allow your attorney to reach the best possible negotiated deal with the prosecution for your situation, you may be able to significantly shorten the prosecutorial process by agreeing to plead guilty or nolo contendere to a single count of DUI-DWI. If this agreement to resolve the case with a negotiated plea is a part of an agreement with the prosecution to recommend a specified punishment, this is presented to the judge as a "negotiated" plea. The judge will either accept the terms of the negotiated plea, or you will be given the opportunity to withdraw your plea and go to trial. Your judge may be willing to accept most of the negotiated conditions, but add some additional or modified punishment, if the negotiated deal is to be accepted by the judge. Again, if you reject this modification to the terms of the negotiated deal, you can still proceed with a trial.

Another kind of plea is sometimes called a "blind" or "open" plea. It may also be called "pleading straight up." This is where no agreement between your attorney and the prosecution can be reached. Instead, you stand before the court, plead guilty (or nolo contendere if this is allowed) and accept the punishment as determined by the judge after hearing from both the prosecution and your attorney. In such situations, the judge will listen to any aggravating or mitigating factors from both attorneys. If you enter into a blind (open) plea, you have no chance to withdraw your plea if you do not like the punishment imposed by the judge during your sentencing.

In about a dozen states, first offenders (as that is defined in your state) may have the option of entering into some sort of "deferred" disposition or some form of withholding judgment of guilt for the DUI-DWI offense. Any such disposition only controls your STATE criminal history since the gatekeepers for your federal criminal history are unconcerned with such deferred adjudications for its record-keeping purposes. **Section 13.8 through 13.10** discusses these matters.

This chapter discusses the "plea" process, when you should strongly consider pleading, and when it is not in your best interest. In the end, the decision of when to accept a plea, and when to opt for a trial, is yours and only yours. An experienced DUI-DWI attorney can set forth the opinions and provide a recommendation based on his or her knowledge and years of experience, but the ultimate decision about going to trial or accepting either type of plea is **YOURS**.

13.1. Getting a handle on your case. In order to properly evaluate your case, your attorney needs to analyze what happened to you during the entire time period surrounding your arrest and detention. Without this information, even the best and most experienced DUI-DWI attorney cannot give you an informed opinion of what you should do. To get full information and all of the police documents and videotapes will require two to four months in most courts.

The first thing your attorney will likely request of you is to have you complete a very detailed questionnaire regarding the day of your arrest, the arrest itself and everything that happened to you until your release from the police station or the jail. It may take you several hours to put all of your impressions and recollections on paper in an organized fashion. Every detail you can uncover could be important. Your attorney may want you to complete this form even before he or she spends any significant amount of time with you in a face-to-face interview.

By having you review the details of your day and evening, your DUI-DWI specialist is making you focus on key facts that need to be documented as soon as possible. He or she knows how critical the smallest details can be to winning your case. The fresher the incident is on your mind, the better you can assist in your defense. Additionally, your ability (or lack of ability) to recall details will reveal a good bit of important information concerning your possible impairment level and the likelihood that you can be used as a witness at trial. [See the Questionnaire form in **Appendix J** for a basic form that covers most subjects related to an arrest and your biographical information.]

While you are taking the time to complete this form, your attorney and his or her staff will try to assure that any administrative license suspension or revocation appeal (request for hearing) is properly filed. Your attorney may not be able to obtain all of your police reports before your initial interview.

Your attorney will generally ask for copies of any video recordings made of both your arrest and or your breath testing (if available). He or she will need to see the results of any blood, breath or urine testing performed on you, including results from any independent test you may have obtained. In some court systems, the prosecutors release this information with no more than a phone call, while in other jurisdictions a court order is required after a formal request is made by your attorney.

Your attorney or his or her staff also investigates the court to which your case has been assigned. Who will be your judge, and who will be the prosecutor? Which key staff people from those offices must be consulted for the case and when will they schedule the arraignment, motions and trial in your DUI-DWI case?

With this initial information in hand, your attorney will likely want to meet with you and recommend possibly hiring a private investigator to assist in the preparation of your case. These investigators are almost always ex-law enforcement officers. They talk to their friends and colleagues on the police force that arrested and processed you. They also go to the scene of your stop, gathering as much helpful information as possible.

The investigator may talk to witnesses other than you. This is why it is critical for you to inform your attorney of all names for potential witnesses with whom you came into contact in the time period surrounding your arrest. A person who has no personal stake in your guilt or innocence (such as a bartender) may be a key witness. These investigators also look for any other avenue of information that might be useful to you, such as locating other video or audio recordings from independent sources.

13.2. Evaluating the "quality" of your case. After all this information has been gathered and digested over a period of weeks, an experienced DUI-DWI attorney can begin to give you some evaluation on the "quality" of your case. How good is the prosecution's case? How good are your defenses? How would you be perceived if called as a potential witness? Will the arresting officer be able to stand up to cross-examination? Can you afford to bring in the best expert witness or witnesses?

Your seasoned DUI-DWI attorney knows how your court has handled cases like yours in the past, and understands either the likely result of a plea, a pre-trial hearing or a trial. All of the above factors go into his or her evaluation of the "quality" of your case. Any recommendation they make to you is based on his or her decades of experience.

13.3. Evaluating the fairness of the assigned judge. Judges are human beings, and most have histories of how they rule on situations like yours. Judges usually have handled criminal cases themselves, often as prosecutors, although this is not a requirement for a person to become a judge. Part of the expertise of your DUI-DWI attorney is being familiar with the judge's tendencies and peculiarities.

Misdemeanors like DUI-DWI are often assigned (at least initially) to lower (entry) level courts, like municipal or traffic courts. This is controlled by your state's laws. If this is the case, a slight chance exists that your assigned judge may have limited criminal law experience when your case is tried before him or her. An experienced DUI-DWI lawyer also knows most of the other trial lawyers in their area, so that they might be able to share knowledge about how this assigned judge may rule on the questions involved in your case.

13.4. Evaluating the prosecutor's experience, "relationships" and "personal charisma." Early on, your case will likely be assigned to a specific prosecutor or particular prosecutorial team. Each prosecutor has his or her own strengths, weaknesses and personality traits. Some are warm and forthright, while others have a tendency to be distant and colder. Some readily release information, while others fight any release of the State's information.

A well-seasoned DUI-DWI attorney will have tried cases like yours against this particular prosecutor, possibly dozens of times. It may not be unusual for each prosecutor to use the same experts, use the same trial techniques, even the same themes to their opening and closing statements. Many new prosecutors follow a printed script that they receive at a State prosecutors' training facility.

It is not uncommon for a prosecutor who may have been assigned to handle your case to have less than five years of experience. Despite having fewer years of experience, the prosecutor likely appears in front of your judge on a very regular basis. This repetitive exposure to the judge often creates a distinct edge for the prosecutor. Some prosecutors, however, aggravate judges and your assigned prosecutor may NOT be a person whom the judge holds in high regard. However, it is unlikely that your prosecutor only tries DUI-DWI cases like your DUI-DWI specialist does. This may give an edge to your criminal defense attorney over the prosecutor.

Because of his or her experience trying cases against your prosecutor, your lawyer's knowledge of and experience with this particular prosecutor adds to his or her ability to make better recommendations to you about your DUI-DWI case. A prospective trial against a skilled prosecutor, who is well respected by the judge and well liked by juries, will affect the recommendation by your attorney about seeking a trial. Your attorney may advise you that this prosecutor's ability to handle jury trials effectively reduces your overall chance of success at trial.

13.5. In your jurisdiction, do you even get a jury trial? Not every court in the American legal system has the ability to offer a trial by jury. A few states have eliminated jury trials for some or all DUI-DWI cases, [633] and others are trying to do so.[634] If you and your DUI-DWI charges are originally in a court that does not allow juries (like a traffic or municipal court), and you want a jury trial, the case file must be transferred to a court that gives you that option (like a circuit, superior, or district court). This may delay your trial by months, but a well-seasoned DUI-DWI attorney will know the benefits and risks of a jury trial verses a bench trial in your state.

The names of these jury-capable courts differ from state to state. For example, in South Carolina, a jury trial may be obtained for misdemeanor cases in some entry level courts (e.g., magistrate's court), but the court of general jurisdiction for felony criminal matters is called the Court of Common Pleas. In Georgia, misdemeanor jury trials in larger cities are relegated to State Courts whereas felonies must be handled ONLY by Superior Courts, whether a jury is requested or not. Your DUI-DWI specialist will know which court is which, and the requirements and procedure to get your case transferred to the best type court for you.

It is a fundamental right for anyone facing any criminal trial with a potential period of incarceration in excess of six months, including misdemeanors like DUI-DWI,[635] to have a jury trial if they want one.[636] To opt out of a jury trial and have only the judge decide your innocence or guilt, you must expressly, intelligently and personally opt out of having a jury trial.[637] In some states, the prosecution can thwart your effort to obtain a bench trial by opting for a jury trial even where you have waived a jury.

Several states have passed laws to eliminate their citizen's rights to a trial by jury by shortening the maximum jail term for a DUI-DWI conviction to six months or less. The United States Supreme Court has determined that the Constitution does not guarantee a jury trial for offenses carrying "short" periods of incarceration.[638] Unfortunately, none of the members of the Supreme Court have ever spent six months sitting in a jail cell.

13.6. Where do you find good jurors and bad jurors in your state? If you reach the trial phase in your DUI-DWI case, you certainly want the best possible jury for your case. You want people who are open and fair-minded and are skeptical of police officers. An

---

[633]**City of Bismarck v. Fettig,** 601 N.W.2d 247 (N.D. 1999); **State v. Ninth Judicial Dist. Court of State of Nev. In and For Douglas County,** 104 Nev. 91, 752 P.2d 238 (Nev. 1988); **State v. Lynch,** 223 Neb. 849, 394 N.W.2d 651 (Neb. 1986); **State v. Nakata,** 76 Hawai'i 360, 878 P.2d 699 (Hawai'i 1994); **Opinion of the Justices (DWI Jury Trials),** 135 N.H. 538, 608 A.2d 202 (N.H. 1992); **State v. Rickerson,** 548 So.2d 86 (La.App. 3 Cir. 1989); **Skinner v. State,** 809 So.2d 782 (Miss.App. 2002).

[634] **State ex rel. Wangberg v. Smith,** 211 Ariz. 101, 118 P.3d 49 (Ariz.App. Div. 1 2005).

[635]**Baldwin v. New York,** 399 U.S. 117, 90 S.Ct. 1914, 26 L.Ed.2d 446 (1970).

[636]In all criminal prosecutions, the accused shall enjoy the right to a speedy and public trial, by an impartial jury of the State and district wherein the crime shall have been committed... U.S.C.A. CONST Amend. VI. [N]or shall any State deprive any person of life, liberty, or property, without due process of law; nor deny to any person within its jurisdiction the equal protection of the laws. U.S.C.A. CONST Amend. XIV.

[637]**McCormick v. State,** 222 Ga. App. 753, 476 S.E.2d 271(1996).

[638]**Blanton v. City of North Las Vegas, Nev.,** 489 U.S. 538, 109 S.Ct. 1289, 103 L.Ed.2d 550 (1989); **City of Bismarck v. Fettig,** 601 N.W.2d 247 (N.D. 1999); **State v. Ninth Judicial Dist. Court of State of Nev. In and For Douglas County,** 104 Nev. 91, 752 P.2d 238 (Nev. 1988); **State v. Lynch,** 223 Neb. 849, 394 N.W.2d 651 (Neb. 1986); **State v. Nakata,** 76 Hawai'i 360, 878 P.2d 699 (Hawai'i 1994); **Opinion of the Justices (DWI Jury Trials),** 135 N.H. 538, 608 A.2d 202 (N.H. 1992); **State v. Rickerson,** 548 So.2d 86 (La.App. 3 Cir. 1989); **Skinner v. State,** 809 So.2d 782 (Miss.App. 2002).

experienced trial attorney will usually make excellent decisions on selecting qualified jurors and excusing jurors who will not give you the "benefit of the doubt."

The process of jury selection is a weekly event in most courts. A number of citizens will be called in for jury duty for the week of your trial. From this large group, between fifteen and thirty are chosen to be a jury "pool" for your misdemeanor trial. Your lawyer will help in the "voir dire" process that seeks to uncover juror bias and (hopefully) eliminates these potential jurors. If your state allows the attorneys to question jurors directly, this process may take hours.

Some states utilize 12 jurors (e.g., California) in both misdemeanor cases and felony cases. Other states (i.e., Georgia) use a six-person misdemeanor jury and a 12-person felony jury. So long as a state utilizes 6 *or more* jurors for misdemeanor cases, the United States Supreme Court has not complained about that.[639] At least one state (Virginia) uses 7 jurors in misdemeanor cases.[640]

After the questioning, each attorney gets to choose in turn which of the jurors to eliminate from your jury. Neither attorney gets to "pick" jurors. Instead, it is a process of elimination of prospective jurors. When all "strikes" have been taken by both attorneys, the remaining jurors make up the jury for your case.

As far as the number of "strikes" available to both attorneys, be aware that two different kinds of "strikes" (or challenges) may be utilized. A "challenge for cause" means the attorney has uncovered clear evidence that this potential juror has indicated either favoritism for one side or the other or antagonism against one side. Each attorney - - - defense and prosecution - - - has an unlimited number of "strikes for cause." The other type of "challenge" or "strike" is peremptory. Each side gets an equal number of these and may eliminate a juror for any reason that is not based on race[641] or gender[642] as the sole or "motivating" cause.

Jury pools are selected from several lists of citizens. In most states, everyone who is a registered voter will be called for jury duty. The list of potential jurors is usually supplemented from other public lists, such as driver's license records or real estate ownership records. Absent a legal excuse that authorizes the judge to excuse a juror from your case, a citizen is expected to serve when called upon.

Experienced trial lawyers know which counties have good jury pools and which ones do not. These attorneys will usually tailor their jury selection questions to the "typical" jurors for that jurisdiction. This flexibility and variation is the trademark of a great advocate.

When a seasoned criminal defense attorney is confronted with a particularly "bad" pool of jurors, he or she will modify or adjust the voir dire questions. The reason for this is to try to eliminate - - - for cause - - - a larger number of "bad" jurors.

13.7. If convicted, who sentences you? If you are convicted of a crime, the court will decide your punishment. This may include time in jail plus additional time on probation. You will be given a monetary fine to pay as well as other required penalties. Due to specific state sentencing guidelines, you must be given at least the minimum mandatory sentence.

---

[639]**Burch v. Louisiana,** 441 U.S. 130, 99 S.Ct. 1623, 60 L.Ed.2d 96 (1979).

[640]**Gardner v. Com.,** 195 Va. 945, 81 S.E.2d 614 (Va. 1954).

[641]**Batson v. Kentucky,** 476 U.S. 79, 106 S.Ct. 1712, 90 L.Ed.2d 69 (1986); **Johnson v. California,** 125 S.Ct. 2410, 162 L.Ed.2d 129 (2005).

[642]**J.E.B. v. Alabama ex rel. T.B.,** 511 U.S. 127, 114 S.Ct. 1419, 128 L.Ed.2d 89 (1994).

In most states, for a DUI-DWI conviction, you are given your sentence by the judge who presides over your trial.[643] In his or her consideration of sentencing, the judge is limited by the determination of guilt or innocence by the jury on each charge.[644]   While you have no constitutional right to have a jury decide your sentence, in a few states it is the jury who decides your punishment.[645] Either way, a well-seasoned DUI-DWI specialist can offer guidance based on his or her years of experience as to what penalties you face. This information may assist you to make a decision about going to trial or accepting a negotiated plea offered by the prosecutor.

13.8. Is a "deferred adjudication," diversion, "CWOF," "PBJ," or a "plea in abeyance" possible? In some states, with some criminal offenses, you are allowed to defer your DUI-DWI charges while you complete a prolonged period of restricted driving privileges, performance of community service hours as well as undergoing drug and alcohol evaluation and treatment. If you successfully complete your program, and commit no further violations of the law during this period, the charges against you might be dropped or not recorded on your state record.   Depending on your jurisdiction, this may be called a deferred adjudication, a diversion program, a PBJ, a continuation without a finding of guilt (CWOF) as used in Massachusetts or some other form of a *plea in abeyance*.

In Maryland, a deferred plea called "PBJ" (probation before judgment) may be available to a person who has a first DUI-DWI in five years. Such a plea carries no points, is not reported to other states and is discretionary with the judge at sentencing after a plea of guilty or being found guilty at a trial.   If a defendant asks for such a plea, he or she must waive the right to pursue an appeal. Some judges are reluctant to grant the special plea to a person who has put the State through a trial and then seeks the special disposition, so having an experienced criminal litigator in Maryland is critical to protect this valuable alternative plea disposition. Drug and alcohol treatment as well as interlock are commonly part of the conditions of such a plea. [MD Code, Criminal Procedure, § 6-220.]

These plea options are typically not offered in the majority of states for the more serious criminal charges.   In a few states one of these options is possible for some DUI-DWI charges.[646] Typically, these options may only be available for a person who has NO prior DUI-

---

[643]**State v. Hanf,** 687 N.W.2d 659 (Minn.App. 2004); North Carolina - N.C.G.S.A. § 20-179, **Field v. Sheriff of Wake County, North Carolina,** 831 F.2d 530 (4th Cir.(N.C.) 1987); Tennessee - **City of Chattanooga v. Davis,** 54 S.W.3d 248 (Tenn. 2001); **U.S. v. Murgas,** 31 F.Supp.2d 245 (N.D.N.Y. 1998); Texas - no constitutional right to have the jury sentence you, although state statute can so provide. **McDonald v. State,** 863 S.W.2d 541 (Tex.App.-Hous. (1 Dist.) 1993).

[644]**Apprendi v. New Jersey,** 530 U.S. 466, 120 S.Ct. 2348, 147 L.Ed.2d 435 (2000).

[645]**Williams v. New York,** 337 U.S. 241, 69 S.Ct. 1079, 93 L.Ed. 1337 (1949); Missouri - V.A.M.S. 557.036; **State v. Long,** 698 S.W.2d 898 (Mo.App. E.D. 1985); Texas - Vernon's Ann.Texas C.C.P. Art. 37.07(2)(b); Arkansas - **Tharp v. State,** 294 Ark. 615, 745 S.W.2d 612 (Ark. 1988).

[646]Texas - Vernon's Ann.Texas C.C.P. Art. 42.12; **Stevens v. State,** 2005 WL 2044533 (Tex.App.-Fort Worth 2005); Utah - U.C.A. 1953 § 53-3-218; **In re Worthen,** 926 P.2d 853 (Utah 1996); Kansas - K.S.A. § 8-1567(m)(5), **State v. Wheeler,** 115 P.3d 794 (Kan.App. 2005); Nebraska - **Polikov v. Neth,** 270 Neb. 29, 699 N.W.2d 802 (2005); Virginia - **Rhodes v. Com.,** 45 Va.App. 645, 613 S.E.2d 466 (2005); Kentucky - **Bailey v. Com.,** 2005 WL 119619 (Ky. 2005); Oregon - **State v. Young,** 196 Or.App. 708, 103 P.3d 1180 (2004); California - **People v. Walters,** 127 Cal.Rptr.2d 267 (Cal.App. 2 Dist. 2002); Ohio - **State v. Hacker,** 2002 WL 1332289 (Ohio App. 2 Dist. 2002); Florida - **State v. Cleveland,** 390 So.2d 364 (Fla.App. 4 Dist. 1980).

DWI convictions, or at least none for the last 5, 7 or 10 years, as allowed by state law. In other states, such alternatives are prohibited.[647]

Your DUI-DWI specialist will know if such an alternative plea is even an option for you. He or she will also know the eligibility requirements for these programs in your state, and tell you the parameters of the program you will have to complete to be considered successful at avoiding the DUI-DWI conviction from being entered on your state record. Be certain to disclose your entire history of traffic and criminal offenses to your attorney because the State will have records of all of your transgressions.

13.9. Is a "first offender" plea an option, to keep your long-term record clean? In some states, if your DUI-DWI conviction is your first ever criminal conviction, by keeping your record clean for a specified period of time following this conviction, all record of this conviction can be expunged from your state criminal record. Because minimum mandatory sentencing for subsequent DUI-DWI offenses is based on prior similar convictions, this is an uncommon option for DUI-DWI convictions. A first offender plea is available in some states,[648] while specifically not available in others.[649] Your DUI-DWI specialist will know if this option is even available to you, and the requirements in your state for you to qualify for such favorable treatment.

13.10. Is a "Nolo" plea or an "Alford" plea available, and will it help you on your DUI-DWI case in avoiding license loss or protecting a job? A plea of nolo contendere (or "no contest") means that while you do not admit to committing the crime, you do not contest the charge either. A "nolo" plea means you are willing to accept the punishment even though you do not acknowledge your guilt for the offense charged.

An "Alford plea" is a guilty plea where you do not admit that you did the act, yet you accept that the prosecution likely has enough evidence with which they could convict you. This plea originated in the United States Supreme Court case of *North Carolina v. Alford*, 400 U.S. 25 (1970). After the *Alford* decision, an "Alford" plea generally has the same effect as a plea of guilty with respect to sentencing. Later use of the conviction as an aggravating factor (if the defendant is later convicted of another offense) is allowed in all courts.

In most states, a nolo plea,[650] or an Alford plea,[651] is allowed for DUI-DWI. In these states, such a plea may help you protect your job or in avoiding an automatic loss of your

---

[647]Tennessee - **State v. Tipton,** 2005 WL 1240174 (Tenn.Crim.App. 2005); Washington - **State ex rel. Schillberg v. Cascade Dist. Court,** 94 Wash.2d 772, 621 P.2d 115 (Wash. 1980); Indiana - **Hoage v. State,** 479 N.E.2d 1362 (Ind.App. 2 Dist. 1985); Georgia - Ga. Code Ann., § 40-6-391(f); **Sims v. State,** 214 Ga.App. 443, 448 S.E.2d 77 (1994).

[648]Kansas - K.S.A. § 8-1567(m)(5);Oregon - **State v. Young,** 196 Or.App. 708, 103 P.3d 1180 (2004); Delaware - 21 Del.C. § 4177B; Florida - West's F.S.A. § 948.08.

[649]Tennessee - **State v. Crudup,** 2005 WL 1378774 (Tenn.Crim.App. 2005); **State v. Tipton,** 2005 WL 1240174 (Tenn.Crim.App. 2005); **Sims v. State,** 214 Ga.App. 443, 448 S.E.2d 77 (1994).

[650]**State v. Gardner,** 119 P.3d 19 (Kan.App. 2005); **State ex rel. Douglas v. Burlew,** 106 Ohio St.3d 180, 833 N.E.2d 293 (2005); **State v. Torok,** 704 N.W.2d 424 (Wis.App. 2005); **Clinton R., Sr. v. State, Dept. of Health & Social Services,** 2005 WL 1926234 (Alaska 2005); **State v. Surette,** 90 Conn.App. 177, 876 A.2d 582 (2005); **Stump v. Johnson,** 217 W.Va. 733, 619 S.E.2d 246 (W.Va. 2005); **Hook v. State,** 2005 WL 1542659 (Tex.App.-Fort Worth 2005); **In re Gaudin,** 899 So.2d 1289 (La. 2005); **Department Of Highway Safety And Motor Vehicles v. Brandenburg,** 891 So.2d 1071 (Fla.App. 5 Dist. 2004); **State v. Lioen,** 106 Hawai'i 123, 102 P.3d 367 (Hawai'i App. 2004); **State v. Puckett,** 2003 WL 21638048 (Tenn.Crim.App. 2003); Georgia - O.C.G.A. § 17-7-95; **People v. Walters,** 127 Cal.Rptr.2d 267 (Cal.App. 2 Dist. 2002).

[651]**State v. Ballard,** 2004 WL 1918723 (Tenn.Crim.App. 2004); **Hanneken v. State,** 149 S.W.3d 543 (Mo.App. E.D. 2004); **Patterson v. Com.,** 2004 WL 2481661 (Ky.App. 2004); **Spriggs v. State,** 152 Md.App.

driver's license. In accident cases, with potential civil claims pending, a nolo contendere plea is usually preferable to a "guilty" plea since a "nolo" plea cannot be introduced in a civil trial as an acknowledgement of guilt, as a guilty plea can. Your DUI-DWI specialist will know the favorable aspects of either of these plea alternatives in your state, and can counsel you on the benefits (or lack thereof) of either of these special pleas.

13.11. Is a reduction to a lesser offense always a good solution? Whether or not a reduction to a lesser offense from the DUI-DWI charges is in your best interest depends on your particular situation. A DUI-DWI specialist knows not only the law and the court in which your charges are pending, but also the likely results of your case. Just as importantly, your attorney has taken the time to get to know you and your personal or work situation.

Some people, due to high security jobs, cannot have even a first lifetime DUI-DWI on their criminal and driving record. A second or subsequent DUI-DWI conviction on your criminal record can be devastating to your life regardless of your job. This may be because having such a conviction costs you your job, limits or takes away your right to drive, restricts you from traveling or limits your ability to care for your family. Your criminal defense specialist can also counsel you about the benefits and the detrimental aspects of delaying the start of your trial, if this option exists in your case. To get a glimpse of some non-judicial complications caused by a DUI-DWI conviction see the author's 1993 article from Trial Magazine: http://www.drunkdrivingdefense.com/publications-articles/drunk-driving-defense.htm.

For some people, accepting a reduction in your case to an offense like reckless driving may also not be in your best interest. In a state that has what is called a "wet" reckless law, any DUI-DWI that gets reduced to a reckless driving offense may cause a driver's license suspension, revocation or restriction. For professionals (e.g., doctors, registered nurses, chiropractors, CPAs, dentists, attorneys) reduced pleas (such as a "wet" reckless in California) may trigger "fitness" hearings that delay or prevent being licensed (or renewing a license) in a particular state.

Your attorney may feel that you have an excellent chance to win the DUI-DWI case against you. While this can never be promised with certainty, part of the reason you hired a DUI-DWI specialist is to obtain this type of expertise. The prosecution may offer you a plea to a reduced criminal charge because he or she knows the DUI-DWI case against you is weak, or missing some critical element or witness.

Punishment issues, such as the threat of more lengthy jail time, are a common concern for most people facing drunken driving charges. For some people, going to jail or having to serve mandatory community service for a lengthy period of time could be devastating. For others, even being on probation can end their job.

For a conviction of any misdemeanor offense (no matter what the misdemeanor), you are at least theoretically facing some jail time. You could face exactly the same punishment if you accept a guilty plea to a lesser charge rather than being found guilty on a DUI-DWI charge. It could be that a negotiated plea to another serious offense offers you no real benefit. Your DUI-DWI specialist will be best able to recommend which alternative is best for you.

62, 831 A.2d 72 (2003); **State v. Bernier,** 2002 WL 1545271 (Minn.App. 2002); **Mansfield v. Colwell Const. Co.,** 242 Ga.App. 669, 530 S.E.2d 793 (2000); **State v. Lutgen,** 606 N.W.2d 312 (Iowa 2000); **People v. Root,** 267 A.D.2d 1103, 701 N.Y.S.2d 227 (N.Y.A.D. 4 Dept. 1999); **State v. Gilder,** 295 Mont. 483, 985 P.2d 147 (1999); **State v. Pusey,** 128 Idaho 647, 917 P.2d 804 (Idaho App. 1996); **State v. Wiisanen,** 158 Wis.2d 353, 462 N.W.2d 551 (Wis.App. 1990).

13.12. How long will a conviction stay on your record? If you plead guilty (guilty, nolo contendere, or enter an "Alford" plea) to DUI-DWI, or if you are subsequently convicted at trial of anything, you will always have this conviction on your criminal record unless your state allows for its removal. Some states specifically provide a statutory method under their state laws for requesting a judge to clear your record of a first DUI-DWI offense.[652] However, this can only be done after a specified period of time and is available only if you commit no other criminal offenses. In other states, your record of a DUI-DWI conviction can never be expunged.[653]

Your DUI-DWI specialist will know exactly the availability of expungement, as well as your options for an expungement. Knowing the possibility of being able to clear your state criminal history may be a key factor in deciding to accept a negotiated plea offer.

Be aware that federal law does not reciprocate and clear your federal "tracking" history of any prior convictions, diversions or deferred adjudications. The NCIC (National Crime Information Computer) meticulously tracks all arrests and all dispositions (i.e., guilty, deferred, first offender, nolo contendere or even a dismissal or acquittal). The federal record is almost never "cleared," regardless of what a state might do with its own internal records.

13.13. Is "merging" or dismissing the other charges of any value? It is very uncommon for you to be facing only a solitary DUI-DWI charge with no other pending charges. If you are, the arrest likely followed a roadblock stop or an accident with no eyewitnesses. Other traffic offenses can be a problem because some of them can carry jail or longer probation terms.

More commonly, when you are charged with DUI-DWI, you are possibly facing another DUI-DWI charge. Many people are simultaneously charged with both a "per se" count (a blood alcohol above a specified level while operating a vehicle) and a "common law" count (operating a vehicle while your mental or physical faculties are impaired due to being under the influence of alcohol).

You may also be facing a DUI-DWI "drugs," or a DUI-DWI "combination of alcohol and drugs" charge. This is in addition to whatever traffic violation or violations you were cited for after your traffic stop. Typical traffic offenses may include a lane violation, speeding or not using your turn signals appropriately when making turns or lane changes.

In some negotiated pleas, the prosecution may be willing to "merge" or dismiss the other charges against you in return for your guilty or nolo contendere plea to at least one of the DUI-DWI charges you face. A dismissal means the other charges pending against you are dropped, or not prosecuted against you. "Merger" of an offense generally refers to a lesser offense, such

---

[652]Kansas - K.S.A. § 8-1567(m)(5);Oregon - **State v. Young,** 196 Or.App. 708, 103 P.3d 1180 (2004); Delaware - 21 Del.C. § 4177B; Florida - West's F.S.A. § 948.08; **Rozier v. Director of Revenue, State of Missouri,** 164 S.W.3d 108 (Mo.App. 2005); **State v. Kern,** 110 P.3d 1056 (Mont. 2005); **State v. Badessa,** 869 A.2d 61 (R.I. 2005); Oregon - O.R.S. § 137.225; **Com., Dept. of Transp. v. B.L.R.W.,** 829 A.2d 716 (2003); **Bruno v. Iowa Dept. of Transp.,** 603 N.W.2d 596 (Iowa 1999); Texas - Vernon's Ann.Texas C.C.P. Art. 55.02; **State v. Manning,** 1996 WL 380642 (Minn.App. 1996); **State v. EDB,** 638 So.2d 1108 (La.App. 1994); **State v. Smythe,** 1992 WL 145004 (Tenn.Crim.App. 1992); **Chamberlain v. Buhrman,** 250 Kan. 277, 825 P.2d 168 (1992); **State ex rel. Crank v. City of Logan,** 178 W.Va. 548, 363 S.E.2d 135 (1987).
[653]**State v. Sandlin,** 86 Ohio St.3d 165, 712 N.E.2d 740 (Ohio 1999); **Truluck v. State,** 2004 WL 3354224 (Del.Super. 2004); **Toia v. People,** 333 Ill.App.3d 523, 776 N.E.2d 599 (2002); Florida - West's F.S.A. § 943.0585; **State v. Orr,** 375 N.W.2d 171 (N.D. 1985); **Lovell v. State,** 283 Ark. 425, 681 S.W.2d 395 (Ark. 1984).

as speeding, being "merged" into the more serious DUI-DWI offense, since driving at high speeds could be an "element" of impaired driving.

Many prosecutors may be willing to merge or dismiss some of your charges. The primary reason for your prosecutor to do this is a desire to close your case without the need for a trial. Certainly, if the prosecution has a rock-solid case, and they feel comfortable of proving every offense, little motivation exists for him or her to offer to merge or dismiss some or all of the less serious offenses. If you have a poor driving history, a build-up of "points" on your driving record may be a strong motivation to seek a merger or dismissal of these other charges.

Thus, it depends on your situation and the specifics of your case as to whether or not trading a dismissal or a merger is good for you. If it is the combined punishment from all of the charges that causes you the greatest fear, then reducing the number of charges against you may be in your best interest. If it is the DUI-DWI conviction that will cause you the most problems, no matter what the other charges against you, then to dismiss or merge the other charges does not make sense in your situation.

Your DUI-DWI specialist will offer guidance to you on this issue, if such an offer is even on the table. Your attorney will know the strengths and weaknesses of your case, and will know your job situation. He or she can best explain the benefits and ramifications of the different options.

13.14. Using a "stipulated bench trial" or "conditional plea" to set up appeal. For strategic reasons, your attorney may recommend that you forego trial and use a "stipulated bench trial" or a "conditional plea" (of guilty, nolo contendere or to accept a deferred adjudication or other favorable "first offender" plea) to set up an appeal of your judge's pre-trial rulings that denied key defense motions. This is done just so that a critical legal point in your case can be decided by a court higher than the trial level court. These higher courts ("appellate courts") routinely refuse to decide whether or not an error has been made in your case until your case is "final." To get your case finalized, your attorney, the prosecutor and the judge may agree to allow your attorney to preserve and later appeal one or more legal issues and to proceed with a stipulated bench trial or a conditional plea. Such a plan saves valuable trial time and allows your attorney to try to undo the conviction on appeal.

Going forward with trial may "undo" the favorable situation for appeal that exists after the trial judge has ruled against you. If you opt for a full-blown trial, this may result in the prosecutor bringing all witnesses to trial. This may "fix" some gap in proof of key evidence that was revealed at a motion hearing when only one or two witnesses testified. Alternatively, your DUI-DWI specialist may seek to minimize jail time (in the event you lose) by not putting forth a three-day jury trial. Some judges will increase punishment if you are unsuccessful at trial. Criminal defense attorneys call the constitutionally-questionable practice of the judge adding jail time to the "normal" sentence after an unsuccessful attempt to obtain acquittal "charging rent."

A stipulated bench trial involves the use of certain evidence (such as testimony at a pre-trial motions hearing) as the State's entire offer of proof on a key issue. As used here, a stipulation is an agreement between the prosecution and your defense attorney relating to the use of this evidence instead of proceeding with trial. The judge may have entered his or her interpretation of the law, even though your attorney has noted on the record his or her objection to the admission of critical evidence or noted his or her disagreement with the judge's order.

A conditional plea is one where you plead guilty, nolo contendere or offer an *Alford* plea (even though you feel you are innocent), reserving the right to appeal a pre-trial ruling to an appellate court. By entering such a plea, your case is closed at the trial court level. You then let the appellate court decide the correctness of the trial judge's ruling.

Using either of these "tools" for framing an appellate ruling can be a wise and effective means to resolve certain difficult DUI-DWI cases. It takes an experienced DUI-DWI attorney to fashion this type of attack for a case that has little chance of success at a jury trial. In utilizing either of these tools, you are betting on an appellate court to eventually find in your favor on the disputed issue. Other strategic advantages may be obtained by the use of such a tactic, such as delaying or deferring the record of conviction being entered on state records or possibly allowing you to continue driving while the appeal goes forward.

13.15. Is punishment going to be worse after trial? It is a common concern that if you go all the way through trial for your DUI-DWI charges, you face a harsher punishment than if you accept a negotiated plea bargain offered by the prosecutor. This may or may not be true depending (at least in part) upon your state's laws. It may depend upon the judge, and whether he or she charges "rent" to exercise your constitutional rights to have a trial. It also may depend upon state law, which may prohibit these types of "retaliatory" actions from occurring.

The sentence for a DUI-DWI conviction or guilty plea must stay within your state's mandated minimum and maximum guidelines. These maximums and minimums are established by each state's statutes, and are based on whether this is your first DUI-DWI offense. Most states allow a judge to have some latitude in meting out sentences.

If you face multiple charges, the maximum cumulative sentence (if found guilty on all counts) is likely to be longer than if you accept a plea bargain to a single count. However, because multiple sentences can and often do run concurrently (the sentence for one charge overlaps or runs during the same time period), the actual amount of jail time you face is usually the same either way. On the other hand, if you are found not guilty of DUI-DWI and most of the serious charges against you, you may only face penalties on the remaining non-serious charges. This sentence should be much more favorable than a DUI-DWI sentence.

An experienced DUI-DWI attorney can give you the best estimate of what you face in each of the different circumstances. If you are unfortunate to be in front of a judge who ignores the constitutional right to seek a trial without fear of paying "rent," remember him or her at the next election and do your best to encourage all of your friends, neighbors and family to vote that judge off the bench.

13.16. Special courts or alternative resolution options may exist for repeat offenders. In the past decade, the concept of utilizing special programs or alternative resolutions for repeat offenders has been implemented in numerous states. These courts or alternative programs usually offer a departure from standard jail sentences for people who have demonstrated a problem with alcohol. Although some jail time is commonly involved, a substantial portion of the usual incarceration term is exchanged for some form of alcohol (or drug) treatment and intensive probation. Intensive probation typically involves a high degree of oversight by the probation officers, including weekly or random drug and alcohol screening.

Many of these special programs have a "work-release" component wherein the repeat offender who is gainfully employed is allowed to go to and from work, assuming transportation can be arranged to assure that the person gets to and from work legally. In some jurisdictions, these programs will be a discretionary option (with the sentencing judge) for accused citizens who lose at trial, while other jurisdictions only offer accused citizens the chance to take such an option INSTEAD of work.

Some people are not well-suited for intensive probation and strict reporting requirements. Such people are usually quick to violate the restrictive conditions and are subsequently jailed for non-compliance. This jail term can sometimes be for the remainder of the probation period. For these people, a shorter jail term and normal non-reporting probation may be preferable to taking the "special court" option.

The experience of a highly qualified DUI-DWI specialist can be extremely valuable in these situations. His or her knowledge of the sentencing patterns of your assigned judge can be crucial in deciding whether to try to win at trial or strongly consider accepting some "alternative resolution" plea offer.

Chapter 14

Motions Practice: How to Challenge the Prosecutor's Ability to Introduce Harmful Evidence against You in Order to Win Your Case.

14.0. Overview of this chapter's purpose. During the time your case is pending, including during any trial, many questions arise that the court is asked to answer. Legal defenses or procedural challenges may be asserted by your attorney, which may cause the State to drop some or all of the charges before or during the trial. The quality and experience level of your attorney makes a tremendous difference in asserting and arguing these challenges.

The prosecutor can also assert motions in certain circumstances. When an attorney asks the court (usually in a written pleading) to do something or to decide something, this is called a "motion." The court either grants or denies the motion, based on both the law established by your state's legislature and the law that has been interpreted by appellate-level courts.

On many issues that are "fact specific," decisions are often rendered based upon the personal integrity and the legal knowledge of your trial judge. In a very real sense, your judge's "opinion" about many issues may shape his or her rulings. Judges are human, too.

Because this is **your** defense for the **criminal charges** against **you**, and you will be receiving a large number of forms (copies of the motions and the judge's decision on each motion) from your lawyer, it is best if you understand what each of these might mean. The purpose of this chapter is not to make you into a lawyer. It is intended to allow you to have a more intelligent conversation with your lawyer at any critical point during the legal proceedings so that you can assert the best possible defense to your charges.

14.1. Challenging the accusatory document. To be held liable for a crime, the government has to inform you of the crime with which you are charged. The document that does that may be called one name in your state and another in a different state, but the author will refer to it as an "accusatory document."[654]

The accusatory document can be as simple as the traffic citation itself, or it may be another particular form. The law of criminal procedure requires that this document be accurate so that the person being accused of the crime may raise an adequate defense to the charges. (If you don't know specifically with what crime or crimes you are being charged with, how can you defend yourself?)

A demurrer (or motion to quash) is an attack by the defendant against this accusatory document. A special demurrer (or special motion to quash) is an attack on the FORM of the document - that the crime with which you are charged cannot be specified on this kind of document or that the document is lacking some essential "part."

A general demurrer (general "motion to quash") is a challenge to the SUBSTANCE of what is written in the document. In other words, this type of motion challenges the accusatory document about whether it contains the correct information relating to stating all the elements of

---

[654]See Section 6.1 of this book for a better explanation of the types of accusatory documents.

the offense rather than just some of the elements. If it is defective, you can ask the judge to throw out the criminal charges against you.

The timing of when to ask for a judicial ruling on motions to quash is very important, so that the prosecutor cannot just redo the paperwork correctly and start over. Your DUI-DWI specialist will be familiar with your state's laws regarding when to file such a motion, how to assert the proper motion to quash (demurrer), and the appropriate time to request a ruling upon it (usually, after "jeopardy" has attached.)

14.2. Statute of limitations challenges. A statute of limitations is the maximum time period determined by your state legislature during which a criminal charge or civil claim may be brought against a defendant. The theory is that if what happened occurred too long ago, it will be too hard to defend against (witnesses may have died, moved or forgotten details). In each state, this length of time is different, and set by the state's legislature.

For some serious crimes, no statute of limitations exists, such as murder. A statute of limitations, or limit, on how long the state can wait to enforce a judgment against a criminal or civil defendant is another type of "limitation" on legal proceedings.[655] With misdemeanors, a one, two or three-year statute of limitations usually applies to misdemeanor DUI-DWI charges.

Although it is very uncommon for a long period of time between you being stopped for a DUI-DWI and you being charged with a crime, if for some reason this happened, your lawyer could bring a motion to dismiss the charges against you based on the statute of limitations being violated. In the majority of states, misdemeanors have a statute of limitations of two years, and this is true for misdemeanor DUI-DWI offenses as well.[656]

14.3. Speedy trial. Unreasonable delay by the State to charge you with a crime can lead to a motion to dismiss or a motion to discharge you from responsibility for the offense. This may occur because the process to bring your case to trial once you are charged has been too slow.[657] Your attorney might be able to get the charges dropped because the prosecution has waited an unreasonable length of time to bring your case to trial. However, these situations are very rare.

Be aware that your state may have a type of state-law speedy trial demand of which you can take advantage. Be aware that the rules of asserting such a filing may mean that you be immediately available for trial on little or no advanced notice. Such a situation may cause problems with your defense, especially if the trial date does not fit the schedule of your out-of-state expert witness.

14.4. Pre-trial motions. The use of pre-trial motions allows your attorney to raise specific concerns and questions of the judge assigned to your case before your trial. In

---

[655]http://dictionary.law.com/default2.asp?typed=statute+of+limitations&type=1

[656]O.C.G.A. §§ 40-13-34 and 17-3-1.

[657]See Section 6.27 of this book. "In all criminal prosecutions, the accused shall enjoy the right to a speedy and public trial..." U.S.C.A. Const. Amend. VI. "In criminal cases, the defendant shall have a public and speedy trial by an impartial jury." GA. Const. Art. 1,§ 1, ¶ XI; Arizona - A.R.S. § 13-114; Colorado - C.R.S.A. § 18-1-405; Connecticut - C.G.S.A. Const. Art. 1, § 8; D.C. Code, 2001 Ed. Article I. Bill of Rights Sec. 106; Florida - West's F.S.A. § 918.015; Illinois - 725 ILCS 5/103-5; Indiana - IC 35-33-7-5; Louisiana - LSA-C.Cr.P. Art. 701; Maryland - MD Constitution, Declaration of Rights, Art. 21; Michigan - M.C.L.A. 768.1; Missouri - V.A.M.S. 545.780; Montana - MCA 46-13-202; Nebraska - Neb.Rev.St. § 29-1205; New York - McKinney's CPL § 30.20; North Dakota - NDCC, 29-19-02; Oklahoma - 22 Okl.St.Ann. § 13; Oregon - O.R.S. § 135.745; South Dakota -SDCL. § 23A-16-3; Tennessee - T. C. A. § 40-14-101; Texas - Vernon's Ann.Texas C.C.P. T. 1, Ch. THIRTY-TWO A; Utah - D.Ut. DUCrimR 57-4; West Virginia - Rule 37.01.

an attempt to better define what issues and facts have to be decided at trial by either the jury or the judge, pre-trial motions may be filed and heard before your trial begins. These concerns and questions are framed by the written motions, and because they typically are ruled upon before the trial starts, they are called pre-trial motions. The answers the judge gives to these questions, called "rulings," often determine whether or not the case even goes to trial and how much negotiating room your attorney has with the prosecution to obtain a reduction of the charges. Pre-trial motions may also assist the parties and the judge to determine an appropriate punishment, in the event of your conviction.

14.5. Motion in limine - Latin for "threshold," a motion in limine is a request made at the start of a trial requesting the judge rule that certain evidence may not be introduced in trial.[658] An easy way to remember what "in limine" means is to think of this motion as being one to LIMIT the other side in some fashion. No "list of possible motions exists inasmuch as these motions are customized to fit each case, and can be raised on hundreds of different "grounds."

14.5.1. Motions in limine are most common and most successful. These motions are very common in criminal trials where the admissibility of evidence is subject to constitutional or statutory limitations, such as suppression of your statements made without the *Miranda* warnings (reading your rights to you).[659] In a litigation-oriented DUI-DWI practice, these are the most common and most successful motions brought before the court. Motions can be asserted either in writing or orally, if your state law does not mandate that the particular type of motion be put in writing.

14.5.2. Purpose of motions in limine. The purpose of a motion in limine is to prevent certain evidence (usually proposed testimony) from ever being mentioned once the case is in front of the jury. If this motion is granted, neither the prosecution nor the defense attorney may mention the prohibited subject.[660] Both sides must caution their witnesses against mentioning or referring to the subject of the prohibited evidence. It must not be brought to the attention of the jury. If a witness violates the judge's order, a mistrial can be granted by the judge, thereby stopping the trial.

14.5.3. Is a pre-trial hearing required? A hearing is when the judge meets with both side's attorneys, usually with a court reporter present. Either side can ask the judge to rule on motions (ask the judge to answer legal questions or to otherwise make a decision) based on testimony from witnesses and other evidence, including oral argument (oral presentations) from the attorneys. Because a motion in limine pertains to prohibiting testimony regarding a specific subject, those subject limits often can be determined with or without a hearing based on the lawyers submitting briefs (written documents that argue their side based on the statutes or prior case law). It is at the judge's discretion (in most jurisdictions) whether or not the lawyers get a chance for a hearing, unless state law mandates that a pre-trial hearing must be held, upon request of either party.

---

[658]http://dictionary.law.com/default2.asp?typed=motion+in+limine&type=1&submit1.x=68&submit1.y=5

[659] http://dictionary.law.com/default2.asp?typed=motion+in+limine&type=1&submit1.x=68&submit1.y=5

[660]**CSX Transportation, Inc. V. Levant**, 200 Ga. App. 856, 410 S.E.2d 299 (1991), rev'd on other grounds, 262 Ga. 313, 417 S.E.2d 320 (1992); **Com. v. Maloney**, 876 A.2d 1002 (Pa. 2005); **Harnett v. State**, 38 S.W.3d 650 (Tex.App.-Austin 2000); **People v. Williams**, 188 Ill.2d 365, 721 N.E.2d 539 (1999); **State v. Clapp**, 135 N.C.App. 52, 519 S.E.2d 90 (1999); **State v. French**, 72 Ohio St.3d 446, 650 N.E.2d 887 (1995); **People v. Sterling**, 209 A.D.2d 1006, 619 N.Y.S.2d 448 (1994); **State v. Miura**, 6 Haw.App. 501, 730 P.2d 917 (1986); **Rosa v. Florida Power & Light Co.**, 636 So.2d 60 (Fla.App. 2 Dist. 1994).

14.6. Motion to suppress. This is a motion (filed on behalf of a criminal defendant) to disallow certain evidence (usually some form of tangible property or "thing") in an upcoming trial from ever being considered by the jury. *Example*: A written confession that the defendant alleges was signed while he was drunk or given to police officers without the benefit of the reading of *Miranda* rights.[661]

14.6.1. Nature of the motion. Motions to suppress have to do with the question of whether evidence (property) that has been seized is admissible at trial or not.[662] These motions determine critical evidentiary issues and "frame" the issues the jury will hear.

14.6.2. Manner of filing. Different than a motion in limine, a motion to suppress generally must be made in writing[663] (not in North Carolina[664]), and the motion also must raise a constitutional issue.[665] You will know that your attorney has made this kind of motion when you get a copy of it.

14.6.3. Is a pre-trial hearing required? The Fourth Amendment of the Constitution of the United States prohibits the taking of anyone's property (a seizure) by the police unless there is a legal basis and specific reason for allowing the taking.[666] [See the most commonly invoked federal constitutional provisions in **Appendix K**]. Some constitutional right is usually at question in a motion to suppress, because it usually involves a seizure by the police or other law enforcement officials. Testimony is typically required by the ones who either ordered the seizure or carried out the seizure.

The hearing is held to determine whether or not the seizure was legally valid. That being the case, a pre-trial hearing is required so that each side may question and counter-question those giving sworn testimony before the judge. Your state may require specific motions to be filed at specific times during the progression of the case, or the issue relating to that motion may be "waived" (given up).

14.6.4. Untimely assertion of motion. Frequently, certain motions must be made at or before arraignment (the court process where you are formally informed of the charges against you by the court and asked to make a plea of either guilty or not guilty) unless special permission of the court is obtained to allow a later filing.[667] In other jurisdictions, motions

---

661

http://dictionary.law.com/default2.asp?typed=motion+to+suppress&type=1&submit1.x=82&submit1.y=9

[662]**Jarrell v. State**, 234 Ga. 410, 216 S.E.2d 258 (1975); **Flores v. State**, 129 S.W.3d 169 (Tex.App.-Corpus Christi 2004); **State v. French**, 72 Ohio St.3d 446, 650 N.E.2d 887 (1995); **People v. Sterling**, 209 A.D.2d 1006 (1994); **State v. Shade**, 110 Nev. 57, 867 P.2d 393 (1994); **Jenkins v. State**, 301 Ark. 20, 781 S.W.2d 461 (1989); **State v. Marshall**, 92 N.C.App. 398, 374 S.E.2d 874 (1988).

[663]**Graves v. State**, 135 Ga. App. 921, 219 S.E.2d 633 (1975); **People v. Mezon**, 80 N.Y.2d 155, 603 N.E.2d 943 (1992); **People v. Lewis**, 71 Cal.App.3d 817, 139 Cal.Rptr. 673 (1977); **State v. Roberts**, 755 S.W.2d 833 (Tenn.Crim.App. 1988); **People v. Thomas**, 120 Ill.App.2d 219, 256 N.E.2d 870 (1969); **State v. Rodriguez**, 115 Or.App. 281, 840 P.2d 711 (1992).

[664]**State v. Satterfield**, 300 N.C. 621, 268 S.E.2d 510 (1980).

[665]**Stanley v. State**, 195 Ga. App. 706, 394 S.E.2d 785 (1990); **State v. Medrano**, 67 S.W.3d 892 (Tex.Crim.App. 2002); **State v. French**, 72 Ohio St.3d 446, 650 N.E.2d 887 (1995); **State v. Shade**, 110 Nev. 57, 867 P.2d 393 (1994).

[666]The right of the people to be secure in their persons, houses, papers, and effects, against unreasonable searches and seizures, shall not be violated... U.S.C.A. Const. Amend. IV.

[667]**Motion to suppress must be asserted at or before arraignment - State v. Gomez**, 266 Ga.App. 423, 597 S.E.2d 509 (2004).

can be filed after arraignment but must be filed a certain number of days (e.g., 30 days) before your trial begins.[668]

14.6.5. *Jackson-Denno* hearings and related challenges. In your case, your lawyer may want to argue that any confession or admission that you made at the time of your DUI-DWI arrest was not voluntary, and if it was not voluntary, then the jury should not be allowed to hear anything about it.[669] This is a very uncommon situation in a DUI-DWI arrest because so much of the evidence is based on either the poor driving that has been observed, the field sobriety tests done by the law enforcement officer at the scene, or the results of any medical/scientific tests. Yet, some officers are very good at tricking people into uttering incriminating statements after custody.

14.7. Double jeopardy. It is against the Fifth Amendment of the United States Constitution for anyone to be held criminally accountable twice for the same issue by the same sovereign.[670] What this means is that you cannot be made to stand trial a second time for any of your actions if the first trial regarding these actions was complete enough to be lawful.

However, several important exceptions to this rule exist. Because each state is a separate sovereign (independent government), as is the federal government, each may try you for the same set of circumstances if your actions are possibly against their law and they had concurrent jurisdiction (legal control) over you or the events at the time they occurred. Second, your legal situation only reaches a level where double jeopardy applies at a certain point in the criminal proceedings. If the trial gets stopped before that (usually due to a "mistrial"), you have no constitutional protection against a second trial in most instances. This is yet another reason to have the best lawyer you can, so that if something happens, they know when to pull the plug on your proceedings (and when not to), to protect your best interests.

If a prosecutor or judge makes an error at your trial, certain facts may block a new trial after a mistrial is granted. These are rare, but provide a total victory for you if it occurs.[671]

14.7.1. Administrative license penalties are not double jeopardy. This is another situation where double jeopardy does not usually apply. Although the hearing at which your driver's license is suspended immediately following a DUI-DWI arrest may seem like a criminal trial, the only question being addressed by such proceeding is whether or not you should lose a property interest (your driver's license).[672]

Your driver's license is not a right that you have, but instead a privilege to drive on public highways from the state that granted it to you. This administrative hearing is a determination if this privilege should be revoked. This is a different issue than is your criminal process, by which your liberty interests are at stake (that is they can put you in jail, put you on probation, or penalize you with fines and community service.)[673] Because there are different interests at

---

[668]**U.S. v. Barajas-Chavez**, 358 F.3d 1263 (10th Cir, 2004).

[669]**Jackson v. Denno**, 378 U.S. 368, 84 S.Ct. 1774, 12 L.Ed.2d 908 (1964).

[670] ... nor shall any person be subject for the same offence to be twice put in jeopardy of life or limb... U.S.C.A. Const. Amend. V.

[671]**Jefferson v. State**, 224 Ga.App. 8, 479 S.E.2d 406 (1996); **Ex parte Bauder**, 974 S.W.2d 729 (Tex.Crim.App. 1998); **State v. Kimsey**, 182 Or.App. 193, 47 P.3d 916 (2002); **People v. Dawson**, 431 Mich. 234, 427 N.W.2d 886 (1988); **Whitmore v. State**, 43 Ark. 271 (1884).

[672]**United States v. Ursery**, 518 U.S. 267, 116 S.Ct. 2135, 135 L.Ed.2d 549 (1996).

[673]**Davidson v. MacKinnon**, 656 So.2d 223 (Fla.App. 5 Dist. 1995); **State v. Sneed**, 8 S.W.3d 299 (Tenn.Crim.App. 1999);

stake, the issue at hand is not the same, and having to go through both proceedings is not double jeopardy.[674] Also see **Section 6.25** of this book.

14.7.2. "Same conduct"– procedural double jeopardy.

If the conduct leading to your arrest was such that you are or could be charged with several different crimes that are all known to the prosecutor (and can all be tried in the same court), then a trial on one issue precludes a subsequent trial on any of the other possible offenses.[675] In other words, if you were speeding at the time of your stop by the police, then found to be possibly DUI-DWI, and then you are tried only for the speeding by a court that could have also heard the DUI-DWI, by a prosecutor who knew about the DUI question, you cannot later be tried on the DUI-DWI.

14.7.3. Prosecution of one offense bars prosecution of others.

If you are charged with more than one crime (different counts), and one or more of these counts are dismissed, the State has the option of appealing the dismissal immediately or proceeding with the prosecution of the other counts. If the prosecution elects to proceed on the remaining counts, you cannot later be tried on the counts that were dismissed (and NOT appealed by the prosecutor) because of double jeopardy.[676]

14.7.4. Municipal v. state prosecutions.

Only certain types of cases can be heard in the different levels or types of court. If you are tried before a court that has a limited ability to hear specific crimes, a court that has a broader or more general ability to consider these types of cases can still try you without a claim of double jeopardy. An example would be if you were charged with following too closely and DUI-DWI, the first charge may be properly brought in a municipal traffic court or a local magistrate judge. Perhaps your state law provides that this court cannot hear drunken driving cases. In such a case, it is possible that the DUI-DWI could be tried later in a Circuit Court, Court of Common Pleas, State Court or Superior Court. Ironically, New York's *trial level* courts of general jurisdiction are called "Supreme Court."

14.7.5. Plea constitutes jeopardy.

Once you plead guilty before a trial judge and this plea is properly recorded and accepted by the judge, this constitutes jeopardy, for which your sentence cannot be changed. Once a guilty plea is entered, you cannot be retried on the charge due to the prosecutor changing his or her mind about the punishment handed down by the judge. The double jeopardy clause assures of the finality of such case dispositions. A few exceptions exist to this general rule, however. If you enter a guilty plea in a court that lacks "subject matter" jurisdiction, the plea can be "vacated" (undone) even after you have been sentenced and punished.[677] Likewise, if multiple charges are lodged against you and you somehow are permitted to enter a guilty plea to one charge, but not the remainder, such action may not prevent a prosecutor pursuing the remaining charge or charges if he or she was unaware of the pending nature of these other charges.[678]

---

[674]**United States v. Ursery**, 518 U.S. 267, 116 S.Ct. 2135, 135 L.Ed.2d 549 (1996); **Ex parte Mata,** 925 S.W.2d 292 (Tex.App.-Corpus Christi 1996); **Davidson v. MacKinnon,** 656 So.2d 223 (Fla.App. 5 Dist. 1995); **State v. Sneed,** 8 S.W.3d 299 (Tenn.Crim.App. 1999); **Murphy v. State,** 267 Ga. 120, 475 S.E.2d 907 (1996), **State v. Brabson,** 976 S.W.2d 182 (Tex.App.-Corpus Christi 1998); **State v. McClendon,** 131 Wash.2d 853, 935 P.2d 1334 (1997); **Baldwin v. Department of Motor Vehicles,** 35 Cal.App.4th 1630 (Cal.App. 1 Dist. 1995); **Schrefler v. State,** 660 N.E.2d 585 (Ind.App. 1996); **Miles v. City of Gulfport,** 735 So.2d 1012 (Miss. 1999).

[675]O.C.G.A. §16-1-7(b).

[676]**State v. Stowe,** 167 Ga. App. 65, 306 S.E.2d 663 (1983).

[677] **Perkins v. State,** 276 Ga. 621, 580 S.E.2d 523 (2003).

[678] **Rowe v. State,** 218 Ga.App. 746, 463 S.E.2d 21 (1995)

14.7.6. Instances where prosecution barred. Your attorney may assert a legal argument in your case that seeks to obtain a ruling from your judge that subsequent prosecution is barred. As noted above, if the subsequent charges against you arose out of the *same transaction* for which you have already been tried, double jeopardy applies, banning the second trial. Other situations might arise, such as your paperwork being drawn up incorrectly by the state, where the prosecutor tries to add charges at an improper time. This can bar a subsequent prosecution if a jury has already been impaneled. As these situations can be legally challenging to your trial court, this is yet another reason to have the best DUI-DWI lawyer possible.

14.7.7. Instances where prosecution not barred. In certain situations, a subsequent prosecution is not barred after your trial has been "terminated" by mistrial. Prosecutors can file what is called a *nolle prosequi* on charges. This is a dismissal. It is usually based upon a decision that to prosecute you at this time is not in the best interest of the government.

In most jurisdictions, so long as the statute of limitations has not expired, the prosecutor can change his or her mind and prosecute you later. If a prior termination of your legal proceedings was proper, or if you are being subsequently charged for a transaction that was not the same as your prior trial, you may be able to be prosecuted.

14.7.8. Direct appeal – when is it available? If your lawyer asserts, at the pretrial hearing, that double jeopardy protections should be applied to your subsequent prosecution (and he or she loses the argument), your lawyer may be able to directly appeal this decision without you having to go through a second trial. The reason for this (where immediate, direct appeal is permitted) is that if the legal issue is decided in your favor, you will walk away from the charges "Scot free."

14.8. Motion to sever — or severance. In criminal trial practice, this is a separating of some part of the overall proceedings by court order, such as separate trials for criminal defendants who were charged with criminal acts that arose from the same incident. Such division of issues in a trial is sometimes also called "bifurcation."

Severance is granted in criminal proceedings when a joint trial might be unfair.[679] In a criminal trial, there may be times when there are two defendants charged with the same crime, and it might be fairer to try them separately rather than together. Believe it or not, when a police officer does not see which person drove the vehicle, he or she may charge both of the people in the vehicle with DUI-DWI. The defense attorneys representing each defendant could then file a motion to sever the trials, which should be granted.

14.9. Plea of autrefois acquittal. "Autrefois" is a French word, now part of English criminal law terminology. It refers to an accused who cannot be tried for a crime because the record shows he has already been subjected to trial for the same conduct and was acquitted. If the accused maintains that the previous trial resulted in conviction, he or she pleads "autrefois convict." "Autrefois attaint" is another similar term; "attainted" for a felony, a person cannot be tried again for the same offense.[680] These types of motions rarely arise in a DUI-DWI practice. Your DUI-DWI specialist will be familiar with how to use these "tools" if the occasion arises in your case.

---

[679]http://dictionary.law.com/default2.asp?selected=1942&bold=sever‖

[680]http://www.law-dictionary.org/AUTREFOIS+ATTAINT,+crim.asp?q=AUTREFOIS+ATTAINT%2C+crim

14.10. Similar transactions. In general, evidence that the defendant has committed a "prior act" that is similar to the one presently charged, is inadmissible. Each defendant is supposed to be tried for the present charges only, and not have his or her character impugned by raising prior conduct. In other words, someone with a long criminal record should not automatically be assumed to have committed another crime.

However, if you or your legal counsel raises some issue of character, what you present can be rebutted by the prosecutor. *Example*: Just because you have 15 prior speeding tickets, that poor driving history cannot normally be presented during the trial phase in a pending speeding case. However, if you take the stand and testify as to just how careful a driver you are, in an attempt to convince the jury you are not prone to drive too fast, the prosecution may introduce evidence of your prior speeding tickets to challenge these claims which were made under oath. You "opened the door" to such impeachment evidence.

Some jurisdictions allow a prosecutor to introduce "prior act" evidence if some *purpose* can be asserted and proven by the prosecutor. For example, if you were alleged to have been the driver of a vehicle involved in a "hit and run" case, and (when the police found your car) you were not at the location of the car, the State may seek to introduce a prior drunk driving conviction to show a consciousness of possible severe consequences if convicted of a repeat offense. If some circumstantial evidence pointed to you as the driver, the trial judge may allow the prosecutor to introduce the prior DUI-DWI as "motive" for not stopping.

14.10.1. Prejudicial impact v. probative value of similar transactions. As with all evidence, the judge performs a balancing act in deciding what is admissible. In the foregoing example about a hit and run case, the judge may not allow the prosecutor to use "similar act" evidence. If evidence is important to the case, it has a prejudicial effect on one of the parties involved, hurting either the State's or the defendant's case. When the State seeks to introduce evidence of "prior acts," the judge balances this harm against how important the information is to prove some "missing" element of the charges you are currently facing. Most states have ruled that unless the defense has "opened the door" for use of prior acts evidence as impeachment, no mention can be made of prior convictions. Georgia stands alone in ignoring traditional constitutional concepts on this point.[681]

14.11. Motion to recuse. This is a request by either the prosecutor or your attorney to have your assigned judge removed and replaced by another judge. This is called a "motion to recuse."

Sometimes the grounds for recusal arise due to a conflict of interest or some other good reason (acquaintanceship with one of the parties, for example).

Recusal also applies to a judge being removed or voluntarily removing himself/herself from a criminal case in which he/she has a conflict of interest, such as friendship or known enmity to the defendant.[682] This is why your attorney may ask you if you personally know any judges, any other lawyers, or have had a bad experience with anyone in the local judiciary before.

14.12. DUI-DWI related affirmative defenses. An affirmative defense is a claim by the defendant that there was either a good reason why he or she committed the criminal act, or that for some reason they were justified in doing the act. If asserted properly, and if accepted by the jury, an affirmative defense constitutes a complete exoneration of the offense

---

[681]**Zaino v. State,** 205 Ga.App. 418, 422 S.E.2d 287 (1992); **Reese v. State,** 252 Ga.App. 650, 556 S.E.2d 150 (2001).

[682]http://dictionary.law.com/default2.asp?typed=recuse&type=1&submit1.x=79&submit1.y=9.

that you have been accused of committing. See **Sections 6.28, 6.29, 6.30, 6.31 and 6.34** for more details on affirmative defenses.

Unlike on Perry Mason where a surprise confession resulted in the defendant being found not guilty, in order for these defenses to be allowed into the argument, your attorney must inform the prosecutor that one of the affirmative defenses will be asserted. If the defendant is going to claim any of these defenses, he or she must notify the prosecutor of this intent a specified number of days before the trial. Once you claim an affirmative defense, the burden shifts to your attorney to put forth some evidence to establish the affirmative defense and then the burden shifts back to the prosecutor to disprove it.

In some jurisdictions, once the defense has properly notified the State of the claimed grounds for an affirmative defense, the State must carry the burden to disprove it.[683] Consult with your DUI-DWI specialist on this issue.

14.13. Obtaining rulings on the record or in writing. In every state, unless you get the judge to make a ruling on the record or in writing, it cannot be appealed. Appellate courts typically only handle errors of law. For you to have an error of law that can be appealed, a legal ruling must be made by the judge in your case. So, your attorney will assert and argue for a ruling that is favorable to you and the prosecutor will oppose this disposition.

For a ruling to be official, it typically has to either be a part of the court reporter's record or be rendered in writing under the judge's signature. "In writing" means the judge produces a signed document memorializing his or her decision. Decisions are placed on the record if the court reporter takes down the decision as a part of the case or hearing transcript. This is yet another reason why you will want a court reporter at any pre-trial hearing or at your trial, even if you have to pay the cost for his or her time to be there.

Assuming any decision in your case goes against you, and this decision makes a significant difference in the evidence in the case, then your only chance to have it appealed (and possibly win your case) is if this decision was either written or a part of the record. Listen to your attorney's advice when he or she counsels you to have a court reporter "take down" every word or ruling that occurs at your legal proceeding.

14.14. Seeking to Block Use of Prior DUI-DWI due to Expungement. The matter of the expunction (expungement) of criminal records of convicted adults is the subject, in most jurisdictions, of specific statutory provisions governing the availability (or lack of availability) of such judicial acts and the procedure for obtaining such relief. Statutory provisions affecting the question must be considered on a state-by-state basis. In some states (e.g., Georgia, South Carolina and Indiana) "expungement" or "expunction" laws are almost unheard of, even when a prosecution against you is dropped or totally dismissed. In others (e.g., California, Texas, New York, Ohio, New Jersey, Pennsylvania and Florida), specific statutory provisions are in place to help clear your state criminal records.[684]

Even in states such as Georgia, that have no meaningful way to clear prior state criminal records, your attorney may counsel you to seek to review any prior uncounseled guilty or nolo contendere pleas for DUI-DWI to see if your constitutional rights were protected in the prior case. If a challenge is available, it will often mean filing a petition for habeas corpus (which is civil in nature, not criminal) in a different court proceeding and seeking to completely

---

[683]**State v. B.H.,** 183 N.J. 171, 870 A.2d 273 (2005); **State v. Strandness,** 684 N.W.2d 516 (Minn.App. 2004).

[684]*Annotation, **Judicial Expunction of Criminal Record of Convicted Adult, 11 A.L.R.4th 956 (1982-2006)***

vacate (remove) the prior conviction from your record. This will require that a separate legal fee and costs related to this proceeding be paid by you.

Chapter 15

The Pros and Cons of Bench Trials

15.0. Purpose of this chapter. What is a "bench" trial? The purpose of this chapter is to understand bench trials. A bench trial is a trial before the judge only, without a jury being present. Instead of the jury deciding the issues of fact (like whether or not you are guilty of driving while intoxicated), it is the judge who makes this decision. This chapter explains the benefits or uses of bench trials that may justify not requesting a jury trial, even when that is an option.

15.1. Who gets to opt for a "bench" trial? Other than in states that have taken away your right to trial by jury, it is always your decision to opt for a bench trial. A few states actually REQUIRE a jury trial unless both the defense and the prosecution "waive" a jury.[685] In states that have jury trials, the prosecution cannot force a bench trial on a defendant who wants a jury trial. It is a fundamental right for a defendant facing any criminal trial, including misdemeanors like DUI-DWI,[686] to have a jury if he or she wants one.[687]

To opt out of a jury trial and have the judge decide guilt, the defendant must expressly, intelligently and personally participate in opting out of the jury trial.[688] If you are in a court that does not have legislative authority to conduct jury trials (an inferior court), and you want a jury, the case must be transferred to a court that permits you to have a trial by jury. This, of course, applies only in states that have not eliminated jury trials for misdemeanor DUI-DWIs. (See **Section 13.5** of this book.)

15.2. Why would your attorney want a non-jury trial? A number of factors go into a decision to have a bench trial rather than try the case before a jury. The first factor goes directly to your attorney's knowledge of the assigned judge's basic sense of fairness. Your experienced DUI-DWI lawyer may personally know of the judge's record, may know the prosecutor, will have tried both bench and jury trials in the court where your trial will be held. Based on this experience, your lawyer may recommend a bench trial. For the author, the true test comes down to this: Can the defendant expect a jury of randomly selected citizens to be any better at deciding this case than this judge?

Other reasons for a bench or a jury trial go to the facts of the case. If strong emotions are involved (someone died in the accident related to your alleged DUI-DWI offense or if people

---

[685]In California and Texas, the prosecutor must agree with having a bench trial. If the prosecutor does not agree, the case must go forward with a jury trial. **People v. Ernst,** 8 Cal.4th 441, 881 P.2d 298 (1994); **State ex rel. Curry v. Carr,** 847 S.W.2d 561 (Tex.Crim.App. 1992).

[686]**Baldwin v. New York,** 399 U.S. 117, 90 S.Ct. 1914, 26 L.Ed.2d 446 (1970); **Byrd v. Stavely,** 113 P.3d 1273 (Colo.App. 2005).

[687]In all criminal prosecutions, the accused shall enjoy the right to a speedy and public trial, by an impartial jury of the State and district wherein the crime shall have been committed... USCA CONST Amend. VI. [N]or shall any State deprive any person of life, liberty, or property, without due process of law; nor deny to any person within its jurisdiction the equal protection of the laws. USCA CONST Amend. XIV.

[688]**McCormick v. State,** 222 Ga. App. 753, 476 S.E.2d 271(1996); **State v. Sonnier,** 461 So.2d 567 (La.App. 3 Cir. 1984); **People v. Redman,** 250 Mich. 334, 230 N.W. 196 (Mich. 1930); **Cleveland v. Fischbach,** 2005 WL 1490118 (Ohio App. 2005); **State v. Liddell,** 672 N.W.2d 805 (Iowa 2003); **People v. Foster,** 107 Cal.Rptr.2d 612 (2001); **State v. Valdobinos,** 122 Wash.2d 270, 858 P.2d 199 (Wash. 1993); **Hanley v. State,** 909 S.W.2d 117 (Tex.App.-Hous. (14 Dist.) 1995).

in the other vehicle suffered significant injuries), or if you have prior DUI-DWI convictions that the jury will learn about at trial, a fair minded judge might be a much better choice than leaving the decision of your guilt or innocence to a jury who may be more easily swayed by your prior driving history rather than the facts and the law. In other situations, an experienced DUI-DWI lawyer may know that the judge scheduled to try your case has a poor "barometer" of guilt or innocence, and is likely to side with the prosecution virtually 100% of the time. All in all, the decision of whether or not to have a jury or a bench trial is why you need the best and most knowledgeable DUI-DWI lawyer you can employ.

15.3. Who is present at a bench trial? Unless otherwise determined by order of the judge, bench trials are just as open to the public as are jury trials. Therefore, there may be an audience. However, most bench trials have no observers other than the lawyers, the witnesses, court personnel, bailiffs and the court reporter.

Otherwise, in a bench trial, you as the defendant and your lawyer will be present. Your lawyer may have a paralegal, an assistant or a secretary with him or her, and these people usually sit just behind your table. You will sit at one of the two tables in the middle of the room, in front of the audience section for the public. The prosecutor will be present and will sit at the other table for legal counsel. Sitting with him or her may be an assistant, an investigator or other people from the prosecutor's office. In some courts, the arresting officer may remain in the court at the prosecutor's table.

The judge will be present, as will a court reporter, both usually sitting at the front of the courtroom. The judge's desk is often elevated, and in the name of security, may be behind a complex platform. Other people from the judge's office, the clerk or a secretary may or may not be present, and they often sit near the judge's bench. The court bailiff (the person who calls witnesses into court from a waiting room or the outer hallway) and a member of the sheriff's department (especially if you are coming to trial from the jail) may also be present in court for security purposes.

Witnesses either for the prosecution or for the defense may be present in the courtroom until just before the trial starts. Either the prosecutor or your lawyer may invoke the "Rule of Sequestration." If invoked, all witnesses who are going to testify must physically leave the courtroom and wait outside. This is done so that their own testimony is not patterned after or "improved" by hearing any other witnesses' testimony. As each witness is called, the bailiff goes to the waiting area and retrieves that witness.

15.4. How long does a bench trial take? A bench trial is almost always shorter in duration than a jury trial. The same witnesses testify, and often the same evidence is admitted to the court. However, because a bench trial is usually two lawyers (the prosecutor and your defense attorney) presenting evidence and testimony to another lawyer (the judge), the flow of information is often quicker and more efficient. This may also be true in the questioning of witnesses and in the presentation of physical evidence.

In addition, because there is no jury, their selection process is eliminated, cutting out several hours in a typical DUI-DWI trial. In a bench trial, no jurors are questioned or sworn in, nor does the judge need to read the jury instructions at the end of the trial, then wait around for a jury to make a decision. This saves many, many hours.

Last, in a bench trial, depending on the circumstances, the opening statement and closing argument of each side may be abbreviated for the judge or totally waived by one or both attorneys. Because the judge knows the fine legal points relating to DUI-DWI law, no lengthy explanations are needed by the attorneys. A jury trial for a DUI-DWI which might take several days is often compressed into a time frame of two to eight hours for a bench trial for the same legal issue.

15.5. What is lost by opting for a bench trial? Certain types of cases such as breath test per se alcohol cases usually are best heard by a jury. In other types of cases, such as a case with a sympathetic defendant, a skilled lawyer can sway a jury better than they might be able to sway a judge. At other times the opposite may be true. In making its decision, a jury can vote "guilty" or "not guilty" on the charges based on a multitude of issues regardless of how the judge words the "instructions" on the law that they must apply to the case. A criminal defense lawyer with strong persuasive skills can often sway a jury to vote "not guilty."

One place that you may lose an edge if you opt for a bench trial is if a potential appeal is needed. Appellate courts are more likely to uphold the judge's determination of guilt absent some blatant error in the judge's rulings on admissibility of evidence.[689]

15.6. What may be gained by choosing a bench trial? Because bench trials are often shorter in duration than are jury trials, they are cheaper if you are paying your lawyer by the hour. Some "flat fee" attorneys also charge less for bench trials in their fee agreements. As noted above, it is often quicker to get a bench trial than to wait for an opening for a jury trial. As mentioned before, some state legislatures have set up the court system to provide for entry-level courts to be non-jury, with an option to move the case to a jury trial court later. In such entry-level courts, your request for a jury trial necessitates a transfer to a court that can empanel a jury to hear your case.

A bench trial is a better option if the key to winning your trial rests upon a "legal" issue being decided in your favor. For example, if all pre-trial issues (that would typically be heard by the judge before a jury is ever impaneled) are heard as part of a bench trial, then a favorable ruling on the mid-trial motion to suppress for an illegal stop will win the entire case, and the prosecutor cannot appeal the judge's decision.

15.7. Who testifies at a bench trial? Typically, the testimony (and who provides it) will be the same at a jury trial and at a bench trial. At times, your attorney may add or delete a witness when a judge hears the case without a jury, but this is the exception rather than the rule.

In a DUI-DWI trial, the question of who will testify for your side can vary from no witnesses at all to calling several witnesses. In their case-in-chief, the prosecution will put up the officer who first decided that your vehicle needed to be stopped, or the witness who first saw you driving in such a way that he or she was suspicious that you were driving under the influence. If another officer administered your field sobriety tests, this officer will testify. If a different officer or chemist did your breath, urine or blood tests, this person will also testify.

In a breath test case, the prosecution may need to have a witness testify concerning the machine's periodic calibration reports, to show that the machine was properly checked for calibration and was in good working order. If you underwent a blood or urine test, the person who drew your blood or watched you urinate as well as the person who actually did the laboratory test may testify. The prosecution may also have other fact witnesses testify if this information may help prove their case against you (such as to confirm that you drove your vehicle into the rear of the witness' pickup truck while the driver was sitting at a red light).

Once the prosecution has rested (finished putting up the evidence and testimony they think is required to convict you of DUI-DWI), your attorney and you will decide whether or not

---

[689]**Kitchens v. State,** 258 Ga.App. 411, 574 S.E.2d 451 (2002).

you should put up evidence. In some cases, you may testify. It is highly likely the two of you will have discussed this alternative extensively before trial, but the final decision is sometimes made in the midst of your trial. Unlike the rules for civil cases, in a criminal trial you cannot be forced to testify.[690] As will be discussed below, the prosecution has the burden of proving you guilty. Therefore, you have no burden of proof and you can remain silent.

Your attorney may also have experts who testify to refute or dispute some or all of what the prosecution's witnesses said on the witness stand. Also, your attorney may have other "fact witnesses" testify as to other issues that might be legally relevant to your arrest. For example, a person who was with you all evening may testify that you drank only two beers over a three hour period, and that you acted totally sober in every way. The order of all of these defense witnesses, including your testimony, if it is offered, will depend on how your attorney and you determine your side of the story is most effectively presented.

After your side (the defense) rests, the prosecution has the option of putting on rebuttal witnesses to testify. These can be some of the same witnesses as they put before the court during their case-in-chief, or they can be new witnesses. This testimony is supposed to refute or dispute anything your defense witnesses said or other documentary evidence your side introduced.

After any rebuttal evidence by the State, you and your lawyer get a chance to rebut anything the prosecution's rebuttal witnesses said, or any new evidence they put before the court. This stage of the case is called "surrebuttal." These may be some of the same witnesses you used during your defense, or they can be new witnesses.

15.8. What is the procedure for conducting a bench trial? The procedure for a bench trial starts with everyone gathering in a courtroom. You and your defense team gather around one table, while the prosecution and their team gathers around another. Once the parties and their attorneys are in court, the judge will enter and take his or her seat at the bench. The bailiff usually announces that the judge is entering the courtroom. When the judge enters the courtroom, it is expected that everyone stand until you are told to take your seat.

Next, the judge and the lawyers present may exchange some banter. Remember, they are all lawyers, and often, they have worked in the same courtroom for years. Instead of becoming annoyed at being left out of the verbal exchange, understand that the more the judge engages in chatter with your lawyer, often the better the two of them know each other. This may be a very positive development toward obtaining a favorable outcome.

The judge will then more formally ask each side if they are ready to proceed. The prosecutor, then your lawyer will answer. If either says no, your trial may be halted. This might mean your charges may be dropped, especially if key witnesses for the prosecution are not present. The judge may grant the prosecutor more time to gather their evidence or a missing witness.

A "yes" answer to the question of whether a party is "ready" can be a critical place at trial. This step in the process is more than a polite gesture or formality. A "yes" answer by either attorney can foreclose (prevent) certain legal issues from being raised later if a legal challenge is made.

If both say "yes," then the prosecutor has the option (but not the obligation) of making the first opening statement. The opening statement is supposed to be an outline of their side of

---

[690]No person ... shall be compelled in any criminal case to be a witness against himself... U.S.C.A. Const. Amend. V.

the case for the judge, laying out the facts the prosecution expects to prove and the evidence they expect to present, without any argument as to your guilt.[691] It is not unusual for the prosecutor to skip this step in a bench trial. Unlike a jury, the judge already knows what the State has to prove.

When the prosecution has completed its opening statement, or if they waive their right to make an opening statement, your lawyer gets his or her chance to do the same thing. He or she may opt to follow the prosecutor's opening immediately and outline the facts he or she expects to prove in your defense. Your attorney may also "reserve" his or her opening statement until the prosecutor "rests," once all of the prosecution evidence is closed. Again, your lawyer is not supposed to argue the case during his or her opening statement. He or she should just set forth the facts the defense expects the evidence to show.

Either side may use visual aids such as a chalkboard or a PowerPoint presentation, as long as they are presenting only the facts they will produce at trial. Such presentations are more common in jury trials than in bench trials. Remember, the judge has likely presided over countless trials and might be annoyed at a long-winded or flashy opening.

At the direction of the judge, the prosecution then calls its first witness. The manner of presenting this testimony is laid out above. In their case-in-chief, the prosecution needs to call witnesses to prove every element of every criminal offense you are facing. This is called their "direct examination" of its witnesses.

Your lawyer will keep track of all this, including everything being said, taking notes. He or she cannot listen to you at the same time. Anything you need to "say" needs to be written down on a pad and placed where your attorney can read your note. Distracting your attorney by tapping on his shoulder and trying to speak to your legal counsel can cost you the case. Write any notes and never try to whisper or talk to your lawyer.

Your lawyer gets to question every witness the prosecution puts on the stand and questions. This is called a "cross examination." After the cross examination of a witness, the prosecution may ask the witness a few follow-up questions that relate to the issues raised by the cross-examination. This is called "re-direct" of the witness. Last, your lawyer has the option of asking this same witness a few final questions, called "re-cross examination."

Because your attorney must be totally focused on these prosecution witnesses, your lawyer will likely advise you not to interrupt him or her when any witness is speaking, no matter how important you think it is. Your lawyer may well have given you a legal pad of your own and a pen for exactly this situation. Write down your concerns, and wait for your attorney to see your notes. At the next break, a discussion can occur, but not while testimony is in progress.

After the prosecution has put forward its case-in-chief, presented all their witnesses and any physical evidence, they "rest." *Resting* means they can no longer put in any further evidence against you, unless your side puts on a defense and the prosecution wants to rebut something one of your witnesses said.

The point in your trial when the prosecution "rests" is an important stage of the case. Once the prosecution rests, if it has not proven every element of each crime of which you are charged, your lawyer may ask the judge to eliminate those unproven charges based on a lack of evidence. This happens when the prosecution forgets to ask the right questions or could not get certain evidence admitted.

---

[691]**Prosecutor's Reference in Opening Statement to Matters Not Provable or Which He Does Not Attempt to Prove as Ground for Relief,** 16 A.L.R.4th 810 (1982-2005); **Franks v. State,** 188 Ga. App. 263, 372 S.E.2d 831 (1988); **U.S. v. Freeman,** 514 F.2d 1184 (10th Cir. 1975).

Two quick examples of such oversight will help explain this. In a DUI-DWI-alcohol *per se* case, the State may need to prove that the breath test was taken within so many hours (usually within 2 or 3 hours) after the driving ended. If overlooked, the *per se* DUI-DWI-alcohol charge should be dismissed or eliminated. Similarly, the prosecutor may fail to prove in an accident case that the alcohol was consumed before the driving ended. The time to raise such omissions in the evidence is at the close of the State's evidence.

If the charges are not eliminated, it is now the defense's turn to put on your witnesses, if any. As noted above, no requirement exists for you to put on any defense or to put up any witnesses. If you and your lawyer do put up any witnesses, the same process of examination, cross examination, re-direct, re-cross examination goes on, with your lawyer switching questioning positions with the prosecution. Again, do not interrupt your lawyer in his or her observation of the prosecution's examination of your witnesses. Write down your concerns and he or she will get them at a break.

Once your attorney has put up (on the witness stand) everyone they want to testify, the defense will rest. As mentioned above, the prosecution then has the option of putting on rebuttal witnesses, and the defense the chance for surrebuttal witnesses, each being examined, cross-examined, rebutted and surrebutted by both sides.

When all the testimony has been offered, both sides get a final chance to talk to the judge in closing arguments. As they have the burden of proof, the prosecution has the option of speaking first. In certain situations the prosecution will simply summarize what they already presented and not say anything further.

It is your constitutional right to have your attorney deliver a closing argument.[692] The purpose of this closing argument is for your attorney to take the facts that have been presented by either side, refer to any controlling legal precedent, and put forward to the judge the best possible reasons why you are **NOT GUILTY** of the charges. This is one of the few chances your lawyer will have to utilize his or her persuasive skills. Do not expect the same impassioned oration from your attorney when he or she is speaking to the judge as might be used at a jury trial.

Last, the judge makes a decision as to your guilt. Unlike with a jury, often this is done right away, or after a very short break. With drunken driving cases, like with most other misdemeanors, if you are found guilty, the judge then sentences you to your punishment at the same proceeding. This is further discussed in Chapter 17. If you are found not guilty, your trial is over, your bond is released and you are "discharged" from responsibility for this crime.

15.9. Is a motion for new trial possible after a bench trial? A motion for a new trial is based on a guilty verdict that is contrary to the evidence, or the principles of justice and equity are strongly and decidedly against the weight of the evidence.[693] It is more common for a motion for a new trial to be sought by the defense in a jury trial. In some cases, a motion for a new trial will be granted by a judge who finds that the decision of the jury goes so strongly against the evidence that it would be unfair to not grant a new trial.

Because it is the judge in a bench trial who makes the decision of guilt based on the evidence presented at trial, it is unlikely to believe that the same judge would change his or her mind. It may happen more often if new evidence is discovered that was unavailable or unreachable prior to the trial. Another possible avenue for your attorney to pursue is to try to convince the trial judge that some important or critical evidentiary ruling that he or she made

---

[692]**Herring v. New York,** 422 U.S. 853, 95 S.Ct. 2550, 45 L.Ed.2d 593 (1975).
[693]O.C.G.A. §§ 5-5-20 and 5-5-21.

was clearly wrong and would likely be reversed if appealed to a higher court. One additional reason for requesting a motion for a new trial after a non-jury finding of guilt could be that your attorney (or a new attorney handling this motion) may raise the issue of your trial attorney's ineffective assistance of counsel during the original trial.

15.10. Is appeal possible after a bench trial? In many jurisdictions, such issues must be first raised by motion for a new trial. Many more opportunities for appeal exist in a jury trial than in a bench trial. For a conviction in a bench trial to be reversed, the trial judge has to have made an error admitting evidence at trial that should not have been admitted. Of course, if you win the trial, the State cannot appeal.

15.11. If you appeal after a bench trial, is punishment deferred? It is possible to apply for a supersedeas bond following a bench trial. [694] When you request a court for this type of order, you are asking that your punishment be "held off" until your appeal has been considered and ruled upon by the appellate court. Most states have such procedures in misdemeanor cases, either as a matter of right or as a discretionary matter, with any "abuse of discretion" by the trial judge being subject to an immediate appeal. In unusual situations, your attorney may need to ask for involvement by an appeals court.[695]

Such a bond is typically a matter of right if the trial was in an inferior court where no jury trial was available, such as a municipal court.[696] The same principle should apply in your state if your state legislation permits (or authorizes) supersedeas bonds in misdemeanor DUI-DWI cases. Be aware that felony convictions will not have the same "automatic" avenue of appeal while holding off the punishment until your appeal is completed.

15.12. Would the accused be more likely to testify at a bench trial? No rule of thumb applies here. In some cases, you may need to testify to explain some factual issue. Your attorney may have decided on a bench trial because some inflammatory issue may be exposed by the evidence. For example, if you made a racial comment to the officer in a moment of anger or rage over your arrest. Jurors may convict you based on your bad behavior while most judges would not let such matters unduly sway them.

15.13. Is there a cost savings by opting for a bench trial? As discussed above, if you have a bench rather than a jury trial, the agreement with your attorney may provide for a lesser fee. However, top DUI-DWI trial lawyers may limit their cases to a fixed number of clients, and ALL cases are handled for a fixed fee. No experienced and dedicated trial lawyer will opt for a bench trial unless he or she is convinced that the bench trial offers a better chance for victory.

15.14. Burden of proof. The "burden of proof" in a bench trial is the same as in a jury trial. "Burden of proof" refers to who has the requirement to prove something. As to criminal charges, the burden of proof is on the prosecution to prove that you are guilty beyond a reasonable doubt. The burden never "shifts" to you to prove your innocence.

15.14.1. Affirmative defenses–the burden to disprove may be on the state. Once a defendant has claimed an affirmative defense (like justification or entrapment), in some

---

[694]http://dictionary.law.com/default2.asp?typed=supersedeas&type=1&submit1.x=81&submit1.y=16.

[695]**Velek v. State (City of Little Rock),** --- S.W.3d ----, 2006 WL 62069 (Ark. 2006); **Knapp v. State,** 223 Ga.App. 267, 477 S.E.2d 621 (1996).

[696]O.C.G.A. §5-4-20.

jurisdictions the burden to prove that this defense lacks a basis is on the prosecution.[697]   In other states, the party asserting the affirmative defense must "come forward" with his or her proof. Then, the prosecutor can seek to disprove the defense.

15.14.2. State's burden to get chemical test results admitted, then the burden shifts to defendant to rebut or explain why an error exists. For any chemical test that was used to determine your blood alcohol level (either blood or breath) or that you had drugs in your system (blood or urine), the prosecutor is first required to prove that the tests were performed in a valid and proper manner.[698]   However, once the prosecutor has met this burden, it is then up to your attorney to prove (to put forth evidence) that these results should not be accepted as being reliable by the judge. In the alternative, your attorney may have a way to argue that the results are totally inadmissible.

15.14.3. Presumptions and inferences. The biggest and most important presumption in any trial is that you are innocent until proven guilty.[699]   This is different than on an appeal of a guilty verdict, where the verdict is presumed to be correct.[700]   Once a breath or blood test result is admitted, a presumption (inference) arises that the law enforcement officer did his or her duty in administering the test and that these duties were performed correctly, until the contrary is shown.[701]   Without doubt, once the State's breath or blood test result is admitted into evidence, your attorney will need some proof (usually by way of an expert witness) that the test result is not reliable or accurate.

15.14.4. Who gets to benefit from inferences? Every state can pass statutes allowing evidentiary "inferences" (presumptions) regarding what any breath or blood test "numbers" mean. In most states, an inference of non-impairment will arise if your test results are at 0.05 grams or below. Most state statutes that deal with these "low" numbers state that "it shall be inferred" (or "it shall be presumed") that the driver was not impaired. In considering the "common law" form of DUI-DWI, this inference of non-impairment applies to both drivers age 21 and older, as well as drivers under age 21. However, drivers under age 21 will face an uphill battle on the underage per se case where a limit of 0.00, 0.01 or 0.02 applies.

---

[697]**State v. Moore,** 237 Ga. 269, 227 S.E.2d 241 (1976); **Hill v. State,** 261 Ga. 377, 406 S.E.2d 470 (1993); **State v. B.H.,** 183 N.J. 171, 870 A.2d 273 (2005); **State v. Strandness,** 684 N.W.2d 516 (Minn.App. 2004).

[698]**State v. Ensey,** 881 A.2d 81 (R.I. 2005); **People v. Mojica-Simental,** 73 P.3d 15 (Colo. 2003); **Department of Highway Safety and Motor Vehicles v. Alliston,** 813 So.2d 141 (Fla.App. 2 Dist. 2002); **People v. Massie,** 305 Ill.App.3d 550, 713 N.E.2d 110 (1999).

[699]Georgia - O.C.G.A. §16-1-5; Arizona - A.R.S. § 13-115; California - West's Ann.Cal.Penal Code § 1096; Colorado - C.R.S.A. § 18-1-402; D.C. Code, 2001 Ed. Article I. Bill of Rights; Idaho - I.C. § 19-2104; Illinois - 720 ILCS 5/3-1; Louisiana - LSA-C.Cr.P. Art. 804; Michigan - MCR 6.610; Minnesota - M.S.A. § 611.02; Nevada - N.R.S. 175.191; Ohio - R.C. § 2901.05; Puerto Rico - T. 34 Ap. II, R. 110; Tennessee - T. C. A. § 39-11-201; Vernon's Ann.Texas C.C.P. Art. 38.03; Utah - U.C.A. 1953 § 76-1-501; Washington - West's RCWA 10.58.020.

[700]**Trammell v. State,** 196 Ga. App. 540, 396 S.E.2d 286 (1990); **State v. Smith,** 122 P.3d 615 (Utah 2005); **Moody v. Com.,** 170 S.W.3d 393 (Ky. 2005); **State v. Lioen,** 106 Hawai'i 123, 102 P.3d 367 (Hawai'i App. 2004); **State v. York,** 318 Mont. 511, 81 P.3d 1277 (2003).

[701]**Sapp v. State,** 184 Ga. App. 527, 362 S.E.2d 406 (1987); Oregon - O.R.S. § 40.135; **State v. Fisher,** 180 N.J. 462, 852 A.2d 1074 (2004); **People v. Martinez,** 22 Cal.4th 106, 990 P.2d 563 (2000); **People ex rel. Raster v. Healy,** 230 Ill. 280, 82 N.E. 599 (1907); **Lamoreaux v. Ellis,** 89 Mich. 146, 50 N.W. 812 (1891).

Similarly, many states have inferences that give the prosecutors an edge when the "number" is 0.08 grams or more. The state law may provide that an inference of impairment would then exist, but that this is subject to being rebutted by the defendant.

These statutory inferences were originally created more than three decades ago to help prosecutors get convictions, because jurors during those years were quick to render "not guilty" verdicts. In truth, a 0.08 BAC level is not supported by medical proof that all individuals are too impaired to drive at such levels. That number was decided upon as a result of many factors, including a changing political climate and an evolving public awareness of the risk of impaired drivers being involved in accidents. (See **Sections 1.1.1 and 1.1.4** of this book for more details of this history.

15.14.5. No presumptions for DUI-DWI drugs. Almost none of the states have statutory presumptions of a driver being under the influence of drugs if your blood or urine tests reveal a certain number (nanograms per milliliter or cubic centimeter) of a particular chemical or drug.[702] Such a law setting forth presumptions on several categories of drugs does exist in Virginia[703] and Nevada,[704] with Ohio and Georgia possibly soon to follow. However, the refusal to take a blood test may be considered evidence creating an inference that the test would have shown the presence of a prohibited substance.[705] Do not confuse these rules relating to "inferences" of impairment by drugs with statutes prohibiting driving with **ANY** amount of a contraband substance in your system (the so-called *per se* drug laws).

---

[702]**Perano v. State**, 167 Ga. App. 560, 307 S.E.2d 64 (1983) [reversed on other grounds, 250 Ga. 704, 300 S.E.2d 668 (1983); **Bennett v. State,** 801 N.E.2d 170 (Ind.App. 2003); **People v. Garofalo,** 181 Ill.App.3d 972, 537 N.E.2d 1166 (1989).

[703]Va. Code Ann. § 18.2-269(A)(4) - cocaine, methamphetamine, 3,4- methylenedioxymethamphetamine and PCP.

[704]NRS 484.379(3).

[705]O.C.G.A. §40-6-392(c).

Chapter 16

Jury Trials: How and When a Jury Trial May be Your Best Option.

16.0. Purpose of this chapter. The purpose of this chapter is to help you understand a jury trial, and how it differs from a bench trial. This chapter will also discuss how trials in the criminal part of your DUI-DWI case differ from your administrative license suspension or revocation hearing that relates to the implied consent advisements and whether you refused or took the state's test that indicated a *per se* violation.

Also discussed in this chapter are examples of when it might be better or worse for your case if you decide to have a jury trial. In most jurisdictions, you can opt for a trial by jury if you want your case to be decided by a jury. In some jurisdictions (i.e., California), the prosecutor also can opt to have a trial by jury even if you want a bench trial.

16.1. When is a jury trial available in your jurisdiction? In almost all states, it is your fundamental right if facing any criminal trial, including misdemeanors like DUI-DWI that carry punishments of up to a year in jail,[706] to have a jury if you want one.[707] To opt out of a jury trial and have the judge decide guilt, you must expressly, intelligently and personally participate in opting out of the jury trial.[708]

Even in the states that afford you the right to opt for a jury trial, not every court has the ability to offer a jury trial. If your case is originally booked in an inferior (entry level) court that does not allow juries (like a traffic court, justice court or a municipal court), and you want a jury, the trial can be transferred to a court that gives you that option (like a circuit or superior court). The names of these courts differ from state to state, and your experienced trial lawyer will know which court is the appropriate court for such transfers.

In some states, the court system is set up to always allow your case an "initial" trial at a non-jury court, with a full right to get a NEW trial at court with a jury trial authority. Mississippi, Arkansas and Alabama are three states with this system. In these states, the SECOND trial (with a jury) will start from scratch, which is called a "de novo" trial.

16.2. When a jury trial is the only option to try to achieve victory. Based on your attorney's knowledge of your case, his or her knowledge of the different courts, prosecutors and judges, and his or her experience with the juries in the jurisdiction in which your DUI-DWI trial will be held, good reasons may exist why a jury trial is your only realistic chance to win your case. Certain types of cases are usually not good candidates for a bench trial. For example, if your case involves a breath test result exceeding the per se limit

---

[706]**Baldwin v. New York,** 399 U.S. 117, 90 S.Ct. 1914, 26 L.Ed.2d 446 (1970).

[707]In all criminal prosecutions, the accused shall enjoy the right to a speedy and public trial, by an impartial jury of the State and district wherein the crime shall have been committed... U.S.C.A. CONST Amend. VI. [N]or shall any State deprive any person of life, liberty, or property, without due process of law; nor deny to any person within its jurisdiction the equal protection of the laws. U.S.C.A. CONST Amend. XIV.

[708]**State v. Vasquez,** 109 Wash.App. 310, 34 P.3d 1255 (2001); **State v. Sonnier,** 461 So.2d 567 (La.App. 3 Cir. 1984); **McCormick v. State,** 222 Ga. App. 753, 476 S.E.2d 271(1996); **Havard v. State,** 925 S.W.2d 290 (Tex.App.-Corpus Christi 1996); **People v. Milbratz,** 323 Ill.App.3d 206, 751 N.E.2d 650 (2001); **State v. Wheeler,** 114 Idaho 97, 753 P.2d 833 (Idaho App. 1988).

and your defense is that your high protein diet may have caused a false, elevated reading, few judges would be likely to give the same credence to your expert as the average juror would. Winning these type cases is very possible at a jury trial. To obtain more information about this defense, see www.theduibook.com/highproteindiet.html.

16.3. Jury trials take longer and typically cost more. As will be discussed below, jury trials involve numerous steps, processes and procedures that are not present in a bench trial. These "steps" include the judge providing some orientation instructions and oaths to jurors, and include selecting the jury (something that can take up to half a day in some DUI-DWI trials). In presenting the case to the jury, the lawyers will almost always take longer to explain things to a jury than they would to the judge. The opening statements and closing arguments are longer and more detailed. A conference between the judge and the attorneys is needed to review all jury instructions that the trial judge will be giving the jurors, plus the actual reading of these instructions can take 30 minutes or more. In addition, the time it takes a jury to deliberate (decide guilt or innocence) can often run from two hours to more than a day.

If you are paying your attorney by the hour, this extra time can add up to significant dollars out of your pocket. Also, in order to explain things to a jury, your lawyer may need to use different expert witnesses, or possibly more than one expert witness, to help bring the jurors "up to speed" about your legal defense. These different or extra experts cost money out of your pocket. Also, if the jury trial is taking a day or more longer than a bench trial, this is time you are in court and not at work yourself making money.

16.4. Jurors decide the case --- not the judge. In a bench trial, the judge decides everything. In a jury trial, the judge still decides issues of law such as whether the breath test is excluded at a pre-trial motion, procedural questions like whether or not a witness should really be considered an expert, or whether or not an objection should be rejected, overruled or sustained (upheld). The jury, on the other hand, makes the decisions as to questions of fact such as who is telling the truth, or whether the evidence in the case justifies a verdict of guilty or not guilty.

16.5. Who will not be allowed to be a juror? The United States Constitution does not forbid states from establishing relevant qualifications for jurors. Therefore, states remain free to restrict jury service to persons holding citizenship in the United States, and limit the jury "pool" to persons meeting specified qualifications of age and educational attainment, and to those possessing great intelligence, sound judgment, and fair character.[709] Under federal law, jurors must be able to speak the English language[710] and to read, write, and understand English with sufficient proficiency to satisfactorily complete the juror qualification form.[711]

---

[709]**Carter v. Jury Commission of Greene County,** 396 U.S. 320, 90 S.Ct. 518, 24 L.Ed.2d 549 (1970). In states that have reduced the maximum jail punishment to six months or less on DUI-DWI offenses, federal law does NOT mandate a jury trial. Such offenses are considered "petty" by the courts. **Blanton v. City of North Las Vegas,** 489 U.S. 538, 109 S.Ct. 1289, 103 L.Ed.2d 550 (U.S.Nev. 1989).

[710]28 USCA §1865(b)(3).

[711]28 USCA §1865(b)(2).

A common requirement or qualification in most states is that a juror be a qualified elector or voter of the county or district in which the trial will be held.[712] If this is the case, because people who have been convicted of a felony in the past may not have regained the right to vote, they may be eliminated from serving on a jury. Most jurisdictions have "jury commissioners" who oversee the county's jury pool, and they search various public databases (such as motor vehicle records or registered voter records) to locate and summon for jury service all eligible and "qualified" residents.

16.6. "Striking" a jury: eliminating the bad jurors. At the start of your jury trial, both the prosecutor and your attorney get a chance to eliminate jurors from a larger pool based on several factors, to form the actual 6 to 12 person jury that will serve for your trial. This concept of "elimination" rather than "picking" jurors may surprise you, since some people think that each lawyer gets to ADD selective jurors to the ultimate panel. Prospective jurors can be eliminated from the jury by the judge or the attorneys either "for cause" or based on a "peremptory challenge." These concepts are explained below.

16.6.1. For cause — unlimited. A challenge **"for cause"** is a request that a prospective juror be dismissed due to a specific and important reason that the person (based upon answers given to questions) cannot be fair, unbiased or capable of serving impartially as a juror. "Cause" may include close acquaintanceship with the parties (you or the prosecutor's staff), one of the attorneys or a witness.

"Cause" may be derived from state statutes that require that certain categories of "employment" will disqualify a prospective juror in a criminal case (i.e., a person who is an active law enforcement officer or the spouse of such an officer). A potential juror's expression of an inability to be unbiased and impartial due to a prior negative experience in a similar case can lead to his or her removal. A potential juror's answers showing an obvious prejudice or an inability to serve due to any mental condition, inability to hear well or a language barrier can lead to exclusion. The judge determines if the person shall be dismissed,[713] but the judge can abuse this discretion, which can cause a reversal of a conviction (if you are convicted).[714]

The judge's discretion is not without limits to his or her rulings, however, and a judge can create reversible error if he or she refuses to remove a juror for cause when statutory grounds based on constitutional fairness (due process) dictate that the juror should have been removed. Some states' decisional law (from appellate cases) are more favorable to the accused than the law in other states. An *unlimited* number of challenges for cause can be raised, disallowing anyone who falls into one of the above categories from serving on your jury.

16.6.2. Peremptory — both sides limited. A peremptory challenge is the right of the prosecutor and the defendant in a jury trial to have a juror dismissed before trial without stating a reason. Experienced trial attorneys develop a sort of "sixth sense" for knowing when a juror is "against" his or her client's case. The decision to remove a juror may come down to a lack of eye contact, negative body language or a reluctance to answer questions fully or "believably."

---

[712]**People ex rel. Murray v. Holmes,** 341 Ill. 23, 173 N.E. 145 (1930); **Sturrock v. State,** 229 Ind. 161, 96 N.E.2d 226 (1951); **State v. County Bd. of Renville County,** 171 Minn. 177, 213 N.W. 545 (1927); **State v. Rasor,** 168 S.C. 221, 167 S.E. 396 (1933).

[713]http://dictionary.law.com/default2.asp?typed=challenge+for+cause&type=1

[714]**Kim v. Walls,** 275 Ga. 177, 563 S.E.2d 874 (2002).

The number of peremptory challenges for each side is controlled by state law, the number of parties on trial in a case (usually only one defendant in a DUI-DWI trial), and in some states, whether it is a misdemeanor or felony. The selection process may be by the use of "silent" strikes, where the list of qualified jurors is passed back and forth between the attorneys, with the prosecutor striking first, then your attorney, and then alternating "strikes." Another method is for the attorneys to either "accept" or "excuse" each juror, starting with number 1 and progressing until a jury of either 6 or 12 is selected (as required by state law).

Peremptory challenges must be based on some other reason than race[715] or gender.[716] Either side can challenge any pattern of eliminating jurors based on race or gender alone, without having a legitimate, identifiable "dislike" about the juror's background or answers during the jury selection questioning session.

16.7. Is jury questioning ("*voir dire*") available? **Voir dire** (vwahr [with a near-silent "r"] deer), loosely translated from French, means "to speak the truth." It is the questioning of prospective jurors by a judge and (in most states) your attorney and the prosecutor. After all questioning and strikes for cause, the two attorneys will begin the final selection of the actual jury.

The voir dire process is available any time a jury is involved in a jury trial.[717] Voir dire is used to determine if a juror is biased and/or cannot deal fairly with the issues involved in a particular kind of case. Without doubt, involving both of the attorneys in the process will result in a much more intelligent selection process. However, not all states allow the attorneys to ask any questions. Ask your DUI-DWI specialist about your state's process.

As mentioned before, each attorney's job is to not allow a juror to serve if he or she has knowledge of the facts, acquaintanceship with parties, witnesses or attorneys, or engages in an occupation that might lead to bias. Furthermore, any juror who has had previous experiences that have left him or her with an indelible "impression" that would cause that juror to favor or disfavor one side can be "struck" from the jury panel for cause.

Actually, one of the unspoken purposes of the voir dire is for the attorneys to get a feel for the personalities and likely personal views of the people on the jury panel. When the attorneys are permitted to actively participate and question the jurors, your chances of acquittal are usually improved, assuming that your attorney's skill at this point of the case is honed.

In some courts the judge asks most, if not all of the questions. In others, the lawyers are given substantial latitude and ample time to ask questions.[718]

Following voir dire, the judge and the attorneys will have a brief conference. Then, after all eliminations for "cause" are established, the remaining panel is "struck." The final jury is the "remainder" after the lawyers utilize their limited number of "strikes" for peremptory challenges.

---

[715]**Batson v. Kentucky,** 476 U.S. 79, 106 S.Ct. 1712, 90 L.Ed.2d 69 (1986); **Johnson v. California,** 125 S.Ct. 2410 (2005).

[716]**J.E.B. v. Alabama ex rel. T.B.,** 511 U.S. 127, 114 S.Ct. 1419, 128 L.Ed.2d 89 (1994).

[717]Alabama - Ala.Code 1975 § 12-16-100; Georgia - O.C.G.A. §15-12-133; California -West's Ann.Cal.C.C.P. § 223; New Mexico - NMRA, Crim. UJI 14-120; Montana - Mont. Co. C.P. R. Rule 1.23; Virginia - Sup.Ct.Rules, Rule 1:21.

[718]http://dictionary.law.com/default2.asp?typed=voir+dire&type=1&submit1.x=25&submit1.y=7

16.8. Background information on jurors: can your attorney get it? Unlike what you may see in the movies or on television, in a jury trial for misdemeanors like DUI-DWI, neither the prosecutor nor the defense attorney typically gets an advance list of potential jurors or more than a few details about the prospective juror's background information. Usually, the list of jurors arrives minutes before (or at the same time as) the selection begins.

As jurors report for jury duty, before they are ever assigned to any trial, they are typically asked to fill out an information sheet, giving such information as their name, age, occupation, marital status, any prior personal litigation experience with the courts (criminal or civil) and possibly if they have prior experience of serving on a jury. The attorneys may each get a brief summary of this information just before the pool of prospective jurors comes into the courtroom. In some instances, the prosecutor may have access to the list before defense counsel gets it, but equal access should exist to both sides.

16.9. How a jury trial can improve your chances on appeal. In almost every DUI-DWI case, opportunities for appellate error will occur more often in jury trials than in bench trials. Because a trial judge is typically required to answer dozens of questions of law and make many pre-trial and mid-trial rulings, a good trial attorney (by raising numerous issues during trial) can create many more opportunities for appeal in a jury trial rather than in a bench trial.[719]

16.10. What if jurors don't tell the truth at *voir dire*? If a prospective juror makes a misstatement during voir dire with no deliberate attempt to mislead, this will not usually authorize a new trial if you are convicted in the first trial.[720] If such an issue is discovered, your attorney may file a motion for a new trial alleging that a juror was not truthful during voir dire. The motion will cause an inquiry into the "good faith" (or lack of good faith) in the misstatement, and the judge will decide the significance of the situation.

16.11. Mistrial can be raised by either attorney or at the judge's initiative. A **mistrial** is the termination of your trial before its normal conclusion due to a procedural error, improper statements by a witness, judge or attorney which prejudice your jury, or an act of misconduct by a juror such as conducting his or her own investigation of some aspect of your case. A mistrial can also occur when there is a deadlock by a jury without reaching a verdict after lengthy deliberation (a "hung" jury).

When situations like this arise, the judge, either on his or her own initiative or upon the motion (request) of one of the parties can "declare a mistrial." If granted, this causes dismissal of the jury. Unless the mistrial was caused by the prosecutor's intentional or inexcusable error, the criminal prosecution will be set for trial again, starting from the beginning.[721]

---

[719]**People v. Gay,** 149 Mich.App. 468, 386 N.W.2d 556 (1986); **Washington v. State,** 2005 WL 435119 (Ala.Crim.App. 2005); **State v. Stierhoff,** 879 A.2d 425 (R.I. 2005); **State v. Muro,** 269 Neb. 703, 695 N.W.2d 425 (2005); **State v. Adams,** 163 S.W.3d 35 (Mo.App. 2005); **Riggs v. State,** 912 So.2d 162 (Miss.App. 2005); **Salazar v. State,** 256 Ga. App. 50, 567 S.E.2d 706 (2002).

[720]**People v. Daoust,** 228 Mich.App. 1, 577 N.W.2d 179 (1998); **People v. Carter,** 36 Cal.4th 1114, 117 P.3d 476 (2005); **Hart v. State,** 173 S.W.3d 131 (Tex.App.-Texarkana 2005); **Highler v. State,** 834 N.E.2d 182 (Ind.App. 2005); **People v. Mateo,** 801 N.Y.S.2d 468 (N.Y.A.D. 4 Dept. 2005); **Gilbert v. State,** 262 Ga. 840, 426 S.E.2d 155 (1993).

[721]http://dictionary.law.com/default2.asp?typed=mistrial&type=1&submit1.x=33&submit1.y=9; **Wilson v. State,** 233 Ga.App. 327, 503 S.E.2d 924 (1998).

A mistrial is only available once a trial has begun, which means after the jury has been impaneled and sworn in.[722] A mistrial is not available once the verdict has been rendered.[723] Your experienced criminal litigator will know all the applicable legal issues relating to your state's rules on mistrials.

16.12. What is a directed verdict (instructed verdict) of acquittal? A motion for directed verdict of acquittal (or an "instructed verdict of acquittal") may be requested by your attorney on any or all of your pending charges once the prosecutor "rests" (ends the presentation of evidence). If granted, this is a ruling by the judge that the evidence demands a verdict of not guilty.[724] This motion is proper where the prosecutor totally fails to present any evidence providing one or more critical aspect(s) of one or more of the charges against you. In a DUI-DWI trial, such a motion might be granted if (in a per se alcohol case) your attorney is able to obtain a legal ruling in the middle of your trial wherein the test result cannot be considered by the jury. In these cases, the judge takes the decision about guilt or innocence away from the jury and instructs or directs an acquittal (not guilty) on that charge (or charges, if more than one of them have been challenged).

If this occurs in your trial, three conclusions to your trial may result. First, the judge may instruct the jurors to totally disregard that "dismissed" offense and any alleged evidence that supported it. Second, your attorney may (where state law allows it) ask that the jurors be released and that the judge alone decide the remaining charges. Third, if your attorney is not convinced the judge will be fair on the remaining "counts" against you, he or she can move for a mistrial on the remaining charges and argue that dismissal of a key charge and the supporting evidence might "taint" the jury's ability to hear the remainder of the trial and not allow that to affect their decision-making on the balance of the charges.

16.13. What happens if you are convicted? If the jury comes back with a verdict of guilty on one or more charges, numerous issues arise. First, in a misdemeanor DUI-DWI jury trial, it is likely that you will be sentenced by the judge (or in some states, by the jury) at the same proceeding. Your attorney may request that the judge "poll" the jurors so as to ask each of them if the verdict was his or her "individual" vote.

Also, your lawyer may consider the value of filing a motion of some type to request that the judge not accept the jury's verdict, or to not make the judge's verdict the judgment of the court. Also, a motion for a new trial may be sought or a motion in arrest of judgment, as facts may dictate. If none of these post-trial motions are viable, your lawyer may simply file a motion to ask the judge to delay imposition of the sentence imposed until an appeal (which may be simultaneously filed by your attorney) is ruled upon by an appellate court. Most states have defined rules on how, when and under what circumstances such a post-conviction motion or appeal will delay imposition of immediate jail time and other sentencing conditions.

16.13.1. Sentencing. Depending on the state in which you are convicted, a minimum sentence is typically set by statute regarding any sentence you could receive for a

---

[722]**State v. Snowden,** 198 La. 1076, 5 So.2d 355 (1941); **People v. Ramey,** 115 Ill.App.2d 431, 253 N.E.2d 688 (1969); **Saucier v. State,** 328 So.2d 355 (Miss. 1976); **Carpenter v. State,** 404 So.2d 89 (Ala.Crim.App. 1980); **Ferguson v. State**, 219 Ga. 33, 131 S.E.2d 538 (1963).

[723]**Com. v. Morocco,** 1985 WL 5743 (Pa.Com.Pl. 1985); **Bolser v. State,** 1997 WL 531177 (Tex.App.-Beaumont 1997); **State v. Jorgensen,** 181 Ga. App. 502, 353 S.E.2d 9 (1987).

[724]**Draper v. State,** 562 P.2d 155 (Okla.Crim.App. 1977); **State v. Howard,** 49 Or.App. 933, 621 P.2d 92 (1980); **LeBlanc v. State,** 826 S.W.2d 640 (Tex.App.-Hous. 1992); **State v. Jones,** 338 Ark. 781, 3 S.W.3d 675 (1999); **State v. Shaw,** 880 So.2d 296 (Miss. 2004); Georgia - O.C.G.A. §17-9-1.

DUI-DWI conviction. A maximum sentence is also set by statute. The sentence handed down must fall between the minimum and maximum.

The minimum and maximum sentence for your state depends on whether this is your first DUI-DWI conviction. If not, the minimum and maximum sentences will likely be higher. The judge or jury often has some discretion. The sentence you will receive for a DUI-DWI conviction will almost invariably include jail time, mandatory attendance of a DUI-DWI school, a fine, and a number of hours of community service. In the past decade, due to new legislation mandating tougher sentencing, alcohol and drug assessment and treatment, plus a possible ignition interlock device are also often part of a sentence.

16.13.2. Appeals/new trial. Depending on what errors may have been committed during trial, your attorney may recommend asking for a new trial or appealing the guilty verdict to a higher court. Although a motion for a new trial is rarely granted, if your attorney believes that his or her actions during trial may have constituted "ineffective assistance of counsel," a motion for a new trial is likely to be required, filed and ruled upon before the issue of ineffectiveness is appealed. Otherwise, the issue of your attorney's "ineffectiveness" may be waived (given up) on any appeal that asks for reversal based on that legal ground. See one example where the author was intentionally ineffective at a jury trial in order to guarantee two clients a new trial at:
www.theduibook.com/citycourt.htm.

16.14. What happens if you are acquitted? If you are acquitted, you walk out of the courtroom with no further legal concerns with regard to the charges you faced. The prosecutor cannot appeal an acquittal by a jury or ask for a mistrial after the verdict has been returned.

16.15. Motions for a new trial: why file one? Other than the issue of ineffective assistance of counsel (**Section 16.13.2**), several reasons may exist to file a motion for a new trial. First, a new trial may be granted by the judge if the verdict is contrary to the evidence and the principles of justice and equity are decidedly and strongly against the weight of the evidence,[725] or if your lawyer was ineffective.[726] Another reason for a new trial would be if new evidence is discovered after the verdict, although the requirements for this are very strict.[727]

16.16. If you assert but lose the motion for a new trial, can you still appeal? Yes. The two processes look at different concerns. If granted, the motion for a new trial is available to you because something significantly unjust happened at trial, and the judge agrees that a new trial without the improper act or evidence is justified without asking an appellate court to review it. An appeal is usually based upon the occurrence of a

---

[725]**Grayson v. Com.,** 47 Va. 712 (Va.Gen.Ct. 1849); **State v. Caper,** 215 N.C. 670, 2 S.E.2d 864 (1939); **Com. v. Thomas,** 278 Pa.Super. 39, 419 A.2d 1344 (1980); **Lane v. State,** 562 So.2d 1235 (Miss. 1990); O.C.G.A. §§5-5-20 and 5-5-21

[726]**Henderson v. State,** 123 Idaho 138, 844 P.2d 1388 (Idaho App. 1992); **State v. Denton,** 2002 WL 31309177 (Tenn.Crim.App. 2002); **State v. Fredrick,** 123 Wash.App. 347, 97 P.3d 47 (2004); **State v. Whipple,** 699 N.W.2d 686 (Iowa App. 2005); **Lewis v. State,** 2003 WL 23095980 (Tex.App.-Fort Worth 2003); **Glover v. State**, 266 Ga. 183, 465 S.E.2d 659 (1996).

[727]**State v. Belgarde,** 289 Mont. 287, 962 P.2d 571 (1998); **State v. Dougan,** 83 S.W.3d 698 (Mo.App. W.D. 2002); **People v. Russell,** 2003 WL 356673 (Mich.App. 2003); **Thomas ex rel. Thomas v. Mississippi Dept. of Public Safety,** 882 So.2d 789 (Miss.App. 2004); **Walker v. State,** 222 Ga. App. 491, 474 S.E.2d 695 (1996).

legal mistake made at trial. While the two overlap, they each have different "aspects" or issues to be considered, and are each considered separately.

16.17. Burden of proof. Burden of proof refers to who (prosecutor or defense) has the requirement to prove something. As to criminal charges, the *burden of proof* is on the prosecution to prove that the defendant is guilty beyond a reasonable doubt. The burden never shifts to the defense on the question of guilt or innocence, but the *burden of persuasion* may shift to the defense on some "evidentiary" matters. For example, if the prosecutor is able to overcome all of your attorney's objections to admissibility of your breath test results of 0.10%, it is up to your attorney to put up some evidence to challenge the accuracy of or cast doubt upon the test results' accuracy or reliability. Usually, even the best cross-examination by your attorney of the State's breath test personnel will not gain an acquittal of a per se DUI-DWI charge, unless you have expert testimony that can refute or cast doubt on the result.

16.17.1. Affirmative defenses–burden to disprove is on the state. Once a defendant has claimed an affirmative defense (like necessity or coercion), the burden to prove that this defense is not a viable challenge may be on the prosecution.[728] Other states, e.g., California and Pennsylvania, put the burden of proof of an affirmative defense on the defense.[729] Check with a DUI-DWI specialist in your state to find out if you are one of the extremely rare individuals with an affirmative defense in a DUI-DWI prosecution.

16.17.2. State's burden to get chemical test results admitted, then shifts to defendant to rebut or explain why an error exists. For any chemical test that was used to determine your blood alcohol level (either blood or breath) or that you had drugs in your system (blood or urine), it is first up to the prosecutor to prove that the tests were performed in a valid manner.[730] However, once the prosecutor has met this burden, and the test result is admitted by the judge into evidence, it is then up to the defendant to prove to the court that these results should not be considered by the judge (inadmissible). If the judge leaves the results in evidence, a defense expert is needed to help convince the jury to disregard the results.

16.17.3. Presumptions and inferences. The biggest and most important presumption in any trial is that the defendant is innocent until proven guilty.[731] This is different than on appeal of a guilty verdict, where the verdict is presumed to be correct.[732]

---

[728]**State v. Poshka,** 210 Ariz. 218, 109 P.3d 113 (2005); **State v. Robbins,** 138 Wash.2d 486, 980 P.2d 725 (1999); **State v. Johnson,** 672 N.W.2d 235 (Minn.App. 2003); **State v. Moore,** 237 Ga. 269, 227 S.E.2d 241 (1976); **Hill v. State,** 261 Ga. 377, 406 S.E.2d 470 (1993).

[729]**Com. v. Collins,** 810 A.2d 698 (Pa. 2002); **City of Cuyahoga Falls v. Scupholm,** 2000 WL 1825067 (Ohio App. 9 Dist. 2000); **State v. Valinski,** 61 Conn.App. 576, 767 A.2d 746 (2001); **State v. Parker,** 417 N.W.2d 643 (Minn. 1988); **State v. Duncan,** 1992 WL 247448 (Ohio App. 7 Dist. 1992).

[730]**State v. Ghylin,** 248 N.W.2d 825 (N.D. 1976); **Schacht v. State,** 154 Neb. 858, 50 N.W.2d 78 (1951); **State v. Peters,** 211 Ga. App. 755, 440 S.E.2d 515 (1994).

[731]**Miles v. State,** 154 S.W.3d 679 (Tex.App.-Hous. 2004); **State v. Resendis-Felix,** 209 Ariz. 292, 100 P.3d 457 (2004); **Imel v. State,** 830 N.E.2d 913 (Ind.App. 2005); **State v. Smith,** 275 Conn. 205, 881 A.2d 160 (2005); Louisiana - LSA-Const. Art. 1, § 16; Georgia - O.C.G.A. §16-1-5.

[732]**People v. Garza,** 35 Cal.4th 866, 111 P.3d 310 (2005); **Wilkins v. State,** 162 Md.App. 512, 875 A.2d 231 (2005); **Wilson v. Com.,** 46 Va.App. 408, 617 S.E.2d 431 (2005); **Emerick v. State,** 172 S.W.3d 867 (Mo.App. S.D. 2005); **State v. Baugh,** 2005 WL 2655035 (Tenn.Crim.App. 2005); **Trammell v. State,** 196 Ga. App. 540, 396 S.E.2d 286 (1990).

There is a presumption by the court that the law enforcement officer did his or her duty and that these duties were performed correctly, until the contrary is shown.[733]

16.17.4. Who gets to benefit from inferences. If you are talking about DUI-DWI from alcohol, depending on your blood level at the time the police check it, either you or the State may benefit from a presumption. Based on laws that exist in most states, if your blood alcohol level is 0.05 grams or less, the jury or judge may infer that you were not under the influence of alcohol at their discretion. If your blood alcohol level was above 0.05 and below 0.08 grams, most states allow neither side an inference as to whether or not you were under the influence of alcohol. If the judge or jury believes that you had a blood alcohol level of 0.08 or greater at the time of driving, an inference of impairment may arise, but this must be subject to being rebutted.

16.17.5. Only Nevada and Virginia have presumptions of impairment for DUI-DWI drugs. So far. Until 2003, no state had attempted to establish quantitative standards for the state having an "inference of impairment" by specified drugs. Before Nevada passed the first per se drug law in 2003,[734] and Virginia passed their statute in 2005,[735] no presumption of being impaired or under the influence arose by virtue of a specific quantitative reading in your blood or urine for specific drugs.[736] Dr. A.W. Jones of Sweden has studied current laws across America and has found that 17 states had passed some form of "per se" drugged driving laws as of May 2006. States had dealt with situations where drugs were the suspected impairing substance and had enacted laws that stated that refusal to take a blood test may be considered evidence creating an inference that the test would have shown the presence of a prohibited substance.[737]

16.18. Motion for directed verdict (instructed verdict) of acquittal. A directed verdict of acquittal (also called an "instructed verdict of acquittal" in some jurisdictions) is a ruling by the judge that the evidence **demands** a verdict of not guilty.[738] An example where this would be true would be where the prosecutor totally failed to put up any evidence that supported a critical aspect of the charges. This type of motion goes to the presence or absence of evidence on a critical issue (such as a missing element of the offense charged), not to the weight of the evidence.

16.18.1. Winning a directed verdict by exclusion of evidence. In a DUI-DWI trial, a directed verdict might occur if for some reason all evidence of your blood test result or breath test result was prohibited from being considered as evidence. This

---

[733]**Beaty v. State**, 1998 WL 151062 (Alaska App. 1998); **Poland v. Department of Motor Vehicles**, 34 Cal.App.4th 1128, 40 Cal.Rptr.2d 693 (1995); **Smith v. Com.**, 44 Va.App. 189, 604 S.E.2d 108 (2004); **Siekierda v. Com., Dept. of Transp., Bureau of Driver Licensing**, 580 Pa. 259, 860 A.2d 76 (2004); **Sapp v. State**, 184 Ga. App. 527, 362 S.E.2d 406 (1987).

[734] NRS 484.379(3).

[735]Va. Code Ann. § 18.2-269(A)(4).

[736]**State v. Frazier**, 2004 WL 1462626 (Tenn.Crim.App. 2004); **State v. Bealor**, 377 N.J.Super. 321, 872 A.2d 1081 (2005); **Perano v. State**, 167 Ga. App. 560, 307 S.E.2d 64 (1983)[reversed on other grounds, 250 Ga. 704, 300 S.E.2d 668 (1983).

[737]**People v. Riola**, 137 Misc.2d 616, 522 N.Y.S.2d 419 (N.Y.Dist.Ct. 1987); **State v. Baldwin**, 109 Wash.App. 516, 37 P.3d 1220 (2001); **State v. Collins**, 166 S.W.3d 721 (Tenn. 2005); Georgia - O.C.G.A. §40-6-392(c).

[738]**Hourigan v. Com.**, 883 S.W.2d 497 (Ky.App. 1994); **State v. Garcia**, 83 N.M. 794, 498 P.2d 681 (1972); **Cook v. Bishop**, 764 P.2d 189 (1988); **State v. Lewallen**, 927 S.W.2d 737 (Tex.App.-Fort Worth 1996); Georgia - O.C.G.A. §17-9-1.

prohibition would likely come about in the middle of your trial because your attorney successfully made a legal argument that this evidence must be excluded.

16.18.2. The judge can decide issue, with or without permitting argument. In instances where a directed verdict is requested by your DUI-DWI attorney, the judge can make an immediate ruling without hearing argument from either attorney. Usually both sides get to argue their respective positions. If the judge grants this motion, this issue or "count" of the accusatory document is taken away from the jury's final decision. Acquittal of that charge is declared by the judge due to a lack of evidence or a failure of proof by the state.

16.18.3. Judge cannot direct jury to return verdict of guilty. In a jury trial, it is the jury who determines the question of your guilt or innocence. If a judge were to direct a jury to return a verdict of guilty, this would be impermissible and excellent grounds for an appeal.[739] Only a few judges ignorant of the law would make such an overt error. Your DUI-DWI specialist, however, must be watchful that a pro-prosecution judge does not "communicate" his or her desire or belief that you are guilty of the DUI-DWI offense or offenses. This type of "telegraphing" of how he or she thinks is usually very subtle.

16.19. The stages of a jury trial. A jury trial follows a set pattern that is similar to many of the steps found in a bench trial. A jury trial, however, has more stages or steps that must be completed in a specific order and fashion. Hence, jury trials usually take longer to complete.

The procedure for a jury trial starts with everyone but the jury gathering in a courtroom. You and your defense team gather around one table, while the prosecution and their team gather around another. Only after everyone else is present does the judge enter. The bailiff usually announces the judge coming in. When the judge enters the courtroom, it is expected for you (and everyone else in the courtroom) to stand until you are told to take your seat.

Next, the judge and the lawyers involved with your case may have some preliminary discussions on whether everyone is ready to proceed, or the judge may ask if any unresolved issues need to be discussed before the jury comes in. Often, some "off the cuff" or lighthearted comments may be made between the attorneys and the judge, so do not be alarmed by this. You need not be annoyed or feel that your attorney is fraternizing with the opponent. The fact that this "familiarity" exists between the judge and your attorney is usually an excellent sign for your case. The more open and related all the attorneys are with each other, the better it will be for your case. (Yes, the judge is one of the attorneys!)

The judge will then more formally ask each side if they are ready to proceed. The prosecutor is typically required to answer first, followed by your attorney. If either says no, your trial is halted so that the judge can look into the cause or the reason for any delay. If it is your side's fault, this may not be good, unless the prosecutor (by his actions or inactions) caused a problem with your lawyer being ready to proceed. If some violation of the discovery rules by the prosecutor has occurred, your charges may be dropped. This may also occur if key witnesses for the prosecution are not present. The judge may grant either

---

[739]**City of Lansing v. Hartsuff,** 213 Mich.App. 338, 539 N.W.2d 781 (1995); **Jacques v. State,** 883 So.2d 902 (Fla.App. 2004); **State v. Dykstra,** 127 Wash.App. 1, 110 P.3d 758 (2005); **State v. Snipes,** 168 N.C.App. 525, 608 S.E.2d 381 (2005); **State v. Froiland,** 910 So.2d 956 (La.App. 5 Cir. 2005); **Richmond v. State,** 174 Ga. App. 498, 330 S.E.2d 427 (1985).

side an "adjournment" or a reset of the trial date if good cause can be shown that justifies the present delay.

If both announce "ready," then the judge will instruct the bailiff to bring the prospective jurors into the courtroom. It is usually a good idea to stand any time the jury enters or leaves the courtroom. This is done out of respect for their position as your "decision-makers."

The bailiff will provide for both the prosecutor and your attorney a brief summary of some personal details of each potential juror. The details deal with job data, marital status, age, etc. The idea behind giving the attorneys some background information is to shorten the process and give both sides some basic information that both lawyers will likely need to know.

Once everyone is again seated, the judge will have some preliminary remarks or "qualifying" questions for the jury. The judge may administer an oath to the jury pool, or may have the clerk do this. Next, the judge may describe for the jury the charges you are facing and the expected duration of the trial. The judge may ask the jurors some questions, either as a group or individually. Assuming that your state laws permit the attorneys for both sides to ask questions, both sides are then permitted to ask additional questions.

The judge will ask the prosecutor to conduct his or her questions of the jury panel. Often, the prosecutor will stand at a podium in the center of the open space in front of the jury. He or she will first introduce him or herself before asking some general questions that have to do with whether or not any member of the jury pool would have trouble being a disinterested and fair juror. These questions are typically of the type that they can be answered with a "yes" or "no," with each member of the pool raising his or her number or hand if they are responding.

Once these general questions are finished and the prosecutor has again taken his or her seat, your attorney will stand up, greet the jurors, introduce him or herself and introduce you. Your attorney may ask you to stand briefly for your introduction. He or she will then ask general questions of the jury pool.

During the questioning by either attorney, the other attorney may object to the form or the content of a question. The judge will make a ruling each time that either allows the question or rejects the question as being a proper area for inquiry. The judge may need to confer with the attorneys at the bench (the judge's elevated desk), or ask the jurors to take a short break outside of the courtroom for purposes of letting both attorneys put all of the details of the challenge or objection "on the record" before making a ruling.

Each attorney may then be allowed to ask each juror individually some very pointed questions, using the information that was divulged during the general questions or taken from the information sheet that each juror completed before coming into court. The prosecution asks his or her individual questions, followed by your attorney, for each potential juror in turn. It is important for you to take notes as to how you think each potential juror is responding, how forthcoming you think each is being, or how favorable you think each might be toward you, based on demeanor or body language. Before making any peremptory "strikes," your attorney will usually take a few minutes to discuss possible jury "strikes" with you and both explain his or her "rationale" for the proposed strikes, and listen to your thoughts.

At any point in the jury selection process, both your attorney and the prosecutor may be called to the front of the courtroom, to stand just in front of the judge's bench. It is likely that this is being done to discuss removing a potential juror from the jury pool "for cause." They may also be speaking about details of the trial, which are matters that the jury need not hear. These conversations are conducted in hushed tones so that the jurors do not hear the discussions. The judge may then excuse these selected jurors, without necessarily telling anyone why they are being excused. At some point, the judge may make a point to state "on the record" which jurors were "struck" for cause, and possibly share the reasons for each strike.

After each of the jurors has been asked the more personal questions by both of the lawyers, the judge may then ask a few more questions to satisfy his or her own curiosity. After this, the jury may be asked by the judge to leave the courtroom, and escorted out by the bailiff. The judge gives the attorneys a limited amount of time to consider which jurors to "strike." The judge may leave the courtroom for a few minutes as well while the attorneys confer with their "team," which includes you.

When the judge returns, each lawyer then gets to utilize a certain number of peremptory "strikes." This means that each attorney is allowed to eliminate a fixed number of the remaining potential jurors for ANY legally valid reason he or she believes would justify excusing a particular juror from the panel. The usual pattern of eliminating jurors starts with the prosecutor going first, followed by the defense, then a second elimination by the prosecution and a second elimination by the defense, and so on.

The bailiff then returns the jury to the courtroom, if they were not already in the courtroom. Once everyone is again seated, the judge tells them who is going to be on the jury, who are going to be alternates and must remain, and which of the potential jurors are excused. Those who are excused leave, and the remaining jurors often rearrange themselves in the jury box as seats open.

This method of jury selection is called the silent strike method. In some jurisdictions, an oral method of each attorney either "excusing" or "accepting" each juror takes place with the prosecutor going first. Again, both sides have limited strikes. The remaining jurors who are not struck are your jury.

The judge then administers yet another oath to the jury. This oath generally has the jurors all confirm that they will fairly and honestly listen to all the evidence, follow the judge's instructions and render a verdict that "speaks the truth" in your case. The bailiff may distribute pads of paper and pens for the jurors to take notes, if the judge authorizes this to be done.

At this point, the procedure for a bench trial and a jury trial are the same. (See **Section 15.8**.) In order to best explain things to the jurors (who are non-lawyers) instead of to the judge, your DUI-DWI specialist may recommend that you use additional expert witnesses, or the questioning of any witness may differ, but the procedure for conducting the trial is the same whether to a jury or to the judge.

It should be noted that because of the greater length of a jury DUI-DWI trial when compared to a bench trial, the judge may take several "comfort" breaks during the proceedings. You may expect a short break every few hours, and for lunch. If your trial appears to be likely to extend several hours beyond 5 PM or so, the judge may decide to adjourn court for the day. The choice on any of these breaks, when they occur and how long they last, is always at the discretion of the judge. The decision of when to adjourn is also left to the judge's discretion.

Both sides get a final chance to talk to the jury in closing arguments. However, before closing arguments begin, the judge will usually need to meet with the attorneys to review what "jury instructions" he or she will be giving to the jury after the closing arguments. These jury instructions (or jury "charges") are the rule of law and procedure that apply to this case and these facts as presented.

Since the prosecution has the burden of proof in criminal cases, the prosecutor will have the option of addressing the jury first and last, as a general rule. Sometimes, the prosecutor will "waive" the initial remarks and save his or her time to conclude the closing argument. This is an advantage, since the prosecutor's words will then be the last thing the jury hears prior to the judge giving them his or her jury instructions.

It is your constitutional right to have an attorney deliver your closing argument.[740] The purpose of this closing argument is for your attorney to take the facts that have been presented by either side, discuss how the facts presented do not provide credible proof of the crime charged, and put forward to the jury the best possible reason why you should not be found guilty. This is one of the few chances your lawyer will have to **ARGUE** on your behalf. More commonly to a jury than before just the judge, your DUI-DWI defense specialist will play an emotion or highlight some issue of how you were treated unfairly during the arrest process.

When both sides have finished, the judge then reads the extensive rules of law that the jury is to apply to the facts that they have heard during your trial. The judge will read the charges against you, word for word. The judge will also read as many as 100 jury instructions to the jury, outlining the jury's duties and the rules of law they are required to follow. This reading of all of the applicable legal rules can run for 20 to 35 minutes in a garden-variety misdemeanor DUI-DWI case, or easily exceed an hour in a felony prosecution.

The jury is then excused and the bailiff leads them to a jury deliberation room. Once there, following the judge's instructions, they elect a foreperson who becomes their spokesperson. The jury then decides your guilt or innocence, taking as much time as they need. With most DUI-DWIs, these deliberations typically take at least an hour.

No correlation exists between the length of the deliberations and the likelihood of an acquittal. Do not ask your attorney to guess what the jurors are "doing back there" or how the case will be decided. The jury makes its decision when they make their decision.

After several hours or even several days, the jurors may decide they are making no progress and send written notice of this to the judge. In some situations, the judge may even ask the jurors if they want to keep trying or go home for the night and resume the next day. The judge may also instruct them to keep trying to reach a verdict. As a last resort, the judge may decide to declare a mistrial.

If the jury comes to a verdict, both sides are notified, and everyone again gathers in the courtroom. Because your lawyer must keep him or herself free for this eventuality, he or she cannot do anything else. Whether you are being billed by the hour or were charged a flat fee, this "unknown" time committed to your case is part of that fee.

The judge enters and takes the bench any time issues relating to the jury are being discussed or handled. Once the judge and attorneys have spoken, the bailiff then brings

---

[740]**Herring v. New York,** 422 U.S. 853, 95 S.Ct. 2550, 45 L.Ed.2d 593 (1975).

the jury into the courtroom. The judge asks the foreperson if the jury has reached a verdict. If they have, the bailiff takes the written verdict from the foreperson and hands it to the judge. The judge will then make certain that the verdict is in the proper form. Then, the verdict is given back to the bailiff so that the foreperson or the bailiff can "publish" it (read it into the record).

Once the verdict is read, either lawyer has the option of requesting the judge to "poll" the jury. This involves the judge asking each juror one at a time, if this is his or her verdict in the jury room, and whether it is still his or her verdict. This process gives a juror the opportunity to speak up if he or she was pressured into voting in a manner he or she did not believe was the correct verdict.

A "not guilty" verdict is final, once entered, absent a rare request for a "polling" of the jury and a recanting by one or more jurors. The State cannot appeal a "not guilty" verdict rendered by your jury. After the "not guilty" verdict is made the order of the court, you are "discharged" of any responsibility for that charge.

A guilty verdict usually leads to a defense request for the jury to be polled. Absent a juror "recanting" his or her vote, the guilty verdict will typically be made the order of the court. Certain rarely used motions may be asserted by your legal team, but these usually only arise when an unusual mid-trial motion was made by the defense attorney and the judge reserved ruling or initially ruled against your attorney's motion, only to later change his or her mind after hearing the guilty verdict. Barring this, some form of post-trial motion or appeal can be pursued. See **Chapter 17** for more details.

If the jury can never agree on a verdict, and their vote must be unanimous and agreed to by all, a mistrial can and eventually will be granted by the judge. This means that the State can start over to try your case before a new jury. Often, these cases get resolved at this point by negotiations between the attorneys for a reduced charge.

If you are found not guilty, your trial is over. With a drunk driving conviction, like with most other misdemeanors, if you are found guilty, the judge (or the jury in a few jurisdictions) then sentences you to your punishment at the same proceeding. Your attorney may or may not have additional things to present or witnesses to testify if it would be appropriate for your sentencing. This is further discussed in Chapter 17.

Chapter 17

The Verdict: Sentencing and Issues Relating to Jail (if convicted), License Loss and Probation Issues after Conviction: What are the Consequences and the Timing of Enforcement of the Sentence?

17.0. The purpose of this chapter. At the end of a trial, the defendant will receive a verdict from the court. Based on this verdict, you may be totally finished with the legal aspects of your case, or you may be facing punishment. In rare cases you may be required to undergo an entirely new trial. This chapter discusses everything that happens from the time the verdict is announced in open court through the possible imposition of punishment.

17.1. Verdict rendered by jury (or judge). A verdict is the decision of guilt or innocence by a jury after a trial. A verdict must be accepted by the trial judge to be final, and then is made an "order" of the court. If the verdict is not in the correct form the judge may reject the verdict. Likewise (in some jurisdictions), if the judge finds the verdict to be contrary to the evidence, the verdict can be overturned. [741]

Usually, the single most important question the jury decides in a DUI-DWI criminal trial is whether or not the defendant is guilty. A **judgment** is different than a verdict. A judgment is a determination of guilt or innocence by a judge sitting without a jury.[742] A "special verdict" is a decision by the jury on the factual questions in the case, leaving the application of the law to those facts to the judge, who makes the final judgment.[743]

A "directed verdict" or "instructed verdict" is a decision made by the trial judge (following a mid-trial motion made by the defense counsel once the prosecution "rests" its

---

[741]**Haddix v. State,** 827 N.E.2d 1160 (Ind.App. 2005); **People v. Seneca Ins. Co.,** 29 Cal.4th 954, 62 P.3d 81 (Cal. 2003); **Com. v. Roth,** 437 Mass. 777, 776 N.E.2d 437 (2002); **Cotten v. State,** 251 Ga.App. 628, 555 S.E.2d 15 (2001); **State v. Lewallen,** 927 S.W.2d 737 (Tex.App.-Fort Worth 1996); **State v. Rollins,** 103 Idaho 48, 644 P.2d 370 (Idaho App. 1982); **Sanders v. State,** 429 So.2d 245 (Miss. 1983); **State v. Benoit,** 131 Vt. 631, 313 A.2d 387 (1973); **State ex rel. Myers v. Brown,** 209 Tenn. 141, 351 S.W.2d 385 (1961); **State v. Williams,** 30 Wash.2d 18, 190 P.2d 734 (1948).

[742]**Johnson v. California,** 541 U.S. 428, 124 S.Ct. 1833, 158 L.Ed.2d 696 (2004); **People v. Salgado,** 353 Ill.App.3d 101, 817 N.E.2d 1079 (2004); **State v. Taylor,** 150 Wash.2d 599, 80 P.3d 605 (2003); **State v. Loye,** 670 N.W.2d 141 (Iowa 2003); **Government of Virgin Islands v. Rivera,** 333 F.3d 143 (3rd Cir.(Virgin Islands) 2003); **City of Maplewood v. Erickson,** 80 S.W.3d 477 (Mo.App. E.D. 2002); **Ridgeway v. State,** 140 Md.App. 49, 779 A.2d 1031 (2001); **Smith v. State,** 786 So.2d 423 (Miss.App. 2001); **Mosqueda v. State,** 936 S.W.2d 714 (Tex.App.-Fort Worth 1996); **People v. Martinez,** 193 Mich.App. 377, 485 N.W.2d 124 (1992); **People v. Karaman,** 4 Cal.4th 335, 842 P.2d 100 (1992); **Burkett v. State,** 131 Ga.App. 177, 205 S.E.2d 496 (1974); **Bozovichar v. State,** 230 Ind. 358, 103 N.E.2d 680 (1952); **Moody v. State,** 160 S.W.3d 512 (Tenn. 2005).

[743]**Dean v. State,** 232 Ga.App. 390, 501 S.E.2d 895 (1998); **People v. Davenport,** 41 Cal.3d 247, 710 P.2d 861 (1985); **State v. Robinson,** 84 Wash.2d 42, 523 P.2d 1192 (1974); **Cook v. State,** 506 S.W.2d 955 (Tenn.Crim.App. 1973); **Tate v. State,** 56 Ariz. 194, 106 P.2d 487 (1940).

case) that there is insufficient evidence of guilt on any particular charge.[744] A "chance verdict" (decided by lot or the flip of a coin)[745] and a "compromise verdict" (based on some jurors voting *against* their beliefs to break a deadlock)[746] are both improper (except in Louisiana[747]), and if discovered, will result in a mistrial (having the verdict thrown out by the judge) or be cause for reversal of the judgment on appeal.

17.1.1. Read and published in open court.

When the jury reaches a verdict as to your guilt or innocence, the foreperson will notify the judge and present the judge with the written and signed form upon which the jury's verdict was rendered. The judge ensures that the form is filled out correctly and signed, then directs the foreperson of the jury (or a bailiff) to read the decision aloud to everyone present in the courtroom. Usually, the judge will ask the defendant and his or her legal counsel to stand and receive the verdict of the jury.

In the law, **publication** is anything made public by print (as in a newspaper, magazine, pamphlet, letter, telegram, computer modem or program, poster, brochure or pamphlet), orally, or by broadcast (radio, television).[748] When the verdict is read by the foreperson in open court, this is known as the verdict being read and "published."

17.1.2. Judge will decide whether to accept it and make it the order of the court.

Once the verdict has been read and published by the foreperson, the judge **must** generally accept the decision of the jury as to guilt or innocence. If the verdict form is defective, however, the judge is not required to accept the verdict. The judge typically makes the verdict the "order" of the court, meaning that under the legal authority of the court, he or she requires that this order be filed with the clerk of the court and that the verdict be complied with.

An **order** is a direction or mandate of a judge or a court that is not a judgment or legal opinion (although both may include an order). An order will contain wording from the judge directing that something be done or that there is prohibition against doing some act.[749] By having to accept the decision of guilt or lack of guilt of the jury, the judge must then enter an order confirming or mandating the "guilty" or "not guilty" status of the defendant. In essence, based totally on the verdict of the jury, the judge is ordering the rest of our society to accept that the defendant is either guilty or not guilty of the crime(s) charged.

17.1.3. Polling the jurors, by either side.

Once the verdict of the jury has been read and published, either the prosecution or defense can ask for the jury to be "polled." This means each juror will have to individually answer that the verdict that was reached was his or her own independent choice. This process was put into place to allow jurors who might feel they were forced, pressured or coerced into "going along with the others" to have an avenue to let this be known, and to ensure that the form the foreperson

---

[744]**State v. Lewallen,** 927 S.W.2d 737 (Tex.App.-Fort Worth 1996); **State v. Garcia,** 83 N.M. 794, 498 P.2d 681 (N.M.App. 1972).

[745]**Reyes v. Seifert,** 125 Fed.Appx. 788 (9th Cir.(Cal.) 2005); **People v. Williams,** 25 Cal.4th 441, 21 P.3d 1209 (2001); **U.S. v. Perez-Pagan,** 1973 WL 14822 (ACMR 1973); **Biebelle v. Norero,** 85 N.M. 182, 510 P.2d 506 (1973); **Ferrara v. State,** 101 So.2d 797 (Fla. 1958); **People v. De Lucia,** 20 N.Y.2d 275, 229 N.E.2d 211 (1967).

[746]**State v. Flowers,** 85 Conn.App. 681, 858 A.2d 827 (2004); **Com. v. Trill,** 374 Pa.Super. 549, 543 A.2d 1106 (1988).

[747]**State v. Odom,** 878 So.2d 582 (La.App. 1 Cir. 2004).

[748]http://dictionary.law.com/default2.asp?selected=1674&bold=publication||

[749]http://dictionary.law.com/default2.asp?selected=1408&bold=order||

puts forth accurately represents the opinion of the entire jury, not just the foreperson. Although rare, this process will occasionally cause a juror to recant, and the verdict becomes a "mistrial" (meaning that the jurors could not unanimously agree).

17.2. Three possible outcomes for each count (each separate charge against you). In a criminal trial, there are only three possible outcomes for each count: not guilty, guilty, and no decision. Each count or criminal charge against the defendant is considered separately. It is not unusual for defendants who have been charged with multiple counts to receive more than one of the possible outcomes in the same overall verdict. Jurors usually resolve charges with "guilty" or "not guilty," but occasionally will be unable to unanimously agree. This results in a "mistrial" of such counts of the case. [See **Section 17.2.3**. below.]

17.2.1. Not guilty — judge discharges you from the case, orders bond released. If the defendant is found not guilty on all charges (or some), the judge discharges the defendant from criminal liability for such offense(s). If the defendant had an appearance bond placed so that he or she could remain out of jail while waiting for trial, this bond is released at this time by order of the judge. The security given for the bond is returned (cash) or released (real estate or the written surety of a commercial bonding company). If the defendant is found not guilty, the prosecutor cannot appeal this decision, nor force the accused to face a new trial.

17.2.2. Guilty — sentencing will follow (by either judge or jury, depending on jurisdiction). If the verdict of the jury or the judgment from the judge is that the defendant is guilty on one, several or all of the counts in a trial, sentencing is usually done immediately after the finding of guilt. In most jurisdictions, the judge imposes the sentence. However, in some jurisdictions (e.g., Texas), and for some other criminal offenses, it is the jury that decides the sentence. In a few states (e.g., Virginia) the jury recommends a sentence and the judge has the final word on imposition of that sentence.

17.2.3. Mistrial declared by judge because the jurors cannot reach unanimous verdict. If the jurors cannot gather enough support for either a guilty or not guilty verdict on any of the counts, they may be considered by the judge to be "deadlocked." If this happens, the judge usually gives them a chance to break the deadlock. If the jury then cannot agree on a verdict, the judge declares a mistrial for that count. This may lead to another trial, or may create a stronger negotiating position for the defense attorney to get a reduced charge. In rare cases, a mistrial may result in total dismissal of the DUI-DWI charges by the prosecutor. This usually only occurs when the "split" in the juror's vote was heavily in favor of acquittal.

17.3. Sentencing (if convicted on any counts) is required to be done. Sentence is both the act of imposing the punishment on a person convicted of a crime and the actual verbalization of what punishment is handed down. A sentence is ordered by the judge, based on the verdict of the jury (or the judge's decision if there is no jury) within the possible range of minimum and maximum punishments set by state law (or federal law, in convictions for a federal crime). In everyday jargon, "sentence" refers to the jail or prison time ordered after conviction, as in, "His sentence was 30 days in the county jail."

Technically, a sentence includes all fines, driving school, license suspension, ignition interlock installation, alcohol and drug assessment and treatment, community service, restitution or other punishment, or terms of probation. Defendants who are first offenders without a prior record may be entitled to have a pre-sentence report by a probation officer based on an investigation of background information and circumstances of the crime, often resulting in a recommendation by the probation officer of an amount of punishment. More commonly, in garden-variety misdemeanor DUI-DWI prosecutions, the sentencing judge will merely ask the prosecutor and the defense attorney for any "aggravation" or "mitigation" evidence before imposing the sentence.

For misdemeanors (like DUI-DWI) the maximum sentence is usually up to 12 months in county jail, but for felonies (major crimes) the jail sentence can range from a year in prison to life imprisonment for DUI-DWI based murder charges (in some states). Almost every jurisdiction has escalating punishment schemes for repeat offender DUI-DWI convictions. [Key provisions of the DUI-DWI laws of each American jurisdiction can be found on-line at http://www.theduibook.com/stateDUIDWIsummaries.htm.]

Under some circumstances the defendant may receive a "suspended sentence," which means the jail portion of the punishment is not imposed if the defendant does not get into other trouble for the period he/she otherwise would have spent in jail or prison. This is often for a period of 12 months.

A "concurrent sentence" is a sentence for one count in the verdict that is served at the same time as the sentence for another count and only lasts as long as the longest term. A "consecutive sentence" is one where the judge "stacks" the jail terms, for each to be served one after another.

An "indeterminate sentence" is one in which the actual release date is not set and will be based on a later review of your prison conduct. In DUI-DWI practice, such sentences are extremely rare.[750]

17.3.1. Merger of lesser offenses with the DUI-DWI offense? "Merger" can have several meanings with regard to DUI-DWI offenses. Certain criminal offenses are integral parts of greater offenses. If a defendant is convicted of the *greater* offense, he or she cannot also be sentenced for the *lesser* offense as well. In a DUI-DWI trial, if the defendant is found guilty of a first degree vehicular homicide (a homicide caused by a drunk driver), the lesser misdemeanor of the DUI-DWI is usually merged into the punishment for the homicide.[751] Reckless driving[752] and public intoxication[753] typically are not lesser-included offenses in a DUI-DWI, so a defendant can be tried and sentenced on both the underlying driving act as well as the felony vehicular homicide.

A defendant convicted of different types of alcohol DUI-DWI (per se and traditional DUI) for the same incident can only be sentenced for one.[754] However, sentencing for separate convictions of DUI-alcohol and DUI-drugs from a single arrest may not be merged.[755]

17.3.2. Evidence in aggravation. "Evidence in aggravation" refers to factors which likely could not be introduced by the prosecutor at the trial in the determination of guilt, but which may be presented by the prosecutor at sentencing and considered by the court in imposing a fair punishment after conviction. Examples of these kinds of aggravating factors include any prior criminal record or possibly facts surrounding the defendant's actions after he or she was confronted by the police or after being placed in custody by the police. Thus,

---

[750]http://dictionary.law.com/default2.asp?typed=sentence&type=1&submit1.x=36&submit1.y=7.

[751]**Carthon v. State**, 248 Ga. App. 738, 548 S.E.2d 649 (2001).

[752]**Barber v. State**, 204 Ga. App. 94, 418 S.E.2d 436 (1992).

[753]**State v. Tweedell,** 209 Ga. App. 13, 432 S.E.2d 619 (1993).

[754]**Tomlin v. State,** 184 Ga. App. 726, 362 S.E.2d 489 (1987).

[755]**Carthon v. State**, 248 Ga. App. 738, 548 S.E.2d 649 (2001).

while it is usually improper for the prosecution to tell the judge or the jury about a defendant's prior DUI-DWIs during the trial itself, the defendant's prior criminal offenses are fair game during sentencing after conviction.

If you have a clean criminal record, this bodes well for you. Unless some type of egregious or outrageous behavior occurred in connection with your DUI-DWI arrest, your sentence should be set at or near the minimums established by law. Types of outrageous behavior may include resisting arrest, verbally abusing the officer, not immediately stopping when emergency lights and siren come on, or such similar negative or dangerous acts.

17.3.3. Evidence in mitigation. "Mitigating circumstances" in criminal law are facts, conditions or circumstances which do not excuse or justify the defendant's criminal conduct, but which may be considered by a judge in deciding what would be fair punishment. The attorney for the defendant usually presents this evidence. For example, if a defendant made elaborate plans to use a designated driver and the plans fell apart, leading him or her to attempt to get home from a remote location, this might carry some weight with some judges.[756] If you lost your job as a result of the DUI-DWI arrest, this also may impact the judge's decision by not assessing a high monetary fine.

This is information that might not be relevant in the determination of a defendant's guilt, but which may be important in a determination of a fair punishment. In a DUI-DWI sentencing, common evidence in mitigation may include evidence of regular attendance of Alcoholics Anonymous meetings, voluntary submittal to alcohol treatment and counseling, pre-sentence performing community service hours as a form of penance, and possibly making restitution for property damage or loss.

17.3.4. Attacks on prior conduct. In DUI-DWI sentencing, your prior criminal conduct can almost always be considered as a part of sentencing. In other words, if you have a prior conviction, for a previous DUI-DWI or even a "deferred plea," and are convicted for a second DUI-DWI offense at a later time, it is likely that the sentence for the second offense will be more severe because of the first conviction or the "deferred adjudication." One avenue of attacking the more severe sentence for the second offense is to either seek to vacate (to remove) the prior conviction or to attack the proposed use of the prior offense, if possible.[757] Such challenges are rare, but can result in saving your driving privileges and possibly reduce jail time by many days or even months.[758]

17.3.5. Incarceration. This means time in custody, whether in a jail, under house arrest or some other form of detention. In some states, the statutory minimum jail time must be served even if other alternative forms of "detention" are imposed.[759] It means the State controls a defendant's freedom of movement. If convicted of a DUI-DWI offense, many jurisdictions require that an offender be led in handcuffs from the courtroom by deputies if the sentence includes jail time. Some courts, however, will delay the start of the

---

[756]http://dictionary.law.com/default2.asp?searched=mitigating+circumstances&type=1.

[757]**Baldasar v. Illinois,** 446 U.S. 222, 100 S.Ct. 1585 (1980), overruled on other grounds by **Nichols v. United States,** 511 U.S. 738, 114 S.Ct. 1921 (1994)**; State v. Norwood,** 2006 WL 668746 (Tenn.Crim.App. 2006)[slip opinion].

[758]**State v. Moran,** 331 Mont. 137, 130 P.3d 164 (Mont. 2006); **State v. Solarski,** 374 N.J.Super. 176, 863 A.2d 1095 (N.J.Super.A.D. 2005); **State v. Hight,** 810 So.2d 1250 (La.App. 2 Cir. 2002); **Berry v. State,** 74 Ark.App. 141, 45 S.W.3d 435 (Ark.App. 2001).

[759]**Pierce v. State,** --- S.E.2d ----, 2006 WL 573790 (Ga.App. 2006); **State v. Dyer,** 275 Ga.App. 657, 621 S.E.2d 615 (2005).

jail sentence. Also, filing an appeal may delay imposition of jail time, if an appeal bond is posted.

17.3.5.1. Maximums and minimums. For a misdemeanor DUI-DWI, the typical maximum period of incarceration is twelve months. However, if convicted of multiple criminal counts from a single driving episode, one or more of which are DUI-DWI offenses, the total amount of incarceration can extend (due to *consecutive* sentences being "stacked") to more than a year, even if all counts are misdemeanors. Also, repeat offense DUI-DWI offenders face FELONY punishment for a third, fourth (or in some states) even a SECOND offense.[760]

Depending on the State, there is typically a minimum amount of time you must spend incarcerated if convicted of a DUI-DWI offense. How much time this minimum is depends on whether this is the first DUI-DWI conviction or a subsequent one and how much time there is between multiple DUI-DWI convictions.   How much additional time any defendant has to serve (beyond what was served immediately after being arrested) at the time of sentencing depends on the judge's discretion. Most jurisdictions give credit for time in jail on the night of your arrest.

17.3.5.2. Alternatives to regular jail time. Depending on state law, there may be alternatives to regular jail time that a judge may consider. Consult with your DUI-DWI specialist on your alternatives. Any "alternative" is at the discretion (choice) of the judge, not the defense attorney. If sentenced to any of these alternatives, the period of incarceration may be longer than what might have been required for "regular" jail time to offset the special benefit of obtaining the alternative sentence. The judge must always keep in mind the need to adequately punish the defendant for his or her acts.

It must be noted that all of these alternatives to jail time have significant "compliance" requirements and "accountability." For example, a judge may permit you to serve all but the minimum jail sentence on probation, but will require random phone monitoring or an ankle bracelet (permitting your movement outside of your home) to be utilized to prove that home detention was followed. For more information on these devices see **http://www.alcoholmonitoring.com/.**   But see this article in the shortcomings of SCRAM devices written by Michigan OWI/DUI guru Patrick T. Barone: **http://www.nacdl.org/public.nsf/01c1e7698280d20385256d0b00789923/dd005fb4046ce e9185257019006b2690?OpenDocument**

Additionally, a judge may require regular drug and alcohol screening to be performed. A violation of **any** of these requirements or criteria likely means a loss of these privileges and that you violated the terms of your sentence. Significant jail time will usually be imposed, rather than allow you to serve your sentence on probation.

One of these detention alternatives may be "work-release." In this case, the defendant is allowed some time off on a daily or regular basis so that he or she can go to work, but must report to the jail to be kept locked up every evening. This may be required for part or all of your sentence, depending on your prior record. Defendants who are

---

[760]Alabama - 4th offense lifetime - Ala.Code 1975 § 32-5A-191; Indiana - 2nd offense within 5 years - IC 9-30-5-3; Mississippi - 3rd in 5 years - Miss. Code Ann. § 63-11-30; Texas - third offense lifetime - V.T.C.A., Penal Code § 49.09; Tennessee - 4th offense lifetime - T. C. A. § 55-10-403; Ohio - 3rd in 6 years, or 5th in 20 years - R.C. § 4511.19; Louisianna - 3rd offense lifetime - LSA-R.S. 14:98; South Carolina – 3rd lifetime - Code 1976 § 56-5-2940; Alaska - 4th lifetime - AS 28.35.030; Florida - 3rd in 10 years - West's F.S.A. § 316.193; New York - 2nd in 10 years may be felony - McKinney's Vehicle and Traffic Law § 1193(c).

allowed this option will typically be tested regularly for alcohol and drugs as a condition of this type of incarceration. Plus, the rules of the facility are strict.

A court may impose this type of incarceration for defendants who are otherwise at low risk to commit further crimes and who have regular jobs that would likely be lost if the defendant were to serve regular jail time. Many judges try not to harm a convicted person's dependents (children and spouse), if possible.

Another form of incarceration may be a weekend jail sentence, where defendants are allowed to work all week, and stay at home all week, then report only to the jail for service of jail time on one or more weekends. This is very uncommon in DUI-DWIs due to the limited bed space at jails on the weekends.

Another kind of alternative incarceration that may be available is house arrest. In this situation, the defendant must physically stay in his or her home, subject to frequent and random confirmation of the detainee's presence at home by the State. Some defendants will be required to wear a form of electronic monitoring device to prove compliance, such as an ankle bracelet. The bracelet will either be "radio-controlled" to prevent you from leaving home, or may be operated by GPS (satellite). Other jurisdictions use technology such as Vis-a-tel® (phone camera plus breathalyzers) to assure compliance. Some use a transdermal device that continuously monitors sweat from a person's skin to detect any use of alcohol. These have come under attack, however.[761]

17.3.6. Fines. A **fine** is a monetary punishment, or money out of the defendant's pocket, that has to be paid to the court, either right away or over a period of time through the probation officer. Often minimum and maximum fines are established by statute, although the judge usually has some discretion of the amount of the fine within the statutory range. Plus, almost all states have "add-ons" such as statutory surcharges or court costs that can add an amount that may equal or exceed the fine amount.[762] How much these minimums and maximums will be depends on the State of the conviction, if this is the first or a subsequent DUI-DWI conviction, and how recent the other DUI-DWI convictions occurred, as compared to the current conviction.

If the fine cannot be paid all at once, the defendant is often given a set term in which to complete the payments. Expect to pay "probation supervision fees" for each month that probation handles processing these payments and assuring that you are complying with other probation terms. If a defendant makes every good faith effort to pay the fine, yet fails due to economic misfortune or family obligations, a judge may convert the fine to community service (where permitted to do so by statute). Do not count on this, since any modification is at the judge's discretion. Be sure to contact your attorney (or probation officer) if you need to seek such a modification.

17.3.7. Probation. **Probation** (called "community control" in some states) is a chance to remain out of jail, but on restricted terms and conditions (*example*: no use of alcohol at all). A probated sentence is given by a judge to a person convicted of a crime instead of requiring that he or she be sent to jail or prison. Probation (rather than straight jail time) is a matter of the judge's discretion. Often a sentence is part jail time with the

---

[761] http://www.1800duilaws.com/article/alcohol_monitoring_ankle_bracelets.asp; **In re Disciplinary Action Against Post,** 686 N.W.2d 529 (Minn. 2004).

[762] $3000 in surcharges - **State v. Alderete,** 2004 WL 431490 (Tex.App.-San Antonio. 2004); Mandatory surcharge of $1000/year for three years – New Jersey - *N.J.S.A.* 17:29A-35b(2)(b).

balance to be served on probation. Violation of probation terms will usually result in the person being sent to jail for all or part of the remaining "probation" term.

Repeat criminals are normally not eligible for probation and are often given more jail time than a first offender. Probation is not the same as "parole," which is a term describing "conditional" freedom after a lengthy term of jail under certain restrictions. This refers to the jail release given to convicted felons at or near the end of their imprisonment period.[763]

Probation can be either "reporting" or "non-reporting." Reporting means the defendant must maintain regular contact (usually physically report, although occasionally by phone or by mail) with the probation officer. Non-reporting means the defendant is officially still under supervision by the court but does not have to make regular contact with a probation officer. Some reporting probation can be converted to non-reporting after a period of time, if all conditions specified by the court have been met.

"Intensive probation" is a term used to describe very strict and harsh reporting and compliance for offenders. Many courts are starting to utilize intensive probation to control every aspect of repeat DUI-DWI offender's lives. Compliance with all of these terms is extremely difficult for some offenders, due to a loss of work time and the inability for the person to drive a vehicle (in many instances).

17.3.7.1. Conditions of probation. Probation should be considered as a gift from a judge, since he or she could have sent the offender to jail for the entire sentence instead. Typically, probation is a non-jail alternative only so long as you comply with all of the many conditions. These conditions usually mean that you pay fines and do all other conditions such as community service, attend DUI school, obtain alcohol and drug evaluation and treatment, not violate any laws while on probation, abstain from drinking any alcohol, follow through with any other court-ordered conditions and report regularly to your probation officer.[764]

17.3.7.2. Community service. This part of the probation is done under supervision by the probation department, which assigns the defendant to various public or non-profit service programs or approves of the type of service done. Almost any public or non-profit program may be accepted, such as church, school or community programs, but typically such programs must be pre-approved by the probation officer before the hours count toward satisfying the sentence. The types of service range from picking up trash, to building homes for the poor, to working in a county, city or state facility. It is very important for both the probation officer and for the defendant serving the sentence to independently keep track of the hours spent, just in case a question arises from the court. Written verification, signed by the community service provider, is almost always mandatory. If your state allows for taping of telephone conversations, you should record and keep a taped copy of all visits and telephone meetings with probation officials. (See **Section 3.2.3** of this book.)

17.3.7.3. Probation supervision fee. Many misdemeanor probation programs are now privatized, meaning they are not run by a governmental agency but are provided by a private company. As a part of the sentence, the defendant can be required to pay both an initial fee and a monthly supervision fee (typically $30 to $50 per month) to the probation company. Failure to pay these fees, for any reason, is a reason the court can use to revoke the probation and require the defendant to spend all or part of the remainder of

---

[763]http://dictionary.law.com/default2.asp?selected=1620&bold=probation||
[764]http://dictionary.law.com/default2.asp?selected=1620&bold=probation||

the sentence in jail. Financial hardship may help you get an extension of time to pay and stay out of jail, but you need to have your proof of this hardship ready.

17.3.7.4. Restitution. **Restitution** is the legal term identifying the repayment to a "victim" of an accident (caused by criminal acts such as a DUI-DWI wreck) the monetary value of any loss. In DUI-DWI cases, this may entail lost wages for an injured person, or medical bills, or both. Restitution for property damage is also a common court-imposed "sentence" condition. Restitution may be a condition of granting a defendant probation or giving him/her a shorter sentence than normal.[765]

17.3.8. Probation revocation. If a defendant violates **any** of the terms of his or her probation, the probated sentence (or a portion of it) can be revoked. All or part of this revocation is done at a hearing before the judge who sentenced you. At this hearing, evidence of the violation must be presented. If you dispute this violation, you can present documentary evidence or testimony at this hearing to refute the claimed violation. One of the challenges your attorney may be able to assert is that the alleged acts triggering the revocation petition are "unrelated" to the crime for which you are serving the probated sentence.[766] The amount of proof at these probation revocation hearings is much less than for a criminal conviction - "preponderance of the evidence" rather than "proof beyond a reasonable doubt."[767] If you lose this hearing, you may spend the remaining time of your probated sentence in jail or some other form of detention.

17.3.9. License suspension. A court has the authority to suspend a defendant's driver's license as a part of a sentence, separate from the license suspension from your state's agency handling the issuance of driver's licenses (e.g. DMV, DPS, BMV, SOS, etc.).[768] The court may also require an ignition interlock device to be installed on any vehicle the defendant will drive. This type of device checks your breath alcohol before the vehicle can be cranked.[769]

Under the laws of the different states, the suspension or revocation of a defendant's driver's license may be mandatory. This is often an immediate and unchangeable function of your state's statutes on a DUI-DWI conviction. The judge is often powerless to "grant" any type of limited driving privileges.

The length of time of this mandatory suspension or revocation is based on any prior DUI-DWI convictions and the length of time between the dates of these convictions. If it is the first DUI-DWI conviction (as determined by your state's laws), your state may allow your license to be returned to you sooner than the entire suspension period. Such early reinstatement will only be available after proving successful attendance of a DUI-DWI School and payment of a fee to reinstate your license.

A defendant's license may also be suspended for a DUI-DWI from drugs rather than alcohol, or possibly for a drug conviction that has nothing to do with the person driving.[770] Each state's rules for drug possession vary. If there are any questions about your license suspension after a "drug" possession or DUI-DWI "drug" conviction, ask your DUI-DWI specialist.

---

[765]http://dictionary.law.com/default2.asp?selected=1831&bold=restitution‖

[766]**U.S. v. Britt**, 332 F.3d 1229 (9th Cir. 2003).

[767]O.C.G.A. § 42-8-34.1.

[768]**AR 190-5; Brock v. State**, 165 Ga. App. 150, 299 S.E.2d 71 (1983).

[769]**State v. Villella**, 266 Ga. App. 499, 597 S.E.2d 563 (2004).

[770]O.C.G.A. § 40-5-75.

17.4. Judge sentences — issues to consider. Judges are supposed to know and follow the law. Every day, they are faced with people who are accused of breaking the law, and passing judgment on them. They see people accused of DUI-DWI every week. An experienced DUI-DWI lawyer knows each judge's tendencies and "peculiarities," and may recommend to you to attend a DUI-DWI school, attend AA meetings, and/or start community service, even before trial. A state can assign the task of sentencing to a judge in DUI-DWI cases.[771]

While you may believe that this is an admission of guilt, this is being done *voluntarily* by you because your attorney is considering what factors may influence the judge (if you are later convicted) to give you a more lenient sentence rather than the maximum penalty. When handing down a sentence, judges appreciate the defendant "taking the initiative" to get treatment and to seek to "change his or her behavior." Even if you consider yourself to not be guilty of any crime, if you are convicted despite all of your attorney's efforts, prior preparation may save your job or may mean the difference between jail time and house arrest.

17.5. Jury sentences — issues to consider. If it is the jury who is providing the sentence, then there are different issues for you and your lawyer to consider. Juries may be swayed either way, harsher or less harsh, by emotions. If you have taken corrective steps that show true remorse and that you have taken responsibility for your actions, you can help. In states with "jury sentencing," a much more significant jail term may be given to you than if a judge passes on your punishment. Do everything before your trial and during trial that your lawyer suggests.

One final note on "sentencing by a jury." Attorneys who specialize in DUI-DWI spend endless hours developing jury selection questions that give some insight on the tendencies of jurors toward lenient sentencing. The preparation, witnesses and presentation of your case to a jury at the sentencing phase will be different from what is presented to a trial judge who is sentencing you. In no place is the experience and special training of a DUI-DWI specialist of greater value than at such a "jury sentencing" hearing.

---

[771]**Williams v. New York,** 337 U.S. 241, 69 S.Ct. 1079, 93 L.Ed. 1337 (1949); **Apprendi v. New Jersey,** 530 U.S. 466, 120 S.Ct. 2348, 147 L.Ed.2d 435 (2000); **Blakely v. Washington,** 542 U.S. 296, 124 S.Ct. 2531, 159 L.Ed.2d 403 (2004).

Chapter 18

Appeal, Motion for New Trial, Supersedeas Bond, Expungement and Other Post-Conviction Issues that Your Attorney May Assert on Your Behalf.

18.0. Purpose of the chapter. Once your trial is over, a finding by the judge or the jury of your guilt will set in motion the occurrence of several important dynamics. Other than possible jail time, the most serious of these consequences is the loss of your driving privileges. In most states, that loss is immediate. In a few states, you may be eligible to obtain a work permit or restricted license of some type.

Most state statutes relating to a drunken driving conviction call for the immediate suspension or revocation of your license, for the criminal conviction. If an administrative license suspension or revocation is already in place, state law will typically provide that this new loss of driving privileges will be tacked on following the administrative suspension, or that any suspension or revocation for the criminal conviction will run at the same time as any remaining administrative license loss.

The "appearance bond" that was posted at the time of your arrest terminates upon a conviction. Therefore, once you are convicted, unless sentencing is postponed until a later time by the judge's order, you are "remanded" (turned over) to the custody of the sheriff to serve any jail time called for by your sentence. However, several options may be available to your attorney at this point that may delay or prevent any immediate jail sentence.

You may decide to take no further steps to fight your case and merely accept the conviction and penalty placed on you, complete the conditions of your sentence including jail time, and move on with your life. You may agree to do this but ask your attorney to ask the court to try to defer your jail sentence for some brief period of time based upon some personal or business need. Another option is for your attorney to file a motion for a new trial to request for your trial judge to review specific legal issues raised and ruled upon at your trial and determine whether errors were made in the court's rulings that justify "vacating" (removing) the conviction and starting over with a new trial. Motions for a new trial will be discussed fully in this chapter.

In rare cases, other motions (e.g., a motion in arrest of judgment) may be pursued by your attorney, based upon the specific facts of your case and legal issues that your attorney raised during your trial. These motions may actually convince the judge to make a ruling that lets you **NOT** be convicted at all, due to the prosecutor's failure to either meet all of his or her required proof at your trial or the prosecutor's failure to properly accuse the charges against you.

A third is to appeal your case to a higher court. If this is done, assuming your conviction is for a simple misdemeanor offense, most courts will allow your attorney to file an application for an appeal bond that lets you stay out of jail. This chapter discusses all options available to your attorney if you decide not to accept your guilty verdict and forego appealing further. Your attorney may opt for a "motion for new trial" over an immediate appeal for certain strategic reasons. (See **Sections 18.2 and 18.2.1** of this book.)

18.1. Having paperwork ready, if an appeal bond will be permitted. Immediately after sentencing, it is possible in some courts to apply for a supersedeas bond.[772] The word "supersedeas is Latin for "you shall desist." This is an order (a writ) issued after your conviction by the trial court that instructs the sheriff to "hold off" enforcement of most aspects of your punishment, most importantly, jail time.[773] The one place, however, that most states do not delay enforcement of your sentence is the imposition of a license suspension or revocation, which often occurs by statutory mandate upon your conviction occurring.

Most experienced DUI-DWI attorneys will have all standard appeal documents prepared for immediate filing in the event you lose the case. Beyond merely having all documents ready to file, your criminal trial specialist will inform you of how to prepare for such a possibility of appeal, including advising you on having funds available to pay an appeal bond. This is important because it may take months for an appeal to be prepared by the clerk's office, and briefs written and argued. The use of a supersedeas bond will also prevent the imposition of other "punishment" while the merits of your appeal are reviewed by the appellate court. Hence, mandatory items of punishment such as community service or alcohol assessment and treatment can be deferred until the appeal has been decided upon. Otherwise, you could be fully punished BEFORE the appeals court has a chance to review the errors by the trial court and possibly overturn your guilty verdict.

18.2. Deciding whether to appeal *or* file a motion for new trial *or* motion in arrest of judgment. Everyone is familiar with the concept of an appeal, which is to have a lower court's decision or verdict reviewed by a higher court. However, other tactical choices might be sought by your attorney rather than going directly to an appeal. When these "other" options are selected, you are not losing or giving up the right to a later appeal if the other tactics are not successful.

A *motion in arrest of judgment* is a special form of post-conviction pleading. It is generally only filed when a jury has found you guilty and some flaw or missing component in the State's case dictates to the trial judge that he or she must overturn your conviction. Perhaps the flaw was that the prosecutor failed to properly "accuse" the case due to a defective accusation. In the alternative, the proof that was introduced at trial may have fallen short of proving each of the several "elements" of the DUI-DWI crime that you were accused of in the written accusatory document.

Although motions in arrest of judgment are rarely available, if granted, your DUI-DWI conviction will be "vacated" (undone) and you will be completely acquitted of the DUI-DWI. A successful motion of this type ends with the judge declaring that the State failed to prove or properly accuse the DUI-DWI offense fully, that jeopardy attached by the trial beginning, and that the jury's verdict cannot stand.

A *motion for a new trial* is a more common pleading that is filed at the trial level (like the motion in arrest of judgment) so that the trial judge is given a chance to "correct" the improper verdict before an appellate court has to review the case. Also, if a claim of "ineffective assistance of counsel" is one of the "errors" cited, many state courts (as well as all federal courts) require that this issue first be raised by motion for new trial, not by direct appeal. Otherwise, this challenge is waived (you give it up as an issue), even if other legal challenges may still be pursued on an appeal.

---

[772]Florida - West's F.S.A. § 924.065; West's F.S.A. § 45.051; Alabama - Ala.Code 1975 § 12-12-73; Michigan - W.D. Mich. LCrR 57; MCR 3.604; Tennesee - T. C. A. § 27-7-104.

[773]http://dictionary.law.com/default2.asp?typed=supersedeas&type=1&submit1.x=81&submit1.y=16

Trial level courts in many jurisdictions have a variety of names. Some lower level non-jury courts may have their rulings reviewed by a "higher" local court, but not one of your state's "courts of appeal." The typical court for such appeals is the superior or circuit court that acts as your state's "court of general jurisdiction" for trial level serious civil and criminal cases. This type of review is in place to allow a more experienced judge to review what has occurred in the "inferior" court proceedings. Depending on your state's laws, a further appeal beyond this is available either by absolute right (direct appeal) or by discretionary appeal (meaning that your attorney has to seek permission at the appellate court to have the higher appellate court agree to review and rule upon the legal issues).

The first level of state appellate courts available in most states are often called the "court of appeals," while the highest state court is typically the "supreme court." Other states may have different names for their appellate courts. This can be confusing to people unfamiliar with the legal system. Your experienced DUI-DWI specialist will help you review your state's courts that handle appeals so you can see what avenues of appeal may exist.

18.2.1. Appeals. Depending on the structure of your state's court system, you may get a non-jury trial first, with an absolute right to appeal any adverse decision and begin all over at a jury trial if you are dissatisfied with the initial trial judge's decision. This system is antiquated and only remains in a few southern states such as Mississippi, Arkansas and Alabama.

In other states, you only get one trial. In a substantial majority of states, you can opt for either a bench or a jury trial. In fewer than a dozen states, this trial must be conducted as a bench trial only for at least first offenses (e.g., New Jersey, Nevada, Hawaii, Louisiana and other states).

Appellate courts are generally in place to review the actions of the lower court that handled your trial. Generally, the focus of an appeal is not to look at issues of "guilt" or "innocence." Instead, the purpose of an appeal is to review *rulings* of the trial court that led to a failure of justice or a misapplication of state law or procedure.

In an appeal of a criminal conviction, you no longer have a presumption of innocence as you did at trial. On appeal, the evidence is reviewed with an inference that the verdict reached was correctly rendered. Appellate courts utilize different "standards of review" in considering a multitude of different types of appellate errors that a trial judge may have committed. Your experienced DUI-DWI attorney will know all these "standards of review" that apply in your state.

Since this is the "focus" of an appeal, these challenges are only successful where timely objections or challenges were made to testimony or evidence (such as your breath test result) that the trial judge allowed the jury to hear as part of your case. Also, any adverse rulings that were made at any pre-trial or mid-trial motions can be appealed. Hence, your attorney's written motions, oral objections or motions, jury challenges for "cause" (meaning that your attorney sought to exclude a juror who was obviously biased) are all possible places that the judge made erroneous rulings that may cause your conviction to be ultimately overturned.

A trial transcript can be from several hundred to more than a thousand pages in length. This transcript contains the "record" of all that was done in the case. All legal challenges contained in the official record offer a chance for review of erroneous rulings. It is these rulings of law made by the judge (at trial or at pre-trial motions) that are the basis of most appeals. Prosecutor errors that are not corrected or properly ruled upon by the judge offer another avenue for reviewing your conviction.[774] It is these pre-trial and mid-trial decisions that form the basis of most successful appeals.

Once your trial is concluded, your attorney generally has a very limited time in which to file an appeal on your behalf. Once this time limit has passed, very rarely will the appellate court hear your challenges made "out-of-time." Instead, the appellate court will simply rule that your appeal is too late.

Once your notice of appeal has been filed, your attorney has to obtain the transcript of your trial or hearing. This will cost you money to get the transcript prepared by the court reporter. The preparation of this record is your expense, generally. Your attorney will then scour the "record" in your case for errors.

Your attorney must also order the clerk's "record" of all documents that were filed before, during and after your trial. This is sent directly by the clerk to the appellate court. This is a certified account of every document filed in the case, including the date and time of filing. This will also carry a fee for preparation, which is also a cost item for you.

Once an appeal is timely and correctly filed, it typically takes anywhere from nine to twenty-four months for the appellate court to render its decision. Your attorney may or may not be asked to present an oral argument to the appellate judges to assist them in making their decision. The trend today is that most appellate courts prefer to only receive written argument, and do not hear oral arguments from the attorneys.

If the initial appellate court does not grant relief from your conviction, you may still have the opportunity (in most states) to bring a form of request for further review to the highest court in your state, typically the state Supreme Court. Your highest court not only looks at the possible errors of law, but may also review the legal reasoning given by the intermediate appellate court. Usually, the request for review by your highest court is a matter of "discretion" and not mandatory by the highest court. Often, these requests or petitions for further review are called "petitions for certiorari." Generally, your state's highest appellate court gets to choose which cases it hears (and more importantly), which it will not.

Once the highest court in your state has either accepted your petition for further review or refused to take the case on certiorari, almost all cases are at the end of the final "review" stage. In rare circumstances, a federal or state "habeas corpus" proceeding may be sought. Almost never is this done in DUI-DWI cases, however.

18.2.2. Motion for a new trial. A motion for a new trial may be granted if the verdict is contrary to the evidence, or if the principles of justice and equity are decidedly and strongly contrary to the jury's guilty verdict.[775] Your DUI-DWI defense attorney may also be able to convince the trial court judge that one or more critical rulings made at trial were incorrect, thereby justifying a new trial. In other words, the trial judge has the discretion to decide that based on the evidence (or lack of evidence) presented at trial, or based upon the judge's erroneous rulings during trial, that the jury's verdict needs to be vacated (removed) so

---

[774]**Bolden v. State**, 272 Ga. 1, 525 S.E.2d 690 (2000); **Jefferson v. State**, 224 Ga.App.8, 479 S.E.2d 406 (1996); **James v. State**, 260 Ga.App. 536, 580 S.E.2d 334 (2003); **Mullinax v. State**, 231 Ga.App. 534, 495 S.E.2d 903 (1998); **Martin v. State**, 257 Ga.App. 435, 571 S.E.2d 459 (2002).

[775]Alabama - Ala.Code 1975 § 12-22-10; Arizona - A.R.S. § 12-2026; Georgia - O.C.G.A. §§ 5-5-20 and 5-5-21; Arkansas - A.C.A. § 16-89-130; Florida - West's F.S.A. § 924.065; California - West's Ann.Cal.Const. Art. 6, § 4; Indiana - Rules App.Proc., Rule 66; Michigan - M.C.L.A. 770.1; Mississippi - **Crowley v. State,** 791 So.2d 249 (Miss.App. 2000); Tennessee - T. C. A. § 27-3-131; Texas - Vernon's Ann.Texas C.C.P. Art. 31.08.

that a new trial can be heard again without such "error" (or errors) being part of the presentation of evidence. If your attorney can point to a clearly erroneous (and reversible) ruling by the trial judge, he or she may prefer to let you have a new trial rather than see the error reported in an appeal that is published for anyone in the world to see.

18.2.3. Motion in arrest of judgment. A motion in arrest of judgment is asking the trial judge to not allow the entry of **any** judgment of you due to a serious technical problem with the evidence that has been produced or possibly a problem with a defective accusatory document that the state produced at trial. To sustain a motion in arrest of judgment, it must typically be based upon the court in question lacking jurisdiction[776] or that the evidence presented at trial is in some respect fatally deficient or defective and (therefore) legally insufficient to support a judgment.[777]

18.3. Extraordinary motion for new trial, based on newly discovered evidence. The granting of a new trial based on newly discovered evidence is very rare. Numerous well-established criteria must ALL exist and be shown to have occurred by the party seeking the extraordinary motion before a new trial will be granted.[778] Failure to show *even one of these requirements* is sufficient to authorize the judge to deny the extraordinary motion for a new trial.

In a nutshell, this "newly discovered" evidence must not only be "new" but also be of such a nature that the new evidence was not known, or could not have been known to the party bringing the motion. The new evidence cannot be merely repetitive or cumulative of what was already presented at the original trial. The new evidence cannot be merely information that will impeach the credibility of a witness who testified at the original trial. The granting of this extraordinary motion for a new trial is left to the discretion of the trial judge, and no appellate relief will be granted to overturn the trial judge's ruling except upon an "abuse of discretion."

18.4. What can the appellate court consider in the appeal, and what can they (or will they) not consider? Appellate courts typically only consider final judgments or decisions.[779] A final judgment is one that disposes of all claims affecting all parties that were brought before the court.[780] Except in extraordinarily rare circumstances, the appellate court will not retry your case, will not weigh evidence, or review the jury's (or the trial judge's)

---

[776]**U.S. v. Lias**, 173 F.2d 685 (4th Cir. 1949); **State v. Williams**, 253 N.C. 337, 117 S.E.2d 444 (1960).

[777]**U.S. v. Lias**, 173 F.2d 685 (4th Cir. 1949); **Demolli v. U.S.**, 144 F. 363 (C.C.A. 8th Cir. 1906); **State v. Willis**, 147 La. 114, 84 So. 514 (1920); **Coblentz v. State**, 164 Md. 558, 166 A. 45 (1933); **State v. Doughtie**, 238 N.C. 228, 77 S.E.2d 642 (1953); **U.S. v. Kurt**, 986 F.2d 309 (9th Cir. 1993); **U.S. v. Treadway**, 748 F.Supp. 396 (W.D.N.C. 1990); **Clampitt v. U.S.**, 6 Indian Terr. 92, 89 SW 666 (Indian Terr. 1905); **Bowman v. State**, 227 Ga. App. 598, 490 S.E.2d 163 (1997); **People v. Jones**, 222 Ill. App.3d 206, 583 N.E.2d 623 (4th Dist. 1991); **State v. Sanford**, 250 Kan. 592, 830 P.2d 14 (1992); **State v. Southern Ry. Co.**, 145 N.C. 495, 59 S.E. 570 (1907).

[778]**People v. Grant**, 470 Mich. 477, 684 N.W.2d 686 (2004); **Miller v. State**, 908 So.2d 1168 (Fla.App. 2005); **State v. McQuary**, 2005 WL 2649166 (Mo.App. 2005); **State v. Shaw**, 705 N.W.2d 620 (S.D. 2005); **State v. Fury**, 2005 WL 2670249 (Tex.App.-Hous. (1 Dist.) 2005); **Timberlake v. State**, 246 Ga. 488, 271 S.E.2d 792 (1980).

[779]**Dixon v. Dixon**, 485 So.2d 742 (Ala.Civ.App. 1986); **Wesley v. Brandon**, 419 So.2d 257 (Ala.Civ.App.1982); **Middleton v. Finney**, 214 Cal. 523, 6 P.2d 938 (1931); **People v. Ross**, 344 Ill.App. 407, 101 N.E.2d 112 (Ill.App. 2 Dist. 1951); **Mertens v. McMahon**, 334 Mo. 175, 66 S.W.2d 127 (1933); **Anderson v. Bothum**, 77 N.D. 678, 45 N.W.2d 488 (1950); **Good v. Hartford Acc. & Indem. Co.**, 201 S.C. 32, 21 S.E.2d 209 (1942); **E.I. du Pont de Nemours & Co. v. Universal Moulded Products Corp.**, 189 Va. 523, 53 S.E.2d 835 (1949).

[780]**Musa v. Adrian,** 130 Ariz. 311, 636 P.2d 89 (1981).

determinations of credibility of witnesses, assuming testimony or documentary evidence was properly introduced at trial.

An appellate court might decide that based on the "legally admissible" evidence, that the finding of guilt was based on legally insufficient evidence to sustain a conviction. This can result from the trial judge improperly overruling objections by your criminal defense attorney or the trial judge not granting a motion for directed verdict of acquittal sought by your attorney. In such a case, the appellate court will reverse your conviction. In some cases, the reversal will also contain language that constitutes an "acquittal," due to the fact that (without the erroneous evidence being introduced) the remaining evidence was insufficient to support the DUI-DWI charge.

Appellate courts are quick to point out that they are not seeing and hearing the actual witnesses. Instead, they review the printed "record" (the transcript and pleadings filed at or before trial). They seldom see any of the physical evidence presented at trial, including any videotapes. The focus of the appellate courts is to look for erroneous trial rulings that either could have clearly affected the outcome or were so significant to the evidence being considered by the jury that likely could have led to the conviction.

As mentioned above, the appellate court only reviews decisions on legal issues made by the trial court. These rulings usually involve the admission of evidence, or the refusal to admit evidence. Sometimes, these rulings involve the granting or denial of oral or written motions, or the overruling or sustaining of objections made by your attorney or the prosecutor in the midst of the trial.[781] As you can see, for you to have a good chance on appeal, your criminal defense attorney must have "created a record" by raising numerous challenges to the evidence being offered against you at trial and requiring the judge to rule on these challenges.

The decision by the appellate court can take many forms. The appellate opinion may briefly review the arguments and "affirm" (uphold) your conviction. The appellate court may review the "challenged" rulings made in the lower court and find that the rulings were of such a nature that justice was denied, and that you walk away free of all charges. The appellate court may also rule that an error was made by the trial judge, but that the error was of a type that will cause a "new trial" to be ordered, free of the erroneous prior ruling. This last type of ruling (if the conviction is overturned) occurs more commonly.

Thus, one of two typical results comes out of an appellate decision from your point of view. One, the court of appeals **affirms** the decision of the trial court. This means the appellate court feels the trial court either "got it right" or was close enough that any error didn't matter. In the other result, the appellate court disagrees with all or part of the lower court's decision. The appellate court may **modify** a lower court's verdict, and change it somewhat to better fit with the law as the appellate court sees fit. This is rare in DUI-DWI cases and other criminal law concerns, however.

If the appellate court determines that the trial court did something wrong, and this error was significant, the most common thing they will do is to reverse the conviction and will instruct the trial court that the evidence that was allowed to be heard by the jury was incorrectly allowed into your case. Such a ruling indicates that the trial judge's error is likely to have had an impact on your jury's verdict of guilty. In such cases, the appellate court will return the case or **remand** it with instructions to the lower court that the erroneous rulings not be made at your retrial.

---

[781] **Taylor v. State,** --- S.E.2d ----, 2006 WL 573803 (Ga.App. 2006).

In a smaller number of "reversals" of convictions, the case cannot be retried. This means that you win your freedom from the DUI-DWI charge after the appellate court makes a finding that your rights were so significantly violated that you cannot be tried again.

18.5. Is my punishment held in abeyance during my appeal? Maybe. The availability of a supersedeas writ or an appeal bond is a function of your state's laws. If it is available, your sentence (or most aspects of it) will be delayed until the appeal is finalized. If not, you will begin your sentence at the discretion of the trial court. In most misdemeanor DUI-DWIs, you have a specific right to be released from jail after posting a reasonable bond pending your appeal. Your knowledgeable DUI-DWI defense attorney will know about the availability of an appeal and deferral of the imposition of punishment in your state.

18.6. Probation oversight or delayed totally until the case is finalized on appeal. If you are convicted of a DUI-DWI offense, and an appeal is sought along with a supersedeas writ or appeal bond application, you may be required to have a probation officer assigned to your case until your appeal is finalized. Depending on the laws of your state, you may have to report periodically (in person or by mail). The probation officer may not need to see you all the time, but may check the state crime information computer weekly or monthly to make sure that you have not violated any new state laws. New violations would authorize your judge to consider imposing new restrictions on your activities or even revoking the supersedeas bond. You may (in some states) need to be monitored through some means of electronic detection (i.e., through an ankle bracelet or an alcohol detection and monitoring system on your home phone) while you remain free on bond.

18.7. License loss is usually immediate, even if other punishment is held off. No matter what other punishment might be delayed due to the start of an appeal process or as a result of filing a motion for a new trial, the loss of your driver's license is not usually held off. If your driver's license was not surrendered and revoked or suspended at the time of your arrest, it will usually be taken at the time of sentencing after your criminal trial. This is usually not a matter of discretion with your trial judge because state law mandates the surrender of any license "upon conviction."

In spite of an appeal or motion for a new trial, your license will usually remain suspended. The determination of when reinstatement can occur depends on your state's laws. Usually, you remain suspended until: (1) you are either found not guilty at a new trial; or (2) the appellate court reverses your original conviction; or (3) the period of suspension or revocation (as set by state law) is completed and all conditions for reinstatement have been met by you. These conditions typically include a showing of completion of driving school (DUI-DWI school), showing proof of automobile insurance and possibly the installation of an ignition interlock device.

18.8. Expungement of a conviction is controlled by statute and by your state's decisional authority. If you are convicted of a DUI-DWI offense, can your criminal record be cleared at a future time? Will your arrest and the record of either your conviction or acquittal follow you forever? Like a lot of answers in the law, this depends on your state's laws.

In several states, including California and Texas, you can seek to have a conviction removed from your **state** record by filing a specific set of documents and paying a filing fee.[782] In others (New York, South Carolina, North Carolina and Georgia), removing a conviction (or even a record of your acquittal) is not possible except under extraordinary circumstances.

---

[782]West's Ann.Cal.Penal Code § 1203.4, Superior Court Fee Schedule; TX - Vernon's Ann.Texas C.C.P. Art. 55.01.

Georgia, for example, has no "expungement" law whatsoever. Ask your DUI-DWI attorney about the applicable law in your jurisdiction.

18.8.1. Some states have a mechanism to routinely clear records. Some states have a specific mechanism, either by statute or by case law to clear your criminal or traffic violation record. If you are found not guilty, a different process may apply.[783] If you are convicted of certain criminal offenses, these records can be cleared from the state's records in many jurisdictions by another legal process after a specified period of time passes. Also, most states require that you get into no further trouble.[784]

If your conviction of a state law has violated your civil rights, then a federal district court likely has the power to expunge your criminal records.[785] These last two options are very, very rare for a DUI-DWI conviction. Moreover, remedies such as these are more likely to happen in felony cases involving issues such as a wrongful conviction based upon defective forensic evidence (i.e., your DNA could not be compared to crime scene evidence in a 1985 rape conviction).

Even if some process exists to clear your record, the chance always exists that not all references to your arrest, accusation, trial, conviction and acquittal cannot be removed form all possible databases. The federal government almost NEVER totally clears all records and computer notations to your criminal arrest record.

For this reason, if you apply for a job with a high-level security clearance in the future, or merely answer background questions on a job application, it is usually best to inform your potential employer about your prior circumstances rather than to chance them finding the record of your conviction. Deception on a job application is usually considered to be worse than the old record of having made a mistake in your past. Clearly, the best report you can make to a prospective employer is that you were merely accused of DUI-DWI, but found NOT GUILTY. Hence, the value of having a top-notch DUI-DWI defense specialist is of paramount importance.

18.8.2. Other states have no statute and poor legal authority to ever remove a prior conviction. Some states have no statutory process to remove the record of your conviction from your criminal record, no matter what the circumstances. Case law in these states consistently rejects removal of a criminal record for a DUI-DWI conviction.[786] A good DUI-DWI specialist will know the options available to you where you have been charged and convicted, and can help you in whatever process is available. Do not expect your attorney to be able to correct a matter that is totally beyond his or her control.

18.9. If new trial is granted by the trial judge or your case is reversed and remanded after an appeal, will a new trial be required? Possibly. When an appellate court reverses (takes away the conviction) and remands (sends the case back to the trial court), they are saying that the trial court made one or more significant errors at your trial. This means that your conviction cannot be upheld. Often, the evidence that was allowed (incorrectly) to be introduced will either be excluded at your new trial or no longer available for use at the new trial.

---

[783]North Carolina - N.C.G.S.A. § 15A-146; Illinois - 20 ILCS 2630/5; Missouri - V.A.M.S. 610.122; Tennessee - T. C. A. § 40-32-101; Ga. Code Ann., §§ 35-3-36 and 35-3-37.

[784]Vernon's Ann. Texas C.C.P. Art. 55.01; West's Ann.California.Penal Code § 1203.4; Washington - RCW 9.95.240; W. Va. Code, 61-11-25 [2000]:1; Rhode Island Gen. Laws 1956, § 12-1.3-1, et seq; Oregon - O.R.S. § 137.225; Ohio - R.C. § 2953.32; Florida - West's F.S.A. § 943.0585.

[785]42 U.S.C. § 1983, **United States v. Sumner**, 226 F.3d 1005 (9th Cir. 2000); **State v. Ambaye**, 616 N.W.2d 256 (Minn. 2000).

[786]Louisiana - LSA-R.S. 44:9(E)(3)(a).

Hence, the prosecutor may not have enough evidence to proceed to a new trial. And a dismissal or a reduction of charges may be mandated.

The prosecutor may also consider that his or her office already took their best shot at you, and is now faced with starting over. This is expensive, and often their witness or witnesses may no longer be available. Plus, your defense attorney will have the benefit of using the detailed, sworn testimony of the police officers available in the transcript of your first trial to impeach these officers at any new trial. Such facts may give your attorney powerful leverage to negotiate with the prosecutor either to dismiss the DUI-DWI charges or seek to reduce the charges to a lesser offense.

18.10. Correcting an error in your sentencing. In rare cases, detailed review of the record in your entry of a guilty plea or in your sentencing after trial can reveal errors made by your judge, the prosecutor or even your own attorney. This type of post-conviction review is best handled by attorneys who specialize in fighting such cases.[787]

Errors may have occurred when the judge mistakenly sentenced you to the wrong code for too long[788] or incorrectly sent you back to jail after the time allowed to do that had already passed or expired.[789] The difficulty of such situations may be to locate and pay a specialist in *habeas corpus* relief, unless family, friends or a court-appointed attorney care enough to try to assist you.

---

[787]Certain attorneys specialize in these matters and will go to any state to handle such appeals. See http://www.georgia.criminal-defense-lawyer.com.

[788]**Landon v. State**, --- S.W.2d ---, 2006 WL 408230 (Tex.App.-Tyler 2006).

[789]**State v. Rompre**, 837 So.2d 453 (Fla.App. 5 Dist. 2002); **Stevenson v. State**, 808 A.2d 1205 (Del.Supr. 2002); **Hebb v. State**, 714 So.2d 639 (Fla.App. 4 Dist. 1998).

Chapter 19

Understanding Habitual Violator (Habitual Offender) Laws

in Relationship to DUI-DWI Laws.

19.0. General purpose to this chapter. Although fewer than half of 1% of all drivers ever become "habitual violators" (also called "habitual offenders"), this topic must be covered in a book for clients facing DUI-DWI charges. While it is legal for others to drive their vehicles if they have a driver's license, once you have been declared a habitual violator because of DUI-DWI convictions (or other serious driving offenses in some jurisdictions), it becomes illegal for you to operate a motor vehicle, even if you somehow obtain a driver's license. This chapter discusses what is required for you to be considered a "habitual violator" and the ramifications of having been placed in this unenviable legal status.

19.1. Statutory wording. A habitual violator usually means any person who has been arrested and convicted within the United States three or more times (of serious driving offenses like DUI-DWI) within a fixed period of time.[790] It does not matter (in most states) if your three DUI-DWI convictions were each in different states.

As mentioned above, several jurisdictions have added other highly dangerous driving convictions to the list of "HV" offenses that can count toward three violations within your state's prescribed "lookback" term of years. Examples of these are attempting to elude a police officer, or striking an occupied vehicle and leaving the scene (hit and run). Your state may have a statute that calls for "HV" status to be possible from ONE driving incident in which ALL THREE serious driving acts occurred and resulted in convictions against you.[791]

19.2. Penalties for causing the death of another while driving "HV" revoked. As would be expected, if you cause the death of another person while driving your vehicle as a habitual violator, the penalty is quite severe.[792] In Georgia, for example, instead of a maximum jail term of 15 years per fatality, the maximum jail term is extended to 20 years if you were driving while "HV."[793] All that is required to receive this severe penalty is to be operating a vehicle and that another person's death occurred in a collision with your vehicle. No causal connection to your poor driving and the death is required.

---

[790]Georgia - 3 in 5 years - O.C.G.A. §40-5-58; Tennessee - 3 in 5 years - T. C. A. § 55-10-603; South Carolina - 3 in 3 years - Code 1976 § 56-1-1020; Florida - 3 in 10 years - West's F.S.A. § 316.193, 3 in 5 years - West's F.S.A. § 322.264; Texas - third time becomes a felony, no time limit - V.T.C.A., Penal Code § 49.09; California - 3 in 10 years - West's Ann.Cal.Vehicle Code § 23566; Colorado - 3 in 7 years - C.R.S.A. § 42-2-202; Delaware - 3 - either 3 or 5 years - 21 Del.C. § 2802; Indiana - 2 in 10 years - IC 9-30-10-4; Washington - 3 in 5 years - West's RCWA 46.65.020; Mississippi - 3 in 5 years - Miss. Code Ann. § 63-11-30(2)(c); Hawaii - 3 in 10 years - HRS § 291E-61.5; Kansas 3 in 5 years - K.S.A. § 8-285; Montana - 3 in 3 years - MCA 61-11-203.

[791]O.C.G.A. § 40-5-1(16.1); **Hollis v. State**, 234 Ga.App. 269, 505 S.E.2d 837 (1998).

[792]Colorado - C.R.S.A. § 18-1.3-401; Delaware - 21 Del.C. § 2810; Indiana - IC 9-30-10-16; Mississippi - 5 years - Miss. Code Ann. § 63-11-30; Tennessee - T. C. A. § 55-10-616; California - West's Ann.Cal.Vehicle Code § 23566; Texas - V.T.C.A., Penal Code § 49.09;

[793]O.C.G.A. §40-6-393.

19.3. The state's burden of proof. The facts that led to your being declared a dangerous driver (being declared an "HV") are of no consequence when you are found behind the wheel of a motor vehicle.[794] Once you have been declared a habitual violator, if you are caught driving or operating any vehicle, the State is not required to address any collateral attacks that your attorney may raise as to why you originally received the habitual violator status. As a general rule, the legitimacy of having been declared "HV" will not be considered in your current prosecution.

19.4. Habitual violator status differs from "recidivist" status. A **recidivist** is a repeat criminal offender who is convicted of a crime after having been previously convicted of this same crime.[795] If you are considered a recidivist, while your penalty for the second conviction for the same crime may be significantly greater due to the existence of a prior offense all that is required to become a recidivist is to break the law a second time. For example, you would be considered a recidivist if you received a second DUI-DWI conviction.

It is a crime for anyone to drive while intoxicated. A habitual violator status differs because you are prohibited by law from doing something that other people can legally do. If you are declared a habitual violator, it is a crime for you to **operate any motor vehicle**, whether sober or intoxicated, for any reason, even though doing so would not be illegal for anyone with a valid license. Simply stated, being declared an "HV" driver makes you totally ineligible to operate **ANY** vehicle for any purpose, at any time, until your privilege to drive has been legally restored in accordance with state law.

19.5. Procuring a license from another state does not cure "HV" status. Once you have been declared a habitual violator, if you operate a motor vehicle in most states, you can be convicted of driving in violation of your habitual violation status even if you somehow obtain a driver's license from another state.[796] Your legal right to drive has been revoked by the state government and procuring a license by any means from another state will not restore your right to operate a vehicle. Your HV status is typically uncovered when your full name, fingerprints, date of birth, social security number or other identifying information is entered into the state's computer database by the police officer at the roadway.

19.6. The origin of predicate offenses leading to "HV" status. You can be determined to be a habitual violator based upon a conviction of DUI-DWI (or any of the other serious offenses proscribed by your state, such as homicide by vehicle, fleeing or attempting to elude, racing, reckless driving, aggressive driving, leaving the scene of an accident or fraudulent or fictitious use of or application for a driver's license) in violation of the laws of any

---

[794]Tennessee - T. C. A. § 55-10-616; **James v. State ex rel. Com'r of Motor Vehicles,** 475 N.E.2d 1164 (Ind.App. 2 Dist. 1985); **West v. Com.,** 14 Va.App. 350, 416 S.E.2d 50 (1992); **People v. Roybal,** 617 P.2d 800 (Colo. 1980); **Upward v. State,** 38 Wash.App. 747, 689 P.2d 415 (1984); **State v. Marcotte,** 124 N.H. 61, 466 A.2d 949 (1983); **State v. Fields,** 809 So.2d 99 (Fla.App. 2 Dist. 2002); **Bollen v. State,** 155 Ga. App. 181, 270 S.E.2d 227 (1980); **Texas Dept. of Public Safety v. Richardson,** 384 S.W.2d 128 (Tex. 1964).

[795]http://dictionary.law.com/default2.asp?typed=recidivist&type=1&submit1.x=38&submit1.y=12; **U.S. v. Morgan,** 354 F.3d 621 (7th Cir.(Wis.) 2003); **State v. Davis,** 203 So.2d 160 (Fla. 1967); **Harris v. Com.,** 26 Va.App. 794, 497 S.E.2d 165 (1998).

[796]**Tootle v. State,** 203 Ga. App. 497, 417 S.E.2d 433 (1992); **Stanek v. State,** 519 N.E.2d 1263 (Ind.App. 3 Dist. 1988); **Walls v. State,** 167 Ga.App. 276, 306 S.E.2d 371 (1983); **Sink v. Com.,** 28 Va.App. 655, 507 S.E.2d 670 (1998); Montana - MCA 61-11-203.

state.[797] Pleas of nolo contendere are considered in most states as a prior offense against you for the purpose of counting toward your habitual violator status,[798] while not in others.[799]

19.7. Declaring a person "HV" is not a criminal proceeding.[800] No fines are imposed as part of the legal notification where you are declared a habitual violator and no loss of any liberty is usually involved. The only result of this proceeding is that you are either given or mailed (by certified mail) a directive from the State where your driver's license was issued that you are not to operate any motor vehicle by virtue of your status as a dangerous driver. However, you may have been punished severely upon your conviction of that third serious driving event.

19.8. Constitutional considerations. Taking away your driver's license is not denying you any of your State or U.S. Constitutional rights. Having a driver's license is only a privilege, not a constitutional or statutory entitlement. As such, this privilege can be continuously reviewed by the state that gave it to you. For good cause, this privilege can be taken away from you. However, because a driver's license becomes an item of "property" once issued, the State cannot take your license away without reason, or without notice and an opportunity to be heard.[801]

Courts across America have recognized a driver's right to due process of law in being able to challenge the legitimacy of the declaration of "HV" status.[802] When taking away your license as a habitual violator, the State acts under its police powers for the protection of the public. So, while the right to hold driving privileges in your state is not guaranteed, nor protected by your legal rights, certain procedural and due process rights still are available.

19.9. The quantum of proof required. Before a state may remove your driver's license from your possession, they must prove certain basic facts supporting their legal action against you. This proof must include your identity as the dangerous driver, identify the dates and type(s) of offenses upon which your conviction was obtained, and include proof of your

---

[797]**Hardison v. Haslam**, 250 Ga. 59, 295 S.E.2d 830 (1982). Georgia - O.C.G.A. §40-5-58; Tennessee - T. C. A. § 55-10-603; South Carolina - Code 1976 § 56-1-1020; Florida - West's F.S.A. § 316.193(3), West's F.S.A. § 322.264; Texas - V.T.C.A., Penal Code § 49.09; California - West's Ann.Cal.Vehicle Code § 23566; Colorado - C.R.S.A. § 42-2-202; Delaware - 21 Del.C. § 2802; Indiana - IC 9-30-10-4; Washington - West's RCWA 46.65.020; Kansas - K.S.A. § 8-285; Montana - MCA 61-11-203.

[798]O.C.G.A. §40-5-63(a)(3); **Sigala v. Campbell**, 130 Fed.App. 129 (9th Cir. 2005); **State v. Domingues,** 106 Hawai'i 480, 107 P.3d 409 (2005); **State v. Foy**, 808 So.2d 735 (La.App. 2001); **Bailey v. State,** 728 So.2d 1070 (Miss. 1997); **State v. Knoff**, 22 Kan.App.2d 85, 911 P.2d 822 (1996); K.S.A. § 8-285; **Teague v. State,** 772 S.W.2d 932 (Tenn.Crim.App. 1988);

[799]**Department of Highway Safety and Motor Vehicles v. Rosenthal**, 908 So.2d 602 (Fla.App. 2 Dist. 2005).

[800]**Johnston v. State**, 236 Ga. 370, 223 S.E.2d 808 (1976); **State v. Boos,** 232 Kan. 864, 659 P.2d 224 (1983); **State v. Perreault**, 113 N.H. 588, 311 A.2d 303 (1973); **State v. Ponce**, 93 Wash.2d 533, 611 P.2d 407 (1980); **State v. Wilson**, 354 So.2d 1077 (La.App. 2 Cir. 1978); **Iowa Dept. of Transp. v. Iowa Dist. Court for Poweshiek County,** 530 N.W.2d 725 (Iowa 1995); **State v. Wilhere,** 653 A.2d 282 (Del.Super. 1994); **Bouldin v. Com.,** 4 Va.App. 166, 355 S.E.2d 352 (1987).

[801]Fifth Amendment, Fourteenth Amendment, U.S.C.A.

[802]**Appeal of Elias,** 70 Pa.Cmwlth. 404, 453 A.2d 372 (1982); **State v. Domingues,** 106 Hawai'i 480, 107 P.3d 409 (2005); **Fetty v. Com., Dept. of Transp., Bureau of Driver Licensing,** 784 A.2d 236 (Pa.Cmwlth. 2001); **State v. Sneed,** 8 S.W.3d 299 (Tenn.Crim.App. 1999); **State v. Anaya,** 123 N.M. 14, 933 P.2d 223 (1996); **State v. Stafford,** 394 So.2d 1287 (La.App. 1 Cir. 1981); **Van Gerpen v. Peterson,** 620 P.2d 714 (Colo. 1980); **Scott v. Hill,** 407 F.Supp. 301 (E.D.Va. 1976); **State v. Fernandez,** 156 So.2d 400 (Fla.App. 2 Dist. 1963).

receipt of a clear notice that you were declared to be a "habitual violator." Often, state law will allow documentary proof of certain certified records, transcripts or return mail receipt cards to supply proof of "service" upon you. Your attorney will probably be aware of current legal challenges based upon hearsay or confrontation grounds.[803]

19.10. Identification of driver. As a minimum, your name and the name of the person the State is attempting to declare a habitual violator must be the same. This is especially true if you deny that the person with the prior violations claimed by the State is you.[804]

19.11. Identification of victim. If you are being prosecuted for felony vehicular homicide in conjunction with your habitual violator status, the State must prove not only your habitual violator status, but also that the victim named in the indictment died as a result of your driving actions.[805] Most states do not require that a DUI-DWI or other serious driving offense be proven to have occurred as the causal connection with the victim's death when you have an "HV" status.

19.12. "Operate" is construed broadly. In most jurisdictions, the law is broadly written to cover both "drive," "operate" and "to be in actual physical control." To "operate" means to "drive" or "to be in actual physical control." This is true even when the physical control falls short of driving.[806]

19.13. Is there a misdemeanor "HV" lesser included offense as a possible plea alternative? Your felony habitual violator statute may also have a lesser-included offense of operating a motor vehicle after revocation of a driver's license but before the issuance of a new license after the term of suspension or revocation is over. This misdemeanor offense may not contain the felony habitual violator element of operating a motor vehicle within the prescribed "lookback" period, as set out in your notice of license revocation or suspension. If you are caught operating a motor vehicle within the stated period during which you are declared to be a habitual violator, you will be charged with the felony. If you have successfully "cleared"

---

[803]**State v. Smith**, 155 Wash.2d 496, 120 P.3d 559 (Wash. 2005); **State v. Leonard**, 915 So.2d 829, (La.App. 1st Cir. 2005).

[804]**State v. Miller,** 608 S.W.2d 158 (Tenn.Crim.App. 1980); **State v. Dawson,** 91 N.M. 70, 570 P.2d 608 (N.M.App. 1977); **State v. Johnson,** 194 Wash. 438, 78 P.2d 561 (1938); **Hill v. State**, 162 Ga. App. 637, 292 S.E.2d 512 (1982): **People v. Coyle,** 88 Cal.App.2d 967, 200 P.2d 546 (Cal.App. 1 Dist. 1948); **State v. Grooms,** 359 N.W.2d 901 (S.D. 1984); **Shapiro v. State,** 233 Ga.App. 620, 504 S.E.2d 719 (1998); **State v. Morin,** 598 A.2d 170 (Me. 1991); **Frazier v. State,** 907 So.2d 985 (Miss.App. 2005); **Brady v. State,** 575 N.E.2d 981 (Ind. 1991); **Montgomery v. State,** 277 Ark. 95, 640 S.W.2d 108 (1982).

[805]**Everett v. State**, 216 Ga. App. 444, 454 S.E.2d 620 (1995); **State v. Campbell,** 189 Mont. 107, 615 P.2d 190 (1980); **State v. Brown,** 996 S.W.2d 719 (Mo.App. W.D. 1999).

[806]J. Pearson, *What Constitutes Driving, Operating, or Being in Control of Motor Vehicle for the Purposes of Driving while Intoxicated State or Ordinance*, 93 A.L.R.3d 7 (1979-2005); Florida - West's F.S.A. § 322.01; Tennessee -T. C. A. § 55-8-101; Texas - V.T.C.A., Transportation Code § 541.001; Missouri - V.A.M.S. 565.002; Wisconsin - W.S.A. 343.305; **Miller v. State**, 202 Ga. App. 414, 414 S.E.2d 326 (1992); **U.S. v. Walker**, 393 F.3d 819 (8th Cir. 2005); **Com. v. Johnson**, 833 A.2d 260, 2003 PA Super 354 (Pa.Super. 2003); **Freeman v. State,** 69 S.W.3d 374 (Tex.App.-Dallas 2002); **People v. Howard,** 100 Cal.App.4th 94, 121 Cal.Rptr.2d 892 (2002); **Com. v. Eckert,** 431 Mass. 591, 728 N.E.2d 312 (2000); **People v. Page,** 266 A.D.2d 733, 698 N.Y.S.2d 774 (N.Y.A.D. 3 Dept. 1999); **State v. Jones,** 714 So.2d 819 (La.App. 1 Cir. 1998); **Lathan v. State,** 707 P.2d 941 (Alaska App. 1985); **Jones v. State,** 461 So.2d 686 (Miss. 1984); **State v. Graves,** 269 S.C. 356, 237 S.E.2d 584 (S.C. 1977); Indiana - IC 9-13-2-47; Washington - West's RCWA 46.61.504 and West's RCWA 46.61.502.

the stated period of HV revocation term, you may be charged with a misdemeanor offense if you are caught driving before you have gotten the state to reissue your license.[807]

19.14. Eligibility for issuance of a license or lack of license is no defense.
It does not matter if you were eligible to get a driver's license anywhere else in determining whether you can be charged with a violation of your habitual violator status.[808] Nor is it a valid legal defense in most states to a charge of being a habitual violator if you have never had a driver's license,[809] although in Kansas, you cannot be convicted of driving as an "HV" if you have never had a valid driver's license.[810]

19.15. Lack of knowledge of "HV" consequences is no excuse.
You do not need to know that you are still considered a habitual violator, or to know of the consequences of your actions by operating any vehicle, to be held responsible for this offense. In most states, merely being found driving or being in actual physical control of any motor vehicle will lead to a felony charge of driving after having been declared (being notified of being) a habitual violator.[811] Your lack of knowledge of this legal status is an adequate defense in a few places.[812]

19.16. "HV" status alone will not elevate a vehicular homicide to murder.
If you have a habitual violator status and you are caught driving with your license revoked, this alone will not constitute the malice element in a malice murder prosecution.[813] Felony murder is a special type of homicide charge that is brought against you where someone died while you were committing a felony. If you are charged with a felony vehicular homicide based on your driving after being notified of your habitual violator status, during the commission of felony fleeing and attempting to elude a police officer, a felony murder charge may be possible.[814]

19.17. The "notice" requirement for "HV" revocation.
Like any other "property" right, before your driver's license can be taken away, you must receive notice of this process to be declared a habitual violator. Much of the appellate litigation in your state on "HV" revocations will typically deal with the State's ability to prove that you were actually notified or "served" with the notice of the total ban of driving privileges. Trial judges commonly allow proof to be used at a hearing or trial that falls short of your right to be confronted with admissible evidence.

---

[807]**Davis v. Com.,** 12 Va.App. 246, 402 S.E.2d 711 (1991); **Travis v. Com.,** 20 Va.App. 410, 457 S.E.2d 420 (1995); **Hyde v. State,** 205 Ga. App. 754, 424 S.E.2d 39 (1992); **People v. Parga,** 964 P.2d 571 (Colo.App. 1998).

[808]**Stanek v. State,** 519 N.E.2d 1263 (Ind.App. 3 Dist. 1988); **Goblet v. State,** 174 Ga.App. 675, 331 S.E.2d 56 (1985); **Bryant v. State,** 182 Ga. App. 609, 356 S.E.2d 698 (1987); **Sink v. Com.,** 28 Va.App. 655, 507 S.E.2d 670 (1998).

[809]**Mays v. State,** 190 Ga. App. 390, 378 S.E.2d 145 (1989); **Carroll v. State,** 761 So.2d 417 (Fla.App. 2 Dist. 2000).

[810]**State v. Logan,** 28 Kan.App.2d 289, 14 P.3d 1193 (2000).

[811]**Com. v. Tharp,** 724 A.2d 368 (Pa.Super. 1999)**; Turner v. State,** 210 Ga. App. 303, 436 S.E.2d 229 (1993).

[812]**Reed v. Com.,** 15 Va.App. 467, 424 S.E.2d 718 (1992); **Bishop v. State,** 638 N.E.2d 1278 (Ind.App. 4 Dist. 1994); **State v. Lewis,** 263 Kan. 843, 953 P.2d 1016 (Kan. 1998); **People v. Parga,** 964 P.2d 571 (Colo.App. 1998).

[813]**Chester v. State,** 262 Ga. 85, 414 S.E.2d 477 (1992).

[814]**People v. Andrews,** 2003 WL 21398293 (Mich.App. 2003); **State v. Archer,** 150 Or.App. 505, 947 P.2d 620 (1997); **State v. Tiraboschi,** 269 Ga. 812, 504 S.E.2d 689 (1998); **Franks v. State,** 636 P.2d 361 (Okla.Crim.App. 1981).

19.17.1. Requirement. Not only must you have received this notice, but the State also has the burden of *proving* that you received it. Some states allow the State to prove that they took such reasonable steps to get the notice to you, that the court can determine this requirement was met.[815] Today, many courts will actually serve the formal notice upon you in the same courtroom that you enter a plea of guilty (or are found guilty) of the third "HV" offense. Another common procedure is for a law enforcement officer to later locate you at home or at work and deliver the notice to you personally.

19.17.2. Due process. Due process is a fundamental constitutional right, which applies before your life, liberty or property is taken away from you by the government. A key component of due process is that you must have notice that it is going to be taken away and that a hearing be made available to you during which you can argue your claim of non-receipt of the requisite notice.[816]

19.17.3. Prima facie proof. "Prima facie proof" is proof that stands by itself.[817] Once such proof is established, the court will accept it as true. If the State shows it mailed notice of your HV status to you by either certified mail or statutory overnight delivery with return receipt requested to your last known address, this is typically prima facie evidence that you received notice of your habitual violator status.[818] Once such a showing is made, it is then up to you to prove otherwise, or to rebut this proof.[819]

19.17.4. No presumption. As noted above, the State has to establish that you received notice of your habitual violator status for you to be punished for operating a motor vehicle again.[820] No assumption exists that just because the State declared you a habitual violator without meeting the above notice requirement that you should be held to this higher standard of legal accountability without the State proving that you received the required notice.

19.17.5. Sufficiency of notice. By whatever method you receive this notice (in person or by mail), the notice must also be unambiguous and not misleading in telling you that you now are considered a habitual violator. This notice is not required to set forth all of the legal consequences if you do drive again after being declared a habitual violator.[821]

---

[815]"No person shall ... be deprived of life, liberty, or property, without due process of law..." U.S.C.A. Const. Amend. V; "No State shall make or enforce any law which shall abridge the privileges or immunities of citizens of the United States; nor shall any State deprive any person of life, liberty, or property, without due process of law..." U.S.C.A. Const. Amend. XIV.

[816]**Powell v. State,** 2005 WL 2051291 (Tenn.Crim.App. 2005); **Richards v. Johnson,** 2005 WL 1528419 (W.D.Va. 2005); **Weaver v. State,** 242 Ga. 8, 247 S.E.2d 749 (1978); **State v. Campbell,** 877 So.2d 112, 2003-3035 (La. 2004); Georgia - O.C.G.A. §40-5-58; Tennessee - T. C. A. § 55-10-610; South Carolina - Code 1976 § 56-1-1030; Colorado - C.R.S.A. § 42-2-204; Delaware - 21 Del.C. § 2806; Indiana - IC 9-30-10-8; Washington - West's RCWA 46.65.065; Montana - MCA 61-11-210.

[817]http://dictionary.law.com/default2.asp?typed=prima+facie&type=1&submit1.x=47&submit1.y=9; **Collins v. State,** 567 N.E.2d 798 (Ind. 1991).

[818]O.C.G.A. §40-5-58(b); **State v. Morin,** 598 A.2d 170 (Me. 1991); **Collins v. State,** 567 N.E.2d 798 (Ind. 1991); **Wallace v. State,** 158 Ga.App. 338, 280 S.E.2d 385 (1981).

[819]**King v. State,** 179 Ga. App. 184, 345 S.E.2d 902 (1986); **Collins v. State,** 567 N.E.2d 798 (Ind. 1991).

[820]**People v. Parga,** 964 P.2d 571 (Colo.App. 1998); **State v. Orr,** 246 Ga. 644, 272 S.E.2d 346 (1980); **Fields v. State,** 679 N.E.2d 898 (Ind. 1997).

[821]**People v. McKnight,** 200 Colo. 486, 617 P.2d 1178 (1980); **Quarles v. State,** 763 N.E.2d 1020 (Ind. Ct. App. 2002); **State v. Woodard,** 387 So.2d 1066 (La. 1980); **State v. Sims,** 335 Or. 269, 66 P.3d 472 (2003).

19.17.6. Service by mail. You can receive this notice in any way approved by your state's law, but the methods by which your state can assure you have received proper notification include regular mail,[822] certified/registered mail, hand delivery, or statutory overnight mail with return receipt to your last known address.[823]

19.17.7. Personal service of notice. The State can also have someone personally serve you with notice. The person who serves this upon you is usually a law enforcement officer such as a state trooper or a deputy sheriff or court-appointed process server. This person will hand you the documents giving you notice of your habitual violator status.[824] This person's sworn affidavit or a court transcript from any court proceeding that clearly shows the delivery of the notice will usually take away any argument that it was served upon you.

19.17.8. Constructive notice. "Constructive notice" is a legal fiction that is imputed or implied by the law to constitute reasonable notice to a person.[825] It is the law's substitute for actual notice, by which the law advises you that because of a special circumstance you should have received notice, and the court will consider that you did receive that notice.[826] In some states, simply being convicted of a specific form of DUI-DWI is enough notice to you that you are now considered a habitual violator. Furthermore, in some jurisdictions, a SINGLE driving event may have had three or more "serious" (HV) offenses that will trigger an "HV" declaration without any other errant driving in your lifetime,[827] while in other states, the offenses must be separated by being separate incidents.[828]

---

[822]**Brown v. State,** 677 N.E.2d 517 (Ind. 1997); **State v. Martinez,** 268 Kan. 21, 988 P.2d 735 (1999); **State v. Morin,** 598 A.2d 170 (Me. 1991); **Collins v. State,** 567 N.E.2d 798 (Ind. 1991); **State v. Moore,** 1992 WL 354194 (Del.Super. 1992); **People v. Calvo,** 847 P.2d 205 (Colo.App. 1992).

[823]O.C.G.A. §40-5-58(b); **Bureau of Motor Vehicles v. Fisher,** 117 Ohio App. 59, 189 N.E.2d 744 (Ohio App. 10 Dist. 1962); **Texas Dept. of Public Safety v. King,** 366 S.W.2d 215 (Tex. 1963); Washington - certified mail - West's RCWA 46.65.065; Iowa - I.C.A. § 321.501;

[824]**State v. Woodard,** 387 So.2d 1066 (La. 1980); **McDonald v. Iowa Dept. of Transp.,** 2002 WL 1331787 (Iowa App. 2002); **Smoot v. Com.,** 18 Va.App. 562, 445 S.E.2d 688 (1994); **Lanier v. State,** 237 Ga. App. 875, 517 S.E.2d 106 (1999); O.C.G.A. § 40-5-58; **Gould v. Director, New Hampshire Div. of Motor Vehicles,** 138 N.H. 343, 639 A.2d 254 (1994); **State v. Moore,** 1992 WL 354194 (Del.Super. 1992); **State v. Blair,** 1991 WL 35743 (Tenn.Crim.App. 1991); **State v. Vahl,** 56 Wash.App. 603, 784 P.2d 1280 (Wash.App. Div. 1, 1990); **State v. Atkinson,** 305 Or. 295, 751 P.2d 784 (1988); **State v. Grundman,** 138 Wis.2d 528, 406 N.W.2d 172 (Wis.App. 1987);

[825]**Amoco Production Co. V. U.S.,** 619 F.2d 1383 (10th Cir. 1980); **Physicians Plus Ins. Corp. V. Midwest Mut. Ins. Co.,** 246 Wis. 2d 933, 632 N.W.2d 59 (2001); **Joseph Bucheck Const. Corp. V. W.e. Music,** 420 So2d 410 (Fla. Dist. Ct. App. 1st Dist. 1982); **Blevins v. Johnson County,** 746 S.W.2d 678 (Tenn. 1988); **Barton v. Cannon,** 94 Idaho 422, 489 P.2d 1021 (1971); **State v. Vahl,** 56 Wash.App. 603, 784 P.2d 1280 (1990); **Reed v. Com.,** 15 Va.App. 467, 424 S.E.2d 718 (1992).

[826]**Butten & Superior Copper Co. V. Clark-Montana Realty Co.,** 249 U.S. 12, 39 S.Ct. 231, 63 L.Ed. 477 (1919); **Hotch v. U.S.,** 14 Alaska 594, 212 F.2d 280 (9th Cir. 1954); **Blevins v. Johnson County,** 746 S.W.2d 678 (Tenn. 1988); **Commercial Credit Corp. V. Duckett,** 114 Vt. 450, 49 A.2d 106 (1946); **Hagin v. Fireman's Fund Ins. Co.,** 88 Ariz. 158, 353 P.2d 1029 (1960); **Salt Lake, G&W Ry. Co. V. Allied Materials Co.,** 4 Utah 2d 218, 291 P.2d 883 (1955).

[827]Georgia - O.C.G.A. §§40-5-63 and 40-6-391 (DUI - less safe); **Hollis v. State,** 234 Ga.App. 269, 505 S.E.2d 837 (1998).

[828]**State v. Ahakuelo,** 5 Haw.App. 205, 683 P.2d 400 (1984); **People v. Jones,** 171 Mich.App. 720, 431 N.W.2d 204 (1988); **State v. Mace,** 133 Idaho 903, 994 P.2d 1066 (Idaho App. 2000); **Crawley v. State,** 423 So.2d 128 (Miss. 1982).

19.18. Penalty. If you are declared a habitual violator, and you are caught operating a motor vehicle, you likely face a very significant punishment. A punishment only becomes "excessive" and unconstitutional if it either is nothing more than a purposeless and needless imposition of pain and suffering or it is grossly out of proportion to the severity of the crime.[829] In that light, an imposition of significant mandatory jail time (without the possibility of any of this spent on probation or parole) for a violation of your habitual violator status is neither barbaric nor excessive.[830] Often, courts justify lengthy sentences based upon the clear danger that a two or three ton guided missile poses when driven by a chronically dangerous driver who has received clear notice of the lack of any legal right to operate that "missile."

19.19. Novel punishment within trial court's discretion. Because the purposes of probation include a trial judge's duty to protect society and to rehabilitate the probationer, in most states, the court's discretion to impose other forms of punishment outside of the norm will not be questioned in the absence of express authority to the contrary.[831] This is not true in others.[832]

19.20. Habitual violator and administrative license loss. In some states, a fixed period of driver's license embargo is automatically placed on your habitual violator status. During this time period you cannot even apply to have this status ended.[833] Administrative hearings relating to taking away your driving privileges have nothing to do with imposition of criminal punishment or a criminal prosecution. Hence, these administrative proceedings have nothing to do with ending or shortening the time period of a non-criminal punishment.

---

[829]**Coker v. Georgia,** 433 U.S. 584, 97 S.Ct. 2861, 53 L.Ed.2d 982 (1997).

[830]Tennessee - 1-4 years -**State v. McGill,** 2004 WL 1580614 (Tenn.Crim.App. 2004) per T.C.A §55-10-616; Alabama - minimum 60 days - **Ex parte Boyd,** 796 So.2d 1092 (Ala. 2001); Georgia - 1-5 years - **Cox v. State,** 241 Ga. 154, 244 S.E.2d 1 (1978); Nebraska - minimum 1 year - **State v. Cook,** 1999 WL 731844 (Neb. App. 1999); North Dakota - minimum 6 months for 4th DUI offense in 7 years - North Dakota CC, 39-08-01; Pennsylvania - 90 days to 2 years -75 Pa.C.S.A. § 1543; South Carolina - no more than 5 years - Code 1976 § 56-1-1100; **People v. McKnight,** 200 Colo. 486, 617 .P.2d 1178 (1980).

[831]Defendant had to place ad in newspaper with his mugshot and a caption of "DUI convicted." - **Lindsay v. State,** 606 So.2d 652 (Fla.App. 4 Dist. 1992); Making the person on probation wear a pink bracelet that said "DUI Convict," **Ballenger v. State,** 210 Ga. App. 627, 436 S.E.2d 793 (1993); Defendant must attend AA meetings and have random urine screens, or serve more jail time - **State v. Lamis,** 139 Ohio App.3d 617, 744 N.E.2d 1260 (Ohio App. 8 Dist. 2000).

[832]Could not have the defendant use a fluorescent license plate stating "convicted DUI" - **People v. Letterlough,** 86 N.Y.2d 259, 655 N.E.2d 146 (1995).

[833]South Carolina - 5 years - Code 1976 § 56-1-1090; Florida - 10 years - West's F.S.A. § 322.28; California - 5 years - West's Ann.Cal.Vehicle Code § 23566; Washington - 7 years - West's RCWA 46.65.070; Hawaii - 1 - 5 years - HRS § 291E-61.5.

Chapter 20

Boating and Flying Under the Influence

and Other Related "Impaired Operation" Laws.

20.0. Purpose of this chapter. Similar to the illegality of driving a motor vehicle under the influence of alcohol, operating a boat or flying while underage or under the influence of drugs or alcohol are also typically illegal. This chapter discusses these situations, and the ramifications of each offense.

During the discussion of each section in this chapter, the law from representative states will be referenced. Not every state has statutes that cover each of the situations discussed. Some states have radically different laws than their neighbors. It is vitally important that you not assume because your state is not specifically mentioned in this section that any "boating under the influence" activity is not illegal, or that any section applies in your state. If you have any question, consult your DUI-DWI specialist who can likely give you best information.

20.1. Boating under the influence or boating while intoxicated (BUI-BWI). Boating under the influence (BUI) or boating while intoxicated (BWI) is treated much like DUI-DWI in most states, and in most circumstances, there are the same possible charges of BUI-BWI as there are DUI-DWI.[834] There is little case law on the subject, because few trials go on to an appeal that would be recorded so as to establish case law. However, because of the similarities between BUI-BWI and DUI-DWI it is likely the courts would apply the same thought process and legal reasoning to both situations.

20.1.1. Statutory wording — common law offense - alcohol. One form of BUI-BWI is a "less safe" offense, where you just have to be adjudged to be less safe because of alcohol while operating a boat. A sample statute regarding this type of offense is that no person shall operate, navigate, steer or drive any moving vessel, or be in actual physical control of any moving vessel, nor shall any person manipulate any moving water skis, moving aquaplane, moving surf board, or similar moving device while under the influence of alcohol to the extent that it is less safe for that person to operate, navigate, steer or drive any moving vessel, moving water skis, moving aquaplane, moving surf board, or similar moving device.[835]

20.1.2. Statutory wording — per se offense — alcohol. Another form of BUI-BWI is a per se offense - that is, it is automatically illegal for you to operate a boat if your blood alcohol level is at a specified level or higher. A sample statute regarding this type of offense is that no person shall operate, navigate, steer or drive any moving vessel, or be in actual physical control of any moving vessel, nor shall any person manipulate any moving water skis, moving aquaplane, moving surf board, or similar moving device while that person's blood alcohol concentration is 0.08 grams[836] or more at any time within three hours after such operating,

---

[834]Alaska - AS 28.35.030(a); Alabama - Ala.Code 1975 § 32-5A-191.3; Michigan - M.C.L.A. 324.80176.

[835]Michigan - M.C.L.A. 324.80176(3); Georgia - O.C.G.A. § 52-7-12(A)(1); Florida - West's F.S.A. § 327.354; Texas - V.T.C.A., Penal Code § 49.06; Texas - V.T.C.A., Penal Code §§ 49.06 and 49.01; Alabama - Ala.Code 1975 § 32-5A-191.3; California - West's Ann.Cal.Harb. & Nav.Code § 655(b); South Carolina - Code 1976 § 50-21-112(A).

[836]Florida - West's F.S.A. § 327.35(1); Texas - V.T.C.A., Penal Code §§ 49.06 and 49.01; Alabama - Ala.Code 1975 § 32-5A-191.3; California - West's Ann.Cal.Harb. & Nav.Code § 655; New York - McKinney's Navigation Law § 49-a(2)(b).

navigating, steering or driving any moving vessel, moving water skis, moving aquaplane, moving surf board, or similar moving device.[837] At least one state still has a 0.10 gram per se level.[838]

20.1.3. Statutory wording — common law offense - drugs.

One form of BUI-BWI is a "less safe" offense where you just have to be adjudged to be less safe because of drugs while operating a boat. A sample statute regarding this type of offense is that no person shall operate, navigate, steer or drive any moving vessel, or be in actual physical control of any moving vessel, nor shall any person manipulate any moving water skis, moving aquaplane, moving surf board, or similar moving device while under the influence of any drug to the extent that it is less safe for that person to operate, navigate, steer or drive any moving vessel, moving water skis, moving aquaplane, moving surf board, or similar moving device.[839]

20.1.4. Statutory wording — per se offense — contraband drugs.

It can be inherently illegal for you to operate a boat if you have specified drugs in your system, such as marijuana or other controlled substances. A sample statute regarding this type of offense is that no person shall operate, navigate, steer or drive any moving vessel, or be in actual physical control of any moving vessel, nor shall any person manipulate any moving water skis, moving aquaplane, moving surf board, or similar moving device while there is any amount of marijuana or a controlled substance in a person's urine, blood or both, including metabolites and derivatives of each, without regard to whether or not there is any alcohol present.[840]

20.1.5. Statutory wording — inhalants or noxious vapors.

It could be argued that any of the above drug statutes that make it illegal to operate a boat but do not specify the particular drugs involved could include the use of an inhalant or a noxious vapor. A few states are more specific and a sample statute reads in part that a person commits the crime of driving while under the influence of an alcoholic beverage, inhalant, or controlled substance if the person operates or drives a motor vehicle or operates an aircraft or a watercraft.[841]

20.1.6. Statutory wording — combination of two or more impairing substances.

Yet another form of BUI-BWI is a "less safe" offense where you just have to be adjudged to be less safe because of any combination of drugs while operating a boat. A sample statute regarding this type of offense is that no person shall operate, navigate, steer or drive any moving vessel, or be in actual physical control of any moving vessel, nor shall any person manipulate any moving water skis, moving aquaplane, moving surf board, or similar moving device while under the combined influence of alcohol and any drug to the extent that it is less safe for that person to operate, navigate, steer or drive any moving vessel, moving water skis, moving aquaplane, moving surf board, or similar moving device.[842]

---

[837]Florida - West's F.S.A. § 327.35(1); Georgia - O.C.G.A. §52-2-12(a)(4).

[838]Michigan - M.C.L.A. 324.80176; Georgia - O.C.G.A. §52-7-12(a)(4); Tennessee - T. C. A. § 69-9-217.

[839]Florida - West's F.S.A. § 327.354; Texas - V.T.C.A., Penal Code §§ 49.06 and 49.01; Alabama - Ala.Code 1975 § 32-5A-191.3; Georgia - O.C.G.A. §52-7-12(a)(2); California - West's Ann.Cal.Harb. & Nav.Code § 655(b); South Carolina - Code 1976 § 50-21-112(A); New York - McKinney's Navigation Law § 49-a(2)(e). **State v. Higgins**, 680 N.W.2d 645 (N.D. 2004).

[840]Florida - West's F.S.A. § 327.354; skiing BUI marijuana - West's F.S.A. § 327.38; Tennessee - T. C. A. § 69-9-217(a); Georgia - O.C.G.A. §52-7-12(a)(5); Texas - V.T.C.A., Penal Code §§ 49.06 and 49.01; South Carolina - Code 1976 § 50-21-112(A); Michigan - M.C.L.A. 324.80176(1).

[841]Alaska - AS 28.35.030(a); Texas - V.T.C.A., Penal Code §§ 49.06 and 49.01.

[842]Alabama - Ala.Code 1975 § 32-5A-191.3(a)(4); California - West's Ann.Cal.Harb. & Nav.Code § 655(b); Georgia - O.C.G.A. §52-7-12(a)(3); South Carolina - Code 1976 § 50-21-112(A).

20.2. "BUI-BWI - prescribed drugs" can call for a higher standard. In some states, if you are taking a drug that has been prescribed for you, the legal standard to be considered BUI-BWI is higher.[843] This is not true in other states.[844] If you have any concerns or questions, consult your DUI-DWI specialist.

In those states with a different standard, the State must usually prove that you were acting in a manner that deviated from "use of your normal faculties." A sample statute would read in part that such people will not be in violation of the BUI-BWI code section unless they were **rendered incapable of operating** (emphasis added), navigating, steering, driving, manipulating or being in actual physical control of a moving vessel, moving water skis, moving aquaplane, moving surf board, or similar moving device safely as a result of using a drug other than alcohol that the person was legally entitled to use.

20.3. "Presumptions" (inferences) arising from test results. In some states, if you are involved in a boating incident where alcohol or drugs may have been involved, there are a couple of presumptions that might arise. In these "presumption" states, there is a presumption that if your blood alcohol is measured at a certain level within a couple of hours of being involved in the incident, your blood alcohol level was illegally high at the time of the incident. This presumption can be overcome by other evidence. A sample statute reads that it is a rebuttable presumption that the person had 0.08 percent or more, by weight, of alcohol in his or her blood at the time of operation of a recreational vessel if the person had an alcohol concentration of 0.08 percent or more in his or her blood at the time of the performance of a chemical test within three hours after the operation.[845]

The second presumption is one of likely guilt or innocence if the State can prove specific blood levels of alcohol or the simple presence of one of the proscribed substances. A sample statute reads in part that upon the trial of any criminal action, or preliminary proceeding in a criminal action, arising out of acts alleged to have been committed by any person who was operating a vessel or manipulating water skis, an aquaplane, or a similar device while under the influence of an alcoholic beverage, the amount of alcohol in the person's blood at the time of the test, as shown by a chemical test of that person's blood, breath, or urine, shall give rise to the following presumptions affecting the burden of proof:

(1) If there was at that time less than 0.05 percent, by weight, of alcohol in the person's blood, it shall be presumed that the person was not under the influence of an alcoholic beverage at the time of the alleged offense.

(2) If there was at that time 0.05 percent or more, but less than 0.08 percent, by weight, of alcohol in the person's blood, that fact shall not give rise to any presumption that the person was or was not under the influence of an alcoholic beverage, but the fact may be considered with other competent evidence in determining whether the person was under the influence of an alcoholic beverage at the time of the alleged offense.

(3) If there was at that time 0.08 percent or more, by weight, of alcohol in the person's blood, it shall be presumed that the person was under the influence of an

---

[843]Georgia - O.C.G.A. §52-7-12(b).

[844]South Carolina - Code 1976 § 50-21-112(A); Tennessee - T. C. A. § 69-9-217; Texas - V.T.C.A., Penal Code §§ 49.10.

[845]Michigan - M.C.L.A. 324.80184; California - West's Ann.Cal.Harb. & Nav.Code § 655(h) and (j); Georgia - O.C.G.A. § 52-7-12(d)(4); South Carolina - Code 1976 § 50-21-114(B); Florida - West's F.S.A. § 327.352.

alcoholic beverage at the time of the alleged offense.[846] Presumption does not equate to absolute proof. Attacks against this kind of presumption (if they are similar to the same presumptions found in a DUI-DWI situation) would likely either have to be against the fact that you were not really operating the boat, or against the scientific accuracy of the test.[847]

20.4. Implied consent. Similar to when you drive your vehicle on a public road, the term implied consent means in this situation that by operating a boat within the State's boundaries, you have impliedly and automatically given your consent to give a sample of your breath, blood or urine for chemical analysis if a law enforcement officer decides to arrest you for something occurring as a result of you operating a boat. A sample statute reads that a person who operates a water device is considered to have given consent to chemical tests or analysis of his breath, blood, or urine to determine the presence of alcohol, drugs, or a combination of both, if arrested for an offense arising out of acts alleged to have been committed while the person was operating or directing the operation of a water device while under the influence of alcohol, drugs, or a combination of both.

A test given must be administered at the direction of the arresting law enforcement officer. The person first must be offered a breath test to determine the alcohol concentration of his blood. If the person is physically unable to provide an acceptable breath sample because he has an injured mouth, is unconscious or dead, or for any other reason considered acceptable by licensed medical personnel, a blood sample may be taken.

If the officer has reasonable grounds to believe the person is under the influence of drugs other than alcohol, the officer may order that a urine sample be taken for testing. If the breath analysis reading is eight one-hundredths of one percent or above by weight of alcohol in the person's blood, the officer may not require additional tests of the person as provided in this chapter.[848]

20.5. Implied consent not withdrawn by death or loss of consciousness. Typically, if you are rendered unconscious, your implied consent for law enforcement to require you to give a blood, breath or urine sample for either drugs or alcohol is not withdrawn. This allows the police to collect evidence that can be used against you following your detention, regardless of your awareness of being tested. One of the most important ramifications of this is that you might not later be able to claim you would have refused to allow a sample to be taken if the police obtain that sample from a blood draw while you are unconscious. If you are unconscious, the police can simply obtain the sample without anyone's permission.[849] In at least one state, this is not true.[850]

---

[846]Michigan - M.C.L.A. 324.80184; California - West's Ann.Cal.Harb. & Nav.Code § 655(h) and (j); Georgia - O.C.G.A. § 52-7-12(d); South Carolina - Code 1976 § 50-21-114(B); Florida - West's F.S.A. § 327.352; Tennessee - T. C. A. § 69-9-217(j)(2); Alaska - AS 28.35.033.

[847]**Lattarulo v. State**, 261 Ga 124, 401 S.E.2d 516 (1991); **Cardenas v. State,** 867 So.2d 384 (Fla. 2004); **State v. Gallichio,** 71 Conn.App. 179, 800 A.2d 1261 (2002); **Hall v. State,** 560 N.E.2d 561 (Ind. App. 2 Dist. 1990); **Sturgeon v. State,** 575 N.E.2d 679 (Ind. App. 1 Dist. 1991); **State v. Klausner,** 194 Ariz. 169, 978 P.2d 654 (Ariz.App. Div. 1 1998); **Bouleware v. State,** 557 So.2d 1320 (Ala.Crim.App. 1989).

[848]Michigan - M.C.L.A. 324.80187; Georgia - O.C.G.A. § 52-7-12(e); South Carolina - Code 1976 § 50-21-114(A)(1); Florida - West's F.S.A. § 327.354; Tennessee - T. C. A. § 69-9-217(d)(1); Alaska - AS 28.35.031; New York - McKinney's Navigation Law § 49-a(7).

[849]Georgia - O.C.G.A. §52-7-12(f); South Carolina - Code 1976 § 50-21-114(D); Alaska - AS 28.35.035;

[850]Tennessee - T. C. A. § 69-9-217(g).

20.6. Refusal admissible into evidence. If you are involved in a boating incident where a law enforcement officer requests that you undergo a breath, urine or blood test, and you refuse, different things occur as a result of this "legal mandate" for testing. This refusal can be used as evidence against you in virtually all cases.[851] In other states, this refusal can also be used to increase criminal penalties,[852] or the refusal itself can be a criminal offense carrying a jail sentence.[853] In some states, there is an automatic monetary fine for any refusal.[854]

20.7. Underage boating under the influence. Much as it is with driving, in most states it is commonly a criminal offense for anyone under the age of 21 to operate a boat with a much lower blood level of alcohol. A typical statute reads that it is an infraction for a person under the age of 21 years who has 0.01 percent or more, by weight, of alcohol in his or her blood to operate any motorized vessel or manipulate water skis, an aquaplane, or a similar device.[855]

20.8. "Nolo contendere" or "Alford" plea — are they allowed? In some states, the ability of a person to be able to enter a plea of nolo contendere, or no contest, is dependant on other factors.[856] In Georgia, no one under the age of 21 can enter a "nolo" plea to BUI.[857]

An "Alford plea" is a guilty plea where you do not admit that you did the act, yet you accept that the prosecution likely has enough evidence with which they could convict you. While there is a distinct scarcity of legal decisions regarding such pleas and BUIs, in general, under Alford, an individual accused of crime may voluntarily, knowingly, and understandably consent to imposition of his sentence even if he is unwilling to admit his participation in acts constituting the crime.[858]

20.9. Child endangerment in a vessel. In some states, it is specifically unlawful to endanger a child in the use of a watercraft. This may be in addition to any other child endangerment statutes in your state's laws. A sample statute reads that "a person who violates this Code section while transporting in a moving vessel or personal watercraft or towing on water skis, an aquaplane, a surfboard or similar device, or a child under the age of 14 years

---

[851]Florida - West's F.S.A. § 327.352; Alaska - AS 28.35.032; New York - McKinney's Navigation Law § 49-a(7)(f); Georgia - O.C.G.A. §52-7-12(g); South Carolina Code 1976 § 50-21-116; Michigan - M.C.L.A. 324.80189. **Bowling v. State** 275 Ga.App. 45, 619 S.E.2d 688 (2005).

[852]California - West's Ann.Cal.Harb. & Nav.Code § 655.5(a).

[853]Alaska - AS 28.35.031.

[854]Florida - West's F.S.A. § 327.35215.

[855]0.02 -Under age 21 - Florida - West's F.S.A. § 327.355(1)(a); Alabama - Ala.Code 1975 § 32-5A-191.3(b); Georgia - O.C.G.A. § 52-7-12(k)(1); New York - McKinney's Navigation Law § 49-b; 0.01 - Under age 21 - California - West's Ann.Cal.Harb. & Nav.Code § 655.6(a).

[856]Michgan - M.C.L.A. 324.80186; M.C.L.A. 324.80197a; South Carolina Code 1976 § 50-21-113; Georgia O.C.G.A. §52-7-12.

[857]O.C.G.A. §52-7-12(k)(2).

[858]**Boykin v. Garrison,** 658 So.2d 1090 (Fla.App. 1995); **Crowe v. State,** 265 Ga. 582, 458 S.E.2d 799 (1995) reconsideration denied, certiori denied, 116 S.Ct. 1021, 516 U.S. 1148, 134 L.Ed.2d 100, rehearing denied 116 S.Ct. 1455, 517 U.S. 1151, 134 L.Ed.2d 573 (1996); **State v. Ray,** 310 S.C. 431, 427 S.E.2d 171 (1993).

is guilty of the separate offense of endangering a child by operating a moving vessel or personal watercraft under the influence of alcohol or drugs."[859]

20.10. Reckless operation of vessel or other water device. Simply being "reckless" in your boat is likely a violation of state law. A sample statute reads that a person who operates any water device in such a manner as to indicate either a willful or wanton disregard for the safety of persons or property is guilty of reckless operation. Reckless operation includes, but is not limited to, weaving through congested vessel traffic at more than idle speed; or jumping the wake of another vessel within two hundred feet of that vessel; or crossing the path or wake of another vessel when the visibility around the other vessel is obstructed; or maintaining a collision course with another vessel or object and swerving away in close proximity to the other vessel or object.[860]

20.11. Homicide by vessel. If someone dies as a result of your operation of a boat, this is likely considered a homicide by most states. A sample statute reads that when the death of a person ensues within three years as a proximate result of injury received by the operation of a boat in reckless disregard of the safety of others, the person operating the boat is guilty of reckless homicide.[861] Like almost all other homicides, this is typically a felony offense, meaning the punishment can be more than a year in prison and may also carry severe fines. Furthermore, multiple deaths can lead to an extremely high bond amount being required, and this is not unconstitutional.[862]

20.12. Feticide by vessel. Some states have a separate criminal offense for causing the death of an unborn child because of your operation of a vessel. This is a felony and involves injury of a pregnant woman in the second or third trimester. A sample statue reads that a person commits the offense of feticide by vessel in the first degree if he or she causes the death of an unborn child. The unborn child must be so far developed as to be capable of survival outside of the womb, which doctors call "quick."[863]

20.13. Serious injury by vessel. Some states have an additional serious (felony) criminal offense if you cause a serious injury through your use of a vessel. What constitutes a serious injury differs from state to state. A sample statute reads that whoever, without malice, shall cause bodily harm to another by depriving him or her of a member of his or her body, by rendering a member of his or her body useless, by seriously disfiguring his or her body or a member thereof, or by causing organic brain damage which renders the body or any member thereof useless shall be guilty of the crime of serious injury by vessel.[864]

20.14. Implied consent warnings. In those states where your consent to be tested for drugs and alcohol is implied by your operating a boat, an advisement of your right to refuse and (if you do test) the consequences of having a per se alcohol limit must be read to

---

[859]Georgia - O.C.G.A. § 52-7-12(l); Illinois - 720 ILCS 5/12-21.6. See **State v. Rennick**, 295 Mont. 97, 983 P.2d 907 (Mont. 1999), where engenderment charges were dropped in exchange for a guilty plea to the BUI-BWI.

[860]Michigan - M.C.L.A. 324.80147; South Carolina Code 1976 § 50-21-111; New York - McKinney's Navigation Law § 45); Georgia - O.C.G.A. §52-7-12.1.

[861]Michigan - M.C.L.A. 324.80176(4); South Carolina Code 1976 § 50-21-115; Florida - West's F.S.A. § 327.35(3)(c); Texas - V.T.C.A., Penal Code §§ 49.08; Georgia - O.C.G.A. §52-7-12.2; Alabama - Ala.Code 1975 § 32-5A-192.

[862]**Cameron v. McCampbell**, 704 So.2d 721 (Fla.App. 4 Dist. 1998).

[863]Florida - West's F.S.A. § 782.09; Georgia - O.C.G.A. §52-7-12.3.

[864]Michigan - M.C.L.A. 324.80176(5); Florida - West's F.S.A. § 327.35(3); Georgia- O.C.G.A. § 52-7-12.4; South Carolina Code 1976 § 50-21-113(B).

you so as to insure that you understand your rights.[865] Different statements may be required to be read depending on your age and your occupation (e.g., a commercial boat captain). The most important thing is that you inform your attorney if anything was read to you regarding your implied consent and what exactly was told to you by the law enforcement officer before any blood, breath or urine samples were taken from you.

20.15. Administrative suspension/revocation of boating (and possibly driving) privileges for refusing to submit to testing. In most states, if you refuse to undergo a breath, urine of blood test at the request of a law enforcement officer following some boating incident, an automatic penalty applies that may be similar to an automatic driver's license suspension for a refusal to take a similar test if stopped while driving.[866] Some states limit the suspension or revocation to boating privileges, while others will take away your driving privileges, too.

20.16. Administrative suspension/revocation of boating (and possibly driving) privileges submitting to testing and being over the legal limit. Similar to losing your driver's license automatically if you are arrested for DUI-DWI, your boating privileges may be automatically suspended if you are arrested for BUI-BWI and you have a positive test for either alcohol or drugs.[867] Some states have no automatic suspension.[868]

20.17. Requesting a hearing — timing and letter requirement. Much like the qualified right you have to a driver's license, the qualified right you have to operate a boat cannot typically be taken away without you having notice and an opportunity to be heard.[869] This is not a criminal hearing. It usually only controls whether or not you lose your right to operate a boat, not any punishment for any crime.

20.18. Term of suspension. The length of this revocation or suspension of boating privileges is state-specific, and usually lasts from 6 months to a year for a first offense.[870] Suspensions are typically longer for subsequent offenses.[871]

20.19. Penalties if convicted. The penalties you face if convicted of BUI-BWI depend on the individual state which convicts you, and if this is your first or a subsequent offense. For first offenses, you typically face up to 6 to 12 months in jail and a fine of up to $2500. In Florida, your vessel is also impounded, whether you own the vessel or whether it was just a boat owned by someone else that you were using.[872]

---

[865]Michigan - M.C.L.A. 324.80181(1)(b); Georgia - O.C.G.A. §52-7-12.5.

[866]South Carolina Code 1976 § 50-21-114 - 180 day boating suspension; Georgia - O.C.G.A. §52-7-12.5(e) - 1 year suspension; Florida - West's F.S.A. § 327.35215 - $500 fine and Florida - West's F.S.A. § 327.359 - up to one year in jail just for the refusal; Tennessee - T. C. A. § 69-9-217(f)(2) - six month suspension; Michigan - 6 months - Michigan - M.C.L.A. 324.80181(1)(b).

[867]Georgia - O.C.G.A. 52-7-12.6 - one year suspension; Tennessee - T. C. A. § 69-9-219 - one year suspension.

[868]Texas.

[869]Georgia - O.C.G.A. §52-7-12.5(g)(1); South Carolina Code 1976 § 50-21-114 (E); Florida - West's F.S.A. § 327.35215.

[870]South Carolina Code 1976 § 50-21-112 - 6 month suspension; Georgia O.C.G.A. 52-7-12.6 - one year suspension; Tennessee - T. C. A. § 69-9-219 - one year suspension.

[871]South Carolina Code 1976 § 50-21-112; Georgia O.C.G.A. 52-7-12.6; Tennessee - T. C. A. § 69-9-219.

[872]The penalties listed here are for first offenses. For subsequent offenses, see the listed statutes. South Carolina Code 1976 § 50-21-112 - Up to $250 fine and up to 30 days in jail; Georgia O.C.G.A. 52-7-12.6 - up to $1000 fine and up to 12 months in jail; Tennessee - T. C. A. § 69-9-219 - Up to $2500 fine, one year and up to 11 months, 29 days in jail; Texas - V.T.C.A., Penal Code §§ 49.06 - Up to $2000 fine and up to

20.20. What constitutes reasonable suspicion to stop a boat, versus stopping a motor vehicle on the highway? The level of your activity for a police officer to have "reasonable suspicion" in order to legally stop you while you are in a boat appears to be less than or the same as what is needed for this same officer to stop you if you were driving your car. An example would be if a law enforcement officer sees you with a can of beer in your hand while you are boating, this equates to reasonable suspicion that you may be BUI and the officer can stop you to check. [873]

20.21. Is reasonable suspicion even required to stop a boat? In some states, "reasonable suspicion"[874] or "probable cause"[875] is needed to stop you in a boat. In other states, such searches can be performed by the police on a public lake without cause.[876] Plus, if the police cause injury to someone on a vessel that is being randomly stopped, they are likely immune from civil liability under an immunity statute.[877]

The same right to stop a vessel without probable cause may not exist, however, on a private lake.[878] While most states have not litigated this question with regard to BUI-BWI, it is likely safest to assume that unlike your home, the police may stop your boat at any time and inspect you and the contents for illegal activity. This is particularly true if you are on the open seas (ocean) on an intercoastal waterway.

20.22. Administrative regulations pertaining to boating use. Unlike any such publishing requirement for DUI-DWI testing rules or regulations, these regulations do not likely apply to BUI-BWI.[879] Check with your local criminal defense attorney to get further information about your jurisdiction.

20.23. Flying under the influence. Similar to driving or boating under the influence of either drugs or alcohol, it is also typically against state law to fly while under the influence. It is also specifically against federal law to operate an aircraft while under the influence of either alcohol or drugs.[880] An example of a state statute reads that it is unlawful for any person who is under the influence of an alcoholic beverage or any drug, or the combined influence of an alcoholic beverage and any drug, to operate an aircraft in the air, or on the ground or water, or to engage in parachuting for sport. No person shall operate an aircraft in the air or on the ground or water who has 0.04 percent or more, by weight, of alcohol in his or

---

180 days in jail; Florida - West's F.S.A. § 327.35 - Up to $500 fine, vessel is impounded and six months in jail; Michigan - M.C.L.A. 324.80177.

[873]**State v. Baker,** 197 Ga. App. 1, 397 S.E.2d 554 (1990); **Maxwell v. State,** 587 So.2d 436 (Ala.Crim.App. 1991).

[874]Michigan - M.C.L.A. 324.80180.

[875]**Com. v. Lehman**, 857 A.2d 686 (Pa.Super. 2004).

[876]**Schenekl v. State**, 996 S.W.2d 305 (Tex.App.-Fort Worth 1999); **Dalton v. State,** 216 Ga. App. 411, 454 S.E.2d 554 (1995); **Peruzzi v. State**, 275 Ga. 333, 567 S.E.2d 15 (2002); **State v. Pike**, 139 N.C.App. 96, 532 S.E.2d 543 (2000); **Maine v. Giles,** 669 A.2d 192 (Me.1996).

[877]**Hayes v. Patrick**, 71 S.W.3d 516 (Tex.App.-Fort Worth 2002).

[878]**Meeks v. State**, 265 Ga.App. 279, 593 S.E.2d 746 (2004).

[879]**State v. Bowen**, 274 Ga. 1, 547 S.E.2d 286 (2001).

[880]14 C.F.R. § 91.17(a) No person may act or attempt to act as a crewmember of a civil aircraft — (1) Within 8 hours after the consumption of any alcoholic beverage; (2) While under the influence of alcohol; (3) While using any drug that affects the person's faculties in any way contrary to safety; or (4) While having .04 percent by weight or more alcohol in the blood. See news article about pilots getting 5 years at: http://www.courttv.com/trials/pilots/072105_sentencing_ctv.html?link=eaf.

her blood.[881] Take notice of the LOWER alcohol standard that applies to everyone, regardless of the age of the pilot.

20.23.1. Federal law also has jurisdiction, so possible double judicial proceedings since two sovereigns. Because many waterways (rivers, lakes, canals) form state boundaries, you could be prosecuted in two or more different courts for the same act of drunken operation of an aircraft. Many flights might originate in one state but fly or land in a different one.

Due to this ability to become subject to the laws of multiple jurisdictions, you could potentially face multiple trials and sentences for any one of your actions. This is because each state and the Federal government are all separate sovereigns, meaning they are independent governments. The concept of double jeopardy prohibiting multiple prosecutions for the same offense only applies when the multiple prosecutions occur within the same sovereign. Thus, if you commit a possible criminal offense like boating or flying while intoxicated, any state may attempt to prove that you violated the law within or above its boundaries when you were boating or flying after drinking or using drugs AND the federal government each could potentially prosecute you for the same actions. These same rules can apply to boating in more than one state's waters.

---

[881]Texas - V.T.C.A., Penal Code §§ 49.05 and 49.01; Georgia - O.C.G.A. § 6-2-5.1(a); Alaska - AS 28.35.030(a); California - 0.04 per se limit - West's Ann.Cal.Pub.Util.Code § 21407.1; South Carolina - 0.04 per se limit - Code 1976 § 55-1-100; Tennessee - T. C. A. § 42-1-201; Michigan - 0.02 per se limit - M.C.L.A. 259.185.

Appendix A

Legal Research Tips

Introduction. Like many professions, lawyers often write and abbreviate in their own language. Appellate cases, books, treatises, periodicals and other commonly used terms and phrases are verbally mentioned and written down in shorthand derived from centuries of law practice. This book is not meant to teach you how to practice law, instead to better understand the legal process so as to help you help your specialized DUI-DWI lawyer with your defense. This appendix will help you understand this legal shorthand, and to seek answers from the numerous sources of legal information available to almost everyone.

The law that the judges tend to follow comes from several sources, statutes and case law. Statutes are the written laws that come from the legislature with the approval (or over the veto) of the executive branch (governor or president). Case law comes from appellate courts interpreting these statutes as they apply to real-life situations. Courts determine what the words of the statutes mean to everyone else.

More than 1000 cases and statutes are cited and used throughout this book, usually quoted in the footnotes of the different chapters. This book is not intended to be an all-inclusive encyclopedia of the law of impaired driving. It is intended to provide an overview and guide to a person facing criminal charges relating to driving while intoxicated. This appendix will help you find these sources, as well as other sources you may locate on your own.

If you are interested in reading the full appellate court opinion for any case cited in this book, it can be found in sets of books called "reports" or "reporters." Because these books are specialized and expensive, local libraries may have only the *regional reporters* or state official reporters which contain your state's cases. Also, many smaller libraries will carry one of the sets of books containing the opinions of the U.S. Supreme Court.

To locate reporters in other jurisdictions, you will likely need to resort to one of the following sources:

(1) A major law school library;

(2) A state law library;

(3) A county law library in major cities; *or*

(4) A major law firm's library.

Today, legal cases and a myriad of other sources of legal authority are available *via* computer modem from one of two major legal research computer systems - - *Westlaw* and *NexisLexis*. For example, despite the author's law office having the largest assemblage of DUI-DWI attorneys in Georgia, our office does 100% of its legal research electronically. To have access to one of these systems, a person must subscribe to the particular service sought. Many attorneys have access to one or both of these systems, *but* access to the system database costs money, as does the phone or cable Internet service required to "connect" with these services' computers.

Although numerous types of legal authority have been cited in this book, the greatest number of references is to **court opinions** (cases) from various state and federal courts across the United States. These "cases" are identifiable by the **bold** name of the case, followed by some numbers and letters, and ending with a date bracketed with parentheses.

Statutory Law. The shorthand for statutory law is often fairly easy to recognize. First, the name of the state is often in the shorthand. As an example, West's Ann.Cal.Pub.Util.Code § 21407.1 is a California statute prohibiting flying under the influence of alcohol. In the midst of the shorthand are the letters "Cal." demonstrating that the statute is from California. The abbreviation "Ann." refers to "annotated," meaning that the statute will be followed by short appellate case blurbs that will identify key reported decisional law that corresponds to the statute that the Legislature enacted. "West's" refers to the largest legal publisher in history, West Publishing Company, which bid for and received the publishing rights for California's legal reporters (as well as numerous other states). The remainder of this citation is indicating that the state of California has a ***public utility code***, under which this particular statute was enacted.

However, a large number of statutes are indicated in this legal shorthand by abbreviations that have no obvious state of origin. As examples, O.C.G.A. stands for the Official Code of Georgia Annotated and R.C.W.A. is the Revised Code of Washington Annotated.

The most obvious way to recognize a shorthand term that indicates that you are probably looking at a statute is seeing the symbol "§" in the midst of the citation. This symbol stands for "section" and typically designates a part of the statute or constitutional provision being cited.

In checking statutes, the *first* number following the statute's name is usually the book or chapter that you will be looking for on the shelf. The remaining numbers are subparagraphs or sections within the main book, title or chapter. Many DUI-DWI laws of most states are covered under the heading "Motor Vehicles," or "Crimes" or "Criminal Offenses."

The letters and numbers associated with the statutory citation designate which part of the statute is being quoted. As an example, O.C.G.A. § 41-4-7(e)(2) means the Official Code of Georgia Annotated, section 41-4-7, part e, subpart 2.

Case law. Case law has its own special shorthand. For example, **"State v. Pike,** 139 N.C.App. 96, 532 S.E.2d 543 (2000)" designates a North Carolina case from their Court of Appeal (not from their Supreme Court) for a decision rendered in the year 2000. A quick glance at this citation will tell an experienced attorney all of this information, so that he or she can track down the case and its "holding" (the legal principles that it establishes), if North Carolina law may help with the attorney's legal arguments.

The first part **"State v. Pike"** tells everyone the parties to the case, the State of North Carolina and a person whose last name is "Pike." In civil cases, there are often more than just the two parties to judicial cases. If so, just the last name of the first party on each side is used to designate the shorthand name of the case. In criminal cases, one of the parties is always some governmental agency, either the "State," the "Commonwealth" (Com), the "People" or some other governmental entity. The other name is the name of the defendant. The first party named in an appellate case is the party that lost at the trial, and is the party bringing the appeal. Because many cases share names, there could be multiple cases of "State v. Pike."

The second two parts of the shorthand designation, those letters and numbers surrounded by commas, designate specific books in series of volumes where the case can be found. Each court has its own series of initial interim reports of the case decisions that are published in soft cover within weeks of the case being decided. These interim paperback versions are put into hard cover volumes of books when enough cases are collected to make an entire book. "139 N.C.App. 96" means the case being sought can be found in the 139th volume of the North Carolina Court of Appeals series, starting on page 96. These designators indicate and specific individual cases. No other case has these same numbers.

The United States has been broken down into numerous regions by West *[see chart below]*, such as Southeast, Northwest, Pacific, etc. West Publishing started its own set of parallel reporters (books) in the late 1800s, and marketed these to attorneys as a more useful tool because West's editors developed a short case summary called "headnotes" at the beginning of each case and later assigned its own proprietary "Key" numbers to each and every legal principle in American law. So, an attorney in Kansas could find a West regional reporter citation from another state with West Key number 433.2 and then see if Kansas had any cases reported under that same Key number. All of the appellate (intermediate appellate and highest courts, such as a state supreme court) courts in each region collectively also report all of their decisions in these volumes. The second set of letters and numbers represent where the same case may also be found in these regional collections. "532 S.E.2d 543" means that this case can be found in volume 532 of the Southeastern series, starting on page 543. These designators indicate the specific individual cases. No two cases share these numbers.

The last designator in the case citation is the year when the decision was rendered. "(2000)" means the case was decided by this court in the year 2000. As a part of this last designator, there may also be letters preceding the year. If present, this indicates the specific court or division of the intermediate appellate court in which the case was decided.

You may have noticed that some of the cases have *two* or *three* number/letter combinations following the case name, separated by commas. When this appears in the citation, it is because the case has been published in more than one reporter. Your local library may have one of these sets of books, but not the other, so these "parallel" references may assist you.

Two facts will help you to expedite your research of these cases. First, numerous cases cited are from the United States Supreme Court. The author has tried to provide you with either the citation from the "official" reporter for that court ("United States Reports"), which is shown as ___U.S.___, or the parallel reporter provided by West Publishing Company (the "Supreme Court Reporter"), which is shown as ___S. Ct.___. These are the reporters that your public library may have if it carries any bound volumes at all. If they have discontinued using the bound books, due to cost, your library may have Internet access to a legal research search engine on-line, but the number of subscriptions at each library may be very limited.

Secondly, as far as *state* cases, the author has always provided the West Publishing Company's citation to the appropriate **regional** reporter, plus given the official state or federal reporter citation in as many cases as possible. Many libraries will carry the West set of books, unless they have gone to total electronic search.

You can identify the appropriate West **regional** reporter by first locating the *state* abbreviation for the case. West has grouped the cases in certain regions into reporters for that **region**. The regional groupings are as follows:

Regional Reporter	Abbreviations	Covering Cases From The Following States
Atlantic	A. *or* A.2d	CT, DE, DC, ME, MD, NH, NJ, PA, RI & VT
North Eastern	N.E. *or* N.E.2dIL	IN, MA, NY & OH
North Western	N.W. *or* N.W.2d	IA, MI, MN, NE, ND, SD & WI
Pacific	P. *or* P.2d	AK, AZ, CA, CO, HI, ID, KS,

	MT, NV, NM, OK, OR, UT, WA & WY

South Eastern	S.E. *or* S.E.2d	GA, NC, SC, VA & WV
South Western	S.W. *or* S.W.2d	AR, KY, MO, TN & TX
Southern	So. *or* So.2d	AL, FL, LA & MS

In addition to the above regional reporters, West also publishes special reporters which provide case opinions from three of our most populous states---NY, CA & IL. Because each of these states has a large volume of cases, such a grouping makes sense. Plus, New York will even publish trial level opinions from some courts, as these cases are rendered.

Generally, these special state reporters will carry decisions from the state's highest court, plus selected other cases from selected lower courts in that state. The sets of books are:

New York Supplement (N.Y.S. *or* N.Y.S.2d)
California Reporter (Cal. Rptr.)
Illinois Decisions (Ill. Dec.)

Search engines. Now that you know what the legal shorthand indicates, how do you find the cases? Attorneys usually subscribe to specific legal search engines such as Westlaw[882] or LexisNexis.[883] In fact, because these services are on-line, these tools are often the first to report decisions from the courts. If reported on one of these services before being published in one of the above series, these citations contain an assigned tracking number, such as "2005 WL 123654." This shorthand means that the case was decided in 2005, and carries the case number of 123654 for the Westlaw service.

These search engines are very powerful, but they cost money. Most attorneys pay a monthly fee, depending on how much of the service they desire to use and how frequently they want to use the service.

The author writes for Thomson-West and uses their ultra-powerful search engine (Westlaw) for research needs. West offers a low-cost trial use of its search engine at: http://www.west.thomson.com/store/product.asp?product%5Fid=Westlaw+subscription+options

LexisNexis also offers free limited search capability for on-line case research at LexisONE at: http://www.lexisone.com/lx1/caselaw/freecaselaw?action=FCLDisplayCaseSearchForm&l1loc=L1E.

For the average person facing the tangled legal bureaucracy, these ongoing expenses can be prohibitive. Other ways exist for searching for full copies of these cases and statutes at minimal or no cost to you. The first of these is to use parts of the above citations in basic search engines like Google,[884] AskJeeves,[885] or Yahoo.[886] Link up to one of these generic search engines, and put one of the sets of designators (names or sets of letters and numbers) into the search field in quotation marks, like "532 S.E.2d 543." If these searches do not take you to the specific case that you want, they will at least take you to places where these cases have either been discussed or cited in discussions of issues involved in these cases.

---

[882]http://www.westlaw.com.

[883]http://www.lexisnexis.com.

[884]http://www.google.com.

[885]http://www.ask.com.

[886]http://www.yahoo.com.

Several free legal search engines such as Lawguru.com,[887] Findlaw.com,[888] and RefDesk.com [889] are available on-line. These are very useful at not only finding specific cases that are cited in this book, but to investigate the legal issues that you face if the issue is either not mentioned in this book or if the statutory or case law of your state is not mentioned in the text. Each of these search engines has its own set of instructions that are available on the different websites.

Search tips. Beyond entering the specific case citation designators into these search engines, if you are attempting to broaden your search, or if the results you get are not answering your questions, try using synonyms to the search terms. Instead of entering "DUI," try "DWI," "driving while intoxicated," "driving under the influence," "operating under the influence," "drunk driving" or "operating while intoxicated." Break out a thesaurus, and add as many of the different words as it takes to get results.

If one of the sites does not yield results, try a second, or a third site. Information that cannot be found on one web site may be readily available on another.

Conclusion. This "thumbnail" sketch of how to do legal research will only introduce you to the subject of legal research. The field of research is immense, and fairly complex. However, for the limited purpose of *finding* cases and statutes, this short explanation should suffice for most readers. If you hit a "dead end," ask the reference librarian for assistance.

You may want to copy selected cases and save them for use in your case or to read again. If the case doesn't make sense to you, this may be a function of the way the judge writes, or it may just be normal "legalese." You will just have to work through the wording and ask an attorney for guidance if you get stumped.

If you want to learn more about sources of legal material and about legal research, we highly recommend either of the following books:

1) Christopher G. Wren and Jill Robinson Wren, *The Legal Research Manual: A Game Plan for Legal Research and Analysis,* 3rd Ed., © 2002 Legal Education Publishing; ISBN: 0916951227.
2) William Statsky, *Legal Research and Writing – West Legal Studies (5th Ed.),* © 1998 Thomson Delmar Learning; ISBN: 0314129014.
3) Stephen Elias and Susan Levinkind, *Legal Research: How to Find & Understand the Law,* © 2004 NOLO Press; ISBN: 1413300588.

Last, there is no substitute for an experienced and well-season DUI-DWI trial attorney. You cannot represent yourself in these complex matters. If you try and fail to find answers to your questions, it is time to seek help from one of these experts.

---

[887] http://www.lawguru.com/.
[888] http://www.findlaw.com/.
[889] http://www.refdesk.com/lawsrch.html.

Appendix B

Glossary

ACCUSATION - The charging document that a prosecutor uses to identify each specific type of crime alleged to have been committed by the defendant. An accusation in a DUI-DWI case is typically several "counts" (each count is written and considered as a separate offense then set forth and described separately in the accusation) that identify in general terms, how, when and in what fashion each offense was committed. In DUI-DWI practice, a person might be accused in alternative "counts" of an accusation with (1) DUI-alcohol (drunk driving), (2) DUI-per se (being above the state's minimum mandatory alcohol blood level), (3) DUI-drugs [impairment from prescribed or illegal (i.e., cocaine) drugs], AND (4) DUI-alcohol AND drugs, by being under the combined impairing effects of both alcohol and some type of drug.

ACQUITTAL - A finding by a judge or jury that a person who was tried for committing a crime is not guilty.

ACUTE INTOXICATION - The term used by medical facilities to refer to intoxication that is "of clinical significance" (potentially fatal). Complications from acute intoxication may include trauma, aspiration (vomit getting into your lungs), delirium, coma, and convulsions, depending on the substance and method of administration.

ADJOURNMENT - Postponing or rescheduling a case or court session until another date or time. In some jurisdictions, this is called a "continuance." Each state's laws control when and under what circumstances an adjournment or continuance is available to either party.

ADJUDICATION - Generally, this term refers to a final judicial (by a court) determination of a decision in a pending case. In juvenile delinquency cases, it is the equivalent of a 'conviction.' In typical criminal cases, "adjudication" refers to the court entering its ruling of guilty or not guilty after a bench trial.

AFFIDAVIT - A written statement of fact that is verified by oath or affirmation before a notary public. These are commonly offered to the court, the judge and the jury to verify some fact or to confirm that some act has been accomplished.

AFFIRMATIVE DEFENSE - Without denying the charge, the defendant raises extenuating or mitigating circumstances such as insanity, necessity, or coercion to avoid civil or criminal responsibility. Another way of thinking of an affirmative defense would be as a valid excuse as to why the crime was committed or why the defendant should not be held to blame for the crime. The defendant usually must prove (or set forth some evidence of) any affirmative defense he/she raises. Court rules or state statutes typically require a defendant to notify the opponent before the trial that an affirmative defense will be asserted.

ALCOHOL - Derived from Arabic. Refers to a wide range of chemicals, whether suited for human consumption or not. The term "alcohol" is often used by lay persons to refer to alcoholic beverages made with ethyl alcohol or ethanol. The usual type of alcohol found in mixed drinks, wine and beer is ethanol. However, the chemical "alcohol" can be part of many products that contain some form of alcohol, often a different form of alcohol besides ethanol, as well as products such as sugarless chewing gum, breath sprays, medicines, mouth washes, cologne or deodorant. See **Appendix E** for a chart showing the wide range of chemicals that make up the alcohol family.

ALFORD PLEA - The so-called *Alford* plea is a form of "guilty" plea in which the defendant does not admit the act, but admits that sufficient evidence exists with which the prosecution could likely convince a judge or jury to find the defendant guilty. Upon receiving an *Alford* plea from a defendant, the court may immediately pronounce the defendant guilty and impose sentence as if the defendant had otherwise been convicted of the crime. However, in many states, such as Massachusetts, a plea that "admits sufficient facts" more typically results in the case being "continued without a finding" (see description below) and later dismissed. It is the appeal of the ultimate dismissal of charges that engenders most pleas of this type. This plea originated in the United States Supreme Court case of *North Carolina v. Alford*, 400 U.S. 25 (1970). After the *Alford* decision, the plea "Alford" plea generally has the same effect as a plea of guilty with respect to sentencing. Later use of the conviction as an aggravating factor (if the defendant is later convicted of another offense) is allowed in all courts.

ALIBI - A "lack of presence" defense. The Defendant need not prove that he was elsewhere when the crime happened; rather, a Prosecutor must *dis*prove a claimed alibi (i.e., Prosecutor must prove beyond a reasonable doubt that the defendant was present). Although rare in DUI-DWI cases, some drivers may not be present after an accident when the police arrive at the scene. In most, if not all, states, the Defendant must notify the prosecution prior to trial if they are going to claim an alibi defense.

APPEAL - A request to take a case to a higher court for review of proceedings in a lower court. No new evidence may be introduced during the appellate process; the reviewing court considers only whether errors occurred during prior proceedings.

APPEARANCE - Although usually associated with an attorney's "entry of appearance" (see below), this word can signify a client's obligation to show up for court at the time, date and place indicated in a summons or other court notification.

APPELLANT - The party appealing an adverse decision or judgment to a higher court.

APPELLATE COURT - A court having jurisdiction over appeals as opposed to a trial court that allows witnesses to testify under oath and enters rulings on admission of documents, exhibits or testimony at the trial.

APPELLATE JURISDICTION - The power and authority of a court (established by state law) to review a case that has already been tried by a lower court.

APPELLEE - The party responding to an appeal filed by the opposite party in a higher court.

ARRAIGNMENT - Typically, the first court appearance after an arrest and release from jail on bond, where the charges are formally read, and one enters his or her plea of guilty or not guilty.

ATTORNEY - A lawyer; one who is licensed to act as a representative for another in a legal matter or proceeding; one who is licensed to practice law. Most attorneys are licensed in and practice in one state.

ATTORNEY-CLIENT PRIVILEGE - In all legal matters, the client (whether or not a party to litigation) has a privilege to refuse to disclose, and to prevent another from disclosing, a confidential communication between client and lawyer. The attorney-client privilege authorizes a client to refuse to disclose, and to prevent others from disclosing, information communicated in confidence to the attorney and legal advice received in return. The objective of the privilege is to enhance the value which society places upon legal representation by assuring the client the opportunity for full disclosure to the attorney, unfettered by fear that others will be informed. While the privilege belongs only to the client, the attorney is professionally obligated to claim it on his client's behalf whenever the opportunity arises unless he has been instructed otherwise by the client.

BAIL - To set free a person arrested or imprisoned (pending trial or resolution of an appeal) in exchange for security such as cash, credit card deposit or real estate. Bail is forfeited if the person fails to appear in court as directed.

BOND - In criminal law, a surety bond puts up money or property that assures the appearance of the defendant or the payment of the defendant's bail if the defendant fails to appear. The person who agrees to be the "surety" is financially obligated to pay the bond if the person fails to appear. The failure to appear will typically cause the judge of the court requiring attendance to issue a "bond forfeiture" order, as well as a warrant for the defendant's arrest.

BLOOD ALCOHOL CONTENT/LEVEL (BAC) OR (BAL) - The amount of alcohol in a person's bloodstream. The adult (age 21 and over) legal limit in drunken driving cases is .08% in all states. For someone under 21, the legal limit is 0.00%, 0.01% or 0.02%, depending on the state the offense is committed in. For persons of any age driving a commercial vehicle, the legal limit is 0.04%.

BLOOD TEST - A test to measure a person's BAC by drawing the blood, usually done in a hospital. Blood tests are often requested where substances other than alcohol are suspected to be impairing the driver in a DUI-DWI case, or where an accident may require that the person suspected of drunk driving is already going to a hospital. In some states, refusal is possible for a person who is capable of refusing. In other states, forcible blood draws are authorized.

BREATH TEST - A test to measure your breath alcohol content, usually done at a police station or a jail. One does not have to agree to blow into a breath machine, and in most cases, one should not agree to do so. Some police jurisdictions also use roadside breath tests, but these are not admissible as evidence in court.

BRIEF - A written document presented to the court by a lawyer that sets forth both the facts of the case and the law which supports the lawyer's case.

BURDEN OF PROOF - This refers to the evidentiary obligation of a party to legal proceedings having to "carry" the burden to prove his or her allegations during a trial. Different levels of proof are required depending on the type of case. This phrase is employed to signify the duty of proving the facts in dispute on an issue raised between the parties in a cause. In criminal cases, as every person is presumed to be innocent until the contrary is proved, the burden of proof rests on the prosecutor to prove each and every element of the charges. After the prosecutor has presented such evidence, the defendant may need to rebut (challenge) the prosecutor's evidence, as a practical matter, even though the burden of proof in criminal cases never shifts to the defendant.

CHARGES - A formal accusation, indictment, or other criminal complaint form used to inform an accused person of the existence of a criminal offense against him or her. These are also sometimes merely called "criminal charges."

CIRCUMSTANTIAL EVIDENCE - A type of indirect evidence that implies something occurred but does not directly prove it. For example, circumstantial evidence that it rained recently can be obtained by a witness testifying that he went into his house at 6:00 p.m. and it was not raining. Later, at 7:30 p.m., he comes outside and the ground, roadways and trees are wet. He did not SEE it rain, but circumstantial evidence says it did.

CITATION - Similar to a unique web site address [URL], this is a legal shorthand method of referring to a particular criminal or civil case that has been decided by a court. Each reported (and some unreported) decisions by appellate and even trial level decisions in some states is given a unique set of alphanumeric identifiers that help attorneys refer to the case so others can look it up and review the ruling by that court. In this book, you will frequently see such cases used as references for legal points that are made either in the text itself or in the footnotes. By copying the case names (State v. Jones) and the numbers and words following (233 N.C. App. 456) as a whole and entering this information into either a legal search engine or into Google, you can find the entire case itself.

CODE - A collection of written laws arranged into chapters, table of contents, and index, and published by legislative authority. For example, the Iowa Code is a collection of laws approved by the Iowa legislature. Abbreviations for statutory provisions in this book may be a byproduct of the "code" citation. Example: Official *Code* of Georgia Annotated is abbreviated O.C.G.A.

COMMON LAW - Law based upon previous decisions of courts or referring to the body of laws passed down from England to America.

CONCURRENT SENTENCE - Upon conviction for multiple crimes, a criminal sentence can be ordered by the judge to be served at the same time as another criminal sentence, rather than one after the other.

CONSECUTIVE SENTENCE - Upon conviction for multiple crimes, criminal sentences that must be served one after the other, rather than at the same time, are called "consecutive" sentences. Consecutive sentences may only be imposed if there is specific statutory authority to do so. In some circumstances, consecutive sentences may be imposed within the judge's discretion (e.g., when a person is convicted of a new offense committed while on parole status). In other circumstances, consecutive sentences are mandatory under state law.

CONTEMPT OF COURT - This phrase refers to any act or conduct that shows disrespect for the court's authority. Contempt usually means a person has failed to obey a court order. Contempt can be punished by a fine or imprisonment. Generally, contempt that can result in jail time must occur within the courtroom or in the presence of the judge. Other forms of contempt are typically punished by fines.

CONTINUANCE - This term refers to postponing or rescheduling a case or court session until another date or time. In some jurisdictions, this is called an "adjournment." Each state's laws control when and under what circumstances an adjournment or continuance is available to either party, and typical rules include being able to prove several criteria exist that justify the Court resetting the case to a future date.

CONVICTION - Finding by a judge or jury that a person is guilty beyond a reasonable doubt of committing a crime.

COPPING A PLEA - See "Plea Bargain" below.

COURT-APPOINTED ATTORNEY - Refers to legal counsel assigned by the court to represent an indigent criminal defendant. A court-appointed attorney is not necessarily a "free" attorney; the court can order that some or all of the attorney's time utilized on behalf of the client be reimbursed. If there is no chance jail time will be imposed on a defendant on a misdemeanor, the judge need not appoint an attorney.

CROSS EXAMINATION - The process of challenging the evidence presented by a witness who is testifying for the opposite side in a trial. The person cross-examining the witness may utilize a series of questions, plus documents and other exhibits (such as videotape) to case doubt on the testimony of the witness. Questions on cross-examination (as opposed to direct examination) can be "leading" (questions that suggest the answer to the witness). Leading questions are not permitted to be asked by the party who offers the witness for providing evidence on their behalf.

DEFENDANT - The person accused of a crime.

DEPOSITION - The testimony of a witness not taken in open court, but given under oath before a court reporter pursuant to authority given by statute or court rule, to take testimony in preparation for trial. Deposition testimony may be introduced as evidence in a court proceeding. Only a few states allow deposition testimony in criminal cases, although depositions are very common in civil cases.

DIRECTED VERDICT - In criminal cases, upon motion made by the defense attorney, a trial judge's directive (order) to a jury to return a specified verdict of "not guilty," usually because the prosecutor failed to prove its case. This type of ruling or order is sometimes called an "instructed verdict of acquittal."

DISTRICT ATTORNEY - A lawyer elected or appointed to serve as a prosecutor for the state in criminal cases. In some jurisdictions, this prosecutor's title is "state" attorney or solicitor. The common abbreviation for the elected District Attorney in a jurisdiction is "DA," while the assistants who work for him/her are "assistant district attorneys" (ADA).

DIVERSION - Also known as adjournment in contemplation of dismissal or conditional dismissal. A program in which a defendant is put on probation for a set period of time and his or her case does not go to trial during that time. If the defendant meets the conditions set by the court, the charge will be dismissed. Diversion is generally only allowed for first offenders, as that term is defined by state law. Some jurisdictions have no statutes authorizing diversion in DUI-DWI cases.

DOCKET - A list or index of cases and case events maintained by the clerk of court. This term can also mean a list of cases on a court calendar for a specific day or term of court.

DOUBLE JEOPARDY - In criminal law, a plea of "double jeopardy" is a procedural defense based upon state and/or federal constitutional rights (and possibly statutory rights in some states) that forbids the government from trying an accused citizen a second time for a crime, after having already been tried for the same crime. In ancient common law, a defendant would plead "*autrefois acquit*" or "*autrefois convict*" which merely meant that the defendant had been acquitted or convicted of the same offense before.

ENTRAPMENT - Entrapment occurs when police engage in impermissible conduct that would induce an otherwise law-abiding person to commit a crime in similar circumstances, or when police engage in conduct so reprehensible that it cannot be tolerated by the court. Entrapment does not occur if the defendant has the propensity to commit the crime, and the police conduct only gives the defendant the opportunity to commit the crime. This defense is almost never viable in a DUI-DWI case.

ENTRY OF APPEARANCE - A document filed by an attorney with the court, and provided to the prosecutor and judge, advising that the attorney has undertaken representation of a specific individual.

EVIDENCE - A fact presented before a court such as a statement of a witness, an object, etc., that bears on or establishes a point in question.

EXCLUSIONARY RULE - This is a court-made rule preventing illegally obtained evidence from being used by the government in its case-in-chief against a criminal defendant. The rule is derived from the 4th and 5th Amendments to the United States Constitution. Some states have enacted state constitutional provisions or state statues to give citizens more protections under state laws that track the protections covered by the federal 4th and 5th Amendments. These state laws can offer more protection than the United States Constitution offers to a citizen.

EXCULPATORY EVIDENCE - Evidence that the Prosecutor may possess that could establish a person's innocence or be used by his or her attorney to prove some fact that could cast doubt upon his or her guilt.

EX-PARTE - A Latin term that means "by or for one party." This refers to situations in which only one party appears before a judge without the adversary being present. Such meetings are highly suspicious, and can result in legal penalties against the party that meets with a judge without the opponent being present or even being notified.

EXPUNGEMENT - A process where a conviction may be set aside either upon the passage of time or the completion of certain conditions. The conviction may or may not be totally removed from all aspects of a criminal record. Not available in some states.

EXTRADITION - EXTRADITE - This is the formal application process whereby the prosecuting authority of one jurisdiction seeks the turnover of a person who has been located in one state to the authorities in another state where that person has been accused of or convicted of a crime. This can also be done between nations, where a person has fled from one country to another to avoid being brought to justice.

FIELD SOBRIETY TESTS - Various roadside exercises that are used by law enforcement officers to determine whether or not a person is likely to have an alcohol content at or above the legal limit. Although police routinely do not advise of the voluntary nature of these evaluations, field sobriety evaluations are optional in almost all jurisdictions. Most experienced attorneys advise their clients against attempting the evaluations due to inconsistent officer training, defective administration of the evaluations, as well as the *subjective* nature of these exercises.

FELONY - A crime considered to be of a graver nature than a misdemeanor and punishable by more than a year in prison. Examples of felonies include murder, kidnapping, manslaughter, burglary, robbery, and certain types of sexual abuse.

HABEAS CORPUS (Petition for) - From the Latin, this translates to "you have the body." A petition for habeas corpus is a petition to bring a person (typically a prisoner) before a court or a judge for a hearing on whether the person is being held or detained illegally. In most common usage, it is directed to and served upon the official person detaining another, commanding that the person produce the body of the prisoner or person detained so the court may determine if such a person had been denied his or her liberty without the process of law.

HEARSAY - A statement made outside of court (i.e., not from the witness stand at the present proceeding) that is offered into evidence not merely to prove that the statement was made but to prove that it was *true*. The reason that hearsay is often kept out of a trial is that it is considered unreliable. Instead of having someone testify about what they heard someone else say, it is much more reliable to have the person who actually made the statement testify. There are dozens of long-established exceptions to the general rule that hearsay statements are inadmissible in court; the exceptions are based on circumstances where the out-of-court statements carry a strong likelihood of trustworthiness (e.g., deathbed statements, self-incriminating statements, statements made to doctors about medical conditions, etc.).

INDICTMENT - A formal accusation of a felony, issued by a grand jury (a special jury of everyday citizens that is assembled to decide if sufficient evidence exists to go forward with the prosecution)

INFORMATION - A formal accusation of crime, based on an affidavit of a person allegedly having knowledge of the offense.

INFRA – Regarding something that is cited as legal precedent later in the same document.

INSTRUCTIONS - Also called "jury instructions" or "jury charges," these are directions given by the judge to the jury concerning the law of the case and on the applicable legal principles that the jury is duty-bound to follow in deciding guilt and innocence.

INTERLOCUTORY - A legal term that means provisional, temporary or preliminary. It applies to legal orders or decrees given by a court before it issues its final decision. An "interlocutory appeal" involves an appeal of a matter within a case before the case is concluded or final.

JURISDICTION - The right and power to interpret and apply the law to a particular case. One definition relates to the authority of a court to hear and rule upon certain types of cases. This is sometimes called "subject matter jurisdiction." This term can also refer to a limitation on the extent of authority or control. By way of example, the law in some states limits the place or geographic area that a police officer can arrest a person to being the area where a crime is committed and observed within the officer's "jurisdiction" (e.g., the City Limits).

JURY - A number of people, selected according to law, and sworn to listen to certain matters of fact and declare the truth based upon evidence presented to them. In a criminal case, panels of 6 to 12 jurors (depending on state law) can hear misdemeanor offense cases, and 12 will typically be required to hear felony cases. It may or may not be required (in a few states) to have a unanimous decision for either a conviction or an acquittal.

JURY SELECTION - Also called, *voir dire*. This is an inquiry of prospective jurors, by the attorneys (in most jurisdictions) and by the judge, to determine if such jurors are fit for jury duty in a given case. Any juror revealing an inability to be impartial to the parties or issues will be stuck (taken off) the jury panel by the judge either by the judge's own action or upon a well-founded motion made by either attorney for removal. Once all questions and answers have ended, each attorney is allowed a given number of arbitrary "strikes" (eliminations) of those on the panel. These are called "peremptory strikes."

MANDAMUS - The name of a writ that is issued from a court of superior jurisdiction, directed to a lower court or a public officer, commanding the performance of a particular act.

MIRANDA WARNING - A four-part warning required to be given by police to a criminal suspect who has been arrested before custodial interrogation can take place. This warning advises the person being detained that he or she does not have to talk to police, that he or she can stop any interrogation at any time and have counsel present, and that his silence will not be held against him, and his right to legal counsel before talking to police. This "phrase" derives from a US Supreme Court decision: *Miranda v Arizona*, 384 US 436 (1966). Over the years, courts at every level have carved dozens of exceptions into the rule so that its effect is watered down.

MISDEMEANOR - Offenses considered less serious than felonies. There are three classes of misdemeanors–simple, serious, and aggravated. Examples of misdemeanors may include simple battery (hitting someone), traffic violations, thefts of property not exceeding a certain value (possibly $500), trespass, and disorderly conduct. Maximum fines for misdemeanors vary from state, but $5000 is usually an upper limit, with many states capping fines at $1000. Typically, the longest prison sentence for being found guilty of a misdemeanor is one year or possibly less.

MISTRIAL - A mistrial is a court ruling made by a trial judge after a jury is impaneled but before the jury is able to reach a decision of innocence or guilt of the defendant on the pending criminal charge(s).

MOTION - An application to the court requesting action or some type of "relief" in a pending case. Usually, a motion addresses an issue that is within the court's discretion to order some form of guidance as to how the trial will proceed. The judge may also order some act to be done or not done by another litigant or participant at trial. In terms of pre-trial motions, these are challenges to certain evidence being presented to the jury (or judge) due to some legal challenge that requires that evidence either be allowed to be used at trial or that it not be considered.

NOLLE PROSEQUI - NOL PROS - The Latin term used in many jurisdictions to describe the prosecutor's voluntary dismissal of one or more pending criminal charges. The court's permission is required for the *nolle prosequi* to be valid. As long as a jury trial has not been started, the entry of a *nolle prosequi* by a court is not an adjudication of the case on the merits (e.g., it is not final and you can be re-accused later).

NOLO CONTENDERE PLEA - A *nolo contendere* plea (also called a *"no contest"* plea) can be entered by criminal defendants facing a realistic prospect of conviction, who do not wish to undergo a trial, and yet are not willing to admit to being responsible for the criminal act charged. Also, defendants may wish to avoid admitting to a tort (a civil personal injury suit arising from an accident in which the injured party seeks monetary damages) or any other type of wrongdoing alleged in the indictment, accusation, uniform traffic citation or information against him/her with a view to possible later civil action.

OPINION - A formal statement by a judge, magistrate or justice (another name used for trial level judges in some states), that sets forth a decision about some aspect of a case or on the legal issues bearing on a case.

ORDINANCE - A law passed by a city, town, parish or county legislative body. Ordinances are of lower significance and reach than state statutes, which control the law across an entire state.

OVERRULE - A judge's decision (usually made during trials or motions hearings) to not allow an objection to prevail. Also, this can refer to a decision by a higher (appellate) court that a lower court's decision was in error.

PARTIES - The persons who are actively concerned in the prosecution or defense of a legal proceeding. In a criminal case, the parties are the State, the United States, or some other governmental entity as the prosecution verses the defendant, the person charged with the crime. The person against whom the crime was committed is typically not a party.

PERJURY - Knowingly making a material false statement while under oath to otherwise tell the truth. Perjury is a crime in all jurisdictions and applies to all witnesses (*i.e.*, it is a crime to lie to the judge or while testifying to the jury.)

PER SE – Latin, meaning "of, in, or by itself or oneself; intrinsically." In DUI-DWI practice, all that the prosecutor needs to prove to obtain a conviction for this type of "DUI-DWI" offense is to successfully introduce the breath, blood or urine test result that meets or exceeds the applicable numerical "level" so as to convince the jury or judge that the result obtained was reliable and trustworthy, as required under state law.

PLEA BARGAIN - This term generally refers to an agreement in a criminal case in which a prosecutor and a defense attorney (acting on his or her client's behalf) arrange to settle the case against the defendant on some negotiated terms and conditions. Typically, all plea bargains are subject to the consent of the trial judge before whom the case is pending. The defendant may agree to plead guilty or *nolo contendere* in exchange for the prosecutor dropping some charges or reducing the recommended punishment aspect of the case to a more favorable level.

PLEADING - A formal statement, generally written, propounding the case of action or the defense of a legal case. Pleadings may also have specific titles such as "Motion to Suppress," "Motion in Limine" or "Discovery Motion," and these are all classified as "pleadings."

PRELIMINARY HEARING - Synonymous with *preliminary examinations;* the hearing given before a magistrate or other judge to determine whether a person charged with a crime should be held or bound over for trial. The level of proof required to be shown at this level of criminal proceedings is very low since the prosecutor typically will not have fully investigated the case. Often, if a person is released on bond, no right to such a hearing exists, or is waived (given up).

PRESUMPTION OF INNOCENCE - The Government has the burden of proving a person charged with a crime guilty beyond a reasonable doubt, and if it fails to do so, the person is (so far as the law is concerned) not guilty. The indictment or formal charge against any person is not evidence of guilt. Indeed, the person is presumed by the law to be innocent until the judge or jury finds them guilty. The law does not require a person to prove his innocence or produce any evidence at all, nor can the government use this silence against a defendant.

PRIMA FACIE - Latin for "at first view." Evidence that is sufficient or plain enough on its face to raise a presumption of fact or to establish the fact in question unless rebutted. So far as can be judged from the disclosure, an accurate fact, presumed to be true unless disproved by some evidence to the contrary.

PRO SE — Latin for "on one's own behalf." A person who represents himself in court alone without the help of a lawyer is said to appear *pro se*.

PROBABLE CAUSE – A legal term of art that means a constitutionally prescribed standard of proof or (in the alternative) may refer to a reasonable ground for belief in the existence of certain facts. Probable cause is the burden of proof necessary for issuance of an indictment or issuance of an accusatory document (*i.e.*, an information or an accusation).

PROBATION - A form of criminal sentence in which an offender agrees to comply with certain conditions imposed by the court rather than being put in jail or prison.

PROOF BEYOND A REASONABLE DOUBT - The highest level of proof in any legal matters, reserved for criminal cases. In order for a criminal defendant to be convicted of a crime, the prosecutor must prove his or her case to the point that the jurors have no reasonable doubts in their minds that the defendant did whatever he or she is charged with having done. The typical jury in criminal cases must be unanimous, but some jurisdictions now allow verdicts on less than unanimous verdicts.

PROSECUTOR - A government lawyer who initiates an accusation against a party suspected of committing a crime; also one who takes charge of a case or performs the function of a trial lawyer in a criminal case on behalf of the state or the people.

PUBLIC DEFENDER - A lawyer employed by the government to represent a person accused of a crime and who cannot afford to hire a lawyer.

REBUTTAL EVIDENCE - Evidence given to explain or disprove facts given in evidence by the opposing party.

RESTITUTION - A legal remedy sometimes allowed by statute under which a person is restored to his or her original position prior to loss or injury. In DUI-DWI accident cases, the laws of many jurisdictions authorize the criminal court disposing of a guilty verdict or plea to order restitution of damages to the "victim" of the DUI-related crash. In these case, the person convicted of having been DUI-DWI, must pay "restitution" to the victim of the accident, to put the victim in the financial position they would have been in if there hadn't been an accident.

RETAINER - A contract between an attorney and his or her client. Preferably (under most state bar rules) these need to be in some written form, but retainers can be oral. The payment of money to the attorney as a "retainer" signifies an agreement for the attorney to act on the person's behalf and to represent the person in the legal matter that is the subject of their "contract." In criminal cases, a retainer is typically a partial payment toward the ultimate, total fee that may be due in the event the case requires filing of a variety of motions and other pleadings, handling administrative license issues, conduction of pre-trial hearings of various types, going to trial or possibly filing an appeal. To avoid confusion on the exact terms and schedule of other payments, retainer agreements should be in writing in virtually all cases.

SENTENCE - Judgment formally pronounced by a judge upon defendant after the defendant's conviction in the criminal prosecution.

SOLICITOR - The prosecutor representing the state if your county or parish has a separate court for trying misdemeanors.

STANDARD OF PROOF - The amount of evidence which a prosecuting attorney in a criminal case must present in a trial in order to win is called the standard of proof. In criminal cases in America, the appropriate standard is the highest legal standard in existence, proof beyond a reasonable doubt.

STATUTE - A law adopted by the legislature.

SUBPOENA - A court-authorized or court-issued form (usually under the seal of the court) ordering a person to be in court at a certain place, hour and time, or "to be punished" for not doing so.

SUPRA – The legal citation for the point just made has already been cited above in the same document.

SUSTAIN - A judge's decision (usually during trial or motions hearings) to allow an objection or motion to prevail.

TESTIMONY - Spoken evidence given by a confident (competent?) witness, under oath, as distinguished by evidence derived by writings, physical exhibits and other sources.

TRIAL INFORMATION (OR ACCUSATION) - A document filed by the prosecutor, which states the charges and evidence against a defendant in a criminal case. See further information under "accusation" in this glossary.

UNIFORM CITATION (OR UNIFORM TRAFFIC CITATION) - A statutory form of a handwritten or digitally created charging document generally used by police officers to accuse a citizen of certain types of offenses. In some states, this method allows a law enforcement officer to issue a traffic citation on certain misdemeanor or traffic infraction cases. Typically, uniform citations are authorized for traffic offenses and other types of violations that are considered less serious offenses. Some states allow the prosecution of DUI-DWI cases on these citations, without the need for the prosecutor to file a formal, computer-generated (or typewritten) accusation or "information" setting forth the charges.

VERDICT - The formal decision or finding made by a jury in a trial after consideration of the evidence presented and applying the rules of law given to the jury by the judge. In a criminal case, for each "count," the jury will render one of three decisions: (1) "guilty," (2) "not guilty" or (3) "can't agree unanimously" (or by whatever non-unanimous standard some state may have rather than unanimous).

VOIR DIRE - French for "to speak truly, to tell the truth." In English, this is called "jury selection." Jury selection is an inquiry of prospective jurors by the attorneys (in most jurisdictions) and by the judge, to determine if prospective jurors are qualified for jury duty in a given case.

WAIVER - This refers to knowingly and intentionally giving up a right. Example: a defendant waives his right to remain silent by agreeing to be interviewed by police. In the legal system, almost any right can be waived, if it is done knowingly and intelligently.

WARRANT - A writ or order issued by a judge or magistrate authorizing an officer of the law to make an arrest, to conduct a search, or to perform some other designated act.

WITNESS - One who testifies to what he or she has seen, heard, or otherwise observed or (in the case of expert witnesses) testifies to his or her professional opinion based on a hypothetical set of facts, treatment records, or statement.

WORK RELEASE - A probation program (alternative to jail sentence) that is available in some jurisdictions wherein the defendant is permitted to maintain employment while residing in jail when not at work. The defendant leaves jail on workdays only for his work hours, plus limited travel time. These programs are not available in some jurisdictions, due to lack of funding for such facilities. Also, some state statutes do not allow DUI-DWI detainees to utilize "work release."

WRIT - An order issued from a court requiring the performance of a specified act, or giving authority and commission to having it done.

Appendix C

Comparison of Fourteen States' Standards of Proof for DUI-DWI

South Carolina[890] - It is unlawful for a person to drive a motor vehicle within this State while: (1) under the influence of alcohol to the extent that the person's faculties to drive are materially and appreciably impaired; (2) under the influence of any other drug or a combination of other drugs or substances which cause impairment to the extent that the person's faculties to drive are materially and appreciably impaired; or (3) under the combined influence of alcohol and any other drug or drugs or substances which cause impairment to the extent that the person's faculties to drive are materially and appreciably impaired. {From: State v. Knuckles, 583 S.E.2d 51 (S.C., 2003)}.

Georgia[891] - (a) A person shall not drive or be in actual physical control of any moving vehicle while: (1) Under the influence of alcohol to the extent that it is less safe for the person to drive;(2) Under the influence of any drug to the extent that it is less safe for the person to drive; (3) Under the intentional influence of any glue, aerosol, or other toxic vapor to the extent that it is less safe for the person to drive; (4) Under the combined influence of any two or more of the substances specified in paragraphs (1) through (3) of this subsection to the extent that it is less safe for the person to drive;

....

(b) The fact that any person charged with violating this Code section is or has been legally entitled to use a drug shall not constitute a defense against any charge of violating this Code section; provided, however, that such person shall not be in violation of this Code section unless such person is rendered incapable of driving safely as a result of using a drug other than alcohol which such person is legally entitled to use.

California[892] - It is unlawful for any person who is under the influence of any alcoholic beverage or drug, or under the combined influence of any alcoholic beverage and drug, to drive a vehicle.

A person is [under the influence of an alcoholic beverage] [under the influence of a drug] [under the combined influence of an alcoholic beverage and a drug] when as a result of [drinking such alcoholic beverage] [and] [using a drug] [his] [her] physical or mental abilities are impaired to such a degree that [he] [she] no longer has the ability to drive a vehicle with the caution characteristic of a sober person of ordinary prudence under the same or similar circumstances.

[If it is established that a person is driving a vehicle [under the influence of an alcoholic beverage] [under the influence of a drug] [under the combined influence of an alcoholic beverage and a drug], it is no defense that there was some other cause which also tended to impair [his] [her] ability to drive with the required caution.][893]

---

[890]§ 56-5-2930. Unlawful to operate motor vehicle while under influence.

[891]O.C.G.A. § 40-6-391. Drivers with ability impaired by alcohol, drugs, or toxic vapor.

[892]§ 23152(a). Driving under influence.

[893]California Jury Instructions--Criminal, January 2005 Edition. The Committee On Standard Jury Instructions, Criminal, Of The Superior Court Of Los Angeles County, California. Part 16. Misdemeanor Instructions, D. Vehicle Code. CALJIC 16.831. Alcohol Or Drug Influenced Driving--"Under The Influence"-- Defined

Delaware[894] - (a) No person shall drive a vehicle: (1) When the person is under the influence of alcohol; (2) When the person is under the influence of any drug; (3) When the person is under the influence of a combination of alcohol and any drug;

(b) In a prosecution for a violation of subsection (a) of this section:
(1) The fact that any person charged with violating this section is, or has been, legally entitled to use alcohol or a drug shall not constitute a defense.
....
(5) "While under the influence" shall mean that the person is, because of alcohol or drugs or a combination of both, less able than the person would ordinarily have been, either mentally or physically, to exercise clear judgment, sufficient physical control, or due care in the driving of a vehicle.
....
(7) "Drug" shall include any substance or preparation defined as such by Title 11 or Title 16 or which has been placed in the schedules of controlled substances pursuant to Chapter 47 of Title 16. "Drug" shall also include any substance or preparation having the property of releasing vapors or fumes which may be used for the purpose of producing a condition of intoxication, inebriation, exhilaration, stupefaction or lethargy or for the purpose of dulling the brain or nervous system.

Maryland[895] - (a)(1) A person may not drive or attempt to drive any vehicle while under the influence of alcohol. (2) A person may not drive or attempt to drive any vehicle while the person is under the influence of alcohol per se.

(b) A person may not drive or attempt to drive any vehicle while impaired by alcohol.

(c)(1) A person may not drive or attempt to drive any vehicle while he is so far impaired by any drug, any combination of drugs, or a combination of one or more drugs and alcohol that he cannot drive a vehicle safely. (2) It is not a defense to any charge of violating this subsection that the person charged is or was entitled under the laws of this State to use the drug, combination of drugs, or combination of one or more drugs and alcohol, unless the person was unaware that the drug or combination would make the person incapable of safely driving a vehicle.

Texas[896] - Definitions. (2) "Intoxicated" means: (A) not having the normal use of mental or physical faculties by reason of the introduction of alcohol, a controlled substance, a drug, a dangerous drug, a combination of two or more of those substances, or any other substance into the body;

Florida[897] - Definition - "Intoxication" means more than merely being under the influence of an alcoholic beverage. Intoxication means that the defendant must have been so affected from the drinking of an alcoholic beverage as to have lost or been deprived of the normal control of either his body or his mental faculties, or both. Intoxication is synonymous with "drunk."

---

[894]§ 4177 Driving a vehicle while under the influence.

[895]§ 21-902. Driving while under the influence or impaired.

[896]§ 49.01.

[897]Standard Jury Instructions in Criminal Cases

New York[898] - 1. Driving while ability impaired. No person shall operate a motor vehicle while the person's ability to operate such motor vehicle is impaired by the consumption of alcohol.

....

3. Driving while intoxicated. No person shall operate a motor vehicle while in an intoxicated condition.

The accepted definition of the offense in New York is derived from case law, not statutory definition. In *People v. Miller*, 373 N.Y.S.2d 312 (N.Y.Town Ct. 1975), this is how "intoxicated" (as well as New York's lesser offense of "driving while ability impaired") are judicially defined: Thus, it determined that operating while 'impaired' was a lesser form of operating while 'intoxicated'.

'Intoxicated', for the purpose of the Vehicle and Traffic Law, has no exact statutory definition. In 1919 the Appellate Division in *People v. Weaver*, 188 App.Div. 395, 401, 177 N.Y.S. 71, 74 defined it as implying 'undue or abnormal excitation of the passions or feelings or the impairment of the capacity to think and act correctly and efficiently, and suggests the loss of normal control over one's faculties.' The court also approved the definition (page 401, 177 N.Y.S. p. 74) that 'intoxicated' means the imbibing in enough liquor 'to render him incapable of giving that attention and care to the operation of his automobile that a man of prudence and reasonable intelligence would give'. These definitions related to Section 290 of the Highway Law, which at that time only prohibited driving while intoxicated.

Since the decision in that case, the Legislature in 1960 saw fit to subdivide this law into the two divisions above described. The Court of Appeals has told us the use of the word 'impaired' intended a lesser degree of criminal culpability than the word 'intoxicated'.

It is interesting to note that the word 'intoxicated' is now defined by Webster's Third New International Dictionary as 'being under the marked influence of an intoxicant'. 'Intoxicate' is defined as 'to execute or stupify by alcoholic drinks or narcotics, especially to the point where physical and mental control is markably diminished'. The Legislature, in amending and enacting this law as recently as 1972, is presumed to use words of current, contemporary meaning (McKinney's Statutes, Section 114). Therefore, this court finds that it was the intention of the Legislature that a person be convicted of driving while intoxicated when it is established that he has consumed enough alcohol so that his physical and mental control are markably diminished; or putting it another way, that his judgment and ability to operate a motor vehicle are adversely affected to a substantial degree.

The word 'impaired' as defined by said dictionary is 'to make worse or lessen'. It would therefore appear that the Legislature intended that the driving of an automobile after the consumption of sufficient alcohol to lessen or impair physical and mental control to any significant degree, constituted a violation of this section. The difference is purely one of degree. If in fact, consumption of alcohol had no significant effect, there would be no criminal violation. If on the other hand, it had an effect to a degree that diminished physical and mental control to a standard less than that would be exercised by a reasonably prudent driver, the driver's ability would be impaired in violation of subsection 1. If loss of control was sufficient to cause a markable or high degree of loss of control, it would be a violation of section 3.

Washington[899] - A driver is under the influence of [alcohol] [or] [any drug] if, as a result of using [alcohol] [or] [any drug], the person's ability to drive a motor vehicle is lessened in any appreciable degree.

---

[898]§ 1192. Operating a motor vehicle while under the influence of alcohol or drugs.

[899]WPI 16.04.01. Under the Influence of Alcohol or Any Drug--Driving a Motor Vehicle.

This instruction and WPI 16.05, Under the Influence of Alcohol--Analysis of Bodily Substance--Intoxication Defense Statute, represent alternative theories for proving a person was under the influence of alcohol or drugs. For a case in which evidence is presented under each theory, then both instructions should be given to the jury with appropriate modification to indicate that the two theories are alternatives.

COMMENT

RCW 5.40.060(1). The statute provides in part that the standard for determining whether the person injured or killed was under the influence of intoxicating liquor or any drug is the same standard set forth in the statute on Driving While Under the Influence. Pursuant to RCW 46.61.502, a person is guilty of driving while under the influence of intoxicating liquor or any drug if the person drives a motor vehicle within this state while the person is either under the influence of or affected by intoxicating liquor or any drug or under the combined influence of or affected by any intoxicating liquor and any drug. Case law interpreting the phase "under the influence" has defined it as meaning "any influence which lessens in any appreciable degree the ability of the accused to handle his automobile." *State v. Lewellyn*, 78 Wn.App. 788, 895 P.2d 418 (1995) (quoting *State v. Hurd*, 5 Wash. 308, 105 P.2d 59 (1940), and *State v. Hansen*, 15 Wn.App. 95, 546 P.2d 1242 (1976)). This definition has been adapted for this instruction which is intended to be used in the case of a person injured or killed while driving a motor vehicle.

Experience with WPI 92.10, Under the Influence Of or Affected By Intoxicating Liquor or Drugs--Definition (the criminal counterpart to this instruction) has shown that the jury may have trouble understanding the word "appreciable." Therefore, it may be desirable when giving this instruction to further instruct the jury that the word "appreciable" is defined as meaning capable of being perceived or noticed. See W. Statsky, Legal Thesaurus/Dictionary (1985).

If intoxication is alleged in an action arising out of a motor vehicle accident, the fact that a driver has consumed intoxicating liquor does not automatically justify instructing the jury on the issue of the driver being under the influence. For cases which review evidence of drinking which is not sufficient to take the issue of intoxication to the jury, see: *Madill v. Los Angeles Seattle Motor Express, Inc.*, 64 Wn.2d 548, 392 P.2d 821 (1964) (complete absence of any evidence that driver was under the influence of or affected by intoxicating liquor at the time of the accident); *White v. Peters*, 52 Wn.2d 824, 329 P.2d 471 (1958) (no evidence of conduct or appearance that driver was under the influence of two drinks consumed earlier in the day prior to or at the time of accident). See the Comment to WPI 12.01, Voluntary Intoxication, for other cases discussing the sufficiency of evidence to take the issue of driver's intoxication to the jury.

Tennessee.[900] (a) It is unlawful for any person to drive or to be in physical control of any automobile or other motor driven vehicle on any of the public roads and highways of the state, or on any streets or alleys, or while on the premises of any shopping center, trailer park or any apartment house complex, or any other premises which is generally frequented by the public at large, while: (1) Under the influence of any intoxicant, marijuana, narcotic drug, or drug producing stimulating effects on the central nervous system; or (2) The alcohol concentration in such person's blood or breath is eight- hundredths of one percent (.08%) or more.

(b) For the purpose of this section, "drug producing stimulating effects on the central nervous system" includes the salts of barbituric acid, also known as malonyl urea, or any compound, derivatives, or mixtures thereof that may be used for producing hypnotic or somnifacient effects, and includes amphetamine, desoxyephedrine or compounds or mixtures thereof, including all

---

[900] T. C. A. § 55-10-401.

derivatives of phenolethylamine or any of the salts thereof, except preparations intended for use in the nose and unfit for internal use.

Mississippi.[901] (1) It is unlawful for any person to drive or otherwise operate a vehicle within this state who (a) is under the influence of intoxicating liquor; (b) is under the influence of any other substance which has impaired such person's ability to operate a motor vehicle; (c) has an alcohol concentration of eight one-hundredths percent (.08%) or more for persons who are above the legal age to purchase alcoholic beverages under state law, or two one-hundredths percent (.02%) or more for persons who are below the legal age to purchase alcoholic beverages under state law, in the person's blood based upon grams of alcohol per one hundred (100) milliliters of blood or grams of alcohol per two hundred ten (210) liters of breath as shown by a chemical analysis of such person's breath, blood or urine administered as authorized by this chapter; (d) is under the influence of any drug or controlled substance, the possession of which is unlawful under the Mississippi Controlled Substances Law; or (e) has an alcohol concentration of four one-hundredths percent (.04%) or more in the person's blood, based upon grams of alcohol per one hundred (100) milliliters of blood or grams of alcohol per two hundred ten (210) liters of breath as shown by a chemical analysis of such person's blood, breath or urine, administered as authorized by this chapter for persons operating a commercial motor vehicle.

Virginia.[902] It shall be unlawful for any person to drive or operate any motor vehicle, engine or train (i) while such person has a blood alcohol concentration of 0.08 percent or more by weight by volume or 0.08 grams or more per 210 liters of breath as indicated by a chemical test administered as provided in this article, (ii) while such person is under the influence of alcohol, (iii) while such person is under the influence of any narcotic drug or any other self-administered intoxicant or drug of whatsoever nature, or any combination of such drugs, to a degree which impairs his ability to drive or operate any motor vehicle, engine or train safely, (iv) while such person is under the combined influence of alcohol and any drug or drugs to a degree which impairs his ability to drive or operate any motor vehicle, engine or train safely, or (v) while such person has a blood concentration of any of the following substances at a level that is equal to or greater than: (a) 0.02 milligrams of cocaine per liter of blood, (b) 0.1 milligrams of methamphetamine per liter of blood, (c) 0.01 milligrams of phencyclidine per liter of blood, or (d) 0.1 milligrams of 3,4-methylenedioxymethamphetamine per liter of blood. A charge alleging a violation of this section shall support a conviction under clauses (i), (ii), (iii), (iv), or (v).

For the purposes of this article, the term "motor vehicle" includes mopeds, while operated on the public highways of this Commonwealth.

Illinois.[903] (a) A person shall not drive or be in actual physical control of any vehicle within this State while: (1) the alcohol concentration in the person's blood or breath is 0.08 or more based on the definition of blood and breath units in Section 11-501.2; (2) under the influence of alcohol; (3) under the influence of any intoxicating compound or combination of intoxicating compounds to a degree that renders the person incapable of driving safely; (4) under the influence of any other drug or combination of drugs to a degree that renders the person incapable of safely driving; (5) under the combined influence of alcohol, other drug or drugs, or intoxicating compound or compounds to a degree that renders the person incapable of safely

---

[901]Miss. Code Ann. § 63-11-30.
[902]Va. Code Ann. § 18.2-266.
[903]625 ILCS 5/11-501.

driving; or (6) there is any amount of a drug, substance, or compound in the person's breath, blood, or urine resulting from the unlawful use or consumption of cannabis listed in the Cannabis Control Act, a controlled substance listed in the Illinois Controlled Substances Act, or an intoxicating compound listed in the Use of Intoxicating Compounds Act.

Alabama.[904] (a) A person shall not drive or be in actual physical control of any vehicle while: (1) There is 0.08 percent or more by weight of alcohol in his or her blood; (2) Under the influence of alcohol; (3) Under the influence of a controlled substance to a degree which renders him or her incapable of safely driving; (4) Under the combined influence of alcohol and a controlled substance to a degree which renders him or her incapable of safely driving; or (5) Under the influence of any substance which impairs the mental or physical faculties of such person to a degree which renders him or her incapable of safely driving.

(b) A person who is under the age of 21 years shall not drive or be in actual physical control of any vehicle if there is .02 percentage or more by weight of alcohol in his or her blood. The Department of Public Safety shall suspend or revoke the driver's license of any person, including, but not limited to, a juvenile, child, or youthful offender, convicted or adjudicated of, or subjected to a finding of delinquency based on this subsection. Notwithstanding the foregoing, upon the first violation of this subsection by a person whose blood alcohol level is between .02 and .08, the person's driver's license or driving privilege shall be suspended for a period of 30 days in lieu of any penalties provided in subsection (e) of this section and there shall be no disclosure, other than to courts, law enforcement agencies, and the person's employer, by any entity or person of any information, documents, or records relating to the person's arrest, conviction, or adjudication of or finding of delinquency based on this subsection.

All persons, except as otherwise provided in this subsection for a first offense, including, but not limited to, a juvenile, child, or youthful offender, convicted or adjudicated of, or subjected to a finding of delinquency based on this subsection shall be fined pursuant to this section, notwithstanding any other law to the contrary, and the person shall also be required to attend and complete a DUI or substance abuse court referral program in accordance with subsection (i).

(c)(1) A school bus or day care driver shall not drive or be in actual physical control of any vehicle while in performance of his or her duties if there is greater than .02 percentage by weight of alcohol in his or her blood. A person convicted pursuant to this subsection shall be subject to the penalties provided by this section except that on the first conviction the Director of Public Safety shall suspend the driving privilege or driver's license for a period of one year.
(2) A person shall not drive or be in actual physical control of a commercial motor vehicle as defined in 49 CFR Part 390.5 of the Federal Motor Carrier Safety Regulations as adopted pursuant to Section 32-9A-2, if there is .04 percentage or greater by weight of alcohol in his or her blood. Notwithstanding the other provisions of this section, the commercial driver's license or commercial driving privilege of a person convicted of violating this subdivision shall be suspended for the period provided in accordance with 49 CFR Part 383.51 or 49 CFR Part 391.15, as applicable, and the person's regular driver's license or privilege to drive a regular motor vehicle shall be governed by the remainder of this section if the person is guilty of a violation of another provision of this section.

(d) The fact that any person charged with violating this section is or has been legally entitled to

---

[904]Ala.Code 1975 § 32-5A-191.

use alcohol or a controlled substance shall not constitute a defense against any charge of violating this section.

Appendix D

Limited Issues Determined at ALS/ALR Hearings

Arizona[905] - For the purposes of this section, the scope of the hearing shall include only the following issue:

1. Whether the officer had reasonable grounds to believe the person was driving or was in actual physical control of a motor vehicle while under the influence of intoxicating liquor.
2. Whether the person was placed under arrest for a violation of § 4-244, paragraph 33, § 28-1381, § 28-1382 or § 28-1383.
3. Whether a test was taken, the results of which indicated the alcohol concentration in the person's blood or breath at the time the test was administered of either:
>   (a) 0.08 or more.
>   (b) 0.04 or more if the person was driving or in actual physical control of a commercial motor vehicle.
4. Whether the testing method used was valid and reliable.
5. Whether the test results were accurately evaluated.

Oklahoma[906] - The hearing before the Commissioner of Public Safety or a designated hearing officer shall be conducted in the county of arrest or may be conducted by telephone conference call. The hearing may be recorded and its scope shall cover the issues of whether the officer had reasonable grounds to believe the person had been operating or was in actual physical control of a vehicle upon the public roads, highways, streets, turnpikes or other public place of this state while under the influence of alcohol, any other intoxicating substance, or the combined influence of alcohol and any other intoxicating substance as prohibited by law, and whether the person was placed under arrest.

1. If the revocation or denial is based upon a breath or blood test result and a sworn report from a law enforcement officer, the scope of the hearing shall also cover the issues as to whether:
a. if timely requested by the person, the person was not denied a breath or blood test,
b. the specimen was obtained from the person within two (2) hours of the arrest of the person,
c. the person, if under twenty-one (21) years of age, was advised that driving privileges would be revoked or denied if the test result reflected the presence of any measurable quantity of alcohol,
d. the person, if twenty-one (21) years of age or older, was advised that driving privileges would be revoked or denied if the test result reflected an alcohol concentration of eight-hundredths (0.08) or more, and
e. the test result in fact reflects the alcohol concentration.

2. If the revocation or denial is based upon the refusal of the person to submit to a breath or blood test, reflected in a sworn report by a law enforcement officer, the scope of the hearing shall also include whether:
a. the person refused to submit to the test or tests, and

---

[905]A.R.S. § 28-1385(I).
[906]47 Okl.St.Ann. § 754(F).

b. the person was informed that driving privileges would be revoked or denied if the person refused to submit to the test or tests.

California[907] - If the department determines in the review of a determination made under Section 13353 or 13353.1, by a preponderance of the evidence, all of the following facts, the department shall sustain the order of suspension or revocation:
(A) That the peace officer had reasonable cause to believe that the person had been driving a motor vehicle in violation of Section 23136, 23140, 23152, or 23153.
(B) That the person was placed under arrest or, if the alleged violation was of Section 23136, that the person was lawfully detained.
(C) That the person refused or failed to complete the chemical test or tests after being requested by a peace officer.
(D) That, except for the persons described in Section 23612 who are incapable of refusing, the person had been told that his or her privilege to operate a motor vehicle would be suspended or revoked if he or she refused to submit to, and complete, the required testing.

Alabama[908] - Upon suspending the license or permit to drive or the privilege of driving a motor vehicle on the highways of this state that is given to a nonresident or any person, or upon determining that the issuance of a license or permit shall be denied to the person, the director or his or her authorized agent shall within three days of suspension notify the person in writing. Upon a request filed by the person within five days from the date of the notice of suspension or denial, the director shall schedule a hearing with notice of the hearing to be provided by certified mail to the person stating the date, time, place, and scope of the hearing. The scope of the hearing shall pertain to all of the following issues:
(1) Whether the law enforcement officer had reasonable grounds to believe the person had been driving a motor vehicle on the public highways of this state while under the influence of the substances enumerated in subsection (a).
(2) Whether the person refused to submit to the test upon request of a law enforcement officer.
(3) Whether the person was informed that his or her privilege to drive would be suspended or denied if he or she refused to submit to the test.

---

[907] West's Ann.Cal.Vehicle Code § 13557(b)(1).
[908] Ala.Code 1975 § 32-6-49.13(f).

Appendix E

Samples of Implied Consent (Informed Consent) Warnings

California[909] - The person shall be told that his or her failure to submit to, or the failure to complete, the required chemical testing will result in a fine, mandatory imprisonment if the person is convicted of a violation of Section 23152 or 23153, and (i) the suspension of the person's privilege to operate a motor vehicle for a period of one year, (ii) the revocation of the person's privilege to operate a motor vehicle for a period of two years if the refusal occurs within 10 years of a separate violation of Section 23103 as specified in Section 23103.5, or of Section 23140, 23152, or 23153, or of Section 191.5 or paragraph (3) of subdivision (c) of Section 192 of the Penal Code that resulted in a conviction, or if the person's privilege to operate a motor vehicle has been suspended or revoked pursuant to Section 13353, 13353.1 or 13353.2 for an offense that occurred on a separate occasion, or (iii) the revocation of the person's privilege to operate a motor vehicle for a period of three years if the refusal occurs within 10 years of two or more separate violations of Section 23103 as specified in Section 23103.5, or of Section 23140, 23152, or 23153, or of Section 191.5 or paragraph (3) of subdivision (c) of Section 192 of the Penal Code, or any combination thereof, that resulted in convictions, or if the person's privilege to operate a motor vehicle has been suspended or revoked two or more times pursuant to Section 13353, 13353.1 or 13353.2 for offenses that occurred on separate occasions, or if there is any combination of those convictions or administrative suspensions or revocations.

Michigan[910] - A person arrested for a crime described in section 625c (1) shall be advised of all of the following:

(*i*) If he or she takes a chemical test of his or her blood, urine, or breath administered at the request of a peace officer, he or she has the right to demand that a person of his or her own choosing administer 1 of the chemical tests.

(*ii*) The results of the test are admissible in a judicial proceeding as provided under this act and will be considered with other admissible evidence in determining the defendant's innocence or guilt.

(*iii*) He or she is responsible for obtaining a chemical analysis of a test sample obtained at his or her own request.

(*iv*) If he or she refuses the request of a peace officer to take a test described in subparagraph (*i*), a test shall not be given without a court order, but the peace officer may seek to obtain a court order.

(*v*) Refusing a peace officer's request to take a test described in subparagraph (*i*) will result in the suspension of his or her operator's or chauffeur's license and vehicle group designation or operating privilege and in the addition of 6 points to his or her driver record.

---

[909]West's Ann.Cal.Vehicle Code § 23612(D).
[910]M.C.L.A. 257.625a(6)(b).

Florida[911] - The person shall be told that his or her failure to submit to any lawful test of his or her breath will result in the suspension of the person's privilege to operate a motor vehicle for a period of 1 year for a first refusal, or for a period of 18 months if the driving privilege of such person has been previously suspended as a result of a refusal to submit to such a test or tests, and shall also be told that if he or she refuses to submit to a lawful test of his or her breath and his or her driving privilege has been previously suspended for a prior refusal to submit to a lawful test of his or her breath, urine, or blood, he or she commits a misdemeanor in addition to any other penalties.

Washington[912] - The officer shall inform the person of his or her right to refuse the breath or blood test, and of his or her right to have additional tests administered by any qualified person of his or her choosing as provided in RCW 46.61.506. The officer shall warn the driver, in substantially the following language, that:

(a) If the driver refuses to take the test, the driver's license, permit, or privilege to drive will be revoked or denied for at least one year; and

(b) If the driver refuses to take the test, the driver's refusal to take the test may be used in a criminal trial; and

(c) If the driver submits to the test and the test is administered, the driver's license, permit, or privilege to drive will be suspended, revoked, or denied for at least ninety days if the driver is age twenty-one or over and the test indicates the alcohol concentration of the driver's breath or blood is 0.08 or more, or if the driver is under age twenty-one and the test indicates the alcohol concentration of the driver's breath or blood is 0.02 or more, or if the driver is under age twenty-one and the driver is in violation of RCW 46.61.502 or 46.61.504.

Georgia[913] - At the time a chemical test or tests are requested, the arresting officer shall select and read to the person the appropriate implied consent notice from the following:
(1) Implied consent notice for suspects under age 21:
"Georgia law requires you to submit to state administered chemical tests of your blood, breath, urine, or other bodily substances for the purpose of determining if you are under the influence of alcohol or drugs. If you refuse this testing, your Georgia driver's license or privilege to drive on the highways of this state will be suspended for a minimum period of one year. Your refusal to submit to the required testing may be offered into evidence against you at trial. If you submit to testing and the results indicate an alcohol concentration of 0.02 grams or more, your Georgia driver's license or privilege to drive on the highways of this state may be suspended for a minimum period of one year. After first submitting to the required state tests, you are entitled to additional chemical tests of your blood, breath, urine, or other bodily substances at your own expense and from qualified personnel of your own choosing. Will you submit to the state administered chemical tests of your (designate which tests) under the implied consent law?"
(2) Implied consent notice for suspects age 21 or over:
"Georgia law requires you to submit to state administered chemical tests of your blood, breath, urine, or other bodily substances for the purpose of determining if you are under the influence of alcohol or drugs. If you refuse this testing, your Georgia driver's license or privilege to drive on the highways of this state will be suspended for a minimum period of one year. Your refusal

---

[911]West's F.S.A. § 316.1932(1)(a)(1)(a).

[912]West's RCWA 46.20.308(2).

[913]Georgia - O.C.G.A. § 40-5-67.1.

to submit to the required testing may be offered into evidence against you at trial. If you submit to testing and the results indicate an alcohol concentration of 0.08 grams or more, your Georgia driver's license or privilege to drive on the highways of this state may be suspended for a minimum period of one year. After first submitting to the required state tests, you are entitled to additional chemical tests of your blood, breath, urine, or other bodily substances at your own expense and from qualified personnel of your own choosing. Will you submit to the state administered chemical tests of your (designate which tests) under the implied consent law?"

(3) Implied consent notice for commercial motor vehicle driver suspects:

"Georgia law requires you to submit to state administered chemical tests of your blood, breath, urine, or other bodily substances for the purpose of determining if you are under the influence of alcohol or drugs. If you refuse this testing, you will be disqualified from operating a commercial motor vehicle for a minimum period of one year. Your refusal to submit to the required testing may be offered into evidence against you at trial. If you submit to testing and the results indicate the presence of any alcohol, you will be issued an out-of-service order and will be prohibited from operating a motor vehicle for 24 hours. If the results indicate an alcohol concentration of 0.04 grams or more, you will be disqualified from operating a commercial motor vehicle for a minimum period of one year. After first submitting to the required state tests, you are entitled to additional chemical tests of your blood, breath, urine, or other bodily substances at your own expense and from qualified personnel of your own choosing. Will you submit to the state administered chemical tests of your (designate which tests) under the implied consent law?"

Appendix F

Types of Alcohol[914]

Alcohols (the chemical class) and chemicals in the same family as alcohol
primary alcohols
methanol
ethanol and ethanol derivatives
ifenprodil
propyl alcohol
butyl alcohol
acetoin
amyl alcohol
hexyl alcohol
octyl alcohol
secondary alcohols
glycol
butanediol
2,3-butanediol
chloral hydrate
polyethylene glycol
polysorbate
propanediol
chloramphenicol
tertiary alcohols
aliphatic alcohols
fatty alcohols
lauryl alcohol
sodium dodecyl sulfate
sodium tetradecyl sulfate
sugar alcohols
glycerin
nitroglycerin
inositol
inositol phosphate
inositol triphosphate
inositol 1,3,4 triphosphate
inositol 1,3,4,5-tetrakiphosphate
inositol 1,4,5-trisphosphate
mannitol
sorbitol
isosorbide
isosorbide dinitrate
xylitol

---

[914]http://etoh.niaaa.nih.gov/AODVol1/aodhqz.htm#ZF2]

Appendix G

Alcoholics Anonymous and Alternatives

Alcoholics or who have any problem with alcohol have the option of involving themselves in a treatment group, which may consist of individual counseling and group therapy. Alcoholics Anonymous (AA) is one of these support groups.[915] "AA" is a worldwide fellowship of men and women who meet together to attain and maintain sobriety. There are no requirements for joining AA, only the need to stop drinking.

Some courts order AA meeting attendance (or suggest this as a means of diminishing other punishment) as mandatory or an optional part of sentencing. For example, a court may diminish other types of punishment at sentencing, if the convicted DUI-DWI driver agrees to attend not fewer than 2 (or 3) AA meetings per week for a specified time period.

In light of this group's size and universal availability, more information may be helpful to know about it. AA was started in 1935 when two men, Bill W. and Dr. Bob S. met in Akron, Ohio to help each other stay sober. Today, AA has grown to over 87,000 groups in more than 130 countries, with more than two million active members. Their motto is "to stay away from one drink at a time, one day at a time."

AA uses the twelve-step method in approaching sobriety:

Step 1. We admitted we were powerless over alcohol - that our lives have become unmanageable.

Step 2. Came to believe that a Power greater than ourselves could restore us to sanity

Step 3. Made a decision to turn our will and our lives over to the care of God as we understood him.

Step 4. Made a searching and fearless moral inventory of our self.

Step 5. Admitted to God, to our self and to other human being the exact nature of our wrongs.

Step 6. Were entirely ready to have God remove all these defects of character.

Step 7. Humbly asked Him to remove our shortcomings.

Step 8. Made a list of all persons we had harmed, and become willing to make amends to them all.

Step 9. Made direct amends to such people wherever possible, except when to do so we would injure them or others.

Step 10. Continued to take personal inventory and when we were wrong promptly admitted it.

Step 11. Sought through prayer and meditation to improve our conscious contact with God as we understood Him, praying only for knowledge or His will for us and the power to carry that out.

Step 12. Having had a spiritual awakening as the result of these steps, we tried to carry this message to alcoholics and to practice these principals in all our affairs.

Newcomers are not forced to follow all of these steps if they are unwilling or unable to do so because of religious or personal beliefs. They will however be asked to keep an open mind, to attend meetings, and to read AA literature describing the AA program.

Alternatives to AA

---

[915]http://www.alcoholics-anonymous.org/?Media=PlayFlash

Other treatment programs may involve counseling with a certified alcohol and drug abuse counselor who is specially trained to help "problem drinkers" find solutions to their reliance on alcohol. These links may help you to locate a nearby counselor: http://dasis3.samhsa.gov/ and http://www.mentalhealth.org/databases/.

Besides the above programs, in cases involving repeat offenders and severe alcoholics, there is a doctor-prescribed medication that may help some people lessen their cravings for alcohol. These medications, when taken with alcoholic beverages, can cause vomiting, nausea, and severe headaches. With larger doses of alcohol, these medications can even lead to death of the person. The idea behind prescribing such drugs is that through classical conditioning the alcoholic begins to subconsciously relate the unpleasant side effects to the consumption of alcohol thereby making his or her drinking become extremely distasteful. A few of these drugs are antabuse, naltrexone, and acamprosate.

Appendix H

Penalties for Refusal to Submit to State-administered Testing of Your Blood, Breath or Urine under Implied (Informed) Consent Laws

State	Statute containing administrative & civil penalties - license loss	Additional criminal penalty/enhancement?
Alabama	Ala.Code 1975 § 32-5-200	No
Alaska	AS 28.35.032	No.
Arizona	A.R.S. § 28-1321	No.
Arkansas	A.C.A. § 5-65-205	No.
California	West's Ann.Cal.Veh. Code § 13353	Code § 23612
Colorado	C.R.S.A. § 42-4-1301.2	No.
Connecticut	C.G.S.A. § 14-227b	No.
Delaware	21 Del.C. § 2741	No.
District of Columbia	DC ST § 50-1905	No.
Florida	West's F.S.A. § 316.1932	West's F.S.A. § 316.1939
Georgia	Ga. Code Ann., § 40-5-67.1	No.
Hawaii	HRS § 291E-65	No.
Idaho	I.C. § 18-8002	No.
Illinois	625 ILCS 5/11-501.1	No.
Indiana	IC 9-30-6-7	No.
Iowa	I.C.A. § 321J.9	No.
Kansas	K.S.A. § 8-1002	No.
Kentucky	KRS § 189A.107	KRS § 189A.105
Louisiana	LSA-R.S. 32:661	LSA-R.S. 32:666
Maine	29-A M.R.S.A. § 2521	29-A M.R.S.A. § 2521
Maryland	MD Code, Transportation, § 16-205.1	No.
Massachusetts	M.G.L.A. 90 § 24	No.
Michigan	M.C.L.A. 257.625f	No.
Minnesota	M.S.A. § 169A.52	No.
Mississippi	Miss. Code Ann. § 63-11-21	No.
Missouri	V.A.M.S. 577.041	No.
Montana	MCA 61-8-402	No.
Nebraska	Neb.Rev.St. § 60-4,164	Neb.Rev.St. § 60-4,164
Nevada	N.R.S. 484.382	No.
New Hampshire	N.H. Rev. Stat. § 265:92	No.
New Jersey	N.J.S.A. 39:4-50.4a	No.
New Mexico	N. M. S. A. 1978, § 66-8-111	No.
New York	McKinney's Vehicle and Traffic Law § 1194	No
North Carolina	N.C.G.S.A. § 20-16.2	No.
North Dakota	NDCC, 39-20-04	No.
Ohio	R.C. § 4511.191	No.
Oklahoma	47 Okl.St.Ann. § 753	No.
Oregon	O.R.S. § 813.100	No.

Pennsylvania	75 Pa.C.S.A. § 1547(b)	No.
Rhode Island	Gen.Laws 1956, § 31-27-2.1	Gen.Laws 1956, § 31-27-2.1
South Carolina	Code 1976 § 56-5-2951	No.
South Dakota	SDCL. § 32-23-18	No.
Tennessee	T. C. A. § 55-10-406	T. C. A. § 55-10-406
Texas	V.T.C.A., Transportation Code § 724.035	No.
Utah	U.C.A. 1953 § 41-6a-520	No.
Vermont	23 V.S.A. § 1205	23 V.S.A. § 1202
Virginia	Va. Code Ann. § 18.2-268.3	Va. Code Ann. § 18.2-268.3
Washington	West's RCWA 46.20.308	No.
West Virginia	W. Va. Code, § 17C-5-7	No.
Wisconsin	W.S.A. 343.305	No.
Wyoming	W.S.1977 § 31-6-107	No.

Appendix I

Checklist of Challenging Forensic

(Blood or Breath) Tests in DUI-DWI Cases

A. Whether the blood sample was timely withdrawn by a person legally qualified to do so.

1. Is there a statutory or administrative requirement that a blood sample be withdrawn within a specified period after a specified event, such as the end of driving?

    a. If so, was the requirement complied with in this case?

    b. What is the penalty, if any, for failing to comply with the time requirement?

    c. When, and how long after the end of driving, was the blood sample withdrawn from the defendant?

    d. Was the blood sample withdrawn within a reasonable period after the end of driving?

2. What are the statutory or regulatory credentials for persons to be allowed to take blood under the state blood-drawing statute?

3. Who withdrew the blood sample from the defendant in this case?

    a. What are the professional credentials or other qualifications of the person who withdrew the blood sample?

    b. If the person who withdrew the blood sample was a nurse, was he or she a registered nurse?

    c. If the person who withdrew the blood sample was not a physician or registered nurse, what training had the person received in blood drawing and how much experience had he or she had in blood drawing?

4. Does the blood-drawing statute or rule contain any locational (e.g., from the test subject's arm) or other requirements related to the withdrawal of blood?

    a. If so, were the requirements complied with in this case?

5. Is there a statutory, administrative rule, or common law requirement to preserve a sample of blood after the completion of chemical testing?

    a. If so, was the requirement complied with in this case?

    b. Where is the preserved sample located?

c. If a sample was not preserved, what is the penalty for failing to do so?

B. **Whether an adequate chain of identification and custody can be established by the prosecution.**

 1. The withdrawal of the blood sample.

  a. Who withdrew the blood sample from the defendant?

  b. Who witnessed the withdrawal of the blood sample from the defendant?

  c. Once the blood was collected in a vial or tube, did the blood collection technician properly invert the blood (not shake it) in accordance with the blood kit package instructions or within accepted industry standards?

  d. What statutory or administrative rule requirements are applicable to the withdrawal of a blood sample for purposes of chemical testing?

  e. Were such requirements complied with in this case?

 2. The sealing of the blood sample.

  a. Who sealed the blood sample after it was withdrawn from the defendant?

  b. Who witnessed the sealing of the blood sample?

  c. What type of seal was applied to the blood sample and how was it affixed?

  d. When, and how long after withdrawal, was the blood sample sealed?

  e. What statutory or administrative rule requirements are applicable to the sealing of a blood sample?

  f. Were such requirements complied with in this case?

 3. The labeling of the blood sample.

  a. Who labeled, or otherwise marked for identification, the defendant's blood sample?

  b. Who witnessed the labeling or marking of the blood sample?

c.   How, and in what manner was the blood sample labeled or marked, according to the person who labeled or marked it?

d.   Exactly what was written or marked on the label or container (upon inspection of the vial or photographs/copies of it)?

e.   How was the label affixed to the container?

f.   When, and how long after withdrawal, was the blood sample labeled or marked for identification?

g.   What statutory or administrative rule requirements are applicable to the labeling of a blood sample?

h.   Were such requirements complied with in this case?

4.   Continuous exclusive custody of the defendant's blood sample prior to shipment to the testing facility.

a.   Who was responsible for and who had possession of the sample at all times between the time of withdrawal and labeling and the time of transportation to the blood testing laboratory/facility?

b.   Where and under what conditions (e.g., locked storage refrigerator with restricted and documented security access) was the sample maintained or stored during this period?

c.   What other persons had access to the sample during this period?

d.   What does the written security log show insofar as handling and retrieval of this sample?

5.   Transportation of the defendant's blood sample to the testing facility.

a.   What is the name and address of the facility where the sample was tested?

b.   In what manner was the sample transported to the testing facility?

c.   If the sample was transported to the testing facility by mail -

On what date was the sample deposited in the mail?

By whom was the sample deposited in the mail?

To what address was the sample mailed?

What type of mail was used (certified mail return receipt requested, first class, etc)?

Was the sample shipped with ice packs or other method of refrigeration?

d. If the sample was transported to the testing facility other than by mail -

What method of transportation was used (e.g., in a police car or by courier)?

Who transported the sample to the testing facility?

Was the sample refrigerated during transportation?

In what part of the vehicle was the blood container stored during transport?

On what date was the sample transported to the testing facility?

Who had access to the sample during transportation?

How many other blood samples were transported to the testing facility at the same time?

6. Receipt of the defendant's blood sample at the testing facility.

a. Who received the sample upon its arrival at the testing facility?

b. On what date and at exactly what time of day was the sample received at (delivered to) the testing facility?

c. Was the blood sample directly delivered to a person at the testing facility, or put in a night box or similar repository?

d. Was any night storage box refrigerated?

e. Who unpacked the sample from its shipping container?

f. Who photographed, copied or otherwise documented the shipping box and its labeling/marking?

g. If an electronic bar code tracking number and label was assigned to this sample, by whom and what method was this done?

h. Exactly what time and date was this done, if a bar code or tracking label was affixed or assigned to this sample?

i. If known, what was the condition of the sample when it arrived at the testing facility?

j.   Who, if anyone, identified the sample upon its arrival at the testing facility and how was it logged in and identified upon being received at the testing facility?

7.   Continuous exclusive custody of the defendant's blood sample at the testing facility until the time of testing.

a.   Where and under what conditions was the sample stored at the testing facility?

b.   What persons had access to the sample at the testing facility?

c.   When was the sample delivered for testing?

d.   Who identified the sample at the time of testing?

e.   How was the sample identified at the time of testing?

f.   How many other blood samples were delivered for testing at the same time?

g.   Where is the documentation for the removal of the sample from the refrigerated storage?

h.   Does the tracking record show when and at what time the remaining sample was returned to storage?

C. Whether a legally authorized and scientifically reliable method of chemical testing was employed.

1.   What method of chemical testing was employed in this case?

2.   Has this method of chemical testing been approved statutorily, administratively or judicially in this state?

3.   Is this method of chemical testing considered reliable for blood testing under generally accepted scientific standards?

4.   Is another method of testing (i.e., a confirmatory test) required under the facts of this case after an initial "presumptive" test?

D. Whether the chemical test involved in this case was properly performed by a qualified person.

1.   What statutory or administrative rule requirements are applicable to the performance of the chemical test employed in this case?

a.   Were such requirements complied with in this case?

b.   Is the state proposing to use documentary proof of the testing person's credentials, or bring the testing person to court to testify?

c.   Is the "qualified person" certified by his/her college degree or by the state crime lab's in-house program, to conduct testing?

2.   Was the chemical test performed in accordance with accepted scientific standards?

    a.   Were the instruments used in the performance of the test properly certified, calibrated, and otherwise qualified for use?

    b.   Were the chemical solutions used in the performance of the test checked for qualitative and quantitative accuracy, either by the person who performed the test or by another qualified person?

    c.   Were the required measurements and calculations properly performed?

    d.   Did a supervising chemist or toxicologist check the work and the conclusions of the lab tech or the toxicologist who conducted the analysis?

3.   What statutory or administrative rule requirements or standards are applicable to persons performing chemical tests on blood samples?

    a.   Is a permit or certificate required?

    b.   Was the permit current as it relates to the date of this analysis?

    c.   Were all administrative requirements complied with in this case?

4.   Was the person who performed the chemical test qualified to do so under accepted scientific standards?

    a.   What is the person's educational background and scientific training? (Track down information on degrees, grades, etc.)

    b.   How many chemical tests of this type has the person performed?

    c.   Prior to being employed at the crime lab (or testing facility) was any similar "forensic" work done by this person?

CHECKLIST FOR DETECTION OF SCIENTIFIC ERROR IN BLOOD TESTING

A. The withdrawal, preservation, and labeling of the defendant's blood sample.

1.   If the traditional method of blood withdrawal and storage was used -

a. What type (including brand name) of sterilizing agent was used to sterilize the defendant's arm, and did it contain alcohol?

b. How much time elapsed between the application of the sterilizing agent and the insertion of the needle?

c. Was the blood collection syringe needle still in its sheath prior to being used to draw blood, or was it exposed and out of its sheath?

d. In what type of facility was the blood sample taken (hospital, physician's office, etc.), and were any odors or fumes noticeably present in the air at the time?

e. How much blood was withdrawn from the detainee for the sample?

f. Was the blood collected from the detainee's forearm or some other location?

g. How much time elapsed between the depositing of the blood sample in the storage container and the capping and sealing of the container?

h. When and exactly how were the blood preservative and the anticoagulant added to the blood sample?

i. What type of blood preservative and anticoagulant were added to the blood sample, and how much of each were added?

j. How, when, and by whom was the blood sample labeled or otherwise marked for identification?

k. What color(s) were the stoppers on any blood collection vials used?

l. If one or more aborted attempts were made to collect the blood, describe in detail all efforts and the cause of each aborted or failed effort.

2. If a blood collection and storage kit was used -

a. What type of blood collection and storage kit was used? (If not known, describe the size, shape and color of the package that you saw.)

b. What instruments, devices and materials were contained in the kit?

c. What instruments, devices or materials not contained in the kit were used in the course of withdrawing, sealing, labeling, and storing the blood sample?

d. What are the exact provisions of any instructions contained in the kit, and to what extent were they followed?

e. If the instructions contained in the kit were not followed to the letter, exactly what procedures were followed?

f. What are the exact provisions of any manufacturer's certificate of instructions contained in the kit?

g. When was the shipment that contained the collection kit used in this case received from the manufacturer, and by whom was it received?

h. Were the kits in that shipment checked or sampled (randomly or otherwise) for compliance with the manufacturer's certificate? If so, give details of how, when and obtain records from such verification.

i. When and by whom was the blood sample withdrawn from the defendant?

j. How, when, and by whom was the defendant's blood sample labeled or otherwise marked for identification?

k. Who was present and acted as a witness to the blood collection process?

l. How much blood was withdrawn from the defendant for the sample?

B. Whether the blood sample obtained from the defendant was representative of the blood needed for testing.

1. How much time elapsed between the commission of the alleged offense and the withdrawal of the blood sample?

2. How much time elapsed between the detainee's last consumption of alcohol and the withdrawal of the blood sample?

3. When did the detainee last operate any motor vehicle that is claimed to have been the basis of the DUI-DWI or BUI-BWI offense?

4. If the defendant was given medical treatment prior to the taking of the blood sample -

a. Was the defendant given any drugs or medication prior to the taking of the blood sample?

b. Was the defendant given any fluids intravenously prior to the taking of the blood sample?

c. Was the defendant given a blood transfusion prior to the taking of the blood sample?

d. Prior to the blood being drawn, was the defendant given any type of medical treatment or emergency care wherein either topical anesthesia or oral medication was administered?

C. Whether the integrity of the blood sample was maintained through the completion of testing.

1. What type of preservative (bacteriastat) was added to the detainee's blood sample, how much was added, and when was it added?

2. What type of anticoagulant was added to the defendant's blood sample, how much was added, and when was it added?

3. When and by what method was the defendant's blood sample sealed, and what type of seal was used?

4. Was the seal on the defendant's blood sample broken, damaged or tampered with at any time prior to the time of testing?

5. Was the defendant's blood sample at any time accessible to persons other than those responsible for its custody?

6. If more than one test was performed on the defendant's blood sample, was the sample sealed and preserved between tests?

7. If additional testing beyond the first analysis was performed, was the blood collected for both analysis from the same vial or from different vials?

D. Whether the defendant's blood sample was properly and accurately tested.

1. If the blood sample was tested by gas chromatography -

   a. Was liquid blood or headspace vapor tested?

   b. If liquid blood was tested -

   How much blood was injected into the chromatograph for each test performed, and how and by whom was it measured?

c.   If headspace vapor was tested -

How and under what conditions was the headspace vapor obtained?

How much headspace vapor was injected into the chromatograph for each test performed, and how and by whom was it measured?

d.   How, when, and by whom was the chromatograph used in testing last calibrated prior to its use in this case?

What was the base liquid and chemical composition of each calibrating sample used?

Who prepared the calibrating samples?

When were the calibrating samples prepared?

e.   What was used as the internal standard for the chromatograph?

What was the concentration of any alcohol contained in the internal standard?

What was the concentration of other chemicals contained in the internal standard?

Who prepared the internal standard, and when was it prepared?

What quantity of internal standard was added to the test sample and how and by whom was it measured?

f.   How many tests were performed on the defendant's blood sample?

g.   What were the chromatograph readings for each test, and how was each reading converted to BAC?

h.   What other substances were found in each sample of blood tested, and what were the chromatograph readings for each substance?

i.   What was the identification number of the chromatograph used in testing?

j.   What was the maintenance record of the chromatograph used in testing?

k.   Did the person who performed the test personally check the composition of each chemical solution used either in directly testing the blood sample or in calibrating any instrument or device used in testing the sample?

l. Who performed the test, and was such person certified or otherwise qualified to do so?

2. If the blood sample was tested by enzymatic oxidation -

a. Who prepared the testing solution, and when was it prepared?

b. What were the contents of the testing solution?

c. What was the concentration of NAD in the testing solution?

d. What quantity of testing solution was used in each test performed?

e. What quantity of blood was added to the testing solution in each test performed?

f. How much NADH was formed in the reaction between the blood and the testing solution?

g. How was the NADH measured?

h. If the NADH was measured photometrically, how and when was the photometric instrument last calibrated prior to its use in this case, and who calibrated it?

i. Was whole blood, blood serum, or blood plasma tested?

If blood serum or plasma was tested, did the test results reported represent the BAC of serum, plasma or the BAC results of whole blood?

If blood serum or plasma was tested and if the reported test results represent the BAC of whole blood, how was the BAC of whole blood calculated? (Find out the multiplication factor utilized.)

j. Was the hematocrit of the defendant's blood checked or ever determined?

k. If an automated instrument was used to test the blood sample, how many other samples were tested in the same run?

l. Who was the manufacturer of any automated instrument or machine used in testing the blood sample, what was its identification number, and what was its maintenance record?

m.   Did the person who performed the test personally prepare or check the composition of each chemical solution used either in directly testing the blood sample or in calibrating any instrument or device used in testing the sample?

n.   Who performed the test, and was such person certified or otherwise qualified to do so? (Check for permit dates – beginning and expiring.)

o.   Is the method of analysis used in this case approved by statute or regulation for use as a forensic test in cases involving allegations of criminal offenses?

3.   If another method of chemical testing was used -

a.   What method of chemical testing was employed?

b.   What procedures were followed, and what type and quantity of chemicals were used?

c.   How was the amount of ethyl alcohol in the blood sample measured?

d.   How, when, and by whom was any photometric or other measuring instrument used in the test last calibrated prior to its use in this case?

e.   Did the person who performed the test personally prepare or check the composition of each chemical solution used either in directly testing the blood sample or in calibrating any instrument or device used in testing the sample?

f.   Who performed the test, and was such person certified or otherwise qualified to do so?

E. Whether adequate steps were taken to detect the presence of random or human error in the performance of the chemical test.

1.   Was more than one test performed on the blood sample?

2.   If only one test was performed on the blood sample, why were other tests not performed?

3.   If more than one test was performed, what were the results of each test?

4.   Is replicate or multiple (duplicate) testing required by statute or administrative rule in this state?

5.   Is the reported result the average or mean of multiple analysis, or the lowest result obtained?

F. Whether adequate steps were taken to detect the presence of systematic error in the laboratory or clinic where the blood sample was tested.

1. When did the laboratory or clinic where the blood sample was tested last participate in a proficiency testing program?

2. Who sponsored the proficiency testing program last participated in by the testing laboratory or clinic, and how many other laboratories or clinics participated in the program?

3. What were the results of the last proficiency testing program?

4. If the testing laboratory or clinic does not participate in proficiency testing programs, what are its reasons for not doing so?

5. Does the testing laboratory or clinic employ any other procedures or practices that are designed to detect the presence of systematic error?

6. Are there statutory or administrative rule requirements pertaining to proficiency testing, and were such requirements complied with in this case?

CHECKLIST FOR DETECTION OF FOUNDATIONAL ERROR IN BREATH TESTING

A. Whether the method of testing used is scientifically accurate and reliable.

1. What type of breath testing instrument was used to test the defendant's breath?

2. Has this instrument been approved either statutorily or administratively in this state?   If so -

   a. By whom was it approved?

   b. When was the instrument most recently approved?

   d. Has the instrument been altered in any way by the manufacturer or by the user since it was last approved?

3. Has this make and model testing instrument been the subject of a product recall or class action litigation based upon any type of malfunction?

4. If the instrument has been factory serviced recently, was the machine checked for calibration accuracy after being shipped back from the factory?

B. Whether the testing equipment used was in proper working order when the test was administered to the defendant.

1.   Is certification by a state agency or officer required for any of the breath testing equipment used in this case?   If so -

   a.   By whom is the certification given?

   b.   What type of certification is required?

   c.   What are the certification standards?

   d.   How often is certification required?

   e.   When was the equipment used in this case most recently certified?

   f.   Has any part or component of the breath testing instrument (including its computer software) been changed or modified since the most recent certification?

   g.   In what manner was the equipment used in this case certified and who certified it?

   h.   If the testing device was also inspected to determine its capability to detect and report interfering substances, give full details on how, when and by what method such verification was conducted.

2.   Is periodic inspection or testing of breath testing equipment required in this state?   If so -

   a.   What agency or officer conducts the inspections or tests?

   b.   How often must the inspections or tests be conducted?

   c.   When was the equipment used in this case last inspected or tested?

   d.   What is the name of the person who conducted the last inspection or test on the equipment used in this case?

   e.   What training and other qualifications are required of persons who conduct such inspections or tests?

   f.   Did the person who last inspected or tested the equipment used in this case possess the required qualifications?

   g.   Is certification required of persons who conduct such inspections or tests?   If so -

By whom is the certification issued?

How often is certification required?

What are the certification standards?

Was the person who last inspected or tested the equipment used in this case properly certified at the time?

h. What components of the breath testing equipment must be inspected or tested?

i. What are the published inspection or testing standards?

j. What were the results of the last inspection or test conducted on the breath testing instrument and the breath-alcohol simulator used in this case?

k. In what manner may proof of compliance with the inspection or testing requirements be entered into evidence at trial?

l. Did the certifying officer or technician strictly comply with the required testing protocol for the breath machine as published by the state?

3. If periodic inspection or testing of breath testing equipment by a state agency or officer is not required, what are the testing or inspection requirements for such equipment?

a. Who is responsible for conducting the periodic inspections or tests?

b. What are the inspection or testing standards?

c. Was the testing equipment properly and timely inspected prior to its use for forensic analysis in this case?

4. What periodic maintenance procedures, if any, are required to be performed on the breath testing equipment used in this case?

a. Were the maintenance procedures properly and timely performed by qualified persons prior to the use of the testing equipment in this case?

b. Were all calibration check test cards provided to verify that the breath device was properly checked?

C. Whether the breath testing equipment was properly operated by a qualified person.

1. Have uniform or official procedures for the operation of the breath testing equipment used in this case been adopted?   If so -

    a. What are the procedures?

    b. In what form have such procedures been implemented (checklist, operating instructions, etc.)?

    c. What forms, lists, or other documents must operators of the testing equipment complete when administering a breath test?

    d. Were the checklists or operating instructions followed by the operator in this case?

    e. Were the required forms or documents contemporaneously completed by the operator?

    f. What is the required length of the period of waiting (deprivation) and observation prior to the taking of a breath sample?

    g. How long was the defendant observed prior to the taking of a breath sample in this case?

    h. Who observed the defendant and in what manner was the observation performed?

2. Is certification or other proof of qualification required of operators of breath testing equipment?   If so -

    a. What are the training and educational requirements to be qualified to be a breath test operator?

    b. What type of certificate or permit is required?

    c. By whom is the certificate or permit issued?

    d. How often must the certificate or permit be renewed?

    e. Had the operator of the breath testing equipment in this case been timely issued a certificate or permit at the time of testing in this case?

    f. Had the operator received the required amount of training?

    g. In what manner may the qualifications of the operator be established in court?

D. Whether the breath test was administered within the required period.

1.   Is there a statutorily or administratively required period within which a breath test must be administered?   If so -

       a.   Upon what event does the time for the required period begin to run?

       b.   What is the length of the period within which the test must be administered?

       c.   Was the test administered to the defendant within the required period in this case?

       d.   What is the penalty for not administering the test within the required period?

2.   Whether or not there is a statutorily or administratively required period for administering a breath test, was the test administered to the defendant within a reasonable period after the end of driving?

CHECKLIST FOR DETECTION OF SCIENTIFIC ERROR IN BREATH TESTING

A. The defense of a lower partition ratio.

1.   Determining the defendant's temperature at the time of testing.

       a.   Was the defendant's temperature taken at or near the time of testing?

           If so, what was the temperature and who took it?

       b.   If the defendant's temperature was not taken at or near the time of testing -

           Was the defendant suffering from injury, illness or disease at the time of testing?

           Had the defendant been exposed to excessive heat or trauma prior to the time of testing?

           Had the defendant taken psychotropic drugs prior to the time of testing?

           Did other factors exist that may have caused the defendant to have had an elevated body temperature at the time of testing?

           Did the defendant receive any medical care or treatment after being incarcerated that may yield a test of body temperature?

c. From the above conditions and factors, what was the defendant's actual or estimated body temperature at the time of testing?

2. Determining the hematocrit of the defendant's blood at the time of testing.

  a. Has a sample of the defendant's blood been tested for hematocrit?

  If so, on what date was it tested and what did the test indicate?

  What was the estimated hematocrit of the defendant's blood at the time of the breath test?

3. Using the defendant's actual or estimated body temperature at the time of the breath test and/or the estimated hematocrit of the defendant's blood at the time of the breath test, what was the defendant's estimated partition ratio at the time of the breath test?

B. The defense of testing during absorption and the rising BAC defense [likely applicable to all traditional (common law) cases and to the per se count in some states].

1. At what time did the defendant commence drinking on the occasion in question?

2. At what time did the defendant cease drinking on the occasion in question?

3. How much alcohol did the defendant consume?

4. Did the defendant consume any food during the course of drinking or within an hour prior to the commencement of drinking? If so -

  a. What type of food was consumed?

  b. How much food was consumed?

  c. When was the food consumed?

5. At what time did the alleged offense occur (i.e., when did the driving episode END)?

6. At what time was the breath or blood test administered to the defendant?

7. Did the defendant consume or take any medication or drugs prior to or during the period of drinking? If so -

  a. What medications or drugs were consumed or taken?

  b. When were the medications or drugs consumed or taken?

8. Was the defendant suffering from disease or illness at the time of drinking?   If so -

    a. Describe the disease or illness.

    b. When did the disease or illness begin?

9. Was the defendant subjected to stress at the time of drinking? If so -

    a. What was the cause of the stress?

    b. When did the stress begin?

10. Did the defendant engage in strenuous physical exercise during or after the period of drinking?   If so -

    a. Describe the exercise.

    b. For how long a period was the defendant engaged in the exercise?

11. Based on the above facts, was the defendant in the absorptive phase of the alcohol distribution process when the breath test was administered?

12. Was the defendant involved in an accident wherein gastric emptying may have been stopped or slowed due to trauma?

    a. Was any hospital test of blood alcohol taken as a part of the treatment?

    b. If a hospital blood test was taken, what time was this blood drawn?

13. Based on the above facts, was the defendant in the absorptive phase of the alcohol distribution process at the time of the alleged offense?

14. Based on the above facts, did the defendant's BAC rise between the time of the offense and the time of testing?

C. Defenses related to the integrity of the breath sample.

1. Whether the breath sample was contaminated by regurgitated contents or gas from the stomach or the esophagus or due to mouth cavity alcohol being trapped.

    a. Did the defendant have any pockets (e.g., from wisdom tooth extraction), tooth cavities or broken fillings at the time of testing?

b. Was the defendant wearing dentures at the time of testing? If so -

Were the dentures upper or lower dentures?

Was the testing officer aware of the dentures?

c. Was denture adhesive used to secure the denture plate(s)? If so, what type and brand of denture adhesive was used?

d. Was the testing officer aware of the presence of dentures or dental plates?

e. If asked by any officer, what did the defendant report as to the time of his or her last drink prior to breath testing?

f. Was the defendant ever permitted to rinse his or her mouth prior to submitting to breath testing?

g. Did the defendant either hold his or her breath or engage in hyperventilation just prior to testing?

h. Was the defendant crying at the time of or during delivery of the breath sample?

2. What was the composition of any denture or plate material?

a. Was the material hard and inflexible or pliable and flexible?

b. Can a sample of the material be tested to see if it retains or absorbs alcoholic beverages?

3. Did the defendant have any active tooth, gum or mouth pain that was being treated with any type of topical medication? If so

a. What type and brand of topical pain ointment, dental packing, dental plug or salve was used?

b. Does the container indicate any alcohol being part of the contents of the pain relief medicine?

c. Are there any other chemicals in the pain relief medication of similar composition or chemical make-up to ethanol?

4. Whether the breath sample was contaminated by stomach alcohol.

a. For how long a period was the defendant observed by the testing officer prior to the taking of the breath sample?

b. Did the defendant burp, belch, hiccup, vomit or otherwise regurgitate any stomach contents or stomach gases during the period of waiting and observation?   If so -

What type of regurgitation activity occurred?

How many times did it occur during this period?

Was the testing officer aware of the regurgitation activity?

If noticed by the testing officer, was a new observation period begun, as required by state law?

Was the defendant's mouth open or closed during the regurgitation activity?

How long before the taking of the breath sample did the regurgitation activity occur?

5. Whether the breath sample was contaminated by non-consumed alcohol.

a. Did the defendant use or consume breath mints, cough drops, lip ointment, breath fresheners, cola drinks or other substances that may have contained alcohol or similar compounds within an hour prior to the administration of the breath test?

b. If so, what was used or consumed and in what amounts?

6. Whether the breath sample was contaminated by acetone or other endogenous substances.

a. Is the defendant a heavy smoker, an alcoholic, or a diabetic?

b. Had the defendant been adhering to a "high protein" or on a low carbohydrate diet at the time of testing?

7. Whether the breath sample was contaminated by inhaled substances.

a. Was the defendant exposed to organic or alcoholic fumes during the 24-hour period prior to testing?   If so -

b. To what type of fumes was the defendant exposed?

c. For how long a period was the defendant exposed?

d. How long prior to testing did the exposure end?

e. What was the degree of the defendant's physical activity during the exposure?

f.   Did the defendant use a functioning respirator or filtration mask while being exposed to the vapor?

8.   Whether the integrity of the breath sample was compromised by the presence of an elevated body temperature.

     a.   What was the defendant's body temperature at the time of testing? (See item A.1 above)

     b.   Did the defendant ever verbally complain of being "too hot" or overheating.

D. The defense of simulator test error.

1.   Was the breath testing instrument used in this case tested on a wet-bath breath-alcohol simulator?   If so -

     a.   When was the wet-bath simulator test performed?

     b.   Who performed the simulator test?

     c.   What were the results of the simulator test?

     d.   Who prepared the alcohol-water solution used in the simulator?

     e.   When was the alcohol-water solution prepared?

     f.   What was the concentration of alcohol in the solution?

     g.   How and where was the alcohol-water solution stored after preparation and before the vapor was ported into the simulator?

     h.   When was the concentration of alcohol in the solution last checked and who checked it?

     i.   When was the solution that was in the simulator at the time of the simulator test inserted into the simulator and how many simulator tests had been run since it was inserted?

     j.   When a simulator test is run, how is the vapor replaced in the simulator?

     k.   At what temperature was the simulator test run?

     l.   When was the simulator last checked for the presence of leakage from seals and was leakage found to exist?

     m.   What qualifications are required of simulator test operators?

n. Did the simulator test operator in this case possess such qualifications?

o. In what manner may the results of a simulator test be introduced into evidence?

p. Was the simulator solution used in testing the breath testing instrument used in this case preserved or destroyed?

q. If preserved, where is it located?

r. When and how was the thermometer in the wet-bath simulator checked for accuracy at being the state-approved mandatory temperature?

E. The defense of faulty dry gas simulator.

1. Was the dry gas simulator purchased from a certified supplier that verifies the contents of its canisters?

2. Did someone at the state verify the contents of the dry gas mixture?

3. Was the dry gas canister kept at a proper temperature and rotated to assure full mixture of the gases?

F. The defense of radio frequency interference.

1. What type and model of breath testing instrument was used in this case?

   a. Has this type of instrument been found by the National Highway Traffic Safety Administration, by its manufacturer, or by any independent testing agency or institution, to be susceptible to radio frequency interference?

   b. Does this instrument have a history locally, of being affected by radio frequency interference?

   c. Did the incident involving radio or cell phone communication in the room containing the breath machine occur while the defendant's testing was being conducted?

2. Had the breath testing instrument used in this case been tested for susceptibility to radio frequency interference?   If so -

   a. By whom was it tested?

   b. When was the test performed?

   c. What type of test was performed?

d.   What were the results of the test?

e.   Were such tests provided by or recommended by the manufacturer of the instrument?

3.   Had the breath testing instrument used in this case been modified to render it less susceptible to radio frequency interference? If so -

a.   What modifications were made?

b.   When were the modifications made?

c.   By whom were the modifications made?

d.   Were such modifications provided by or recommended by the manufacturer of the instrument?

4.   If the instrument has not been modified to render it less susceptible to radio frequency interference, have such modifications been recommended by the manufacturer of the instrument?

5.   Was a police radio in operation within 150 feet of the breath testing instrument at the time of the administration of the defendant's breath test?   If so -

a.   Where was the radio located?

b.   At what frequency was the radio being operated?

c.   What was the name of the person (or a description of the person) who was operating the radio?

6.   Was the breath testing instrument used in this case equipped with a radio frequency interference detector? If so, was the detector connected and in full operating condition?

7.   Do administrative rules or regulations exist that deal with prevention of possible radio frequency interference in breath testing instruments?

a.   If so, were such rules or regulations complied with in this case?

b.   What steps, if any, did the breath test operator take to confirm that all electronic devices had been turned off prior to breath testing?

G. Defenses related to the preservation of a sample of the defendant's breath.

1.   Are the police required to preserve a sample of the defendant's breath?

2.   Was a sample of the defendant's breath preserved in this case?   If so -

a.   Where is the sample located?

b.   For how long a period must the sample be preserved by the police?

c.   For how long a period will the sample be suitable for chemical testing?

3.   If a sample of the defendant's breath was not preserved, was replicate testing performed?

     a.   If so, what were the results of each test?

     b.   If not, is replicate testing required in this state or jurisdiction?

H. Replicate tests being correlated.

1.   Did the breath test operator obtain two sequential inhalations of breath that were within numerical agreement to within +/- 0.020?

2.   Did one inhalation report as a numerical value and the other report as being insufficient (or similar designation of the delivered sample being deficient)? If so

     a.   Did the breath test operator offer a new opportunity to re-test and provide two sequential samples?

     b.   In the event of physical inability to deliver a replicate test, did the breath test operator offer an alternative method of testing (e.g., blood testing) which requires no physical ability to deliver a long, continuous, fixed exhalation?

APPENDIX J

SAMPLE CLIENT QUESTIONNAIRE

CONFIDENTIAL INFORMATION

{Please complete every part of this form to the best of your ability, and be 100% truthful in every response. The sooner you complete this form, the better your memory will be about the incident and all the important facts surrounding your case. Your detailed answers to these questions will be the primary source of information that we use to try to evaluate your opportunities for successfully challenging the state's case against you. Lack of information greatly impedes our ability to discover winning defenses or jury arguments. All personal data will be kept confidential. Take sufficient time to complete this questionnaire, and use extra sheets of paper to supplement your responses wherever necessary. However, don't delay in returning the questionnaire since "time" can be an important factor in your case.}

⇩⇩⇩⇩ IMPORTANT QUICK REFERENCE DATA ⇩⇩⇩⇩

NAME AND HOME ADDRESS: Own / Rent / Live with Someone **Full Name:** Street **City** **State** **ZIP**	HOME PHONE ☐ * ( ) - CELL PHONE ☐ * ( ) -	WORK PHONE ☐ * ( ) - ext. PAGER NUMBER ☐ * ( ) -
OTHER MAILING ADDRESS: (to be used for mail in this case) **Street** **City** **State** **ZIP** **Email Address (if any):**	**If a different address was put on your citation, show that address here:** **Street** **City** **State** **ZIP**	

☐ *Speak with client only*

CLIENT INTAKE QUESTIONNAIRE

[1] BASIC

Nickname or Name You Prefer To Be Called:

Birth Date: /   /   Age: Birth Place:

Social Security Number   -   -

Preferred Telephone Number to use in order to reach you:

[2] *LICENSE*

Have you ever had your license suspended or revoked for any period of time, in any jurisdiction?   Yes / No

If "yes," answer these questions for each suspension/revocation:

When?

    a)   What court proceeding or traffic "event" caused it?

    b)   How long were you without all privilege to drive a vehicle?

    c)   Did you ever get a LIMITED or "work" permit during the suspension/revocation?

[3] *EMPLOYMENT*

Employer: Employer Address:

Job Title: How Long?

Duties:

Annual Income: ☐ Under $25,000   ☐ $25,000 to $50,000   ☐ Over $50,000

Prior Employment (past 5 years)

How long were you at each job?

Any problems with present employment or plans to change jobs?

Vehicle required for your employment?

Would you be fired, restricted in duties, passed over for promotion or demoted

                         (a) If convicted of DUI-DWI? ☐

                         (b) If your license is suspended? ☐

                         (c) If suspended, but you had a "work permit"? ☐

Do you drive a company-owned vehicle?

Does your company's insurance carrier insure you?

Do you ever have to "prove" insurability in order to drive a "company" car annually or periodically?

How many miles do you drive to/from/at work on a routine day?

How many *total* miles driven each week (business and personal miles)?

Is public transportation (taxi cabs; subway; buses) readily available to you?

What are the possibilities that you could relocate to another state IF ABSOLUTELY NECESSARY to protect your right to drive?

Do you have "security clearance" issues at work?

[4] *HEALTH & FAMILY INFORMATION*

Weight at time of arrest: Height:

General health conditions:

Any orthopedic problems, physical disabilities or prior surgery (in your lifetime)?

On arrest date, any *prescribed medication* taken by you daily or periodically?

If so, what?

Any *non-prescription medicine*, supplements, vitamins taken on arrest date by you daily or periodically?

Specific *health problems*, especially as it may relate to gastric or digestive issues?

Prior head trauma (i.e., concussions, car accidents where unconscious) at ANY time, from ANY cause, in your lifetime?

Circle all that apply: Diabetes / Hypoglycemia / Hyperglycemia / Gastric Reflux / Hiatal Hernia / Ulcers / Hepatitis / Cirrhosis / Emphysema / Lung Disorder / ADHD / ADD / Dyslexia / Meniere's Disease / Vertigo

Please supply some basic "background" information on your family and basic educational history below:

Family Connections	City, State	Occupation/School	Phone number *
Father (if living):			
Mother (if living):			
Brother/Sister:			
Brother/Sister:			
Brother/Sister:			
Brother/Sister:			
Adult Children:			
Child #1:			
Child #2:			
Child #3:			
Child #4:			

Your Educational Institutions	City, State	Graduate ?
High School:		Yes / No
College or Trade School:		Yes / No
Professional Degree (s)		Yes / No
Other Post-Graduate Education:		Yes / No

List any honors or special recognitions at ANY educational institution mentioned above:

[5] *EFFECTS OF A POSSIBLE CONVICTION*

What effect would a conviction have on you *personally*?

Would a conviction affect *your marriage (relationship)*?

Do you ever need to rent a ***rental car***, for personal or business use?

If "yes," if you were convicted of DUI-DWI or if your license was suspended with NO driving privileges, would denial of access to rental vehicles (Avis, Hertz) affect you or your business?

If so, explain:

If you are a "preferred" member of any car rental companies, list all below:
(e.g., Hertz #1, Thrifty "Blue Chip," etc.)

In what ways would a DUI-DWI conviction or license suspension affect your employment or professional standing?   Explain:

Are you involved in any "domestic" (divorce, child custody, etc.) case or judicial dispute that a DUI-DWI conviction or license suspension might negatively impact or affect?

If so, explain:

Are you on any Executive Committees or Boards, such as a Board of Directors for a publicity-traded stock, or a non-profit Board?

Are you a United States citizen? Yes / No (circle one) If not, please provide your immigration attorney's name and phone number below.

Are you in the United States on: ☐ a "green" card, ☐ a temporary work permit, or ☐ a temporary visa (if here on visa, what classification?)

If so, give details:

If you *are "licensed" by any state or federal authority to fly, operate a specialized motor vehicle (e.g., CDL license for commercial vehicles) or to operate a watercraft or vessel,* give all special licenses or permits below.

If you are "licensed" by any state or federal authority *to practice a profession or engage in any regulated industry* with annual licensing, give all special licenses or permits below.

Do you ever need to *travel outside the continental United States* (i.e., Canada, Mexico, Europe, Asia), such that any travel limitations imposed by other nations from a DUI-DWI conviction could affect you?

With whom did you talk to *within the last 3 hours* before arrest?

Name	Address/Phone/Cell	Relationship/Location	Employer

Was anyone *with you* when you were arrested?

If so, full name, address, and home, cell and work phone numbers:

What was his/her condition (sober, drinking, impaired, passed out, etc.) when you were arrested?

Was this person permitted to drive the vehicle home for you?

If not permitted to drive the vehicle, was this person "screened" for alcohol impairment in any way?

Did anyone (including the above-named person) observe or overhear any portion or aspect of the police traffic "stop," questioning, "field tests," or conversation at or during arrest?

Names, addresses, and telephone numbers (cell and home):

Name	Address	Phone

Did the police *allow* someone else to come to the scene to drive the vehicle away from the scene, or to move the vehicle at all? Yes/No   If "yes," Who:

From the point you departed driving, how far did you drive the vehicle before the police stopped you?

Traffic conditions you encountered on roadways that you drove upon prior to being arrested:

Stop lights?   How many?

Working properly?   Caution lights?

Weather conditions? (*be specific*)

County stopped in: Street stopped on:

Nearest crossing street or highway exit:

[6] *ROADBLOCKS*

(Complete *only* if stopped at a roadblock)

Was arrest at roadblock or "license check"?

How far ahead did you see the roadblock?

How long did you wait in line before getting to an officer who asked you questions?

Did the officer who first questioned you tell you what the PURPOSE of the roadblock was?

Were you given any advance *notice* of the roadblock (i.e., was the roadblock well-marked and visible from flares, fluorescent cones, emergency lights)?

If so, give details:

Were **any visible signs** indicating "roadblock ahead" or similar advisement of a "checkpoint" as you approached the roadblock location? Yes/No.   If yes, what did it say?

How many police *cars* did you see?

Did any have their emergency lights on? Yes/No.   If so, how many?

Did any officer reach inside your car with his or her hand (with a portable breath tester) **_OR_** using a flashlight-type device **_OR_** put his or her head inside your window?

Did more than one officer give you field tests **_OR_** interrogate you?

How many police *officers* did you see at the roadblock location (total number)?

In the direction you were traveling, were **_all_** cars being stopped (at least briefly, for "screening" of all drivers)?

[7] *DRIVER'S LICENSE AND INITIAL QUESTIONING BY THE OFFICER*
(ALL DRIVERS COMPLETE THIS SECTION)

Any ***restrictions on your license*** when you were stopped?

If so, were these restrictions being complied with when you were stopped?

Where was your plastic license when you first began looking for it?

If you did not have your "plastic" license in your possession at the time of the "stop," give details about where the license was, and why it was not in your possession?

What were the ***officer's first words*** to you when he/she encountered you? (Be exact)

What did you say in response to this question?

What happened next, in terms of dealing with your possible "impairment" or testing?

Did the officer comment on your breath "smelling like alcohol," or similar words?

Were any ***containers of alcohol visible*** to the officer as he/she stood outside your vehicle?

Did the officer comment about or question you about any ***open or empty alcohol containers***?

If so, what type, and were they full and unopened, partially full (seal broken) or empties?

Did the officer confiscate these containers, for use as "evidence" against you in this case?

Had you "masked" the smell of your breath with food, coffee, gum, candy, breath spray, breath strips, etc., to cover the smell of alcohol?

If so, how or what did you use and when did you put it in your mouth?

Was any other suspicious or illegal item or items (i.e., guns, bullets, other weapons, rolling papers, bong, baggies, marijuana pipe or "roaches") visible *from outside your car* when the police approached your vehicle?

If so, give details:

[8] INSURANCE AND REGISTRATION

Did officer ask for proof of insurance?

Did you produce proof of insurance before officer asked for it?

In what state was the insurance issued?   Was it *your* insurance?

Insurance Company: Policy No.:

Did the officer ask for your vehicle registration papers?

What was the state of registration?

{NOTE: If charged with "no insurance" or "no proof of insurance" bring a copy of proof of insurance with you to your first interview}

[9] FIELD SOBRIETY TESTS OR ROADSIDE SOBRIETY TESTS
(ALL DRIVERS COMPLETE THIS SECTION)

Did the officer *direct* you (or "*request*" you) to perform any coordination or roadside sobriety tests?

Exactly *when* (how many minutes, seconds after getting out of car) were you first requested to (told to) perform these tests?

What was the *exact wording used* by the officer in making this "request or demand"?

Did the officer ask you *any preliminary questions about your physical limitations, prior injuries, prior surgery or impairments or present illnesses/medications* before beginning to "test" you?

Have you *EVER* suffered any concussion, head trauma or brain surgery during your lifetime?

Before you began doing *any* of the field sobriety tests (including the hand-held breath tester), were you under the impression that you were "in custody" or "not free to leave"?

If "yes," *give details why you felt that you were not free to leave*:

Was there anything about this traffic stop that led you to believe that this was not going to be a "brief" encounter with the police, but that you were going to be detained for a more prolonged period of time?

If "yes," give *specific* facts or reasons for this belief (e.g., "took my license and never returned it," or said "you're not going anywhere after this," etc.):

If so, what questions did you ask, and how did the officer respond to what you said?

Describe your shoes (if wearing any) during field sobriety tests:

Were your shoes: **On / Off? (Select one) [During the field sobriety "agility" tests]**

Were any street lights above or near your location to illuminate the field test area? Yes/No

Describe the lighting in the area where you were trying to perform the field tests:

Before doing *any or all* of these field tests, did you EVER request to call an attorney?

When asked to try to do these field evaluations, did you EVER hesitate, decline or ask if you were *required to do these evaluations*?

Where were the lights in relation to your field tests (including any automobile headlights)? Give detailed description:

Were any flashing emergency lights "on" or ant "wigwags" (alternating high and low beam lights) "on" any police cars when you attempted to do the field tests.

Name each of the eye tests, alphabet tests, agility or coordination tests that you performed *in the order given*, and how did you do?

[NOTE: This question is *not* directed to any hand-held breath testing device used, which has its own section below.]

Test Type (Describe what was done)	*Officer Said* I Did OK/ Failed/No Comment	*I Thought* I Did OK/ Failed/Don't Know
1		
2		
3		
4		

<u>Road or shoulder conditions where field tests were given:</u> (circle your selections)

Level / Sloping   Smooth / Rocky Wet / Dry   Grassy / Dirt   Holes/ Ruts
Wide / Narrow   Windy / Calm   Line to Walk/ No Line to Walk   Raining/ Snowing
Hot /Cold

<u>Other conditions:</u>

Eyeglasses: **On / Off /NA**   *Contact Lenses:* **In / Out**   *Emotions:* **Crying/ Nervous / Shaky**

Traffic: **Interstate Speeds / Heavy / Other** _____

Distractions at "field sobriety testing" location?   Yes/No   What?

Were any bystanders or other people gathered around? Yes/No   If "yes," how many?

Temperature: Humidity: Moonlight?

If you were asked to recite the *alphabet (or part of the alphabet),* when was the last time you had said your ABC's before the night/day of arrest?

Did the officer say the complete ABC's **<u>OR</u>** the same "partial" alphabet requested of you before asking you to do it?

On *any other "verbal" tests* that you were asked to perform (such as counting backward), had you ever attempted to do that task before being asked to perform it on the day/night of your arrest? When?

Were you shaking or "quivering" when you were being given the agility tests?

Did the officer *demonstrate* any or all of the tests *before* you did them?

Did the officer advise you <u>what you had to do</u> on each test *to* **pass** *it*?

Did the officer ever indicate to you that these agility tests were *100% voluntary or optional*?

What compelled you or caused you to attempt to perform these **<u>voluntary</u>** field sobriety tests?

Did the officer ever make any statement of encouragement or make a promise to you that **if you passed these tests** that he/she *would let you go home?*

Did the officer ever indicate (***in any manner or fashion***) that by **<u>not</u>** taking the roadside field sobriety tests **<u>OR</u>** the portable breath alcohol tester, that you would *either* lose your license, *or* be subjected to immediate arrest *or* would be convicted of DUI-DWI simply for refusing?

Did you ever *blow into* a hand-held breath alcohol tester *at the scene* of the stop?

If so, were you permitted to **SEE** the digital reading that the tester indicated?

If so, what was the reading? _____ If "two" samples were taken, 2nd sample: _____

If *not* permitted to see it, did the officer *tell you* the result?

What did he/she say about the result?

Were you asked or required to "blow" *more than one test* on the hand-held breath machine?

Did the officer ever make any statement or promise to you that *if you passed the hand-held breath test* that he/she would let you go home?

Did the officer ever advise you that the hand-held test is *100% voluntary*, and that you had a right to refuse to take that hand-held test *without **any** penalty or loss of license befalling you*?

Did the officer ever indicate (*in any manner or fashion*) that by not blowing into the hand-held alcohol tester that you would either lose your license **OR** be subject to immediate arrest?

At what point during the arrest process was the hand-held breath test given to you? (List all times, if more that once):

Was there *any physical or vocal resistance by you* or interference with the officer's arrest procedures *by others* while you were being detained or when you were arrested?

Did you ever advise *any* of the officers that you came in contact with, *either* at the arrest scene, *or* at the testing site *or at jail*, that you wanted an independent test of your blood, breath or urine?

[10] *ARREST*

Were you *ever* told you were "under arrest" or similar wording to indicate that you were going to jail?

When, and by whom?

Were you told *exactly* what you were being *arrested for*?

If the officer told you one offense (e.g., "DUI-DWI"), did he/she also advise you about being charged *with the other traffic offenses* for which you were ticketed?

What was the last thing you said (or did) before the officer told you that you were under arrest?

What was the officer's *exact wording* to you about your being placed under arrest?

Did you *ever lose your composure* and begin using profanity or speak disparagingly to the officers that you dealt with?

[11] *IMPLIED CONSENT RIGHTS*

Assuming that you *were* read (or given) your implied consent rights *at ANY point in time,* did the warnings she/he read include any of the *three* versions of the following language? If you were under 21, the *first* warning should have been read. If you were operating a commercial vehicle when stopped, the *second* warning should have been read.

Yes / No / Not Certain (select one)   [NOTE: This applies to a Georgia case].

Implied Consent Notice / SUSPECTS UNDER AGE 21

Georgia law requires you to submit to state-administered chemical tests of your blood, breath, urine, or other bodily substances for the purpose of determining if you are under the influence of alcohol or drugs.

If you refuse this testing, your Georgia driver's license or privilege to drive on the highways of this state will be suspended for a period of one year. Your refusal to submit to the required testing may be offered into evidence against you at trial.

If you submit to testing and the results indicate a blood alcohol concentration of 0.02 grams or more, your Georgia driver's license or privilege to drive on the highways of this state may be suspended for a minimum period of one year.

After first submitting to the required state tests, you are entitled to additional chemical tests of your blood, breath, urine, or other bodily substances at your own expense and from qualified personnel of your own choosing.

Will you submit to the state administered chemical tests of your ***(Designate which tests)*** *under the implied Consent Law?*

Yes / No / Not Certain (select one)

Implied Consent Rights/COMMERCIAL DRIVER SUSPECTS

Georgia law requires you to submit to state-administered chemical tests of your blood, breath, urine, or other bodily substances for the purpose of determining if you are under the influence of alcohol or drugs.

If you refuse this testing, you will be disqualified from operating a commercial motor vehicle for a minimum period of one year. Your refusal to submit to the required testing may be offered into evidence against you at trial.

If you submit to testing and the results indicate the presence of any alcohol, you will be issued an out-of-service order and will be prohibited from operating a motor vehicle for 24 hours. If the results indicate a blood alcohol concentration of 0.04 grams or more, you will be disqualified from operating a commercial motor vehicle for a minimum period of one year.

After first submitting to the required state tests, you are entitled to additional chemical tests of your blood, breath, urine, or other bodily substances at your own expense and from qualified personnel of your own choosing.

Will you submit to the state administered chemical tests of your ***(Designate which tests)*** *under the implied Consent Law?*

Yes / No / Not Certain (select one)

Implied Consent Rights/ALL OTHER SUSPECTS

Georgia law requires you to submit to state-administered chemical tests of your blood, breath, urine, or other bodily substances for the purpose of determining if you are under the influence of alcohol or drugs.

If you refuse this testing, your Georgia driver's license or privilege to drive on the highways of this state will be suspended for a period of one year. Your refusal to submit to the required testing may be offered into evidence against you at trial.

If you submit to testing and the results indicate a blood alcohol concentration of 0.08 grams or more, your Georgia driver's license or privilege to drive on the highways of this state may be suspended for a minimum period of one year.

After first submitting to the required state tests, you are entitled to additional chemical tests of your blood, breath, urine, or other bodily substances at your own expense and from qualified personnel of your own choosing.

Will you submit to the state administered chemical tests of your ***(Designate which tests)*** *under the implied Consent Law?*

When you heard these words, ***did you understand these warnings*** and the penalties and consequences stated by the officer?

What was your interpretation of the words the officer read to you?

At the time these warnings from the small card were read to you, (or otherwise told to you) had the officer told you *or otherwise let you know* by his/her conduct (**example**: *handcuffs*) ***that you were under arrest for DUI-DWI?***

Explain:

What were you doing (or what was "going on" around you) at the time that the officer was giving you these implied consent warnings?

If you <u>took</u> the officer's official breath test(s) [at a police station, jail or in the "Batmobile"], answer the following three questions:

(1) Did the officer "speed read" or hurry the reading of these warnings?

(2) Did you realize that you had an ***absolute right to refuse*** the State-administered test?

(3) ***Did you ever stop, hesitate or verbally or physically decline to submit to this test,*** before finally submitting to it? Yes / No

If so, state exactly why you "changed your mind." (Be specific)

If you believed then or if you now believe that the reading of these advisements was deficient or misleading ***in any way***, please give details why:

Other than the wording given to you from the applicable "warning" on the preceding pages, did the officer ***say anything else or elaborate or explain your obligation to submit to the official chemical sobriety test or the penalties which would befall you if you refused to submit to it?***

If "yes," give the exact wording used by officer:

Did you ever request to call or consult with an attorney?

Did you ever ***express any doubt*** about the reliability or accuracy of a "breath" test device?

Did you **EVER** advise *any* of the officers that you came in contact with, at the arrest scene, at the testing site or at jail, (*anyone, anytime, any place*) that you wanted an independent test of your blood, breath or urine?

If so, give exact details and time that this was done:

[12] *MIRANDA WARNINGS*

[**NOTE:** *Don't confuse this "warning" with the Implied Consent Rights in the previous section.*] Were you given your *Miranda* warnings *at any time*? ["You have the right to remain silent. You have the right to an attorney. If you want an attorney, and can't afford one, the court will appoint one for you," etc.?]

If so, *by whom* were these read, *where were they read to you* and (most importantly) *WHEN*?

[13] *CONVERSATION AFTER ARREST*

What did the officer say to you or ask you first *after* you were arrested?

Precisely what was said or asked next and by whom?

Were you struck, pushed, injured, ridiculed, verbally abused or physically "roughed up" by the officer(s) when you were arrested?

If so, describe:

Did either you or the police officer ever use profanity toward each other? (Describe in detail what was said and when it occurred).

Did you ever complain of the cuffs being too tight on your wrists?

[14] *CAR TOWING OR REMOVAL FROM SCENE*
[Complete Applicable Parts of This Section]

Make of vehicle: Year: Model:

What happened to the vehicle you were driving?

Was it towed away?   By what tow service?

Were you present when it was taken (towed) from scene?

What were you doing (or where were you) when the tow truck *arrived*?

Did the tow truck operator observe any of your "sobriety" testing?

Did you speak to the tow operator?

Did you get a copy of the tow operator's report?

Did you have to sign a towing permission form?

Was your car searched before being towed? Yes/No

Were you present when it was searched? Yes/No

Was anything removed or later was found to be "missing" from your vehicle?

Was your vehicle "ransacked" when you picked it up?

If so, describe in detail:

If you had a cell phone available, did the officer ever offer to let you call someone to come get your car, **or** offer to let you call an attorney **or** offer an alternate tow company of your choosing?

If "yes," *how long after you were "arrested"* did the tow truck arrive?

Did you ever hear or notice the officer requesting a "transport" or "tow" vehicle on his/her two-way radio?

If "yes," when did you hear this?

Did the arresting officer stay at the scene until the vehicle was towed away?

[15] *AT STATION/JAIL/TESTING FACILITY*

Did you see a clock when you arrived at the jail?   Time:

How many other officers there?   Conversation with anyone?

Who?

Before you took the State's official breath test, were you **asked any health or environmental contamination questions,** such as "Are you taking medication?" "Are you a diabetic?" "Do you have false teeth or a bridge?" or "Have you been around any paint vapors or other chemicals today?"

If so, what were you asked, and what was your response to these "screening" questions?

Did anyone require you to open your mouth to look for objects or gum inside your mouth?

Searched?   Fingerprinted?   Videotaped?

Was a "mug shot" taken of you?

Did you sign any papers at the jail?

If so, what type of papers?

Did the arresting or testing officer make any *statements about you* or *about the circumstances of your arrest* or *about your alcohol "reading,"* or anything else of significance to anyone?

Did the arresting officer (or *any* officer) *ask you about prior DUI-DWI offenses* or comment to you that your computer record showed *prior* DUI-DWI(s)?

Without being asked about this, *did you say anything to the officer about prior DUI-DWIs* that you previously had received?

If "yes," give details:

Was the **arresting officer** *physically present* in the room where you were given the test, and did he/she *keep you in view the entire time* that you were at the testing facility?

Explain:

Did he/she or any other officer(s) *in the testing room have their cell phone, walkie-talkie or portable radios* on their belt or shoulder when they were in the testing room?

While in the room where the testing was being conducted, did you ever *hear* or *observe* an officer (*any* officer) use radio equipment or a cell phone in communicating with the dispatcher or with other officers?

If "yes," give details:_

Was anyone smoking in or around the breath testing room prior to **or** during the time you were being tested?

Did any other officers make comments to the arresting officer **or** testing officer **or** to YOU?

What did they say?

Were you permitted to go to the rest room? <u>Yes/No</u> (circle one)

If "yes;" ***when***?

Permitted to make a telephone call?   If "yes," when was this permitted?

To whom did you place a call?

Were you allowed to go to the rest room, smoke, drink water or put ***anything*** into your mouth within 20 minutes ***before*** the test was administered?

If so, give details:

[16] BREATH TESTS

[Sections 16 & 17 should be completed by you ONLY if you were administered a <u>breath, blood</u> <u>or urine</u> test at a police precinct/jail or a mobile testing van by the police after your arrest. If you were <u>not</u> taken to a breath machine and (upon arrival there) <u>asked to blow into the</u> collection tube, mark this box ☐ with an "X," and skip these sections.]

Testing officer's/operator's name:

Officer's/Operator's police agency:

Officer/Operator present when you arrived?

Did officer/operator arrive afterwards?   When?

Did the operator *turn on* the breath machine and wait several minutes before asking you to "blow" into it?

Did you ever hear the breath machine give any computer-generated "beeps" or "chirps" *before* or *during* your testing?

Did the testing officer ***ever PRINT OUT one test card*** and insert another?

If "yes," what do you recall hearing, and when did you hear it?

When did the **testing** officer/operator begin "observing" you prior to the breath test starting?

Was this observation continuous and uninterrupted?

Where was the arresting officer during this time?

Time of *first* test: Reading:

Time of *second* test: Reading:

396

Time of *third* test (if given): Reading:

Witnesses to your breath tests? Who?

Approximate room temperature in the breath test room and lighting conditions:

Did anyone ask you about false teeth, "bridge" work or dental plates?

Details:

Did you have a "fever" or elevated body temperature when being tested?

If so, was the elevated body temperature from: Sick? Dancing? Exercising? Sunbathing?

Indicate other cause:

Are you a smoker? Yes/No. If yes, when did you LAST SMOKE prior to the breath testing?

Did you smoke while being transported to the breath testing location, or upon arrival there?
Did you have any difficulty performing the breath test?

If so, give details:

If a repeat "blow" was required on the official chemical sobriety test (***not*** the hand-held test), was the **mouthpiece** *changed* each time?

In the 12 hours immediately prior to being tested on a breath machine, were you exposed to (i.e., breathe or work with) solvents, glues, cleaning solutions, paints, acetone (such as nail polish remover), mineral spirits or any similar caustic or aromatic products?

If so, describe:

Did you have an "air bag" deploy in your vehicle before your breath test?
If so, was your clothing covered with a powdery chemical?

[17] CONVERSATION WITH BREATH TESTING OPERATOR
(Applies to anyone who was taken before a breath machine operator)

Did the breath-testing operator ask you any questions? What?

Did the breath test operator give you any instructions or explain how the machine worked or how you were to "blow" into the machine?

What?

Did the breath testing officer/operator ever show you his/her **permit** to operate the machine?

Was the arresting officer present and observing *all* procedures at *all* times during the testing procedures?

When you gave the breath sample, was your body in an upright position (perpendicular to the floor), or *were you leaning forward* to reach the mouthpiece from a sitting or standing position?

Describe in detail:

Did you get to *see* the numerical reading on the machine's digital readout?   Explain:

[18] *BLOOD OR URINE TESTS*

[This section should only be completed if you were given a blood / urine test by the police.]

Where were you taken to obtain the blood/urine test?

Who took you for a blood/urine test?

When did this occur, in relation to your time of arrest?

Had you already given a breath sample before being taken for a blood/urine test?

Did you consent to having this blood/urine sample taken from you?

What were you told or asked by the police in order to obtain your consent for this sample to be taken from you?

Who drew (took) your blood (urine) sample?

Were you *required* to sign any forms before the nurse/doctor/technician would take your blood/urine?

If so, what did you sign?

Did the person who took your blood sample use any type of cloth or swab to cleanse the surface of your skin *before* taking the sample?

If so, please describe what was done to prepare the skin:

As the needle was removed from your arm, did the person who took the sample hold a swab or cloth over the puncture site?

What happened to the blood/urine sample after it was collected from you? (Be as specific as possible)

Were you told *(or were you under the impression)* that if the police took a blood or urine test that you could not request your own independent test of your blood, urine, or breath, by a different medical or laboratory provider?

Describe (in detail) the type container (i.e., square cardboard box **or** metal cylindrical tube) your blood/urine was placed into, and the vials and color of the stoppers in the vials.

[19] *RIGHT TO COUNSEL*

Were you *ever* advised by anyone that you had the right to consult with an attorney?

By whom?   When?   Your response?_____

Did *you* **ever** *ask* to call an attorney?   Did you know a number?

Did you have the opportunity to make the phone call?   If so, *when*?

Were you provided access to a phone book or "411" service?

If you were denied the right to call an attorney before deciding whether to take the State's test, did the officer (or anyone at the station) explain *why* you were being denied access to legal counsel?

Were you physically able to read that night (i.e., coherent and not impeded or restrained)?

Who told you that you could call an attorney?   When?

When were you told you could make a phone call to anyone else, if you desired?

Did the police cooperate with you in providing phone access?

If not, **or** if you were delayed in being provided phone access, **or** if the police limited your calls, give details:

Could you talk privately?   Were the police listening in on your conversation?

[20] *FORMS SIGNED*

Did you ever sign your name?   What documents did you sign and why?

Did you ever *refuse* to sign your name on any document?

What forms did you refuse to sign?

Why did you refuse?

Did you ever sign (or were you asked to sign) a form or temporary driving permit or other documents relating to SUSPENSION of your license or right to drive for either *refusing* to take the State's test _OR_ for taking the State's test and having a result of above the legal limit? Yes/NO *[We need a copy of this form, if applicable]*.

[21] *VIDEO OR AUDIO TAPING*

Do you know if a video or audiotape was made at the arrest scene **OR** at the testing site?

Any clue(s) (i.e., officer mentioned it) that a video tape *may* have been being made?

Explain:

Did you know that a video tape was being made *when* it was being made?

[22] *RELEASE FROM JAIL*

What was date of release?   /   /   @ Time: :   **AM/ PM** (Eastern Daylight Time)

Did you sign for your own release, or pay your own bond?   Yes / No

If not, were you released *to someone* (commercial bondsman, friend, or a family member)?

Who?   Relationship to you?

Phone Number: (   )_____   **- Cell number (   )_____**

Full Address:

How did that person know to come to assist you?

Any conversation with him/her on the phone near the time of your arrest?

What did you talk about?

Was there any discussion about getting an independent test once you were released from jail?

If so, give details:

Did you sign any forms for the bond?   **[If so, provide copies.]**

[23] *ACCIDENT*

[This section is to be completed <u>ONLY IF</u> an accident of some type has occurred in connection with your DUI-DWI arrest.]

Were you involved in an accident?

How many cars were involved?

Describe accident:

Were you inside your vehicle when the officer *first arrived* on the scene?

    Was your vehicle "running"? Yes / No

    Were the keys in the ignition? Yes / No   If not, where were the keys?

    If "no," give details of *where you were* in relationship to the vehicles:

    Were other persons from your vehicle there, too?

After the accident, did you *ever* leave the immediate area (for any purposes, such as to call a tow truck, call police, locate a pay phone, etc.)?

If so, give details of how long you were gone, where you went, why you left, etc.:

Were there any injuries or death to any other person(s)?

If so, give full details on separate sheet.

Did an **airbag** deploy inside your vehicle?

If "yes," give details of how it affected you:

401

Did the arresting officer make it clear to you at what point of the investigation that he/she was terminating the *ACCIDENT* investigation and BEGINNING the *CRIMINAL* investigation for suspected drunk driving against you?

Give details about what questions the police asked, by whom, and at what location they asked the questions:

Did the officer ever ask you about what you had had to drink that day/night?

Did the officer ever ask WHEN you consumed any alcohol that day/night?

Were you given any Miranda advisements before the officer(s) began to question you?

Prior to this case, *had you EVER been the driver of a vehicle in which another person [passenger, person(s) in other car, pedestrian(s)] were injured or killed?*

If so, give details:

[24] *DRIVING AND CRIMINAL RECORD*

Have you had a prior DUI-DWI in your **LIFETIME---ANYWHERE**?

If so, when?   City   State

Case No. or Citation No.:

Court that handled case: The _____ Court of _____ (County, State)

Any other DUI-DWI convictions (including *Nolo Contendere* pleas) **during your lifetime**, *anywhere*? **(List ALL in detail)**

{*NOTE:* The prosecutor *will have this information*, and we must know the entire history to be able to properly analyze your chances at trial.}

If any *other* serious driving offenses, drug-related offenses, or alcohol-related *anywhere*, list all below, including court, city, state and date (month and year) of arrest:

{*NOTE:* **We are especially interested in any offenses that** *began as a DUI-DWI* **and were reduced or changed to another offense**}:

Ever involved in an accident involving death or serious injury regardless of whether DUI-DWI involved?

If so, fully state the circumstances:

Arresting Officer in prior case (s)?   Agency:

Represented by an attorney in each case?

If so, who?

Was a plea entered?:   *Did you have a Trial?*

Result?

Have you ever been declared a "habitual violator" (HV) offender, for your prior driving offenses?

If so, give the date you were sentenced:

Were you on "HV" status when this incident occurred?

What court?   Judge's name:

Prior attorney's name and phone number:

Are you presently on probation for prior DUI-DWI?

Where:

On probation for *any other* **offense(s)?**

If so, give details:

Was your license under suspension in any jurisdiction when arrested in this case?

Give details as to what court, why suspended, etc.:

Were you driving on a "work permit," HV *probationary* license, or other *restricted* license when this incident occurred?

Prior Driving Suspension (whether in effect now or not)?

Prior SERIOUS Traffic Violations in ANY jurisdiction at ANY time in the past (racing, attempting to elude an officer, hit and run, leaving the scene of an accident, etc.). [Show offense(s) below and approximate date(s) of occurrence]

Prior *Minor* Traffic Violations [show offense(s) and approximate date(s) of occurrence].

Prior criminal record of *any* type (not already mentioned), especially *alcohol-related* or *drug-related* charges, such as underage possession of alcohol, open container violation, possession of marijuana, public intoxication:

[25] *OTHER ATTORNEYS*

Prior to coming to us for legal assistance, did you consult with any other attorney(s) about the present DUI-DWI case?

If so, with whom did you consult?

Have you either hired another attorney **or** *paid a partial fee to another attorney for this case?*

What advice (regarding a possible plea or about challenging this case) were you given by such other attorney(s)?

Do you understand that you are free to follow that attorney's advice (or any other attorney's advice), and that you are in no way bound to use our legal services in your case unless you hire us?

[26] *REFUSAL OF THE STATE'S BREATH, BLOOD, OR URINE TESTS*

[Complete this section ONLY IF you REFUSED (or allegedly refused) to submit to the State's breath, urine or blood tests as requested by the arresting officer.]

What actions were taken or statements were made by the police officer to you *just prior to your alleged refusal* to take the state's test(s)?

Why did you refuse (or why did the officer *claim* that you refused) the State's test(s):

In what way (or with what words or *conduct*) did you (allegedly) refuse the State's test?

Were you aware that your Georgia license (or privilege to drive on Georgia's highways for out-of-state licensees) would be *suspended* for one year by administrative action *for refusing to submit* to the State's test(s)?

Do you wish for us to handle your license suspension hearings (assuming that a timely appeal has been filed)?

Do you understand that these ***administrative*** proceedings are *separate* proceedings from your DUI-DWI and any other pending ***criminal*** (traffic) offenses?

Have you provided us with everything you have received from your State's driver's licensing agency or from the arresting officer?

Do you understand that you have (had) a *very short* amount of time in which to appeal a proposed administrative suspension?

Have you received any WRITTEN FORM or notification from the arresting officer or from your State's driver's licensing agency notifying you of a proposed suspension or revocation of your privilege to drive?

If so, have you filed a timely appeal (or had our office assist you in doing it)?

Have you checked with your State's driver's licensing agency by telephone or ON-LINE to see if your license is valid at this time?

Did you have to get an ignition interlock device put on your vehicle as a condition or bail, or prior to being allowed to recover your vehicle?

When did you recover your car and start to be able to use it again?

Did you have to get anyone else (e.g., your employer or family members) to assist in getting your vehicle back after it was impounded?

What was the total towing and storage charge for your vehicle?

[27] *OTHER CHARGES FROM SAME INCIDENT*

What is the citation number on your DUI-DWI ticket?

[If you were charged with *any other traffic offenses or crimes*, give the following information on EACH separate offense]:

1. Offense:

Citation Number _____:

a) Describe the driving or activities that led to this charge being made against you:

b) Were you aware that you committed this offense?

If "No" give details to explain:

c) Any witnesses or evidence relating to this offense that supports your claim of innocence?

Explain:

2. Offense:

Citation Number _____:

a) Describe the driving or activities that led to this charge being made against you:

b) Were you aware that you committed this offense?

If "No" give details to explain:

c) Any witnesses or evidence relating to this offense that supports your claim of innocence?

Explain:

3. Offense:

    Citation Number _____ :

    a) Describe the driving or activities that led to this charge being made against you:

    b) Were you aware that you committed this offense?

    If "No" give details to explain:

    c) Any witnesses or evidence relating to this offense that supports your claim of innocence?

    Explain:

4. Offense:

    Citation Number _____ :

    a) Describe the driving or activities that led to this charge being made against you:

    b) Were you aware that you committed this offense?

    If "No" give details to explain:

    c) Any witnesses or evidence relating to this offense that supports your claim of innocence?

    Explain:

[If additional citations or offenses, list the applicable information on a separate sheet].

To the best of my knowledge and belief, the foregoing information is true and correct.

_____

Signature

Dated:_____

Thank you for completing the questionnaire. Now, we need to get certain ESSENTIAL copies of documents relating to your case. WE NEED THEM *WITH* THE QUESTIONNAIRE, so don't omit sending them. A list of the requested items is below:

IMPORTANT NOTE: When returning these forms, if you have not already supplied me with *copies* of the following, please do so:

1) Copies of all traffic citations that you received after being arrested;

2) Copies of any "breath test" machine tape;

3) Copies of any incident report or arrest report from the case, if you have obtained one;

4) Copies of any accident report from the case, if you have obtained one;

5) Copies of any bond release forms relating to your case;

6) Copies of any "personal items" inventory forms (jail intake or documents received upon release from jail/custody) you received in connection with your arrest;

7) Copies of any other documents, receipts or other papers of any type whatsoever that you or your family/friends/bondsman received that day/night. This includes copies of any checks written by you (if applicable).

8) A copy of all tow company records (if applicable);

9) A copy of the license suspension form (front and back) completed by the police at the time you were jailed (if applicable);

10) Copies of other examples of your signature, for *comparison* purposes (*example:* copies of old canceled checks, letters, etc.);

11) VERY IMPORTANT! A copy of your previous driving history from your State driver's licensing office. NOTE: Obtain the LONGEST report available from each state, but at least Five (5) years in length. Some drivers will need to seek reports from more than one state. For non-resident licensees, check with your state for costs and method of requesting the report. Go to this website for a link to your state's DMV/DPS/BMV: www.drunkdrivingdefense.com/national/dps-offices.htm. We have provided you with a phone number and address for every state.

12) On any previous DUI-DWI offenses or habitual violator advisements, make copies of all prior documents that are in your possession relating to any aspect of such case(s).

13) If you did not have your PROOF OF INSURANCE when arrested, bring proof with you when you come to our office (or mail it to us, if you consult with us by phone.

14) If you have your driver's license, please copy it and bring (or mail) it to our office.

15) If you were taking any prescribed medications, bring copies of your pharmacist's records of these prescribed medications with you (or mail us copies).
   NOTE: I only need *copies*. Do NOT send me your originals. *You* need them.

APPENDIX K

SELECTED PROVISIONS FROM THE UNITED STATES CONSTITUTION

Preamble

WE THE PEOPLE of the United States, in Order to form a more perfect Union, establish Justice, insure domestic Tranquility, provide for the common defence, promote the general Welfare, and secure the Blessings of Liberty to ourselves and our Posterity, do ordain and establish this CONSTITUTION for the United States of America.

* * * *

[The Fourth, Fifth, Sixth and Seventh Amendments were adopted in 1791.]

Amendment IV

The right of the people to be secure in their persons, houses, papers, and effects, against unreasonable searches and seizures, shall not be violated, and no Warrants shall issue, but upon probable cause, supported by Oath or affirmation, and particularly describing the place to be searched, and the persons or things to be seized.

* * * *

Amendment V

No person shall be held to answer for a capital, or otherwise infamous crime, unless on a presentment or indictment of a Grand Jury, except in cases arising in the land or naval forces, or in the Militia, when in actual service in time of War or public danger; nor shall any person be subject for the same offence to be twice put in jeopardy of life and limb; nor shall be compelled in any criminal case to be a witness against himself, nor be deprived of life, liberty, or property, without due process of law; nor shall private property be taken for public use, without just compensation.

* * * *

Amendment VI

In all criminal prosecutions the accused shall enjoy the right to a speedy and public trial, by an impartial jury of the State and district wherein the crime shall have been committed, which district shall have been previously ascertained by law, and to be informed of the nature and cause of the accusation; to be confronted with the witnesses against him; to have compulsory process for obtaining witnesses in his favor, and to have the Assistance of Counsel for his defence.

Amendment VII

In suits at common law, where the value in controversy shall exceed twenty dollars, the right of trial by jury shall be preserved, and no fact tried by a jury shall be otherwise re-examined in any Court of the United States, than according to the rules of the common law.

* * * *

[The Fourteenth Amendment was adopted in 1868. Section One of this five-section Amendment pertains to matters covered in this book].

Amendment XIV

Section 1. All persons born or naturalized in the Unites States, and subject to the jurisdiction thereof, are citizens of the United States and of the State wherein they reside. No State shall make or enforce any law which shall abridge the privileges or immunities of citizens of the United States; nor shall any State deprive any person of life, liberty, or property, without due process of law; nor deny to any person within its jurisdiction the equal protection of the laws. ...

* * * *

[The Eighteenth Amendment was passed by Congress, and adopted by the requisite number of States in 1919, following years of protests by anti-alcohol activists such as Carrie Nation. In 1933, due to widespread public resentment and violation of the law, it was repealed by the Twenty-First Amendment, which follows below.]

Amendment XVIII

Section 1. After one year from the ratification of this article the manufacture, sale, or transportation of intoxicating liquors within, the importation thereof into, or the exportation thereof from the United States and all territory subject to the jurisdiction thereof for beverage purposes is hereby prohibited.

Section 2. The Congress and the several States shall have concurrent power to enforce this article by appropriate legislation.

Section 3. This article shall be inoperative unless it shall have been ratified as an amendment to the Constitution by the legislatures of the several States, as provided in the Constitution, within seven years from the date of the submission hereof to the States by the Congress.

Amendment XXII

Section 1. The eighteenth article of amendment to the Constitution of the United States is hereby repealed.

Section 2. The transportation or importation into any State, Territory, or possession of the United States for delivery or use therein of intoxicating liquors, in violation of the laws thereof, is hereby prohibited.

Section 3. This article shall be inoperative unless it shall have been ratified as an amendment to the Constitution, within seven years from the date of the submission hereof to the States by the Congress.

* * * *

[The last amendment to have been passed in this country is the Twenty-Sixth Amendment, which was adopted in 1971].

* * * *

Amendment XXVI

<u>Section 1.</u> The rights of citizens of the United States, who are eighteen years of age or older, to vote shall not be denied or abridged by the United States or any state on account of age.

<u>Section 2.</u> The Congress shall have the power to enforce this article by appropriate legislation.

Biographical Sketch of

William C. Head, Atlanta, GA

Senior Partner of *Head, Thomas, Webb & Willis, LLC*, based in Atlanta, GA

BOARD CERTIFIED AS A SPECIALIST IN DUI DEFENSE BY THE NATIONAL COLLEGE FOR DUI DEFENSE, INC.

Mr. Head was named *"Top DUI Lawyer in America"* by the National College for DUI Defense, Inc., at Harvard Law School in July of 2003. Mr. Head is a frequent seminar lecturer on DUI law, criminal trial practice and on legal issues surrounding the use of alcohol and drugs. He serves as National Editor of the *DWI Journal.* He and his firm **[Head, Thomas, Webb & Willis, LLC]** are *"av" rated (highest)* with Martindale-Hubbell, America's oldest and most respected attorney rating service. Martindale-Hubbell has also named Mr. Head and his firm to *"The Bar Registry of Pre-Eminent Attorneys"* for the past six years. He is the author of four books on DUI-related issues including *101 Ways to Avoid a Drunk Driving Conviction* (©Maximar Publishing Company 1991) which he co-authored with Reese I. Joye of North Charleston, SC. The second edition of this book (with **202** WAYS to Avoid a Conviction) will be released in July of 2006. He completed the first ever national, in-depth book on DUI-DWI law written for clients called *The DUI Book*, published in May, 2006

He is the author of *The Georgia DUI Trial Practice Manual* (©Thomson-West 1996-2006). In addition, he is the author of (1) "Georgia Jurisprudence," vol. 20, ch. 35, part 8, "Automobile Traffic Offenses: Driving Under the Influence," 1995 Lawyers Co-op Publishing Co., Rochester, NY; (2) *Medical-Legal Aspects of Alcohol (4th Edition)*, "Defense of Driving Under the Influence Cases," 2003, Lawyers & Judges Publishing Co., Tucson, AZ; (3) Update Editor, *An Introduction to Law in Georgia, "Behind the Wheel,"* (1995 Update), Carl Vinson Institute of Government of the University of Georgia (text on legal rights for Georgia high school students) (4) The author of *"Five Myths About Defending Accused Drunk Drivers,"* ATLA Trial Magazine, vol. 29, no. 3, p. 64, 3/93. Mr. Head's law practice is limited to the defense of contested DUI, drug offense and vehicular homicide cases. For 15 years, Mr. Head has coordinated a statewide network of more than 80 Georgia DUI attorneys who regularly share cutting-edge information on Georgia DUI practice.

In January 2000, former Gov. Roy Barnes appointed Mr. Head to a national symposium dealing with "Aggressive Driving." The Symposium was coordinated by *NHTSA (National Highway Traffic and Safety Administration)* in Washington, DC. He was elected National Chairman of the 200+ member Symposium. In connection with this, he made a presentation to the Lifesavers 2000 Conference in March 2000. Mr. Head was one of the original twelve Regents who started the *National College for DUI Defense, Inc* in 1995. He is a retired Regent at this time. He also holds *"Life Member"* status in the NACDL, GACDL, and SCACDL. He is also a member of the ATLA, the ABA, the Atlanta Bar Association, and the Gwinnett County Bar Association and is founder of two national web sites for DUI-DWI trial attorneys, **www.DrunkDrivingDefense.com** and **www.DUI-DWI.com**. He is certified to operate an **Intoxilyzer 5000** breath testing instrument and owns the model of the Intoxilyzer 5000 used in Georgia. He also received factory certification to operate the **BAC Datamaster** infrared breath testing instrument in 2004.

He has produced a 90-minute videotape on crime laboratory testing methods and procedures in conjunction with the University of Tennessee Medical School, Department of Toxicology in April of 2000. Mr. Head holds a certificate of completion for the Robert F. Borkenstein Course on *Alcohol, Drugs, and Highway Safety: Testing, Research, and Litigation* based out of Indiana University at Bloomington and is a provisional member of the International Association for Chemical Testing (IACT) as well as member of the jurisprudence section of the American Academy of Forensic Scientists (AAFS).

In 1994, Mr. Head sponsored the first training program in America that enabled defense attorneys to be certified practitioners in the NHTSA standardized field sobriety tests [SFSTs]. He also sponsored the first certification course for defense attorneys for the Intoxilyzer 5000 breath machine in 1996. He then sponsored the first 40-hour certification course that allowed defense attorneys to become certified as SFST instructors. In 1998, he sponsored and enrolled in a comprehensive Blood and Urine Testing training seminar held in Lake Tahoe. In 2005, he sponsored the first DRE Overview Course for criminal defense attorneys and the first SFST Advanced Update Course for attorneys. He is not only an SFST instructor now, but helps teach other defense attorneys (including public defenders at no cost) every year.

In the cover story for *Atlanta Magazine* (March, 2000), Mr. Head was recognized as the state's "best DUI lawyer" based upon a survey of Georgia lawyers. He has also been named one of Georgia's *"Super Lawyers"* every year that this designation has been awarded by Law & Politics Magazine. He has also been named as one of Georgia's *"Legal Elite"* by *Georgia Trend Magazine*. He also oversees more than a dozen web sites for his law firm, including **www.CriminalDefenseAdvice.com**, **www.Absolutely-Not-Guilty.com**, and **www.GeorgiaCriminalDefense.com**. Mr. Head can be reached at wchead@mindspring.com.

413

INDEX

U

V

W

X

Y

Z